CRIMINAL EVIDENCE

FOR LAW ENFORCEMENT OFFICERS

• • • • • • • • •

LARRY E. HOLTZ   FIFTH EDITION

D0814052

LexisNexis®
Gould Publications™

ISBN: 1-4224-0350-5

Editorial Office
701 East Water Street, Charlottesville, VA 22902-7587
(800)446-3410

www.lexisnexis.com

Customer Service: 800/833-9844

Publication Number: 29160   Product Number: 29160-11

Preface

The criminal law of evidence plays an integral part in the day-to-day enforcement responsibilities of virtually all public police officials, private security officials and other criminal justice practitioners and, as such, must be clearly understood. Indeed, before a particular item can earn the title of "evidence," it must, at some point in time, be recognized by the investigating officer as having not only a logical connection to the offense under investigation but also a legally significant one.

When a law enforcement official formally accuses an individual of committing a criminal offense, that officer will often be called upon to account for his or her accusations in a criminal court of law. At trial, the officer's criminal accusations must always be supported by evidence that is (a) legally obtained, (b) legally sufficient, (c) logically and legally relevant, and (d) competent. While all investigations of a criminal nature seek the ultimate and ideal result of a valid criminal conviction, as we all know—perhaps all too well—the impenetrable barrier to that ultimate result is "reasonable doubt," that type of doubt which arises from the evidence admitted, tainted evidence which has been excluded, or, even more simply, from a general lack of evidence. In this respect, the competent investigator will strive to eliminate the possibility of "tainted" evidence or "lack of evidence" by (a) responding to the crime scene as quickly as possible; (b) protecting the scene and the evidence within it from outside contamination; (c) thoroughly and meticulously examining the crime scene for physical evidence; (d) identifying the relevant evidence present; and (e) collecting, preserving and maintaining proper custody of the evidence for trial.

It is therefore critical for patrol officers and security officers in general, and criminal investigators or detectives in particular—each of whom may, at some point in a criminal investigation, have the responsibility of locating, identifying, protecting, collecting, or preserving evidence—to understand the body of rules, cases, statutes and constitutional provisions which form the basis of that portion of the criminal law of evidence which significantly impacts upon the professional performance of their duties. Indeed, it is the entire body of the law of evidence which regulates the admission into the courtroom of the criminally probative aspects of the enforcement official's case against the accused.

Table of Contents

CHAPTER 3. PRESERVATION OF / ACCESS TO EVIDENCE

CHAPTER 4. WITNESSES: EXPLORING TESTIMONIAL AND DOCUMENTARY EVIDENCE

CHAPTER 5. EYEWITNESS IDENTIFICATION EVIDENCE

CHAPTER 6. PROOF IN CRIMINAL CASES

APPENDIX

SAMPLE CASE

1{MIRANDA v. ARIZONA
Supreme Court of the United States
384 *U.S.* 436, 86 *S.Ct.* 1602 (1966) }3
2

QUESTION: Are self-incriminating statements elicited from an individual during incommunicado interrogation in a police-dominated atmosphere without full warnings of constitutional rights admissible in evidence? ⌐4

ANSWER: NO. "[T]he prosecution may not use statements, whether exculpatory or inculpatory, stemming from custodial interrogation of the defendant unless it demonstrates the use of procedural safeguards effective to secure the privilege against self-incrimination." {*Id.* at 1612.}7 ⌐5

RATIONALE: In this landmark decision, the United States Supreme Court clarifies its holding in *Escobedo v. Illinois,* 378 *U.S.* 478, 84 *S.Ct.* 1758 (1964), and provides "concrete constitutional guidelines for law enforcement agencies and courts to follow." {*Miranda* at 1611.}8

Initially, the Court defines "custodial interrogation" to "mean questioning initiated by law enforcement officers after a person has been taken into custody or otherwise deprived of his freedom of action in any significant way." *Id.* at 1612. As for the procedural safeguards to be employed, the Court requires that: ⌐6

> Prior to any questioning, the person must be warned that he has the right to remain silent, that any statement he does make may be used as evidence against him, and that he has a right to the presence of an attorney, either retained or appointed. The *defendant may waive* effectuation of *these rights, provided the waiver is made voluntarily, knowingly, and intelligently.* If, however, he indicates in any manner and at any stage of the process that he wishes to consult with an attorney before speaking there can be no questioning. Likewise, if the individual is alone and indicates in any manner that he does not wish to be interrogated, the police may not question him.
>
> * * * }9

Id. [Emphasis added.] }10

x

Reading Guide

EXPLANATION

1. *NAME OR TITLE OF CASE.*
2. *CASE CITATION:*
   Number on left = volume of book.
   Number on right = page number where case begins.
   If blank, (e.g., ___ U.S. ___) the case has not been published as of the printing date of the Handbook.

MEANINGS OF ABBREVIATIONS BETWEEN NUMBERS:

FEDERAL CASES:
   Texts which report cases from the U.S. Supreme Court:
   U.S. = United States Reports.
   S.Ct. = Supreme Court Reporter.
   L.Ed.2d = Lawyer's Edition of the U.S. Supreme Court Reports; Second Edition.
   U.S.L.W. = United States Law Week
   Texts which report cases from other (lower) federal courts:
   F.Supp. = Federal Supplement. (Cases generally from the Federal District Courts)
   F.2d = Federal Reporter; Second Edition. (Cases generally from the Federal Circuit Courts of Appeal)

NEW JERSEY CASES:
   N.J. = New Jersey Reports. (Cases from the New Jersey Supreme Court)
   N.J.Super. = New Jersey Superior Court Reports. (Cases from the New Jersey Superior Court, Appellate and Trial Divisions)

MISC. STATE CASES:
   A.2d = Atlantic Reporter; second edition (Cases from: CT, DE, DC, ME, MD, NH, NJ, PA, RI, VT)
   N.E.2d = North Eastern Reporter; second edition (Cases from: IL, IN, MA, NY, OH)
   N.W.2d = North Western Reporter; second edition (Cases from: IA, MI, MN, NE, ND, SD, WI)
   P.2d = Pacific Reporter; second edition (Cases from: AK, AZ, CA, CO, HI, ID, KS, MT, NV, NM, OK, OR, UT, WA, WY)
   So.2D = Southern Reporter; second edition (Cases from: AL, FL, LA, MS)
   S.E.2d = South Eastern Reporter; second edition (Cases from GA, NC, SC, VA, WV)
   S.W.2d = South Western Reporter; second edition (Cases from: AR, KY, MO, TN, TX)

3. *DATE CASE WAS DECIDED.*
4. *QUESTION OR ISSUE PRESENTED.*
5. *ANSWER TO THE QUESTION OR ISSUE PRESENTED* (Is normally the case "holding" or "rule of law.")
6. RATIONALE: The extended explanation for the rule of law.
7. *"SHORTHAND" CITATION FORMS:*
   "Id."— used to indicate a reference to a case or authority cited immediately preceding the present use.
   NOTE, MODIFICATION OF USE OF *Id.*: Unless otherwise specified, when the use of *Id.* refers the reader back to the CITATION immediately following the CASE TITLE, the reference shall *only* refer to the text cited immediately before the date. For example, *"Id. at 1612"* refers the reader to page 1612 of volume 86 of the Supreme Court Reporter. (*See* 1 and 2.)
8. OTHER "SHORTHAND" CITATION FORMS:
   "Miranda at 1611"— Periodically used instead of *Id.* for clarification. Either of these "shorthand" citation forms shall be used when the case speaks of, or refers to, more than one case or authority. The purpose is to clarify exactly which case or authority is being cited.
   "Supra"—Refers you back to a case or authority already cited in full. For example, "as was held in *Escobedo v. Illinois, supra,* ..."; or more simply, "as was held in *Escobedo, supra,* ...".
   "Infra"—Used in the same manner as *supra,* but instead of referring you "back," it refers you "ahead."
9. *OMITTED WORDS:*
   The ellipsis, "* * *," is used to indicate that unnecessary words have been omitted.
10. *BRACKETED MATERIAL:*
    Consists of material added or changed by the Author. In this sample, the emphasis by italic type in the last paragraph has been added by the Author.

Dedicated
To the memory of the law enforcement officers
Who made the ultimate sacrifice while
Making our world a safer place.

Chapter 1

THE LAW OF EVIDENCE
AND THE
ADVERSARY SYSTEM

§1.1. THE LAW OF EVIDENCE: BASIC PRINCIPLES AND DEFINITIONS

§1.1(a). What is Evidence?

In our everyday affairs, we all use evidence to help us make decisions and form judgments. The use of evidence may be as simple as looking out the window in the morning to see what the weather is like, and then making a decision as to what to wear based on this "evidence." Businesses follow the market, examine trends and sales statistics, and then use this "evidence" to formulate a strategy for advertising and marketing. Doctors examine patients, conduct tests, and analyze the results to make a judgment, based on this "evidence," as to the most appropriate course of treatment or therapy. Teachers ask questions, administer formal exams, and analyze student responses as "evidence" of whether a particular teaching strategy is effective.

In the criminal justice arena, law enforcement officials gather as much evidence as possible. The evidence may be used to (1) prove a fact; (2) support a particular theory or proposition; (3) disprove a contrary theory or proposition, such as an alibi; (4) provide probable cause for an arrest; or (5) support the lodging of criminal charges.

"Evidence" may, therefore, be defined as all the means by which any alleged matter of fact—any proposition of fact—is established as true. "Criminal evidence" consists of any form of proof or probative matter, formally presented by the prosecution or the defense at a legal proceeding, through the medium of (1) witnesses, (2) physical objects, (3) documents, or (4) demonstrative exhibits, for the purpose of establishing as true a given fact proposition. When an item is offered as evidence in a legal proceeding, that item should demonstrate, confirm, clarify, or ascertain the truth of a disputed fact for either the prosecution or the defense. In this respect, the item offered should help persuade a reasonable mind that a particular fact proposition is or is not true.

§1.1(b). Sufficiency of Evidence: The Decision to Prosecute

If enough evidence has been gathered to support an arrest and the filing of criminal charges, the target of the investigation—the accused—will be taken into custody, and the matter will be referred to the prosecuting attorney. The prosecutor must then decide whether the evidence is sufficient to warrant moving forward with a criminal prosecution.

The prosecutor is not obligated to proceed with all the charges originally filed by the police. In fact, the prosecutor may decide that the evidence supports none of the charges, and may decline to prosecute entirely. In order to dismiss charges already filed, the prosecutor will, depending on the jurisdiction, either move for, recommend, or enter on the record a *"nolle prosequi."* Through the legal device of *nolle prosequi*, the prosecuting attorney makes a formal declaration or motion on the record that he or she will not prosecute the matter further, whether as to some of the charges, all of the charges, some of the persons accused, or altogether. On the other hand, the prosecutor may decide, based on a close examination of the evidence and supplemental investigation, that additional charges or more serious charges should be lodged against the accused.

These determinations represent the exercise of *"prosecutorial discretion"*—the official authority or power to decide in good faith whether to prosecute or to refrain from prosecution. In this regard, the prosecuting attorney has the duty, in each case, to examine with care and accuracy the available evidence, the law and the facts, and the applicability of each to the other, and to intelligently weigh the chances of successful conclusion of the prosecution. Naturally, such discretion must be exercised in accordance with established principles of law, fairly, wisely, and with skill and reason. It includes consultation and collaboration with other law enforcement and criminal justice officials, and produces a decision regarding a course of action or non-action, in light of what is right under the circumstances as a matter of law and policy.

There are many factors which impact on the decision to prosecute. In addition to administrative concerns, such as caseload and the availability of prosecutorial resources, the following factors impact on the decision to prosecute:

(1) whether the offense is serious enough to warrant prosecution;

(2) if a victim is involved, whether the victim is cooperative, the nature and extent of the victim's involvement in the offense, and the relationship of the victim to the accused;

(3) the accused's degree of criminal culpability;

(4) whether the accused was directly or marginally involved in the crime;

(5) the nature and extent of the accused's criminal history;

(6) whether the accused was cooperative;

(7) any assistance rendered by the accused in the apprehension or prosecution of other offenders, or in the prevention of other offenses;

(8) the availability of diversionary programs and the accused's amenability to such programs;

(9) whether, given the nature of the offense and the offender, the prosecution would do more harm than good; and

(10) public policy concerns, including the deterrence value of the prosecution in preventing future offenses by others, and the fostering of the community's sense of security and confidence in the criminal justice system.

Perhaps the single most important factor impacting upon the decision to prosecute is whether there is sufficient, admissible, and reliable evidence in the case to prove each and every element of the alleged criminal offense beyond a reasonable doubt. More often than not, prosecutors will decline prosecution due to "case weakness" or insufficient proof to convict. A weak case may result from problems related to witnesses and/or physical evidence. Some witnesses fail to appear for court; others may be reluctant, may be uncooperative, or may simply refuse to testify. Some witnesses lack credibility, perhaps due to substance abuse problems, criminal records, or criminal involvement. Physical evidence problems may be traced to missing fingerprints, a missing weapon or instrument of the crime, or the absence of scientific analyses or medical evidence. In some cases, the prosecution may not be permitted to use certain evidence because it was obtained by the police in violation of the Constitution.

Insufficient proof to convict may also result from the significant difference in legal standards between what the police need to arrest—probable cause—and what the prosecutor needs to convict—proof beyond a reasonable doubt. To best counteract the dangers of insufficient proof and to increase the percentage of cases that may be prosecuted, law enforcement officials should consider performing post-arrest investigative activities, and coordinating those activities with the prosecutor's staff.

---

§1.1(c). Probative Matter and the Law of Evidence

If something is "probative," it tends to prove something. The term "probative matter" refers to those evidentiary items which have the ability to prove, or the effect of proving, desired facts. It includes all of those things which contribute to establishing an alleged fact as true. Once an alleged fact is established as true, it is said to have been "proved." It is clear, therefore, that "evidence" is not synonymous with "fact" or "proof." Evidence may be ambiguous (subject to different interpretations), false (exaggerated or fabricated), or modified (by forgetfulness, inattention, or faulty perception). On the other hand, an "established" fact proposition may be considered the truth, the consequence, or end result of the presentation of evidence; it is also dependent upon the evidence. In a criminal case, the presentation of evidence may directly prove a fact, be just strong enough to compel a conclusion of fact, or just strong enough, or weak enough for that matter, to raise a reasonable doubt. Thus, evidence is the medium or vehicle of proof; it is the means by which the facts are established. Proof is the end result—the final conclusions drawn from the presentation of all the evidence. As illustrated in Figure 1-1, each slice of the pie represents an item of evidence, while the entire pie may constitute proof of guilt.

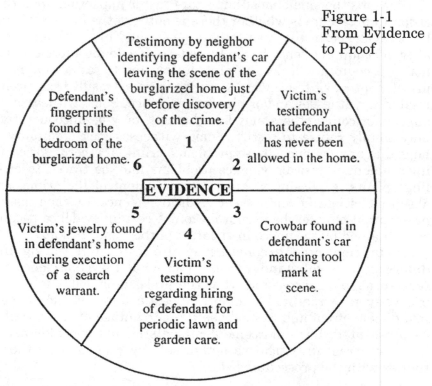

Figure 1-1
From Evidence
to Proof

The entire body of rules, statutes, standards, and constitutional provisions by which the admission of proof at a legal proceeding is regulated is called the "law of evidence."

_____

§1.1(d). Triers of Fact and Law

In a criminal case, the responsibility for discovering the truth lies with the judge or jury. If the case is to be tried before a jury, the jurors, in their role as "triers of fact," review all the evidence—testimony, exhibits, documents, etc.—which has been admitted during the trial in order to make a decision as to the guilt or innocence of the accused. The judge, as "trier of law," determines, by application of the law and rules of evidence, the admissibility of evidence, that is, what evidence the jury may consider in its decision-making process. The judge will also instruct the jury on the relevant law and caution the jury to avoid reaching a verdict colored by passion, sympathy, bias, or prejudice. Thus, the jurors decide all questions of fact and the judge decides all questions of law. The jurors will also determine, in accordance with the judge's instructions, the value, weight, and effect of the evidence presented to them, including the credibility of witnesses. In a non-jury trial, the judge performs both functions.

---

§1.1(e). Admissibility

The concept of "admissibility" is the touchstone of the law of evidence. It protects the trier of fact (judge or jury as the case may be) from hearing, seeing, or otherwise considering improper evidence. The rules of admissibility protect the trier of fact from matters which (a) have no bearing on the case, (b) are a needless waste of the court's time, (c) are unreliable or untrustworthy, (d) create a substantial danger of unfair prejudice to the defendant, or (e) are too confusing or misleading for the jury.[1] Admissibility questions are legal matters which are decided by the judge, and these decisions are generally made out of the presence of the jury. The answers to such questions determine whether or not the material offered as evidence "gets in" to the courtroom, that is, whether the evidence will be "received" by the court "*in* evidence"—in a word, whether the evidence is *admissible*.[2]

---

§1.1(f). Limited Admissibility

Most of the law of evidence relates to whether probative material should be considered "admissible" in court—whether or not the item offered should be received "in evidence." One portion of the law, however, relates to the question of *what permissible use* can be made of the particular item of evidence once it is ruled to be admissible.[3]

---

[1] *See e.g., Fed.R.Evid.* 403.

[2] *See generally Fed.R.Evid.* 104.

[3] *See e.g., Fed.R.Evid.* 105 ("When evidence which is admissible as to one party or for one purpose but not admissible as to another party or for another purpose is admitted, the court, upon request, shall restrict the evidence to its proper scope and instruct the jury accordingly.").

For example, a prior, out-of-court statement made by a witness may be ruled to be admissible for one purpose but not another. Consider the witness who takes the stand and testifies on cross-examination that she distinctly remembers that the defendant did not go through the red traffic light immediately before the traffic accident. The prosecution then puts on a rebuttal witness who testifies that he heard the first witness say, a substantial time after the accident, "Gee, I wonder if anyone else saw this guy go through that red light ?" In such cases, the jury may be instructed that it may not consider the testimony by the rebuttal witness as substantive proof that the defendant actually did go through the red light (an impermissible use because it is hearsay), but only as bearing on the credibility of the first witness' statement on cross-examination when she said that the defendant did not go through the red light (the permissible use).

In the same vein, evidence may be admitted for use against one party, but not as against another, in which event the judge, if requested, will instruct the jury to consider the evidence "only as to the party against whom it is admissible."[4] Because of the substantial danger of unfair prejudice, such instructions have been held insufficient to "insure against misuse by the jury of the confessions or admissions of a codefendant who does not take the stand when the confessions or admissions implicate the defendant. A violation of the Sixth Amendment right to confront witnesses results."[5] Thus, in *Bruton v. United States,*[6] the Court ruled that Bruton's Sixth Amendment right of confrontation was violated by the introduction of his non-testifying codefendant's confession, at their joint trial, naming Bruton as a participant in the crime. The right of confrontation will not be violated, however, when, with proper limiting jury instructions, a nontestifying codefendant's confession is redacted to eliminate any and all references to the defendant.[7]

---

§1.1(g). Weight of the Evidence

Once an item has been ruled to be admissible, the trier of fact (also known as the factfinder) is then free to attach whatever "weight" to the item of evidence that he or she believes is appropriate under the circumstances. The fact that some probative matter has been admitted or received "in evidence" only means that the judge has determined that it is worthy of consideration. The trier of

---

[4] 1 McCormick, *Evidence* §59 (West 4th ed. 1992).

[5] *Id.* at 237.

[6] 391 *U.S.* 123, 88 *S.Ct.* 1620 (1968).

[7] *Richardson v. Marsh,* 481 *U.S.* 200, 107 *S.Ct.* 1702 (1987).

fact is then free to assess the persuasiveness or believability of the evidentiary item, and attach to it a great deal of weight, some weight, very little weight, or no weight at all.

---

§1.1(h). Law Enforcement and the Law of Evidence

The law of evidence plays an integral part in the day-to-day enforcement responsibilities of all law officers, and, as such, must be clearly understood. Indeed, before a particular item can earn the title of "evidence," it must, at some point in time, be recognized by the investigating officer as having not only a logical connection to the criminal offense under investigation but also a legally significant one. Moreover, a law enforcement officer who formally accuses an individual of committing a criminal offense, will often be called upon to account for his or her accusations in a criminal court of law.

At trial, the officer's criminal accusations must always be supported by evidence which is (a) legally obtained, (b) legally sufficient, (c) logically and legally relevant, and (d) competent. While all investigations of a criminal nature seek the ultimate and ideal result of a valid criminal conviction, as we all know—perhaps all too well—the impenetrable barrier to that ultimate result is "reasonable doubt," that type of doubt which arises from the evidence admitted, tainted evidence which has been excluded or the lack of evidence in general.[8] In this respect, the competent law enforcement officer will strive to eliminate the possibility of "tainted" evidence or the "lack of evidence" by (a) responding to the crime scene as quickly as possible; (b) protecting the crime scene and the evidence within it from outside contamination; (c) thoroughly and meticulously examining the crime scene for physical evidence; (d) identifying the relevant evidence present; and (e) collecting and preserving the evidence for trial.

It is therefore critical for patrol officers in general, and criminal investigators or detectives in particular—each of whom may, at some point in a criminal investigation, have the responsibility of locating, identifying, protecting, collecting, or preserving evidence—to understand the body of rules, statutes and constitutional provisions which form the basis of that portion of the criminal law of evidence which significantly impacts upon the professional performance of their duties. Indeed, it is the entire body of the law of evidence which regulates the admission into the courtroom of the criminally probative aspects of the law enforcement officer's case against the accused.

---

[8] *See e.g., Johnson v. Louisiana*, 406 *U.S.* 356, 360, 92 *S.Ct.* 1620, 1624 (1972) ("reasonable doubt" in criminal trials "arises from the evidence or lack of evidence").

STATE v. PATTON
Superior Court of New Jersey, Appellate Division
362 *N.J.Super.* 16, 826 A.2d 783 (App.Div. 2003)

CARCHMAN, J.A.D.

During the early morning hours of August 10th, "police found the lifeless body of Gloria Deen Hoke in an alley in Camden. In the early evening of the same day, the Camden police, acting on an anonymous tip of a 'man with a gun,' stopped, searched and arrested defendant Ronald Patton on a weapons offense and took him to police headquarters. During the ensuing nineteen hours between the time of defendant's arrest and the commencement of interrogation, law enforcement officers fabricated an account of Hoke's murder. A law enforcement officer, posing as an eyewitness, was 'interviewed' on an audiotape that was later played to defendant who, despite his early denials of involvement, upon hearing the audiotape, confessed to the murder. The fabricated audiotape, identified as such, was later introduced into evidence at trial, and defendant was convicted of murder and related offenses. His motion to suppress the confession and objection to the use of the fictitious audiotape at trial were denied as was his challenge to the initial arrest and search." *Id.* at 18.

"We reverse. We hold that law enforcement officers may not fabricate evidence to prompt a confession and later introduce that police-fabricated evidence at trial to support the voluntariness of the confession." *Id.*

"The dominant issue on this appeal is the propriety and use of the police-fabricated audiotape prompting the confession. This issue implicates two considerations: the voluntariness of the confession and whether the use of such evidence both in the interrogation process and thereafter at trial comports with both Federal and State Constitutional protections." *Id.* at 27.

"Over the last century, police interrogation procedures evolved from the use of physical force to extract confessions to the modern day use of psychologically coercive techniques. * * * The shift away from physically coercive police practices began in the 1930s in response to several studies, the most prominent of which was the Wickersham Report to Congress, National Commission on Law Observance and Enforcement, Report No. 11, *Lawlessness in Law Enforcement* (1931) (Wickersham Report), decrying the use of brutality and 'third degree' techniques to extract confessions. * * *" *Patton* at 28.

"By the 1960s, studies indicated that while police in some jurisdictions continued to use physical force, the majority practice was to use psychologically-coercive methods to extract confessions, including the use of trickery." *Id.*

"To address such interrogation methods, the United States Supreme Court mandated in *Miranda*[9] that for police to obtain a voluntary confession, they must inform suspects subject to custodial interrogation of their rights, including the right to remain silent and the right to an attorney. * * * While *Miranda* focused on informing suspects of their rights, it did not address the propriety or use of the psychologically coercive techniques it deplored, once suspects validly waived their rights." *Id.* at 29.

Other decisions have addressed the issue, and the use of psychological coercion including trickery and deceit by police has received judicial sanction. Without defining the limits of such conduct, the Supreme Court has upheld certain forms of trickery. *See Frazier v. Cupp*, 394 *U.S.* 731, 89 *S.Ct.* 1420 (1969) (holding confession was voluntary where police lied to defendant that his co-defendant had implicated him in the crime); *see also Miller v. Fenton*, 474 *U.S.* 104, 106 *S.Ct.* 445 (1985) (upholding confession obtained after an hour long interrogation, where the police lied about evidence they had against defendant, expressed sympathy toward defendant by indicating suspect was not a criminal and should receive psychiatric help, and where the suspect collapsed in a state of shock immediately after confessing)." *Patton* at 29.

"Other Federal and State courts have similarly tolerated the use of trickery after a suspect has waived his *Miranda* rights permitting, among other forms of deceit, police falsely advising a defendant that the police possess incriminating evidence inculpating defendant for the alleged offense. *See, e.g., Sovalik v. State*, 612 *P.*2d 1003 (Alaska 1980) (telling the defendant that his fingerprints were found at the crime scene); *State v. Cobb*, 566 *P.*2d 285 (Ariz. 1977) (same); *State v. Jackson*, 304 S.E.2d 134 (N.C. 1983) (same); *State v. Register*, 476 *S.E.*2d 153 (S.C. 1996) (defendant's tires and shoes matched impressions and prints found at murder scene and DNA linked him to crime). *And see Hopkins v. State*, 311 A.2d 483 (Md.App. 1973) (co-defendant made a statement incriminating defendant); *State v. Stubenrauch*, 503 *S.W.*2d 136 (Mo.App. 1973) (same); *Commonwealth v. Jones*, 457 Pa. 423, 322 A.2d 119 (Pa. 1974) (same). *See also Holland v. McGinnis*, 963 *F.*2d 1044 (7th Cir. 1992) (eyewitness linked defendant to crime scene); *People v. Pendarvis*, 10 *Cal.Rptr.* 625 (Ct.App. 1961) (pharmacist identified defendant accused of forging a prescription for narcotics); *In re D.A.S.*, 391 A.2d 255 (D.C. 1978) (victim had identified defendant); *State v. Manning*, 506 *So.*2d 1094 (Fla.Dist.Ct.App. 1987) (medical records indicated defendant had same venereal disease as victim); *State v. Boren*, 224 *N.W.*2d 14 (Iowa 1974) (father accused of incest was told that daughter had passed a lie detector test); *Springer v. Commonwealth*, 998 *S.W.*2d 439 (Ky. 1999) (police told defendant that

---

[9] 384 *U.S.* 436, 86 *S.Ct.* 1602 (1966).

they had been taping her telephone calls and began to play actual recording of phone calls, which actually did not contain any incriminating information); *State v. Norfolk,* 381 *N.W.*2d 120 (Neb. 1986) (police referenced a non-existent autopsy report)." *Patton* at 30-31.

"This case presents a different circumstance than the other trickery cases. Thematic throughout most of the legion of cases approving the use of trickery and false representations by police officers is the common fact that the falsity emanates from the 'voice' of the officer. The teachings of these cases support a view that a police officer in the interrogation process may, by the officer's statements, make misrepresentations of fact or suggest that evidence in the form of reports or witnesses exist that will implicate a suspect. That the 'voice' of the misrepresentation is the police officer is a distinguishing factor between these decisions and those questioning the use of police-fabricated tangible evidence, the issue in this case." *Id.* at 32.

"The use of police-fabricated evidence to induce a confession has been addressed in other jurisdictions. In *State v. Cayward,* 552 *So.*2d 971 (Fla.Dist.Ct.App. 1989), the police fabricated two scientific reports, one on stationery of the Florida Department of Criminal Law Enforcement, the other on stationery of a scientific testing organization, 'Life Codes, Inc.,' indicating that semen stains on the victim's underwear came from defendant. The police presented the reports to defendant during their interrogation, and some time later during the interview, defendant confessed. Noting that police deception does not render a confession involuntary *per se*, the court held that 'the police overstepped the line of permitted deception,' answering the question 'whether there is a qualitative difference between the verbal artifices deemed acceptable and the presentation of the falsely contrived scientific documents challenged here,' in the affirmative. In rendering its decision, the court focused on both constitutional and practical considerations. It first noted:

> It may well be that a suspect is more impressed and thereby more easily induced to confess when presented with tangible, official-looking reports as opposed to merely being told that some tests have implicated him. If one perceives such a difference, it probably originates in the notion that a document which purports to be authoritative impresses one as being inherently more permanent and facially reliable than a simple verbal statement. * * *

> We think, however, that both the suspect's and the public's expectations concerning the built-in adversariness of police interrogations do not encompass the notion that the police will knowingly fabricate tangible documentation or physical evidence against an individual. Such an idea brings to mind the horrors of

less advanced centuries in our civilization when magistrates at times schemed with sovereigns to frame political rivals. This is precisely one of the parade of horrors civics teachers have long taught their pupils that our modern judicial system was designed to correct. Thus we think the manufacturing of false documents by police officials offends our traditional notions of due process of law under both the federal and state constitutions.

Patton at 33. [Citations omitted.]

"Addressing practical concerns, the court noted that police-fabricated evidence was dangerous:

Unlike oral misrepresentations, manufactured documents have the potential of indefinite life and the facial appearance of authenticity. A report falsified for interrogation purposes might well be retained and filed in police paperwork. Such reports have the potential of finding their way into the courtroom.

*   *   *   *

We are further concerned that false documents retained in police or state attorney's files might be disclosed to the media as a result of the public records law. A suspect's reputation could be unwittingly yet unfairly and permanently marred and his right to a fair trial jeopardized by the media's innocent reporting of falsified documents.

We can also conceive of an unintended scenario where a manufactured document, initially designed only for use in interrogation, might be admitted as substantive evidence against a defendant. Although one hopes that such an error would be discovered in preparation for trial, the reality of our courts' heavy caseloads is that counsel and trial judges routinely accept as true documents which appear to be reliable reports from known government and private agencies.

We shudder to think of the impact that questionable authenticity of court records might have not only on the trial level, but on the appellate level. We are routinely presented with documents in court files which we must assume to be genuine. To sanction the manufacturing of false documents, which have the potential of being admitted as substantive evidence, would severely diminish our confidence in relying upon facially valid documents in court files.

Id.

11

"The court finally noted that it was concerned with public perception of the police and fashioned a *per se* rule against such tactics stating that police-fabricated evidence 'has no place in our criminal justice system.' " *Id.* at 33-34. [Citation omitted.]

We agree with the approach of *Cayward* and "hold that the circumstances presented here—the fabrication of evidence by police to elicit a confession and admission of that evidence at trial—violates due process, and any resulting confession is *per se* inadmissable." *Id.* at 46.

"We hold that law enforcement and the public would best be served by a 'bright-line' rule precluding the use of police-fabricated evidence that later finds its way into the trial. Such 'bright-line' rules serve to protect the constitutional rights of suspects while providing a clear procedure for police to follow that should produce consistent results." *Id.* at 48.

"We recognize that the rule here invalidates a confession to a murder, yet on balance, the sanctity of our constitutional protections for all remains paramount. As a noted jurist observed: 'The quality of a nation's civilization can be largely measured by the methods it uses in the enforcement of its criminal law.' Walter V. Schaefer, *Federalism and State Criminal Procedure*, 70 Harv. L. Rev. 1, 26 (Nov. 1956) * * *. His cogent observation was echoed by the former Director of the Federal Bureau of Investigation who said:

> We can have the Constitution, the best laws in the land, and the most honest reviews by courts; but unless the law enforcement profession is steeped in the democratic tradition, maintains the highest in ethics, and makes its work a career of honor, civil liberties will continually—and without end—be violated. . . . The best protection of civil liberties is an alert, intelligent and honest law enforcement agency. There can be no alternative. [J. Edgar Hoover, Civil Liberties and Law Enforcement: The Role of the FBI, 37 Iowa L. Rev. 175, 177 (1952).]

Patton at 48-49.

"In sum, we hold that the use of police-fabricated evidence to induce a confession that is then used at trial to support the voluntariness of a confession is *per se* a violation of due process. We deem it in the same class and nature as [] physical coercion * * *. The trial judge erred in denying the motion to suppress." *Id.* at 49.

"We recognize that our decision barring the use of fabricated evidence effectively denies the right of the State to use defendant's confession to a murder. However, adherence to constitutional precepts cannot cease simply because the result is unfavorable to law enforcement * * *. There is a more significant principle at stake: due process." *Id.* at 53.

---

§1.2. THE ADVERSARY SYSTEM OF AMERICAN JURISPRUDENCE

The **Sixth Amendment** to the United States Constitution provides in pertinent part:

> In all criminal prosecutions, the accused shall enjoy the right to a speedy and public trial, by an impartial jury * * * and to be informed of the nature and cause of the accusation; to be confronted by the witnesses against him; to have compulsory process for obtaining witnesses in his favor, and to have the Assistance of Counsel for his defence.

The Constitution additionally commands that, "No person shall be * * * deprived of life, liberty, or property, without due process of law[,]" by either the federal or any state government.[10]

The constitutional provisions set forth above have been consistently interpreted by the courts as an express guarantee that criminal convictions in this country will be the product of an *adversarial process*, rather than the one-sided investigation and determination by the prosecutor or district attorney.[11] The American adversarial process, known also as the adversary system of American jurisprudence,[12] is grounded at the foundation of a system of criminal justice which is accusatorial in nature. It is accusatorial by virtue of the fact that once sufficient evidence exists, the government accuses an individual of a criminal offense and then bears the burden of proving the individual guilty of that offense.

§1.2(a). The "Presumption of Innocence" and the "Reasonable Doubt" Standard

The adversary system may be likened to a 1000-meter rowing race, wherein the defendant's boat is sitting on the water at the 700-meter mark. At the zero-meter mark we find the prosecution's boat standing ready to row. Once the signal is given, this "uneven" contest begins; and it is readily apparent that the prosecution has a heavy burden, not only at the start of the race, but throughout the contest. The prosecution must catch up with the defendant's boat, overtake it, and cross the finish line first. Here, the individual rowing the prosecution's boat has an extremely heavy burden from the outset of the contest and, as is evident, will maintain that heavy burden throughout the entire contest.

---

[10] *U.S.Const. amends.* V & XIV.

[11] *See e.g., Nix v. Williams*, 467 U.S. 431, 453, 104 *S.Ct.* 2501, 2514 (1984).

[12] The term "jurisprudence" is generally defined as the "science of law."

13

Such is the burden the prosecution has at a criminal trial. The prosecution has, and must maintain throughout the trial, the burden of proving the defendant guilty *beyond a reasonable doubt*. The uneven nature of the adversarial trial proceeding—the defendant's lead at the beginning of the contest—is premised upon an important assumption which constitutes the hallmark of the adversary system of American jurisprudence. This assumption, referred to by many as the *"presumption" of innocence,* provides that a criminal defendant *is presumed innocent until proven guilty beyond a reasonable doubt.* This principle describes the law's requirement that, in the absence of facts to the contrary, it is to be assumed that a person's conduct upon a given occasion was lawful. The "presumption of innocence" also reminds the jurors that they must eliminate from their minds all suspicion that arises from a defendant's arrest, indictment, arraignment, or continued custody, and to reach their conclusion solely from the legal evidence presented at trial.[13]

The prosecution is not required, however, to prove its case beyond all possible doubt or beyond a shadow of a doubt, or to a mathematical certainty; nor must it demonstrate the complete impossibility of innocence. On the other hand, reasonable doubt contemplates neither a "grave uncertainty" nor an "actual substantial doubt."[14] The type of doubt envisioned by the law may not be an imaginary or fanciful doubt invented by a juror for the purpose of avoiding an unpleasant verdict. As one court explained, "reasonable doubt"

> is not a mere possible doubt, because everything relating to human affairs, and depending on moral evidence, is open to some possible or imaginary doubt. It is that state of the case which, after the entire comparison and consideration of all the evidence, leaves the minds of the jurors in that condition that they cannot say they feel an abiding conviction, to a moral certainty, of the truth of the charge.[15]

Stated another way, "reasonable doubt" is not vague, nor is it speculative. At a minimum, a "reasonable doubt" is "one based upon 'reason.' "[16] It is that type of doubt which would cause persons of reasonable prudence to hesitate or refrain from acting upon matters

---

[13] *See generally Taylor v. Kentucky,* 436 *U.S.* 478, 485 (1978). *See also id.* at 483 ("The principle that there is a presumption of innocence in favor of the accused is the 'undoubted law, axiomatic and elementary, and its enforcement lies at the foundation of the administration of our criminal law.' ") (quoting *Coffin v. United States,* 156 *U.S.* 432, 453 (1895)); *Estelle v. Williams,* 425 *U.S.* 501 (1976).

[14] *Cage v. Louisiana,* 498 *U.S.* 39, 111 *S.Ct.* 328, 329 (1990).

[15] *Commonwealth v. Webster,* 59 *Mass.* (5 *Cush.*) 295, 320 (1850).

[16] *Jackson v. Virginia,* 443 *U.S.* 307, 317 (1979).

of importance to themselves.[17] The doubt must arise solely from the evidence or lack of evidence presented. If jurors have a reasonable doubt, they must enter a verdict of "not guilty."

As quoted in *United States v. Alston,*[18] and *United States v. Cummings,*[19] here are two forms of model jury instructions related to the "burden of proof," the "presumption of innocence," and "reasonable doubt":

Jury Instruction
BURDEN OF PROOF — PRESUMPTION OF INNOCENCE

Every defendant in a criminal case is presumed to be innocent. This presumption of innocence remains with the defendant throughout the trial unless and until he is proven guilty beyond a reasonable doubt. The burden is on the government to prove the defendant guilty beyond a reasonable doubt. This burden of proof never shifts throughout the trial. The law does not require a defendant to prove his innocence or to produce any evidence. Unless the government proves beyond a reasonable doubt that the defendant has committed every element of the offense with which he is charged, you must find him not guilty.

Jury Instruction
PRESUMPTION OF INNOCENCE — BURDEN OF PROOF —
REASONABLE DOUBT

The law presumes a defendant to be innocent of crime. Thus a defendant, although accused, begins the trial with a "clean slate"— with no evidence against him. And the law permits nothing but legal evidence presented before the jury to be considered in support of any charge against the accused. So the presumption of innocence alone is sufficient to acquit a defendant, unless the jurors are satisfied beyond a reasonable doubt of the defendant's guilt after careful and impartial consideration of all the evidence in the case. It is not required that the government prove guilt beyond all possible doubt. The test is one of reasonable doubt. A reasonable doubt is a doubt based upon reason and common sense—the kind of doubt that would make a reasonable person hesitate to act. Proof beyond a reasonable doubt must, therefore, be proof of such a convincing character that you would be willing to rely and act upon it unhesitatingly in the most important of your own affairs. The jury will remember that a defendant is never to be convicted on mere suspicion or conjecture. The burden is always upon the prosecution to prove guilt beyond a reasonable doubt. This burden never shifts to

---

[17] *Bishop v. United States,* 71 *App.D.C.* 132, 137-138, 107 *F.*2d 297, 303 (D.C.Cir. 1939). *See also Holland v. United States,* 348 *U.S.* 121, 140 (1954).

[18] 551 *F.*2d 315, 318-319 (D.C. Cir. 1976).

[19] 468 *F.*2d 274, 280 (9th Cir. 1972).

a defendant; for the law never imposes upon a defendant in a criminal case the burden or duty of calling any witnesses or producing any evidence. A reasonable doubt exists whenever, after careful and impartial consideration of all the evidence in the case, the jurors do not feel convinced to a moral certainty that a defendant is guilty of the charge. So, if the jury views the evidence in the case as reasonably permitting either of two conclusions—one of innocence, the other of guilt—the jury should of course adopt the conclusion of innocence.

IN RE WINSHIP
Supreme Court of the United States
397 *U.S.* 358, 90 *S.Ct.* 1068 (1970)

Mr. Justice BRENNAN delivered the opinion of the Court.

* * * * *

"This case presents the single, narrow question whether proof beyond a reasonable doubt is among the 'essentials of due process and fair treatment' required during the adjudicatory stage when a juvenile is charged with an act which would constitute a crime if committed by an adult. * * * [The defendant,] a 12-year-old boy, had entered a locker and stolen $112 from a woman's pocketbook." *Id.* at 1070.

"The requirement that guilt of a criminal charge be established by proof beyond a reasonable doubt dates at least from our early years as a Nation. The 'demand for a higher degree of persuasion in criminal cases was recurrently expressed from ancient times, [though] its crystallization into the formula "beyond a reasonable doubt" seems to have occurred as late as 1798. It is now accepted in common law jurisdictions as the measure of persuasion by which the prosecution must convince the trier of all the essential elements of guilt.' * * * Although virtually unanimous adherence to the reasonable-doubt standard in common law jurisdictions may not conclusively establish it as a requirement of due process, such adherence does 'reflect a profound judgment about the way in which law should be enforced and justice administered.'" *Id.* at 1071. [Citations omitted.]

"[I]t has long been established that proof of a criminal charge beyond a reasonable doubt is constitutionally required. * * * Mr. Justice Frankfurter stated that '[i]t is the duty of the Government to establish * * * guilt beyond a reasonable doubt. This notion—basic in our law and rightly one of the boasts of a free society—is a requirement and a safeguard of due process of law in the historic, procedural content of "due process."' * * * In a similar vein, [this Court has said] that '[g]uilt in a criminal case must be proved beyond a reasonable doubt and by evidence confined to that which long experience in the common-law tradition, to some extent embodied in the Constitution, has crystallized into rules of evidence consistent with that standard. These rules are historically grounded rights of our system, developed to safeguard men from dubious and unjust convictions, with resulting forfeitures of life, liberty and property.' " *Id.* at 1071-72. [Citations omitted.]

"The reasonable-doubt standard plays a vital role in the American scheme of criminal procedure. It is a prime instrument for reducing the risk of convictions resting on factual error. The standard provides concrete substance for the presumption of innocence—that bedrock 'axiomatic and elementary' principle whose 'enforcement lies at the foundation of the administration of our criminal law.' * * * '[A] person accused of a crime * * * would be at a severe disadvantage, a disadvantage amounting to a lack of fundamental fairness, if he could be adjudged guilty and imprisoned for years on the strength of the same evidence as would suffice in a civil case.' " *Id.* at 1072. [Citations omitted.]

"The requirement of proof beyond a reasonable doubt has this vital role in our criminal procedure for cogent reasons. The accused during a criminal prosecution has at stake interests of immense importance, both because of the possibility that he may lose his liberty upon conviction and because of the certainty that he would be stigmatized by the conviction. Accordingly, a society that values the good name and freedom of every individual should not condemn a man for commission of a crime when there is reasonable doubt about his guilt." *Id.*

"Moreover, use of the reasonable doubt standard is indispensable to command the respect and confidence of the community in applications of the criminal law. It is critical that the moral force of the criminal law not be diluted by a standard of proof that leaves people in doubt whether innocent men are being condemned. It is also important in our free society that every individual going about his ordinary affairs have confidence that his government cannot adjudge him guilty of a criminal offense without convincing a proper fact-finder of his guilt with utmost certainty." *Id.* at 1072-73.

"Lest there remain any doubt about the constitutional stature of the reasonable-doubt standard, we explicitly hold that the Due Process Clause protects the accused against conviction except upon proof beyond a reasonable doubt of every fact necessary to constitute the crime with which he is charged." *Id.* at 1073.

"The same considerations that demand extreme caution in fact-finding to protect the innocent adult apply as well to the innocent child. * * * We therefore hold * * * 'that where a 12-year-old child is charged with an act of stealing * * * the case against him must be proved beyond a reasonable doubt.' " *Id.* at 1073, 1075.

CHAMBERS v. MISSISSIPPI
Supreme Court of the United States
410 *U.S.* 284, 93 *S.Ct.* 1038 (1973)

Mr. Justice POWELL delivered the opinion of the Court.

* * * * *

"The right of an accused in a criminal trial to due process is, in essence, the right to a fair opportunity to defend against the State's accusations. The rights to confront and cross-examine witnesses and to call witnesses in one's own behalf have long been recognized as essential to due process. Mr. Justice Black, writing for the Court in In re Oliver, 333 U.S. 257, 273, 68 S.Ct. 499, 507 [] (1948), identified these rights as among the minimum essentials of a fair trial:

> A person's right to reasonable notice of a charge against him, and an opportunity to be heard in his defense—a right to his day in court—are basic in our system of jurisprudence; and these rights include, as a minimum, a right to examine the witnesses against him, to offer testimony, and to be represented by counsel."

Id. at 1045.

"[The right to challenge the State's evidence and t]he right of cross-examination [are] more than [] desirable rule[s] of trial procedure. [They are] implicit in the constitutional right of confrontation, and help [] assure the 'accuracy of the truth-determining process.' [They are] indeed, '[] essential and fundamental requirement[s] for the kind of fair trial which is this country's constitutional goal.'" *Id.* at 1046.[20] [Citations omitted.]

---

§1.3. BURDENS OF PROOF & PRODUCTION

It is clear from the preceding sections that in any criminal trial, the prosecution bears the burden of proving the guilt of the accused, that is, proving each essential element of the offense charged beyond a reasonable doubt. The burden of proof in this regard is also known as the "burden of persuasion." At no time does

---

[20] See also *California v. Green*, 399 *U.S.* 149, 90 *S.Ct.* 1930 (1970), where the Court explained that an accused's Right of Confrontation "(1) insures that the witness will give his statements under oath—thus impressing him with the seriousness of the matter and guarding against the lie by the possibility of a penalty for perjury; (2) forces the witness to submit to cross-examination, the 'greatest legal engine ever invented for the discovery of truth'; [and] (3) permits the jury that is to decide the defendant's fate to observe the demeanor of the witness in making his statement, thus aiding the jury in assessing his credibility." *Id.* at 158, 90 *S.Ct.* at 1935 (quoting 5 Wigmore § 1367).

the burden shift to the defendant to prove his or her innocence, or disprove any of the essential elements of the offense charged.[21]

The prosecution does not, however, bear the burden of disproving the existence of an affirmative defense (*e.g.*, self defense), unless and until there is some evidence supporting such a defense.[22] Thus, while the prosecution ultimately bears the burden of proof in a criminal trial, the defendant may, at times, bear the burden of production—the burden of going forward or presenting some evidence demonstrating the possible existence of such a defense. If the defendant meets his or her "burden of production," the burden then shifts to the prosecution to prove beyond a reasonable doubt the absence of the defense alleged.[23]

MULLANEY v. WILBUR
Supreme Court of the United States
421 U.S. 684, 95 S.Ct. 1881 (1975)

Mr. Justice POWELL delivered the opinion of the Court.

"The State of Maine requires a defendant charged with murder to prove that he acted 'in the heat of passion on sudden provocation' in order to reduce the homicide to manslaughter. We must decide whether this rule comports with the due process requirement, as defined in *In re Winship*, * * * that the prosecution prove beyond a reasonable doubt every fact necessary to constitute the crime charged." *Id.* 1882-83.

"The Maine law of homicide, as it bears on this case, can be stated succinctly: Absent justification or excuse, all intentional or criminally reckless killings are felonious homicides. Felonious homicide is punishable as murder—*i.e.*, by life imprisonment—unless the defendant proves by a fair preponderance of the evidence that it was committed in the heat of passion on sudden provocation, in which case it is punished as manslaughter—*i.e.*, by a fine not to exceed $1,000 or by imprisonment not to exceed 20 years. The issue is whether the Maine rule requiring the defendant to prove that he acted in the heat of passion on sudden provocation accords with due process." *Id.* at 1886.

---

[21] *See Martin v. Ohio*, 480 *U.S.* 228, 107 *S.Ct.* 1098 (1987); *Patterson v. New York*, 432 *U.S.* 197, 97 *S.Ct.* 2319 (1977).

[22] *See generally* 9 Wigmore, *Evidence* §§2501, 2502, 2514 (Chadbourn rev. 1981).

[23] *See United States v. Bailey*, 444 *U.S.* 394, 100 *S.Ct.* 624 (1980) (defendant bears burden of production respecting duress and necessity); *Rook v. Rice*, 783 *F.*2d 401 (4th Cir. 1986) (defendant bears burden of production respecting self-defense and heat of passion). *See also State v. Finn*, 257 *Minn.* 138, 100 *N.W.*2d 508 (1960) (insanity); *State v. Church*, 169 *N.W.*2d 889 (Iowa 1969) (intoxication).

"[At common law,] the early English authorities * * * held that once the prosecution proved that the accused had committed the homicide, it was 'incumbent upon the prisoner to make out, to the satisfaction of the court and jury' 'all . . . circumstances of justification, excuse, or alleviation.' * * * Thus, at common law the burden of proving heat of passion on sudden provocation appears to have rested on the defendant." *Id.* at 1887.

"In this country[, and particularly] in the past half century, the large majority of States have [abandoned the common law rule] and now require the prosecution to prove the absence of the heat of passion on sudden provocation beyond a reasonable doubt. * * * [Therefore,] the clear trend has been toward requiring the prosecution to bear the ultimate burden of proving this fact." Id. at 1888.

"[It is argued that] *Winship* should not be extended to the present case[; that] the absence of the heat of passion on sudden provocation is not a 'fact necessary to constitute the *crime*' of felonious homicide in Maine." *Id.* [Emphasis in original.]

"This analysis fails to recognize that the criminal law of Maine, like that of other jurisdictions, is concerned not only with guilt or innocence in the abstract but also with the degree of criminal culpability. Maine has chosen to distinguish those who kill in the heat of passion from those who kill in the absence of this factor. Because the former are less 'blameworth[y],' * * * they are subject to substantially less severe penalties. By drawing this distinction, while refusing to require the prosecution to establish beyond a reasonable doubt the fact upon which it turns, Maine denigrates the interests found critical in Winship." Id. at 1888-89. [Citation omitted.]

"*Winship* is concerned with substance rather than * * * formalism. The rationale of that case requires an analysis that looks to the 'operation and effect of the law as applied and enforced by the state,' * * * and to the interests of both the State and defendant as affected by the allocation of the burden of proof." *Id.* at 1890. [Citation omitted.]

"In *Winship* the Court emphasized the societal interests in the reliability of jury verdicts[.] * * * These interests are implicated to a greater degree in this case than they were in *Winship* itself[,] * * * [and] in one respect the protection afforded those interests is less here. In *Winship* the ultimate burden of persuasion remained with the prosecution, although the standard had been [unconstitutionally] reduced to proof by a fair preponderance of the evidence. In this case, by contrast, the State has affirmatively shifted the burden of proof to the defendant. The result, in a case such as this one where the defendant is required to prove the critical fact in dispute, is to increase further the likelihood of an erroneous murder conviction. Such a result directly contravenes the principle articulated in *Speiser v. Randall*, 357 *U.S.* 513, 525-526, 78 *S.Ct.* 1332, 1342 [] (1985):

[W]here one party has at stake an interest of transcending value—as a criminal defendant his liberty—th[e] margin of error is reduced as to him by the process of placing on the [prosecution] the burden . . . of persuading the factfinder at the conclusion of the trial[.]"

Mullaney at 1890-91.

"It has been suggested * * * that because of the difficulties in negating an argument that the homicide was committed in the heat of passion the burden of proving this fact should rest on the defendant. No doubt this is often a heavy burden for the prosecution to satisfy. The same may be said of the requirement of proof beyond a reasonable doubt of many controverted facts in a criminal trial. But this is the traditional burden which our system of criminal justice deems essential." *Id.* at 1891.

"[P]roving that the defendant did not act in the heat of passion on sudden provocation is similar to proving any other element of intent; it may be established by adducing evidence of the factual circumstances surrounding the commission of the homicide. And although intent is typically considered a fact peculiarly within the knowledge of the defendant, this does not, as the Court has long recognized, justify shifting the burden to him " *Id.*

"Nor is the requirement of proving a negative unique in our system of criminal jurisprudence. Maine itself requires the prosecution to prove the absence of self-defense beyond a reasonable doubt. * * * Satisfying this burden imposes an obligation that, in all practical effect, is identical to the burden involved in negating the heat of passion on sudden provocation. Thus, we discern no unique hardship on the prosecution that would justify requiring the defendant to carry the burden of proving a fact so critical to criminal culpability." *Id.*

"Maine law requires a defendant to establish by a preponderance of the evidence that he acted in the heat of passion on sudden provocation in order to reduce murder to manslaughter. Under this burden of proof a defendant can be given a life sentence when the evidence indicates that it is *as likely as not* that he deserves a significantly lesser sentence. This is an intolerable result in a society where, to paraphrase Mr. Justice Harlan, it is far worse to sentence one guilty only of manslaughter as a murderer than to sentence a murderer for the lesser crime of manslaughter. * * * We therefore hold that the Due Process Clause requires the prosecution to prove beyond a reasonable doubt the absence of the heat of passion on sudden provocation when the issue is properly presented in a homicide case." *Id.* at 1892. [Citation omitted; emphasis in original.]

Chapter 2

THE
FORMS OF EVIDENCE

§2.1. GENERAL CONSIDERATIONS

There are a countless number of items which may be offered as evidence in a formal legal proceeding, and no list could ever be all-inclusive. It is useful, however, not only in a legal sense but in a practical sense, to categorize items of evidence into four forms: (1) Real Evidence (the actual physical, tangible objects themselves); (2) Documentary Evidence (writings); (3) Demonstrative Evidence (exhibits); and (4) Testimonial Evidence (oral testimony given by a witness at a formal proceeding). While some texts list a fifth form—"tangible-testimonial" evidence, to cover hybrids such as a deposition or a court transcript of a witness' prior testimony—this form nonetheless may be considered a special form of documentary evidence, for it certainly documents or memorializes prior testimony for use at a subsequent proceeding.

---

§2.2. REAL EVIDENCE

Real evidence (also called physical evidence) consists of the actual physical or tangible item which had some role in, or connection to, the crime or incident. It may be produced in court and seen or examined by the trier of fact (judge or jury). It is not a representation, reproduction or recreation; it is the "real thing." In a criminal case, real evidence may include physical, concrete objects and traces found at crime scenes, on the person or clothing of suspects, victims or witnesses, or at any other location so long as the physical object or trace item is in some way connected to the commission of the offense or any other relevant consideration relating to the offense.[1] In a "real" sense, whenever a human being comes into contact with a particular place or another human being, *something* is always left and *something* is always taken. It is up to the crime-scene investigator to find out what that "something" is.

---

[1] *See Commonwealth v. Ballem*, 386 *Pa.* 20, 26-27, 123 *A.2d* 728, 732 (1959), *cert. denied*, 352 *U.S.* 932, 77 *S.Ct.* 235 (1956) ("Pistols, fruits of the crime, clothing, parts of the body of the person killed, everything pertaining to the crime which will aid the jury in its consideration of the (alleged) crime and the guilt or innocence of the accused, is admissible.").

By way of example, explosives, guns and ammunition, poisons, knives, clubs, razor blades and other weapons or instrumentalities connected to the commission of the offense, along with dust, debris, hairs, fibers, glass or wood fragments, paint chips, and the like, may be considered real evidence. Also included within the category of real evidence are fingerprints, palmprints, footprints, tire marks, tool impressions, accelerants, blood, saliva, semen stains, bite marks, and similar traces left at crime scenes, on victims or on suspects.

Closely connected to the subject of real evidence are the principles surrounding the "chain of custody" of real evidence, and three additional concepts which have become common currency in this subject area: (a) the "instrumentality of the crime," (b) the "fruits of the crime," and (c) "contraband." Moreover, closely intertwined with the question of admissibility of real evidence is the issue of "prejudicial impact versus probative value."

---

§2.2(a). Chain of Custody

The evidentiary "chain of custody" may be defined as the testimonial and documentary link which establishes the authenticity of real or physical evidence. It proves that the physical item of evidence offered in court has a rational connection to the case by establishing (a) that it is the same item which was seized and taken into custody at the time of its initial discovery, and (b) that it is in the same or substantially the same condition as when found.[2] The custodial chain must demonstrate a *continuity of possession* sufficient to eliminate any suggestion that the item of real evidence offered at court is not the original or, if it is, has not in any way been tampered with or otherwise compromised. As one court put it, "where the incriminating object has passed out of the possession of the original receiver and into the possession of others, the 'chain of possession' must be established to avoid any inference that there has been substitution or tampering."[3] This is especially true where

---

[2] Courts have, however, held admissible weapons found at the crime scene notwithstanding the fact that no witness can positively identify the weapon as the instrument of the crime. For example, in *Commonwealth v. Ford*, 451 *Pa.* 81, 301 *A.*2d 856 (1973), the knife used to stab the victim to death had been washed and put away in the kitchen. At trial, a 12-inch kitchen knife was admitted in evidence even though no witness could identify it as the actual murder weapon. The Court ruled, "Weapons, instruments and articles found in the possession of the accused at the time of his arrest, although not identified as those actually used, but similar thereto, or which from the circumstances of the finding, justify an inference of the likelihood of their having been used, are admissible." *Id.* at 85, 301 *A.*2d at 857-58. *See also Nelson v. United States*, 601 *A.*2d 582, 597 (D.C.App. 1991) (victim's inability to identify the precise knife used in the assault "affected only its evidentiary weight, not its admissibility").

[3] *State v. Brown*, 99 *N.J.Super.* 22, 27, 238 *A.*2d 482 (App.Div. 1968).

the contested evidence is fungible, and not readily distinguishable by a unique feature or other identifying mark.[4]

Before a court will allow an item of real evidence to be received "in evidence," the party offering it must show that *the item is what it purports to be*. This requirement, considered by the courts to be an "inherent logical necessity," demonstrates the legal relationship of the evidence to the case.[5] It is also considered to be a legal necessity because of the human tendency to accord great weight to physical items of evidence.

"While the proper foundation for the admission of such real evidence requires a showing of an *uninterrupted chain of possession*, it is not necessary for the party introducing such evidence to negate every possibility of substitution or change in condition between the event and the time of trial[.]"[6] Rather, the question for the court will always be whether there exists a "reasonable probability" that "no tampering has occurred," that is, a "reasonable probability" that the evidence is "in substantially the same condition" as when it was collected.[7] Whether or not the chain of custody has been sufficiently demonstrated is a matter which is left to the sound discretion of the trial judge.

To ensure the sufficiency of the chain of custody, along with the proper identification of the physical item of evidence in court, law enforcement officials should strictly adhere to standard operating procedures relating to the collection and identification of physical evidence. In this respect, the time and date of the discovery of the item of evidence, along with a precise description of where and by whom it was located should be carefully documented. Moreover, the item itself (or its container when necessary) should be properly marked, labeled or tagged to permit easy identification many months later in court. This marking should occur the moment the item is taken into custody or as soon thereafter as is reasonably possible. In addition, if the particular item is turned over to another official for safekeeping or delivery to the station, the evidence

---

[4] *See State v. Woitkowski*, 136 *N.H.* 134, 136, 612 *A.2d* 1317, 1318 (1992) ("Generally, drug evidence is fungible," and its authentication requires "a testimonial tracing of the item's 'chain of custody' * * *.").

[5] *Brown* at 27.

[6] *Id*. (emphasis added).

[7] *Id*. at 28. *See also United States v. Abreu*, 952 *F.2d* 1458, 1467 (1st Cir. 1992); *United States v. Howard-Arias*, 679 *F.2d* 363, 366 (4th Cir. 1982) ("precision in developing the 'chain of custody' is not an ironclad requirement, and the fact of a missing link does not prevent the admission of real evidence"); *United States v. Ortiz*, 966 *F.2d* 707, 716 (1st Cir. 1992) (gaps in the chain of custody affect only the weight to be accorded the evidence); *State v. Greene*, 209 *Conn*. 458, 479, 551 *A.2d* 1231 (1988) (State's burden is satisfied by showing there is a reasonable probability that the item has not been changed in any important respect.); *State v. Moscillo*, 649 *A.2d* 57, 59 (*N.H.* 1994) (State need only establish the chain of custody "with sufficient completeness as to render it reasonably improbable that the original item has been tampered with.").

lockup, or some other place, this transfer must be meticulously documented, and, at the very least, such documentation should contain the place, date and time of the transfer, the identity of the persons involved in the transfer and the exact location where the evidence was stored after transfer. *In all cases, the number of individuals who handle or control the physical evidence should be kept to a minimum.*

EX PARTE HOLTON
Supreme Court of Alabama
590 *So.*2d 918 (1991)

INGRAM, Justice.

Danny Ray Holton was convicted of selling cocaine and was sentenced to 21 years in prison. In this appeal, he claims that the State failed to sufficiently prove the chain of custody of the cocaine allegedly sold by him to Alcoholic Beverage Control Board Officer Yvonne Bedgood.

"At trial, the State presented the following testimony: Bedgood testified that she had received the cocaine from Holton. She testified that she put the cocaine into a plastic bag, which, she said, she put into an envelope. She testified that she sealed the envelope and put her initials on it and then turned the envelope over to Governor Jackson, a narcotics investigator with the Dothan Police Department. Jackson testified that he put tape over the seams of the envelope and that he also initialed the envelope. He further testified that he put the envelope in the police locker, to which only he had access. He testified that he later gave the envelope to Ray Owens, a Dothan police officer, to transport to the forensic laboratory. He stated that the envelope was in the same condition when he gave it to Owens as it was when he placed it in the locker." *Id.* at 919.

"The next person to testify was Joe Saloom, the director of the forensic laboratory in Enterprise. He testified that he had received the item from Owens and that when he received the envelope, it was sealed. Owens did not testify." *Id.*

"Holton argues that Owens's testimony is an essential link in the State's chain of custody and that, without such testimony, the cocaine was inadmissible. The State contends that the lack of testimony from Owens merely 'weakens' the chain and creates a question of credibility, rather than one of admissibility. * * * This opinion sets forth an analysis to be followed in deciding whether a proper chain of custody has been shown." *Id.*

As a general matter, "the State must establish a chain of custody without breaks in order to lay a sufficient predicate for admission of evidence. * * * Proof of this unbroken chain of custody is required in order to establish sufficient identification of the item and continuity of possession, so as to assure the authenticity of the item. In order to establish a proper chain, the State must show to a 'reasonable probability that the object is in the same condition as, and not substantially different from, its condition at the commencement of the chain.' " *Id.* at 919-20. [Citation omitted.] "Because the proponent of the item of demonstrative evidence has the burden of showing this reasonable probability, we require that the proof be shown on the record with regard to the various elements discussed below." *Id.* at 920.

"The chain of custody is composed of 'links.' A 'link' is anyone who handled the item. The State must identify each link from the time the item was seized. In order to show a proper chain of custody, the record must show each link and also the following with regard to each link's possession of the item: '(1) the receipt of the item; (2) the ultimate disposition of the item, *i.e.*, transfer, destruction, or retention; and (3) the safeguarding and handling of the item between receipt and disposition.' " *Id.* [Citation and internal marks omitted.]

"If the State, or any other proponent of demonstrative evidence, fails to identify a link or fails to show for the record any one of the three criteria as to each link, the result is a 'missing' link, and the item is inadmissible. If, however, the State has shown each link and has shown all three criteria as to each link, but has done so with circumstantial evidence, as opposed to the direct testimony of the 'link,' as to one or more criteria or as to one or more links, the result is a 'weak' link. When the link is 'weak,' a question of credibility and weight is presented, not one of admissibility." *Id.*

"In this case, Owens failed to testify as to his action regarding the envelope. However, the record reflects his receipt of the item; he received the item from Jackson, who testified that he had given the envelope to Owens. Also, Owens's ultimate disposition of the item appears in the record through the testimony of Saloom, who testified that he received the item from Owens. Therefore, the only criterion left to analyze is the handling and safeguarding by Owens." *Id.*

"Again, Owens did not testify; thus, there is no direct evidence of his handling of the item. However, both Jackson and Saloom testified that the envelope was sealed when given to and when taken from Owens. A sealed envelope was adequate circumstantial evidence to establish the handling and safeguarding of the item by Owens to treat the item as authenticated. Although the lack of Owens's direct testimony 'weakens' the chain, the testimony of Jackson and Saloom prevented a break in the chain. The cocaine was properly admitted by the trial court, and the jury could decide how much weight to give the evidence, given the lack of direct testimony from Owens." *Id.*

"Circumstantial evidence is generally sufficient to authenticate the item sought to be entered into evidence, except when there appears to be evidence that the item of evidence was tampered with or that a substitution was made while the item was in the custody of the link who has failed to appear and testify." *Id.*

"In this case, there is no suggestion that Owens tampered with or made a substitution as to the item he was to deliver. Thus, we hold that as to the envelope containing the cocaine the State established a chain of custody sufficient to authenticate that item." *Id.*

TURNEY v. UNITED STATES
District of Columbia Court of Appeals
626 A.2d 872 (1993)

ROGERS, Chief Judge.
[Defendant Reginald Turney appeals his conviction of possession of cocaine. He argues that the trial court should have granted his motion for judgment of acquittal because the government failed to prove beyond a reasonable doubt that the drugs admitted in evidence at trial were the same drugs recovered from him at the time of his arrest.] "The crux of [defendant's] contention is that, because the prosecutor only asked each of the police officers who handled the drugs whether the exhibit was 'the same or similar to' the drugs recovered by the same police from [defendant] on [the day of the crime,] the evidence was insufficient to sustain his conviction for possession of cocaine on that date." *Id.* at 873. *This Court disagrees with defendant's contention.*

"Because drugs are fungible, the government was required to prove that the material seized from [defendant] by the police and thought to be illegal drugs was the same material analyzed by the chemist and found to be cocaine. *See generally* Thomas A. Mauet, FUNDAMENTALS OF TRIAL TECHNIQUES 186-87 (1980) ("Where an object cannot be uniquely identified through the senses, a chain of custody must be established to demonstrate that it is the same object that was previously found."). Typically, this is accomplished by having a police officer identify his or her initials on the envelope into which he or she has placed the material obtained from the seizing officer or other officer on the scene. *See e.g., Tompkins v. United States,* 272 A.2d 100, 103 (D.C. 1970) (envelope containing syringe with heroin traces identified through testimony by expert witness that his signature and signature of officer who received the item from another officer who found item at scene were on the envelope; envelope was inside of heat-sealed envelope); *United States v. Santiago,* 534 F.2d 768, 769-70 (7th Cir. 1976) (chain sufficiently established where agent testified that he affixed seal with his name on it to envelope containing drugs and placed the envelope in safe)." *Turney* at 873-74.

"In [this] case, the prosecutor did not follow this procedure. Although it was clear that there was a signature on the heat-sealed envelope, the prosecutor did not ask Officer Hassen, who performed a field test on the drugs, whether his initials or signature appeared on the heat-sealed envelope into which he testified he placed the drugs. Instead, the prosecutor asked Officer Hassen (and every other officer who handled the drugs) whether or not the drugs in the envelope were 'the same or similar' to the drugs he had received from Officer Norris, who in turn had received them from Officer Rivera, who found the drugs in [defendant's] clothing." *Id.* at 874.

"Nevertheless, the government maintains that it met its burden to prove the chain of custody by having the three officers who handled the drugs each testify as to whom he received them from and passed them to, accounting for the drugs up until the time they were placed in the heat-sealed envelope and secured for analysis by the chemist. Thus, Officer Rivera testified that he handed the drugs to Officer Norris, who testified that he radioed a request for a field test. Officer Hassen testified that he responded to this call and received the drugs from Officer Norris. After testing the drugs, Hassen took them to the police station where he prepared the evidence envelope, filled out the necessary paperwork, and placed the drugs in the heat-sealed envelope.* During direct examination, the prosecutor held up a clear plastic bag containing a white rock substance and asked each of the officers if it looked 'the same or similar' to the bag that Officer Rivera recovered from [defendant]. Each officer replied that it did." *Id.*

"Although better practice would suggest that at trial the government use the signature-initial identification procedure that the police routinely follow, as in *Tompkins, supra,* 272 A.2d at 103, we agree that the government presented sufficient evidence to establish the chain of custody of the drugs. Each officer who handled the drugs recovered from [defendant] testified about his handling of them. No link in the chain was missing. *See Ford v. United States,* 396 A.2d 191, 194-95 (D.C. 1978) (when physical evidence is in control of government, a presumption arises that it has been handled properly); *Rosser v. United States,* 313 A.2d 876, 880 (D.C. 1974) (once the government has established an 'unbroken chain of custody as a matter of reasonable probability,' defendant must present evidence of tampering) * * *.

"Consequently, it was up to [defendant] to rebut the presumption, established at the close of the government's case in chief, that the government had established an unbroken chain of custody by showing that the drugs had been tampered with or that the drugs

---

*Defendant has not challenged the custody of the drugs after they were placed inside the heat-sealed envelope.

allegedly seized from [defendant] were indistinguishable from other exhibits of illegal drugs handled by the officers on the same day and that, hence, there was a defect in a link in the chain. * * * [Defendant] did not do this. Indeed, the only testimony on whether the drugs had been tampered with was the government's expert testimony that the drugs had been handled in accordance with the chain of custody Get rid of this or procedures of the Metropolitan Police Department." *Id.* at 874.

"Accordingly, we affirm the judgment of conviction." *Id.* at 875.

NOTE

In *In re D.S.*, 747 A.2d 1182 (D.C. App. 2000), D.S., a juvenile, was adjudicated delinquent for the possession of a prohibited weapon, a sawed-off shotgun, and possession of an unregistered firearm. In the appeal following his adjudication of delinquency, D.S. argued that the prosecution failed to demonstrate that the shotgun admitted into evidence was the one taken from him on the night in question. In rejecting this contention, the court explained:

> A chain of custody for real evidence must be established if: (1) the item is not readily identifiable; (2) the item is readily identifiable but the witness neglected to note the characteristics that make the item readily identifiable; or (3) the item is susceptible to alteration by tampering or contamination. * * * One way that chain of custody can be shown is by having a police officer initial the evidence. * * * [It should be] noted that evidence of a break in the chain of custody affects only the weight to be given to that evidence by the factfinder.

Id. at 1187.

> In this case, Officer Key testified that the weapon admitted into evidence at trial was the weapon that they recovered from D.S. the night he was placed under arrest. Officer Mable likewise identified the weapon as the one Officer Key had taken from D.S. Officer Mable further testified that he had scratched his initials onto the gun and placed it in a locker at the Seventh District station house. D.S. argues that there is a break in the chain of custody because it is unclear when Officer Mable's initials were scratched onto the gun. Even assuming this to be true, as stated above, evidence of a break in custody only affects the weight to be given to the evidence. This court has stated that when physical evidence is in the hands of government the presumption arises that it has been properly handled. * * * [Moreover,] once the government has established an

"unbroken chain of custody as a matter of reasonable probability," defendant must present evidence of tampering. * * * D.S. failed to rebut this presumption * * *.

Id. at 1187-88.

---

§2.2(b). Instrumentality of the Crime
The "instrumentality of the crime" is the criminal's "tool of the trade," and consists of any object or implement used to effectuate the commission of the offense. For example, in an aggravated assault, the instrumentality of the crime might be a gun, knife, baseball bat, or other weapon; in a burglary, it might be a crowbar or other burglar tool; in an auto theft, it might be a lock-jock; in a bank robbery it might be a machine gun; and so on.

---

§2.2(c). Fruits of the Crime
The "fruits of the crime" are the criminal's "bounty," and consist of the proceeds of the criminal act. Examples might include a stereo stolen in a burglary, money received from the sale of narcotics or stolen goods, a shoplifted candy bar, or the money stolen during the course of a bank robbery.

---

§2.2(d). Contraband
The term "contraband" encompasses all of those items which are unlawful to possess in and of themselves. Anything which, under the law, is unlawful to possess under any circumstances is contraband. Thus, controlled dangerous substances such as cocaine, heroin, L.S.D., etc., may be considered contraband. Contraband may also incorporate such weapons as sawed-off shotguns, hand grenades, machine guns, switchblade knives, and so on.

To bring all the concepts together, consider the case of a robber entering the First National Bank, threatening the bank tellers with a machine gun, and then stealing $50,000 in cash. The money stolen would represent the "fruit of the crime." The machine gun would be considered the "instrumentality of the crime"; it would also be "contraband."

---

§2.2(e). The Significance and Usefulness of Real or Physical Evidence

The significance and usefulness of any particular type of real or physical evidence will vary from case to case, depending on the material elements of the crime under investigation and the necessary proofs for prosecution.

For example, a suspect's fingerprint at a crime scene can be a very significant piece of physical evidence used to establish his presence at the scene. In fact, a single fingerprint under certain circumstances can stand alone to establish "probable cause" for an arrest or "proof beyond a reasonable doubt" for a conviction. Conversely, if the suspect had "innocent access" to the crime scene (a legitimate right to be there), the presence of his fingerprints at the scene may have no significance. Thus, although the history and origin of a piece of physical evidence may be established from a scientific examination, the key to its usefulness may only be uncovered through the testimony of the victim or witness.*

To determine the significance and usefulness of a given item of real or physical evidence, the item should be examined as to its class and individual characteristics. In this regard, the potential value of an item of real or physical evidence lies in the investigator's ability to establish a connection between the evidence and a suspect, victim, the crime scene, or a material element of the crime.

Class characteristics

Aspects or features of physical evidence that are common to a group of objects or persons are termed "class characteristics." For example, examination of a shoeprint left at the scene of a crime might establish the brand name of the shoe from the inscription located on the shoe's heel. The evidence reveals that whoever left the print wears, for example Bostonian shoes, or Florsheim shoes. This is a class characteristic. As such, the evidence may only be placed in a broad category or class; an individual identification cannot be made because of the possibility of more than one source for the evidence. Clearly, the greater number of class characteristics that can be associated with the item of evidence, the smaller the class or possible range of sources exist. Examples of this type of evidence include automobiles identified only by make, model or color, shoeprints in cases where microscopic or unique markings are insufficient for individual identification, glass fragments too small to be matched to broken edges, and unremarkable, non-distinct tool marks.

---

*Mauriello, *Criminal Investigation Handbook: Strategy, Law and Science*, at 10-7 (Matthew Bender 2004).

Individual characteristics

Aspects of an item of physical evidence that identifies its source with a high degree of probability is termed "individual characteristics." The unique ability to establish individuality—to provide a nexus to a particular person or source—distinguishes this type of physical evidence from that possessing only class characteristics. Individual characteristics make an object different from all others within its class, identifying it as unique to the exclusion of all others. Some examples of evidence with individual characteristics include DNA, fingerprints, palm prints and footprints. In addition, upon closer examination, individual characteristics may come to light from uniquely worn or damaged shoeprints, spent ammunition, toolmarks, tire tracks, teeth marks, handwriting, etc.

While physical evidence that allows for individualization is of more value than that offering only class characteristics, the latter type is still important to the prosecution. A substantial amount of class-characteristic evidence tying a suspect, weapon or tool in the suspect's possession to the crime enhances the government's case. In addition, class characteristic evidence may be of such an unusual nature that its value nears that of individual-characteristic evidence. Finally, class-characteristic evidence can also be useful in excluding a particular person from a list of suspects.

---

§2.2(f). Negative Evidence

There are many cases in which the *absence of evidence*—negative evidence—can be just as compelling as real evidence. For example, when an officer engages in a crime-scene search or an area search for the purpose of locating possible suspects or physical objects, the officer is gathering evidence. If the search is productive, whatever the officer finds—the positive or real evidence—will most certainly be reported and documented. If the search is not productive, however, whatever the officer does *not* find—the "negative evidence"—should also be reported and documented. At trial, testimony related to this *negative* evidence may assist the prosecution by serving to counter defenses raised by the accused. In this respect, consider the case where a defendant, charged with murder, raises the defense of "self-defense," alleging that the victim provoked the attack with a weapon, but discarded the weapon *before* the police arrived. If the prosecution can present testimony from those officers who responded to, and searched, the area of the crime, and such testimony establishes not only that the immediate area of the crime scene was thoroughly searched but also an area beyond the crime scene, covering a distance beyond which the victim could have possibly thrown a weapon, the defendant will naturally have a very difficult time establishing self-defense.

§2.2(g). Prejudicial Impact Versus Probative Value

In most cases, properly collected, preserved and authenticated real evidence is admissible in court. If, however, the nature of the evidence is inflammatory, that is, its introduction in evidence would create a substantial risk of unfair prejudice to the defendant, it may be excluded. In such a case, courts must determine whether a likelihood exists that the item of real evidence will arouse the jury's prejudice, hostility or sympathy for one side without regard to the probative value of the evidence. Once the court concludes that the probative value of an item of real evidence outweighs its prejudicial impact, the evidence will be admitted.[8]

PEOPLE v. JENNINGS
Supreme Court of Illinois
252 Ill. 534, 96 N.E. 1077 (1911)

The opinion of the Court was delivered by

CARTER, C.J.

[Defendant, Thomas Jennings, was found guilty of the murder of Clarence Hiller, and was sentenced to death. At the time of the murder, Mr. Hiller lived with his wife and four children in a two-story frame house on West 104th Street in Chicago. The evidence established that on the night in question, defendant broke into the Hiller residence at about 2:25 a.m., and after a confrontation with Mr. Hiller, shot Mr. Hiller twice. Hiller died a few moments later. The investigation uncovered that a short time before the murder, the Hiller's residence had been painted; that the back porch was the last part of the house that was painted; and that entry by the intruder was gained through a rear window of the kitchen. Near the window was the porch, the freshly painted railing of which the intruder leaned on to facilitate entry. On the railing in the fresh paint, police discovered the imprint of four fingers of a person's left hand. Thereafter, officials from the Chicago Police Identification Bureau removed the railing and made enlarged photographs of the prints. At trial, four witnesses testified, over the objection of defendant's counsel, that in their opinion the prints on the railing matched the prints taken from defendant's fingers.]

Defendant argues that "the evidence as to the comparison of the photographs of the finger marks on the railing with the enlarged finger prints of [defendant] * * * is not admissible under the common-law rules of evidence, and as there is no statute in this state authorizing it, the court should have refused to permit its introduction." *Id.* at 1081.

---

[8] *See Fed.R.Evid.* 403 (Relevant evidence "may be excluded if its probative value is substantially outweighed by the danger of unfair prejudice * * *.").

"While the courts of this country do not appear to have had occasion to pass on the question, standard authorities on scientific subjects discuss the use of finger prints as a system of identification, concluding that experience has shown it to be reliable. * * * These authorities state that this system of identification is of very ancient origin, having been used in Egypt when the impression of the monarch's thumb was used as his sign manual, that it has been used in the courts of India for many years and more recently in the courts of several European countries; that in recent years its use has become very general by the police departments of the large cities of this country and Europe; that the great success of the system in England, where it has been used since 1891 in thousands of cases without error, caused the sending of an investigating commission from the United States, on whose favorable report a bureau was established by the United States government in the war and other departments." *Id.* at 1081-82.

"Four witnesses testified for the state as to the finger prints. [Each of the witnesses had extensive education and experience with the subject of finger print identification.] All of these witnesses testified * * * as to the basis of the system and the various markings found on the human hand, stating that they were classified from the various forms of markings, including those known as 'arches,' 'loops,' 'whorls' and 'deltas.' " *Id.* at 1082.

"We * * * hold from the evidence of the four witnesses who testified, and from the writings we have referred to on this subject, that there is a scientific basis for the system of finger print identification, and that the courts are justified in admitting this class of evidence; that this method of identification is in such general and common use that the courts cannot refuse to take judicial cognizance of it. Such evidence may or may not be of independent strength, but it is admissible, the same as other proof, as tending to make out a case." *Id.*

[Defendant also argued that it was unnecessary, and therefore improper, to admit "expert" testimony on the subject of finger print identification.]

"Expert testimony is admissible when the subject matter of the inquiry is of such a character that only persons of skill and experience in it are capable of forming a correct judgment as to any facts connected therewith. * * * [W]here[, however,] the court or jury can make their own deductions[, expert testimony will not be permitted.]" *Id.* at 1082.

"[T]he classification of finger print impressions and their method of identification is a science requiring study. While some of the reasons which guide an expert to his conclusions are such as may be weighed by any intelligent person with good eyesight from such exhibits as we have here in the record, after being pointed out to him by one versed in the study of finger prints, the evidence in question does not come within the common experience of all men of common education in the ordinary walks of life, and therefore the court and jury were properly aided by witnesses of peculiar and special experience on this subject." *Id.* at 1082-83.

NOTE

1. *People v. Jennings* is one of the nation's first reported appellate cases on the subject of fingerprint identification evidence.

2. The scientific basis of fingerprint identification evidence is the uniqueness of the fingerprint. The likelihood of two people having the same fingerprints is about as low as 1 out of 10^{60} (10 followed by 60 zeros). Ingraham and Mauriello, *Police Investigation Handbook* §10.05[1] (Matthew Bender 1992). "Add the additional odds of having two people with the same fingerprint at the same place and time and with the ability to commit the same crime, and it becomes clear that fingerprints are a unique form of personal identification." *Id.*

3. *Convictions resting solely on fingerprint evidence.* Generally, "a conviction may be based solely upon fingerprint evidence as long as the attendant circumstances establish that the object was generally inaccessible to the defendant and, thus, a jury could rationally find beyond a reasonable doubt such object had been touched during the commission of the crime." *State v. Watson,* 224 *N.J.Super.* 354, 361, 540 *A.*2d 875 (App.Div. 1988). A majority of jurisdictions follow the rule that "proof of an accused's fingerprints found in a place where a crime was committed under such circumstances that they could only have been imprinted at the time of the offense is sufficient proof of identity * * * to sustain a conviction." *Id.* at 359. *See also State v. Carter,* 118 *Ariz.* 562, 578 *P.*2d 991 (1978); *State v. Thorpe,* 188 *Conn.* 645, 453 *A.*2d 88 (1982); *State v. Pryor,* 306 *So.*2d 675 (La. 1975); *Commonwealth v. LaCorte,* 373 *Mass.* 700, 369 *N.E.*2d (1977); *State v. Ouellette,* 125 *N.H.* 602, 484 *A.*2d 1148 (1984); *Ricks v. Commonwealth,* 218 *Va.* 523, 237 *S.E.*2d 810 (1977).

Courts disagree, however, over the amount or quality of evidence which is necessary to prove that the fingerprints were impressed at the time of the crime. Some jurisdictions require the State to exclude every other reasonable hypothesis other than that the defendant's fingerprints were imprinted at the time of the offense. *See e.g., Solis v. People,* 175 *Colo.* 127, 485 *P.*2d 903 (1971); *Musgrove v. State,* 3 *Md.App.* 54, 237 *A.*2d 804 (1968). Other jurisdictions require that the prosecution prove only that the object upon which the fingerprints were found was generally inaccessible to the defendant and, as a result, were probably touched during the commission of the crime. *See e.g., United States v. Lonsdale,* 577 *F.*2d 923, 927 (5th Cir. 1978); *United States v. Jones,* 433 *F.*2d 1107, 1108-09 n.10 (D.C.Cir. 1970); *State v. Carter,* 118 *Ariz.* 562, 563, 578 *P.*2d 991, 992 (1978).

---

§2.3. DOCUMENTARY EVIDENCE

Documentary evidence is similar to real evidence in the sense that the item may be a physical or tangible object which can be seen or examined by the trier of fact. In most cases, however, it does not constitute the *actual* or real item of evidence. Rather, this type of evidence represents, depicts, portrays, or *documents* a particular physical or tangible item's existence or appearance at a relevant time. Additionally, documentary evidence may be used as a memorialization of certain events, actions, procedures or prior testimony. Examples may include photographs, computer print-outs, police reports, laboratory reports, medical reports, x-ray photographs, written statements, video or audio recordings, depositions, court transcripts, and the like.

STATE v. DRIVER
Supreme Court of New Jersey
38 *N.J.* 255, 183 *A.*2d 655 (1962)

The opinion of the Court was delivered by

FRANCIS, J.

* * * * *

"Some questions have been raised as to the admissibility in general of sound recordings." * * *

"At the present time the great weight of authority throughout the country sanctions the use of sound recordings where the matter contained therein is competent and relevant. * * * We adopt that view. As a condition to admissibility, however, the speakers should be identified and it should be shown that (1) the device was capable of taking the conversation or statement, (2) its operator was competent, (3) the recording is authentic and correct, (4) no changes, additions or deletions have been made, and (5) in instances of alleged confessions, that the statements were elicited voluntarily and without any inducement." *Id.,* 38 *N.J.* at 287.

"A [recording] which catches the actual voice of an accused and of his questioner, may be an invaluable aid to a court and jury where the issue of voluntariness of a confession is raised. * * * In fact, the recording may be more satisfactory and persuasive evidence than the written and signed document. In all situations, however, the trial judge should listen to the recording out of the presence of the jury before allowing it to be used. In this way he can decide whether it is sufficiently audible, intelligible, not obviously fragmented, and, also of considerable importance, whether it contains any improper and prejudicial matter which ought to be deleted." *Id.* at 287-88.

NOTE

1. *Authentication of documentary evidence.* As a general rule, before a documentary item of evidence may be received by a court, it must be "authenticated," that is, shown to be "genuine"—whether it is an original document, a copy, or some other documentary representation. In the case of written documents, the proponent of the document may establish its authenticity through a witness who can identify the document, the handwriting or any signatures affixed thereto. The witness should also be able to testify as to whether the document is presently in the same or substantially the same condition as it was when relied upon or made. *See generally Fed.R.Evid.* 901.

If the witness is not the person who created or signed the document, a court may accept, for authentication purposes, the *lay opinion* of anyone who is familiar with the handwriting of the person in question or who saw it being written or signed. In addition, a written document may be authenticated by the testimony a *handwriting expert*. This would normally require the expert to be provided with a handwriting sample of the person who allegedly made the document so that the expert may compare the characteristics found in the sample with those in the questioned document.

In the case of photographs, motion pictures or videotapes, the proponent need only establish, through the use of a witness with knowledge of the event or scene, that the photograph or video accurately portrays what it purports to portray; that it "fairly and accurately represents" the object, person or place as it existed at, or sufficiently close to, the relevant time. Significantly, there is no requirement that the photographer be produced as a witness.

2. *The "best evidence" rule.* The "best evidence" of a writing, recording or photograph is, of course, the original writing, recording or photograph, not a copy. In this respect, *Fed.R.Evid.* 1002 provides: "To prove the content of a writing, recording, or photograph, the original writing, recording or photograph is required, except as otherwise provided[.]" An "original" of a writing or recording is "the writing or recording itself or any counterpart intended to have the same effect by a person executing or issuing it." *Fed.R.Evid.*

1001(3). "An 'original' of a photograph includes the negative or any print therefrom. If data are stored in a computer or similar device, any printout or other output readable by sight, shown to reflect the data accurately, is an 'original.' " *Id.*

There are, however, a number of exceptions to the best evidence rule. For example, *Fed.R.Evid.* 1003 allows for the admission of a "duplicate" to the same extent as the original "unless (1) a genuine question is raised as to the authenticity of the original or (2) in the circumstances it would be unfair to admit the duplicate in lieu of the original." "Duplicate" is defined as "a counterpart produced by the same impression as the original, or from the same matrix, or by means of photography, including enlargements and miniatures, or by mechanical or electronic re-recording, or by chemical reproduction, or by other equivalent technique which accurately reproduces the original." *Fed.R.Evid.* 1001(4). *See also Fed.R.Evid.* 1004 (original not required when lost or destroyed in the absence of bad faith, when no original can be obtained, when it is in the possession of the party against whom it is offered under certain circumstances, or when the writing, recording or photograph is not closely related to a controlling issue).

STATE v. BUNTING
Superior Court of New Jersey, Appellate Division
187 *N.J.Super.* 506, 455 *A.2d* 531 (1983)

PER CURIAM.

* * * * *

"Defendant [] challenges the admission into evidence of a film. The film was a type of surveillance used by banks and some late night retail stores, which is activated in an unobtrusive manner by the store clerk during an occurrence such as a robbery. In this particular case, defendant, as a participant in an armed robbery of a retail store, was photographed during the commission of the offense by the activation of a camera located above the cash register. The camera was activated by the store clerk when he moved a money clip located within the register." *Id.*, 187 *N.J.Super.* at 508.

"[T]he film is offered as independent evidence depicting the circumstances of the robbery and the identity of defendant in the store on that occasion." *Id.*

"The question of admissibility of films in a criminal action has never been established in this State. The general rule in other jurisdictions is that films are ordinarily admissible in criminal trials. * * * No reason has been advanced to prohibit their admissibility in this State and we see no reason to do so. The authentication of a film which purports to portray an actual criminal event taking place would not require the same type of authentication as in [a case in which the film is being offered to illustrate, or in conjunction with, the testimony of an expert witness]." *Id.* at 508, 509.

"In a Maine case, *State v. Young*, 303 *A*.2d 113 (Me.Sup.Ct. 1973), the court held that film evidence which is introduced as independent evidence of the crime, should be admitted without corroborative testimony by an eyewitness if the film is otherwise authenticated. [] Here, the film was introduced as independent probative evidence and no corroboration by witnesses Wyatt and Brownfield, the clerks, was required. In *Young*, the Maine court adverted to the credible testimony in the case which supplied the necessary authentication there:

> "[T]he State introduced the testimony of the bank manager as to the installation and field of view of the camera; the testimony of an employee of the surveillance company which installed the camera as to the method of triggering the operation of the camera, and of the periodic testing of the camera; testimony of the person who removed the exposed film; testimony of the person who developed the film; testimony of each of the law enforcement officers who had custody of the film from the time it was taken from the camera until the time of trial; and testimony of the bank teller as to the activation of the camera during the robbery."

Bunting at 509 (quoting *Young* at 116).

"Here, the facts supporting the trial court's admission of the film absent eyewitness corroboration are very similar to those approved by the *Young* court. Specifically, the State introduced Wyatt's testimony regarding the installation and view of the camera; the testimony of Mr. Restaino, the loss/security representative for Quick Check, as to the camera's operation and his own 'periodic testing' of the camera, as well as his removal of the film; the testimony of Officer Ferrante as to the film's chain of custody subsequent to the robbery, to which defendant stipulated, and finally, Wyatt's testimony regarding activation of the camera by removing the clip during the robbery." *Id.* at 509-10.

"There is little likelihood that the film was other than that exposed on the night in question or that it is otherwise an inaccurate representation of the events it purports to show. It was properly admitted as independent evidence." *Id.* at 510.

---

§2.4. DEMONSTRATIVE EVIDENCE

Demonstrative evidence is illustrative evidence; it illustrates, shows or exhibits—by way of reconstruction, recreation or enactment—the actual event or real thing. It is different from real evidence for it has no evidential or probative value by itself, but serves only as a visual or auditory aid to assist the factfinder in understanding other evidence. Demonstrative evidence may include diagrams, charts, maps, models, movies, audio-visual aids, crime-scene mockups, experiments and other courtroom demonstrations. In the discretion of the judge, courtroom demonstrations may be permitted to show that a person or an object acts or behaves in a particular way. At a minimum, the party offering this type of evidence—whether a demonstration or re-enactment of a real event, or a visual aid such as an illustration or model of a real thing—must establish that the evidence (a) fairly and accurately demonstrates what it purports to demonstrate, and (b) will be helpful to the factfinder's understanding of some important issue in the case.

PEOPLE v. RANSOM
Appellate Court of Illinois, Fourth District
319 *Ill.App.*3d 915, 746 *N.E.*2d 1262 (2001)

PRESIDING JUSTICE STEIGMANN delivered the opinion of the court.

After a jury trial, defendant, Darren Ransom, was convicted of attempted murder, home invasion, and armed robbery. In this appeal, he argues, among other things, that the trial court erred by allowing the State to present testimony regarding the use of a hammer as demonstrative evidence.

"Specifically, he contends that the use of the hammer was (1) unnecessary because a hammer is a 'familiar object' and (2) inflammatory." *Id.* at 921. As a general matter, "[c]ourts look favorably upon the use of demonstrative evidence, because it helps the jury understand the issues raised at trial. "The overriding considerations in admitting demonstrative evidence are relevancy and fairness. The question of the admissibility of such exhibits is a matter within the trial court's discretion and will be disturbed only on a showing of clear abuse." *Id.* at 921. [Citations omitted.]

"Here, the State's expert witness testified that [the victim's] injuries were consistent with those that would result from blows inflicted by a hammer similar to the one the State presented. This testimony might have laid to rest any doubts the jury held regarding whether [the victim's] description of the attack was consistent with the injuries she received. Given the other extensive and sometimes gruesome evidence of the brutality of the attack and the injuries [she] suffered, we hold that the State's use of the hammer as demonstrative evidence was not so inflammatory as to unfairly prejudice defendant and the trial court did not abuse its discretion by allowing it." *Id.*

PEOPLE v. COOK
Appellate Court of Illinois, First District
279 *Ill.App.*3d 718, 665 *N.E.*2d 299 (1996)

JUSTICE BUCKLEY delivered the opinion of the court.

Defendant, Haywood Cook, was convicted of possession of a stolen motor vehicle and criminal trespass to a motor vehicle. Among the issues raised in this appeal was "whether the trial court erred in allowing a peeled steering column to be used as demonstrative evidence." *Id.* at 720-21.

At the suppression hearing, Officer McNulty testified that at about 4:15 a.m., on the day in question, "he and two other officers were in an unmarked squad car when they noticed a white 1985 Oldsmobile Cutlass with a broken taillight. They followed the vehicle for about one mile during which time they ran a license plate check on the Cutlass and determined it to be registered to Orville Jackson, a 73-year-old man who had not reported the car stolen. Officer McNulty testified that the Cutlass stopped at a gas station at 71st and Halsted. He testified that the officers pulled up parallel to the Cutlass, one or two feet away on the passenger side. He stated that he observed defendant, whom he ascertained to be younger than 73 years old, in the driver's seat. He also testified that the car was still running although there was no key in the ignition, the steering column was peeled, the driver's side window was broken out, and a screwdriver and a mallet were on the floor of the vehicle. Officer McNulty also testified that defendant did not know the license plate number of the car. The officers then took defendant out of the car and placed him under arrest." *Id.* at 721.

At trial, Officer McNulty further testified "that in order to start a vehicle without a key, it is necessary to bypass the locking mechanism and that this is usually done by peeling the steering column. As he explained the process of peeling a steering column, he used a peeled steering column manufactured by General Motors to demonstrate the process. Defendant objected, and the trial court allowed the peeled column to be used for demonstrative purposes, but would not allow it into evidence. The jury found defendant guilty of possession of a stolen motor vehicle and criminal trespass to a vehicle." *Id.* at 722.

Defendant claims "that the trial court erred in allowing Officer McNulty to use a peeled steering column provided by General Motors as demonstrative evidence while he explained the process of peeling the steering column." *Id.* at 725.

"The purpose of demonstrative evidence is to aid the trier of fact in interpreting, understanding, and weighing other evidence or testimony. * * * The decision of whether to allow a witness to use a demonstrative aid is within the sound discretion of the trial court * * *. Defendant's contention that the steering column used during Officer McNulty's testimony was prejudicial, and used only for dramatic effect, is without merit. The record indicates that Officer McNulty used the exhibit to illustrate the process he was simultaneously describing. The trial court's ruling that the exhibit was informative as an illustration was not an abuse of discretion. Furthermore, given the corresponding testimony of the officer and the other evidence presented in the trial, this demonstrative aid was not prejudicial to defendant." *Id.*

NOTE

See also United States v. Aldaco, 201 *F.*3d 979 (7th Cir. 2000) (prosecution allowed to use a replica of the destroyed shotgun as demonstrative evidence); *United States v. Towns,* 913 *F.*2d 434, 446 (7th Cir. 1990) (allowing admission of a gun and ski mask identified by eyewitnesses "as being similar to those possessed by the robbers" for "the limited demonstrative purpose of providing examples of the gun and ski mask" used in the robbery); *United States v. Salerno,* 108 *F.*3d 730, 742-43 (7th Cir. 1997) (allowing the use of a scale model of a crime scene as demonstrative evidence).

STATE v. GEAR
Superior Court of New Jersey, Appellate Division
115 *N.J.*Super. 151, 278 A.2d 511 (1971)*

PER CURIAM.
[Immediately before defendant's arrest for the possession of lottery slips, he managed to destroy the "water soluble" slips of paper by throwing them in a plastic container filled with water. As soon as the slips of paper hit the water, they disintegrated.]
"The single argument advanced is that it was error to permit Detective McManus, who participated in defendant's apprehension and arrest, to testify as to tests he had made with water-soluble paper before trial and to perform a demonstration with such paper in the presence of the jury. The basis of this argument is that the witness could not say whether the paper he used was similar to that allegedly used by defendant." *Id.*, 115 *N.J.Super.* at 153.
[At trial,] "the prosecution requested permission to conduct a test, using water-soluble paper with numbers written on it, the

---

*aff'd, 59 *N.J.* 270, 281 A.2d 532 (1971).

purpose being to show the ultimate result when the paper was placed in water. The defense objected[, contending] that the State would have to show that the paper used was identical to the paper found in the container[.]" *Id.*

"McManus was [] permitted to testify before the jury that he had seen water-soluble paper demonstrated before and had made tests in his office to determine just what happened with such paper. In every case the results were the same as when he tried to recover the paper from the container at the scene of the arrest; the paper would break up in his hand, flake, become sticky and pasty, and disintegrate completely when he attempted to remove it. * * * [T]he judge ruled that he would allow the demonstration to proceed, whereupon McManus left the stand and placed water-soluble paper, on which numbers had been written, into a jar filled with water. The jury then filed past the jar to see what happened. Some 2 1/2 minutes after placing the paper in the jar McManus tried to remove the paper and it dissolved in his hand. The 2 1/2 minutes approximated the time [which elapsed at the scene of defendant's arrest]." *Id.*

"The only purpose of [the detective's] testimony and demonstration was to show, as the prosecution stated, that 'there exists a paper that will dissolve when placed in water.' For this there was no need of testimony as to the exact ingredients and chemical composition. The demonstration was obviously for the purpose of being helpful to a clear understanding of the detective's testimony. * * * McManus had said that defendant possessed lottery slips on water-soluble paper. By showing the jury the use of such paper he fulfilled the requirement that the demonstration must be substantially the same as that described in his testimony." *Id.* at 154.

"A demonstration of the type here under attack lies in judicial discretion and *may be justified because it tends to enlighten the jury on an important point*." *Id.* at 154-55. [Emphasis added.]

NOTE

But see State v. LiButti, 146 *N.J.Super.* 565, 370 *A.2d* 486 (App.Div. 1977), where the court held it to be error for a trial court in an arson case to permit the prosecutor to rebut a defense expert's testimony regarding the time it would take to pour gasoline, lacquer and paint thinner out of ten-gallon containers, by performing a demonstration during closing argument to the jury, whereby the prosecutor poured water from a five-gallon container into another receptacle while timing the flow of liquid with a Pulsar watch. According to the Appellate Division, "[t]he demonstration should not have been permitted." *Id.,* 146 *N.J.Super.* at 572.

It was clearly performed for the purpose of providing evidential rebuttal of [the defendant's expert's] testimony. Ordinarily it is discretionary with the court as to allowing an experiment to be performed in the jury's presence. Demonstrations or experiments may be justified on the ground that they tend to enlighten the jury on an important point. "But caution and prudence should govern in each instance, depending upon the circumstances and the character of the demonstration." * * * The demonstration must be performed within the scope of the evidence in the case. * * *

It is difficult to understand why the prosecuting attorney did not use the receptacle which had been marked in evidence as a substantial representation of those which [had] been used in connection with setting the fire. * * *

[S]uch demonstrations must take place during the taking of testimony or the presentation of evidence, so as to permit an opportunity for cross-examination * * * prior to final argument. * * *

Id. at 572-73. [Citations omitted.]

TAYLOR v. UNITED STATES
District of Columbia Court of Appeals
601 A.2d 1060 (1991)

The opinion of the Court was delivered by

FARRELL, Associate Judge.
[Taylor and Lawrence appeal from their convictions for armed robbery. The robbery occurred at the end of an unsuccessful undercover drug buy. Before being robbed at gunpoint, however, the undercover officer managed to record the conversations between him and Taylor. Taylor argues that the trial judge erred in refusing to allow him to conduct a demonstration of his voice without taking the witness stand and being subjected to cross-examination.]
"The purpose of the proposed voice exemplar was to allow the jury to compare Taylor's voice with the voice of the gunman on the tape made by the device in [the officer's] car. Taylor's counsel suggested that the format for the demonstration be 'to play the tape and to have Mr. Taylor speak the words that he hears on the tape.' Counsel argued that because [Taylor] would only recite the words used by the gunman on the tape 'from the well of the court,' he would not be testifying and thus would not waive his Fifth Amendment privilege against self-incrimination. The trial judge rejected the proposed demonstration, ruling that [Taylor] could provide the jury with the opportunity to hear his voice only if 'he's going to be on the stand and under oath.' " *Id.* at 1065.
"The basis for the judge's ruling was his assumption that the voice demonstration would amount to giving testimony." *Id.* at 1065-66.
"We cannot accept this underlying premise. As the government concedes in its brief, a voice exemplar is demonstrative, not

testimonial evidence. That principle is well established. * * * The government can compel an accused to provide a voice exemplar without violating the privilege against self-incrimination since a person's voice is 'an identifying physical characteristic outside [Fifth Amendment] protection.' * * * A voice exemplar carries no communicative or otherwise testimonial component; it serves only to demonstrate the inherent physical properties of a particular voice. * * * We see no reason, in principle, for denying a defendant the right to offer similar non-testimonial evidence without waiving Fifth Amendment protections. Therefore, the judge could not properly exclude the voice exemplar on the ground that Taylor refused to take the witness stand and submit to cross-examination about his involvement in the crime." *Id.* at 1066. [Citations omitted.]

NOTE

See also *Gilbert v. California*, 388 *U.S.* 263, 267, 87 *S.Ct.* 1951, 1953 (1967) (a person's voice is "an identifying physical characteristic outside [Fifth Amendment] protection"); *United States v. Dionisio*, 410 *U.S.* 1, 6-7, 93 *S.Ct.* 764, 767-68 (1973) (a voice exemplar is demonstrative evidence); *United States v. Williams*, 704 *F.*2d 315, 320 (6th Cir. 1983) (a "defendant compelled to give a live voice exemplar is not" compelled to give testimonial evidence).

STATE v. MAYBERRY
Supreme Court of New Jersey
52 *N.J.* 413, 245 *A.*2d 481 (1968)

The opinion of the Court was delivered by

JACOBS, J.
"The defendants were convicted of murder in the first degree[.] * * * As part of its case, the State called a tavern owner who had sold [defendant] Kestner the 32.20 revolver and the German Mauser. He was shown a gun which was marked Exhibit S-26 and was asked how it compared with the 32.20 he had sold to Kestner. He replied that it was the same type, make and caliber but that it was not as new or as dark as the gun he had sold. [Defendant] Mayberry testified that S-26 was 'very similar' to the gun he was carrying on the night of the killing. When on cross-examination he was shown S-26 and was asked how it compared to his gun he said, 'it looks just like it.' When the State offered S-26 in evidence the defendants objected. In response, the Prosecutor urged that it was being received in evidence with proper instructions since it was not intended to be the murder weapon but only 'a similar weapon.' In overruling the objection, the court instructed the jury that the ex-

hibit was not intended as the gun that was used 'because there was testimony to the effect by Mayberry that he did throw the gun away and this was not the gun.' " *Id.*, 52 *N.J.* at 435.

"We find neither error nor prejudice in the admission of S-26 as a gun similar to but not the actual gun used in the killing." *Id.*

NOTE

See also United States v. Golden, 671 *F.*2d 369, 371-72 (10th Cir. 1982) (upholding admission of a "flashlight similar to that used" in the assault, a "seven-cell kel-light").

RILEY v. UNITED STATES
District of Columbia Court of Appeals
647 A.2d 1165 (1994)

KING, Associate Judge.
[Following a jury trial, defendant Julian Riley was convicted of armed assault with intent to kill, armed mayhem, possession of a firearm during a crime of violence, carrying a pistol without a license, and perjury. The evidence at trial indicated that Riley, during a street fight with the victim, Pernell Gibson, shot Gibson at point-blank range in the face. During the course of Gibson's trial testimony, the prosecution asked him to show his injury to the jury. Defendant's objection was overruled.]

*   *   *   *

In this appeal we "find no merit in [defendant's] contention that the trial court erred when it allowed Gibson to remove his eye patch and show his eye socket to the jury. He contends exposing the wound to the jury was inflammatory * * *. The government maintains that his display 'properly demonstrated the permanency of Gibson's injury—an element of mayhem while armed—and was real evidence of his disfigurement.' " *Id.* at 1172.

"The decision whether to admit demonstrative evidence is within the trial court's sound discretion. * * * After viewing Gibson's disfigurement out of the jury's presence and finding that it was neither 'gory' nor 'attractive,' the trial judge permitted Gibson to display his wound on the ground that the government is required to prove 'permanent disabling injury' for a mayhem charge. Although we have not previously considered whether bodily demonstrations are permitted in criminal cases, we see no significant difference between Gibson's display of his injury on one hand and the admission of a photograph of that same injury on the other hand. Photographs are admissible 'so long as they have some probative value and are not intended solely to inflame the jury." *Id.*

"Thus, we hold that if in the sound discretion of the trial court, the probative value outweighs the prejudicial impact, the display of injuries to the body is admissible. * * * Being satisfied the trial court properly weighed probativeness versus prejudice, we conclude there was no abuse of discretion in allowing the victim to display his wound to the jury." *Id.* at 1173.

---

§2.4(a). Crime-Scene Sketches

Another form of demonstrative evidence is the crime-scene sketch. These sketches provide "a graphic display of the crime scene (in whole or in part) with accurate measurements of distances between objects."[9] Crime-scene sketches are said to assist in (1) accurately portraying the physical facts of the incident; (2) relating the sequence of events at the scene; (3) establishing the precise location and relationship of objects and evidence at the scene; (4) helping to create a mental picture of the scene for those not present; (5) interviewing and interrogating persons connected with the crime or incident; (6) creating a permanent record of the scene; and (7) presenting the case in court.[10]

Crime-scene sketches differ from crime-scene photographs in several respects. First, from an evidentiary point of view, crime-scene photographs fall into the category of documentary evidence. Yet, while photographs have the capacity to reproduce the scene in detail, and are extraordinarily valuable at crime scenes, they may, at times, tend to distort distances and relationships between objects and evidence at the scene. Also, photographs do not show items behind other items and do not show measurements or accurate distances between objects and evidence. On the other hand, crime-scene sketches provide "a clear and concise description of all pieces of evidence at the crime scene, the relationship of items to each other, the distances between objects and the movement of witnesses and suspects."[11] In addition, unnecessary detail at a crime scene can be eliminated or reduced on a sketch, allowing for each crime-scene sketch to demonstrate precise areas of interest.

---

[9] Mauriello, *Criminal Investigation Handbook: Strategy, Law and Science* (Matthew Bender 1998), at 7-17.

[10] Bennett and Hess, *Criminal Investigation* (West/Wadsworth 1998), at 54.

[11] *Mauriello* at 7-17.

§2.4(a)(1). Rough Sketches and Formal or "Finished" Sketches

The preliminary or "rough" crime-scene sketch is drawn by the investigator or crime-scene technician as he or she takes field notes. It is the first diagram of the scene and is generally not drawn to scale. Naturally, during the rough-sketching process, evidence should not be disturbed or moved from its original position until photographs and accurate measurements are taken. In this respect, as a matter of evidence law, an object that has been once moved cannot be returned to its *exact original* position without raising serious credibility issues.

Later, the formal, more detailed or "finished" crime-scene scaled drawing is drafted from the investigator's field notes, "rough" sketches and photographs of the scene. It is recommended that both the rough and finished sketches be preserved, as both may constitute evidence at a later court hearing.[12]

§2.4(a)(2). Types of sketches

The rectangular-coordinate method of sketching is an easy method for locating objects and evidence in a square or rectangular room. This method employs two adjacent walls as fixed points from which distances are measured at right angles. Objects are located by measuring from one wall at right angles and then from the adjacent wall at right angles.[13]

The baseline method is another coordinate measurement technique which establishes a baseline from one fixed point to another. This method requires that a straight line be drawn from one fixed point to another, from which measurements are taken at right angles. Measurements are then taken along the baseline to a point at right angles to the object to be portrayed.[14]

The triangulation sketch is used most often in outdoor settings where there are no readily identifiable reference points, such as edges of fields or roads to use as baselines. Triangulation sketching employs "straight-line measures from two fixed objects to the evidence to create a triangle with the evidence in the angle formed by the two straight lines The degree of the angle formed at the location of the object or evidence can then be measured with a protractor."[15]

The projection sketch is a two-dimensional diagram which depicts the full crime scene with all relevant objects in the area. The distance between each object is shown.

---

[12] *Id.* at 7-18.

[13] *Bennett and Hess* at 60.

[14] *Id.*

[15] *Id.* at 62.

The cross-projection sketch is helpful when it is necessary to locate objects on walls or show the relationship between evidence on the floor and evidence on the walls. Where most sketches will show the crime scene in two dimensions, the cross-projection method of sketching portrays the scene in three dimensions to allow a better analysis of the evidence. The cross-projection sketch of a room is drawn as though the viewer is straight above it, looking down at it. "In effect, the room is flattened out much like a box cut down at the four corners and opened out flat."[16] The floor and walls are then presented as though they were one flat surface.

The schematic sketch is useful to illustrate a significant chain of events, for example, the path of a bullet, or movement of suspects, victims or vehicles.[17]

The elevation sketch is used when a vertical illustration of the crime scene is necessary. Such a sketch is helpful when an outside area with hills and valleys, or a two-story building must be shown.[18]

---

§2.5. TESTIMONIAL EVIDENCE

Essentially, **testimonial evidence**, as the term implies, consists of oral testimony given in court, or at some other formal hearing in anticipation of a court proceeding, by a witness under oath. Testimonial evidence is also referred to as *viva voce* evidence, or that form of evidence which flows from the words provided by the mouth of a living human being—the "living voice." The testimony may be factual or, in the appropriate set of circumstances, opinion.

As a general rule, "[e]very person is competent to be a witness."[19] There are, however, four basic attributes that all persons must have in order to be "competent" to testify as a witness in court:

(1) the ability to accept and appreciate the obligation to testify truthfully;

(2) perception;

(3) recollection; and

(4) the ability to communicate.

---

[16] *Id.*

[17] *Mauriello* at 7-22.

[18] *Id.* at 7-23.

[19] *See Fed.R.Evid.* 601.

First and foremost, the witness must take an oath or affirmation prior to giving testimony, and have the capacity to sincerely understand the nature and consequences of the oath or affirmation. This requires an appreciation of the obligation to testify truthfully and to know and understand the difference between telling the truth and lying. Although the rules of evidence do not specify any particular form or specific language that must be contained in an oath or affirmation, the rules do provide that "[b]efore testifying, every witness shall be required to declare that the witness will testify truthfully, by oath or affirmation administered in a form calculated to awaken the witness' conscience and impress the witness' mind with the duty to do so."[20] The oath or affirmation is not a form of evidence. Rather, it is a vehicle used by the courts to strongly advise a witness of his or her duty to tell the truth and of the punishment in store for the witness should he or she testify falsely. If the proposed witness refuses either to take an oath or make an affirmation, the witness should not be allowed to testify.

Second, the witness must have had the capacity to observe or in some way perceive the event in question. This demonstrates not only the relevance of the witness' proposed testimony but also that the witness has personal knowledge of the event in question. In the absence of direct, personal (first-hand) knowledge of the event, the witness must demonstrate that he or she has particular or specialized knowledge, training, experience or education which would provide a relevant and competent basis for the witness' proposed testimony.

Next, the witness must have the capacity to recollect, to remember, the event in question. In this respect, lapses in memory would seriously draw into question the witness' competence to provide testimony relating the events in question.

Finally, the witness must have the capacity to communicate in some reasonably understandable manner what he or she previously observed or perceived, or in the case of opinion testimony, the ability to relate information in a clear and understandable manner and in such a way as will be helpful to the factfinder.[21]

---

[20] *Fed.R.Evid.* 603.

[21] *See e.g., Fed.Rs.Evid.* 602 & 603.

Chapter 3

PRESERVATION OF / ACCESS TO EVIDENCE

§3.1. GENERAL CONSIDERATIONS

In *Brady v. Maryland,*[1] the United States Supreme Court made it clear that the Due Process Clause of the Fourteenth Amendment provides a criminal defendant with the privilege to request and obtain from the prosecution favorable evidence that is material either to the guilt of the defendant or relevant to the punishment to be imposed.[2] Questions arise, however, as to whether and to what extent, as a matter of due process, law enforcement officials must retain, protect and preserve evidence for defendants when the evidence *might* be potentially useful to the defense.

§3.2. CASES AND MATERIALS

CALIFORNIA v. TROMBETTA
Supreme Court of the United States
467 U.S. 479, 104 S.Ct. 2528 (1984)

Mr. Justice MARSHALL delivered the opinion of the Court.

"[T]he question presented is whether the Due Process Clause requires law enforcement agencies to preserve breath samples of suspected drunk drivers in order for the results of breath-analysis tests to be admissible in criminal prosecutions." *Id.* at 2530.

---

[1] 373 *U.S.* 83, 83 *S.Ct.* 1194 (1963).

[2] *Brady* at 87, 83 *S.Ct.* at 1196. *See also United States v. Bagley*, 473 *U.S.* 667, 105 *S.Ct.* 3375 (1985); *United States v. Agurs*, 427 *U.S.* 97, 103-07, 96 *S.Ct.* 2392, 2397-99 (1976); *Moore v. Illinois*, 408 *U.S.* 786, 794-95, 92 *S.Ct.* 2562, 2567-68 (1972). A court's review of the failure of the State to disclose evidence favorable to the accused will necessarily focus on the "cumulative effect of all such evidence suppressed by the government," and "the prosecutor remains responsible for gauging that effect regardless of any failure by the police to bring favorable evidence to the prosecutor's attention." *Kyles v. Whitley*, 514 *U.S.* 419, 115 *S.Ct.* 1555, 1560 (1995). If, on appeal, a court should determine that the net effect of the evidence withheld by the State raises a reasonable probability that its disclosure would have produced a different result, the defendant would be entitled to a new trial. Id. It is, therefore, the duty of each individual prosecutor "to learn of any favorable evidence known to the others acting on the government's behalf, including the police." *Id.*, 115 *S.Ct.* at 1567.

"The Omicron Intoxilyzer (Intoxilyzer) is a device used in California to measure the concentration of alcohol in the blood of motorists suspected of driving while under the influence of intoxicating liquor. The Intoxilyzer analyzes the suspect's breath." *Id.*

"In unrelated incidents in 1980 and 1981, each of the [defendant]s in this case was stopped [for] drunken driving[, and each] submitted to an Intoxilyzer test. Each [defendant] registered a blood-alcohol concentration substantially higher than 0.10 percent." *Id.*

"Prior to trial in municipal court, each [defendant] filed a motion to suppress the Intoxilyzer test results on the ground that the arresting officers had failed to preserve samples of [defendant]s' breath. Although preservation of breath samples is technically feasible,[3] California law enforcement officers do not ordinarily preserve breath samples, and made no effort to do so in these cases. [Defendant]s each claimed that, had a breath sample been preserved, he would have been able to impeach the incriminating Intoxilyzer results." *Id.* at 2530-31.

"Under the Due Process Clause of the Fourteenth Amendment, criminal prosecutions must comport with prevailing notions of fundamental fairness. We have long interpreted this standard of fairness to require that criminal defendants be afforded a meaningful opportunity to present a complete defense. To safeguard that right, the Court has developed 'what might loosely be called the area of constitutionally-guaranteed access to evidence.' * * * Taken together, this group of constitutional privileges delivers exculpatory evidence into the hands of the accused, thereby protecting the innocent from erroneous conviction and ensuring the integrity of our criminal justice system." *Id.* at 2532. [Citation omitted.]

"A defendant has a constitutionally protected privilege to request and obtain from the prosecution evidence that is either material to the guilt of the defendant or relevant to the punishment to be imposed. * * * Even in the absence of a specific request, the prosecution has a constitutional duty to turn over exculpatory evidence that would raise a reasonable doubt about the defendant's guilt." *Id.*

"Less than clear from our access-to-evidence cases is the extent to which the Due Process Clause imposes on the government the additional responsibility of guaranteeing criminal defendants access to exculpatory evidence beyond the government's possession.

---

[3] "The California Department of Health has approved a device, known as an Intoximeter Field Crimper-Indium Tube Encapsulation Kit (Kit), which officers can use to preserve samples. [] To use the Kit, a suspect must breathe directly into an indium tube, which preserves samples in three separate chambers. * * * The breath trapped in each chamber can later be used to determine the suspect's blood-alcohol concentration through the use of a laboratory instrument known as a Gas Chromatograph Intoximeter * * *. Because the suspect must breathe directly into the indium tube, the Kit cannot be used to preserve the same breath sample used in an Intoxilyzer test." *Trombetta* at 482 n.3, 104 *S.Ct.* at 2530 n.3.

"[W]e have suggested that the [g]overnment * * * [must not] hamper a criminal defendant's preparation for trial." *Id.*

"We have, however, never squarely addressed the government's duty to take affirmative steps to preserve evidence on behalf of criminal defendants. The absence of doctrinal development in this area reflects, in part, the difficulty of developing rules to deal with evidence destroyed through prosecutorial neglect or oversight. Whenever potentially exculpatory evidence is permanently lost, courts face the treacherous task of divining the import of materials whose contents are unknown and, very often, disputed. * * * Moreover, fashioning remedies for the illegal destruction of evidence can pose troubling choices. In nondisclosure cases, a court can grant the defendant a new trial at which the previously suppressed evidence may be introduced. But when evidence has been destroyed in violation of the Constitution, the court must choose between barring further prosecution or suppressing * * * the State's most probative evidence." *Id.* at 2533.

"To the extent that [defendant]s' breath samples came into the possession of California authorities, it was for the limited purpose of providing raw data to the Intoxilyzer.[4] The evidence to be presented at trial was not the breath itself but rather the Intoxilyzer results obtained from the breath samples. * * * [Defendant]s here seek the breath samples in order to challenge incriminating test results produced with the Intoxilyzer." *Id.*

"Given our precedents in this area, we [do not believe] that the State's failure to retain breath samples for [defendant]s constitutes a violation of the Federal Constitution. To begin with, California authorities did not destroy [defendant]s' breath samples in a calculated effort to circumvent the disclosure requirements established by *Brady v. Maryland*[.] In failing to preserve breath samples for [defendant]s, the officers here were acting 'in good faith and in accord with their normal practice' * * *. The record contains no allegation of official animus towards [defendant]s or of a conscious effort to suppress exculpatory evidence." *Id.*

"More importantly, California's policy of not preserving breath samples is without constitutional defect. *Whatever duty the Constitution imposes on the States to preserve evidence, that duty must be limited to evidence that might be expected to play a significant role in the suspect's defense. To meet this standard of constitutional materiality, * * * evidence must both possess an exculpatory value that was apparent before the evidence was destroyed, and be of such a nature that the defendant would be unable to obtain comparable evidence by other reasonably available means.* Neither of these conditions is met on the facts of this case." *Id.* at 2534. [Emphasis added.]

---

[4] "We accept the California Court of Appeal's conclusion that the Intoxilyzer procedure brought [defendant]s' breath samples into the possession of California officials." *Id.* at 488 n.7, 104 *S.Ct.* at 2533 n.7.

"Although the preservation of breath samples might conceivably have contributed to [defendant]s' defenses, a dispassionate review of the Intoxilyzer and the California testing procedures can only lead one to conclude that the chances are extremely low that preserved samples would have been exculpatory. * * * In all but a tiny fraction of cases, preserved breath samples would simply confirm the Intoxilyzer's determination that the defendant had a high level of blood-alcohol concentration at the time of the test. Once the Intoxilyzer indicated that [defendant]s were legally drunk, breath samples were much more likely to provide inculpatory than exculpatory evidence." *Id.*

"Even if one were to assume that the Intoxilyzer results in this case were inaccurate and that breath samples might therefore have been exculpatory, it does not follow that [defendant]s were without alternative means of demonstrating their innocence. [The record discloses a] limited number of ways in which an Intoxilyzer might malfunction: faulty calibration, extraneous interference with machine measurements, and operator error. * * * [Defendant]s were perfectly capable of [exploring and] raising these issues without resort to preserved breath samples." *Id.*

"We conclude, therefore, that the Due Process Clause of the Fourteenth Amendment does not require that law enforcement agencies preserve breath samples in order to introduce the results of breath-analysis tests at trial."[5] *Id.* at 2535.

ARIZONA v. YOUNGBLOOD
Supreme Court of the United States
488 *U.S.* 51, 109 *S.Ct.* 333 (1988)

Chief Justice REHNQUIST delivered the opinion of the Court.

"[Defendant] Larry Youngblood was convicted by a Pima County, Arizona, jury of child molestation, sexual assault, and kidnapping. The Arizona Court of Appeals reversed his conviction on the ground that the State had failed to preserve semen samples from the victim's body and clothing. * * * We granted certiorari to consider the extent to which the Due Process Clause of the Federal Constitution requires the State to preserve evidentiary material that might be useful to a criminal defendant." *Id.* at 334.

---

[5] "State courts and legislatures, of course, remain free to adopt more rigorous safeguards governing the admissibility of scientific evidence than those imposed by the Federal Constitution. *See e.g., Lauderdale v. State*, 548 *P.*2d 376 (Alaska 1976); *City of Lodi v. Hine*, 107 *Wis.*2d 118, 318 *N.W.*2d 383 (1982)." *Trombetta* at 491 n.12, 104 *S.Ct.* at 2535 n.12.

"On October 29, 1983, David L., a 10-year-old boy, attended a church service with his mother. After he left the service at about 9:30 p.m., the boy went to a carnival behind the church, where he was abducted by a middle-aged man of medium height and weight. The assailant drove the boy to a secluded area near a ravine and molested him. He then took the boy to an unidentified, sparsely furnished house where he sodomized the boy four times. Afterwards, the assailant tied the boy up while he went outside to start his car. Once the assailant started the car, albeit with some difficulty, he returned to the house and again sodomized the boy. The assailant then sent the boy to the bathroom to wash up before he returned him to the carnival. He threatened to kill the boy if he told anyone about the attack. The entire ordeal lasted about 1 1/2 hours." *Id.*

"After the boy made his way home, his mother took him to Kino Hospital. At the hospital, a physician treated the boy for rectal injuries. The physician also used a 'sexual assault kit' to collect evidence of the attack. The Tucson Police Department provided such kits to all hospitals in Pima County for use in sexual assault cases. Under standard procedure, the victim of a sexual assault was taken to a hospital, where a physician used the kit to collect evidence. The kit included paper to collect saliva samples, a tube for obtaining a blood sample, microscopic slides for making smears, a set of Q-tip like swabs, and a medical examination report. Here, the physician used the swab to collect samples from the boy's rectum and mouth. He then made a microscopic slide of the samples. The doctor also obtained samples of the boy's saliva, blood, and hair. The physician did not examine the samples at any time. The police placed the kit in a secure refrigerator at the police station. At the hospital, the police also collected the boy's underwear and T-shirt. This clothing was not refrigerated or frozen." *Id.* at 334-35.

"Nine days after the attack, on November 7, 1983, the police asked the boy to pick out his assailant from a photographic lineup. The boy identified [defendant] as the assailant[, who was ultimately] arrested on December 9, 1983." *Id.* at 335.

"On November 8, 1983, Edward Heller, a police criminologist, examined the sexual assault kit. He testified that he followed standard department procedure[, and determined that] sexual contact had occurred. * * * [He then] placed the assault kit back in the refrigerator." *Id.*

"[Defendant] was indicted on charges of child molestation, sexual assault, and kidnapping. The State moved to compel [defendant] to provide blood and saliva samples for comparison with the material gathered through the use of the sexual assault kit, but the trial court denied the motion on the ground that the State had not obtained a sufficiently large semen sample to make a valid comparison. The prosecutor then asked the State's criminologist to perform an ABO blood group test on the rectal swab sample in an attempt to

ascertain the blood type of the boy's assailant. This test failed to detect any blood group substances in the sample." *Id.*

"In January 1985, the police criminologist examined the boy's
clothing for the first time. He found one semen stain on the boy's
underwear and another on the rear of his T-shirt. The criminologist
tried to obtain blood group substances from both stains using the
ABO technique, but was unsuccessful. He also performed a P-30
protein molecule test on the stains, which indicated that only a
small quantity of semen was present on the clothing; it was incon-
clusive as to the assailant's identity. The Tucson Police Department had just begun using this test, which was then used in
slightly more than half of the crime laboratories in the country." *Id.*

"[Defendant]'s principal defense at trial was that the boy had
erred in identifying him as the perpetrator of the crime. In this
connection, both a criminologist for the State and an expert witness
for [defendant] testified as to what might have been shown by tests
performed on the samples shortly after they were gathered, or by
later tests performed on the samples from the boy's clothing had
the clothing been properly refrigerated." *Id.*

"The jury found [defendant] guilty as charged, but the Arizona
Court of Appeals reversed the judgment of conviction[, * * * finding that the destruction of the evidence in this case worked] a denial of due process. * * * The Supreme Court of Arizona denied the
State's petition for review, and we granted certiorari. * * * We now
reverse." *Id.*

"Decision of this case requires us again to consider 'what might
loosely be called the area of constitutionally-guaranteed access to
evidence.' * * * In *Brady v. Maryland,* 373 *U.S.* 83, [87,] 83 *S.Ct.*
1194[, 1196] (1963), we held 'that the suppression by the prosecution
of evidence favorable to the accused upon request violates due process where the evidence is material either to guilt or to punishment,
irrespective of the good faith or bad faith of the prosecution.' * * * In
United States v. Agurs, 427 *U.S.* 97, [111,] 96 *S.Ct.* 2392[, 2401]
(1976), we held that the prosecution had a duty to disclose some evidence of this description even though no requests were made for it,
but at the same time we rejected the notion that a 'prosecutor has a
constitutional duty routinely to deliver his entire file to defense counsel.' * * * [S]ee also Moore v. Illinois, 408 U.S. 786, 795, 92 S.Ct. 2562,
2568 [] (1972) ('We know of no constitutional requirement that the
prosecution make a complete and detailed accounting to the defense
of all police investigatory work on a case.')." *Youngblood* at 336.

"There is no question that the State complied with *Brady* and
Agurs here. The State disclosed relevant police reports to [defen-
dant], which contained information about the existence of the swab
and the clothing, and the boy's examination at the hospital. The
State provided [defendant]'s expert with the laboratory reports and
notes prepared by the police criminologist, and [defendant]'s expert
had access to the swab and to the clothing." *Id.*

"If [defendant] is to prevail on federal constitutional grounds, then, it must be because of some constitutional duty over and above that imposed by cases such as *Brady* and *Agurs*. * * * In th[is] case, the likelihood that the preserved materials would have enabled the defendant to exonerate himself appears to be greater than it was in [*California v.*] *Trombetta*, but here, unlike in *Trombetta*, the State did not attempt to make any use of the materials in its own case in chief."* *Id.*

"The Due Process Clause of the Fourteenth Amendment, as interpreted in *Brady*, makes the good or bad faith of the State irrelevant when the State fails to disclose to the defendant material exculpatory evidence. But we think the Due Process Clause requires a different result when we deal with the failure of the State to preserve evidentiary material of which no more can be said than that it could have been subjected to tests, the results of which might have exonerated the defendant. Part of the reason for the difference in treatment is found in the observation made by the Court in *Trombetta* * * * that '[w]henever potentially exculpatory evidence is permanently lost, courts face the treacherous task of divining the import of materials whose contents are unknown and, very often, disputed.' Part of it stems from our unwillingness to read the 'fundamental fairness' requirement of the Due Process Clause * * * as imposing on the police an undifferentiated and absolute duty to retain and preserve all material that might be of conceivable evidentiary significance in a particular prosecution. We think that requiring the defendant to show bad faith on the part of the police both limits the extent of the police's obligation to preserve evidence to reasonable bounds and confines it to that class of cases where the interests of justice most clearly require it, *i.e.*, those cases in which the police themselves by their conduct indicate that the evidence could form a basis for exonerating the defendant. *We therefore hold that unless a criminal defendant can show bad faith on the part of the police, failure to preserve potentially useful evidence does not constitute a denial of due process of law.*" *Id.* at 337. [Emphasis added.]

"In this case, the police collected the rectal swab and clothing on the night of the crime; [defendant] was not [located and therefore not] taken into custody until six weeks later. The failure of the police

---

* *Trombetta* speaks of evidence whose exculpatory value is 'apparent.' * * * The possibility that the semen samples could have exculpated [defendant] if preserved or tested is not enough to satisfy the standard of constitutional materiality in *Trombetta*. Moreover, we made clear in *Trombetta* that the exculpatory value of the evidence must be apparent '*before* the evidence was destroyed.' * * * Here, [defendant] has not shown that the police knew the semen samples would have exculpated him when they failed to perform certain tests or to refrigerate the boy's clothing; this evidence was simply an avenue of investigation that might have led in any number of directions. The presence or absence of bad faith by the police for purposes of the Due Process Clause must necessarily turn on the police's knowledge of the exculpatory value of the evidence at the time it was lost or destroyed." *Youngblood* at 336-37 n. *. [Court's emphasis.]

to refrigerate the clothing and to perform tests on the semen samples can at worst be described as negligent. None of this information was concealed from [defendant] at trial, and the evidence—such as it was—was made available to [defendant]'s expert who declined to perform any tests on the samples. The Arizona Court of Appeals noted in its opinion—and we agree—that there was no suggestion of bad faith on the part of the police. It follows, therefore, from what we have said, that there was no violation of the Due Process Clause." *Id.*

"The Arizona Court of Appeals also referred * * * to the State's 'inability to quantitatively test' certain semen samples with the newer P-30 test. If the court meant by this statement that the Due Process Clause is violated when the police fail to use a particular investigatory tool, we strongly disagree. The situation here is no different than a prosecution for drunk driving that rests on police observation alone; the defendant is free to argue to the finder of fact that a breathalyzer test might have been exculpatory, but the police do not have a constitutional duty to perform any particular tests." *Id.* at 338.

"The judgment of the Arizona Court of Appeals is . . . *REVERSED.*"

FIELD / ROUGH NOTES

KILLIAN v. UNITED STATES
Supreme Court of the United States
368 *U.S.* 231, 82 *S.Ct.* 302 (1961)

Mr. Justice WHITTAKER delivered the opinion of the Court.

[An indictment was returned against defendant in the United States District Court for the Northern District of Illinois, charging him with two counts of false swearing. Defendant was found guilty on both counts. During the course of defendant's trial, a question arose as to the F.B.I. agents' destruction of the notes taken during interviews with one of their informants, a witness for the government at trial. The agents' notes documented the informant's oral account of his expenses.]

"[T]he Solicitor General contends that * * * [the defendant] is not entitled to * * * a new trial, because the true facts are that the F.B.I. agents' notes covering [the informant's] oral reports of expenses were not in existence at the time of trial, [but the information contained in those notes,] and the receipts signed by [the informant,] * * * [which contain] the same information, in much greater detail, w[ere] given to [defendant] in the witness' narrative statements that were produced and delivered to his counsel at the trial[.]" *Id.* at 307.

"[T]he Solicitor General tells us * * * that * * * his interrogation of the F.B.I. agents has disclosed that, after they incorporated the data contained in their notes of [the informant's] oral reports into the receipts to be signed by him, the agents destroyed the notes in accord with normal practice, and hence those notes were not in existence at the time of [defendant's trial]." *Id.*

"For these reasons, the Solicitor General contends that * * * no error, at least no prejudicial error, resulted from the nonproduction of the F.B.I. notes * * * at the trial." *Id.* at 308.

"In opposition, [defendant] argues that the claimed destruction of the agents' notes admits the destruction of evidence that may have been helpful to him and deprives him of his right[] * * * to due process of law, and therefore the judgment should be reversed." *Id.*

"As to [defendant's] contention that the claimed destruction of the agents' notes admits the destruction of evidence, deprives him of legal rights and requires reversal of the judgment, it seems appropriate to observe that almost everything is evidence of something, but that does not mean that nothing can ever safely be destroyed. If the agents' notes of [the informant's] oral reports of expenses were made only for the purpose of transferring the data thereon to the receipts to be signed by [the informant], and if, after having served that purpose, they were destroyed by the agents in good faith and in accord with their normal practice, it would be clear that their destruction did not constitute an impermissible destruction of evidence nor deprive [defendant] of any right. Those are the factual representations made by the Solicitor General. Whether they are true can be determined only upon a hearing in the District Court." *Id.*

"Accordingly, we vacate the judgment and remand the cause to the District Court for a hearing confined to the issues raised by the Solicitor General's representations as stated in this opinion." *Id.* at 309.

NOTE

1. *See also Wright v. State*, 501 *P.*2d 1360, 1371 (Alaska 1972) (police department's pre-trial act of destroying police captain's notes taken during interview with a prospective government witness found to be "in good faith, without the intent to avoid production," and therefore "not a ground for reversal"); *United States v. Comulada*, 340 *F.*2d 449, 451 (2nd Cir. 1965) (destruction of notes, which an officer thought were no longer useful in the case, did not constitute a basis for reversal). *State v. Zenquis*, 251 *N.J.Super.* 358, 370, 598 *A.*2d 245 (App.Div. 1991) (officer's destruction of his notes "did not impair the defendant's ability to defend"; approving, however, an instruction to the jury that if it found that the officer destroyed his notes at a time when he knew the case was proceeding to trial, it

could infer that the notes contained information inconsistent with the witness's trial testimony). *But see United States v. Lonardo*, 350 *F*.2d 523 (6th Cir. 1965) (case reversed because federal agents destroyed their original notes in an apparent attempt to avoid the production required under the Jencks Act).

2. An officer's testimony concerning the destruction of his or her rough notes should be positive and deliberate. Consider the following:

CROSS-EXAMINATION

By Mr. Defense Attorney:

Q. Now officer, you were taught in the police academy to always take field notes, were you not ?

A. We were taught to take field notes whenever the situation reasonably permits the taking of notes.

Q. Officer, you were dispatched to the alleged crime scene ?

A. Yes.

Q. You arrived at the scene quickly ?

A. Yes I did.

Q. You spoke with several persons there ?

A. Yes.

Q. Well, that situation certainly was one which provided an opportunity for the taking of field notes, wasn't it ?

A. Yes.

Q. You took field notes, didn't you officer ?

A. Yes.

Q. Now officer, you were taught in the police academy to include every important fact in your notes, weren't you ?

A. We were taught that the purpose of the field notes is to help refresh our recollection for the writing of the formal incident or investigation report.

Q. Your notes documented what the witnesses at the scene told you ?

A. Yes.

Q. You gave those notes to the prosecutor ?

A. No.

Q. No ? What did you do with your notes ?

A. After carefully and meticulously incorporating the information contained in the notes into my formal report, I discarded them.

Q. You threw them away ?

A. Yes I did.

Q. Why did you throw them away ?

A. The rough notes are made for the purpose of facilitating the writing of the formal police report. After the information contained in the rough notes is carefully transferred into the formal report, the rough notes are discarded as a matter of standard practice and procedure.

3. As a matter of standard practice and procedure, a number of federal agencies and circuit courts require the retention of certain "rough notes" prepared by a government agent. The following cases are illustrative.

UNITED STATES v. VELLA
United States Court of Appeals
562 *F.*2d 275 (3rd Cir. 1977)

PER CURIAM.

"In this appeal from his conviction of conspiracy and operating an illegal gambling business in violation of federal law, [defendant, Peter Vella,] contends that the district court erred in refusing to exclude the testimony of two F.B.I. agents who had destroyed the rough notes of interviews they held with Vella. [Defendant] claims that the written notes constituted statements producible under the Jencks Act, 18 *U.S.C.* § 3500, and that their destruction (a) deprived him of a full and fair opportunity to cross-examine the agents, and (b) violated the principles of *Brady v. Maryland*, 373 *U.S.* 83, 83 *S.Ct.* 1194 [] (1963)." *Vella* at 275.

"A similar contention was made before this court in *United States v. Harris*, 560 *F.*2d 148 (3rd Cir. 1977), in which this court stated:

> At argument of this case, counsel for the Government stated to the court that it is now the policy of the Federal Bureau of Investigation to preserve rough notes of interviews. We accept this representation and, accordingly, do not meet the issue insofar as it affects future conduct of F.B.I. agents.* *See United States v. Harrison*, 173 *U.S.App.D.C.* 260, 524 *F.*2d 421 (1975).

"To avoid future misunderstandings, we specifically adopt the precepts announced in *United States v. Harrison* * * * as the law in this circuit[:] the rough interview notes of F.B.I. agents should be kept and produced so that the trial court can determine whether

---

* In its brief, the government pointed out that "the FBI is now attempting to set up procedures where rough notes will be preserved in the future." *Vella* at 275-76 n.1.

the notes should be made available to the [defendant] under the rule of *Brady v. Maryland*[.]" *Vella* at 276.

"For the purposes of the present appeal, we have determined that in light of the other evidence in the record, as well as the apparent good faith administrative decision which led to the destruction of the notes, the error must be considered harmless." *Id.*

UNITED STATES v. AMMAR
United States Court of Appeals
714 *F.*2d 238 (3rd Cir. 1983)

SLOVITER, Circuit Judge.

* * * *

Defendants "contend that the district court erred in failing to strike the testimony of DEA Agent Schmotzer or to declare a mistrial after it was revealed that Schmotzer had destroyed the handwritten drafts of his reports. These contained, [among other things], Schmotzer's accounts of his meetings and telephone conversations with the [defendants] while Schmotzer was posing as a heroin buyer. [Defendants] contend that their destruction violated the Jencks Act, 18 *U.S.C.* § 3500, which requires that 'statements' of a government witness relating to the subject matter of his testimony be produced by the government upon motion of the defendant." *Id.* at 258.

"In analyzing this issue, it is important to distinguish between three categories of documents: (1) contemporaneous rough notes taken by a government agent of meetings, conversations, or interviews during the course of his or her investigation; (2) the agent's subsequently prepared drafts of his reports of these incidents; and (3) the final report signed by the agent. In *United States v. Vella*, * * * we held with regard to the first category that 'the rough interview notes of F.B.I. agents should be kept and produced so that the trial court can determine whether the notes should be made available to the [defendant] * * *. No question under *Vella* arises here. Schmotzer taped some of the conversations, had only rough notes of others, and had no contemporaneous record of still others. The tape recordings were made available to [defendants] and were played at trial. The rough notes of the conversations were turned over to the defendants. The final typed, signed reports were also made available to defendants." *Ammar* at 258-59.

"The issue in this case is thus confined to the second category of materials referred to above. [Defendants] claim they were entitled to the handwritten drafts of Schmotzer's reports, on the theory that some of those were the most nearly contemporaneous record of the events at issue." *Id.* at 259.

"Under the Jencks Act, the government must produce written statements made by a witness which are 'signed or otherwise adopted or approved by him.' 18 *U.S.C.* § 3500(e)(1). Ordinarily, rough drafts of an agent's report which are subsequently typed verbatim would not be a producible 'statement.' * * * On the other hand, [we have] recognized that a report draft which 'was at least in a form sufficiently acceptable to the agent that he allowed it to be reviewed by his superior' might have been 'adopted or approved' by the agent and hence fall within the Jencks Act. * * *" *Id.*

"Although in most cases a rough draft may not be a Jencks Act 'statement,' we believe the same rationale which underlay our decision in *Vella* directing retention of rough notes is also applicable to handwritten drafts of agents' reports. We therefore hold that, hereafter, the government must retain and, upon motion, make available to the district court, both the rough notes and the drafts of reports of its agents to facilitate the district court's determination whether they should be produced. This requirement should impose no undue burden on the government."* *Id.* at 259 n.19.

"In this case, * * * the handwritten drafts were not shown to Schmotzer's supervisor. Thus, there would have been no basis to find that Schmotzer had 'adopted or approved' them, a predicate to [a determination] that the handwritten drafts were 'statements' under the Jencks Act." *Id.*

"Furthermore, Schmotzer testified that he compared the typewritten reports with the handwritten drafts and determined that they were substantially identical before he destroyed the handwritten drafts. There is no basis for concluding that the destruction was in bad faith. Thus, even were these drafts Jencks Act material, their destruction would have constituted harmless error." *Id.* at 259-60.

UNITED STATES v. RAMOS
United States Court of Appeals
27 *F.*3d 65 (3rd Cir. 1994)

LEWIS, Circuit Judge.

"We confront, once again, a problem which no court, trial or appellate, should have to face in this circuit. Although we have unequivocally required since 1977 that government agents preserve rough notes of interviews with prospective trial witnesses, * * * this case presents yet another instance in which notes were destroyed. We do not reverse here because it is apparent to us that the destroyed notes did not constitute Jencks Act or *Brady* material and

---

* The court has been advised "that the DEA itself has adopted regulations requiring the retention of draft reports, at least in cases where no contemporaneous notes were taken."

that the officers who destroyed them acted in good faith. Nonetheless, we take this opportunity to emphasize that the fortuitous mix of legal and factual circumstances which might excuse the destruction of notes * * * are few and far between. We should not encounter such cases in the future." *Id.* at 66-67.

Defendants "Maria and Elizabeth Ramos, mother and daughter, were convicted of conspiracy to distribute cocaine and cocaine base, possession of cocaine with intent to distribute and related charges arising out of their involvement in a family-operated drug ring." *Id.* at 67.

"At trial, the government's case against the Ramoses was supported by the testimony of 13 co-conspirators who cooperated pursuant to plea agreements. * * *" *Id.*

"Detective James Moffit and his partner, Sergeant Gerald Logan, interviewed the cooperating witnesses and took notes during their initial debriefings, or 'proffers,' in late 1990 or 1991. Both were long-time Philadelphia police officers who began working with the federal government on this investigation in the fall of 1989, in association with the federal Drug Enforcement Administration ('DEA'). Logan described himself as being 'assigned' to the DEA; Moffit termed his position as one in which he was 'detailed' or 'cross-designated' to the DEA. * * * Both had been 'sworn in' by the DEA and were issued DEA credentials." *Id.*

"It is undisputed that Moffit and, apparently, Logan destroyed their notes after they prepared summary reports[. Defendants] contend that this destruction mandated suppression of the officers' testimony or a mistrial, both of which the district court denied." *Id.*

"The Jencks Act requires that after each government witness has testified on direct examination, the government must produce to the defense 'any statement' made by the witness which relates to his or her testimony. In *Brady* [*v. Maryland*], the Supreme Court held that due process required that the government produce all 'exculpatory' evidence, which includes both 'materials . . . that go to the heart of the defendant's guilt or innocence and materials that might affect the jury's judgment of the credibility of a crucial prosecution witness.' " *Id.* at 68.[6]

In *United States v. Vella* "we held that 'the rough notes of F.B.I. agents should be kept and produced so that the trial court can determine whether the notes should be made available to the [defendant] under the rule of *Brady* . . . or the Jencks Act.' * * * *See also United States v. Ammar* [] (extending rule to require preservation of rough drafts of agents' reports) * * *. Since then, the DEA has apparently adopted an internal policy requiring such retention. * * * But we need not decide whether our holding in *Vella* or the

---

[6] Quoting *United States v. Hill*, 976 *F.*2d 132, 143-45 (3rd Cir. 1992). See also *Giglio v. United States*, 405 *U.S.* 150, 154, 92 *S.Ct.* 763, 766 (1972). In *Moore v. Illinois*, 408 *U.S.* 786, 92 *S.Ct.* 2562 (1972), the Court explained that "[a] valid *Brady* complaint contains three elements: (1) the prosecution must suppress or withhold evidence, (2) which is favorable, and (3) material to the defense."

DEA's policy was followed in this case; there is simply no question that they were not. Instead, the only question before us is: what should be done about a clear failure to follow established rules and policy ?" *Ramos* at 68. [Citations omitted.]

"In *Vella* and *Ammar*, we explained the requirement in such unambiguous terms that it would be futile to try to elucidate further here, for what we meant cannot be stated more clearly. * * *" *Id.*

"A careful reading of both *Vella* and *Ammar*, however, suggests that we did not imply a rule which would automatically preclude evidence based upon destroyed rough notes, without regard for other considerations. * * * [T]he mere fact that *Vella* and *Ammar* each established rules for the government to follow does not suggest that we intended the automatic suppression of evidence when those rules are violated." *Id.* at 69. Rather, " 'unless a criminal defendant can show bad faith on the part of the police, failure to preserve potentially useful evidence does not constitute a denial of due process of law.' " *Id.*[7]

"In this case, since the [defendants] raised *Brady* and Jencks Act issues, we will first proceed to analyze whether either *Brady* or Jencks Act material might have been present in the destroyed notes. Only after ascertaining that it was not present will we move on to a good faith analysis." *Id.*

"We may quickly dispose of the Jencks Act issues. The Jencks Act requires a court, upon motion of the defendant and after direct examination of a government witness, to order the United States to produce to the defense 'any statement . . . of the witness in [its] possession . . . which relates to the subject matter as to which the witness has testified.' 18 *U.S.C.* § 3500(b). Leaving aside 'statements' which are transcriptions or recordings of grand jury testimony, a 'statement' within the meaning of the Jencks Act is:

> (1) a written statement made by said witness and signed or otherwise adopted by him; [or]
>
> (2) a stenographic, mechanical, electrical, or other recording, or a transcription thereof, which is a substantially verbatim recital of an oral statement made by said witness and recorded contemporaneously with the making of such oral statement; * * *

18 *U.S.C.* § 3500(e)

Ramos at 69.

"The destroyed notes fall into neither of these categories. They clearly do not constitute 'statements' of the cooperating coconspirators, for they are neither 'substantially verbatim recitals' of what those witnesses said during their proffers nor writings which they signed or otherwise adopted or approved. * * * Nor are they 'statements' of Moffit or Logan, for they are by no means

---

[7] Quoting *Arizona v. Youngblood*, 488 *U.S.* 51, 58, 109 *S.Ct.* 333, 337 (1988).

'substantially verbatim' recitals of anything Moffit or Logan said. Further, * * * they do not constitute writings which the officers later adopted in any way. * * * Accordingly, we conclude that the destroyed notes did not constitute Jencks Act material." *Id.* at 69-70.

"The *Brady* issue is more complex. * * * [I]t is impossible to know for certain whether or not rough notes which have been destroyed would have been exculpatory, or whether their exculpatory nature would have been apparent to the agents at the time of the destruction, because they are no longer here for us to see, to analyze, to interpret. Whatever truths might have been gleaned from them, and whatever contributions these truths might have offered to the doing of justice, were destroyed along with the notes themselves. * * *" *Id.* at 70.

"Nevertheless, the mere possibility that the destroyed notes might have included *Brady* material, without more, is insufficient to implicate such concerns. '[U]nless a defendant is able to raise at least a colorable claim that the investigator's discarded rough notes contained evidence favorable to [him] and material to his claim of innocence or to the applicable punishment—and that such exculpatory evidence has not been included in any formal interview report provided to defendant—no constitutional error of violation of due process will have been established.' " *Id.* at 71. [Citation omitted.]

"In this case, the defendants have offered nothing beyond their speculation that the agents' notes might have contained *Brady* material. In response, the government indicated that Moffit had incorporated everything contained within the notes into the [summary reports]. * * * There was no suggestion by anyone in a position to know (that is, the witnesses or the officers) that the [summary reports] differed in any way from the oral proffers that would have been reflected in the destroyed notes. * * * [Defendants] have not raised a colorable claim that the destroyed notes contained exculpatory material that was material to their defense and was not included within the DEA [summary reports]. Therefore, we conclude that the destruction of the notes did not constitute a *Brady* violation." *Id.*

"It is undisputed that Moffit and Logan destroyed their notes in good faith. They are Philadelphia police officers, not DEA agents, and Moffit testified that the federal practice of retaining records of a cooperating-witness interview is 'completely different' from the Philadelphia police department's. * * * In the Philadelphia police department, at least at the time the events with which we are concerned took place, the officers 'consider[ed notes] sensitive material' that they 'don't leave . . . around at all.' [] Philadelphia police officers retain the reports they draft based upon their notes but destroy the notes." *Id.*

"Moreover, Moffit received no special training and no orientation for his work with the DEA. * * * [He] was not told to preserve the notes he used in compiling the [summary reports]." *Id.* at 71-72.

"We are well aware of the critical contribution the DEA and its agents make to the national effort to control illegal drug trafficking and to combat illegal drug use. * * * But we cannot approve of the way in which Moffit and, presumably, Logan were trained. It is regrettable that the DEA failed to instruct officers affiliated with it to preserve the rough notes taken at proffer sessions, particularly after we have made it abundantly clear that it is required to do so and its own internal guidelines mandate that it do so. Our affirmance in this case is in no way intended to encourage or to permit lax compliance with the dictates of due process under the guise of good-faith ignorance. To the contrary, we expect more of the government." *Id.* at 72.

"In conclusion, because the destroyed notes did not constitute Jencks Act materials, there is nothing beyond speculation to indicate that they contained *Brady* material, and the officers clearly acted in good faith in destroying them, we will affirm the district court's denial of [defendants'] motion for suppression or, in the alternative, a mistrial. The judgment of conviction is affirmed." *Id.*

COMMONWEALTH v. OWENS
Supreme Court of Pennsylvania
427 *Pa.Super.* 379, 629 *A.2d* 150 (1993)

POPOVICH, Judge.

[Defendant was convicted of speeding. The state trooper clocked him traveling 96 miles per hour in a 55 mile-per-hour zone. At the time of the stop, defendant asked the trooper to show him the radar reading. The trooper refused defendant's request.]

"[Defend]ant contends that according to *Brady v. Maryland*, 373 *U.S.* 83, 83 *S.Ct.* 1194 [] (1963), [he] had a right to see the radar reading when the trooper stopped him for speeding. We disagree." *Id.*, 629 *A.2d* at 152.

"The United States Supreme Court held in *Brady*, that suppression by the prosecution of evidence favorable to an accused upon request violates due process where the evidence is material either to guilt or punishment. * * * The holding in *Brady* applies to evidence that is requested during or following discovery and is withheld by the prosecution. The case is not applicable to the present situation in which a person requests to view immediately a police officer's radar [reading]." *Id.*

"Presently, [defend]ant is asking us to rule that a police officer must justify stopping a person for speeding at the time of the stop. However, the law does not provide support for [defend]ant's argument. [A police officer] is not required to allow a suspect to view the radar at the time he was stopped. Rather, the Common-wealth must prove beyond a reasonable doubt the following to sustain a conviction for speeding: '(1) that an accused was driving in excess of the applicable speed limit, (2) that the speed timing device was approved by the Department of Transportation, and (3) that it had been tested for accuracy by an approved testing station.' * * * [Defend]ant does not dispute that the Commonwealth sustained its burden of proving these elements." *Id.* [Citation omitted.]

"[Defend]ant was fully informed of the charges against him. He received notice of the charges and had an opportunity to be heard. * * * Accordingly, we find that [defend]ant was not denied a due process right when Trooper Long refused to allow [defend]ant to see the radar."* *Id.*

---

* "We note that to allow every individual who is stopped for speeding to enter the police car to view the radar would not be workable." *Id.* at 152 n.4.

Chapter 4

WITNESSES:
EXPLORING TESTIMONIAL AND DOCUMENTARY
EVIDENCE

§4.1. OPINION TESTIMONY

Historically, witnesses were held to the requirement that their testimony relate only the "facts they personally know," not their "inferences, conclusions or opinions."[1] Over time, however, the rule against opinion testimony has been tempered by such countervailing interests as "expediency" and "convenience,"[2] coupled with a dose of common sense and logic. Today, the law recognizes that in many cases, testimony in the form of an opinion is not only unavoidable but necessary and, at times, desirable.[3]

It is clear, therefore, that testimony comes in two varieties: factual and opinion. When the testimony is factual in nature, the witness must testify from personal knowledge. When the testimony is in the form of an opinion, its admissibility will normally require a preliminary determination by a court as to the "type" of witness from which it flows. In this respect, witnesses who offer their opinions have been classified as (a) lay witnesses, (b) skilled witnesses or (c) expert witnesses.

§4.1(a). Lay Witnesses

As a general rule, a lay witness may give his or her opinion "in matters of common knowledge and observation."[4] *Fed.R.Evid.* 701 sets forth the principles to be applied to opinion evidence offered by lay witnesses. It provides:

> If the witness is not testifying as an expert, the witness' testimony in the form of opinions or inferences is limited to those opinions or inferences which are (a) rationally based on the perception of the witness,

---

[1] *See* 1 McCormick, *Evidence* §11 (West 4th ed. 1992).

[2] 1 McCormick, *Evidence* §11. McCormick further explains that the factors of "expediency" and "convenience" have been recognized by many courts under the guise of the "so-called 'short-hand rendition' rule." *Id.* at 44. This rule incorporates "the practice of admitting 'opinions' where they can be justified as 'short-hand renditions' of a total situation, or as 'statements of collective facts.' " *Id.* at 44 n.16. (citations omitted).

[3] In all cases, "[t]he admissibility of opinion evidence rests within the discretion of the trial court." *State v. Labrutto*, 114 *N.J.* 187, 197, 553 *A.*2d 335 (1989).

[4] *State v. Labrutto, supra*, 114 *N.J.* at 197.

and (b) helpful to a clear understanding of the witness' testimony or the determination of a fact in issue, and (c) not based on scientific, technical, or other specialized knowledge within the scope of Rule 702.

The first requirement of the rule is that the lay witness must have "actual knowledge, acquired through his or her senses, of the matter to which he or she testifies."[5] This is called the "first-hand knowledge or observation" requirement.[6] In addition, the opinion of the lay witness must help the factfinder understand the witness' testimony or determine a fact in issue. The third, and most recent requirement, is that the lay witness' opinion must not be based on "scientific, technical, or other specialized knowledge," which would otherwise require the opinion of an "expert."[7]

It is up to the trial court to determine when an opinion or inference embodied in a lay witness' testimony begins to cross the line into a complicated, technical subject; and that line is not always clear.[8] By requiring the trial court to closely examine proposed lay witness opinion testimony by reference to the "scientific, technical, and other specialized knowledge" component of the rules governing expert testimony, Rule 701 ensures that a party will not evade the expert witness disclosure requirements set forth in *Fed.R.Crim.P.* 16 by simply calling an expert witness in the guise of a layperson.[9]

Rule 701 does not distinguish between expert and lay *witnesses*, but rather, between expert and lay *testimony*. In this respect, it is possible for the same witness to provide both lay and expert testimony in a single case. For example, in *United States v. Figueroa-Lopez*,[10] the court determined that a law enforcement officer could testify that the defendant was "acting suspiciously," without being qualified as an expert, but that the rules on expert testimony were

---

[5] Advisory Committee's Note, 56 *F.R.D.* 183, 281.

[6] *Id.*

[7] As explained by the Advisory Committee, "Rule 701 has been amended to eliminate the risk that the reliability requirements set forth in Rule 702 will be evaded through the simple expedient of proffering an expert in lay witness clothing. Under the amendment, a witness' testimony must be scrutinized under the rules regulating expert opinion to the extent that the witness is providing scientific, technical, or other specialized information to the trier of fact."

[8] *See e.g., United States v. Fleishman*, 684 *F.*2d 1329 (9th Cir. 1982) (undercover officer's testimony that the defendant was "acting as a lookout" may have been either a lay opinion or an expert opinion).

[9] *See e.g., United States v. Figueroa-Lopez*, 125 *F.*3d 1241, 1246 (9th Cir. 1997) (law enforcement agents testifying that the defendant's conduct was consistent with that of a drug trafficker could not testify as lay witnesses; to permit such testimony under Rule 701 "subverts the requirements" of the Federal Rules of Criminal Procedure). In this respect, *Fed.R.Crim.P.* 16(a)(1)(G) provides in pertinent part: "At the defendant's request, the government must give to the defendant a written summary of any testimony that the government intends to use under Rules 702, 703, or 705 of the Federal Rules of Evidence during its case-in-chief at trial. * * * The summary provided under this subparagraph must describe the witness's opinions, the bases and reasons for those opinions, and the witness's qualifications."

[10] 125 *F.*3d 1241 (9th Cir. 1997).

applicable where the officer further testified on the basis of extensive experience that the defendant was using "code words" to refer to drug quantities and prices.[11]

Accordingly, any part of a witness' testimony that is based upon scientific, technical, or other specialized knowledge is governed by the standards of Rule 702 and the corresponding disclosure requirements of the Federal Rules of Criminal Procedure.

---

§4.1(b). Skilled Witnesses

Law enforcement officers are generally permitted "to testify as lay witnesses, based on their personal observations *and their long experience* in areas where expert testimony might otherwise be deemed necessary."[12] Thus, in cases in which a police witness may not qualify as an "expert" *per se*, the officer may offer, upon a properly laid and sufficient foundation setting forth his or her training and experience, his or her "skilled" opinion based on personal observations.[13]

STATE v. LABRUTTO
Supreme Court of New Jersey
114 *N.J.* 187, 553 *A.2d* 335 (1989)

The opinion of the Court was delivered by

GARIBALDI, J.
"Police officers are usually the first witnesses to arrive at the scene of an automobile accident. Before physical evidence at the scene is removed, distorted, or tampered with, they have the unique opportunity to observe it. The primary issue in this appeal is whether an investigating state trooper, not qualified as an expert, may testify about the vehicles' point of impact based on his own observations. We hold that the state trooper's testimony is admissible under *Evid.R.* 56(1)."[14] *Id.*, 114 *N.J.* at 191.

---

[11] *Id.* at 1246.

[12] *Labrutto* at 198. (emphasis added).

[13] *Labrutto* at 200-01. Many courts place this type of testimony in the "lay opinion" category. It is, however, more appropriate to recognize the existence of a third category, the "skilled" witness, in light of the additional foundation required for such testimony, namely, that the witness have a reasonable degree of training and experience to offer a "skilled" opinion. *See e.g., Harris v. District of Columbia*, 601 A.2d 21, 25 (D.C.App. 1991) (the additional foundation for "lay opinion" testimony that a person was under the influence of drugs "is that the witness have had a reasonable degree of experience in observing persons who are under the influence of narcotics").

[14] *N.J.Evid.R.* 56(1) is this state's equivalent of *Fed.R.Evid.* 701.

"The admissibility of opinion evidence rests with the discretion of the trial court. Our review of this record establishes that the trial court properly admitted Trooper Mutter's non-expert point of impact opinion testimony * * *." *Id.* at 197.

"[I]n order to admit lay opinion the trial court must determine first that the witness' opinion is 'rationally based' on the witness' personal perception, and then that the opinion will be helpful to an understanding of the witness' testimony or the case in general." *Id.* at 198.

"Courts in New Jersey have permitted police officers to testify as lay witnesses, based on their personal observations and their long experience in areas where expert testimony might otherwise be deemed necessary." *Id.*

"We find no reason why an investigating police officer should not be allowed to testify as a non-expert based on his own observations regarding the point of impact of two vehicles in an automobile accident case. We find no merit in the position that the police officer's opinion on the point of impact should be excluded because it invades the province of the jury, or that the officer's testimony is unnecessary because the average juror can readily determine the point of impact from the officer's description of the physical evidence. Nor do we agree that only a police officer who is qualified as an accident-reconstruction expert can give his opinion of the point of impact." *Id.* at 199.

"We acknowledge that there may be some cases in which determining the point of impact of a collision will involve such complicated technical and scientific evidence that only a qualified reconstruction expert could rationally form an opinion about the point of impact. We anticipate that such complicated cases seldom will occur, and leave it to the trial courts to determine the necessity of having expert testimony in such cases." *Id.* at 199-200.

"Our holding that a police officer who is not qualified as an accident-reconstruction expert may testify based on his own observations of the point of impact is supported by many out-of-state cases. Most hold that an experienced police officer may properly testify on his or her *'skilled'* or 'expert' opinion of the point of impact based on personal observations of physical evidence such as skid marks and debris found at the scene of an accident. * * * These cases hold that it is unnecessary for the officer to possess a formal certificate qualifying him as an accident-reconstruction expert in order to offer his *'skilled'* or 'expert' opinion *so long as he is experienced and schooled in investigating motor vehicle accidents.*" *Id.* at 200. [Citations omitted; emphasis added.]

"Several other recent out-of-state cases hold that a police officer may testify as a lay witness and need not qualify as an expert to testify about the point of impact based on his personal observations.

Most of those cases, nonetheless, consider the officer's experience to determine if a proper foundation had been laid for the officer's opinion." *Id.* at 200. [Citations omitted.]

In this case, "Trooper Mutter was not presented as a qualified accident-reconstruction expert. He did, however, have training and substantial experience in accident investigation, having been involved in the investigation of over 400 motor-vehicle accidents in his seven years as a state trooper. Moreover, he based his point-of-impact opinion on personal observations at the scene of the accident." *Id.* at 201.

"Trooper Mutter, together with his partner, Trooper Mikoljczyk, arrived shortly after the accident. For over two hours he conducted his own investigation of the scene. He observed the weather and visibility, the location of the cars, the damage to the cars, the location of Mr. Pignatelli's body, the defendant's condition, the tire marks in the grass and their direction, the uprooted grass and location of the debris, and the distance between the scuff marks in the grass and the location of defendant's vehicle. He made notes at the site, which he later incorporated into his police report. He also made a diagram incorporating his personal observations. He ordered police photographs. These observations provided sufficient evidence on which to base an opinion about the point of impact." *Id.*

"All these observations were disclosed to the jury. The trooper's opinion did not rest on any unknown assumptions. He was subject to extensive cross-examination, and his testimony was challenged by [the] defendant's expert[.] Mutter's testimony did not remain unchallenged or accepted because he was a police officer." *Id.* at 202.

"Accordingly, we conclude that the trial court properly admitted Trooper Mutter's point-of-impact testimony as it met both requirements of *Evid.R.* 56(1), namely, it was rationally based on what he observed at the scene of the accident and it was helpful to the jury's full comprehension of the facts in question." *Id.*

NOTE

1. *An officer's personal knowledge, training and experience: The foundation.* Naturally, before a law enforcement officer may testify as a "skilled" witness, a preliminary determination will be made by the court as to whether the police witness possessed, at the relevant time, the requisite personal qualifications, education, training and experience.

2. Once the court determines that the prospective police witness is sufficiently trained and experienced, subject to *Fed.R.Evid.* 602 (the personal knowledge requirement), the officer may testify as to his or her "skilled" opinion on a wide variety of matters.

(a) High crime areas. See Trentacost v. Brussel, 164 *N.J.Super.* 9, 20, 395 *A.*2d 540 (App.Div. 1978), *aff'd* 82 *N.J.* 214, 412 *A.*2d 436 (1980), where, in a case involving a tenant's suit against her landlord to recover for injuries sustained when she was mugged in the hallway of her apartment building, the court allowed the investigating detective to testify that the apartment building was located in a high-crime neighborhood. The court held the testimony admissible under *Evid.R.* 56(1), noting that the officer had investigated approximately 75-100 crimes (including numerous muggings) in the neighborhood over a three-year period.

(b) Individuals "under the influence."

(i) Drugs. See State v. Jackson, 124 *N.J.Super.* 1, 304 *A.*2d 565 (App.Div. 1973), where the court ruled that a police detective was competent to testify, as a "non-expert," that in his opinion he had observed the defendant under the influence of narcotics. Noting that the detective's background included advanced training in the field of narcotics and participation in 75-100 narcotics arrests, the court concluded that a lay witness, such as the police detective in this case, "if sufficiently experienced and trained, may testify generally as to the observable reaction of drug users and [to] the technique of the use." *Id.,* 124 *N.J.Super.* at 4. *See also Harris v. District of Columbia,* 601 *A.*2d 21, 25, 26 (D.C.App. 1991) ("because an adequate foundation was laid, the trial court did not err in allowing Officer Grooms to testify that [defendant] appeared to be under the influence of drugs"); *State v. Lesac,* 231 *Neb.* 718, 722, 437 *N.W.*2d 517, 519 (1989) (law enforcement officers could give opinions that defendant was under the influence of drugs because their opinions "were rationally based on those witnesses' perceptions and were obviously helpful to the determination of a fact in issue"); *State v. Lindley,* 286 *N.C.* 255, 258-59, 210 *S.E.*2d 207, 210 (1974) ("[A] patrol officer with five years' experience in enforcement of the motor vehicle laws * * * is competent to express an opinion, based on the conditions he observed and on the knowledge gained from interrogation of defendant, that defendant was under the influence of some drug").

(ii) Alcohol. It is well accepted that in drunk-driving prosecutions, a properly qualified police officer witness may offer his or her opinion that the defendant was drunk based on the officer's observations of the defendant's performance on certain balance tests. *State v. Morton,* 74 *N.J.Super.* 528, 531-32, 181 *A.*2d 785 (App.Div. 1962), *aff'd* 39 *N.J.* 512, 189 *A.*2d 216 (1963). "Even a lay witness lacking special expertise may give opinion evidence concerning whether an individual is intoxicated." *State v. Phillips,*

213 *N.J.Super.* 534, 545 n.6, 517 *A.2d* 1204 (App.Div. 1986) (refer-ring to "such well-known indicia" as "watery eyes, imbalance, an odor of alcohol or like symptoms"). *See also Harris v. District of Columbia, supra* at 24 ("It has long been established * * * that police officers [] may testify to their opinion whether the driver of a vehi-cle appeared to be under the influence of alcohol").

(c) Voice comparisons. See State v. Perez, 150 *N.J.Super.* 166, 375 *A.2d* 277 (App.Div. 1977), where the investigating detec-tive was held competent to testify, as a "non-expert," that in his opinion the voice of the defendant taken from a voice exemplar matched a voice in a taped telephone conversation. In this case, the jury was also permitted to hear the taped conversation and the voice exemplar.

(d) Footprint identification. In *State v. Johnson,* 120 *N.J.* 263, 576 *A.2d* 834 (1990), a fingerprint expert testified at trial that a "footprint" found at the scene had been made by defendant's sneaker. Defendant argued that it was error to admit such testi-mony without first qualifying the fingerprint expert as "an expert specifically trained in footprint identification." *Id.* at 293. The Court disagreed.

Preliminarily, the Court reminded that "[a] lay witness may give an opinion on matters of common knowledge and observation." *Id.* at 294. In the case of footprint identification, " 'shoe-print pat-terns are often "readily recognizable and well within the capabili-ties of a lay witness to observe. No detailed measurements, no sub-tle analysis or scientific determination is needed." ' " *Id.* [Citations omitted.] As a result, the Court concluded that "footprint identifi-cation is an area in which lay-opinion testimony is acceptable[.]" *Id.* at 295. The prosecution may not, however, attempt to bolster the credibility of such testimony, as it did in this case, by qualify-ing the witness as a fingerprint expert for the primary purpose of relying on the officer's qualifications as a fingerprint expert to en-hance the credibility of his conclusions about the shoeprint identifi-cation. *Id. See also State v. Gerald,* 113 *N.J.* 40, 53-54, 61, 549 *A.2d* 792 (1988) (medical examiner and state police forensic chemist permitted to testify to sneaker pattern similarities); *State v. Bruzzese,* 94 *N.J.* 210, 215, 239, 463 *A.2d* 320 (1983) (footprint-identification testimony permitted by police detective who person-ally observed similarity between footprint at crime scene and shoe in defendant's room).

§4.1(c). Expert Witnesses

Expert testimony, in criminal cases, is usually introduced when the trier of fact (judge or jury) needs assistance in ascertaining the significance or the character of physical or other forms of evidence, and, more generally, when such testimony would assist the trier of fact in understanding or deciding an issue in the case. Indeed, the fundamental reason for permitting expert testimony is that the average juror is not capable of dealing with a subject that is not a matter of common knowledge.

The admission of expert opinion testimony is regulated generally by the rules of evidence. In this respect, *Fed.R.Evid.* 702 provides:

> If scientific, technical, or other specialized knowledge will assist the trier of fact to understand the evidence or to determine a fact in issue, a witness qualified as an expert by knowledge, skill, experience, training, or education, may testify thereto in the form of an opinion or otherwise, if (1) the testimony is based upon sufficient facts or data, (2) the testimony is the product of reliable principles and methods, and (3) the witness has applied the principles and methods reliably to the facts of the case.

Expert witnesses need not have direct personal knowledge of the event in question. As explained by the United States Supreme Court in *Daubert v. Merrell Dow Pharmaceuticals, Inc.,*[15] unlike an ordinary witness, "an expert is permitted wide latitude to offer opinions, including those that are not based on first-hand knowledge or observation."[16] The information, "facts or data in the particular case upon which an expert bases an opinion or inference may be * * * made known to the expert at or before the hearing."[17] Moreover, there is no prohibition against an expert giving an opinion which embraces an ultimate issue in the case.[18] The testimony provided by the expert must be "not only relevant, but reliable,"

---

[15] 509 *U.S.* 579, 113 *S.Ct.* 2786 (1993).

[16] *Id.* at 592, 113 *S.Ct.* at 2796.

[17] *Fed.R.Evid.* 703. This rule further provides: "If of a type reasonably relied upon by experts in the particular field in forming opinions or inferences upon the subject, the facts or data need not be admissible in evidence in order for the opinion or inference to be admitted. Facts or data that are otherwise inadmissible shall not be disclosed to the jury by the proponent of the opinion or inference unless the court determines that their probative value in assisting the jury to evaluate the expert's opinion substantially outweighs their prejudicial effect."

[18] *Fed.R.Evid.* 704(a). An exception to this so-called "ultimate issue" rule may be found at *Fed.R.Evid.* 704(b), which would prohibit expert psychiatric testimony on the ultimate issue of a criminal defendant's mental state or condition. Such testimony would be limited to presenting and explaining the psychiatrist's diagnosis, "such as whether the defendant had a severe mental disease or defect and what the characteristics of such a disease or defect, if any, may have been." *H.R. Report* 98-1030, 98th Cong., 2d Sess., p. 230; 1984 *U.S.Code Cong. & Ad.News* 232 (Legislative History).

and trial judges are charged with the responsibility of acting as gatekeepers to exclude unreliable expert testimony.[19]

The "expert witness" rule imposes four basic requirements for the admission of expert testimony: (1) the proposed testimony or evidence must concern a subject matter requiring either "scientific," "technical," or "specialized" knowledge beyond the basic understanding of the average juror; (2) the proposed testimony or evidence must be supported by "appropriate validation," *i.e.*, it must be reliable; (3) the witness must have sufficient expertise to offer the intended testimony; and (4) the proposed testimony or evidence must be relevant— it must assist the trier of fact to understand the evidence or to determine a fact in issue.[20]

To assess the scientific validity, relevance, and reliability of proposed scientific expert testimony, "the trial judge must determine at the outset, pursuant to Rule 104(a), whether the expert is proposing to testify to (1) 'scientific,' 'technical' or 'other specialized' knowledge that (2) will assist the trier of fact to understand or determine a fact in issue. This entails a preliminary assessment of whether the reasoning or methodology underlying the testimony is scientifically valid and whether that reasoning or methodology properly can be applied to the facts in issue."[21] Although many factors may bear on this inquiry, the Court in *Daubert* set forth a non-exclusive "checklist" for trial courts to use:

> (1) whether the expert's technique or theory can be (and has been) tested;

---

[19] *Daubert* at 589, 113 *S.Ct.* at 2795. *See also General Electric Co. v. Joiner*, 522 *U.S.* 136, 142, 118 *S.Ct.* 512, 517 (1997) ("[W]hile the Federal Rules of Evidence allow district courts to admit a somewhat broader range of scientific testimony than would have been admissible under *Frye*, they leave in place the 'gatekeeper' role of the trial judge in screening such evidence."). The *Frye* test focused primarily on whether the proposed expert testimony concerned a scientific principle which had gained "general acceptance" in the relevant scientific community. *Frye v. United States*, 54 *App.D.C.* 46, 293 *F.* 1013, 1014 (1923).

[20] *See Daubert* at 590-92, 113 *S.Ct.* at 2795-96. Of course, expert testimony that meets these four criteria is still subject to other rules of evidence. For example, the probative value of the expert's testimony must not be substantially outweighed by the danger of unfair prejudice, confusion of the issues, misleading the jury, or by considerations of undue delay, waste of time, or needless presentation of cumulative evidence. *See Fed.R.Evid.* 403. *See also Fed.Rs.Evid.* 703, 706; *Daubert* at 595, 113 *S.Ct.* at 2797-98.

[21] *Daubert* at 592-93, 113 *S.Ct.* at 2796. *See also Kumho Tire Co. v. Carmichael*, 526 *U.S.* 137, 141, 119 *S.Ct.* 1167, 1171 (1999) (Clarifying that this inquiry "applies not only to testimony based on 'scientific' knowledge, but also to testimony based on 'technical' and 'other specialized' knowledge.").

(2) whether the technique or theory has been subject to peer review and publication; [22]

(3) what the known or potential rate of error of the technique or theory is when applied;

(4) what standards or controls were used or maintained; and

(5) whether the technique or theory has been generally accepted in the scientific community.[23]

The inquiry should be a "flexible one."[24] "Its overarching subject is the scientific validity—and thus the evidentiary relevance and reliability—of the principles that underlie a proposed submission; and its focus must be solely on the principles and methodology, not on the conclusions that they generate."[25]

---

[22] Publication is only one element of peer review, but it is not an indispensable prerequisite of admissibility. "The fact of publication (or lack thereof) in a peer reviewed journal thus will be a relevant, though not dispositive, consideration in assessing the scientific validity of a particular technique or methodology on which an opinion is premised." *Daubert* at 593-94, 113 *S.Ct.* at 2979. *See also Kannankeril v. Terminix Int'l., Inc.*, 128 *F*.3d 802, 809 (3rd Cir. 1997) (holding that the lack of peer review or publication was not dispositive where the expert's opinion was supported by "widely accepted scientific knowledge").

[23] *Daubert* at 593-594, 113 *S.Ct.* at 2796-97. *See also Kumho Tire Co., supra,* at 152, 119 *S.Ct.* at 1176 (*Daubert* requires the trial court to exercise its gatekeeping duty and assure itself that the expert "employs in the courtroom the same level of intellectual rigor that characterizes the practice of an expert in the relevant field").

[24] The list of factors set forth in *Daubert* "was meant to be helpful, not definitive." *Kumho Tire Co. v. Carmichael*, 526 *U.S.* 137, 151, 119 *S.Ct.* 1167, 1175 (1999). In this respect, a trial court *may* consider one or more of these factors "when doing so will help determine that testimony's reliability. But, as the Court stated in *Daubert*, the test of reliability is 'flexible,' and *Daubert's* list of specific factors neither necessarily nor exclusively applies to all experts or in every case. Rather, the law grants a [trial] court the same broad latitude when it decides *how* to determine reliability[.]" *Id.* at 141-42 119 *S.Ct.* 1167, 1171 (1999) (court's emphasis). *See also General Electric Co. v. Joiner*, 522 *U.S.* 136, 142-43, 118 *S.Ct.* 512, 517 (1997) ("while the Federal Rules of Evidence allow district courts to admit a somewhat broader range of scientific testimony than would have been admissible under *Frye*, they leave in place the 'gatekeeper' role of the trial judge in screening such evidence"). In *Joiner*, the Court adopted an "abuse of discretion" standard for appellate courts to apply in reviewing a trial court's decision to admit or exclude expert testimony. *Id.* at 139, 118 *S.Ct.* at 515.

[25] *Daubert* at 594-95, 113 *S.Ct.* at 2979. Since the Court's decision in *Daubert*, other factors have been cited as relevant in making the reliability determination. *See e.g., General Elec. Co. v. Joiner*, 522 *U.S.* 136, 146, 118 *S.Ct.* 512, 519 (1997) (whether the expert has unjustifiably extrapolated from an accepted premise to an unfounded conclusion; recognizing that a "court may conclude that there is simply too great an analytical gap between the data and the opinion proffered").

STATE v. ODOM
Supreme Court of New Jersey
116 *N.J.* 65, 560 *A.2d* 1198 (1989)

QUESTION: Once a law enforcement officer at trial is qualified as an expert on the subject of illegal drugs, their possession, distribution and packaging, may that officer then testify that in his opinion the facts and circumstances surrounding the possession of the controlled dangerous substances at issue indicated that they were possessed by the defendant not for personal use but with an intent to distribute them ?

ANSWER: YES. As long as the police "expert does not express his opinion of defendant's guilt but simply characterizes defendant's conduct based on the facts in evidence in light of his specialized knowledge, the [expert's opinion—that possession of the drugs was for the purpose of distribution—] is not objectionable even though it embraces ultimate issues that the jury must decide." *Id.*, 116 *N.J.* at 79. "Moreover, such an opinion is permissible although it is expressed in terms that parallel the language of the statutory offense when that language also constitutes the ordinary parlance or expression of persons in everyday life." *Id.*

RATIONALE: In late January, officers from the Paterson Police Department executed a search warrant at a North Main Street residence. Defendant, Ernest Odom, and a juvenile were present at the residence. During the search, the officers found a clear plastic bag containing eighteen vials of cocaine in crack form in the pillowcase on defendant's bed. No other drugs or drug paraphernalia were found. Odom was subsequently charged with possession of a controlled dangerous substance, cocaine, and possession with the intent to distribute.

"At trial, the State offered Detective Sergeant Ronald Tierney as an expert in illegal narcotics. * * * Detective Tierney had been a member of the Paterson Police force for sixteen and one-half years and had served with the narcotics squad for nine and one-half years. He had participated in over 8,000 investigations and had made approximately 4,000 narcotics arrests. The detective had also been involved in over 400 crack investigations and had spoken with crack dealers on over fifty occasions. He had arrested over 100 individuals distributing crack and had executed twenty search warrants where crack and crack paraphernalia were seized. In the past he had been qualified 1,000 times as an expert in trials involving narcotics distribution." *Id.* at 69. Consequently, the trial court found Detective Tierney qualified to testify as an expert.

"The detective then testified about the packaging of crack, its street value, characteristics, and use. He was asked to assume the following facts, [which were brought out at trial], to be true: that a search warrant was executed, that eighteen vials of crack were found in a pillowcase in a bed in which defendant was found sleeping, that $24.00 was found in the apartment and that no other drug paraphernalia was found. He was asked based on his experiences and such facts if he had an opinion 'whether Ernest Odom possessed 18 vials of crack for his own use or possessed them with the intent to distribute them.' * * * Detective Tierney stated that it was his opinion that the drugs were possessed with an intent to distribute them." *Id.*

Detective Tierney then explained the basis for his opinion. "He detailed the procedures for crack processing and packaging, the estimated value of a vial of crack, and the addictive impact of the drug. The detective also stated that the lack of paraphernalia relating to personal drug use was another factor considered in forming his opinion, noting that distribution of crack required no paraphernalia." *Id.* Defendant was found guilty as charged.

In the appeal which followed, defendant argued that the trial court erred when it allowed Detective Tierney to testify to his opinion that defendant possessed the drug with the intent to distribute. *The New Jersey Supreme Court disagreed.*

Speaking for the Court, Justice Handler preliminarily pointed out that "the opinion of a duly-qualified expert may be presented to a jury if it will genuinely assist the jury in comprehending the evidence and determining issues of fact. The admissibility of expert testimony turns not on 'whether the subject matter is common or uncommon or whether many persons or few have knowledge of the matter, but [on] whether the witnesses offered as experts have peculiar knowledge or experience not common to the world which renders their opinions founded on such knowledge or experience any aid to the court or jury in determining the questions at issue.' " *Id.* at 70. [Citations omitted.] "Thus, *the opinion of an expert can be admitted in evidence if it relates to a relevant subject that is beyond the understanding of the average person of ordinary experience, education, and knowledge. If the expert's testimony on such a subject would help the jury understand the evidence presented and determine the facts, it may be used as evidence.* The witness offered as an expert must, of course, be suitably qualified and possessed of sufficient specialized knowledge to be able to express such an opinion and to explain the basis of that opinion. * * * Once it is determined that this testimony will genuinely aid the jury, it can be admitted." *Id.* at 71. [Emphasis added.]

In a case such as this, it is clear "that the jury will normally need the insight of an expert to explain the significance of the properties, packaging, and value of illegal drugs." *Id.* at 76. Moreover, under the circumstances of this case, "the subject of intent or purpose in connection with the possession of unlawful drugs is a matter of specialized knowledge of experts." *Id.* The Court concluded, therefore, "that the testimony of the expert covered a subject beyond the understanding of average persons and was genuinely helpful to the jury in understanding the evidence presented and determining the important issues of fact." *Id.*

An expert may not, however, express a direct opinion that the defendant is guilty of the crime charged. "The determination of facts that serve to establish guilt or innocence is a function reserved exclusively to the jury." *Id.* at 77. In this respect, the Court found that "Detective Tierney did not express an opinion that defendant was guilty of the crime charged." *Id.* Rather, "the detective's opinion was based exclusively on the surrounding facts relating to the quantity and packaging of the drugs and their addictive quality, as well as the absence of drug-use paraphernalia; his explanation of these facts was clearly founded on his experience and specialized knowledge as an expert. The conclusion he drew—that possession of these drugs was for the purpose of distribution—was similarly derived from his expertise." *Id.* at 78-79.

Accordingly, "as long as the expert does not express his opinion of defendant's guilt but simply characterizes defendant's conduct based on the facts in evidence in light of his specialized knowledge, the opinion is not objectionable even though it embraces ultimate issues that the jury must decide." *Id.* at 79. *See also State v. Kelly,* 97 *N.J.* 178, 208, 478 *A.*2d 364 (1984) (allowing an expert to testify about areas of specialized knowledge if that testimony will assist the trier of fact to understand the evidence or determine a fact in issue, even if that opinion embraces an ultimate issue to be determined by the jury). "Moreover, such an opinion is permissible although it is expressed in terms that parallel the language of the statutory offense when that language also constitutes the ordinary parlance or expression of persons in everyday life." *Odom* at 79. The expert may not, however, express his opinion in such a way as to emphasize that he believes the defendant is guilty of the crime charged under the statute. This would be highly improper. *Id.* at 80.

The Court concluded, therefore, that Detective Tierney's expert opinion in this case was properly admitted. "It covered a subject that was within the specialized knowledge of the expert, and thus beyond the understanding of persons of average knowledge, education, and experience; therefore it was reasonably required to assist the jury in understanding the evidence and determining the facts. Further, although expressed in terms of ultimate issues of fact, namely, whether drugs were possessed with the intent to distribute, the expert's opinion did not impermissibly constitute the expression of a view that defendant was guilty of the crime charged." *Id.* at 81.

NOTE

1. *Standards governing expert testimony.* During the course of its opinion in *State v. Odom*, the Court stated that the hypothetical question posed by the State and answered by the expert had several problems, particularly the improper incorporation of the defendant's name in the hypothetical. The Court instructed that hypothetical questions "should be carefully phrased to refer only to the testimony and evidence adduced 'about the manner of packaging and processing for use or distribution, the significance of various quantities and concentrations of narcotics, the roles of various drug paraphernalia, characteristics of the drugs themselves, the import of circumstances surrounding possession, the conduct of the possessor and the manner in which drugs may be secreted or otherwise possessed for personal use or distribution.' Once this foundation has been laid, the expert should then be presented with a hypothetical question through which he or she can advise the jury of the significance of these facts on the issue of possession. Having set forth this information in the form of a hypothetical, the expert may be asked if, based on these assumed facts, he or she has an opinion whether the drugs were possessed for personal use or for the purpose of distribution." *Id.* at 81-82. [Citation omitted.]

"It is also essential that the jury be advised, following the presentation of the expert's opinion, of the basis for that opinion. The hypothetical question should clearly indicate that it is the witness' opinion that is being sought and that that opinion was formed assuming the facts and circumstances adduced only at trial. It is important that the witness, and the jury, understand that the opinion cannot be based on facts that are not in evidence." *Id.* at 82.

"In addition, to the extent possible, the expert's answer should avoid the precise terminology of the statute defining the criminal offense and its necessary elements. While ordinary expression and plain language should not be distorted, statutory language should be paraphrased. * * * Further, the defendant's name should not be used." *Id.*

"Finally, the trial court should carefully instruct the jury on the weight to be accorded to and the assessment of expert opinion testimony. It should be emphasized that the determination of ultimate guilt or innocence is to be made only by the jury." *Id.*

2. *Police officer testifying as principal fact witness and expert* An arresting officer, if properly qualified, may testify as an expert as well as a fact witness. As one court explained:

> The use of fact witnesses as experts is an ordinary incident of many trials. It occurs regularly with doctors, accountants and other professionals who are produced because of their personal knowledge of the controversy and are utilized as experts to

render explanations and opinions which will aid the fact finder in areas beyond their normal knowledge or experience.

State v. Jackson, 278 *N.J.Super.* 69, 75, 650 A.2d 385 (App.Div. 1995). Use of a police officer with personal knowledge of an observed narcotics transaction to testify both as an eyewitness and an expert has been met with specific judicial approval. *See United States v. Soto*, 885 *F.*2d 354, 360 (7th Cir. 1989); *United States v. Young*, 745 *F.*2d 733, 760 (2nd Cir. 1984), *cert. den. sub nom., Myers v. United States*, 470 *U.S.* 1084, 105 *S.Ct.* 1842 (1985); *Channer v. State*, 94 *Md.App.* 356, 617 A.2d 1092, 1097 (1993).

COMMONWEALTH v. BROWN
Superior Court of Pennsylvania
408 *Pa.Super.* 246, 596 A.2d 840 (1991)

The opinion of the Court was delivered by

BROSKY, *Judge.*

In early April, plain-clothes Officer McClain, assigned to investigate possible illegal sales of controlled substances, was standing at the intersection of 54th and Berks Streets in Philadelphia, when he heard and observed a man yell to and approach defendant. The officer watched and listened as defendant and the other man engaged in a brief conversation, arguing over the "pricing of something." Defendant then handed the other man "a large amount of United States currency," and the man handed defendant a plastic bag which contained what was subsequently determined to be 13.02 grams of crack cocaine. Defendant was arrested and a search incident thereto uncovered, in addition to the crack cocaine, one hundred pink vial caps, eighteen empty plastic vials, a box of single-edge razor blades and $800 in cash.

At trial, Officer McClain provided detailed testimony regarding his observations of defendant and the seizure of the crack cocaine and drug paraphernalia. Thereafter, the Commonwealth called Philadelphia Police Officer John Boucher to the stand to testify as an expert. Officer Boucher "was a narcotics investigator and had participated in approximately 1,600 seizures of cocaine and/or crack cocaine. He had received extensive training regarding the packaging and distribution of cocaine, crack cocaine and other controlled substances and had served as an expert witness in over 600 cases that involved the 'packaging and distribution' of cocaine and/or crack cocaine." *Id.* at 841.

The prosecuting attorney asked Officer Boucher "to give his opinion, based upon his expertise regarding the packaging and distribution of crack cocaine and Officer McClain's testimony describing the

85

cocaine and drug paraphernalia seized from [defendant], regarding whether [defendant] possessed all of the seized items for his personal use or rather with the intent to deliver or distribute the cocaine." *Id.* Boucher testified that, "in his opinion, 'the items were possessed with the intent to deliver to others.' * * * Officer Boucher then proceeded to justify his opinion." *Id.* at 841-42. The officer explained

> that the cost for 13.02 grams of crack cocaine would be approximately $800 to $1000. [] He stated that if a user, as opposed to a dealer, possessed that amount of cash to spend for crack cocaine "he would buy . . . cocaine hydrochloride, which is . . . powdered cocaine, and make his own crack." [] Boucher also stated that this could be accomplished by placing the cocaine hydrochloride and baking soda in boiling water and then collecting the residue through a paper coffee strainer; once the residue cools it constitutes crack cocaine. [] This simple procedure allows a user to double the amount of crack cocaine that he has to satisfy his habit. [] Boucher also stated that a user would not have possessed eighteen empty vials; once a user consumes the contents of a vial he then discards the vial. [] Officer Boucher further stated that the razor blades are used by a dealer to cut small chunks from the larger mass of crack cocaine and place them into individual vials. []

Id. at 842.

In the appeal following his judgment of sentence, defendant argued that the trial court erred when it permitted Officer Boucher to give expert testimony regarding defendant's intent to deliver the cocaine that he possessed. According to defendant, the officer's opinion testimony "usurped the function of the factfinder" since the officer's testimony was related to the "ultimate issue . . . in the case." *Id.* at 841. Moreover, defendant argued that the element of "intent to deliver" was, in this case, "well within the ordinary knowledge and understanding of the average person," and, hence, no expert testimony was necessary. *Id. The Superior Court disagreed.*

" 'Generally speaking, the admission of expert testimony is a matter left largely to the discretion of the trial court * * *. If a witness has * * * specialized knowledge on the subject under investigation[, he or] she may testify, and the weight to be given [the] testimony is for the trier of fact.' " *Id.* at 842. [Citation omitted.]

> "Although the witness must demonstrate some particular knowledge or skill, there is no requirement that a witness acquire that knowledge as a result of formal schooling; expertise acquired by experience is expertise nonetheless. The determination

of whether a witness is a qualified expert involves two inquiries: When a witness is offered as an expert, the first question the trial court should ask is whether the subject on which the witness will express an opinion is so distinctly related to some science, profession, business or occupation as to be beyond the ken of the average layman. If the subject is of this sort, the next question the court should ask is whether the witness has sufficient skill, knowledge, or experience in that field or calling as to make it appear that his opinion or inference will probably aid the trier in his search for the truth."

Id. (quoting *Palmer v. Lapp*, 392 *Pa.Super.* 21, 27-28, 572 A.2d 12, 15-16 (1990)).

"A witness may testify to an ultimate issue only in those instances where the admission will not cause confusion or prejudice." *Id.* Moreover, "[e]xpert testimony will be admitted only if it is based upon facts which are of record. ∗ ∗ ∗ This requirement enables the factfinder to determine whether to accept or reject the opinion testimony, based upon, [among other things], whether it believes the facts upon which the opinion is based." *Id.* at 842-43.

The Superior Court has already held that " '[e]xpert opinion testimony is admissible concerning whether the facts surrounding the possession of controlled substances are consistent with an intent to deliver rather than with an intent to possess it for personal use.' " *Id.* at 843 (quoting *Commonwealth v. Ariondo*, 397 *Pa.Super.* 364, 383, 580 A.2d 341, 350-51 (1990)). Such testimony is proper so long as the officer's expert opinion (that the defendant possessed the drugs with the intent to deliver) does not follow—and therefore is not based on—prior testimony which related that the defendant was observed *selling* drugs. *See Commonwealth v. Carter*, 403 *Pa.Super.* 615, 617, 589 A.2d 1133, 1134 (1991) (finding error in the admission of an officer's expert opinion testimony that defendant was "dealing narcotics," when the testimony followed on the heels of testimony given by that same officer that he observed the defendant sell heroin to three different individuals). When the expert opinion does follow testimony recounting a police observation of the defendant *selling* drugs, a court may find the expert opinion testimony to be "cumulative and prejudicial" for the facts so presented would be easily assessed by an ordinary layperson who may then make the necessary inferences from those facts. *Id.* at 617, 589 A.2d at 1134. Thus, the assistance of an expert would not be necessary. *Brown* at 844.

In this case, the police testified "that they observed [defendant] *buy* the drug[; and this testimony could not have] prejudice[d] a defendant charged with possession with intent to deliver since the Commonwealth could only rely upon the quantity and packaging of the drug, the presence of paraphernalia, etc., to prove beyond a reasonable doubt that a defendant intended to deliver the drug." *Id.* Moreover, "[t]he expert's testimony could not have been cumulative since there was no prior testimony regarding any sales of drugs that [defendant] may have made." *Id.* Thus, "any prior testimony regarding a defendant's purchase of drugs would not preclude subsequent police expert opinion testimony regarding the defendant's possession with intent to deliver." *Id.*

Finally, it is clear that Officer Boucher's expert testimony "involved subject matter [] beyond the appreciation of the average layperson, who would not be cognizant of the significance of the quantity and form of the cocaine, the empty vials, the single-edge razor blades and the quantity of United States currency seized from [defendant]." *Id.*

STATE v. SUMMERS
Supreme Court of New Jersey
176 *N.J.* 306, 823 *A.*2d 15 (2003)

The opinion of the Court was delivered by

VERNIERO, J.

"A jury convicted defendant of multiple drug charges, including possession and distribution of a controlled dangerous substance (CDS). The question before us is whether the State's expert witness intruded on the jury's fact-finding role by expressing what defendant argues was an impermissible opinion on guilt. Specifically, the expert expressed the view that facts presented in a hypothetical (modeled on identical facts adduced at trial) were indicative of drug distribution." *Id.,* 176 *N.J.* at 308.

"On the evening of April 20th, an Atlantic City narcotics detective, Sam Dickson, conducted a surveillance operation of a known drug area on Texas Avenue near the boardwalk. Facing north in an unmarked police vehicle, Detective Dickson used a pair of binoculars to view the street. At about 8:45 p.m., the detective observed a man, later identified as defendant David Summers, walking southbound toward the officer. * * * Using his binoculars, Detective Dickson observed defendant stop briefly. Two men greeted defendant. The detective saw one of the men, later identified as co-defendant Peter Dyer, engage defendant in a conversation that lasted only a few seconds (from his vantage point, the detective could not determine whether the third man participated in the conversation). Thereafter, the three men crossed over to the street's east side and stood before an abandoned home. Defendant and Dyer then walked to the home's porch area, which Detective Dickson described as 'a concrete pad.' The detective observed defendant holding out his palm with an object in it. He further observed Dyer proffer to defendant what appeared to be folded currency. The detective was approximately 100 to 150 feet away from the parties when he viewed that exchange." *Id.* at 308-09.

"After receiving certain objects from defendant, Dyer returned to the street's west side with the objects in his right hand. Believing that he had witnessed a drug transaction, Detective Dickson radioed for backup officers and directed them to apprehend defendant and the third man, leaving the detective to apprehend Dyer. The detective exited his car as Dyer approached. Before the detective could identify himself as a police officer, Dyer placed the objects in his mouth. The detective ordered Dyer to open his mouth and spit them out. Dyer complied and spat out four baggies of a white-rocky substance. By then, the other officers had arrived and apprehended defendant and the third man." *Id.* at 309.

"Based on a conversation with Dyer, Detective Dickson asked one of the backup officers, Joseph Falcone, whether he (the officer) had recovered a cigarette pack from defendant. Detective Falcone confirmed that he had retrieved the cigarette pack and that when he had opened it, he found the following items: a medium-size bag with the number 1212 and an apple imprinted on it, and 50 smaller plastic bags of identical size and shape with a white rocky substance in them. Detective Falcone also testified that he had recovered from defendant nine $20 bills, five $10 bills, four $5 bills, six $1 bills, in addition to numerous coins, for a total of $262. The detective also retrieved an activated pager found on defendant. Because the police found no drugs on the third man, they released him at the scene. The white rocky substance found in the baggies later tested positive for cocaine. A grand jury charged defendant with multiple drug offenses * * *." *Id.* at 309-10.

At trial, "Detective Donna Price, who had not participated in the surveillance or arrest of defendant, testified at his trial as an expert in narcotics. On direct examination, the assistant prosecutor posed the following hypothetical to Detective Price:

> Atlantic City police are conducting a surveillance in the area of the beach block of Texas Avenue. It's approximately 8:45 at night * * *. During the course of their surveillance they see three males. There is one male walking, and then he is approached by two other males. There is a brief conversation between the first male and one of the other males, very brief, approximately twenty seconds. After that the males leave one side of the street and go to an abandoned house up on a cement pad. At that point the third male separates himself, and the first male and the second male appear to be in conversation.

> At one point the second male has an object in his hand which he shows to the first male. We'll call him S-1. And S-1 looks at what S-2 has in his hand. At that point S-2 hands S-1 the objects, and S-1 hands S-2 money. At that point the two separate. S-1 is later stopped by the police, and while he's being stopped he puts what he got in his

mouth. He is told to spit it out, which he does. The police recover four small zip-loc baggies containing cocaine.

The other male, S-2, is then stopped a short distance away, and recovered from him is a cigarette box containing 50 small zip-loc baggies. He has $262 on him, as well as an activated pager. The baggies found on the second male are identical to the baggies found on the buyer.

The second male that was with S-2 is at a distance apart from him and has no drugs on him. The cigarette box is recovered from S-2's person. The other person was not charged; he was released. This happened on the beach block of Texas Avenue in Atlantic City.

Do you have an opinion as to whether S-2 in this hypothetical . . . possessed those drugs for his own use or for distribution?

Id. at 310-11.

"In response, Detective Price expressed her view that S-2 in the hypothetical possessed the drugs for distribution and not for personal use. She based that opinion on the fact that no paraphernalia was found on S-2, that S-2 had $262 in various paper currencies and coins, and that S-2 had a large bag with smaller bags containing cocaine. * * * The jury found defendant guilty of all the [drug] charges.* * *." *Id.* at 311.

In this appeal, defendant argues that the hypothetical posed to Detective Price and the detective's response to it were improper. *The Supreme Court disagreed.*

The legal principles governing this dispute are well settled and straightforward. Generally,

the opinion of an expert can be admitted in evidence if it relates to a relevant subject that is beyond the understanding of the average person of ordinary experience, education, and knowledge. If the expert's testimony on such a subject would help the jury understand the evidence presented and determine the facts, it may be used as evidence. The witness offered as an expert must, of course, be suitably qualified and possessed of sufficient specialized knowledge to be able to express such an opinion and to explain the basis of that opinion. * * * Once it is determined that this testimony will genuinely aid the jury, it can be admitted. * * *

Id. at 312.

" 'Testimony in the form of an opinion or inference otherwise admissible is not objectionable because it embraces an ultimate issue to be decided by the trier of fact.' *N.J.R.E.* 704. Such testimony, however, still is subject to exclusion if the risk of undue prejudice substantially outweighs its probative value." *Id.* at 312.

"Courts widely agree that expert testimony about drug-trade practices is admissible, although case law varies in terms of the permissible extent and nature of such testimony. * * * The underlying rationale in allowing expert testimony is that jurors normally require 'the insight of an expert to explain the significance of the properties, packaging, and value of illegal drugs.' * * * [Indeed, it would be] 'unreasonable to assume that the average lay person called to serve as a juror would necessarily know what a person who possesses [a certain quantity of drug] was going to do with it.' " *Id.* [Citations omitted.]

There are set guidelines "for the appropriate use of a hypothetical question in a drug case. The question must be limited to the facts adduced at trial. The prosecutor may ask the expert to express an opinion, based on those facts, whether the drugs were possessed for distribution or for personal consumption. The expert should inform jurors of the information on which the opinion is based, and must avoid parroting statutory terminology whenever possible. * * * Obviously, the expert must walk a fine line. His or her opinion can be expressed in terms of ultimate issues of fact, namely, whether drugs were possessed with the intent to distribute, but it cannot contain an explicit statement that 'the defendant is guilty of the crime charged under the statute.' Finally, trial courts should instruct the jury in respect of the proper weight to be given to the expert's opinion, reminding jurors that the ultimate decision concerning a defendant's guilt or innocence rests solely with them." *Id.* at 314-15. [Citations omitted.]

"In applying the above tenets, we observe first that the parties do not dispute that the expert in this case properly was qualified in the field of narcotics. Moreover, the assistant prosecutor limited her hypothetical to facts presented at trial. In response, the witness expressed the view that the drugs were possessed 'for distribution' rather than for S-2's 'own use.' She did not, however, refer to defendant explicitly, nor did she refer to statutory law or express a view that an illegal drug transaction in fact had occurred. [T]he witness also recounted the basis of her opinion. She explained that the parties exchanged an object for currency, that the encounter was brief, and that the drugs were packaged in fifty small bags. She further noted that the bags in the buyer's possession and those in the seller's possession were similar, that the drugs were concealed in a pack of cigarettes, that the exchange took place in a high-crime area, and that there was an absence of drug paraphernalia." *Id.* at 315.

"When asked about the money recovered from the second male in the hypothetical, the detective commented, 'that's telling me he was distributing drugs.' When asked about the matching baggies carried by the alleged buyer and seller, she stated, 'that would tell me that S-2 was distributing them, if they are the same type of

packaging.' Those comments are sustainable as part of a hypothetical that did not refer to defendant by name and did not ask the
witness to offer an explicit opinion on defendant's guilt. That the
hypothetical was detailed in form did not itself render it impermissible[.] Although it was declarative in nature and embraced ultimate issues that the jury had to decide, the detective's testimony
[was nonetheless proper.]" *Id.* at 315-16.

"We find no error in the admission of the expert's testimony * * *. Detective Price's opinion was highly probative of the
distribution offenses and necessary to assist members of the jury,
who presumably were unschooled in the drug trade. * * * [T]he expert's testimony uniquely aided the jury. It did so by helping jurors
to understand how drugs are packaged, priced, concealed, and sold
consistent with distribution in high-crime areas." *Id.* at 316-17.

"We acknowledge that some courts in other jurisdictions flatly
forbid expert testimony concerning intent in a drug case, concluding that it constitutes an impermissible opinion on a defendant's
guilt. *See, e.g., United States v. Boyd,* 55 *F.*3d 667, 670 (D.C. Cir.
1995) (concluding that such testimony is improper 'even though
posed as a hypothetical'). [We remain convinced, however, that our
approach is sound.] To hold otherwise would deprive jurors of valuable assistance as they discharge their important and often difficult responsibilities." *Id.* at 317.

NOTE

1. *Illegal drugs.* Generally, courts recognize that the nature,
purpose and scope of the possession of illegal drugs is a subject
within the specialized knowledge of law-enforcement experts and
not something known to the average juror. *See State v. Perez,* 218
N.J.Super. 478, 485, 528 *A.*2d 56 (App.Div. 1987) (testimony of a
police expert, that in his opinion defendant possessed the drugs
with the intent to distribute, upheld, concluding that "it is unreasonable to assume that the average lay person called to serve as a
juror would necessarily know what a person who possesses 4.4
ounces of 56% pure cocaine was going to do with it"); *State v. Binns,*
222 *N.J.Super.* 583, 592, 537 *A.*2d 764, *certif. denied,* 111 *N.J.* 624,
546 *A.*2d 540 (1988) (upholding the testimony of a State's narcotics
expert that "[t]wo people in possession of approximately two and a-
half ounces of cocaine at the purity level of [] approximately 36
percent, based on an economic factor it would be my opinion based
on my knowledge and training that they possessed that cocaine
with the intent to redistribute it for profit."); *State v. Toro,* 229
N.J.Super. 215, 225, 551 *A.*2d 170 (1988) (upholding the admissibility of an expert's opinion that the defendant's possession of 501
grams of 65% pure free-base cocaine was indicative of one "in the
business of distribution of cocaine").

2. *Possession with the intent to distribute.* Once a defendant is charged with possession of a particular controlled dangerous substance with the intent to distribute, the Government bears the burden of establishing sufficient proof of the possessor's "specific intent" to distribute the contraband, and it may do so "by either direct or circumstantial evidence." *United States v. Brett*, 872 *F.*2d 1365, 1370 (8th Cir. 1989). *See also United States v. Matra*, 841 *F.*2d 837, 841 (8th Cir. 1988). In the absence of direct evidence of distribution, a court must infer a possessor's intent to distribute from the circumstantial evidence produced by the prosecution which tends to demonstrate an inference of such an intention. *United States v. Franklin*, 728 *F.*2d 994, 998 (8th Cir. 1984). Expert law-enforcement testimony is most helpful in this regard.

Expert testimony on the subject of a defendant's possession with the intent to distribute is permitted so long as the testimony relates information that is not within the common knowledge of the average lay person and is helpful in assisting the trier of fact to understand the evidence or determine a fact in issue. Persons permitted to testify as expert witnesses about controlled dangerous substances and narcotics activities will usually have several years of experience in drug-related fields and advanced training in the detection and recognition of controlled substances. *United States v. Franklin, supra* at 998 n.8; *United States v. Pugliese*, 712 *F.*2d 1574, 1581 (2d Cir. 1983); *United States v. Carson*, 702 *F.*2d 351, 369 (2d Cir. 1983). *See also Gray v. United States*, 600 *A.*2d 367, 368 (D.C.App. 1991).

Once the expert witness is properly qualified, many courts will permit the witness to testify about the characteristics, processing and packaging of narcotics, their street value, average dosage unit, usage and whether the circumstances surrounding a particular individual's possession demonstrate possession for sale rather than personal use. *See e.g., State v. Keener*, 520 *P.*2d 510 (Ariz. 1974) (en banc); *State v. Carreon*, 729 *P.*2d 969 (Ariz.Ct.App. 1986); *People v. Douglas*, 193 *Cal.App.*3d 1691, 239 *Cal.Rptr.* 252 (Ct.App. 1987); *State v. Avila*, 353 *A.*2d 776, 780-781 (Conn. 1974); *Hinnant v. United States*, 520 *A.*2d 292, 293 (D.C. 1987); *State v. Olsen* 315 *N.W.*2d 1, 6-7 (Iowa 1982); *State v. Montana*, 421 *So.*2d 895 (La. 1982); *Commonwealth v. Nichols*, 356 *N.E.*2d 464, 468-469 (Mass. 1976); *State v. Odom*, 116 *N.J.* 65, 78-79 (1989); *Commonwealth v. Johnson*, 517 *A.*2d 1311 (Pa.Super. 1986).

(a) *Quantity.* Quantity is perhaps the foremost indicator; the intent to distribute may, in some cases be inferred "solely" from the possession of a large quantity of drugs. *United States v. La-Guardia*, 774 *F.*2d 317, 320 (8th Cir. 1985). *See also United States v. Koua Thao*, 712 *F.*2d 369, 371 (8th Cir. 1983) (154.74 grams of opium); *United States v. Vergara,* 687 *F.*2d 57, 62 (5th Cir. 1982) (intent to distribute found from defendant's possession of five ounces of heroin, valued at that time at $8,500); *United States v. DeLeon,* 641 *F.*2d 330, 335 (5th Cir. 1981) (294 grams of cocaine); *United States v. Love,* 599 *F.*2d 107, 109 (5th Cir. 1979) (26 pounds of marijuana); *United States v. Edwards,* 602 *F.*2d 458, 470 (1st Cir. 1979) (200 grams of heroin); *United States v. Muckenthaler,* 584 *F.*2d 240, 247 (8th Cir. 1978) (147.09 grams of cocaine); *United States v. Echols,* 477 *F.*2d 37, 40 (8th Cir. 1973) (199.73 grams of cocaine); *United States v. Mather,* 465 *F.*2d 1035, 1037-38 (5th Cir. 1972) (197.75 grams of cocaine). *Cf. Chapman v. United States,* 500 *U.S.* 453, 111 *S.Ct.* 1919, 1926, 1929 (1991) (when calculating the weight of LSD for punishment purposes, the weight of the blotter paper or other carrier medium used to distribute the drug is included in the calculation of the total weight of the drug; defendant's mandatory minimum sentence of five years affirmed where, even though weight of the pure LSD was under the statutory requirement (50 milligrams), the combined weight of the LSD and blotter paper (5.7 grams) triggered the mandatory minimum sentence).

The absence of the requisite intent may at times be inferred where only a small amount of the controlled substance is discovered. *See e.g., Commonwealth v. Gill,* 490 *Pa.* 1, 415 *A.*2d 2, 4 (1980) (small amount of controlled substance held consistent with personal use, not distribution). In fact, it has been held that "[p]roof of possession of a small amount of a controlled substance, standing alone, is an insufficient basis from which an intent to distribute may be inferred." *United States v. Washington,* 586 *F.*2d 1147, 1153 (7th Cir. 1978) (possession of 1.43 grams of cocaine). *See also Turner v. United States,* 396 *U.S.* 398, 422-23, 90 *S.Ct.* 642, 655-656 (1970) (possession of 14.68 grams of 5% pure cocaine held insufficient to demonstrate an intent to distribute); *United States v. Bailey,* 691 *F.*2d 1009, 1019 n. 13 (11th Cir. 1982) (possession of 3.4 grams of cocaine held insufficient to raise an inference of intent to distribute); *United States v. Oliver,* 523 *F.*2d 1252, 1253 n.1 (5th Cir. 1975) (possession of 1.84 grams of 16.8% pure cocaine held to be too small an amount to demonstrate an intent to distribute); *Bentley v. Cox,* 508 *F.Supp.* 870, 877 (E.D. Va. 1981) (possession of 73 grams of marijuana held consistent with possession for personal use).

(b) Purity. "Purity level is another factor properly considered with respect to intent to distribute." *Brett, supra,* 872 *F.* 2d at 1370. *See also United States v. Burns,* 624 *F.*2d 95, 102 (10th Cir. 1980); *United States v. Blake,* 484 *F.*2d 50, 58 (8th Cir. 1973) (possession of 14.3 grams of 17.3% pure heroin, a bottle of quinine, a mirror, two playing cards, and testimony that the purity level exceeded the average street purity level supported an inference that the drug

was not possessed merely for personal use); *State v. Perez*, 218 *N.J.Super.* 478, 482, 528 *A.2d* 56 (App.Div. 1987) (possession of 124.6 grams of 56% pure cocaine, 70 grams of which were free base, supported inference of intent to distribute).

(c) *Paraphernalia*. The presence or absence of drug paraphernalia can be significant. While the presence of a razor, mirror and straw along with a small amount of cocaine would certainly be indicative of personal use, a larger amount of the drug and no paraphernalia could suggest possession for the purpose of distribution. On the other hand, possession of a small amount of the drug together with a substantial quantity of paraphernalia, such as boxes of new vials, scores of new plastic baggies or sensitive weighing scales may suggest the presence of an intent to distribute. *See e.g., United States v. Staten*, 581 *F.2d* 878, 886 (D.C.Cir. 1978) ("intent to distribute may be inferred from possession of drug-packaging paraphernalia"); *United States v. Fitzgerald*, 719 *F.2d* 1069, 1072 (10th Cir. 1983) (possession of 33 grams of 70% pure amphetamine and 25 grams of 47% pure cocaine, found along with sensitive weighing scales supported an inference of an intent to distribute); *United States v. Burns*, 624 *F.2d* 95, 102 (10th Cir. 1980) (possession of 100% pure cocaine along with weighing equipment supported inference of an intent to distribute); *United States v. Hollman*, 541 *F.2d* 196, 199 (8th Cir. 1976) (possession of heroin packaged in 127 separate foil packets held consistent with an intent to distribute).

The presence of cutting agents coupled with the possession of a controlled substance whose physical characteristics permit dilution in this way leads to a reasonable inference that the drug is not merely possessed for personal use. *United States v. Franklin*, 728 *F.2d* 994, 999 (8th Cir. 1984). *See also United States v. Marszalkowski*, 669 *F.2d* 655, 662 (5th Cir. 1982) (possession of 38.2 grams of at least 84% pure cocaine along with cutting substance, a large amount of cash and a weapon justified inference of intent to distribute); *State v. Binns*, 222 *N.J.Super.* 583, 593, 537 *A.2d* 764 (App.Div. 1988) (baking soda and gram scale seized along with 62.96 grams of cocaine, 22.91 grams of which were free base, found indicative of distribution); *United States v. James*, 494 *F.2d* 1007, 1030 (D.C.Cir. 1974) (possession of significant amounts of glassine bags, assorted cutting and weighing paraphernalia, and address books containing notations in terminology used in the drug-trafficking trade supported an inference of an intent to distribute).

(d) *Presence of large sums of cash*. The unexplained presence of large sums of cash in connection with other evidence of drug dealing has been considered as probative of prior drug sales. *See e.g., United States v. Tramunti*, 513 *F.2d* 1087, 1105 (2d Cir. 1975);

Marszalkowski, supra, 669 *F.*2d at 662. In order to successfully present this indicator of an intent to distribute, the prosecution must demonstrate a sufficient nexus between the money and the controlled substance.

(e) Location. At times, smaller quantities of a controlled substance may still sustain an inference of the intent to distribute when the quantity of drug possessed is "highly unusual" in the context of the location at which the possessor is found. *See e.g., United States v. Ramirez-Rodriquez,* 552 *F.*2d 883 (9th Cir. 1977) (prison inmate's possession of 10 grams of cocaine, calibrated at its pure level, supported inference of an intent to distribute when that quantity of cocaine was "very unusual" in the context of the prison setting and prison authorities on prior occasions almost never found any narcotics in that quantity).

(f) Presence of firearms. "[T]he presence of a firearm, generally considered a tool of the narcotics dealer's trade, also is evidence of an intent to distribute." *Brett, supra,* 872 *F.*2d at 1370; *Marszalkowski, supra,* 669 *F.*2d at 662; *United States v. Moses,* 360 *F.Supp.* 301, 303 (W.D.Pa. 1973) (possession of weapon and heroin packaged in a manner commonly used in street distribution sustained an inference of an intent to distribute).

(g) Possessor addicted to same or different drug. The question whether the possessor is addicted to the drug found in his possession is another consideration in determining whether there is sufficient evidence of an intent to distribute. On the one hand, "[a] finding of addiction may support an inference that a larger quantity of the drug may be kept for personal use." *Ramirez-Rodriquez* at 885. On the other hand, evidence that demonstrates that a defendant is addicted to a substance other than the one found in his possession may support an inference that the drug possessed was for distribution.

3. *Expert testimony that a defendant fits the "drug courier profile."* The 'drug courier profile' is an abstract of characteristics found to be typical of persons transporting illegal drugs." *Florida v. Royer,* 460 *U.S.* 491, 494 n.2, 103 *S.Ct.* 1319, 1322 n.2 (1983). While not an end in itself, the "drug courier profile" is an effective means or investigative tool utilized by trained law enforcement officers as a systematic method of recognizing characteristics repeatedly found among those who traffic in illicit drugs. The profile has also been described as "the collective or distilled experience of narcotics officers concerning characteristics repeatedly seen in drug smugglers." *Id.* at 525 n.6, 103 *S.Ct.* at 1339 n.6 (Rehnquist, J., dissenting). However, the use of drug courier profiles as substantive evidence

that a defendant possessed a quantity of drugs with the intent to distribute has been "severely criticized." *United States v. Belton-Rios*, 878 *F*.2d 1208, 1210 (9th Cir. 1989). Where the prosecution engages in a point-by-point examination of an expert, with specific references to the defendant's characteristics as fitting the typical "drug courier profile," for the purpose of offering such testimony as substantive evidence of the defendant's guilt (*i.e.*, because the defendant fits the profile he must have possessed the drugs for distribution purposes rather than personal use), the tactic has been held to be error. *See United States v. Quigley*, 890 *F*.2d 1019, 1023-24 (8th Cir. 1989) (while the expert "did not directly say that he thought Quigley was guilty of the offense charged because he fit the profile, that was the clear implication of his testimony[, and t]his use of drug courier profile evidence was error"); *United States v. Hernandez-Cuartas*, 717 *F*.2d 552, 555 (11th Cir. 1983) ("Although this information is valuable in helping drug agents to identify potential drug couriers, we denounce the use of this type of evidence as substantive evidence of a defendant's innocence or guilt.").

But see United States v. Belton-Rios, supra, where the court held that such testimony could be used in rebuttal to refute specific attempts by the defense to suggest innocence based on the particular characteristics described in a drug courier profile. *Note also* that in *Quigley* and *Hernandez-Cuartas,* both defendants' convictions were affirmed; in *Quigley* because "the error, in the context of all the evidence, was harmless," *id.* at 1024, and in *Hernandez-Cuartas* because the testimony admitted was used "purely for background material" on how and why the defendant was stopped and searched. *Id.* at 555.

UNITED STATES v. DIAZ
United States Court of Appeals
25 *F*.3d 392 (6th Cir. 1994)

QUESTION: May the police rely on a trained and certified narcotics detection dog as probable cause for a search ?

ANSWER: YES. "[T]he police properly may rely on a trained and certified dog as probable cause for a search." *Id.* at 393. "A positive indication by a properly-trained dog is sufficient to establish probable cause for the presence of a controlled substance." *Id.* at 393-94. If, however, a positive dog reaction is to support a determination of probable cause, "the training and reliability of the dog must be established." *Id.* at 394.

RATIONALE: Acting on information received from a suspected drug courier at the Detroit airport, drug agents located Diaz's car at the Colonial Motel in Taylor, Michigan. Wayne County Deputy Sheriff Kris Dennard responded to the motel's parking lot with her partner, "Dingo," a narcotics detection dog. Dingo "alerted" on the car, and a subsequent search uncovered one hundred pounds of marijuana located in the car's trunk.

In the appeal following his unsuccessful motion to suppress, Diaz contended that the government failed to establish the dog's training and reliability, and thus the agents lacked probable cause to search the car. *The United States Court of Appeals for the Sixth Circuit disagreed.*

"A positive indication by a properly-trained dog is sufficient to establish probable cause for the presence of a controlled substance." *Id.* at 393-94. In this case, Diaz does not challenge the proposition that a narcotics detection dog's alert can establish probable cause, but challenges the training and reliability of the drug detection dog, Dingo.

"For a positive dog reaction to support a determination of probable cause, the training and reliability of the dog must be established." *Id.* at 394. Because the courts "have not definitively addressed the issue of the quality or quantity of evidence necessary to establish a drug detection dog's training and reliability[,]" this court looked "to analogous principles of evidence law for guidance on this issue." *Id.*

> As with evidence generally, trial judges have broad discretion in determining the admissibility of expert evidence. * * * Similarly, an expert's qualification is a question that lies within the trial judge's discretion. * * * The court considers the proffered expert's education and experience in determining if he is qualified. * * * Formal education is not always necessary to qualify an expert; practical skill and experience may suffice. [Above all,] "the expert's knowledge of the subject matter [must be] such that his opinion will likely assist the trier of fact in arriving at the truth." * * * When an expert has been qualified, other evidence, including the testimony of other experts, that contradicts or undermines the testimony of the expert affects that expert's credibility, not his qualifications to testify.

Id. [Citations omitted.]

Those principles, found the court, are "useful guides in evaluating the training and reliability of a drug detection dog for the purpose of determining if probable cause exists based on the results of the dog's sniff." *Id.*

> When the evidence presented, whether testimony from the dog's trainer or records of the dog's training, establishes that the dog is generally certified as a drug detection dog, any other evidence,

including the testimony of other experts, that may detract from the reliability of the dog's performance properly goes to the "credibility" of the dog. Lack of additional evidence, such as documentation of the exact course of training, similarly would affect the dog's reliability. As with the admissibility of evidence generally, the admissibility of evidence regarding a dog's training and reliability is committed to the trial court's sound discretion.

Id.

At the hearing on Diaz's motion to suppress, Deputy Sheriff Dennard, Dingo's trainer and handler, testified that

> she and Dingo successfully attended an eight-week training school in which both learned techniques for the detection of controlled substances, including marijuana, cocaine, and heroin; that as part of the training, Dingo was subjected to "live" search tests (in which drugs were present) and "dead" search tests (in which drugs were not present, but plastic bags and live animals sometimes were); that to gain certification, Dingo was required to successfully "indicate" narcotics on fourteen "live" targets; that Dingo would "indicate" by barking, biting, and scratching, but occasionally would "alert" by coming to a standstill in order to scent more intently; that Dingo was certified; that she and Dingo have passed recertification tests every year since their original training in 1989; that she and Dingo have had occasion to search for the presence of drug odors on approximately 1500 occasions; that on at least one occasion, Dingo indicated the presence of illegal substances but none was found, although there was evidence that drugs had been present among the items to which Dingo had positively responded; that she ran Dingo around a test car before scenting Diaz's car to avoid unduly suggesting to the dog a specific place to indicate; and that Dingo indicated on Diaz's car but not on the test car. The district court found Dennard's testimony to be credible.

Id. at 394-95.

Diaz presented the testimony of a former police officer who trains drug detection dogs and their handlers and who has testified on a number of occasions regarding the reliability of dog sniffs. This "expert" relied on defense counsel's description of Dennard's testimony. "He never visited Dingo's school, never spoke with Dingo's trainer or with Dennard, and had never seen Dingo in action." *Id.* at 395. Diaz's expert testified that "barking and biting may indicate a dog's frustration over not detecting any drug odors; that Dingo's reliability was compromised by [according to this expert's knowledge of Dingo's training] failing to be trained on 'dead' targets; and that, because Dennard knew which car was suspected, she may have unconsciously cued Dingo, and thus Dingo's indication might have been tainted." *Id.*

Diaz therefore contended that the finding by the court below "that Dingo was a reliable drug detection dog was clearly erroneous * * *." *Id.* Diaz argued that "the government could not establish Dingo's reliability because Dennard failed to bring the dog's training and performance records to court and so was unable to answer precisely how many searches Dingo had done and how many times drugs were or were not discovered when Dingo indicated." *Id.* He further contended that "the search was unreliable because of the possibility * * * of unconscious cuing by Dennard. Finally, Diaz argue[d] that Dennard and Dingo were improperly trained, as evidenced by Dennard's taking Dingo's barking and biting as a positive indication when [his expert] says it may mean frustration at the failure to detect odors and by Dennard's failure to define 'alert' and 'dead target' in the same manner as [his expert]." *Id.* The court found Diaz's contentions unpersuasive.

Dennard testified as to her and Dingo's training, certification, and experience. The district judge heard the testimony and made a credibility determination: Dennard was believable. Her testimony supports a finding that Dingo was trained and reliable. After reviewing the testimony, we are not left with a definite and firm conviction that a mistake has been made.

Furthermore, [the defense expert's] objections simply appear unpersuasive. The fact that [he] is a former police officer and now a drug detection trainer does not detract from Dennard's qualifications. As to the issue of false positive indications, Dennard admitted that there had been times when Dingo had alerted yet no drugs were found. She then described one such instance at an airport search. She explained that although there were no drugs present, the owner of the suitcase on which Dingo had alerted admitted that she had been smoking "weed" all weekend and that the scent could have remained in her clothing found in the suitcase. Diaz infers from this that there had been false positive indications and that therefore Dingo was not reliable. [This court disagrees. B]ased on Dennard's testimony, Dingo was reliable and the single incident described did not detract from this reliability. *In any event, a very low percentage of false positives is not necessarily fatal to a finding that a drug detection dog is properly trained and certified.* * * *

Regarding the failure to prove Dingo's training and reliability with training and performance records, this court has indicated that testimony is sufficient to establish a dog's reliability in order to support a valid sniff. * * * While training and performance documentation would be useful in evaluating a dog's reliability, here the testimony of Dennard, Dingo's handler, sufficiently established the dog's reliability.

United States v. Trayer, 898 F.2d 805, 809 (D.C.Cir. * * * 1990), noted that "less than scrupulously neutral procedures, which create at least the possibility of unconscious 'cuing,' may well jeopardize the reliability of dog sniffs," but upheld the district court's determination that cuing had in fact not occurred. Here, similarly, although there was a possibility of unconscious cuing because Dennard knew which was the suspected car, the district court found that Dennard had not done anything differently between the sniffs of the test car and the suspected car and thus the chance of cuing was reduced. * * *

Finally, Dennard did define "alert" and testified that Dingo was in fact trained with "dead targets," although she did not use term "dead target." She also explained that Dingo was trained to bark, bite, and scratch when he indicated. In any event, she testified that, on this search, Dingo indicated by scratching alone. This supports the district judge's finding that Dingo was not frustrated as Diaz contends, but, instead, reliable.

Id. at 395-96. [Emphasis added.]
Accordingly, this court accepts the findings of the court below that "Dingo was trained and reliable." *Id.* at 396. "Therefore, there was probable cause to search Diaz's car, because a valid dog sniff indicated the presence of a controlled substance." *Id.*

---

§4.2. THE HEARSAY EVIDENCE RULE

The **hearsay evidence rule** may be simply stated: "Hearsay is inadmissible."[26] The more difficult question is, of course: What is hearsay?

The *Federal Rules of Evidence* provide:

Rule 801. Definitions.

* * * *

(c) **Hearsay.** "Hearsay" is a statement, other than one made by the declarant while testifying at the trial or hearing, offered in evidence to prove the truth of the matter asserted.

---

[26] *Fed.R.Evid.* 802.

Stripped to its essentials, "hearsay" may be defined as an out-of-court statement offered (in court) to prove the truth of the matter asserted within the statement. The "out-of-court statement" encompasses not only an "oral or written assertion" but also "nonverbal conduct of a person, if it is intended by the person as an assertion."[27] The person who makes the out-of-court statement is called the "declarant."[28]

The language in the rule referring to a "statement, other than one made by the declarant while testifying at the trial or hearing," is generally taken to mean an "out of court" statement made by a declarant, which is thereafter repeated or offered by a witness for evidentiary purposes at a court proceeding. As the definition of "statement" indicates, the out-of-court statement need not be limited to oral declarations. It may include written statements which the prosecution or the defense wishes to introduce into evidence through the testifying witness, or out-of-court (nonverbal) expressive conduct which the witness wishes to recount on the witness stand. For example, a witness' act of pointing to identify a suspect in a lineup "is clearly the equivalent of words, assertive in nature, and [will] be regarded as a statement."[29]

Assuming that a witness' testimony does recount an "out-of-court statement," that does not mean that the testimony is hearsay. A second question must be answered: What is the "relevance" of the out-of-court statement? To qualify as hearsay, the out-of-court statement must be offered for one purpose only—to prove the truth of the matter asserted within the statement. If the statement is offered for any other purpose—other than to prove its truth—it is not hearsay. Thus, if a witness testifies that while he and his wife were riding as passengers in a bus, his wife said to him, "Look, there's a sign up ahead that says, 'Speed Limit—25 m.p.h.,' " the statement is not hearsay if offered only to prove that, at the time of the event, there was nothing wrong with his wife's eyesight. If, however, the statement is offered to prove that there was in fact a sign up ahead which stated, "Speed Limit—25 m.p.h.," the statement is hearsay and is inadmissible unless it comes within one of the recognized exceptions to the hearsay evidence rule.

---

[27] *Fed.R.Evid.* 801(a). *Advisory Committee's Note*, 56 *F.R.D.* 183, 293.

[28] *Fed.R.Evid.* 801(b).

[29] *Advisory Committee's Note*, 56 *F.R.D.* 183, 293.

CHAMBERS v. MISSISSIPPI
Supreme Court of the United States
410 *U.S.* 284, 93 *S.Ct.* 1038 (1973)

Mr. Justice POWELL delivered the opinion of the Court.

*   *   *   *

"The hearsay rule, which has long been recognized and re-spected by virtually every State, is based on experience and grounded in the notion that untrustworthy evidence should not be presented to the triers of fact. Out-of-court statements are tradi-tionally excluded because they lack the conventional indicia of reli-ability: they are usually not made under oath or other circum-stances that impress the speaker with the solemnity of his state-ments; the declarant's word is not subject to cross-examination; and he is not available in order that his demeanor and credibility may be assessed by the jury." *Id.* at 1047.

---

§4.2(a). Hearsay and Criminal Cases

The hearsay evidence rule is applicable in both civil and criminal cases. In a criminal case, however, hearsay that is offered against a defendant under an exception from the hearsay rule may sometimes be excluded because its admission would violate the defendant's right "to be confronted with the witnesses against him" under the Sixth Amendment of the United States Constitution, or under a par-allel state constitutional provision. As a result, when hearsay is of-fered against a defendant in a criminal case, the defendant may raise three separate objections: (1) admission of the evidence would violate the hearsay rule; (2) admission of the evidence would violate the defendant's right to confront the witnesses against him under the Sixth Amendment; and, where applicable, (3) admission of the evidence would violate the defendant's right of confrontation under a parallel state constitutional provision.

CALIFORNIA v. GREEN
Supreme Court of the United States
399 *U.S.* 149, 90 *S.Ct.* 1930 (1970)

JUSTICE WHITE delivered the opinion of the Court.

*   *   *   *

"While it may readily be conceded that hearsay rules and the Confrontation Clause are generally designed to protect similar values, it is quite a different thing to suggest that the overlap is complete and that the Confrontation Clause is nothing more or less than a codification of the rules of hearsay and their exceptions as they existed historically at common law. Our decisions have never established such a congruence; indeed, we have more than once found a violation of confrontation values even though the statements in issue were admitted under an arguably recognized hearsay exception." *Id.* at 155-56.

"The converse is equally true: merely because evidence is admitted in violation of a long-established hearsay rule does not lead to the automatic conclusion that confrontation rights have been denied. Given the similarity of the values protected, however, the modification of a State's hearsay rules to create new exceptions for the admission of evidence against a defendant will often raise questions of compatibility with the defendant's constitutional right to confrontation." *Id.* at 156.

"Such questions require attention to the reasons for, and the basic scope of, the protections offered by the Confrontation Clause. The origin and development of the hearsay rules and of the Confrontation Clause have been traced by others and need not be recounted in detail here. It is sufficient to note that the particular vice that gave impetus to the confrontation claim was the practice of trying defendants on 'evidence' which consisted solely of *ex parte* affidavits or depositions * * *, thus denying the defendant the opportunity to challenge his accuser in a face-to-face encounter in front of the trier of fact." *Id.*

"Our own decisions seem to have recognized at an early date that it is this literal right to 'confront' the witness at the time of trial that forms the core of the values furthered by the Confrontation Clause:

> "The primary object of the constitutional provision in question was to prevent depositions or *ex parte* affidavits, such as were sometimes admitted in civil cases, being used against the prisoner in lieu of a personal examination and cross-examination of the witness in which the accused has an opportunity, not only of testing the recollection and sifting the conscience of the witness, but of compelling him to stand face to face with the jury in order that they may look at him, and judge by his demeanor upon the stand and the manner in which he gives his testimony whether he is worthy of belief."

Id. at 157-58 [Citation omitted.]

"Viewed historically, then, there is good reason to conclude that the Confrontation Clause is not violated by admitting a declarant's out-of-court statements, as long as the declarant is testifying as a witness and subject to full and effective cross-examination. This conclusion is supported by comparing the purposes of confrontation with the alleged dangers in admitting an out-of-court statement. Confrontation: (1) insures that the witness will give his statements under oath—thus impressing him with the seriousness of the matter and guarding against the lie by the possibility of a penalty for perjury; (2) forces the witness to submit to cross-examination, the 'greatest legal engine ever invented for the discovery of truth'; [and] (3) permits the jury that is to decide the defendant's fate to observe the demeanor of the witness in making his statement, thus aiding the jury in assessing his credibility. * * *" *Id.* at 158.

CRAWFORD v. WASHINGTON
Supreme Court of the United States
541 *U.S.* 36, 124 *S.Ct.* 1354 (2004)

JUSTICE SCALIA delivered the opinion of the Court.

*   *   *   *

Defendant "Michael Crawford stabbed a man who allegedly tried to rape his wife, Sylvia. At his trial, the State played for the jury Sylvia's tape-recorded statement to the police describing the stabbing, even though he had no opportunity for cross-examination. * * * The question presented is whether this procedure complied with the Sixth Amendment's guarantee that, '[i]n all criminal prosecutions, the accused shall enjoy the right . . . to be confronted with the witnesses against him.' " *Id.* at 1356-37.

The Sixth Amendment's Confrontation Clause applies to both federal and state prosecutions. At issue in this case is the admissibility of "an unavailable witness's out-of-court statement." *Id.* at 1357. Earlier cases have determined that such a statement "may be admitted so long as it has adequate indicia of reliability—*i.e.*, it falls within a 'firmly rooted hearsay exception' or bears 'particularized guarantees of trustworthiness.' " *Id. See e.g., Ohio v. Roberts,* 448 *U.S.* 56, 100 *S.Ct.* 2531 (1980).

This approach, as set forth in *Roberts,* "departs from [] historical principles * * * in two respects. First, it is too broad: It applies the same mode of analysis whether or not the hearsay consists of *ex parte* testimony. This often results in close constitutional scrutiny in cases that are far removed from the core concerns of the Clause. At the same time, however, the test is too narrow: It admits statements that do consist of *ex parte* testimony upon a mere finding of reliability." *Id.* at 1369.

"Members of this Court and academics have suggested that we revise our doctrine to reflect more accurately the original understanding of the Clause." *Id.* In this case, Silvia Crawford's statement is clearly testimonial. It is also clear that there was no prior opportunity for cross-examination of it.

"Where testimonial statements are involved, we do not think the Framers meant to leave the Sixth Amendment's protection to the vagaries of the rules of evidence, much less to amorphous notions of 'reliability.' * * * Admitting statements deemed reliable by a judge is fundamentally at odds with the right of confrontation. To be sure, the Clause's ultimate goal is to ensure reliability of evidence, but it is a procedural rather than a substantive guarantee. It commands, not that evidence be reliable, but that reliability be assessed in a particular manner: by testing in the crucible of cross-examination. The Clause thus reflects a judgment, not only about the desirability of reliable evidence (a point on which there could be little dissent), but about how reliability can best be determined[.]" *Id.* at 1370.

"The *Roberts* test allows a jury to hear evidence, untested by the adversary process, based on a mere judicial determination of reliability. It thus replaces the constitutionally prescribed method of assessing reliability with a wholly foreign one. * * * Dispensing with confrontation because testimony is obviously reliable is akin to dispensing with jury trial because a defendant is obviously guilty. This is not what the Sixth Amendment prescribes." *Id.* at 1370-71.

"The unpardonable vice of the *Roberts* test, however, is not its unpredictability, but its demonstrated capacity to admit core testimonial statements that the Confrontation Clause plainly meant to exclude." *Id.*

"*Roberts'* failings were on full display in the proceedings below. Sylvia Crawford made her statement while in police custody, herself a potential suspect in the case. Indeed, she had been told that whether she would be released 'depend[ed] on how the investigation continues.' In response to often leading questions from police detectives, she implicated her husband in [the] stabbing and at least arguably undermined his self-defense claim. Despite all this, the trial court admitted her statement, listing several reasons why it was reliable. In its opinion reversing, the Court of Appeals listed several *other* reasons why the statement was *not* reliable. Finally, the State Supreme Court relied exclusively on the interlocking character of the statement and disregarded every other factor the lower courts had considered. The case is thus a self-contained demonstration of *Roberts'* unpredictable and inconsistent application." *Id.* at 1372.

"We readily concede that we could resolve this case by simply reweighing the 'reliability factors' under *Roberts* and finding that Sylvia Crawford's statement falls short. But we view this as one of those rare cases in which the result below is so improbable that it reveals a fundamental failure on our part to interpret the Constitution in a way that secures its intended constraint on judicial discretion. Moreover, to reverse the Washington Supreme Court's decision after conducting our own reliability analysis would perpetuate, not avoid, what the Sixth Amendment condemns. The Constitution prescribes a procedure for determining the reliability of testimony in criminal trials, and we, no less than the state courts, lack authority to replace it with one of our own devising." *Id.* at 1373.

"Where nontestimonial hearsay is at issue, it is wholly consistent with the Framers' design to afford the States flexibility in their development of hearsay law—as does *Roberts*, and as would an approach that exempted such statements from Confrontation Clause scrutiny altogether. Where testimonial evidence is at issue, however, the Sixth Amendment demands what the common law required: unavailability and a prior opportunity for cross-examination. We leave for another day any effort to spell out a comprehensive definition of 'testimonial.' Whatever else the term covers, it applies at a minimum to prior testimony at a preliminary hearing, before a grand jury, or at a former trial; and to police interrogations. These are the modern practices with closest kinship to the abuses at which the Confrontation Clause was directed." *Id.* at 1374.

"In this case, the State admitted Sylvia's testimonial statement against [defendant], despite the fact that he had no opportunity to cross-examine her. That alone is sufficient to make out a violation of the Sixth Amendment. *Roberts* notwithstanding, we decline to mine the record in search of indicia of reliability. Where testimonial statements are at issue, the only indicium of reliability sufficient to satisfy constitutional demands is the one the Constitution actually prescribes: confrontation. The judgment of the Washington Supreme Court is reversed, and the case is remanded for further proceedings not inconsistent with this opinion.

It is so ordered.

---

§4.2(b). The Vice of Hearsay

One of the classic ways hearsay is explained to students undertaking a consideration of the law of evidence is to ask each student to picture in his or her mind's eye the problem a prosecutor encounters in an armed robbery prosecution when the State's principal eyewitness is so ugly and repulsive that no juror would ever listen to the witness, let alone believe the witness' testimony. One solution would be to lock the repulsive witness in a closet and hire a professional, articulate and appealing individual to take the witness stand and testify before the jury. Because the good-looking witness has no knowledge of the armed robbery, each time the prosecutor asks a pertinent question, the witness must leave the stand, go to the closet where the repulsive eyewitness is waiting, and ask him the same question. After the repulsive eyewitness tells the good-looking witness the answer, the good-looking witness returns to the witness stand and repeats the answer for the jury.

Certainly, this method of dealing with such a repulsive witness is innovative; but the vice of hearsay, that is, the inability of the defendant to confront the evidence against him—to cross-examine the principal eyewitness to the armed robbery—is readily apparent.

As a general rule, *hearsay is inadmissible* at most court proceedings. The rule "is premised on the theory that out-of-court statements are subject to particular hazards. The declarant might be lying; he might have misperceived the events which he relates; he might have faulty memory; his words might be misunderstood or taken out of context by the listener. And the ways in which these dangers are minimized for in-court statements—the oath, the witness' awareness of the gravity of the proceedings, the jury's ability to observe the witness' demeanor, and, most importantly, the right of the opponent to cross-examine—are generally absent for things said out of court."[30]

Nonetheless, the rules of evidence "also recognize that some kinds of out-of-court statements are less subject to these hearsay dangers."[31] Over the course of time, therefore, a number of hearsay exceptions have developed "to allow admission of hearsay statements made under circumstances that tend to assure reliability and thereby compensate for the absence of the oath and opportunity for cross-examination."[32] This development has been formally codified in *Fed.R.Evid.* 802, which prohibits the admission of hearsay evidence *unless it falls within one of the many recognized exceptions.*[33] Yet, before deciding whether the evidence fits within one of the many recognized hearsay exceptions, a preliminary question must be addressed: *Is it hearsay ?*

UNITED STATES v. SALLINS
United States Court of Appeals
993 *F.*2d 344 (3rd Cir. 1993)

COWEN, Circuit Judge.

"A jury convicted defendant Steven Sallins on one count of possession of a firearm by a convicted felon * * *. Sallins claims that the district court erred by admitting hearsay evidence of a police radio dispatch and a police computer record detailing the contents of a call to

---

[30] *Williamson v. United States*, 512 *U.S.* 594, 598, 114 *S.Ct.* 2431, 2434 (1994).

[31] *Williamson*, 114 *S.Ct.* at 2434.

[32] *See Chambers* at 298-99, 93 *S.Ct.* at 1047.

[33] *Fed.R.Evid.* 802 provides that "[h]earsay is not admissible except as provided by these rules or by other rules prescribed by the Supreme Court pursuant to statutory authority or by Act of Congress." *See also Fed.Rs.Evid.* 803(1) through 803(24) and 804(b)(1) through 804(b)(5).

911. Because we agree that the contents of the police radio dispatch and the police computer record were inadmissible hearsay, we will reverse Sallins' conviction and remand for a new trial." *Id.* at 345.

"At trial, Philadelphia Highway Patrol Officer Antonio Santiago testified that on January 25, 1991, at approximately 7:00 p.m., he and his partner, Officer Mark Howard, received a police radio dispatch. Over defense counsel's objection, Santiago revealed the contents of the radio call by stating that, as a result of the call, he proceeded to the 2500 block of North Franklin Street looking for a black male, wearing all black clothing, who was carrying a gun. Howard, who testified after Santiago, also told the jury that the radio call prompted him to look for a black male, with all black clothing, carrying a gun." *Id.*

"Officer Santiago testified that as he turned onto North Franklin Street at a high rate of speed, he observed a black male, dressed in all black clothing, later identified as Sallins, walk quickly along the sidewalk. As the police car neared Sallins, he turned his head and looked in the officers' direction. Sallins then threw down what appeared to be a gun and ran. The two officers continued down the block, stopped, and exited the police car. While Howard chased and apprehended Sallins, Santiago went to the area where Sallins had been walking and retrieved a gun from underneath a car parked near the sidewalk." *Id.*

"On cross-examination of Santiago, defense counsel questioned whether the audio tape of the communication between the dispatcher and the police car had been preserved. Santiago responded that he was not sure. The government later called as a witness Kimberly Casey, a police officer assigned to the police radio room. Over defense counsel's objection, the government was permitted to introduce the contents of a radio room computer record, which revealed that on January 25, 1991, at approximately 7:00 p.m., a call was received via 911 stating that there was a black male, wearing all black clothing, carrying a gun on the 2500 block of North Franklin Street. The government argued that it was offering Casey's testimony to rebut any intimation by defense that the police radio call never occurred." *Id.* at 345-46.

"Sallins first claims that the contents of the message received by Santiago and Howard over police radio was inadmissible hearsay. Hearsay is a statement, other than one made by the declarant while testifying at trial, offered in evidence to prove the truth of the matter asserted. *Fed.R.Evid.* 801(c). The government argues that the radio dispatch was not hearsay because it was not offered to prove the truth of the matter asserted—that there was in fact a black male dressed in all black with a gun on the 2500 block of North Franklin Street. According to the government, the contents of the radio call were introduced only as background to explain why the officers went to North Franklin Street and acted as they did. Whether evidence is hearsay is a question of law * * *." *Id.* at 346.

"[C]ourts have admitted testimony by police officers or government agents revealing information received out-of-court for the limited purpose of establishing background for the officers' actions. * * * While officers generally should be allowed to explain the context in which they act, the use of out-of-court statements to show background has been identified as an area of 'widespread abuse.' " *Id.* [Citation omitted.]

> "In criminal cases, an arresting or investigating officer should not be put in the false position of seeming just to have happened upon the scene; he should be allowed some explanation of his presence and conduct. His testimony that he acted 'upon information received,' or words to that effect, should be sufficient. [The officer should not be] allowed to relate historical aspects of the case, replete with hearsay statements in the form of complaints and reports, on the ground that he was entitled to give the information upon which he acted. The need for the evidence is slight, and the likelihood of misuse great."

Id. [Citation omitted.]

"Whether a disputed statement is hearsay frequently turns on the purpose for which it is offered. If the hearsay rule is to have any force, courts cannot accept without scrutiny an offering party's representation that an out-of-court statement is being introduced for a material non-hearsay purpose. Rather, courts have a responsibility to assess independently whether the ostensible nonhearsay purpose is valid." *Id.*

"The facts of the present case undermine the government's position that testimony regarding the police radio call was admissible as background to explain why Santiago and Howard went to North Franklin Street and arrested Sallins. First, to the extent that any background was needed to explain why Santiago and Howard sped onto North Franklin Street, the government simply could have elicited testimony that the officers were responding to a radio call or information received. Second, no background beyond what the officers testified they observed was necessary to help the jury understand why Santiago and Howard pursued and arrested Sallins. Santiago stated that when Sallins looked toward the marked police car, he threw down what looked like a gun and ran. Santiago also testified that he recovered a gun from the very location where he believed he saw Sallins throw one. This testimony was more than sufficient to explain why Santiago and Howard acted as they did. Additional background was unnecessary." *Id.* at 346-47.

"Not only was the testimony regarding the radio call inadmissible to show background, it clearly was not offered for that purpose. The absence of a tenable non-hearsay purpose for offering the contents of the police radio call establishes that the evidence could have been offered only for its truth value." *Id.* at 347.

"Repeatedly, the government used the contents of the radio call to prove the truth of the matter asserted, that there was a black man wearing all black clothes with a gun at the place and time in question, as well as to establish the implied fact that Sallins was the man with the gun. Because the details of the radio call were offered for their truth value, the testimony was hearsay and should have been excluded." *Id.*

"Because the officers' testimony as to the contents of the radio dispatch was not admissible in the first place, additional evidence of the 911 call was not admissible to corroborate the earlier testimony." *Id.* at 348.

"For the foregoing reasons, we will reverse the district court's judgment of conviction and remand for a new trial." *Id.* at 349.

NOTE

1. *Statements which produce subsequent conduct.* In *State v. Douglas*, 204 *N.J.Super.* 265, 498 *A.*2d 364 (App.Div. 1985), the court explained that "the hearsay rule is not violated when a police officer explains the reason he approached a suspect or went to the scene of the crime by stating that he did so 'upon information received.' * * * Such testimony has been held to be admissible to show that the officer was not acting in an arbitrary manner or to explain his subsequent conduct. However, when the officer becomes more specific by repeating what some other person told him concerning a crime by the accused, the testimony then violates the hearsay rule. * * * Moreover, the admission of such testimony violates the accused's Sixth Amendment right to be confronted by witnesses against him. * * * When the logical implication to be drawn from a witness' testimony is that a nontestifying witness has given the police evidence of the accused's guilt, the testimony should be disallowed as hearsay." *Id.*, 204 *N.J.Super.* at 272. *See also Commonwealth v. Palsa*, 521 *Pa.* 113, 555 *A.*2d 808, 810-11 (1989) (arresting or investigating officer's testimony that he acted "upon information received" or words to that effect, is sufficient); *State v. Beattie*, 596 *A.*2d 919, 922 (Vt. 1991) (officer's testimony that he had been told by a passing motorist that there was a person "asleep, passed out, or even dead behind the wheel of a van" in a parking lot held not to be hearsay for "it was not offered for the truth of the matter asserted"; "it was offered to prove only that the officer thought he had reason to approach defendant's van"); *United States v. Love*, 767 *F.*2d 1052, 1063 (4th Cir. 1985) ("out of court statement is not hearsay if it is offered for the limited purpose of explaining why a government investigation was undertaken").

2. *Elaborating upon the "information received."* Elaborating upon the "information received," that is, going beyond what is necessary to demonstrate that the law enforcement officer did not act in an arbitrary manner, violates a defendant's right to confront his accuser

and the rule against hearsay. For example, while it may be proper for an officer to testify that the police went to a specific location based "upon information received," it would be improper for an officer to testify that the police went to that location to investigate "a male beating a female" call. *See e.g., State v. Vandeweaghe*, 827 A.2d 1028, 177 *N.J.* 229, 240-41 (2003).

(a) In *Commonwealth v. Yates*, 531 *Pa.* 373, 613 A.2d 542 (1992), the Court ordered a new trial for the defendant because the hearsay statements contained in the officers' testimony at trial not only demonstrated the reason why the officers had arrived at a particular location but also suggested that the defendant had been involved in "drug dealing." The officers' testimony set forth the reason why they responded to the 600 block of Brushton Avenue. Each stated that an informant notified him that "a large black male," *i.e.*, defendant, was "dealing drugs" at that location. *Id.*, 613 A.2d at 543. According to the Court, those statements were "highly incriminating," they contained "specific assertions of criminal conduct," and "were likely to have been understood by the jury as providing substantive evidence of guilt," particularly in light of the fact that defendant had been charged with possession of cocaine, and possession with intent to deliver. *Id.* The Court emphasized:

> "It is the prosecutor's duty to avoid the introduction of out-of-court statements that go beyond what is reasonably necessary to explain police conduct." In the present case, the prosecution could easily have explained the course of police conduct without introducing the informant's incriminating statements regarding [defend]ant's drug dealing. [The] officers could simply have testified that they acted "upon information received," or words to that effect.

Yates at 543. [Citation omitted.]

(b) In *State v. Baker*, 228 *N.J.Super.* 135, 549 A.2d 62 (App.Div. 1988), the trial court permitted a police officer's testimony identifying his confidential informant (who had died of an overdose prior to trial) as the owner and operator of the car in which the defendants were occupants when it was stopped by the police. The officer further testified that it was this informant who had provided the telephone tip which led to the arrest of the defendants for the possession of heroin.

Finding this testimony to constitute "inadmissible hearsay," the Superior Court, Appellate Division, first recognized that "the hearsay rule does not bar a police witness from testifying that he approached a suspect or went to the scene of a crime 'upon information received' where the evidence is not offered to prove that the information received was true but only that 'the officer was not acting in an arbitrary manner or to explain his subsequent conduct.' " *Id.*, 228 *N.J.Super.* at 139. [Citation omitted.] However, according to the court, "[t]here is seldom any justification for admitting such evidence where the defendant does not claim that the police acted arbitrarily in approaching him." *Baker* at 139-140. "Where the only reason for referring to a tip is to place before the trier of fact, directly or indirectly, the truth of an informer's incriminating statement, the evidence is inadmissible hearsay and also violates the defendant's Sixth Amendment right to confront the informer." *Id.* at 140. Additionally, "evidence from which the content of a tip may be inferred is as inadmissible as the tip itself." *Id.*

In this case, "when the police witness identified the owner and operator of the car as the source of the tip, he in effect advised the jury that [the informant] had told him that defendants knowingly possessed the heroin hidden in the car. The inference is irresistible that [the informant] tipped off the police to advise them of defendants' criminal conduct and not just his own." *Id.* at 139. Significantly, because the informant's incriminating hearsay statement was placed before the jury by inference, "its impact was essentially the same as it would have been had [the informant's] words been quoted directly." *Id.* As a result, "[t]he import of the officer's testimony here was not simply to identify [the driver of the vehicle] as the informer. The fact that [the driver] was the informer formed the basis for a reasonable but inadmissible inference that he gave the police a statement that incriminated defendants." *Id.* at 140.

3. *Other statements not offered for their truth.* So long as the probative effect of an out-of-court statement may be accomplished without the need for any reliance upon the truth of the matter asserted within the statement, the hearsay rule is not implicated.

(a) *Statements which have independent legal significance—"verbal acts."* There are many statements which, when offered at trial, have legal significance independent of their truth. The mere utterance of the statement calls forth certain legal obligations or rights, or produces certain legal consequences. For example, an objection posed (in a "false public alarm" or "reckless endangerment" prosecution) to a witness' testimony that, "In the movie theater, the defendant yelled, 'Oh my, there's a fire !' " would not be sustained on hearsay grounds, for the statement is being offered only to show that the defendant spoke the operative words, not to prove the truth of the matter asserted within the statement (that there *was* a fire in the theater). Thus, when a witness testifies that someone said something to him and the purpose is not to show that what was said was true but that the statement was made, the testimony is not hearsay but instead a "verbal act."

(b) Statements which demonstrate knowledge. Similarly, an out-of-court statement will not be considered hearsay when it is repeated in court merely to show that an individual had knowledge of a certain event, fact or condition. For example, if a witness wishes to testify that he heard the driver of an automobile tell the defendant passenger that there was an ounce of cocaine in the trunk of the car, the statement would not constitute hearsay when offered solely to prove that the defendant had knowledge of the presence of the contraband.

(c) Inquiries. In *United States v. Oguns*, 921 *F*.2d 442 (2nd Cir. 1990), federal agents were in the process of searching defendant's apartment when the phone rang. One of the agents answered the phone. During the course of the ensuing conversation, the unidentified caller asked to speak to defendant. The agent told the caller that defendant had gone to the store. The caller then asked, "Have the apples arrived there ?" After this statement was introduced at trial, the government introduced further testimony that narcotics traffickers often use such code words when discussing drugs on the telephone. The "apples" in this case referred to over 1400 grams of heroin. Defendant argued on appeal that the evidence of the question asked during the telephone call to his apartment was hearsay and was improperly admitted. The circuit court of appeals disagreed.

According to the court, " '[a]n inquiry is not an "assertion," and accordingly is not and cannot be a hearsay statement.' * * * Because a question cannot be used to show the truth of the matter asserted, the dangers necessitating the hearsay rule are not present." *Id.* at 449. [Citation omitted.] *See also United States v. Detrich*, 865 *F*.2d 17, 20-21 (2nd Cir. 1988). The court concluded, therefore, that the government legitimately used the phone call as circumstantial evidence of the defendant's knowledge and intent regarding the drug importation and distribution charges.

4. *Nonhuman evidence.* "Does it violate the rule against hearsay when a police witness on the stand testifies that radar equipment 'said' that the defendant was driving his automobile at 90 miles an hour ? Is violence done to the rule when a meter maid testifies that the parking meter 'said' the defendant's allotted time had expired ? * * * Are these machines all out-of-court declarants within the meaning of the [] hearsay rule ?

"On the theory that machines, unlike some humans, lack a conscious motivation to tell lies, and because the operation (including the accuracy and reliability) of machines can be explained by human witnesses who are then subject to probing cross-examination by opposing counsel, the law permits so-called nonhuman hearsay." Waltz, *Criminal Evidence* (1975), 70.

---

§4.3. HEARSAY EXEMPTIONS AND EXCEPTIONS

The hearsay evidence rule primarily functions to effectuate the policy of requiring that testimony be given in open court, under oath, and subject to cross-examination.[34] Problems arise, however, from the wide variation in the reliability of evidence which, by definition, is classified as hearsay. Over the years, the solution has been found in the "recognition of numerous exceptions where it has been thought that 'circumstantial guarantees of trustworthiness' justified departure from the general rule excluding hearsay."[35] The following sections explore some of the more common hearsay exceptions encountered by law enforcement and criminal justice officials.

---

§4.3(a). Admissions and Confessions

An out-of-court statement offered against a party, which is the party's own statement, is admissible in a court proceeding.[36] If the statement contains facts which are incriminating or adverse to the interest of its maker, it is an "inculpatory admission."[37] When the statement contains a sufficient amount of "admissions" to warrant the conclusion that its maker is guilty of a criminal offense, it may then be said to be a "confession." An admission or confession made by a criminal defendant is generally subject to a preliminary determination by a judge as to its admissibility at a hearing outside

---

[34] 2 McCormick, *Evidence* §253 (West 4th ed. 1992), at 130.

[35] *Id.* [Citation omitted.]

[36] *Fed.R.Evid.* 801(d)(2)(A). While many jurisdictions treat admissions and confessions as hearsay exceptions, the federal rules do not classify such statements as hearsay. Under the federal rules, admissions and confessions are exempted from the category of hearsay "on the theory that their admissibility in evidence is the result of the adversary system rather than satisfaction of the conditions of the hearsay rule." *Advisory Committee's Note*, 56 *F.R.D.* 183, 296.

[37] It is not, however, necessary that the statement be incriminating to be admissible. "Admissions include any statement made by and offered against a party opponent." *State v. Bernier*, 597 A.2d 789, 791 (Vt. 1991). "They need not be against the declarant's interest when made." *Id.* at 791. *See also United States v. Leal*, 781 *F.*2d 1108, 1111 (5th Cir. 1986) (defendant's out-of-court statements were admissible because they were relevant; "a party's words, offered against him, form an exclusion to the definition of hearsay").

the presence of the jury.[38] In such a hearing, the burden is on the prosecution to establish the admissibility of the statement.[39]

---

§4.3(a)(1). Authorized, Adoptive and Vicarious Admissions

A statement offered against a party is admissible if it is the party's own statement made in a "representative capacity," or if it is a statement of which "the party has manifested an adoption or belief in its truth," or if it is "a statement by a person authorized by the party to make a statement concerning the subject."[40] A statement offered against a party is also admissible if it is "a statement by the party's agent or servant concerning a matter within the scope of the agency or employment, made during the existence of the relationship."[41]

For example, "[a] partner is an agent of the partnership for the conduct of the firm's business. Accordingly, when the existence and scope of the partnership have been proved, the statement of a partner made in the conduct of the business of the firm is receivable as the admission of the partnership."[42]

---

§4.3(a)(2). Implied Admissions

An admission need not be express or articulated in order to qualify as such. An admission by conduct may be just as evidential as an admission by word. In this respect, many acts committed by criminal defendants, which run contrary to innocence, that is, acts or conduct which constitute "circumstantial evidence" of a defendant's "consciousness of guilt and hence of the fact of guilt itself,"[43] may be admissible as an "implied admission." A number of acts have been held

---

[38] *See Fed.R.Evid.* 104(c) ("Hearings on the admissibility of confessions shall in all cases be conducted out of the hearing of the jury."). In some jurisdictions, a confession is treated as a "statement against interest." *See e.g., State v. White*, 158 *N.J.* 230, 238, 729 *A.*2d 31 (1999) ("[A] statement in which a party confesses to having committed a crime subjects the declarant to criminal liability, and therefore constitutes a statement that is against interest.").

[39] *Id. See also Jackson v. Denno*, 378 *U.S.* 368, 376-377, 391, 84 *S.Ct.* 1780-81, 1788 (1964) (a criminal defendant has a constitutional right "at some stage in the proceedings to object to the use of the confession and to have a fair hearing and a reliable determination on the issue of voluntariness, a determination uninfluenced by the truth or falsity of the confession," along with a "resolution of disputed facts upon which the voluntariness issue may depend").

[40] *See Fed.R.Evid.* 801(d)(2)(A)-(C).

[41] *See Fed.R.Evid.* 801(d)(2)(D).

[42] 2 McCormick, *Evidence* §259 (West 4th ed. 1992), at 164.

[43] 2 McCormick, *Evidence* §263, at 181.

to constitute circumstantial evidence of a defendant's "consciousness of guilt." These include: attempting to bribe arresting officers; flight from the scene of the crime, the police or the jurisdiction; concealment of whereabouts or identity; the destruction or fabrication of evidence; shaving off a beard; refusing to submit to physical examination; threatening an opposing witness; and even attempted suicide.[44]

---

§4.3(b). Statements of Co-conspirators

Statements made by a co-conspirator are admissible against the accused if the statements are made "during the course and in furtherance of the conspiracy,"[45] and there is evidence demonstrating the existence of the conspiracy. In this regard, each co-conspirator is considered a representative, agent or partner of the other for the purpose of furthering or accomplishing a particular unlawful act, and any statements made in connection thereto are admissible as a representative admission against any one of the co-conspirators. The rule requires proof that (1) a conspiracy was in existence, (2) the statements made by the co-conspirator(s) were made while the conspiracy was continuing, and (3) the statements in some way furthered the unlawful venture.[46]

---

[44] *See generally id.* at 181-94. *See also United States v. Ballard,* 423 *F.*2d 127, 133 (5th Cir. 1970). A number of courts engage in a multi-step analysis to determine the probativeness of flight evidence. For example, in *United States v. Myers,* 550 *F.*2d 1036 (5th Cir. 1977), the court held that the probative value of flight evidence "depends upon the degree of confidence with which four inferences can be drawn: (1) from the defendant's behavior to flight; (2) from flight to consciousness of guilt; (3) from consciousness of guilt to consciousness of guilt concerning the crime charged; and (4) from consciousness of guilt concerning the crime charged to actual guilt of the crime charged." *Id.* at 1049. *See also United States v. Dillon,* 870 *F.*2d 1125, 1126-29 (6th Cir. 1989); *United States v. Peltier,* 585 *F.*2d 314, 323 (8th Cir. 1978).

A vast majority of jurisdictions analogize attempted suicide to flight. *See* 2 Wigmore, *Evidence* §276 (Chadbourn rev. 1979), at 131 (attempted suicide may be interpreted as "an attempt to flee and escape forever from the temporal consequences of one's misdeeds"); *State v. Mitchell,* 450 *N.W.*2d 828, 831 (Iowa 1990) (in a kidnapping and rape case, evidence of defendant's attempted suicide while in a police squad car en route to jail was admissible to show his guilty state of mind); *State v. Brown,* 128 *N.H.* 606, 615-16, 517 *A.*2d 831 (1986) (just as a jury may consider flight after a crime, it may also consider attempted suicide as indicating a consciousness of guilt); *State v. Mann,* 132 *N.J.* 410, 422, 625 *A.*2d 1102 (1993) ("As with flight, the evidence must be sufficient to support the inference that a defendant's attempted suicide is evidence of consciousness of guilt.").

[45] *Fed.R.Evid.* 801(d)(2)(E).

[46] *See United States v. Patton,* 594 *F.*2d 444 (5th Cir. 1979) (upholding admissibility of a co-conspirator's statement that two other members of the conspiracy told him that marijuana was being purchased for the defendant); *United States v. Fielding,* 645 *F.*2d 719, 727 (9th Cir. 1981) (mere narrative statements which do not further the objectives of the conspiracy, such as those designed to induce others to join the conspiracy held inadmissible as not made in furtherance of the conspiracy). *Compare State v. Bird,* 238 *Kan.* 160, 177, 708 *P.*2d 946, 960 (1985) (co-conspirator's statement need only be relevant to the unlawful venture, it need not be made in furtherance of it).

§4.3(c). Prior Inconsistent Statements

Under the federal rules, a statement is "not hearsay" if the declarant testifies and is subject to cross-examination concerning the statement, and the statement is "inconsistent with the declarant's testimony, and was given under oath subject to the penalty of perjury at a trial, hearing, or other proceeding, or in a deposition[.]"[47]

COMMONWEALTH v. BRADY
Supreme Court of Pennsylvania
510 *Pa.* 123, 507 *A.2d* 66 (1986)

The opinion of the Court was delivered by

LARSEN, *Justice.*

[Early one September morning in 1980, Tina Traxler was awakened by her boyfriend (defendant) and was persuaded to go for a ride with him. After riding around for awhile, the car was run into a ditch alongside a dirt road by defendant, who was unable to get the car free. Defendant and Tina began walking back towards town and saw the Wilson Manufacturing plant. They climbed the fence surrounding the building and entered through a side door. While defendant was attempting to pry open a dollar bill change machine, a security guard approached. A scuffle ensued, during which defendant stabbed the guard. Leaving the security guard for dead, defendant and Tina left the plant. Later that evening, Tina gave a tape-recorded statement to the police detailing the events leading to the stabbing of the guard. At trial, however, she recanted her statement and testified that she was with defendant at the time of the murder, but they were not at the scene of the crime and defendant did not commit the murder.]

"We granted the Commonwealth's petition * * * to reconsider this Court's long-standing rule that prior inconsistent statements of a non-party witness at trial cannot be used as substantive evidence to prove the truth of the matters asserted therein but may only be used for the limited purpose of impeaching the credibility of the witness. We now discard this antiquated rule and hold that such statements may be used as substantive evidence where the declarant is a witness at trial and available for cross-examination." *Id.* at 67.

"Until now, this Court has adhered to the 'orthodox' rule limiting the use of such prior inconsistent statements of a non-party witness to impeachment. * * * This rule has been widely discredited by most legal scholars and commentators that have considered its efficacy." *Id.* at 68.

"Upon further reflection and consideration of the shortcomings of the orthodox rule, as clearly illustrated by the circumstances of this

---

[47] *Fed.R.Evid.* 801(d)(1)(A).

case, we reject that rule and embrace the modern rule as the law of this Commonwealth. The traditional view is that a prior statement of a witness is hearsay if offered to prove the truth of the matters asserted therein. The orthodox rule deems hearsay generally, and prior inconsistent statements specifically, too unreliable to be admitted as substantive evidence because the declarant was (1) not under oath, (2) not subject to cross-examination at the time the statement was made, and (3) not in the presence of the trier of fact when the statement was made. * * * Each prong of this threefold requirement has been logically and thoroughly debunked by the scholars and by the growing number of jurisdictions adopting the modern rule governing prior inconsistent statements of non-party witnesses by statute, rule or case law." *Id.* at 68-69.

"The simple fact is that 'the usual dangers of hearsay are largely nonexistent where the witness testifies at trial.' * * * By hypothesis in these situations, the out-of-court declarant is now a witness *in court* where he or she is placed under oath, subject to cross-examination and observation by the finder of fact. * * * Indeed, the cross-examination to which a recanting witness is subjected will likely be meaningful and vigorous since the witness is already 'on the spot' in having to explain the discrepancies between the earlier statements and direct testimony, or deny that the earlier statements were made at all." *Id.* at 69. [Citations omitted; court's emphasis.]

"Earlier decisions expressed some concern that the cross-examination was not contemporaneous with the out-of-court declaration. * * * This concern is unfounded for, as the United States Supreme Court has observed, the 'most successful cross-examination at the time the statement was made could hardly hope to accomplish more than has already been accomplished by the fact that the witness is now telling a different, inconsistent story.' *California v. Green*, [399 *U.S.* 149, 159, 90 *S.Ct.* 1930, 1935 (1970)]." *Brady* at 69.

"The availability of cross-examination at trial also assures a meaningful opportunity for the trier of fact to observe the declarant who has been called upon and sworn as a witness and questioned as to the discrepancy between the prior statement and the direct testimony. The trier of fact may bring to bear his or her sensory observations, experience, common sense and logic upon the witness to assess credibility and to determine the truth and accuracy of both the out-of-court declarations and the in-court testimony." *Id.*

"We are persuaded that the modern view is the better, more principled view. As we have seen, the hearsay concerns are virtually nonexistent where the out-of-court declarant is a witness in a judicial proceeding. On the other hand, the damage done to the integrity of the fact-finding process by continued adherence to the orthodox rule would be significant." *Id.* at 70.

"Accordingly, we reverse this Court's previous position and hold that otherwise admissible prior inconsistent statements of a declarant who is a witness in a judicial proceeding and is available for cross-examination may be used as substantive evidence to prove the truth of the matters asserted therein." *Id.*

"We * * * hold that the tape-recorded statement was properly admitted as substantive evidence. The out-of-court declaration was rendered under highly reliable circumstances assuring that they were voluntary, knowing and understanding. Moreover, the declarant testified at trial * * * and was extensively questioned by both the prosecutor and defense counsel as to the respective validity of each statement and as to the discrepancy between them. The jury had more than adequate opportunity to observe the witness' demeanor, hear her testimony and explanations and assess her credibility. Under these circumstances, the trial court did not err in allowing Tina Traxler's tape-recorded statement to be introduced as substantive evidence." *Id.* at 71.

---

§4.3(d). Prior Consistent Statements

In limited circumstances, a prior statement of a witness, which is *consistent* with his or her courtroom testimony, is admissible to strengthen the credibility of the witness' testimony where the witness' truthfulness has been attacked. The federal rules provide that a statement is "not hearsay" if the declarant testifies and is subject to cross-examination concerning the statement, and the statement is "consistent with the declarant's testimony and is offered to rebut an express or implied charge against the declarant of recent fabrication or improper influence or motive[.]"[48]

"The prevailing common-law rule for more than a century before the adoption of the Federal Rules of Evidence was that a prior consistent statement introduced to rebut a charge of recent fabrication or improper influence or motive was admissible if the statement had been made before the alleged fabrication, influence, or motive came into being, but it was inadmissible if made afterwards."[49] This "temporal requirement" has been held to be embodied in Rule 801(d)(1)(B).[50]

---

[48] *Fed.R.Evid.* 801(d)(a)(B). There is no requirement, however, that the declarant actually be cross-examined concerning the statement. The declarant need only be *available* for cross-examination. *See United States v. Piva*, 870 *F*.2d 753, 758 (1st Cir. 1989); *United States v. Vest*, 842 *F*.2d 1319, 1329 (1st Cir. 1988).

[49] *Tome v. United States*, 513 *U.S.* 150, 156, 115 *S.Ct.* 696, 700 (1995). *See also Ellicott v. Pearl*, 35 *U.S.* (10 Pet.) 412, 439 (1836) ("[W]here the testimony is assailed as a fabrication of a recent date . . . in order to repel such imputation, proof of the *antecedent* declaration of the party may be admitted.") (emphasis added).

[50] *Tome, supra*, 115 *S.Ct.* at 700. *See also id.* at 705 (Rule 801(d)(1)(B) "permits the introduction of a declarant's consistent out-of-court statements to rebut a charge of recent fabrication or improper influence or motive only when those statements were made before the charged recent fabrication or improper influence or motive.").

In *Tome v. United States*,[51] the Court emphasized that the admissibility of a prior consistent statement

> is limited to those statements offered to rebut a charge of "recent fabrication or improper influence or motive" * * *. Prior consistent statements may not be admitted to counter all forms of impeachment or to bolster the witness merely because she has been discredited. * * * The Rule speaks of a party rebutting an alleged motive, not bolstering the veracity of the story told.

> This limitation is instructive, not only to establish the preconditions of admissibility but also to reinforce the significance of the requirement that the consistent statements must have been made before the alleged influence, or motive to fabricate arose. That is to say, the forms of impeachment within the Rule's coverage are the ones in which the temporal requirement makes the most sense. Impeachment by charging that the testimony is a recent fabrication or results from an improper motive is, as a general matter, capable of direct and forceful refutation through introduction of out-of-court consistent statements that predate the alleged fabrication, influence or motive. A consistent statement that predates the motive is a square rebuttal of the charge that the testimony was contrived as a consequence of that motive. * * *[52]

Under the federal rules, prior consistent statements are admitted as substantive evidence.[53] A number of jurisdictions, however, permit the introduction of such evidence only in rebuttal.[54] In this respect, the Pennsylvania Supreme Court, in *Commonwealth v. Hutchinson*,[55] explained that the use of prior consistent statements

> as a means to rehabilitate the credibility of an impeached witness' testimony is severely limited; and such statements are admissible only if it is alleged that the witness' present testimony is recently fabricated or a result of corrupt motives. * * * Furthermore, evidence of such statements is "admissible only in rebuttal

---

[51] 513 *U.S.* 150, 115 *S.Ct.* 696 (1995).

[52] *Tome* at 701.

[53] *Advisory Committee's Note*, 56 *F.R.D.* 183, 296. "Noting the 'troublesome' logic of treating a witness' prior consistent statements as hearsay at all (because the declarant is present in court and subject to cross-examination), the Advisory Committee decided to treat those consistent statements, once the preconditions of the Rule were satisfied, as nonhearsay and admissible as substantive evidence, not just to rebut an attack on the witness' credibility." *Tome* at 701.

[54] *See e.g., Commonwealth v. Polston*, 420 *Pa.Super.* 233, 616 *A.2d* 669, 674 (1992) ("The purpose of the evidence is to 'rehabilitate' a witness's credibility after it has been challenged, not to prove the truth of the matter it asserts.").

[55] 521 *Pa.* 482, 556 *A.2d* 370 (1989).

and then only for the purpose of showing that that which the witness now testifies to has not recently been fabricated." * * *

Ordinarily, that one has always said the same thing is subsumed in their testimony and need not be buttressed by evidence of prior consistency, unless that consistency, by allegation of recent fabrication, is challenged. When challenged, evidence of prior and continued consistency may be offered. * * *

As to [a] further restriction upon admissibility, the statement must have been made at a time "before its ultimate effect on the *question trying* could have been foreseen[, that is,] * * * before any corrupt motive ha[d] arisen."[56]

Thus, absent an allegation of a recent fabrication or corrupt motive, evidence of a prior consistent statement is not required and will not be permitted, for it is essentially "cumulative and repetitious."[57]

---

§4.3(e). Dying Declarations

Long before the law recognized a rule against hearsay, dying declarations were received by the courts due to a widespread belief that there was a "special likelihood of truthfulness [in] deathbed statements."[58] In 1789, one court explained that the general principle upon which dying declarations are admitted in court is that "they are declarations made in extremity, when the party is at the point of death, and when every hope of this world is gone; when every motive to falsehood is silenced, and the mind is induced by the most powerful considerations to speak the truth; a situation so solemn, and so awful, is considered by the law as creating an obligation equal to that which is imposed by a positive oath administered in a Court of Justice."[59]

---

[56] *Hutchinson* at 487-88, 556 *A.*2d at 372 (citations omitted; emphasis in original). *See also Commonwealth v. Polston,* 420 *Pa.Super.* 233, 616 *A.*2d 669, 674-75 (1992); *Commonwealth v. Rodgers,* 472 *Pa.* 435, 456, 372 *A.*2d 771, 780-81 (1977).

[57] *Hutchinson* at 487-88, 556 *A.*2d at 372. *See also Commonwealth v. Smith,* 518 *Pa.* 15, 540 *A.*2d 246, 258 (1988) (prior consistent statements admissible to rebut a "suggestion of corrupt motives or recent fabrication"); *Commonwealth v. Polston,* 420 *Pa.Super.* 233, 616 *A.*2d 669, 674-75 (1992) (prior consistent statements may be "admitted only in rebuttal if the witness's testimony has been challenged as recent fabrication"); *Commonwealth v. Smith,* 402 *Pa.Super.* 257, 586 *A.*2d 957, 963-64 (1991).

[58] 2 McCormick, *Evidence* §310 (4th ed. 1992), at 324.

[59] *Rex v. Woodstock,* 1 *Leach* 500, 168 *Eng.Rep.* 352 (K.B. 1789) (Opinion by Chief Baron Eyre).

SHEPARD v. UNITED STATES
Supreme Court of the United States
290 *U.S.* 96, 54 *S.Ct.* 22 (1933)

Mr. Justice CARDOZO delivered the opinion of the Court.

[Defendant, Charles Shepard, a major in the medical corps of the United States Army, was convicted of the murder of his wife, Zenana Shepard, at Fort Riley, Kansas, a United States military reservation. Defendant was sentenced to life imprisonment.]

"The crime is charged to have been committed by poisoning the victim with bichloride of mercury. The defendant was in love with another woman, and wished to make her his wife." *Id.* at 23.

"The evidence complained of * * * [consisted of] a conversation in the absence of the defendant between Mrs. Shepard, then ill in bed, and Clara Brown, her nurse. The patient asked the nurse to go to the closet in the defendant's room and bring a bottle of whisky that would be found upon a shelf. When the bottle was produced, she said that this was the liquor she had taken just before collapsing. She asked whether enough was left to make a test for the presence of poison, insisting that the smell and taste were strange. And then she added the words, "Dr. Shepard has poisoned me." *Id.*

"The conversation was proved [by the testimony of the nurse]. * * * [In addition, the nurse testified that Mrs. Shepard] said she was not going to get well; she was going to die." *Id.*

"She said, 'Dr. Shepard has poisoned me.' * * * The voice of the dead wife was heard in accusation of her husband, and the accusation accepted as evidence of guilt. If the evidence was incompetent, the verdict may not stand." *Id.*

"[In this Court, the government argues] that what was said by Mrs. Shepard was admissible as a dying declaration. * * * To make out a dying declaration, the declarant must have spoken without hope of recovery and in the shadow of impending death. The record furnishes no proof of that indispensable condition." *Id.*

"We have said that the declarant was not shown to have spoken without hope of recovery and in the shadow of impending death. Her illness began on May 20. She was found in a state of collapse, delirious, in pain, the pupils of her eyes dilated, and the retina suffused with blood. The conversation with the nurse occurred two days later. At that time her mind had cleared up, and her speech was rational and orderly. There was as yet no thought by any of her physicians that she was dangerously ill, still less that her case was hopeless. To all seeming she had greatly improved, and was moving forward to recovery. * * * Not till about a week afterwards was there a relapse, accompanied by an infection of the mouth, renewed congestion of the eyes, and later hemorrhages of the bowels. Death followed on June 15." *Id.* at 24.

"Nothing in the condition of the patient on May 22 gives fair support to the conclusion that hope had been lost. * * * Indeed, * * * she said to one of her physicians, though her condition was then grave, 'You will get me well, won't you ?' Fear or even belief that illness will end in death will not avail of itself to make a dying declaration. There must be 'a settled hopeless expectation' * * * that death is near at hand, and what is said must have been spoken in the hush of its impending presence. * * * Despair of recovery may indeed be gathered from the circumstances if the facts support the inference. * * * There is no unyielding ritual of words to be spoken by the dying. Despair may even be gathered, though the period of survival outruns the bounds of expectation. * * * What is decisive is the state of mind. Even so, the state of mind must be exhibited in the evidence, and not left to conjecture. The patient must have spoken with the consciousness of a swift and certain doom." *Id.* [Citations omitted.]

"What was said by this patient was not spoken in that mood. There was no warning to her in the circumstances that her words would be repeated and accepted as those of a dying wife, charging murder to her husband, and charging it deliberately and solemnly as a fact within her knowledge. To the focus of that responsibility her mind was never brought. She spoke as one ill, * * * not [] as one dying, announcing to the survivors a definitive conviction, a legacy of knowledge on which the world might act when she had gone." *Id.*

Apart from these defects in the declaration—that death was not imminent and that hope was still alive—is another concern, namely, that "homicide may not be imputed to a defendant on the basis of mere suspicions, though they are the suspicions of the dying. To let the declaration in, the inference must be permissible that there was knowledge or the opportunity for knowledge as to the acts that are declared. * * * The form [of the declaration] is not decisive, though it be that of a conclusion, a statement of the result with the antecedent steps omitted. * * * 'He murdered me,' does not cease to be competent as a dying declaration because in the statement of the act there is also an appraisal of the crime. * * * One does not hold the dying to the observance of all the niceties of speech to which conformity is exacted from a witness on the stand. What is decisive is something deeper and more fundamental than any difference of form. The declaration is kept out if the setting of the occasion satisfies the judge, or in reason ought to satisfy him, that the speaker is giving expression to suspicion or conjecture, and not to known facts. * * * In this case, the ruling that there was a failure to make out the imminence of death and the abandonment of hope relieves us of the duty of determining whether it is a legitimate inference that there was the opportunity for knowledge. We leave that question open." *Id.* at 24-25.

PEOPLE v. SARZANO
Court of Appeals of New York
212 N.Y. 231, 106 N.E. 87 (1914)

PER CURIAM.

[Defendant was convicted of the murder of Saverio Gragnanello, aka Salvitas Greniera. He shot Gragnanello on November 17, 1912, at Buffalo. Gragnanello died January 22, 1913, as a result of the shooting.]

"The trial court erred in receiving in evidence as a dying declaration the statement made by the deceased on November 17, 1912, after he had been taken to the hospital. The statement was made to Dr. George B. Stocker, who was the deputy medical examiner for Erie County. Dr. Stocker told the deceased 'that his condition was critical, and we expected he would die from the way he was, and we wanted his statement for use later.' 'I talked to him and told him the condition he was in and that he was going to die, and I wanted an ante mortem statement for purposes that might arise later.' The deceased said, 'All right,' he would give it, and made statements, which were written down and read to him by Dr. Stocker. The written statement was:

> *Dying declaration of Salvitas Greniera made on the 17th day of November, 1912, at Emergency Hospital in the city of Buffalo, county of Erie, to Geo. B. Stocker, deputy medical examiner of said county.*
>
> *He says: I consider my condition critical, and am under the influence of an impression that I am about to die, and have no hopes of my recovery from the effects of my wound. I make this statement under that impression.*
>
> *I live at 164-8 Erie Street and am a saloon-keeper by occupation. My wife was in back of saloon and this man Mike by name and I do not know his last name went back to this room and I went back there and asked him what he wanted and told him to go out. He drew a gun and said he would shoot me. I asked him what he wanted to shoot for and again told him to go out. He immediately shot me five times. Then he ran out of the back door. I never had any trouble with him before. He was not drunk. This was between seven and eight o'clock tonight.*
>
> *His*
> *Salvitas   X   Greniera*
> *mark*

Id. at 87.

"The learned district attorney seems confident that the statement was admissible. He points out the [] wounds; that the deceased was about to undergo an operation; that a doctor told him he was in a critical condition, and they did not expect him to live; and that he stated he was under the influence of an impression or under an impression that he was about to die. The statements of the district attorney must, however, be modified in these particulars: There is no proof that the deceased knew that he was about to undergo an operation, or that the person talking to him was a doctor, or that he stated that he was under the impression that he was about to die. The statement was upon a printed blank, and the only affirmative statements of the deceased it contains are those including and following the words, 'I live at 164-8 Erie street.' Above those, the blanks of the printed form were properly filled, and the entire statement was read to him, and he said it was true." *Id.* at 88.

"The principle upon which dying declarations are received in evidence is that the mind, impressed with the awful idea of approaching dissolution, acts under a sanction equally powerful with that which it is presumed to feel by a solemn appeal to God upon an oath. The declarations, therefore, of a person dying under such circumstances are considered as equivalent to the evidence of the living witness upon oath. * * * Safety in receiving such declarations lies only in the fact that the declarant is so controlled by a belief that his death is certain and imminent that malice, hatred, passion, and other feelings of like nature are overwhelmed and banished by it. The evidence should be clear that the declarations were made under a sense of impending death without any hope of recovery. * * * Statements made by a doctor to and accepted by a declarant that there was no chance of his recovering are admissible. * * * If the declarant thinks there is a slight chance of living, the declarations are inadmissible. * * * The mere fact that the doctor told declarant that recovery was impossible is insufficient. There must be proof that the declarant believed it and had no hope of recovery. * * * Declarant's certainty that he is about to die and lack of all hope of recovery may be proven by his express language or conduct, or inferred from his physical condition and obvious danger, or evidence of his acquiescence in the opinions of doctors or others stated to him, or other adequate circumstances." *Id.*

"In the present case the preliminary proof was too slight and indefinite to justify the admission of the statement. The transaction, apart from the wounds, was this: A strange man said to the deceased when received at the hospital that his condition was critical and he was going to die, and they wanted an ante mortem statement for purposes that might arise later, and the deceased said 'All right,' he would give it * * *. The declarant did not ask for wife, children, friends, or priest or by word or act indicate that he believed his death certain and imminent. He did not say or show that he believed he would not recover and was without any hope whatsoever of living. It would be extending the rule beyond the decision in any case we have read or found, and we think beyond safety, to approve the reception in evidence of the statement." *Id.*

NOTE

1. In *Donnelly v. State*, 26 *N.J.L.* 463, *aff'd* 26 *N.J.L.* 601 (E. & A. 1857), the prosecution's evidence revealed that

> the deceased died from a wound inflicted with a sharp instrument on the left side of the neck or throat, six inches in depth, perforating the *aesophagus*, severing the jugular vein and a branch of the carotid artery, and inflicting other internal injury; that the wound in its nature was very dangerous, and the possibility of recovery from it very doubtful; that in point of fact the deceased died from the effect of the wound soon after its infliction; that the wound was inflicted while the deceased was in bed; that after receiving the injury, he had raised the cry of murder, and had followed the murderer through an adjoining room into the hall, bleeding very profusely; that a few steps from the door of the room, through which he had passed into the hall, he had fallen or stopped, and had there lost a large quantity of blood; that he thence returned toward his room, and entering the outer room adjoining his own, had fallen or laid himself upon the bed, from which he never rose; that Mr. Smith, the proprietor of the house, the first person who entered the room, and who came soon after hearing the alarm, found him upon the bed bleeding very profusely. Upon entering the room, the wounded man threw up his hands, called the witness by name and repeated that he had been stabbed; that he had been murdered; that his throat had been cut. The witness then stated, "I asked him who by; he said Donnelly, your book-keeper."

Id. at 498-99. [Italic in original.]

According to the court, the following facts were dispositive: "[1] that the deceased had received a most dangerous wound, from which recovery was very improbable, which was [2] likely very soon to prove mortal, and [3] from which, in fact, the injured man died * * *. [4] [T]he statement was voluntarily made immediately after the injury, * * * [5] the declaration was made within ninety minutes of his death, and [6] was preceded by a declaration that he was murdered." *Id.* at 499.

Finding the evidence admissible as a dying declaration, the court declared:

Was not the statement made under a sense of impending death ? Is there any evidence to warrant the belief that at that time or at any time afterwards, he had the least expectation or hope of recovery ? It is not necessary that the party injured should state, at the time of making the declaration[], that [it was] made under a sense of impending death. It is enough, if it satisfactorily appears in any mode that the declaration was made under that sanction. It may be directly proved by the express language of the declarant, but it may also be inferred from his evident danger, or the opinion of his attendants stated to him, or from his conduct or other circumstances of the case, all of which are resorted to in order to ascertain the state of the declarant's mind at the time of making the declaration[].

Id. at 499-500.

2. In *People v. Little*, 371 *N.Y.S.*2d 726 (Yates Co. Ct. 1975), the declarant, a New York State police officer, was brought to the emergency room of Soldiers and Sailors Memorial Hospital at approximately 7:00 p.m. on Sunday, June 30, 1974, in a state police car. He had been wounded at a cottage owned by the defendant near Dresden, New York. He had been wounded by a shotgun. "His upper right chest had been laid open and some internal organs were exposed." *Id.* at 730. At a pretrial hearing, a village police officer testified that he spoke with the declarant, who was, at the time, lying in the back seat of the police car outside the hospital. Declarant identified himself to the village officer, stated that he had been wounded by a shotgun and identified defendant as his assailant. The declarant told the officer that he thought he had shot defendant; that he had tried to knock defendant's gun aside, but missed it and at that point defendant shot him. When the declarant told the village officer that he hurt in his chest and arm, the officer assured him that help was on the way and went with him when he was taken by stretcher into the emergency room. The village officer further testified that declarant "was shakey and his body shuddering, but his voice was strong and he was moaning and crying out in pain asking for medication." *Id.* When declarant asked how badly he had been hit, the officer assured him he would be o.k., and that a doctor was coming.

Finding none of the declarant's statements to the village officer admissible as a dying declaration, the court observed:

> The rationale or justification for the admissibility of a dying declaration as an exception to the hearsay rule lies in the high degree of probability of trustworthiness that is assured when one speaks at a time when he believes that his death is certain and impending. * * * The declarant must have made his declaration

under a sense of impending death and without any hope of recovery which are here not shown.

Id. at 730-31.

Declarant's surgery lasted from 7:40 p.m. on Sunday, June 30, to approximately 3:00 a.m. on Monday, July 1. Later that Monday, Investigator Hammond of the New York State Police visited the declarant. He testified to the following conversation:

> [A]t approximately 1:15 when I went into the room to check on his condition and see how he was doing, he appeared to have failed quite a bit from the previous time I had seen him * * *. I asked him how he was feeling and he said, "Not very good." I said, "What do you mean ?" He said, "I don't think I am going to make it." I said, "What do you mean ?" He said, "I can't live. I am shot too bad." I said, "Ray, are you sure you are not going to live ?" He said, "Yes, I can't make it. I am shot too bad." I said, "Ray, as a police officer, you know what a dying declaration is ?" He said, "Yes." I said, "If you are absolutely convinced you are not going to live, I think I should take a dying declaration from you." I said, "I have the questions made out to make up the start of the dying declaration." I said, "I would like to ask them, will you answer them ?" He said, "Yes." At that point I had the notebook in my pocket. I took the notebook out and began reading off the questions. They were previously written. I just wrote in his answers in long-hand underneath the questions.

Id. at 732-33.

"The questions had been prepared at 7:30 that morning and were standard questions used in state police procedure for taking dying declarations." *Id.* at 733. The 1:20 p.m. declaration read as follows:

Q. What is your name ?

A. Ray Dodge.

Q. Where do you live ?

A. R.D. #1, Almond.

Q. Do you believe that you are about to die ?

A. Yes, I'm shot bad.

Q. Have you any hope of recovery from the effects of the injury you have received ?

A. No, I can't live, I'm shot too bad.

Q. Are you willing to make a true statement of the manner by which you received the injuries from which you are now suffering ?

A. Yes.

129

Q. What happened ?

A. I went to Little's cottage, knocked on the door and called out, "Mr. Little." He said, "Who's there ?" I said, "Trooper Dodge." He said, "Come on in." I opened the screen door, the other door was open and I went in. He was laying for me. He meant to kill me. The lights were out. He stuck his gun through the door and shoved it open with the barrel. He just jumped out at me. I tried to grab his gun, but he shot me in the gut. I was going to coldcock him, but when he shot me it slammed me up against the wall. He shot me twice. The second shot nicked my arm. I shot him. He meant to kill me. He knew who I was. I had talked to him earlier. He came from behind the partition.

Id. at 733-34.

Ruling that most of the statements made to Investigator Hammond were admissible in evidence as a dying declaration, the court reasoned:

The narrative of the declaration bears upon the facts and circumstances of declarant's death and declarant, if now living, would be competent as a witness. The evidence also shows that declarant was *in extremis* from his mortal wounds, particularly after the noticeable change in his physical condition * * *.

The grievous chest wound described was of such a nature that the wounded man must have realized his situation. The loss of feeling in his feet complained of after noon, together with his complaint of severe pain and his generally deteriorating physical condition evidence the apprehension of death without hope in declarant's mind that he expressed when he made the 1:20 p.m. declarations to the investigator beyond conjecture.

Proof of the actual danger of death and giving up hope of recovery by the declarant at the time of his declaration may be proved like any other fact and can be inferred from the existing and surrounding circumstances. * * *

[C]ross-examination brought out that every state police officer is instructed on the legal requirements of a dying declaration and that is, of course, expected to be the case. * * *

It is true that this encounter between two trained and disciplined officers may lack the spontaneity of a layman's declaration in the awesome knowledge of impending death.

But contemplating this serious business of dying, we are afforded and apply the same established rule of evidence. Did the declarant subjectively sense impending death without any hope of recovery ? This is the vibrant requisite which the law requires to waive the solemnity of an oath and to receive the decedent's testimony without cross-examination.

[T]he declaration made to Investigator [] Hammond at 1:20 p.m. * * * satisfies the standards of a dying declaration * * *.

Id. at 734-35.

The court qualified its ruling, however, by striking the following language from the dying declaration: "He was laying for me" and the two references, "He meant to kill me." According to the court, "these three statements in the declaration are conclusory and would not be proper testimony by the declarant, if living, for the reason that they invade the province of the jury to determine the facts of the case." *Id.* at 736.

3. In *Commonwealth v. Griffin*, 453 *Pa.Super.* 657, 684 *A.*2d 589 (1996), in the early morning hours, defendant, along with four associates, hired a van to facilitate a robbery. Defendant had a .45 caliber handgun with him, and one of his associates carried a 9mm Tec-9 semi-automatic handgun. The victim, Lavearn Miller, was hired by the group to drive them to the site of the robbery. Just before arriving at their destination, however, Miller said, "I don't want to do it now." Miller continued driving, now in the direction of the local police station. Defendant, thinking that Miller was going to turn them in to the police, reached over from the front passenger seat and shifted the van into park. Miller became frightened, quickly exited the vehicle and ran down the street. "A shot entered his left arm, which severed a major artery and ultimately caused his death." *Id.*, 684 *A.*2d at 591.

After being shot, Miller continued to run towards the police station. Just as he arrived at the station, Miller collapsed on the sidewalk. Several officers found him lying face down and bleeding profusely. One officer asked Miller who shot him, and Miller identified the defendant.

In this appeal, defendant argued that the trial court erred by admitting into evidence the statement of the dying victim identifying defendant as his assailant. The Superior Court found no error in its admission.

"A statement may be considered a dying declaration, and hence admissible notwithstanding its hearsay attributes, if the declarant identifies his attacker, the declarant believes he is going to die, []death is imminent, and the death actually results." *Id.* at 592.

The testimony regarding Miller's statement identifying defendant as his attacker came from three police officers who arrived at the scene shortly after the victim was shot. The first officer testified that when she approached the victim, he appeared to be scared and excited, "profusely bleeding," and going in and out of consciousness. The officer asked what had happened to him, and Miller said that he was shot. When she asked, "Who did it?", Miller answered, "Aaron."

Id. Miller was then heard to say, "Just let me die." A second officer at the scene indicated that he could not hear what Miller said to the first officer, but testified that Miller said to him, "Please get me to the hospital." The third officer testified that he heard Miller being asked who shot him, and heard Miller say, "Aaron Griffin." *Id.*

Ruling that the victim's statement qualified as a "dying declaration," the court explained:

> It is clear that the victim was aware of his impending death: he was bleeding profusely, lying in a large pool of his own blood, was lapsing in and out of consciousness, and said, "Just let me die." Our Supreme Court has held that the best evidence of the victim's state of mind regarding his impending death is a statement from the victim. * * * [S]*ee Commonwealth v. Stickle*, 484 *Pa.* 89, 398 *A.*2d 957 (1979) (statement by victim, "I'm going to die" showed requisite state of mind). [Indeed, the victim is not required] to be injured in the head or a vital organ in order for him to have a sense of impending death. * * *

> To be admissible, "a dying declaration must be based on observations of the declarant and may not merely be an expression of opinion based on reflection or reasoning." * * * However, "dying declarations which contain inferences and conclusions of the declarant from facts which he knows or observes but does not state may be admissible." * * * Contrary to [defendant's] suggestion, proof of the victim's actual observation of the facts declared is not required; instead, what needs to be shown is that the victim had the *opportunity* to observe the facts he declares. * * * This rule stems from the absence of proof inherent in a dying declaration: a victim who makes a statement that qualifies as a dying declaration is [] not available to describe in court what observations and inferences formed the basis of his statement. * * * It is only when it is clear that the victim had no opportunity to observe the facts that he declares that a dying declaration is inadmissible for want of personal knowledge. * * *

> Certainly, [in this case,] there was opportunity for the victim to turn around and observe who was shooting at him.

Id. at 592-93. [Citations omitted; court's emphasis.]

The *Federal Rules of Evidence* authorize the introduction of a dying declaration under certain circumstances.

Rule 804(b). Hearsay Exceptions; Declarant Unavailable. The following are not excluded by the hearsay rule if the declarant is unavailable as a witness:

* * * *

(2) Statement under belief of impending death. In a prosecution for homicide or in a civil action or proceeding, a statement made by a declarant while believing that the declarant's death was imminent, concerning the cause or circumstances of what the declarant believed to be impending death.

There are a number of preconditions which must be satisfied before a court will receive a dying declaration in evidence.

1. The case in which the dying declaration was made must be either a homicide prosecution or a civil action or proceeding;[60]

2. The declaration must relate to the cause or circumstances of the declarant's believed imminent death.

3. The declarant's statement must be made at a time when he or she believed that death was imminent, which may be established by:[61]

a. the nature and extent of the injury,

b. the condition of the declarant,

c. any statements or impressions by the declarant demonstrating his or her sense of impending death, or

d. any notice given to the declarant by others that death was imminent;

---

[60] The common law originally limited the rule to statements made by a homicide victim. The federal rule expands the use of the dying declaration to civil actions and proceedings "where the stakes do not involve possible imprisonment[.]" *Report of House Committee on the Judiciary*, 1974 *U.S.Code Cong. & Ad.News* 7075, 7089. Some states prohibit use of the rule in civil proceedings but extend the rule to cover all criminal proceedings. *See e.g., N.J.Evid.R.* 804(b)(2).

[61] The common law had required both that the declarant's statement be made while he or she was aware that death was near and certain, and that there was no hope of recovery. *See e.g., Shepard v. United States*, 290 *U.S.* 96, 54 *S.Ct.* 22 (1933). *See also Bratton v. Bond*, 408 *N.W.*2d 39 (Iowa 1987) (decedent had hope of recovery when he told the defendant (his wife) who shot him that he was going to divorce her). The federal rules and a number of states have loosened the "no hope of recovery" standard. *See* 2 McCormick, *Evidence* §310 (4th ed. 1992), at 326. *See also Johnson v. State*, 579 *P.*2d 20 (Alaska 1978) ("all hope of recovery" standard found too demanding; "awareness of the probability of impending death" standard held sufficient to create solemnity and to remove motives for fabrication).

4. The declarant must have had first-hand, personal knowledge of the cause or circumstances of his or her believed imminent death;[62] and

5. The declarant must die or otherwise be unavailable as a witness.[63]

---

§4.3(f). Statements Against Interest

A statement or declaration against one's pecuniary, proprietary or penal interest is a recognized exception to the rule against hearsay. Such statements are admissible because the assertion of a fact which is "distinctly against one's interest is unlikely to be deliberately false or heedlessly incorrect."[64] The exception recognizes "the commonsense notion that reasonable people, even reasonable people who are not especially honest, tend not to make self-inculpatory statements unless they believe them to be true."[65] Thus, such statements against interest are deemed inherently trustworthy and reliable. *Fed.R.Evid.* 804(b)(3) defines a "statement against interest" as:

> A statement which was at the time of its making so far contrary to the declarant's pecuniary or proprietary interest, or so far tended to subject the declarant to civil or criminal liability, or to render invalid a claim by the declarant against another, that a reasonable person in the declarant's position would not have made the statement unless believing it to be true. A statement tending to expose the declarant to criminal liability and offered to exculpate the accused is not admissible unless corroborating circumstances clearly indicate the trustworthiness of the statement.

---

[62] The requirement of first-hand or personal knowledge is found in *Fed.R.Evid.* 602. *See also Jones v. State,* 52 *Ark.* 345, 12 *S.W.* 704 (1889) (because the declarant could not see who shot him, his statement identifying the shooter could not have been based on personal knowledge, and was therefore properly excluded).

[63] Under the federal rules, "unavailability" is not limited to death. *See Fed.R.Evid.* 804(a). Therefore, the amount of time which passes between the dying declaration and death, should it occur, is not dispositive of the declaration's admissibility. Some states, however, still require that the declarant be unavailable *because of his or her death. See e.g., N.J.Evid.R.* 804(b)(2). *See also People v. Parney,* 98 *Mich.App.* 571, 296 *N.W.*2d 568 (1979) (victim's actual death required). Even those states that have historically held to this requirement have not required death to follow on the heels of the declaration. *See e.g., Emmett v. State,* 195 *Ga.* 517, 25 *S.E.*2d 9 (1943) (decedent's survival of over three months not fatal to declaration's admissibility).

[64] *Rudisill v. Cordes,* 333 *Pa.* 544, 549, 5 *A.*2d 217, 219 (1939).

[65] *Williamson v. United States,* 512 *U.S.* 594, 598-99, 114 *S.Ct.* 2431, 2435 (1994). *See also id.* at 2437 ("[T]he very fact that a statement is genuinely self-inculpatory * * * is itself one of the 'particularized guarantees of trustworthiness' that makes a statement admissible under the Confrontation Clause.") (citation omitted). *See also State v. White,* 158 *N.J.* 230, 238, 729 *A.*2d 31 (1999) ("The statement against interest exception is based on the theory that, by human nature, individuals will neither assert, concede, nor admit to facts that would affect them unfavorably.").

In order to qualify as a declaration against interest, it must first be shown that the person who made the statement, the declarant, is unavailable at the time of trial. A witness will be deemed "unavailable" when (1) the witness is dead or unable to testify because of physical or mental illness or infirmity, or memory loss; (2) the witness has invoked the privilege against self-incrimination or another recognized privilege; (3) the witness refuses to testify; or (4) the party seeking to introduce the witness' statement has made a good-faith effort to locate and obtain the witness' presence at trial, but was unsuccessful at doing so.[66]

The "unavailability" requirement was highlighted in *Commonwealth v. Goldman,*[67] a case in which the defendant was prosecuted for receiving stolen property. At trial, the prosecution introduced a statement made by defendant's wife to the police that, "I know we shouldn't have bought the computer because it was probably stolen." According to the prosecution, this statement qualified as an exception to the rule against hearsay, for it was an admission against penal interest. Rejecting that view, the court ruled that the statement was inadmissible hearsay because the defendant's wife was not "unavailable" at the time of trial. In fact, his wife was sitting in the courtroom at the time the statement was sought to be introduced, and, contrary to the prosecution's theory, there was no reason to believe defendant's wife would invoke the marital privilege.

Next, it must be shown that the statement was against the declarant's penal, pecuniary or proprietary interests at the time it was made. "Statement," in this regard, is construed narrowly to encompass only self inculpatory statements. Rule 804(b)(3) "does not allow admission of non-self-inculpatory statements, even if they are made within a broader narrative that is generally self-inculpatory," and "this is especially true when the statement implicates someone else."[68]

---

[66] *See Fed.R.Evid.* 804(a). Under the Sixth Amendment, the test for unavailability is broad: a witness is unavailable if the prosecution has made a good-faith effort to introduce its evidence through the live testimony of the witness, and through no fault of its own, is prevented from doing so. *See Ohio v. Roberts,* 448 *U.S.* 56, 74, 100 *S.Ct.* 2531, 2543 (1980) (the "ultimate question is whether the witness is unavailable despite good-faith efforts undertaken prior to trial to locate and present that witness"); *California v. Green,* 399 *U.S.* 149, 90 *S.Ct.* 1930 (1970) (although physically present in the courtroom, witness was unavailable for Sixth Amendment purposes when the state made every effort to introduce its live testimony through its witness but witness claimed lack of memory).

[67] 422 *Pa.Super.* 86, 618 *A.*2d 1029 (1993).

[68] *Williamson v. United States, supra,* 114 *S.Ct.* at 2435. In this respect, Justice O'Connor observed: "The fact that a person is making a broadly self-inculpatory confession does not make more credible the confession's non-self-inculpatory parts. One of the most effective ways to lie is to mix falsehood with truth, especially truth that seems particularly persuasive because of its self-inculpatory nature." *Id.*

§4.3(g). Prior Identifications

When a law enforcement officer testifies that on a prior occasion the victim pointed to the accused and said, "That's the person that robbed me at gunpoint," the officer's testimony is hearsay. Yet, if the victim is present in the courtroom, testifies as to the prior identification and is available for cross-examination, the rules of evidence permit the admission of the officer's testimony. In this respect, *Fed.R.Evid.* 801(d)(1) exempts from the rule against hearsay certain prior identifications made by a witness. In pertinent part, the rule provides that a statement is "not hearsay" if "[t]he declarant testifies at the trial or hearing and is subject to cross-examination concerning the statement, and the statement is * * * one of identification of a person made after perceiving the person[.]"[69]

PEOPLE v. GOULD
Supreme Court of California
354 *P.*2d 865 (1960)

The opinion of the Court was delivered by

TRAYNOR, Justice.

[Defendant Jewell Gould appeals his conviction of burglary in the second degree. The evidence revealed that the victim, Mrs. Fenwick, interrupted a burglary taking place at her apartment. As she approached her apartment, she saw a man standing on her steps outside her door and found the door slightly ajar. Inside her apartment she noticed a second man who shouted, "Go into the bedroom and stay there." As soon as she entered her bedroom, the burglars stole about $15 from her purse and fled.

About an hour later, Officer Brewer arrived and showed Mrs. Fenwick an array of seven to ten photographs. She selected Gould's photograph as the man inside her apartment. When asked to identify him at trial, however, Mrs. Fenwick had some difficulty.]

"Mrs. Fenwick pointed out Gould as having 'some features but not all of the features' of the man she saw inside her apartment, and added that he seemed thinner than the burglar. She stated that she was unable to point out anyone in the courtroom as the man she saw on the steps. * * * Officer Brewer testified on cross-examination, however, that Mrs. Fenwick was sure of her identification[] of the photograph[on the day of the crime]." *Id.* at 866.

"Gould contends that the trial court erred in admitting evidence that Mrs. Fenwick identified his photograph shortly after the crime. He asserts that Mrs. Fenwick did not identify him at the trial and that evidence of an extra-judicial[, *i.e.*, a prior, out-of-court,] identification is

---

[69] *Fed.R.Evid.* 801(d)(1)(C).

admissible only to corroborate an identification made at the trial by the same witness." *Id.* at 867.

"Mrs. Fenwick testified that Gould had 'some features but not all of the features' of the burglar. She stated that 'the man who was in my apartment seemed to have—he was a heavy man; he had rather fat cheeks and this man is very thin.' Gould testified that after his arrest he became 'very ill' and that he had 'hernia trouble,' but he denied that he had lost weight. Mrs. Fenwick also testified that 'it is awfully hard for me to point to someone after all of this time, saying that that is the person who looks like that person, because my memory is rather vague about it now.' Although her testimony did not amount to an identification, the evidence of her extra-judicial identification was nevertheless admissible." *Id.*

"Evidence of an extra-judicial identification is admissible, not only to corroborate an identification made at the trial, * * * but as independent evidence of identity. Unlike other testimony that cannot be corroborated by proof of prior consistent statements unless it is first impeached, * * * evidence of an extra-judicial identification is admitted regardless of whether the testimonial identification is impeached, because the earlier identification has greater probative value than an identification made in the courtroom after the suggestions of others and the circumstances of the trial may have intervened to create a fancied recognition in the witness' mind. * * * The failure of the witness to repeat the extra-judicial identification in court does not destroy its probative value, for such failure may be explained by loss of memory or other circumstances. The extra-judicial identification tends to connect the defendant with the crime, and the principal danger of admitting hearsay evidence is not present since the witness is available at the trial for cross-examination." *Id.*

Accordingly, "Gould's contentions are without merit and his conviction must be affirmed." *Id.* at 870.

NOTE

1. In *United States v. Owens,* 484 *U.S.* 554, 108 *S.Ct.* 838 (1988), the defendant argued that "Rule 802 of the Federal Rules of Evidence bars testimony concerning a prior, out-of-court identification when the identifying witness is unable, because of memory loss, to explain the basis for the identification." *Owens* at 840. While Rule 802 would, in fact, render an out-of-court statement inadmissible as hearsay, "it is ultimately Rule 801(d)(1)(C) that determines whether Rule 802 is applicable." *Owens* at 841 n. 1. In this respect, Rule 802 sets forth the general statement that: "Hearsay is not admissible except as [otherwise] provided by these rules[.]" Rule 801(d) delineates certain exemptions from the general hearsay prohibition, defining those statements which are "not hearsay." Specifically, Rule 801(d)(1)(C) provides: "A statement is not hearsay if [t]he declarant testifies at the trial or hearing and is subject to cross-examination concerning the statement,

and the statement is * * * one of identification of a person made after perceiving the person[.]"

According to the Court, the phrase "subject to cross-examination concerning the statement" encompasses the *Owens* set of circumstances. "Ordinarily, a witness is regarded as 'subject to cross-examination' when he is placed on the stand, under oath, and responds willingly to questions." *Id.* at 844. Naturally, trial-court limitations on the scope of cross-examination "or assertions of privilege by the witness may undermine the process to such a degree that meaningful cross-examination within the intent of the rule no longer exists. But that effect is not produced by the witness' [] assertion of memory loss—which * * * is often the very result sought to be produced by cross-examination, and can be effective in destroying the force of the prior statement. Rule 801(d)(1)(C), which specifies that the cross-examination need only 'concer(n) the statement,' does not on its face require more." *Owens* at 844.

Significantly, "the House Report on the Rule noted that since, '(a)s time goes by, a witness' memory will fade and his identification will become less reliable,' minimizing the barriers to admission of more contemporaneous identification is fairer to defendants and prevents 'cases falling through because the witness can no longer recall the identity of the person he saw commit the crime.' " *Owens* at 844 (quoting H.R.Rep. No. 94-355, p. 3 (1975)). Thus, it seems that Rule 801(d)(1)(C) "was in part directed to the very problem here at issue: a memory loss that makes it impossible for the witness to provide an in-court identification or testify about details of the events underlying an earlier identification." *Owens* at 844.

Accordingly, the Court held that Rule 802 of the Federal Rules of Evidence is not "violated by admission of an identification statement of a witness who is unable, because of memory loss, to testify concerning the basis for the identification." *Id.* at 845.

2. For a more extensive discussion of eyewitness identification evidence, *see generally* Chapter 5.

---

§4.3(h). Excited Utterance

"A statement relating a startling event or condition made while the declarant was under the stress of excitement caused by the event or condition[]" is admissible as an exception to the rule against hearsay, notwithstanding the fact that the declarant may be available as a witness.[70] Known historically as the "*res gestae*," the excited

---

[70] *Fed.R.Evid.* 803(2). The theory of this exception "is simply that circumstances may produce a condition of excitement which temporarily stills the capacity of reflection and produces utterances free of conscious fabrication." *Advisory Committee's Note*, 56 *F.R.D.* 183, 303.

utterance will be admissible when, as a spontaneous response to a startling event or occurrence, the declarant makes a statement describing or explaining it. The statement should be made while the declarant is still under the stress of a nervous excitement caused by the event or occurrence at issue, in reasonable proximity to the event and without opportunity to deliberate or fabricate. The excited utterance does not, however, need to be perfectly contemporaneous with the startling event. The critical inquiry is whether the utterance was made during the course of "a continuing state of excitement that contraindicates fabrication and provides trustworthiness."[71] "An automobile accident, pain or an injury, an attack by a dog, a fight, or even seeing a photograph in a newspaper all may qualify."[72]

UNITED STATES v. GOLDEN
United States Court of Appeals
671 *F*.2d 369 (10th Cir. 1982)

The opinion of the Court was delivered by

McKAY, Circuit Judge.

"Bobby Ray Golden, a police officer in Nowata, Oklahoma, was convicted by a jury of violating 18 *U.S.C.* §242, which makes criminal the willful deprivation of constitutional rights by any person acting under color of law." *Id.* at 370.

"[T]he victim was stopped by Officer Golden for allegedly running a red light at 2:00 a.m. In the ensuing discussion, Officer Golden hit the victim with his flashlight, causing severe injuries that required eight stitches." *Id.* at 371.

"Mr. Golden alleges that the trial court erroneously admitted into evidence testimony concerning the victim's statements to his grandmother pursuant to the excited utterance exception to the hearsay rule. *Fed.R.Evid.* 803(2)." *Id.*

"An excited utterance is an exception to the general rule that hearsay testimony is not admissible into evidence. It is defined as '[a] statement relating a startling event or condition made while the declarant was under the stress of the excitement caused by the event or condition.' * * * The evidence shows that after the altercation, the victim drove twelve miles to his grandmother's house at speeds of approximately 120 miles per hour. Upon his arrival, he related what had happened to him and said he feared for his life. [Golden] argues

---

[71] *State v. Lyle*, 73 *N.J.* 403, 413 (1977). *See also Gross v. Greer*, 773 *F*.2d 116 (7th Cir. 1985) (frightened 14-year-old's statement made almost fifteen hours after murder held admissible as an excited utterance, given the fact that the child was found under bed clothes in an apartment with the victim's body).

[72] 2 McCormick, *Evidence* §272 (4th ed. 1992), at 217. [Citations omitted.]

that the trial court erred in admitting this testimony because the conversation was hearsay and occurred too remote in time from the assault to fall within the excited utterance exception. However, the victim's statement to his grandmother occurred within fifteen minutes of the startling event, immediately after a high-speed flight from the scene of the assault. The facts presented indicate that there was no reason to suspect that the victim was no longer 'under the stress of excitement caused by the event' when he spoke with his grandmother. Therefore, the court did not err in admitting testimony concerning this conversation under the excited utterance exception to the hearsay rule." *Id.*

NOTE

1. In his classic statement of the theory which underlies the admissibility of spontaneous statements, Wigmore has written:

> This general principle is based on the experience that, under certain external circumstances of physical shock, a stress of nervous excitement may be produced which stills the reflective faculties and removes their control, so that the utterance which then occurs is a spontaneous and sincere response to the actual sensations and perceptions already produced by the external shock. Since this utterance is made under the immediate and uncontrolled domination of the senses, and during the brief period when considerations of self-interest could not have been brought fully to bear by reasoned reflection, the utterance may be taken as particularly trustworthy (or, at least, as lacking the usual grounds of untrustworthiness), and thus as expressing the real tenor of the speaker's belief as to the facts just observed by him; and may therefore be received as testimony to those facts.

6 Wigmore, *Evidence* §1747 (3d ed. 1940), at 135. [Footnote omitted.]

2. In *State v. Williams*, 214 *N.J.Super.* 12, 518 A.2d 234 (App.Div. 1986), the victim, Carol Brown, was walking to her home in Camden at approximately 3:00 a.m., after an evening out. As she walked past an alley, a man jumped out at her, grabbed her around the neck, and told her "not to holler." A struggle began and the assailant stabbed her at least nine times. Brown was ultimately able to break free and run for help to a nearby house, where she collapsed. The assailant fled.

Camden Police Officer Sunkett, at the time of dispatch, was only a block from the scene. He was the first to arrive after the incident, and, upon arrival, noting that Brown was bleeding, asked her what had happened. Brown stated, "(s)omebody cut me." She then "told Sunkett that she did not know who her attacker was. Sunkett then called for an ambulance. In his police report Sunkett stated that

Brown said the attacker was 'pulling on her clothes'; he noted the attack as a possible rape attempt." *Id.*, 214 *N.J.Super.* at 16.

At trial, the judge would not permit Officer Sunkett to testify as to the contents of his report. On appeal, the court held this to be in error.

"While the exact amount of time which elapsed between the attack and Sunkett's arrival is unclear, Sunkett was only a block away from the scene when he received the call to which he immediately responded. He was the first person to arrive and speak to Brown who * * * was in a 'daze of shock.' " *Id.* As a result, the court viewed "Brown's statement to Sunkett [as one] made under circumstances indicating the presence of a continuing state of excitement that contraindicates fabrication, provides trustworthiness and justifies admission under the rule." *Id.* at 19-20.

Accordingly, Officer Sunkett's testimony repeating Brown's statement as to the attacker "pulling on her clothes" was admissible as an excited utterance. *Id.* at 19.

---

§4.3(i). Present Sense Impression

"A statement describing or explaining an event or condition made while the declarant was perceiving the event or condition, or immediately thereafter[,]" is admissible as an exception to the rule against hearsay, notwithstanding the fact that the declarant may be available as a witness.[73] This exception covers statements relating "nonexciting" events that the declarant was perceiving while making the statement.

BOOTH v. STATE
Court of Appeals of Maryland
306 *Md.* 313, 508 *A.2d* 976 (1986)

The opinion of the Court was delivered by

McAULIFFE, Judge.

"John E. Booth was convicted in the Circuit Court for Baltimore City of the premeditated murder and armed robbery of James Edward ("Pie") Ross[.] * * * [W]e granted certiorari to consider the question of the admissibility of evidence under the present sense impression exception to the hearsay rule." *Id.* at 977.

"At trial, the State proffered evidence that Regina Harrison telephoned Ross between 5:30 and 6:00 p.m. on the day of his murder. Harrison testified that Ross said he was getting ready to prepare

---

[73] Fed.R.Evid. 803(1).

dinner and was going to ask his company, a girl named Brenda, to leave. Harrison said she then heard the door at Ross' home open and questioned Ross as to who was there. Ross told Harrison that Brenda was talking to 'some guy' behind the door. According to Harrison, the general tone of the conversation was normal and Ross did not sound nervous or anxious." *Id.*

"Booth objected to the testimony of Harrison on the ground that it was impermissible hearsay. The trial judge admitted the testimony, concluding that it fell within the present sense impression exception to the hearsay rule." *Id.*

"The present sense impression exception has its origins in what was known as the 'res gestae' exception to the hearsay rule. The term 'res gestae'[, literally meaning, "things done,"] came into usage in discussion of admissibility of declarations in the early 1800s. * * * As Professor McCormick points out, the term is more generic than particular and includes within its definition four distinct exceptions: declarations of present bodily condition; declarations of present mental states and emotions; excited utterances; and declarations of present sense impressions. * * * Although the term res gestae is now condemned in academic circles, the exceptions included within its definition are recognized by most scholars." *Id.* at 977-78 & n.2. [Citations omitted.]

Regarding the present sense impression, one commentator has explained:

> A statement by a person as to external events then and there being perceived by his senses is worthy of credence for two reasons. First, it is in essence a declaration of a presently existing state of mind, for it is nothing more than an assertion of his presently existing sense impressions. As such it has the quality of spontaneity. . . . Second, since the statement is contemporaneous with the event, it is made at the place of the event. Consequently, the event is open to perception by the senses of the person to whom the declaration is made and by whom it is usually reported on the witness stand. The witness is subject to cross-examination concerning the event as well as the fact and content of the utterance, so that the extra-judicial statement does not depend solely upon the credit of the declarant.

Id. at 979. [Citation omitted.]

"The underlying theory of this exception is that 'substantial contemporaneity of event and statement negative the likelihood of deliberate or conscious misrepresentation.' *Advisory Committee Note, Fed.R.Evid.* 803(1). The Note further states that 'in many, if not most, instances precise contemporaneity is not possible, and hence a slight lapse is allowable.' Although the Note does not state that the witness must be the declarant, it indicates that 'if the witness is not the declarant, he may be examined as to the circumstances as an aid in evaluating the statement.' Finally, the Note limits the permissible subject matter under the exception to a 'description or explanation of the event or condition, the assumption being that spontaneity, in the absence of a startling event, may extend no farther.' " *Id.* at 979.

"The content of the statement with which we are concerned in this case, at least when coupled with the evidence of what Harrison heard in the background, offered sufficient evidence that Ross was describing events he was personally witnessing, and that his description of those events was being given contemporaneously with their occurrence. There were no extrinsic circumstances indicating to the contrary. [Consequently,] the trial judge properly admitted the * * * statement pursuant to the present sense impression exception to the hearsay rule." *Id.* at 985.

NOTE

"[S]tatements of perception substantially contemporaneous with an event are highly trustworthy because: (1) the statement being simultaneous with the event, there is no memory problem; (2) there is little or no time for calculated misstatement; and (3) the statement is usually made to one who has equal opportunity to observe and check misstatements." J. Weinstein & M. Berger, *Weinstein's Evidence*, §803(1)[01] (1985). [Footnote omitted.] The present sense impression "has been viewed with favor by those who fear that excitement—such as that required by the excited utterance exception—operates to impair the accuracy of perception. The exception is useful in admitting statements uttered minutes before the event in question and before the declarant was aware that something startling was about to happen." *Id.*

Binder has further explained that the declarant of a present sense impression

> need not be excited or otherwise emotionally affected by the event or condition. The trustworthiness of the assertion arises from its timing. The requirement of contemporaneousness, or near contemporaneousness, reduces the chance of premeditation [fabrication] or loss of memory.
>
> If you turn on your radio during a baseball game, you will be inundated by present sense impressions. The utterances of the sportscaster describing and explaining what he observes on the playing field as it is taking place are [clearly] present sense impressions. But the sportscaster's between-innings or postgame analysis would not qualify for this hearsay exception, for lack of contemporaneity.

D.Binder, *Hearsay Handbook* 89 (2d ed. supp. 1985).

§4.3(j). Statements of Mental, Emotional, or Physical Condition

"A statement of the declarant's then existing state of mind, emotion, sensation, or physical condition (such as intent, plan, motive, design, mental feeling, pain, and bodily health), but not including a statement of memory or belief to prove the fact remembered or believed * * *," is admissible as an exception to the rule against hearsay, notwithstanding the fact that the declarant may be available as a witness.[74]

§4.3(k). Statements for Purposes of Medical Diagnosis or Treatment.

"Statements made for purposes of medical diagnosis or treatment and describing medical history, or past or present symptoms, pain, or sensations, or the inception or general character of the cause or external source thereof as reasonably pertinent to diagnosis or treatment" are admissible as exceptions to the rule against hearsay, notwithstanding the fact that the declarant may be available as a witness.[75]

§4.3(*l*). The Fresh Complaint Rule

Typically applied in sexual abuse cases, the "fresh complaint" rule permits proof that the violated victim complained within a reasonable time to someone to whom he or she "would ordinarily turn for sympathy, protection and advice."[76] Historically, there have been three principles under which proof of a "fresh complaint" may be offered. First, "as an explanation of a 'self contradiction' which would result from the absence of a complaint."[77] In this respect, if no testimony were offered with regard to the complaint, the jury might naturally assume that none was made; it is therefore only fair that the prosecution be permitted to counteract this natural assumption by showing that the victim did in fact make a complaint. Under this principle, the complaint, but not its details, is admissible, and impeachment of the witness is not a prerequisite.[78] Second, the fresh complaint may be offered to rehabilitate a witness after he or she has been impeached, by demonstrating that, consistent with his or her testimony, the witness made the

---

[74] Fed.R.Evid. 803(3).

[75] Fed.R.Evid. 803(4).

[76] *State v. Balles*, 47 *N.J.* 331, 338, 221 A.2d 1 (1966).

[77] *Id.* at 338.

[78] *See* 4 Wigmore, *Evidence* § 1136 (Chadbourn rev. 1972).

complaint shortly after the incident. Under this principle, the details of the complaint are admissible.[79] Third, the fresh complaint will be admitted as a *res gestae* statement so long as the requirement of spontaneity is met; "here the details are admissible and impeachment is not material."[80]

In *Commonwealth v. Freeman*,[81] the theory underlying the admissibility of the fresh complaint was explained as follows:

> Evidence of the alleged victim's "hue and cry" following rape has long been admissible at common law. Hue and cry is thought to follow rape like smoke follows fire. Proof of the former is circumstantial evidence of the latter. Conversely, [the] unexplained lack of evidence of hue and cry that one might expect to ensue from rape casts doubt on the existence of the rape itself. * * *
>
> Fresh complaints of rape, undetailed, are a particular form of hue and cry that provides significant circumstantial support for the alleged victim's subsequent testimony that she was raped. Such fresh complaints are classified evidentially as prior consistent statements. * * *
>
> The general rule is that a prior consistent statement of a witness is admissible only after the witness' testimony has been attacked, expressly or impliedly, as a recent fabrication. * * * However, in the special circumstances of a rape case, the testimony of a woman that she was raped is automatically vulnerable to attack by the defendant as recent fabrication in the absence of evidence of hue and cry on her part. This justifies a special evidential rule permitting introduction of her fresh complaints in the prosecution's case in chief.[82]

The fresh complaint rule has several limitations. First, when offered for the purpose of meeting in advance a self-contradiction in the victim's conduct, the details of the victim's out-of-court statements used to prove the fresh complaint are limited to the fact that the complaint was made and only such additional facts as are necessary to identify the occurrence complained of with the crime charged.[83] In addition, the victim's statement must be "self-motivated" and not extracted by coercive interrogation.

---

[79] *State v. Balles*, supra, 47 N.J. at 338.

[80] *Id.* at 347-48.

[81] 295 *Pa.Super.* 467, 441 *A.*2d 1327 (1982).

[82] *Commonwealth v. Freeman, supra*, 441 *A.*2d at 1332.

[83] *Commonwealth v. Pettiford*, 265 *Pa.Super.* 466, 468, 402 *A.*2d 532, 533 (1979). *See also Commonwealth v. Green*, 487 *Pa.* 322, 328, 409 *A.*2d 371, 374 (1979) (all-encompassing statement by the investigating officer held inadmissible since it went beyond identifying the fact that the complaint was made and its nature).

STATE v. J.S.
Superior Court of New Jersey, Appellate Division
222 N.J.Super. 247, 536 A.2d 769 (1988)

QUESTION: In the below set of circumstances, was the testimony of either Mrs. S. or Mrs. M. properly received in evidence as a "fresh complaint" ?

CIRCUMSTANCES: During an overnight visit with her father (defendant), 11-year-old C. was sexually assaulted by him. One or two days later, C. related the incident to her close friend, 10-year-old S., who then repeated it to her mother. Mrs. S. informed C.'s mother, Mrs. M., of the incident.

At trial, Mrs. S. was permitted to testify that after conversing briefly with S., she questioned C., "who told her that defendant had 'inserted his fingers inside of her.'" *Id.*, 222 *N.J.Super.* at 251. Mrs. S. obtained this information by first asking C. what had happened. C. did not volunteer the information. Mrs. M. was permitted to testify that through extensive questioning, she learned that during C.'s visit with defendant, "defendant came in and out of the bedroom 'feeling her body, putting his fingers in her vagina.'" *Id.* at 251. It was also brought out that "C.'s disclosure to her mother, Mrs. M., 12 days after the alleged assault," was the "total product of Mrs. M.'s questioning." *Id.* at 253. Mrs. M. testified that C. "'wouldn't talk. She cried * * * and wouldn't say hardly anything at all. I had to ask her, you know, about the events, and she would just say yes or no.'" *Id.*

ANSWER: NO. "[T]o qualify as a [fresh] complaint the victim's statement must at least be self-motivated and not extracted by interrogation." *Id.* at 253.

RATIONALE: The fresh complaint rule permits "the State to show in a sexual assault prosecution that the victim complained of the act within a reasonable time to one to whom she would ordinarily turn for sympathy, protection or advice." *Id.* at 251. This rule is also applicable in child abuse cases.

In this case, C.'s statement was not "part of the *res gestae*," nor was the State attempting to "rehabilitate" an impeached witness. Rather, "[t]he fresh complaint theory with which we are here concerned is that which authorizes such testimony to 'repel any inference that because the victim did not complain no outrage had in fact transpired.' * * * On this basis, only those details of the complaint which are necessary to show the nature of the complaint may be admitted." *Id.* at 252. [Citation omitted.]

Although the methods employed here were "certainly understandable," the court's concern focused on "whether the child's out-of-court responses satisfy the exacting standards for admissibility under a rule of evidence which permits such testimony only to demonstrate that the victim made a 'complaint[,' that is,] an 'expression of grief, pain or resentment . . . something that is the cause or subject of protest or outcry. . . .'" *Id.* at 253. [Citation omitted.] Therefore, according to this court, "to qualify as a complaint the victim's statement must at least be self-motivated and not extracted by interrogation." *Id.*

"In permitting the adult witnesses to testify to the child's statement that defendant had felt her breasts and had penetrated her vagina, the court's ruling exceeded the necessities of the case to the prejudice of defendant. All that was needed was enough to show that the child did not suffer the outrage in silence. Professor Wigmore states it thus:

> (1) *Only the fact of the complaint, not the details.* The purpose is to negative the supposed inconsistency of silence by showing that there was not silence. Thus the gist of the evidential circumstances is merely non-silence, *i.e.,* the *fact* of a complaint, but the fact only. That she complained of a rape, or an attempt at rape, is all that principle permits; the further terms of her utterance (except so far as to identify the time and place with that of the one charged) are not only immaterial for the purpose, but practically turn the statement into a hearsay assertion, and as such it is inadmissible (except on the third theory). [4 Wigmore, *Evidence,* (Chadbourn rev. 1972), §1136 at 307.]

J.S. at 254. [Emphasis added.]

As can therefore be seen, the "purpose" of the fresh complaint "rule is to allow the State to meet in advance the negative inference which would be drawn from the absence of evidence that the victim reported the incident to one to whom she would naturally turn for comfort and advice." *Id.* at 256. The complaint is not "admitted to 'bolster' the victim's credibility," nor should it be considered " 'as corroboration of the victim's assertion that she was assaulted.' " *Id.* at 256-257. [Citation omitted.]

Accordingly, the court set forth the following principles to govern the "receipt of fresh complaint testimony where it is offered, not to rehabilitate the credibility of an impeached victim or as proof of an excited utterance, but to rebut in advance the assumption that the victim failed to report the fact that she had been defiled.

> *First,* details of the offense should be confined to those minimally necessary to identify the subject matter of the victim's complaint.

> *Second,* the court should specify for the jury in its instructions the particular testimony to which the fresh complaint rule applies.

Third, the jury should be informed that the testimony was allowed only to show that within a reasonable time the victim reported the criminal event to one in whom she would naturally confide under the circumstances, not for the truth of the victim's complaint.

Fourth, the purpose of the rule should be explained as one which enables the State to meet in advance the internal contradiction which might appear from an apparent failure of the victim to make such a complaint; the explanation should be given in language which does not fail to inform the jurors that its use is confined to neutralizing the inference that might otherwise be drawn that her behavior was inconsistent with a claim of sexual abuse. Reference to the complaint as "supporting" or "bolstering" her credibility should not be made.

J.S. at 257. [Emphasis added.]

On the basis of the evidence presented in this case, the court concluded that "the substance of what was related by C. to the adult witnesses, C.'s mother and Mrs. S., did not constitute a 'complaint'. [Moreover,] the testimony given by these two witnesses was excessively detailed in relating what was said by C. [As a result,] the error in receiving the foregoing testimony was clearly capable of producing an unjust result and therefore mandates a reversal of the conviction." *Id.* at 252.

---

§4.3(m). Statements By a Child Relating a Sexual Assault. The "Tender Years" Exception

Recognizing that children may be too frightened and embarrassed to talk about sexual abuse, numerous state courts have adopted flexible approaches in applying the fresh complaint guidelines to complaints of children who allegedly have been sexually abused. In particular, courts have liberally interpreted the allowable period of time between the assault and the child's description of it,[84] the allowable amount of detail contained in the complaint, and have permitted the complaint to be extracted by questioning.[85] "In addition, a growing number of states have enacted specific hearsay exceptions to cover the situations where children are involved as witnesses or victims."[86]

---

[84] 2 McCormick, *Evidence* §272.1 (4th ed. 1992), at 224.

[85] *State v. Bethune*, 121 *N.J.* 137, 578 *A.2d* 364 (1990).

[86] 2 McCormick, *Evidence* §272.1 (4th ed. 1992), at 224. *See also State v. Myatt*, 237 *Kan.* 17, 21, 697 *P.2d* 836, 841 (1985).

Representative of this new exception, sometimes called the "na-ivete" or "tender years" exception to the hearsay rule,[87] is Pennsylvania's statute:

42 Pa.C.S. §5985.1. Statements by a child describing a sexual assault.

(a) General Rule.—An out-of-court statement made by a child victim or witness, who at the time the statement was made was 12 years of age or younger, describing indecent contact, sexual intercourse or deviate sexual intercourse performed with or on the child by another, not otherwise admissible by statute or rule of evidence, is admissible in evidence in any criminal proceeding if:

(1) The court finds, in an *in camera* hearing, that the evidence is relevant and that the time, content and circumstances of the statement provide sufficient indicia of reliability.

(2) The child either:
    i. testifies at the proceeding; or
    ii. is unavailable as a witness and there is corroborative evidence of the act.

(b) Notice required.—A statement otherwise admissible under subsection (a) shall not be received into evidence unless the proponent of the statement notifies the adverse party of the proponent's intention to offer the statement and the particulars of the statement sufficiently in advance of the proceeding at which the proponent intends to offer the statement into evidence to provide the adverse party with a fair opportunity to prepare to meet the statement.[88]

NOTE

1. *Delayed complaints and child victims.* In *Commonwealth v. Lane,* 521 *Pa.* 390, 555 *A.2d* 1246 (1989), the Court recognized that consideration should be given to factors inherent in prosecutions involving child victims which may explain the delay without drawing into question the credibility of the child.

The untimely complaint might be made in order to protect the truly guilty party, as in the case of a child blaming an innocent party for the wrongdoing of a parent. It might be the act of revenge against the accused prompted by dislike or by an unrelated dispute between either the minor complainant and the accused or, possibly, between the family of the minor complainant and the

---

[87] *See e.g., State v. D.R.,* 109 *N.J.* 348, 537 *A.2d* 667 (1988).

[88] In *Commonwealth v. Hanawalt,* 419 *Pa.Super.* 411, 615 *A.2d* 432, 435 (1992), the court held that the provisions of 42 *Pa.C.S.* §5985.1 do not violate the Confrontation Clause of either the Sixth Amendment to the United States Constitution or Article I, Section 9 of the Pennsylvania Constitution.

accused. *It is also possible that the immaturity of the victim would cause the child not to appreciate the offensiveness of the encounter and the need for its prompt disclosure.*

Id. at 398, 555 *A.*2d at 1250. [Emphasis added.]

In *Commonwealth v. Snoke*, 525 *Pa.* 295, 580 *A.*2d 295 (1990), a five-year-old child was the victim of a sexual assault by her father. Immediately after the assault, he told her that this would be "their little secret." The child revealed the incident five months later after viewing a film at her elementary school dealing with sexual assault. The film explained to the children the difference between a "good touch" and a "bad touch." According to the Court:

> Where no physical force is used to accomplish the reprehensible assault, a child victim would have no reason to promptly complain of the wrong-doing, particularly where the person involved is in a position of confidence. Where such an encounter is of a nature that a minor victim may not appreciate the offensive nature of the conduct, the lack of a complaint would not necessarily justify an inference of a fabrication. As the testimony reveals in this case, the child had no reason to question the character of the conduct until her subsequent viewing of a film depicting this type of conduct. It is also significant that the party involved in the behavior was her father whom she would naturally trust and accept his judgment as to the propriety of the act. The encouragement by the father to maintain the confidence as to this incident also dilutes any inference drawn merely from a delayed complaint. In this setting the absence of an immediate outcry would not in and of itself warrant an inference that the event was a recent fabrication and, therefore, a charge to that effect was properly denied by the trial court.

Id., 580 *A.*2d at 299.

2. In 1988, the New Jersey Supreme Court proposed a similar hearsay exception in *State v. D.R.*, 109 *N.J.* 348, 537 *A.*2d 667 (1988). In *D.R.*, the defendant was convicted of aggravated sexual assault, sexual assault, and endangering the welfare of a child. His victim was his 2 1/2-year-old granddaughter. At trial, the child was deemed to be incompetent to testify, and as a result, one of the main witnesses against defendant was a Dr. Martin Krupnick, a clinical psychologist specializing in the field of incest and childhood sexual assaults. Dr. Krupnick's trial testimony related statements made to him by defendant's granddaughter and included a description of the child's use of anatomically-correct dolls to facilitate her ability to express herself and relate the details of the sexual assault.

In the appeal following his convictions, defendant argued that it was error for the trial court to permit the use of the doctor's hearsay testimony. The Supreme Court observed:

> We are in full agreement with the Appellate Division's conclusion that the difficult problems of proof in child sexual abuse cases would be alleviated by a modification of the hearsay rule that addresses the admissibility of out-of-court victim statements such as the one at issue. * * * [S]o significant a modification of the Rules of Evidence[, however,] should be adopted in accordance with the prescribed statutory procedure[.]

Id., 109 *N.J.* at 351-52.

All who have addressed the problems of proof in child sexual abuse prosecutions "appear to agree that the testimony by the victim is often the indispensable element of the prosecution's case. * * * Typically, in such cases the assailant is a close relative, a member of the household, or a trusted acquaintance. Acts of child abuse are seldom committed in the presence of anyone other than the perpetrator and the victim. Frequently, there is no visible physical evidence that acts of sexual molestation have occurred. Absent a confession, the victim's account of the sexual abuse may be the best and sometimes the only evidence that a sexual assault has taken place." *Id.* at 358-359.

Here, the Court recognized that "a child victim's spontaneous out-of-court account of an act of sexual abuse may be highly credible because of its content and the surrounding circumstances. Young children, having no sexual orientation, do not necessarily regard a sexual encounter as shocking or unpleasant, and frequently relate such incidents to a parent or relative in a matter-of-fact manner. * * * Several commentators have observed that child victim accounts of incidents of sexual abuse are highly reliable." *Id.* at 359-360.

Nonetheless, "the reliability of in-court testimony of a young child victimized by a sexual assault is often affected by the stress of the courtroom experience, the presence of the defendant, and the prosecutor's need to resort to leading questions." *Id.* at 360. Moreover, "the lapse of time between the sexual assault and the trial can affect the child's ability to recall the incident. In cases where the accused is a member of the child's family or household, the victim may be urged or coerced to recant. In general, the courtroom setting is intimidating to children and often affects adversely their ability to testify credibly." *Id.*

Significantly, recent years have seen a major "increase in media coverage and public awareness of the problems of child sexual abuse. This heightened public sensitivity to the frequency of child sexual abuse has provoked a widespread criticism and re-examination of evidence rules and trial procedures affecting the prosecution of child sex abuse cases." *Id.* Thus, in response, the American Bar Association (ABA) has set forth its recommendations for the admissibility of a child victim's statements in such a case, numerous states have enacted statutes specifically designed to modify the hearsay rule to permit admission into evidence of a child's out-of-court statement, provided that the statement is determined to be reliable, and many state and federal courts have authorized the use of such hearsay statements under the residual hearsay exception.

Accordingly, based on the recommendation of its supreme court, New Jersey adopted an exception to its rule against hearsay which authorizes, in certain circumstances, the admissibility of a child's out-of-court statement concerning acts of sexual abuse. *See N.J.Evid.R.* 804(b)(8).

3. In *Idaho v. Wright*, 497 *U.S.* 805, 110 *S.Ct.* 3139 (1990), the federal Supreme Court held inadmissible, under the Confrontation Clause, a doctor's testimony relating statements made to him by a 2 1/2-year-old female victim in response to questions he asked regarding an alleged sexual assault. At the time of trial, the State successfully introduced the doctor's testimony under Idaho's residual hearsay exception. Finding the admission of such testimony in violation of the Confrontation Clause, the Supreme Court preliminarily noted that "Idaho's residual hearsay exception * * * under which the challenged statements were admitted * * * is not a firmly rooted hearsay exception for Confrontation Clause purposes. Admission under a firmly rooted hearsay exception satisfies the constitutional requirement of reliability because of the weight accorded longstanding judicial and legislative experience in assessing the trustworthiness of certain types of out-of-court statements. * * * The residual hearsay exception, by contrast, accommodates ad hoc instances in which statements not otherwise falling within a recognized hearsay exception might nevertheless be sufficiently reliable to be admissible at trial." *Id.*, 110 *S.Ct.* at 3147.

> Hearsay statements admitted under the residual exception, almost by definition, therefore do not share the same tradition of reliability that supports the admissibility of statements under a firmly rooted hearsay exception. Moreover, were we to agree that the admission of hearsay statements under the residual exception automatically passed Confrontation Clause scrutiny, virtually every codified hearsay exception would assume constitutional stature, a step this Court has repeatedly declined to take.

Id. at 3148.

"The crux of the question presented" here in *Wright*, therefore, is whether the State, as the proponent of evidence presumptively barred by the hearsay rule and the Confrontation Clause, has carried its burden of proving that the child's incriminating statements to the doctor "bore sufficient indicia of reliability to withstand scrutiny under the Clause." *Id.* According to the Court, because the child's hearsay statements do not fall within a firmly rooted hearsay exception, they are presumptively unreliable and inadmissible for Confrontation Clause purposes, "and 'must be excluded, at least absent a showing of particularized guarantees of trustworthiness.'" *Id.* [Citation omitted.]

The doctor in this case failed to record the interview. He asked leading questions, "and questioned the child with a preconceived idea of what she should be disclosing." *Id.* On cross-examination, the doctor acknowledged that a picture he drew to facilitate his questioning of the child victim had been discarded. He also stated that "although he had dictated notes to summarize the conversation, his notes were not detailed and did not record any changes in the child's affect or attitude." *Id.* at 3144.

"Viewing the totality of the circumstances surrounding the [child's] responses to [the doctor's] questions," the Court held "that the State [] failed to show that the [child's] incriminating statements to the pediatrician possessed sufficient 'particularized guarantees of trustworthiness' under the Confrontation Clause to overcome" the "presumption of inadmissibility accorded accusatory hearsay statements not admitted pursuant to a firmly rooted hearsay exception." *Id.* at 3152, 3153.

During the course of its opinion, the Court agreed with the State's contention that a finding of "particularized guarantees of trustworthiness" should be based on a consideration of the totality of the circumstances surrounding the making of the statement. The Court rejected the contention, however, that the consideration should include other evidence presented at trial that corroborates the truth of the statement. According to the Court,

* * * we think the relevant circumstances include only those that surround the making of the statement and that render the declarant particularly worthy of belief. * * * To be admissible under the Confrontation Clause, hearsay evidence used to convict a defendant must possess indicia of reliability by virtue of its inherent trustworthiness, not by reference to other evidence adduced at trial. * * *

In short, the use of corroborating evidence to support a hearsay statement's "particularized guarantees of trustworthiness" would permit admission of a presumptively unreliable statement by bootstrapping on the trustworthiness of other

evidence at trial, a result we think at odds with the requirement that hearsay evidence admitted under the Confrontation
Clause be so trustworthy that cross-examination of the declarant would be of marginal utility.

Id. at 3148-50.

---

§4.3(n). Recorded Recollection

"A memorandum or record concerning a matter about which a
witness once had knowledge but now has insufficient recollection to
enable the witness to testify fully and accurately, shown to have
been made or adopted by the witness when the matter was fresh in
the witness' memory and to reflect that knowledge correctly," is
admissible as an exception to the rule against hearsay.[89] The purpose of this exception is "not to refresh the memory of a witness
who then testifies with his testimony becoming evidence. Its purpose is to provide that recorded recollection, which satisfies certain
requirements, may be used as evidence when the witness now has
insufficient recollection to testify."[90]

There are four requirements that must be met: (1) the witness
must have personally observed the event or circumstances referred
to in the writing; (2) the writing must have been made or seen by
the witness at a time when the witness' recollection of the event
was fairly fresh; (3) the witness must be able to testify that at the
time the writing was made he or she knew that its contents were
true and accurate; and (4) the witness must have no present recollection of the event, other than his or her testimony to the matters
previously set forth in (1) through (3).[91]

---

[89] *Fed.R.Evid.* 803(5).

[90] 11 J. Moore, *Evidence* §803(5)[5] (2nd ed. 1982).

[91] *See* 3 Wigmore, *Evidence* §§744, 745 (Chadbourn rev. 1970); *Dennis v. Scarbor-
ough*, 360 *So.*2d 278 (Ala. 1979); *Commonwealth v. Galvin*, 27 *Mass.App.Ct.* 150, 535
*N.E.*2d 623 (1989). *But see State v. Sutton*, 253 *Or.* 24, 450 *P.*2d 748 (1969) (permitting
the introduction into evidence of a breathalyzer checklist notwithstanding the officer's
seemingly refreshed recollection, finding the checklist to be more trustworthy).

STATE v. SCALLY
Court of Appeals of Oregon
758 P.2d 365 (1988)

GRABER, Judge.

"Defendant appeals his conviction for driving under the influence of intoxicants. [] He argues that the court erred in admitting testimony, under [the recorded recollection exception], from the arresting police officer. We affirm." *Id.* at 365.

"At trial, the officer testified to circumstances surrounding the stop and the arrest of defendant. He had no present recollection of several questions that he had asked or of the answers that defendant had given. However, that information was contained in the police report that the officer had prepared shortly after the arrest. The court allowed him to read the pertinent portion of the report to the jury." *Id.*

"Defendant first argues that OEC 803(8)(b) bars the officer's testimony. The police report itself is inadmissible under OEC 803(8)(b).[92]

Whether it can be read aloud as a recorded recollection, under OEC 803(5), has not been decided in Oregon. OEC 803(5) and OEC 803(8)(b) are almost identical to their federal counterparts. * * * For that reason, decisions construing the parallel federal rules are persuasive." *Id.* at 366.

"The purpose of [Fed.R.Evid.] 803(8)(B) is to bar police reports as a *substitute* for testimony of the officer. *United States v. Sawyer*, 607 F.2d 1190, 1193 (7th Cir. 1979)[.] When the officer testifies, the danger of unreliability is minimized, because the trier of fact has the opportunity to weigh credibility and to consider the circumstances surrounding the preparation of the report. *United States v. King*, 613 F.2d 670, 673 (7th Cir. 1980). As a result, under [Fed.R.Evid.] 803(5), law enforcement officers have been allowed to read their reports into the record when they lack a sufficient present recollection to testify from memory." *Scally* at 366. [Court's emphasis.]

"Defendant next argues that he was denied his right of confrontation, in violation of the Sixth Amendment and Article I, section 11 of the Oregon Constitution. The argument is unpersuasive. Defendant had an opportunity effectively to cross-examine the officer, who

---

[92] OEC 803(8) provides that these things are admissible despite the rule against hearsay:

> Records, reports, statements or data compilations, in any form, of public offices or agencies, setting forth:
>
> * * *
>
> (b) Matters observed pursuant to duty imposed by law as to which matters there was a duty to report, excluding, however, in criminal cases matters observed by police officers and other law enforcement personnel * * *."

Id. at 366 n.2. [Court's emphasis.]

was the author of the police report. The application of [*Fed.R.Evid.*] 803(5) does not violate defendant's [right of confrontation]." *Id.*

"Defendant relies entirely on *United States v. Oates*, 560 *F.*2d 45 (2nd Cir. 1977), for his argument to the contrary. There, the court held that the government could not introduce a report as a substitute for testimony from an unavailable witness. The present case is distinguishable, because here the officer testified, subject to cross-examination, and because the report itself was not offered." *Id.*

"We agree with the reasoning of *United States v. Sawyer, supra,* and *United States v. King, supra,* and hold that, notwithstanding OEC 803(8)(b), OEC 803(5) permits an officer who testifies in a criminal trial to read relevant parts of his report into the record when he has insufficient present recollection to testify fully and accurately. That procedure does not violate defendant's right to confrontation." *Scally* at 366-67.

"Affirmed."

HENRY v. STATE
Court of Appeals of Maryland
324 *Md.* 204, 596 *A.*2d 1024 (1991)

CHASANOW, Judge.

[Ian George Constantine Henry was tried and convicted in the Circuit Court for Prince George's County of five counts of murder, six counts of use of a handgun in the commission of a crime of violence, and one count each of attempted murder, assault with intent to murder, conspiracy to murder, conspiracy to rob, robbery with a deadly weapon, and theft over $300.00. The jury returned two sentences of death.]

Jereen Brown was one of the many State's witnesses who testified at trial. Brown testified that, on the night in question, "while she was returning to her apartment in the same building where the murders occurred, she saw two men emerging from the building. The men quickly passed by her and almost knocked her down. When asked whether one of those men was now present in the courtroom, Ms. Brown replied, 'I can't remember.' She responded identically when asked to give a detailed description of the two men she saw the evening of [the murders]. The State's Attorney then attempted to refresh Ms. Brown's memory with a written statement that she had given to police in the early morning hours [following the crime], detailing what she had seen on the night of the murders. She stated that, although her memory was fresh when she originally made the statement to the police, rereading the statement on the witness stand did not refresh her recollection of the events. Over Henry's objection, the court admitted the [written] statement into evidence. Henry now asserts that the statement was inadmissible hearsay, and its admission into evidence resulted in reversible error." *Id.* at 1041.

"It is an obvious conclusion that Ms. Brown's written statement to the police is hearsay: it was an out-of-court statement offered to prove the truth of the matter asserted. The crucial question then becomes whether an exception to the hearsay exclusion applies." *Id.*

"A writing is admissible under the exception for past recollection recorded if:

(1) The witness had first-hand knowledge of the matters recorded in the writing;

(2) The witness' present recollection is impaired and cannot be fully refreshed, so that the writing will provide more accurate information than the witness' testimony to present recollection;

(3) The writing was made or adopted by the witness at or near the time of the event recorded; [and]

(4) At that time, the witness or another recorded the facts correctly or the witness recognized as correct the facts recorded.

Id. at 1041-42. [Citations omitted.]

"Under this exception, a written recollection is admissible into evidence. * * * Ms. Brown's written statement fulfills the appropriate criteria and is admissible as a past recollection recorded." *Id.* at 1042.

NOTE

Present recollection refreshed versus past recollection recorded. The recorded recollection exception to the rule against hearsay should be considered in conjunction with the principles which govern refreshing a witness' *present* recollection. One commentator summarized these principles as follows.

[W]hen a witness evinces an inability to remember, interrogating counsel may attempt to revive the witness's memory by producing a writing (or some other item) intended to induce recollection. If [counsel] succeeds in restoring the witness's memory so that the latter can testify from present recollection, the only evidence received by the court is the witness's testimony, not the writing. The writing serves the limited purpose of aiding memory; consequently, the counsel who used the writing for this narrow purpose has no right to introduce it into evidence. Under these circumstances, which are usually designated "present recollection refreshed," there is no hearsay difficulty because no "off-the-stand" assertion is offered for its truth. The witness testifies

157

from present (revived) memory just as if he had not experienced a temporary inability to recall the event in question.

A different situation is encountered when the witness's memory cannot be revived satisfactorily and an earlier writing, authored or previously verified by the witness, is offered *in lieu* of his present testimony. If the proponent introduces the writing for a purpose which requires the trier to accept the truth of the assertions it contains, the writing is hearsay: the cross-examiner neither can cross-examine the writing, nor can he interrogate the witness about the details of the events described in it, since the witness is unable to recall these. Under these circumstances, admissibility must rest upon the use of some exception to the hearsay rule. If the witness can provide a foundation which attests to the accuracy of the writing by reason of its timely and accurate preparation, the present exception for recorded recollection will suffice.[93]

BAKER v. STATE
Court of Special Appeals of Maryland
35 *Md.App.* 593, 371 *A.*2d 699 (1977)

MOYLAN, Judge.
[This appeal addresses the question of what to do when a police officer takes the witness stand and says, "I don't remember." The subject is that of Present Recollection Revived, also known as Present Recollection Refreshed.

Defendant, Teretha Baker, was convicted by a Baltimore City jury of first-degree murder and robbery. Her main contention in this appeal is that the trial judge erred by refusing to allow her attorney to refresh the present recollection of a key police witness by showing him a report written by a fellow police officer.]

"The ultimate source of most of the evidence implicating the [defendant] was the robbery and murder victim himself, Gaither Martin, a now-dead declarant * * *. When Officer Bolton arrived at the crime scene, the victim told him that he had 'picked these three ladies up . . . at the New Deal Bar'; that when he took them to their stated destination, a man walked up to the car and pulled him out; that 'the other three got out and proceeded to kick him and beat him.' It was the assertion made by the victim to the officer that established that his money, wallet and keys had been taken. The critical impasse, for

---

[93] Lilly, *An Introduction to the Law of Evidence* §7.14 (2nd ed. West 1987), at 260. [Emphasis in original.] *See also United States v. Edwards,* 539 *F.*2d 689 (9th Cir. 1976).

present purposes, occurred when the officer was questioned, on cross-examination, about what happened en route to the hospital. The officer had received a call from Officer Hucke, of the Western District, apparently to the effect that a suspect had been picked up. Before proceeding to the hospital, Officer Bolton took the victim to the place where Officer Hucke was holding the [defendant]. The [defendant], as part of this cross-examination, sought to elicit from the officer the fact that the crime victim confronted the [defendant] and stated that the [defendant] was not one of those persons who had attacked and robbed him. [When Officer Bolton could not remember the confrontation, defendant's attorney, in an effort to refresh Bolton's memory,] attempted to show him the police report relating to that confrontation and prepared by Office Hucke. [Defendant's attorney] was consistently and effectively thwarted in that attempt:

BY MR. HARLAN:

Q. Do you have the report filed by Officer Hucke . . . ?

[OFFICER BOLTON:] Right, I have copies.

Q. Okay.

MR. DOORY: I would object to that, Your Honor.

THE COURT: I will sustain the objection. This is not his report.

BY MR. HARLAN:

Q. Can you look at this report and refresh your recollection as to whether or not you ever had the victim in a confrontation with Mrs. Baker?

MR. DOORY: Objection, Your Honor.

MR. HARLAN: He can refresh—

THE COURT: Well, he can refresh his recollection as to his personal knowledge. That's all right.

[OFFICER BOLTON:] That is what I am saying. I don't know who it was that we confronted really.

BY MR. HARLAN:

Q. All right. Would you consult your report and maybe it will refresh your recollection.

THE COURT: I think the response is he doesn't know who—

MR. HARLAN: He can refresh his recollection if he looks at the report.

THE COURT: He can't refresh his recollection from someone else's report, Mr. Harlan.

MR. HARLAN: I would object, Your Honor. Absolutely he can.

THE COURT: You might object but—

MR. HARLAN: You are not going to permit the officer to refresh his recollection from the police report ?

THE COURT: No. It is not his report.

* * * *

Id. at 700-01.

"On so critical an issue as possible exculpation from the very lips of the crime victim, [defendant] was entitled to try to refresh the memory of the key police witness. She was erroneously and prejudicially denied that opportunity." * * * The trial judge in this case erroneously measured the legitimacy of the effort to revive present recollection against the more rigorous standards for [past recollection recorded]." *Id.* at 702.

"It is, of course, hornbook law that when a party seeks to introduce a record of past recollection, he must establish 1) that the record was made by or adopted by the witness at a time when the witness did have a recollection of the event and 2) that the witness can presently vouch for the fact that when the record was made or adopted by him, he knew that it was accurate. * * * Had the [defendant] sought to offer the police report as a record of past recollection on the part of Officer Bolton, it is elementary that she would have had to show, [] that the report had either been prepared by Officer Bolton himself or had been read by him and that he can now say that at that time he knew it was correct. Absent such a showing, the trial judge would have been correct in declining to receive it in evidence." *Id.*

"When dealing with an instance of Past Recollection Recorded, the reason for the rigorous standards of admissibility is quite clear. Those standards exist to test the competence of the report or document in question. Since the piece of paper itself, in effect, speaks to the jury, the piece of paper must pass muster in terms of its evidentiary competence." *Id.*

"Not so with Present Recollection Revived! By marked contrast to Past Recollection Recorded, no such testimonial competence is demanded of a mere stimulus to present recollection, for the stimulus itself is never evidence. Notwithstanding the surface similarity between the two phenomena, the difference between them could not be more basic. *It is the difference between evidence and non-evidence.* [" 'In the one instance, the witness stakes his oath on his present memory; in the other, upon his written recital of things remembered in the past.' "] * * * When we are dealing with an instance of Present Recollection Revived, the only source of evidence is the testimony of the witness himself. The stimulus may have jogged the witness' dormant memory, but the stimulus itself is not received in evidence." *Id.* at 702-03 & n.5. [Court's emphasis; citations omitted.]

"The catalytic agent or memory stimulator is put aside, once it has worked its psychological magic, and the witness then testifies on the basis of the now-refreshed memory. The opposing party, of course, has the right to inspect the memory aid, be it a writing or otherwise, and even to show it to the jury. This examination, however, is not for the purpose of testing the competence of the memory aid (for competence is immaterial where the thing in question is not evidence) but only to test whether the witness's memory has in truth been refreshed." *Id.* at 703.

If a writing is used, "the writing need not be that of the forgetful witness himself, need not have been adopted by him, need not have been made contemporaneously with or shortly after the incident in question, and need not even be necessarily accurate. The competence of the writing is not in issue for the writing is not offered as evidence but is only used as a memory aid." *Id.* at 704.

"When the writing in question is to be utilized simply 'to awaken a slumbering recollection of an event' in the mind of the witness, the writing may be a memorandum made by the witness himself, 1) even if it was not made immediately after the event, 2) even if it was not made of firsthand knowledge and 3) even if the witness cannot now vouch for the fact that it was accurate when made. It may be a memorandum made by one other than the witness, even if never before read by the witness or vouched for by him." *Id.* [Citation omitted.]

"Not only may the writing to be used as a memory aid fall short of vigorous standards of competence required of a record of past recollection, the memory aid itself need not even be a writing. What may it be? It may be anything. It may be a line from Kipling or the dolorous refrain of 'The Tennessee Waltz'; a sniff of hickory smoke; the running of the fingers across a swatch of corduroy; the sweet carbonation of a chocolate soda; the sight of a faded snapshot in a long-neglected album. All that is required is that it may trigger [the witness's memory]. It may be anything that produces the desired testimonial prelude, 'It all comes back to me now.' " *Id.* at 704-05.

Accordingly, "it is quite clear that in this case, the appropriate effort of the [defendant] to jog the arguably dormant memory of the key police witness on a vital issue was unduly and prejudicially restricted." *Id.* at 706.

"Judgments reversed; case remanded for a new trial[.]"

---

§4.3(o). Records of Regularly Conducted Activity. (Business Records)

"A memorandum, report, record or data compilation, in any form, of acts, events, conditions, opinions, or diagnoses, made at or near the time by, or from information transmitted by, a person with knowledge, if kept in the course of a regularly conducted business activity, and if it was the regular practice of that business activity to make the memorandum, report, record, or data compilation, all as shown by the testimony of the custodian or other qualified witness, unless the source of information or the method or circumstances of preparation indicate lack of trustworthiness," is admissible as an exception to the rule against hearsay, notwithstanding the fact that the declarant may be available as a witness.[94]

The justification for a hearsay exception for regularly kept records lies in the notion that "[u]nusual reliability is furnished by the fact that regularly kept records typically have a high degree of accuracy."[95]

JOHNSON v. LUTZ
Court of Appeals of New York
253 *N.Y.* 124, 234 *N.Y.S.* 328, 170 *N.E.* 517 (1930)

HUBBS, J.

"This action is to recover damages for the wrongful death of the plaintiff's intestate, who was killed when his motorcycle came into collision with the defendants' truck at a street intersection. There was a sharp conflict in the testimony in regard to the circumstances under which the collision took place. A policeman's report of the accident filed by him in the station house was offered in evidence by the defendants under section 374-a of the Civil Practice Act, and was excluded. The sole ground for reversal urged by the appellants is that said report was erroneously excluded. That section reads: 'Any writing or record, whether in the form of an entry in a book or otherwise, made as a memorandum or record of any act, transaction, occurrence or event, shall be admissible in evidence in proof of said act, transaction, occurrence or event, if the trial judge shall find that it was made in the regular course of any business, and that it was the regular course of such business to make such memorandum or record at the time of such act, transaction, occurrence or event, or within a reasonable time thereafter. All other circumstances of the making of such writing or record, including the lack of personal knowledge by the entrant or maker, may be shown to affect its weight, but they shall not affect its admissibility. The term business shall include business, profession, occupation and calling of every kind.' " *Id.* at 517.

"Prior to the decision in the well-known case of *Vosburgh v. Thayer*, 12 *Johns* 461, decided in 1815, shopbooks could not be introduced in evidence to prove an account. The decision in that case established that they were admissible where preliminary proof could be made that there were regular dealings between the parties; that

---

[94] *Fed.R.Evid.* 803(6).

[95] 2 McCormick, *Evidence* §286 (4th ed. 1992), at 264-65.

the plaintiff kept honest and fair books; that some of the articles charged had been delivered; and that the plaintiff kept no clerk. At that time it might not have been a hardship to require a shopkeeper who sued to recover an account to furnish the preliminary proof required by that decision. Business was transacted in a comparatively small way, with few, if any, clerks. Since the decision in that case, it has remained the substantial basis of all decisions upon the question in this jurisdiction prior to the enactment in 1928 of section 374-a, Civil Practice Act." Id. at 517-18.

"Under modern conditions, the limitations upon the right to use books of account, memoranda, or records, made in the regular course of business, often resulted in a denial of justice, and usually in annoyance, expense, and waste of time and energy. A rule of evidence that was practical a century ago had become obsolete. The situation was appreciated, and attention was called to it by the courts and text-writers. * * *" *Id.* at 518.

"The report of the Legal Research Committee of the Commonwealth Fund, published in 1927, * * * dealt with the question * * * [and,] based upon extensive research, pointed out the confusion existing in decisions in different jurisdictions. It explained and illustrated the great need of a more practical, workable, and uniform rule, adapted to modern business conditions and practices. The [report discusses] the pressing need of a rule of evidence which would 'give evidential credit to the books upon which the mercantile and industrial world relies in the conduct of business.' * * * [T]he committee proposed a statute to be enacted in all jurisdictions. In compliance with such proposal, the Legislature enacted section 374-a of the Civil Practice Act in the very words used by the committee." Id.

"It is apparent that the Legislature enacted section 374-a to carry out the purpose announced in the report of the committee. That purpose was to secure the enactment of a statute which would afford a more suitable rule of evidence in the proof of business transactions under existing business conditions." *Id.*

"In view of the history of section 374-a and the purpose for which it was enacted, it is apparent that it was never intended to apply to a situation like that in th[is case]. The memorandum in question was not made in the regular course of any business, profession, occupation, or calling. The policeman who made it was not present at the time of the accident. The memorandum was made from hearsay statements of third parties who happened to be present at the scene of the accident when he arrived. It does not appear whether they saw the accident and stated to him what they knew, or stated what some other persons had told them." *Id.*

"The purpose of the Legislature in enacting section 374-a was to permit a writing or record, made in the regular course of business, to be received in evidence without the necessity of calling as witnesses all of the persons who had any part in making it, provided the record was made as a part of the duty of the person making it, or on information imparted by persons who were under a duty to impart such information. The amendment permits the introduction of shopbooks without the necessity of calling all clerks who may have sold different items of account. It was not intended to permit the receipt in evidence of entries based upon voluntary hearsay statements made by third parties not engaged in the business or under any duty in relation thereto. * * * 'It is a proper qualification of the rule admitting such evidence that the account must have been made in the ordinary course of business, and that it should not be extended so as to admit a mere private memorandum, not made in pursuance of any duty owing by the person making it, or when made upon information derived from another who made the communication casually and voluntarily, and not under the sanction of duty or other obligation.' " *Id.* [Citation omitted.]

"An important consideration leading to the amendment was the fact that in the business world credit is given to records made in the course of business by persons who are engaged in the business upon information given by others engaged in the same business as part of their duty." *Id.*

" 'Such entries are dealt with in that way in the most important undertakings of mercantile and industrial life. They are the ultimate basis of calculation, investment, and general confidence in every business enterprise. Nor does the practical impossibility of obtaining constantly and permanently the verification of every employee affect the trust that is given to such books. It would seem that expedients which the entire commercial world recognizes as safe could be sanctioned, and not discredited by courts of justice.' " *Id.* [Citation omitted.]

"The Legislature has sought by the amendment to make the courts practical. It would be unfortunate not to give the amendment a construction which will enable it to cure the evil complained of and accomplish the purpose for which it was enacted. In construing it, we should not, however, permit it to be applied in a case for which it was never intended." *Id.* at 519.

"The judgment should be affirmed with costs." *Id.*

CARDOZO, C.J., and POUND, CRANE, LEHMAN, KELLOGG, and O'BRIEN, JJ., concur.

NOTE

All participants in the making of the record must be under a "business duty." It has been held that the person supplying the information and the person entering the information into the business record both act in the regular course of business. *See e.g., United States v. Baker,* 693 *F.*2d 183 (D.C.Cir. 1982); *United States v. Yates,* 553 *F.*2d 518 (6th Cir. 1977).

§4.3(p). Public Records and Reports

Even though the declarant may be available as a witness, the hearsay rule will not bar the admission of "[r]ecords, reports, statements, or data compilations, in any form, of public offices or agencies, setting forth (A) the activities of the office or agency, or (B) matters observed pursuant to duty imposed by law as to which matters there was a duty to report, excluding, however, in criminal cases matters observed by police officers and other law enforcement personnel, or (C) in civil actions and proceedings and against the Government in criminal cases, factual findings resulting from an investigation made pursuant to authority granted by law, unless the sources of information or other circumstances indicate lack of trustworthiness."[96]

As can be seen from clauses (B) and (C), this exception for public records and reports does not permit the prosecution to introduce investigative reports or other reports of law enforcement officers against the accused without producing the officer in court as a witness. Regarding reports of an evaluative nature, clause (C) "is very specific: they are admissible only in civil cases and against the government in criminal cases in view of the almost certain collision with confrontation rights which would result from their use against the accused in a criminal case."[97] The limitations of clauses (B) and (C) will not, however, "be extended to other hearsay exceptions if the maker is produced in court as a witness and subject to cross-examination."[98]

---

[96] *Fed.R.Evid.* 803(8).

[97] *Advisory Committee's Note*, 56 F.R.D. 183, 311. In one of the first appellate interpretations of these provisions, the court in United States v. Oates, 560 F.2d 45 (2nd Cir. 1977), declared:

> [I]n criminal cases reports of public agencies setting forth matters observed by police officers and other law enforcement personnel and reports of public agencies setting forth factual findings resulting from investigations made pursuant to authority granted by law cannot satisfy the standards of any hearsay exception if those reports are sought to be introduced against the accused. Inasmuch as the chemist's documents here [identifying the substance seized from defendant as heroin,] can be characterized as governmental reports which set forth matters observed by law enforcement personnel or which set forth factual findings resulting from an authorized investigation, they were incapable of qualifying under any of the exceptions to the hearsay rule specified in FRE 803 and 804.

Id. at 84. Subsequent cases have, however, tempered the *Oates* decision by ruling that such reports may be admissible when the declarant is produced in court, subject to cross-examination, and the record qualifies under *Fed.R.Evid.* 803(6) or 803(5). *See e.g., United States v. King*, 613 F.2d 670 (7th Cir. 1980); *United States v. Hayes*, 861 F.2d 1225 (10th Cir. 1988); *United States v. Sawyer*, 607 F.2d 1190 (7th Cir. 1979).

[98] 2 McCormick, *Evidence* §296 (4th ed. 1992), at 294.

UNITED STATES v. ENTERLINE
United States Court of Appeals
894 *F.*2d 287 (8th Cir. 1990)

BEAM, Circuit Judge.

"[Defendant] Enterline appeals from his conviction by a jury on two counts of transporting in interstate commerce a motor vehicle, knowing that it was stolen, * * * and on two counts of possessing with the intent to sell a motor vehicle, knowing that its identification number had been removed or otherwise altered[.]" *Id.*

"Enterline challenges the testimony of Edward Satterfield, a Special Agent of the F.B.I., based in Little Rock, Arkansas. Satterfield participated in the investigation * * * and was present at Enterline's residence * * * when law enforcement officers executed a search warrant. As part of that search, officers from the auto theft unit of the Tulsa Police Department seized several vehicle identification number plates, as well as shipping manifests, from vehicles on Enterline's property. Satterfield then ran a computer check on the identification numbers, and found that several of the vehicles had been reported stolen. Satterfield testified that the computer report indicated that three vehicles * * * had been reported stolen, and that two vehicles * * * had been renumbered. * * * Enterline argues on appeal * * * that the testimony was hearsay and not admissible through any exception in the rules. We disagree, since Satterfield's testimony from the computer report, while hearsay, was admissible under the public records exception, Federal Rule of Evidence 803(8)(B)." *Id.* at 289.

"Satterfield derived his conclusion that several cars on Enterline's property were reported stolen from a computer report comparing the identification numbers given to Satterfield with vehicle identification numbers from all cars reported stolen. The computer report is clearly hearsay, since it is an out of court statement offered to prove the truth of the matter asserted—that the cars on Enterline's property were reported stolen. The report nevertheless qualifies as a public record within Rule 803(8)(B)." *Id.*

"The hearsay exception for public records is based on both the necessity for admitting such records and their inherent trustworthiness. * * * Indeed, were the computer record not admissible as a public record to prove that the cars were reported stolen, the difficulty of proving that simple fact would be enormous. Thus, this circuit has admitted, for example, under Rule 803(8), certified documents from the Missouri Department of Revenue to prove ownership of an automobile. *See United States v. King*, 590 *F.*2d 253, 255 (8th Cir. 1978) * * *. Our concern is thus not whether the public records exception applies in this case, but whether the computer report falls within the exclusion found in Rule 803(8)(B) for matters observed by law enforcement officers in a criminal case. We hold that it does not." *Id.* at 289-90.

"It is clear that the exclusion concerns matters observed by the police at the scene of the crime. Such observations are potentially unreliable since they are made in an adversary setting, and are often subjective evaluations of whether a crime was committed. * * * The exclusion seeks to avoid admitting an officer's report of his observations in lieu of his personal testimony of what he observed. 'In adopting this exception, Congress was concerned about prosecutors attempting to prove their cases in chief simply by putting into evidence police officers' reports of their contemporaneous observations of crime.' * * * Similarly, this circuit [has] explained, * * * that Rule 803(8)(B) contains an exclusion for criminal cases because police reports are not 'reliable evidence of whether the allegations of criminal conduct they contain are true.' " *Id.* at 290. [Citations omitted.]

"Thus, the subject matter of the public record or report determines its admissibility; the exclusion applies only to 'matters observed by police officers and other law enforcement personnel.' Other circuits have found that reports not containing matters observed by officers in an adversarial setting do not fall within the exclusion to Rule 803(8)(B). [*See e.g., United States v. Orozco,* 590 *F.*2d 789, 793 (9th Cir. 1979) (computer report generated by United States Customs officials, containing vehicle license numbers of cars crossing the Mexican border, held admissible as a public record); *United States v. Quezada,* 754 *F.*2d 1190, 1194 (5th Cir. 1985) (deportation warrant containing record made by agent that defendant had departed the country held admissible as a public record at a proceeding in which defendant was charged with illegal re-entry into the United States).] Thus, '[i]n the case of documents recording routine, objective observations, made as part of the everyday function of the preparing official or agency, the factors likely to cloud the perception of an official engaged in the more traditional law enforcement functions of observation and investigation of crime are simply not present.' " *Enterline* at 290 (quoting *Quezada* at 1194).

"Similarly, the facts of this case are not within the purpose of the exclusion. The computer report does not contain contemporaneous observations by police officers at the scene of a crime, and thus presents none of the dangers of unreliability that such a report presents. Rather, the report merely contains, and is based on, facts: that cars with certain vehicle identification numbers were *reported* to have been stolen. Neither the notation of the vehicle identification numbers themselves nor their entry into a computer presents an adversarial setting or an opportunity for subjective observations by law enforcement officers. The officers were not recording their observations of crime, but were recording facts presented to them. Thus, the computer compilation, while hearsay, is simply not a report susceptible to the dangers which the exclusion set forth in Rule 803(8)(B) was designed to avoid. Accordingly, we find no error in the district court's admission of Satterfield's testimony." *Id.* at 290-91. [Court's emphasis.]

STATE v. MATULEWICZ
Supreme Court of New Jersey
101 *N.J.* 27, 499 *A.*2d 1363 (1985)

PER CURIAM.

"The issue raised by the defendant, Stanley A. Matulewicz, focuses upon whether a State Police chemist's laboratory report, identifying a controlled dangerous substance as marijuana, may be admitted as either a 'business entry' pursuant to the hearsay exception in Evidence Rule 63(13) or a 'report and finding' of a public official consistent with Evidence Rule 63(15)(a). * * * We conclude that in the absence of an evidentiary record relating to the foundation requirements underlying these rules, the issue as to the admissibility of a State Police chemist's report under either evidentiary rule cannot be resolved." *Id.*, 101 *N.J.* at 28-29.

"Evidence Rule 63(13) [sets forth] three preliminary conditions to the admissibility of evidence pursuant to this hearsay exception. First, the writing must be made in the regular course of business. Second, it must be prepared within a short time of the act, condition or event being described. Finally, the source of the information and the method and circumstances of the preparation of the writing must justify allowing it into evidence." *Id.* at 29.

"[The basis underlying] Evidence Rule 63(13) [is] the theory 'that records which are properly shown to have been kept as required normally possess a circumstantial probability of trustworthiness, and therefore ought to be received in evidence.' * * * However, this general acceptance of reliability will not attach if 'the trial court, after examining them [the records] and hearing the manner of their preparation explained, entertains serious doubt as to whether they are dependable or worthy of confidence.' " *Id.* at 29-30. [Citations omitted.]

"The factual record below is devoid of evidence that would elucidate the 'method and circumstances' involved in the preparation of the forensic chemist's laboratory report. Consequently, proofs should be adduced to reflect [1] the relative degrees of objectivity and subjectivity involved in the procedure; [2] the regularity with which these analyses are done; [3] the routine quality of each analysis; [4] the presence of any motive to single out a specific analysis for the purpose of rendering an untrustworthy report, and [5] the responsibility of each State Police chemist to make accurate and reliable analyses." Id. at 30.

"[T]he admissibility of the State Police chemist's report must be informed by an evidential record that addresses all relevant factors. While the factors mentioned are certainly relevant, they are not intended to be exhaustive. A trial court may properly require proof regarding additional concerns as to the indicia of trustworthiness necessary to justify admissibility under Evidence Rule 63(13)." Id. at 31.

"Similarly, in considering the admissibility of the forensic chemist's report under Evidence Rule 63(15)(a), these circumstances of reliability must also be addressed. * * * While justification for admission differs from Evidence Rule 63(13), in this case the declarant's status as a 'public official' may give rise to the presumption of trustworthiness. Nevertheless, the concern for reliability remains paramount." Id.

"Evidence Rule 63(15)(a) sanctions the admissibility of the factual observations that are disclosed in the report of a 'public official;' but it does not in particular contexts authorize the admissibility in evidence of the opinions or conclusions expressed in such a report." *Id.*

"[I]n the absence of an evidential record focusing upon the quality and nature of the chemist's report, including that which is denominated an opinion or conclusion, it cannot be determined whether * * * such a report comports with Evidence Rule 63(15)(a)." Id. at 32.

"Accordingly, we remand this case for retrial[.]" *Id.*

NOTE

Computer printouts and sentencing. In *State v. Carey,* 232 *N.J.Super.* 553, 557 A.2d 1036 (App.Div. 1989), the court rejected a drunk-driving defendant's hearsay challenge to a computer printout indicating that he was a second offender. During the course of its opinion, the court explained that

> there are two phases to every criminal and quasi-criminal matter: (1) the determination of guilt or innocence and (2) the imposition of sentence. The rules of evidence apply to the former but are relaxed as to the latter. For example, N.J.S.[] 2C:44-4d provides that "[a]ny prior conviction may be proved by any evidence, including fingerprint records made in connection with arrest, conviction or imprisonment, that reasonably satisfies the court that the defendant was convicted." (Emphasis supplied). Our case law likewise provides that "there is no need to restrict the State's presentation at the sentencing hearing to testimony admissible under the strict rules of evidence. The court may consider any evidence which, from its content, nature and manner of presentation is inherently reliable, trustworthy and credible." * * *
> The rules of evidence apply to the determination of the innocence or guilt of defendant, not the sentencing phase where the judge must, of necessity, consider all relevant information in imposing a proper, legal and just sentence. * * *

Id., 232 *N.J.Super.* at 555, 556-57. [Citations omitted.]

Accordingly, in light of the sentencing posture of the proceedings and the court's recognition of the fact that "[c]omputer-generated material has reached general acceptance in both the private and public sector and has been used by the courts not only on sentencing matters but as substantive evidence in criminal and civil proceedings," *id.* at 555, it held that the computer print-out "was properly used in the sentencing phase" of Carey's drunk-driving prosecution. *Id.* at 558.

---

§4.3(q). Prior Testimony

If the declarant is unavailable as a witness, the hearsay rule will not exclude prior testimony of the declarant which was "given as a witness at another hearing of the same or a different proceeding, or in a deposition taken in compliance with law in the course of the same or another proceeding, if the party against whom the testimony is now offered, or, in a civil action or proceeding, a predecessor in interest, had an opportunity and similar motive to develop the testimony by direct, cross, or redirect examination."[99]

---

§4.3(r). Judgment of Previous Conviction

"Evidence of a final judgment, entered after trial or upon a plea of guilty (but not upon a plea of nolo contendere), adjudging a person guilty of a crime punishable by death or imprisonment in excess of one year, is admissible as a hearsay exception, even though the declarant is available as a witness. A judgment of conviction may be used "to prove any fact essential to sustain the judgment, but not including, when offered by the Government in a criminal prosecution for purposes other than impeachment, judgments against persons other than the accused. The pendency of an appeal may be shown but does not affect admissibility."[100]

---

[99] *Fed.R.Evid.* 804(b)(1). *See also Fed.R.Evid.* 804(a) (defining "unavailability").

[100] *Fed.R.Evid.* 803(22).

§4.3(s). Hearsay Within Hearsay

"Hearsay included within hearsay is not excluded under the hearsay rule if each part of the combined statements conforms with an exception to the hearsay rule provided in these rules."[101]

This exception to the rule against hearsay recognizes that in some circumstances hearsay contained within hearsay may be admissible if both hearsay statements qualify as either an exemption or exception to the rule. For example, if a witness to a startling event immediately reports the facts of the event to a police officer who immediately records the witness' statements pursuant to the officer's business duty, the business record exception would permit introduction of the officer's report and the excited utterance exception would permit the introduction of the witness' statements.[102]

---

§4.4. CHARACTER EVIDENCE

MICHELSON v. UNITED STATES
Supreme Court of the United States
335 *U.S.* 469, 69 *S.Ct.* 213 (1948)

Mr. Justice JACKSON delivered the opinion of the Court.

"In 1947 [] Michelson was convicted of bribing a federal revenue agent. The government proved a large payment by [the] accused to the agent for the purpose of influencing his official action. The defendant, as a witness on his own behalf, admitted passing the money but claimed it was done in response to the agent's demands, threats, solicitations, and inducements. It is enough for our purposes to say that determination of the issue turned on whether the jury should believe the agent or the accused." *Id.* at 216.

"On direct examination of defendant, his own counsel brought out that, in 1927, he had been convicted of a misdemeanor having to do with trading in counterfeit watch dials. On cross-examination it appeared that in 1930, in executing an application for a license to deal in second-hand jewelry, he answered 'No' to the question whether he had theretofore been arrested or summoned for any offense." *Id.*

"Defendant called five witnesses to prove that he enjoyed a good reputation. Two of them testified that their acquaintance with him extended over a period of about thirty years and the others said they had known him at least half that long. A typical examination in chief was as follows:

---

[101] *Fed.R.Evid.* 805.

[102] Lilly, *An Introduction to the Law of Evidence* §7.17 (2nd ed. West 1987), at 267.

'Q. Do you know the defendant Michelson ?

     A. Yes.

'Q. How long do you know Mr. Michelson ?

     A. About 30 years.

'Q. Do you know other people who know him ?

     A. Yes.

'Q. Have you had occasion to discuss his reputation for honesty and truthfulness and for being a law-abiding citizen ?

     A. It is very good.

'Q. You have talked to others ?

     A. Yes.

'Q. And what is his reputation ?

     A. Very good.' "

Id.

"These are representative of answers by three witnesses; two others replied, in substance, that they have never heard anything against Michelson." *Id.*

"On cross-examination, four of the witnesses were asked, in substance, this question: 'Did you ever hear that Mr. Michelson on March 4, 1927, was convicted of a violation of the trademark law in New York City in regard to watches ?' This referred to the twenty-year-old conviction about which defendant himself had testified on direct examination. Two of them had heard of it and two had not." *Id.*

"To four of these witnesses the prosecution also addressed the question the allowance of which, over defendant's objection, is claimed to be reversible error: 'Did you ever hear that on October 11, 1920, the defendant, Solomon Michelson, was arrested for receiving stolen goods ?' None of the witnesses appears to have heard of this." *Id.*

"The trial court asked counsel for the prosecution, out of presence of the jury, 'Is it a fact according to the best information in your possession that Michelson was arrested for receiving stolen goods ?' Counsel replied that it was, and to support his good faith exhibited a paper record which defendant's counsel did not challenge." *Id.* at 216-17.

"The judge also on three occasions warned the jury * * * of the limited purpose for which this evidence was received." *Id.* at 217.

"Defendant[] challenges the right of the prosecution so to cross-examine his character witnesses. The Court of Appeals held that it was permissible. The opinion, however, points out that the practice has been severely criticized and invites us, in one respect, to change the rule. Serious and responsible criticism has been aimed * * * at the common-law doctrine on the whole subject of proof of reputation or character." *Id.* at 217-18.

"Courts that follow the common-law tradition almost unanimously have come to disallow resort by the prosecution to any kind of evidence of a defendant's evil character to establish a probability of his guilt. Not that the law invests the defendant with a presumption of good character, * * * but it simply closes the whole matter of character, disposition and reputation on the prosecution's case-in-chief. The State may not show defendant's prior trouble with the law, specific criminal acts, or ill name among his neighbors, even though such facts might logically be persuasive that he is by propensity a probable perpetrator of the crime. The inquiry is not rejected because character is irrelevant; on the contrary, it is said to weigh too much with the jury and to so overpersuade them as to prejudice one with a bad general record and deny him a fair opportunity to defend against a particular charge. The overriding policy of excluding such evidence, despite its admitted probative value, is the practical experience that its disallowance tends to prevent confusion of issues, unfair surprise and undue prejudice." *Id.* at 218-19.

"But this line of inquiry firmly denied to the State is opened to the defendant because character is relevant in resolving probabilities of guilt. He may introduce affirmative testimony that the general estimate of his character is so favorable that the jury may infer that he would not be likely to commit the offense charged. This privilege is sometimes valuable to a defendant for this Court has held that such testimony alone, in some circumstances, may be enough to raise a reasonable doubt of guilt and that in the federal courts a jury in a proper case should be so instructed. *Edgington v. United States,* 164 *U.S.* 361, 17 *S.Ct.* 72 * * *." *Id.* at 219.

"When the defendant elects to initiate a character inquiry, another anomalous rule comes into play. Not only is he permitted to call witnesses to testify from hearsay, but indeed such a witness is not allowed to base his testimony on anything but hearsay. What commonly is called 'character evidence' is only such when 'character' is employed as a synonym for 'reputation.' The witness may not testify about defendant's specific acts or courses of conduct or his possession of a particular disposition or of benign mental and moral traits; nor can he testify that his own acquaintance, observation, and knowledge of defendant leads to his own independent opinion that defendant possesses a good general or specific character, inconsistent with commission of acts charged. The witness is, however, allowed to summarize what he has heard in the community, although much of it may have been said by persons less qualified to judge than himself. The evidence which the law permits is not as to the personality of defendant but only as to the shadow his daily life has cast in his neighborhood. This has been well described in a different connection as 'the slow growth of months and years, the resultant picture of forgotten incidents, passing events, habitual and daily conduct, presumably honest because disinterested, and safer to be trusted because prone to suspect. * * * It is for that reason that such general repute is permitted to be proven. It sums up a multitude of trivial details. It compacts into the brief phrase of a verdict the teaching of many incidents and the conduct of years. It is the average intelligence drawing its conclusion.' " *Id.* [Citation omitted.]

"While courts have recognized logical grounds for criticism of this type of opinion-based-on-hearsay testimony, it is said to be justified by 'overwhelming considerations of practical convenience' in avoiding innumerable collateral issues which, if it were attempted to prove character by direct testimony, would complicate and confuse the trial, distract the minds of jurymen and befog the chief issues in the litigation." *Id.*

"Thus, the law extends helpful but illogical options to a defendant. Experience taught a necessity that they be counterweighted with equally illogical conditions to keep the advantage from becoming an unfair and unreasonable one. The price a defendant must pay for attempting to prove his good name is to throw open the entire subject which the law has kept closed for his benefit and make himself vulnerable where the law otherwise shields him. The prosecution may pursue the inquiry with contradictory witnesses to show that damaging rumors, whether or not well-grounded, were afloat— for it is not the man that he is, but the name that he has which is put in issue. Another hazard is that his own witness is subject to cross-examination as to the contents and extent of the hearsay on which he bases his conclusions, and he may be required to disclose rumors and reports that are current even if they do not affect his own conclusions.* It may test the sufficiency of his knowledge by asking what stories were circulating concerning events, such as one's arrest, about which people normally comment and speculate. Thus, while the law gives defendant the option to show as a fact that his reputation reflects a life and habit incompatible with commission of the offense charged, it subjects his proof to tests of credibility designed to prevent him from profiting by a mere parade of partisans." *Id.* at 220.

"To thus digress from evidence as to the offense to hear a contest as to the standing of the accused, at its best opens a tricky line of inquiry as to a shapeless and elusive subject matter. At its worst it opens a veritable Pandora's box of irresponsible gossip, innuendo and smear. * * * Growth of urban conditions, where one may never know or hear the name of his next-door neighbor, have tended to limit the use of these techniques and to deprive them of weight

---

* "A classic example in the books is a character witness in a trial for murder. She testified she grew up with defendant, knew his reputation for peace and quiet, and that it was good. On cross-examination she was asked if she had heard that the defendant had shot anybody and, if so, how many. She answered, 'Three or four,' and gave the names of two but could not recall the names of the others. She still insisted, however, that he was of 'good character.' The jury seems to have valued her information more highly than her judgment, and on appeal from conviction, the cross-examination was held proper. *People v. Laudiero*, 192 *N.Y.* 304, 309, 85 *N.E.* 132." *Michelson* at 220 n.16.

with juries. * * * [C]ourts of last resort have sought to overcome danger that the true issues will be obscured and confused by investing the trial court with discretion to limit the number of such witnesses and to control cross-examination. Both propriety and abuse of hearsay reputation testimony, on both sides, depend on numerous and subtle considerations, difficult to detect or appraise from a cold record, and therefore rarely and only on clear showing of prejudicial abuse of discretion will Courts of Appeal disturb rulings of trial courts on this subject." *Id.* at 220-21.

"Wide discretion is accompanied by heavy responsibility on trial courts to protect the practice from any misuse. The trial judge was scrupulous to so guard it in the case before us. He took pains to ascertain, out of presence of the jury, that the target of the question was an actual event, which would probably result in some comment among acquaintances if not injury to defendant's reputation. He satisfied himself that counsel was not merely taking a random shot at a reputation imprudently exposed or asking a groundless question to waft an unwarranted innuendo into the jury box." *Id.* at 221.

"The question permitted by the trial court, however, involves several features that may be worthy of comment. Its form invited hearsay; it asked about an arrest, not a conviction, and for an offense not closely similar to the one on trial; and it concerned an occurrence many years past." *Id.*

"Since the whole inquiry, as we have pointed out, is calculated to ascertain the general talk of people about defendant, rather than the witness' own knowledge of him, the form of inquiry, 'Have you heard ?' has general approval, and 'Do you know ?' is not allowed." *Id.*

"A character witness may be cross-examined as to an arrest whether or not it culminated in a conviction, according to the overwhelming weight of authority. This rule is sometimes confused with that which prohibits cross-examination to credibility by asking a witness whether he himself has been arrested." *Id.*

"An arrest without more does not, in law any more than in reason, impeach the integrity or impair the credibility of a witness. It happens to the innocent as well as the guilty. Only a conviction, therefore, may be inquired about to undermine the trustworthiness of a witness." *Id.* at 222.

"Arrest without more may nevertheless impair or cloud one's reputation. False arrest may do that. Even to be acquitted may damage one's good name if the community receives the verdict with a wink and chooses to remember defendant as one who ought to have been convicted. A conviction, on the other hand, may be accepted as a misfortune or an injustice, and even enhance the standing of one who mends his ways and lives it down. Reputation is the net balance of so many debits and credits that the law does not attach the finality to a conviction when the issue is reputation, that is given to it when the issue is the credibility of the convict." *Id.*

"The inquiry as to an arrest is permissible also because the prosecution has a right to test the qualifications of the witness to bespeak the community opinion. If one never heard the speculations and rumors in which even one's friends indulge upon his arrest, the jury may doubt whether he is capable of giving any very reliable conclusions as to his reputation." *Id.*

"In this case the crime inquired about was receiving stolen goods; the trial was for bribery. * * *." *Id.*

"The good character which the defendant had sought to establish was broader than the crime charged and included traits of 'honesty and truthfulness' and 'being a law-abiding citizen.' Possession of these characteristics would seem as incompatible with offering a bribe to a revenue agent as with receiving stolen goods. The crimes may be unlike, but both alike proceed from the same defects of character which the witnesses said this defendant was reputed not to exhibit. It is not only by comparison with the crime on trial but by comparison with the reputation asserted that a court may judge whether the prior arrest should be made a subject of inquiry. By this test the inquiry was permissible. It was proper cross-examination because reports of his arrest for receiving stolen goods, if admitted, would tend to weaken the assertion that he was known as an honest and law-abiding citizen. The cross-examination may take in as much ground as the testimony it is designed to verify. To hold otherwise would give defendant the benefit of testimony that he was honest and law-abiding in reputation when such might not be the fact * * *." *Id.*

"The inquiry here concerned an arrest twenty-seven years before the trial. Events a generation old are likely to be lived down and dropped from the present thought and talk of the community and to be absent from the knowledge of younger or more recent acquaintances. The court in its discretion may well exclude inquiry about rumors of an event so remote, unless recent misconduct revived them. But two of these witnesses dated their acquaintance with defendant as commencing thirty years before the trial. Defendant, on direct examination, voluntarily called attention to his conviction twenty years before. While the jury might conclude that a matter so old and indecisive as a 1920 arrest would shed little light on the present reputation and hence propensities of the defendant, we cannot say that, in the context of this evidence and in the absence of objection on this specific ground, its admission was an abuse of discretion." *Id.* at 222-23.

"[W]e think defendants in general and this defendant in particular have no valid complaint at the latitude which existing law allows to the prosecution to meet by cross-examination an issue voluntarily tendered by the defense." *Id.* at 223.

"We end, as we began, with the observation that the law regulating the offering and testing of character testimony may merit many criticisms. England and some states have overhauled the practice by statute." *Id.*

"The law of evidence relating to proof of reputation in criminal cases has developed almost entirely at the hands of state courts of last resort, which have such questions frequently before them. This Court, on the other hand, has contributed little to this or to any phase of the law of evidence, for the reason, among others, that it has had extremely rare occasion to decide such issues * * *." *Id.*

"We concur in the general opinion of courts, textwriters and the profession that much of this law is archaic, paradoxical and full of compromises and compensations by which an irrational advantage to one side is offset by a poorly reasoned counterprivilege to the other. But somehow it has proved a workable even if clumsy system when moderated by discretionary controls in the hands of a wise and strong trial court." *Id.* at 223-24.

The judgment is *AFFIRMED.*

Fed.R.Evid. **404. Character Evidence Not Admissible to Prove Conduct; Exceptions; Other Crimes.**

(a) Character evidence generally. Evidence of a person's character or a trait of character is not admissible for the purpose of proving action in conformity therewith on a particular occasion, except:

(1) Character of accused. Evidence of a pertinent trait of character offered by an accused, or by the prosecution to rebut the same, or if evidence of a trait of character of the alleged victim of the crime is offered by an accused and admitted under Rule 404(a)(2), evidence of the same trait of character of the accused offered by the prosecution;

(2) Character of alleged victim. Evidence of a pertinent trait of character of the alleged victim of the crime offered by an accused, or by the prosecution to rebut the same, or evidence of a character trait of peacefulness of the alleged victim offered by the prosecution in a homicide case to rebut evidence that the alleged victim was the first aggressor;

(3) Character of witness. Evidence of the character of a witness, as provided in rules 607, 608, and 609.

*   *   *   *

STATE v. BUDIS
Supreme Court of New Jersey
125 *N.J.* 519, 593 A.2d 784 (1991)

The opinion of the Court was delivered by

POLLOCK, J.

* * * * *

"Once again we turn to the perplexing problems surrounding the reporting and prosecution of child sexual abuse. * * * Child sexual abuse cases raise many of the same vexatious questions raised in the prosecution of other types of sexual assault. Like rape victims, victims of such abuse may feel ashamed or guilty about the assault. Victims of both kinds of assault may be intimidated by a trial, especially cross-examination about the details of the event. Consequently, both rape and child sexual abuse have been underreported. * * * The trial of both kinds of cases poses difficult problems of proof for the prosecution and the defense. Generally, the act occurs in private, with only the victim and the assailant present. In the absence of independent witnesses, the case often turns on an assessment of the credibility of the participants, an assessment better left to the trier of fact. Our primary function is to provide guidelines for making that assessment." *Id.*, 125 *N.J.* at 528.

"In response to problems surrounding the reporting and prosecution of sexual assault cases, legislatures throughout the United States, including New Jersey, have enacted rape shield laws. * * * Those laws represent a legislative response to the common law rule permitting cross-examination of a rape victim about her prior sexual conduct. Such conduct was traditionally considered evidence of the victim's inclination to consent to sexual intercourse and of her lack of moral character and credibility. * * * Because of the 'character assassination' of the victim, rape trials sometimes degenerated to embarrassing invasions of the victim's privacy." *Id.* at 528-29.

"One of the primary purposes of the statutes is to protect rape victims from excessive cross-examination, thereby encouraging them to report the abuse. * * * The statutes also guard against the improper use of evidence of the victim's prior sexual experience. * * * Thus, in addition to protecting victims of sexual assault, rape-shield statutes preserve the integrity of trials. * * * By ensuring that juries will not base their verdicts on prejudice against the victim, the statutes enhance the reliability of the criminal justice system.

"Consistent with these policies, *N.J.S.[]* 2C:14-7 limits exceptions to the admission of evidence of a victim's previous sexual conduct in prosecutions for sexual assault and criminal sexual contact. When a defendant seeks to offer such evidence for any purpose, the trial court must, under the statute, weigh the probative value of the evidence against its prejudicial effect." *Id.* at 529.

"The statute [requires the trial court, upon such application, to] conduct

> a hearing in camera to determine the admissibility of the evidence. If the court finds that evidence offered by the defendant regarding the sexual conduct of the victim is relevant and that the probative value of the evidence offered is not outweighed by its collateral nature or by the probability that its admission will create undue prejudice, confusion of the issues, or unwarranted invasion of the privacy of the victim, the court shall enter an order setting forth with specificity what evidence may be introduced and the nature of the questions which shall be permitted. * * * [*N.J.S.[]* 2C:14-7(a).]

In addition, the statute prescribes the circumstances under which the trial court may consider the evidence to be relevant. The court may find evidence of prior sexual conduct relevant only if 'it is material to negating the element of force or coercion or to proving that the source of the semen, pregnancy or disease is a person other than defendant.' *N.J.S.[]* 2C:14-7(c). For all other purposes, the statute declares evidence of prior sexual conduct irrelevant. To this extent, the statute differs from *Federal Rule of Evidence* 412, which, in addition to permitting evidence of past sexual behavior to show the source of semen or injury, permits such evidence if 'constitutionally required.' *Fed.R.Evid.* 412(b)(1), (2)." *Id.* at 529-30.

Fed.R.Evid. 404. **Character Evidence Not Admissible to Prove Conduct; Exceptions; Other Crimes.**

*   *   *   *   *

(b) Other crimes, wrongs, or acts. Evidence of other crimes, wrongs, or acts is not admissible to prove the character of a person in order to show action in conformity therewith. It may, however, be admissible for other purposes, such as proof of motive, opportunity, intent, preparation, plan, knowledge, identity, or absence of mistake or accident, provided that upon request by the accused, the prosecution in a criminal case shall provide reasonable notice in advance of trial, or during trial if the court excuses pretrial notice on good cause shown, of the general nature of any such evidence it intends to introduce at trial.

UNITED STATES v. COPELIN
United States Court of Appeals
996 *F*.2d 379 (D.C.Cir. 1993)

MIKVA, Chief Judge.

"Warren Ricardo Copelin appeals his conviction on one count of unlawful distribution of cocaine. He argues that the district court erred by permitting the government to cross-examine him concerning his three positive drug tests for cocaine while on pretrial release." *Id.* at 380. [Mr. Copelin's conviction stemmed from his sale of two rocks of cocaine to an undercover District of Columbia police officer.]

[At trial, over the objection of defense counsel, the trial judge permitted the prosecutor to proceed with the following line of questioning:]

> Q. Now, Mr. Copelin, isn't it true that as a condition of your release pending trial in this case, you were required to report to the Pretrial Services Administration for drug testing?
>
> A. Yes.
>
> Q. And isn't it true that you tested positive for cocaine on June 13th, 1991?
>
> A. Yes.
>
> Q. And you tested positive for cocaine on June 14th, 1991?
>
> A. Yes.
>
> Q. And you tested positive for cocaine on June 21st, 1991?
>
> A. I don't recall that one.
>
> Q. You don't recall that one?
>
> A. No sir.
>
> Q. But despite having tested positive for cocaine on at least two occasions, you're telling the ladies and gentlemen of the jury that you have never seen cocaine except on television?
>
> A. It could be anywhere. I never seen it, never used it.

Id. at 382.

"[A]lthough 'prior bad acts' evidence is not admissible to show a defendant's propensity to commit the crime at issue, there are circumstances under which a court may admit such evidence. * * * [A]n attempt to impeach through contradiction a defendant acting as a witness is indisputably a legitimate reason to introduce evidence of other crimes or wrongs. * * * If 'bad acts' evidence is offered for this reason, it is admissible unless 'its probative value is substantially outweighed by the danger of unfair prejudice' * * *." *Id.* at 382. [Citation omitted.]

"Mr. Copelin's admission as to the positive drug tests clearly tended to contradict his earlier assertion that he had only seen drugs on television. Mr. Copelin responded to the government's initial queries by denying that he had ever had any direct acquaintance with narcotics. It was consequently proper for the district court to permit the government to impeach Mr. Copelin by attempting to demonstrate that this statement was false." *Id.*

NOTE

1. A trial court's decision to allow the government to impeach the defendant's credibility with evidence of "prior bad acts" normally carries with it the responsibility to give the jury an immediate cautionary instruction. Evidence of a prior bad act is not introduced as "substantive" evidence; rather, it is used solely for impeachment. Consequently, the jury should be instructed that the evidence by definition has no direct bearing on any substantive issue at trial, but solely on the credibility of the witness on the stand. Such a limiting instruction ensures that the jury does not cross the boundary between the witness' credibility and substantive issues in its assessment of the prior bad act. *See id. at* 384-386. *See also United States v. Bobbitt*, 450 *F*.2d 685, 691 (D.C.Cir. 1971).

2. Every list of acceptable purposes for "other crimes" evidence begins with the classic five purposes identified by the mnemonic acronym "MIMIC"—1) Motive, 2) Intent, 3) absence of Mistake, 4) Identity, and 5) Common scheme or plan. *State v. Faulkner*, 314 *Md.* 630, 634, 552 *A*.2d 896 (1989).

   (a) Motive. Typically, motive is not a formal element of a crime. Instead, it is a circumstantial fact that in some cases may help to prove guilt. For example, "Which of the weekend guests had a motive to poison the baroness?" *Emory v. State*, 101 *Md.App.* 585, 647 *A*.2d 1243, 1254 (Md.App. 1994). "Other crimes" evidence may be admissible to establish motive in a variety of ways. " 'Evidence of another crime has been admitted to show the likelihood of defendant having committed the charged crime because he needed money, sex, goods to sell, was filled with hostility, sought to conceal a previous crime, or to escape after its commission.' " *Id.* [Citation and footnotes omitted.] *See also Veney v. State*, 251 *Md.* 182, 199-200, 246 *A*.2d 568 (1968) (evidence of armed robbery and of shooting of one police officer by defendant was admissible to show motive for murder of second police officer who tried to arrest him).
   Motive overlaps with a number of other acceptable purposes for introducing "other crimes" evidence. In this respect, showing that a defendant had a motive to commit a crime may also help "to establish that he had the requisite intent to commit the crime. Showing which suspect had a motive to commit a crime, moreover, also

helps to establish the identity of the criminal. Furthermore, the demonstrated possession of a motive helps to show that the criminal act was *neither a mistake nor an accident.*" *Emory* at 1254. [Court's emphasis.]

(b) Intent. Except in crimes of strict liability, intent is a formal element in every criminal trial. Courts generally admit evidence of a prior crime which tends to undermine the defendant's innocent explanation for his actions resulting in the charged offense. In this respect, the more often a similar act has been done, the less likely it is that it could have been done innocently.

(c) Absence of Mistake or Accident. "The analysis is the same with respect to absence of mistake or accident." *Emory* at 1255.

"If the defendant admits that he or she took no action, but claims to have done so unintentionally or by mistake, so that allegations of, for example, forgery, fraud, embezzlement, or malice are unfounded, the prosecution may offer evidence of his or her similar prior wrongs, acts, or crimes. * * *

"Similarly, the defendant may claim the harm he or she is alleged to have caused was not at his or her hands, but was the result of an independent accident. Evidence of prior similar acts is then admissible to show lack of mistake or accident. For example, if a defendant charged with child abuse contends that the child's injuries were caused by an accidental fall, evidence of prior beatings of the child by the defendant will be admissible."

Id. [Citation omitted.]

(d) Identity. "Other crimes" evidence may be admissible if it demonstrates any of the following:

[1]"the defendant's presence at the scene or in the locality of the crime on trial;"

[2]"that the defendant was a member of an organization whose purpose was to commit crimes similar to the one on trial;"

[3]"the defendant's identity from a handwriting exemplar, 'mug shot,' or fingerprint record from a prior arrest, or his identity through a ballistics test;"

[4]"the defendant's identity from a remark made by him;"

[5]"the defendant's prior theft of a gun, car or other object used in the offense on trial;"

[6]"that the defendant was found in possession of articles taken from the victim of the crime on trial;"

[7]"that the defendant had on another occasion used the same alias or the same confederate as was used by the perpetrator of the present crime;"

[8] "that a peculiar *modus operandi* used by the defendant on another occasion was used by the perpetrator of the crime on trial;"

[9]"that on another occasion the defendant was wearing the clothing worn by or was using certain objects used by the perpetrator of the crime at the time it was committed;"

[10]"that the witness' view of the defendant at the other crime enabled him to identify the defendant as the person who committed the crime on trial."

State v. Faulkner, 314 *Md.* 630, 637-40, 552 *A.*2d 896 (1989).

The court in *Faulkner* characterized the *"modus operandi"* phenomenon or "signature crime" evidence as simply a subset of the identity exception. *See id.* at 637-38. To establish identity, one commentator has explained that the introduction of *modus operandi* is permissible to prove

other crimes by the accused so nearly identical in method as to earmark them as the handiwork of the accused. Much more is demanded than the mere repeated commission of crimes of the same class, such as repeated murders, robberies or rapes. The pattern and characteristics of the crimes must be so unusual and distinctive as to be like a signature.

1 McCormick, *Evidence* §190 (4th ed. 1992), at 801-03. [Footnotes omitted.] Thus, if on prior occasions the defendant had used " 'a unique way of defeating a burglar alarm, and the same method was used by the perpetrator of the crime with which he is charged, the evidence may be admitted as proof of identity.' " *Emory v. State, supra* at 1257. [Citation omitted.] *See also United States v. Barrett*, 539 *F.*2d 244 (1st Cir. 1976) (evidence admissible to show familiarity with sophisticated means of neutralizing burglar alarms).

Commonwealth v. Hughes, 521 *Pa.* 423, 555 *A.*2d 1264 (1989), presents a prime example of "signature crime" evidence. In *Hughes*, the defendant was on trial for the March 1, 1979, rape and murder of Rochelle G., a nine-year-old girl. During the trial, the prosecution offered into evidence the testimony of 12-year-old Marie O.

Marie O. testified that the defendant raped her on January 5, 1980. The prosecution established the following similarities between the two crimes:

(1) Both crimes involved young females [Rochelle was nine; Marie was twelve]; (2) both victims were non-Caucasian [Rochelle was Black; Marie was Spanish]; (3) both crimes occurred during the daytime; (4) both crimes took place within a four-block radius; (5) both crimes took place within a five-minute walk from [defendant's] home; (6) both crimes involved circumstances in which the victim was lured or strong-armed off the street; (7) both victims were taken to upstairs bedrooms of vacant buildings; (8) in both crimes, the assailant ordered the victims to undress; (9) both crimes involved rape, other sex acts[,] and manual strangulation; and (10) both crimes involved circumstances in which the accused and the victims were previously acquainted.

Id. at 459, 555 *A*.2d at 1282.

In addition, the prosecution presented evidence that at the Rochelle G. crime scene, the letters "PEA" were burned into the ceiling; and when the defendant was arrested for Rochelle's murder, the police noticed the letters "PEANUT" burned into defendant's bedroom ceiling. At Marie O.'s trial, Marie testified that she knew the defendant as "Peanut" in the community.

Based on the foregoing, the Court did not hesitate to conclude that the crime scenario represented the defendant's signature.

(e) Common scheme or plan. "Wrongful acts planned and committed together may be proved in order to show a continuing plan or common scheme." *Emory* at 1257. The crimes must, however, "so relate to each other that proof of one tends to establish the other." *State v. Jones*, 284 *Md*. 232, 243, 395 *A*.2d 1182 (1979). In order to establish "the existence of a common scheme or plan, it is necessary to prove that the various acts constituting the offenses naturally relate to one another by time, location, circumstances and parties so as to give rise to the conclusion that they are several stages of a continuing transaction." *Id. See also Commonwealth v. Swinson*, 426 *Pa.Super.* 167, 626 *A*.2d 627, 632 (1993) (When the common scheme or plan embraces the commission of two or more crimes, the crimes should be "so related to each other that proof of one tends to prove the others.").

Fed.R.Evid. **405. Methods of Proving Character.**

(a) Reputation or opinion. In all cases in which evidence of character or a trait of character of a person is admissible, proof may be made by testimony as to reputation or by testimony in the form of an opinion. On cross-examination, inquiry is allowable into relevant specific instances of conduct.

(b) Specific instances of conduct. In cases in which character or a trait of character of a person is an essential element of a charge, claim, or defense, proof may also be made of specific instances of that person's conduct.

Fed.R.Evid. **406. Habit; Routine Practice.**

Evidence of the habit of a person or of the routine practice of an organization, whether corroborated or not and regardless of the presence of eyewitnesses, is relevant to prove that the conduct of the person or organization on a particular occasion was in conformity with the habit or routine practice.

STATE v. RADZIWIL
Superior Court of New Jersey, Appellate Division
235 N.J.Super. 557, 563 A.2d 856 (1989)*

SKILLMAN, J.A.D.
"The significant issue presented by this appeal is whether evidence that a defendant regularly became intoxicated every weekend at a particular bar is admissible as evidence of a habit to prove that defendant was intoxicated at the time of the automobile collision which resulted in his conviction for aggravated manslaughter and death by auto. We conclude that such evidence was properly admitted under the circumstances of this case." *Id.*, 235 *N.J.Super.* at 561.

"Defendant's conviction was based on an automobile collision which occurred at the intersection of Route 537 and Paint Island Spring Road in Freehold Township slightly past midnight on November 25, 1984. * * * [T]he only real issues at trial were whether defendant operated his vehicle recklessly by consciously disregarding a substantial and unjustifiable risk that injury or death would result, [] and thus was guilty of death by auto, [] or recklessly 'under circumstances manifesting extreme indifference to human life' and thus was guilty of aggravated manslaughter[.]" *Id.* at 561-63.

"Evidence of defendant's intoxication at the time of the accident was relevant to these issues. Our courts have concluded that a jury may infer that an individual who drives while intoxicated is consciously disregarding the risk of an accident and acting with extreme indifference to human life. * * * However, the prosecutor

---

* *aff'd o.b.*, 121 *N.J.* 527, 582 A.2d 1003 (1990).

lacked direct evidence of defendant's intoxication, because he left the scene of the accident. Therefore, to prove that defendant was intoxicated at the time of the accident, the prosecutor offered testimony by Bernie D'Zurella, the bartender at Rova Farms from 1981 to the end of 1985, that defendant came to Rova Farms just about every weekend until the end of November 1984, and that he always got drunk shortly after arriving. D'Zurella also said that defendant would regularly become loud and obnoxious and that he would be forced to escort him outside the bar." *Id.* at 563.

"Defendant argues that D'Zurella's testimony as to defendant's regular weekend intoxication at Rova Farms was inadmissible evidence of a character trait. He relies upon the rule which prohibits the prosecutor from introducing evidence of a character trait of the defendant unless the defendant offers evidence of good character. [] However, '[e]vidence of habit or custom whether corroborated or not is admissible to prove conduct on a specified occasion in conformity with the habit or custom.' * * * Therefore, the admissibility of D'Zurella's testimony regarding defendant regularly becoming intoxicated at Rova Farms on weekends turns on whether that conduct constitutes a character trait or a habit." *Id.* at 563-64. [Citations omitted.]

Professor McCormick aptly explains the difficulty of distinguishing between character and habit evidence:

> The two are easily confused. People sometimes speak of a habit for care, a habit for promptness, or a habit of forgetfulness. They may say that an individual has a bad habit of stealing or lying. Evidence of these "habits" would be identical to the kind of evidence that is the target of the general rule against character evidence. Character is a generalized description of a person's disposition, or of the disposition in respect to a general trait, such as honesty, temperance or peacefulness. Habit, in the present context, is more specific. It denotes one's regular response to a repeated situation. If we speak of a character for care, we think of the person's tendency to act prudently in all the varying situations of life—in business, at home, in handling automobiles and in walking across the street. A habit, on the other hand, is the person's regular practice of responding to a particular kind of situation with a specific type of conduct. Thus, a person may be in the habit of bounding down a certain stairway two or three steps at a time, of patronizing a particular pub after each day's work, or of driving his automobile without using a seatbelt. The doing of the habitual act may become semi-automatic, as with a driver who invariably signals before changing lanes.
>
> Evidence of habits that come within this definition has greater probative value than does evidence of general traits of character. Furthermore, the potential for prejudice is substantially less. By and large, the detailed patterns of situation-specific behavior that constitute habits are unlikely to provoke such sympathy or antipathy as would distort the process of

evaluating the evidence. [*McCormick, Evidence*, § 195 at 574-575 (3d ed. 1984)]

Id. at 564.

"We are satisfied that this is one of those relatively uncommon cases in which defendant's intoxication was shown to occur with sufficient regularity in a specific situation to justify its admission as evidence of habit. D'Zurella testified that defendant came to Rova Farms nearly every weekend and that he invariably became intoxicated shortly after his arrival there. Since the crime occurred on a weekend and defendant admitted to the investigating officers that he was at Rova Farms that evening, the trial court properly admitted evidence of defendant's regularly becoming intoxicated at Rova Farms to prove that defendant was intoxicated at the time of the crime." *Id.* at 565-66.

NOTE

The probative value of "habit evidence to prove intoxication on a given occasion depends on the 'degree of regularity of the practice and its coincidence with the occasion.'" *Reyes v. Missouri Pacific Railroad Co.*, 589 *F*.2d 791, 795 (5th Cir. 1979). *See also State v. Wadsworth*, 210 *So*.2d 4 (Fla. 1968) (evidence of defendant's habit of purchasing vodka three times a week properly admitted as corroborating evidence of his intoxication at the time of the alleged vehicular manslaughter).

Fed.R.Evid. 607. Who May Impeach. The credibility of a witness may be attacked by any party, including the party calling the witness.

Fed.R.Evid. 608. Evidence of Character and Conduct of Witness.

(a) Opinion and reputation evidence of character. The credibility of a witness may be attacked or supported by evidence in the form of opinion or reputation, but subject to these limitations: (1) the evidence may refer only to character for truthfulness or untruthfulness, and (2) evidence of truthful character is admissible only after the character of the witness for truthfulness has been attacked by opinion or reputation evidence or otherwise.

(b) Specific instances of conduct. Specific instances of the conduct of a witness, for the purpose of attacking or supporting the witness' character for truthfulness, other than conviction of crime as provided in rule 609, may not be proved by extrinsic evidence.[103] They may, however, in the discretion

---

[103] "Extrinsic evidence is evidence offered through other witnesses, rather than through cross-examination of the witness himself or herself." *United States v. McNeill*, 887 *F*.2d 448, 453 (3rd Cir. 1989).

of the court, if probative of truthfulness or untruthfulness, be inquired into on cross-examination of the witness (1) concerning the witness' character for truthfulness or untruthfulness, or (2) concerning the character for truthfulness or untruthfulness of another witness as to which character the witness being cross-examined has testified.

The giving of testimony, whether by an accused or by any other witness, does not operate as a waiver of the accused's or the witness' privilege against self-incrimination when examined with respect to matters which relate only to character for truthfulness.

UNITED STATES v. ABEL
Supreme Court of the United States
469 U.S. 45, 105 S.Ct. 465 (1984)

Mr. Justice REHNQUIST delivered the opinion of the Court.

"[Defendant] John Abel and two cohorts were indicted for robbing a savings and loan in Bellflower, Cal. * * * The cohorts elected to plead guilty, but [defendant] went to trial. One of the cohorts, Kurt Ehle, agreed to testify against [defendant] and identify him as a participant in the robbery." *Id.* at 466.

"[Defendant] informed the District Court at a pretrial conference that he would seek to counter Ehle's testimony with that of Robert Mills. Mills was not a participant in the robbery but was friendly with [defendant] and with Ehle, and had spent time with both in prison. Mills planned to testify that after the robbery Ehle had admitted to Mills that Ehle intended to implicate [defendant] falsely, in order to receive favorable treatment from the Government. The prosecutor in turn disclosed that he intended to discredit Mills' testimony by calling Ehle back to the stand and eliciting from Ehle the fact that [defendant], Mills, and Ehle were all members of the 'Aryan Brotherhood,' a secret prison gang that required its members always to deny the existence of the organization and to commit perjury, theft, and murder on each member's behalf." *Id.*

"We hold that the evidence showing Mills' and [defendant]'s membership in the prison gang was sufficiently probative of Mills' possible bias towards [defendant] to warrant its admission into evidence." *Id.* at 467.

"Both parties correctly assume * * * that the question is governed by the Federal Rules of Evidence. But the Rules do not by their terms deal with impeachment for 'bias,' although they do expressly treat impeachment by character evidence and conduct, Rule 608, by evidence of conviction of a crime, Rule 609, and by showing of religious beliefs or opinion, Rule 610." *Id.*

"Before the present Rules were promulgated, the admissibility of evidence in the federal courts was governed in part by statutes or Rules, and in part by case law. * * * This Court had held in *Alford v. United States*, 282 *U.S.* 687, 51 *S.Ct.* 218 [] (1931), that a trial court must allow some cross-examination of a witness to show bias. * * * Our decision in *Davis v. Alaska*, 415 *U.S.* 308, 94 *S.Ct.* 1105 [] (1974), holds that the Confrontation Clause of the Sixth Amendment requires a defendant to have some opportunity to show bias on the part of a prosecution witness." *Abel* at 468.

"[W]e think it unlikely that [the drafters of the Federal Rules of Evidence] intended to scuttle the evidentiary availability of cross-examination for bias. One commentator, recognizing the omission of any express treatment of impeachment for bias, prejudice, or corruption, observes that the Rules 'clearly contemplate the use of the above-mentioned grounds of impeachment.' E. Cleary, *McCormick on Evidence* §40, p. 85 (3d ed. 1984). Other commentators, without mentioning the omission, treat bias as a permissible and established basis of impeachment under the Rules. * * *" *Abel* at 468.

"We think this conclusion is obviously correct. Rule 401 defines as 'relevant evidence' evidence having any tendency to make the existence of any fact that is of consequence to the determination of the action more probable or less probable than it would be without the evidence. Rule 402 provides that all relevant evidence is admissible, except as otherwise provided by the United States Constitution, by Act of Congress, or by applicable rule. A successful showing of bias on the part of a witness would have a tendency to make the facts to which he testified less probable in the eyes of the jury than it would be without such testimony." *Id.*

"The Courts of Appeals have upheld use of extrinsic evidence to show bias both before and after the adoption of the Federal Rules of Evidence. * * *" *Id.*

"We think the lesson to be drawn from all of this is that it is permissible to impeach a witness by showing his bias under the Federal Rules of Evidence just as it was permissible to do so before their adoption." *Id.* at 468-69.

"Ehle's testimony about the prison gang certainly made the existence of Mills' bias towards [defendant] more probable. Thus it was relevant to support that inference. Bias is a term used in the 'common law of evidence' to describe the relationship between a party and a witness which might lead the witness to slant, unconsciously or otherwise, his testimony in favor or against a party. Bias may be introduced by a witness' like, dislike, or fear of a party, or by the witness' self-interest. Proof of bias is almost always relevant because the jury, as finder of fact and weigher of credibility, has historically been entitled to assess all evidence which might bear on the accuracy and truth of a witness' testimony. The 'common law of evidence' allowed the showing of bias by extrinsic evidence, while requiring the cross-examiner to 'take the answer of the witness' with respect to less favored forms of impeachment." *Id.* at 469.

"Mills' and [defendant]'s membership in the Aryan Brotherhood supported the inference that Mills' testimony was slanted or perhaps fabricated in [defendant]'s favor. A witness' and a party's common membership in an organization, even without proof that the witness or party has personally adopted its tenets, is certainly probative of bias." *Id.*

"[T]he *type* of organization in which a witness and a party share membership may be relevant to show bias. If the organization is a loosely knit group having nothing to do with the subject matter of the [case], the inference of bias arising from common membership may be small or nonexistent. If the prosecutor had elicited that both [defendant] and Mills belonged to the Book of the Month Club, the jury probably would not have inferred bias * * *. The attributes of the Aryan Brotherhood—a secret prison sect sworn to perjury and self-protection—bore directly not only on the fact of bias but also on the source and strength of Mills' bias. The tenets of this group showed that Mills had a powerful motive to slant his testimony towards [defendant], or even commit perjury outright." *Id.* at 470. [Court's emphasis.]

"[Accordingly,] the evidence of Mills' membership in an organization having the tenets ascribed to the Aryan Brotherhood * * * was * * * admissible to show bias." *Id.* at 471.

UNITED STATES v. FOSHER
United States Court of Appeals
568 *F.*2d 207 (1st Cir. 1978)

TUTTLE, Circuit Judge.

"[D]efendant, Michael Fosher, was indicted for armed robbery of a federally insured bank and assault of bank employees with a dangerous weapon. Following a three-day jury trial, defendant was convicted of both offenses. He did not testify in his own defense. On appeal, defendant contends that the district court committed reversible error by admitting into evidence a 'mug shot' taken of him in connection with an earlier and unconnected arrest. Because the probative value of the mug shot in identifying defendant as one of the robbers was outweighed by the potential prejudice flowing from its admission into evidence, we conclude that the defendant is entitled to a new trial. Accordingly, we reverse." *Id.* at 208.

"The Commercial Bank and Trust Company is located in a small shopping center adjacent to and to the rear of a 'Value King' supermarket. On the morning of the robbery, government witness, Albert Rankin, made a business call at the supermarket, parking his automobile in front of the store. At approximately 10:20 a.m., some ten minutes before the robbers struck, Mr. Rankin * * * came face-to-face with two individuals [in the parking lot,] one of whom he later identified as the defendant. * * * Following this brief, five-second encounter, Rankin returned to the Value King and was unable to observe the men enter or depart the bank." *Id.* at 209.

"A short time after the robbery, Rankin accompanied a police detective to the [] police station where Rankin executed a written account of the events * * * and provided a description of the individual whose face he had seen. Later in the day, * * * Rankin assisted local FBI agents in constructing a composite sketch." *Id.*

"[S]ome 10 days after the robbery * * *, Agent Cullen displayed to Rankin an array of eight mug shots, from which Rankin selected a single picture. This photograph, which had been taken of defendant at some point in the past, supposedly depicted the man Rankin saw near the bank." *Id.*

"At trial, Mr. Rankin described his chance encounter outside the bank and his various sessions with the police and FBI. On direct examination, Rankin not only testified with respect to a prior corporeal identification, but also made a positive in-court identification of defendant. Apparently not content with this identification testimony, the government proceeded to question Rankin concerning his pretrial photographic identification. * * * [T]he government [then] tendered into evidence the mug shot of defendant and the remaining seven mug shots viewed by Rankin." *Id.* at 209-210.

"On cross-examination, defendant's counsel launched a vigorous assault on virtually every aspect of Rankin's identification testimony. [Among the various arguments, defendant's counsel urged] at a bench conference that

> [the] pictures [were] obviously mugshot-type pictures taken from a police mugshot collection. And although . . . the numbers [were] blacked out, . . . the clear inference . . . [was] that [the defendant] and others in the pictures had been in trouble before.

These protestations proved unsuccessful, and the mug shots were admitted into evidence." *Id.* at 210.

"It is a basic tenet of our jurisprudence that evidence of a criminal defendant's prior criminal acts, which are not charged in the indictment or information, is inadmissible when the defendant elects not to testify. * * * This is but a specific instance of the broader prohibition against permitting the government initially to place the defendant's character in issue." *Id.* at 211-12.

"[T]he jury is required to determine a defendant's guilt or innocence of the crime charged solely on the basis of evidence relevant to that particular crime. A conviction should not be permitted because the jury believes the defendant to be a person of bad character or because of a notion that since he committed some other crime, he must also have committed the crime for which he is being tried. The wisdom and soundness of the rule are beyond dispute." *Id.* at 212.

"As is often the case, however, the general rule is not absolute. Several well-circumscribed exceptions exist as a result of judicial and legislative pragmatism. The current approach, embodied in the Federal Rules of Evidence, provides that

> [e]vidence of other crimes, wrongs, or acts is not admissible to prove the character of a person in order to show that he acted in conformity therewith. *It may, however, be admissible for other purposes, such as proof of motive, opportunity, intent, preparation, plan, knowledge, identity, or absence of mistake or accident.*

Fed.R.Evid. 404(b). [Court's emphasis.] Rule 404(b) is not exclusionary. Rather, it permits the introduction of prior-crimes evidence *unless* the sole purpose for the offer is to establish the defendant's propensity for crime. * * * The admissibility inquiry, however, involves not simply a pigeonholing of proffered evidence within one or several of the specified categories. The problems of minimizing the dangers of prejudice without extensive sacrifice of relevant evidence cannot be resolved satisfactorily by resort to so mechanical a process. The task is one of balancing, and if the probative value of the evidence does not outweigh the prejudice to the defendant that may result from its admission, such evidence must be excluded." *Id.* at 212-13.

"As an initial proposition, we recognize that mug shots from a police department 'rogues' gallery' are generally indicative of past criminal conduct and will likely create in the minds of the jurors an inference of such behavior.

> The double-shot picture, with front and profile shots alongside each other, is so familiar, from "wanted" posters in the post office, motion pictures and television, that the inference that the person involved has a criminal record, or has at least been in trouble with the police, is natural, perhaps automatic.

Barns v. United States, [] 365 *F.*2d 509, 510-11 ([Fed. Cir.] 1966). The government, however, often finds it necessary to introduce such photographs as part of its effort to identify the defendant and thereby prove its case. Indeed, the evidentiary value of a pretrial photographic identification is extremely high. * * * These conflicting interests—the government's need to introduce such evidence to prove its case, and the defendant's right to freedom from the possibility of conviction based on suspicion of other crimes— have created difficulties for the district courts * * *. While each decision necessarily has turned on the particular factual setting presented, we discern several general principles from our reading of the cases." *Fosher* at 213.

"In most instances, mug shots have been introduced to buttress or corroborate a witness' in-court identification, because of either doubts created during cross-examination, * * * or a witness' hesitancy or inability to make a positive identification during trial. * * * This court previously has approved of both tactics. * * * While the precise timing of the introduction has caused the courts little concern, that factor constitutes an integral component of a broader and more critical inquiry—the government's need to introduce such photographs. The cases instruct that where other credible evidence is available to identify the defendant as the perpetrator of the crime charged, a substantial risk is involved in the introduction of mug shots." *Id.*

"[A critical question] concerns the physical appearance of the photographs themselves. Since it is the inference of prior criminal behavior created in the minds of the jurors which is sought to be avoided, the visual message conveyed by a photograph assumes heightened importance. In an area of the law fraught with necessarily imprecise standards, most courts have held that it is error for the prosecution, over objection, to display to jurors police photographs which, because of police or prison identification numbers or other written notations, clearly convey the fact of prior trouble with the law. * * * On the other hand, assuming the requisite probative value can be found, most courts have concluded that it is permissible to introduce such photographs over defense opposition if all incriminating indicia are concealed or removed. * * * This presupposes, of course, that the photographs are masked in a competent fashion, outside the presence of the jury." *Id.* at 214.

"A final factor found to weigh heavily in the balance is the manner in which the photographic evidence is introduced. Comments or actions in connection with the proffer of a mug shot, which could lead the jury to infer that there is something extremely damaging or suspicious about the photograph itself, may inject reversible error into the trial." *Id.*

"Our careful consideration of [numerous] cases reveals that no court has yet adopted a *per se* rule to govern the introduction of mug-shot photographs. Because of the sensitive and competing interests involved, such an approach certainly would prove unsatisfactory. We do conclude, however, that there will normally exist three prerequisites to a ruling that the admission of these photographs does not amount to an abuse of discretion:

1. The Government must have a demonstrable need to introduce the photographs; and

2. The photographs themselves, if shown to the jury, must not imply that the defendant has a prior criminal record; and

3. The manner of introduction at trial must be such that it does not draw particular attention to the source or implications of the photographs.

* * * While it should be clear to all, we reiterate that this test presupposes that the photographs themselves are relevant to a material issue at hand. *See Fed.R.Evid.* 404(b)." *Id.* at 214-15.

"The test we have outlined is a difficult one to apply, requiring as it does an inherently imprecise determination of the impressions conveyed to jurors through photographic evidence. In the circumstances of this case, however, in which the evidence of defendant's guilt was less than overwhelming, we hold that the district court abused its discretion in admitting a photograph which on its face implied prior criminal conduct on defendant's part. While the photograph was not without probative value, this value was substantially outweighed * * * in the circumstances of this case, especially as the pictures could easily have been modified so as to avoid characteristics which would cause the jury to identify the defendant as having a prior record. The masking that was attempted was so inartful and incomplete as merely to invite the jury's attention to these prejudicial matters." *Id.* at 216-17.

REVERSED and REMANDED for a new trial.

UNITED STATES v. WILLIAMS
United States Court of Appeals
739 *F.*2d 297 (7th Cir. 1984)

FLAUM, Circuit Judge.

"This is an appeal from a conviction following a jury trial in which the defendant was found guilty on four counts of transporting stolen motor vehicles in interstate commerce * * *." *Id.* at 298.

"Several years ago, the Federal Bureau of Investigation (FBI) established an undercover business in southern Missouri. This business purchased salvaged wrecked automobiles from insurance companies and sold the public Vehicle Identification Number (VIN) tags to persons who then used them to retag stolen automobiles and sell them. The purpose of the FBI operation was to investigate and identify persons involved in the retagging of stolen automobiles in the St. Louis, Missouri, area. As a result of this FBI investigation, the defendant was implicated in a scheme involving the theft, retagging, and resale of four automobiles." *Id.*

"[One] error alleged by the defendant occurred during the testimony of one of the prosecution's witnesses, a detective with the St. Louis Police Department. The prosecutor asked the detective whether the defendant was known by any aliases. The defense counsel objected, but the trial court permitted the detective to state that he knew the defendant as 'Fast Eddie.' The defendant contends that this testimony caused him undue prejudice and should not have been permitted." *Id.* at 299.

"The defendant argues not only that 'Fast Eddie' is a nickname suggesting a bad character, but also that the fact that a police detective stated that he knew the defendant as 'Fast Eddie' intimated to the jury that the defendant was known to be involved in criminal activity. * * * The government responds by contending that 'Fast Eddie' is a 'neutral' name that did not suggest that the defendant had a criminal reputation or background * * *." *Id.*

"We find it self-evident that the testimony of a police detective stating that he knew the defendant as 'Fast Eddie' might suggest to the jury that the defendant had some sort of history of, or reputation for unsavory activity. We also agree with the defendant that the detective's testimony should have been excluded from evidence as more prejudicial than probative. As many courts have recognized, a prosecutor may introduce evidence of a defendant's aliases or nickname if this evidence aids in the identification of the defendant or in some other way directly relates to the proof of the acts charged in the indictment. *See e.g., United States v. Kalish*, 690 *F.*2d 1144, 1155 (5th Cir. 1982) [] (defendant's alias admissible where it was used to conceal identity from arresting officer). * * * In [this] case, however, the detective's testimony about the defendant's nickname was completely unrelated to any of the other proof against the defendant. The prosecution's only possible purpose in eliciting the testimony was to create an impression in the minds of the jurors that the defendant was known by the police to be an unsavory character or even a criminal. Thus, the detective's statement was tantamount to testimony about a defendant's character that is proffered to show the probability that the defendant acted in conformity with that character in a particular case. This type of evidence, of course, is not permitted in the prosecution's case-in-chief, on the theory that it causes defendants undue prejudice and denies defendants the opportunity to defend against the particular charges against them. *Fed.R.Evid.* 404(a); *Michelson v. United States* * * *. Therefore, it was improper for the prosecutor to elicit the gratuitous testimony about the defendant's nickname, and the testimony should not have been permitted." *Williams* at 299-300.

"We [further] hold that on the facts of this case the testimony concerning 'Fast Eddie' was unduly prejudicial to the defendant's defense * * * since the defendant's only defense was that he did not know that the vehicles that he was transporting were stolen. It is quite possible that this would be viewed as an unlikely story when told by someone known to the police as 'Fast Eddie.' The testimony also was particularly prejudicial because no other evidence relating to the defendant's character, reputation, or criminal past was introduced at trial. The court had ruled prior to trial that evidence of an earlier criminal conviction would be admissible to impeach the defendant's credibility as a witness. However, the defendant elected not to take the stand, and this evidence never was introduced. Thus, by the time the case was submitted to the jury, the detective's testimony about 'Fast Eddie' had gained significance as the only evidence relating to the defendant's character, reputation, or background." *Id.* at 300-01.

"Accordingly, we vacate the defendant's conviction and remand for a new trial." *Id.* at 301.

Fed.R.Evid. **609. Impeachment by Evidence of Conviction of Crime.**

(a) General rule. For the purpose of attacking the credibility of a witness,

> **(1)** evidence that a witness other than an accused has been convicted of a crime shall be admitted, subject to Rule 403, if the crime was punishable by death or imprisonment in excess of one year under the law under which the witness was convicted, and evidence that an accused has been convicted of such a crime shall be admitted if the court determines that the probative value of admitting this evidence outweighs its prejudicial effect to the accused; and

> **(2)** evidence that any witness has been convicted of a crime shall be admitted if it involved dishonesty or false statement, regardless of the punishment.

(b) Time limit. Evidence of a conviction under this rule is not admissible if a period of more than ten years has elapsed since the date of the conviction or of the release of the witness from the confinement imposed for that conviction, whichever is the later date, unless the court determines, in the interests of justice, that the probative value of the conviction supported by specific facts and circumstances substantially outweighs its prejudicial effect. However, evidence of a conviction more than 10 years old as calculated herein, is not admissible unless the proponent gives to the adverse party sufficient advance written notice of intent to use such evidence to provide the adverse party with a fair opportunity to contest the use of such evidence.

(c) Effect of pardon, annulment, or certificate of rehabilitation. Evidence of a conviction is not admissible under this rule if (1) the conviction has been the subject of a pardon, annulment, certificate of rehabilitation, or other equivalent procedure based on a finding of the rehabilitation of the person convicted, and that person has not been convicted of a subsequent crime which was punishable by death or imprisonment in excess of one year, or (2) the conviction has been the subject of a pardon, annulment, or other equivalent procedure based on a finding of innocence.

(d) Juvenile adjudications. Evidence of juvenile adjudications is generally not admissible under this rule. * * *

(e) Pendency of appeal. The pendency of an appeal therefrom does not render evidence of a conviction inadmissible. Evidence of the pendency of an appeal is admissible.

STATE v. SANDS
Supreme Court of New Jersey
76 *N.J.* 127, 386 *A.*2d 378 (1978)

The opinion of the Court was delivered by

SCHREIBER, J.

* * * * *

"We granted [defendant's] petition for certification limited to the question of admissibility of prior convictions to attack credibility." *Id.*, 76 *N.J.* at 132.

"At common law a criminal defendant could not testify on his own behalf. * * * This prohibition existed irrespective of the qualifications of a witness[.] The qualifications of a witness were declared by the Legislature in a statute enacted on June 7, 1799, which provided

> [t]hat no person, who shall be convicted of blasphemy, treason, murder, piracy, arson, rape, sodomy, or the infamous crime against nature, committed with mankind or beast, polygamy, robbery, conspiracy, forgery, or larceny of above the value of six dollars, shall, in any case, be admitted as a witness, unless he or she be first pardoned; and no person, who shall be convicted of perjury, of subornation of perjury, although pardoned for the same, shall be admitted as a witness in any case. * * *

The 1799 statute did not affect the general disqualification of a criminal defendant to testify on his own behalf. It applied to any witness as distinguished from a defendant who had been convicted of one of the enumerated crimes." *Id.* at 134.

"In 1871, the Legislature finally lifted the common law prohibition against a criminal defendant's testifying on his own behalf. * * * Therefore, until 1871, a defendant could not testify even if he had not been convicted of any of the crimes listed in the 1799 act." *Id.*

"In 1874 the 1799 act was repealed. As a result, between 1871 and 1874, a criminal defendant, like any other witness, could testify provided he had not been convicted of any of the offenses listed in the 1799 act, and, if he did testify, prior convictions would not be used to affect his credibility. * * * [T]he 1874 act was intended to remove the harsh disability imposed by the 1799 statute on persons convicted of the enumerated crimes[, but as interpreted, allowed for the use of any] prior convictions for impeachment[.]" *Id*. at 135.

"[In this case we now determine that *not] every criminal conviction is automatically admissible under all circumstances to affect the credibility of a criminal defendant*." Id. at 138. [Emphasis added.]

"It is [] well established that a trial judge has broad discretion in controlling the scope of cross-examination to test credibility[, and] * * * it seems reasonable to conclude that a similar discretion [exists] in connection with prior conviction evidence." *Id*. at 140-42.

"We hold that whether a prior conviction may be admitted into evidence against a criminal defendant rests within the sound discretion of the trial judge. His discretion is a broad one which should be guided by the considerations which follow. Ordinarily, evidence of prior convictions should be admitted and the burden of proof to justify exclusion rests on the defendant." *Id*. at 144.

"*The key to exclusion is remoteness. Remoteness* cannot ordinarily be determined by the passage of time alone. *The nature of the convictions will probably be a significant factor. Serious crimes, including those involving lack of veracity, dishonesty or fraud, should be considered as having a weightier effect* than, for example, a conviction of death by reckless driving. In other words, a lapse of the same time period might justify exclusion of evidence of one conviction, and not another. *The trial court must balance the lapse of time and the nature of the crime to determine whether the relevance with respect to credibility outweighs the prejudicial effect to the defendant*. Moreover, it is appropriate for the trial court in exercising its discretion to consider intervening convictions between the past conviction and the crime for which the defendant is being tried. *When a defendant has an extensive prior criminal record, indicating that he has contempt for the bounds of behavior placed on all citizens, his burden should be a heavy one in attempting to exclude all such evidence*. A jury has the right to weigh whether one who repeatedly refuses to comply with society's rules is more likely to ignore the oath requiring veracity on the witness stand than a law abiding citizen. If a person has been convicted of a series of crimes through the years, then conviction of the earliest crime, although committed many years before, as well as intervening convictions, should be admissible." *Id*. at 144-45. [Emphasis added.]

"In summary then, we hold that [the rules of evidence do] not mandate that every prior conviction be admitted into evidence to affect credibility. The trial judge shall admit evidence of criminal convictions to affect credibility of a criminal defendant unless in his discretion he finds that its probative force because of its remoteness, giving due consideration to relevant circumstances such as the nature of the crime, and intervening incarcerations and convictions, is substantially outweighed so that its admission will create undue prejudice. By recognizing this discretionary power in the trial judges, we shall have removed an obstacle 'in their conscientious efforts to insure fair trial and do justice.' " *Id.* at 147. [Citation omitted.]

PASHMAN, J., concurring.

"I join with the forward looking opinion of the Court. * * * Nevertheless my uneasiness over the amount of discretion vested in the trial judge by the Court prompts me to note my views on that issue separately." *Id.* at 147-48.

"[] I believe that where the defendant has maintained an unblemished criminal record for ten consecutive years since release from confinement or other sentencing conditions of a given prior offense, the burden should shift to the State to justify the admission of such a remote conviction. Placing the burden on the State would be appropriate as it would limit the discretion of the judge and would also protect a defendant from automatically risking what is effectively a form of double jeopardy for a mistake for which he was long before held accountable by society." *Id.* at 149-50.

"In determining whether to admit evidence of prior convictions a trial judge must be mindful of one overriding consideration. He should ask himself whether admission of defendant's prior convictions for impeachment purposes will deny that defendant a trial focused only on the crime he is presently accused of committing by improperly deflecting the jury's consideration to his perceived evil character. In a close case the ever-present danger that such prejudice will result from admitting a prior conviction should tip the scales in favor of exclusion. A defendant deserves a trial on the merits, not on his past demerits." *Id.* at 150.

STATE v. BRUNSON
Supreme Court of New Jersey
132 *N.J.* 377, 625 A.2d 1085 (1993)

The opinion of the Court was delivered by

STEIN, J.

"*N.J.S.[]* 2A:81-12 permits the introduction into evidence of a witness' prior convictions for the purpose of affecting the credibility of that witness. We interpreted that statute in *State v. Sands* * * *. In *Sands*, we set forth broad guidelines for trial courts to follow in deciding whether the probative value of a prior conviction with respect to credibility outweighs the likelihood that its admission will create undue prejudice." *Id.*, 132 *N.J.* at 379.

"In this case we consider whether admission into evidence of defendant's prior convictions for offenses similar to the charged offenses unfairly prejudiced defendant. We also consider whether evidence of prior convictions similar to charged offenses generally should be 'sanitized' by limiting the evidence of prior similar-crime convictions so that the jury is not informed of the substantial similarity of the prior crime to the charged crime." *Id.*

[Defendant was indicted for the possession of a controlled dangerous substance, cocaine, the possession of that substance with the intent to distribute, resisting arrest, and hindering apprehension or prosecution.]

"At a pre-trial hearing, the State indicated that if defendant were to testify, it would offer defendant's prior convictions to impeach his credibility. In 1987, defendant had pleaded guilty to possession of a controlled dangerous substance, possession of a controlled dangerous substance with intent to distribute, and theft. * * * Over defendant's objections, the trial court ruled that defendant's prior convictions would be admissible to impeach defendant's credibility if he were to testify." *Id.* at 381-82.

"Defendant did not testify at trial. He was advised by counsel that he had a right to testify and that the State could introduce his prior convictions to affect his credibility." *Id.* at 382.

"The jury returned a 'guilty' verdict on all counts. * * *

"*N.J.S.[]* 2A:81-12 is based on the widespread belief that a criminal conviction is probative of a witness' credibility. * * * '[T]here is a basis in reason and experience why one may place more credence in the testimony of one who has lived within the rules of society and the discipline of the law than in that of one who has so demonstrated antisocial tendency as to be involved in and convicted of serious crime.' " *Id.* at 384.

"Although prior-conviction evidence is effective in impeaching a defendant's credibility, concern frequently is raised about the extent to which juries consider that evidence as proof of guilt. Commentators generally agree that the use of prior-conviction evidence is fraught with a high risk of prejudice, and they express skepticism about the effectiveness of an instruction to the jury to limit its use of the evidence to an assessment of defendant's credibility. * * * Critics of prior-conviction impeachment evidence are concerned with a jury's tendency to convict a defendant if it knows the defendant previously has committed a crime. As one commentator explains, 'The theory of "limited use" under which such explosive evidence is put before the jury fails to correspond to the actual effect of the evidence even in the minds of the most sober and conscientious jurors.' * * * The risk that juries will use such evidence for an impermissible purpose is particularly high if the prior conviction is for a similar crime. * * * Nevertheless, the rationale for admitting prior-conviction evidence is that the jury is able to follow a trial court's limiting instruction and consider evidence of a prior conviction only to assess a defendant's credibility and not consider such evidence in assessing the likelihood of his or her guilt." *Id.* at 385-86. [Citations omitted.]

200

"Professors Wissler and Saks conducted a study of jurors' use of prior-conviction evidence * * *. Wissler & Saks, *On the Inefficacy of Limiting Instructions*, 9 *J.L.Hum.Behav.* 37, 39 (1985). They concluded that prior-conviction evidence did not affect significantly the predisposition of jurors to doubt the credibility of criminal defendants. However, their study determined that the rate of conviction varied depending upon the type of crime previously committed, the highest conviction rate resulting when the prior crime was the same as the charged offense. * * * Those results corroborated the findings of several earlier studies." *Id.* at 386-87. [Citations omitted.]

"Other jurisdictions have acknowledged and attempted to address the problem presented when a defendant previously has been convicted of a similar offense. One approach has been to exclude evidence of a prior conviction if it is similar to the offense charged and other convictions are available to impeach a defendant. * * *" *Id.* at 387.

"Several courts have allowed the prosecution to introduce evidence of a criminal defendant's prior conviction of a crime similar to the charged offense without permitting evidence of the specific crime, a procedure often referred to as 'sanitization.' * * * Sanitization of a defendant's prior convictions allows the jury to use evidence of such convictions to assess credibility; however, exclusion of any evidence describing the specific offense reduces the risk of impermissible use by the jury." *Id.* at 387-88.

"The rule in this state for admission of prior convictions to affect credibility does not distinguish between crimes that involve dishonesty and those that do not. The analogous federal rule and several similar state formulations mandate the admission of evidence of crimes involving dishonesty and false statements and permit the introduction of other felony convictions if the probative value outweighs the prejudicial effect. * * * The New Jersey Legislature * * * thus expressed its view that any prior conviction has probative value with respect to a criminal defendant's credibility." *Id.* at 388.

"In *Sands, supra*, we held that trial courts should admit evidence of a prior criminal conviction unless, because of its remoteness, its probative force on the issue of the defendant's credibility is substantially outweighed by the prejudicial effect of its admission." *Brunson* at 390.

"The introduction into evidence of a similar prior conviction to impeach a testifying defendant is doubtless highly prejudicial, and that prejudice is unlikely to be cured by a limiting instruction. A limiting instruction imposes on a juror the difficult burden of distinguishing the subtle difference between the impermissible use of prior-conviction evidence to assess the likelihood of a defendant's guilt, and the permitted use of the same evidence to assess that defendant's credibility. Nevertheless, just as the State may impeach the credibility of a defendant who has been convicted of a dissimilar crime, the State is entitled to impeach the credibility of a criminal defendant who previously has been convicted of a similar crime." *Id.* at 391.

"To accommodate those competing principles, we modify our ruling in *Sands* and hold that in those cases in which a testifying defendant previously has been convicted of a crime that is the same or similar to the offense charged, the State may introduce evidence of the defendant's prior conviction limited to the degree of the crime and the date of the offense but excluding any evidence of the specific crime of which defendant was convicted. That method of impeachment will insure that a prior offender does not appear to the jury as a citizen of unassailable veracity and simultaneously will protect a defendant against the risk of impermissible use by the jury of prior-conviction evidence. The balance struck adequately vindicates the State's interest in using the prior conviction to cast doubt on the defendant's credibility without subjecting defendant 'to the extraordinary prejudice that follows if the prior crime was specifically named or described.' " *Id.* at 391-92. [Citation omitted.]

"A defendant wary of jury speculation about the unspecified offense may introduce evidence of the nature of the prior conviction. Sanitization of prior-conviction evidence of similar crimes merely limits the scope of the prosecution's cross-examination of a defendant to the date, degree, and number of similar prior convictions. A defendant may choose to waive the protection afforded by that limitation." *Id.* at 392.

"Prior to defendant's trial in [this] case, the court ruled admissible for impeachment purposes defendant's prior convictions for possession of a controlled dangerous substance, possession of a controlled dangerous substance with intent to distribute, and theft. Defendant contends that to avoid the prejudicial effect of the introduction into evidence of the two similar prior convictions, he did not testify at trial." *Id.* at 393.

"Because that pre-trial ruling is in conflict with the rule we now adopt for admission of evidence of prior similar convictions, we reverse defendant's conviction and remand for a new trial." *Id.*

"[In sum, t]o impeach the credibility of a testifying defendant, the State may introduce into evidence only the number, degree, and date of the defendant's prior similar convictions. When a defendant has multiple prior convictions, some of which are similar to the charged offense and some of which are dissimilar, the State may introduce evidence only of the date and degree of crime of all of the defendant's prior convictions, but cannot specify the nature of the offenses. Alternatively, the State may introduce without limitation evidence of only the dissimilar convictions. * * *" *Id.* at 394.

Chapter 5

EYEWITNESS IDENTIFICATION EVIDENCE

§5.1. INTRODUCTION

As a general principle of constitutional criminal procedure, the Fifth Amendment command that "[n]o person * * * shall be compelled in any criminal case to be a witness against himself[,]" "does not protect a suspect from being compelled by the State to provide 'real or physical evidence.'"[1] Instead, the privilege against self-incrimination "protects an accused only from being compelled to testify against himself, or otherwise provide the State with evidence of a testimonial or communicative nature."[2] In order "to be testimonial, an accused's communication must itself, explicitly or implicitly, relate a factual assertion or disclose information. Only then is a person compelled to be a 'witness' against himself."[3]

Over time, the United States Supreme Court has held that certain acts, though incriminating, are not within the Fifth Amendment privilege. For example, a suspect may be compelled to furnish a blood sample,[4] to provide a handwriting exemplar,[5] or a voice exemplar,[6] to stand in a lineup,[7] and to wear particular clothing.[8] In each of these cases, the Court held that the Fifth Amendment privilege was not implicated because the suspect was not required "to disclose any knowledge he might have," or "to speak his guilt."[9] Rather, "[i]t is the 'extortion of information from the accused,' * * * the attempt to force him 'to disclose the contents of his own mind,' * * * that implicates the Self-Incrimination Clause."[10]

---

[1] *Pennsylvania v. Muniz,* 496 *U.S.* 582, 110 *S.Ct.* 2638, 2643 (1990).

[2] *Schmerber v. California,* 384 *U.S.* 757, 761, 86 *S.Ct.* 1826, 1830 (1966).

[3] *Doe v. United States,* 487 *U.S.* 201, 210, 108 *S.Ct.* 2341, 2347 (1988).

[4] *Schmerber, supra,* 384 *U.S.* at 765, 86 *S.Ct.* at 1832.

[5] *Gilbert v. California,* 388 *U.S.* 263, 266-267, 87 *S.Ct.* 1951, 1953 (1967).

[6] *United States v. Dionisio,* 410 *U.S.* 1, 7, 93 *S.Ct.* 764, 768 (1973).

[7] *United States v. Wade,* 388 *U.S.* 218, 221-222, 87 *S.Ct.* 1926, 1929 (1967).

[8] *Holt v. United States,* 218 *U.S.* 245, 252-253, 31 *S.Ct.* 2, 6 (1910).

[9] *Wade* at 222-223, 87 *S.Ct.* at 1929-1930.

[10] *Doe, supra,* 108 *S.Ct.* at 2348. (citations omitted).

Accordingly, the Fifth Amendment privilege to be free from self-incrimination is a "bar against compelling 'communications' or 'testimony,' but * * * compulsion which makes a suspect or accused the source of 'real or physical evidence' does not violate it."[11] For purposes of this chapter, then, causing a suspect or an accused to stand for a showup or lineup, or placing a photograph of a suspect or an accused in a photographic array, does not implicate the Fifth Amendment privilege to be free from self-incrimination. The method or procedure, however, if employed in an unnecessarily suggestive manner, can nonetheless have constitutional ramifications.

The Fourteenth Amendment to the United States Constitution provides in pertinent part:

> No State shall * * * deprive any person of life, liberty, or property, without *due process of law;* * * * [Emphasis added.]

and it is the Due Process Clause which will invalidate an unnecessarily suggestive eyewitness identification.

While each case will be considered on its own facts, a court will nonetheless invalidate an in-court eyewitness identification when it follows a pretrial identification procedure which was "so impermissibly suggestive as to give rise to a very substantial likelihood of irreparable misidentification."[12] Here, the relationship between suggestiveness and misidentification becomes significant, for as the degree of suggestiveness increases, the likelihood of misidentification similarly increases.

The "very substantial likelihood of irreparable misidentification" standard is the general determining factor of whether an "in-court identification would be admissible in the wake of a suggestive out-of-court identification[.]"[13] When the word "irreparable" is deleted, we come to the "standard for the admissibility of testimony concerning the out-of-court identification itself."[14] Thus, it is this substantial "likelihood of misidentification which violates a defendant's right to due process,"[15] which then forms the basis for the exclusion of the identification as evidence in court.

The admissibility of eyewitness identification evidence may be challenged by a defendant prior to trial, or outside the presence of the jury, at a proceeding called a *"Wade* hearing."[16] It is the defendant's

---

[11] *Schmerber* at 764, 86 *S.Ct.* at 1832.

[12] *Simmons v. United States,* 390 *U.S.* 377, 384, 88 *S.Ct.* 967, 971 (1968).

[13] *Neil v. Biggers,* 409 *U.S.* 188, 198, 93 *S.Ct.* 375, 381 (1972).

[14] *Id.* at 198, 93 *S.Ct.* at 381.

[15] *Id.* at 198, 93 *S.Ct.* at 381, 382.

[16] *United States v. Wade,* 388 *U.S.* 218, 87 *S.Ct.* 1926 (1967).

burden, however, to establish the need for such a hearing. The defendant must preliminarily show the court "some evidence" of impermissible suggestiveness before he or she would be entitled to the hearing.[17] If the defendant satisfies his or her preliminary burden of producing some evidence of impermissible suggestiveness, a *Wade* hearing is held and the judge must first decide whether the suggestive out-of-court identification procedure was in fact "impermissibly" suggestive. If it is determined that the identification procedure was impermissibly suggestive, the prosecution has the burden of establishing that the identification had a source independent of the police-conducted identification procedure. The court must then decide, based on the factors listed below, whether the suggestive out-of-court identification procedure will result in a very substantial likelihood of misidentification in court. If so, the court will disallow any evidence related to, or testimony concerning the out-of-court identification.

The ultimate inquiry will always turn on whether the eyewitness identification, in light of the totality of the circumstances, was "reliable."[18] "Reliability," then, is "the linchpin in determining the admissibility of identification testimony[,]"[19] and it may be assessed by examining such factors as:

[1. T]he opportunity of the witness to view the criminal at the time of the crime [including items such as length of time viewed, lighting, whether face-to-face or side view, or, whether casual observer or direct victim of the crime[;][20]

[2. T]he witness' degree of attention[;][21]

[3. T]he accuracy of the witness' prior description of the criminal[;][22]

[4. T]he level of certainty demonstrated by the witness at the confrontation[;][23] and

[5. T]he length of time between the crime and the confrontation.[24]

---

17 *Watkins v. Sowders*, 449 *U.S.* 341, 101 *S.Ct.* 654 (1981).

18 *Neil v. Biggers, supra*, 409 *U.S.* at 198, 93 *S.Ct.* at 382.

19 *Manson v. Brathwaite*, 432 *U.S.* 98, 114, 93 *S.Ct.* 2243, 2253 (1977).

20 *Neil v. Biggers, supra*, 409 *U.S.* at 199, 93 *S.Ct.* at 382.

21 *Id.* at 199, 93 *S.Ct.* at 382.

22 *Id.*

23 *Id.*

24 *Id.*

Although many commentators explain "that eyewitness evidence is inherently suspect and that suggestive procedures may prejudicially affect the ultimate identification," it is also true that in criminal actions an eyewitness' identification may be the most crucial evidentiary part of the case.[25] Significantly, many prosecutions can be proved *only* through the use of the testimony of an eyewitness.

---

§5.2. PRELIMINARY ISSUES

An eyewitness identification takes place when a person, place or object is later recognized, or "identified," by one or more persons as being the same person, place or object which had been previously drawn into question. The subsequent recognition or identification may be made by:

> (1) a direct one-on-one examination of the actual person, place or object—the "showup";

> (2) a viewing of a photographic array—the "photo lineup"; or

> (3) a viewing of a corporeal group of individuals—the "in-person lineup."

Significantly, whether the identification procedure is conducted live or by means of photographs, the law will focus upon, as the previous section has illustrated, two concepts: "reliability" and "suggestiveness."

Another preliminary issue concerns the documentation of an eyewitness identification procedure. Whether or not an identification is made, law enforcement officials should make a complete record of the identification procedure to the end that the event may, if necessary, be reconstructed at court. The identity of persons participating in a lineup should be recorded, and the lineup itself should be photographed. In addition, whenever an identification is made or attempted on the basis of photographs, a record should be made of the photographs exhibited, and, where feasible, the entire photographic array should be preserved intact. This practice permits the prosecution to address or combat any subsequent allegations of impropriety during the eyewitness identification process.

---

[25] W. LaFave & J. Israel, *Criminal Procedure*, §7.4 at 320 (1985).

UNITED STATES v. CREWS
Supreme Court of the United States
445 *U.S.* 463, 100 *S.Ct.* 1244 (1980)

Mr. Justice BRENNAN delivered the opinion of the Court.

"We are called upon to decide whether in the circumstances of this case, an in-court identification of the accused by the victim of a crime should be suppressed as the fruit of the defendant's unlawful arrest." *Id.* at 1246.

During the course of an investigation into several armed robberies occurring in the women's restroom on the grounds of the Washington Monument, police developed grounds to suspect that defendant, 16-year-old Keith Crews, was the perpetrator. Under the pretense of taking him into custody as a suspected truant, an officer of the United States Park Police transported him to police headquarters, where officers questioned Crews, took his picture, telephoned his school, and then released him. Crews was not formally arrested at this time, nor was he charged with any offense.

The next day, the police showed the first robbery victim an array of eight photographs, including one of Crews. Although she had previously viewed over 100 pictures of possible suspects without identifying any of them as her assailant, she immediately selected Crews' photograph as that of the man who had robbed her. Three days later, one of the other victims made a similar identification. Prior to the photo-lineup procedures (immediately after the crimes), the robbery victims provided the police with detailed descriptions of their assailants. Each description matched the physical appearance of Crews. Crews was again taken into custody, and at a court-ordered lineup was positively identified by the two women who had made the photographic identifications.

At trial, the court disallowed the introduction by the government of any evidence related to the photographic and lineup identifications, ruling that each was the product of an arrest without probable cause.

The critical issue in this case is "whether in the circumstances of this case, an in-court identification of the accused by the victim of a crime should be suppressed as the fruit of defendant's unlawful arrest." *Id.* at 1246.

As a general rule, the exclusionary rule operates to prohibit the use at trial of direct, as well as indirect, products of Fourth Amendment violations. "[T]he exclusionary sanction applies to any 'fruits' of a constitutional violation—whether such evidence be tangible, physical material actually seized in an illegal search, items observed or words overheard in the course of the unlawful activity, or confessions or statements of the accused obtained during an illegal arrest and detention." *Id.* at 1249.

"In the typical 'fruit of the poisonous tree' case, however, the challenged evidence was acquired by the police after some initial Fourth Amendment violation[.] * * * Thus, most cases begin with the premise that the challenged evidence is in some sense the product of illegal governmental activity." *Id.* at 1249-50. [Emphasis added.]

Eyewitness identification cases are, however, a bit different. "A victim's in-court identification of the accused has three distinct elements. First, the victim is present at trial to testify as to what transpired between her and the offender, and to identify the defendant as the culprit. Second, the victim possesses knowledge of and the ability to reconstruct the prior criminal occurrence and to identify the defendant from her observations of him at the time of the crime. And third, the defendant is also physically present in the courtroom, so that the victim can observe him and compare his appearance to that of the offender." *Id.* at 1250. In this case, none of these three elements has come into existence through the exploitation of Crews' unlawful arrest.

In this case, the robbery victim's presence in the courtroom at [defendant's] trial was surely not the product of any police misconduct. She had notified the authorities immediately after the attack and had given them a full description of her assailant. The very next day, she went to the police station to view photographs of possible suspects, and she voluntarily assisted the police in their investigation at all times. Thus, this is not a case in which the witness' identity was discovered or her cooperation secured only as a result of an unlawful search or arrest of the accused. Here, the victim's identity was known long before there was any official misconduct, and her presence in court is thus not traceable to any Fourth Amendment violation.

Nor did the illegal arrest infect the victim's ability to give accurate identification testimony. Based upon her observations at the time of the robbery, the victim constructed a mental image of her assailant. At trial, she retrieved this mnemonic representation, compared it to the figure of the defendant, and positively identified him as the robber. [As the Government put it, the witness' mental image may be compared to "an undeveloped photograph of the robber that is given to the police immediately after the crime, but which becomes visible only at the trial."] No part of this process was affected by [defendant's] illegal arrest.

This is not to say that the intervening photographic and lineup identifications—both of which are conceded to be suppressible fruits of the Fourth Amendment violation—could not under some circumstances affect the reliability of the in-court identification and render it inadmissible as well. Indeed, given the vagaries of human memory and the inherent suggestibility of many identification procedures, just the opposite may be true. But in the present case[,] * * * the witness' courtroom testimony rested on an independent recollection of her initial encounter with the assailant, uninfluenced by the pretrial identifications[.] * * * In short, the victim's capacity to identify her assailant in court neither resulted from nor was biased by the unlawful police conduct committed long after she had developed that capacity.

Id. at 1250-51 & n.16.

Defendant cannot claim that he is immune from prosecution simply because his appearance in court was precipitated by an arrest without probable cause. "An illegal arrest, without more, has never been viewed as a bar to subsequent prosecution, nor as a defense to a valid conviction." *Id.* at 1251. Defendant "is not himself a suppressible 'fruit,' and the illegality of his detention cannot deprive the Government of the opportunity to prove his guilt through the introduction of evidence wholly untainted by the police misconduct." *Id.* at 1251. In this respect, "a defendant's face can[not] be a suppressible fruit of an illegal arrest." *Id.* at 1253.

[I]n this case the record plainly discloses that prior to his illegal arrest, the police both knew [defendant's] identity and had some basis to suspect his involvement in the very crimes with which he was charged. * * * In short, the Fourth Amendment violation in this case yielded nothing of evidentiary value that the police did not already have in their grasp. Rather, [defendant's] unlawful arrest served merely to link together two extant ingredients in his identification. The exclusionary rule enjoins the Government from benefitting from evidence it has unlawfully obtained; it does not reach backward to taint information that was in official hands prior to any illegality.

Id. at 1252. [Emphasis added.]

Accordingly, the pretrial identification obtained through use of the photograph taken during defendant's illegal arrest cannot be introduced in evidence; "but the in-court identification is admissible * * * because the police's knowledge of [defendant's] identity and the victim's independent recollection[] of him both antedated the unlawful arrest and were thus untainted by the constitutional violation." *Id.* at 1253.

§5.3. SHOWUPS

NEIL v. BIGGERS
Supreme Court of the United States
409 *U.S.* 188, 93 *S.Ct.* 375 (1972)

QUESTION: In the wake of a suggestive showup procedure, what factors will a court consider to determine whether the suggestive nature of the showup created a substantial likelihood of misidentification, thereby requiring the exclusion at trial of any evidence relating to the showup ?

ANSWER: Under the totality of the circumstances, a witness' identification may be deemed "reliable" even though the showup procedure was suggestive. In order to determine whether a suggestive out-of-court confrontation gave rise to a likelihood of misidentification, a court will consider such factors as:

    (1) "the opportunity of the witness to view the criminal at the time of the crime,"

    (2) "the witness' degree of attention,"

    (3) "the accuracy of the witness' prior description of the criminal,"

    (4) "the level of certainty demonstrated by the witness at the confrontation,"

    (5) "the length of time between the crime and the confrontation," and

    (6) whether the witness was a "casual observer" or the victim of the crime.

Id. at 382.

RATIONALE: Whenever a suggestive out-of-court identification procedure is challenged by a defendant, a court will conduct an inquiry into whether the suggestive procedure gave rise to a likelihood of misidentification at a future court proceeding. If the court determines that the showup procedure was unnecessarily suggestive and the likelihood of misidentification is substantial, it may disallow the admission of the out-of-court identification, along with any evidence relating to it, at trial, in order to safeguard the defendant's right to due process of law. Respecting the relationship between "suggestiveness" and "misidentification," the Court stated that "the primary evil to be avoided is 'a very substantial likelihood of irreparable misidentification.' While the phrase was coined as a standard for determining whether an in-court identification would be admissible in the wake of a suggestive out-of-court identification, with the deletion of 'irreparable' it serves equally well as a standard for the admissibility of testimony concerning the out-of-court identification itself. It is the likelihood of misidentification which violates a defendant's right to due process[.] * * * Suggestive confrontations are disapproved because they increase the likelihood of misidentification, and unnecessarily suggestive ones are condemned for the further reason that the increased chance of misidentification is [a given]." *Id.* at 381-382.

"[T]he admission of evidence of a showup without more," however, "does not violate due process." *Id.* at 382. Moreover, "unnecessary suggestiveness alone" does not automatically require the exclusion of the out-of-court identification procedure. *Id.* Rather, the central question is whether, "under the 'totality of the circumstances[,]' the identification was *reliable* even though the confrontation procedure was suggestive." *Id.* [Emphasis added.]

In this case, defendant was convicted of rape and sentenced to 20 years' imprisonment. The evidence presented at two separate hearings* established that on January 22, the victim, a practical nurse, was accosted by defendant in her home at the doorway leading to her kitchen. The victim testified that a youth with a butcher knife

> "* * * grabbed me from behind, and grappled—twisted me on the floor. Threw me down on the floor.
> "Q. And there was no light in that kitchen ?
> "A. Not in the kitchen.
> "Q. So you couldn't have seen him then ?
> "A. Yes, I could see him, when I looked up in his face.
> "Q. In the dark ?
> "A. He was right in the doorway—it was enough light from the bedroom shining through. Yes, I could see who he was."

Id. at 379.

"When the victim screamed, her 12-year-old daughter came out of her bedroom and also began to scream. The assailant directed the victim to 'tell her [the daughter] to shut up, or I'll kill you both.' She did so, and was then walked at knifepoint about two blocks along a railroad track, taken into a woods, and raped there. She testified that 'the moon was shining brightly, full moon.' After the

---

* To decide this case, the Supreme Court considered the evidence which was presented at defendant's jury trial and at his habeas corpus hearing.

rape, the assailant ran off, and she returned home, the whole incident having taken between 15 minutes and half an hour." *Id.*

Subsequently, the victim described her attacker to the police as "being fat and flabby with smooth skin, bushy hair and a youthful voice." *Id.* at 380. She reported that he was "between 16 and 18 years old and between five feet ten inches and six feet tall, as weighing between 180 and 200 pounds, and as having a dark brown complexion." *Id.*

"On several occasions over the course of the next seven months, she viewed suspects in her home or at the police station, some in lineups and others in showups, and was shown between 30 and 40 photographs." *Id.* At no time did she positively identify any of the individuals that were shown to her. Thereafter, on August 17, almost seven months after the attack, the police called the victim to the station to view defendant, who was being detained on another charge. "In an effort to construct a suitable lineup, the police checked the city jail and the city juvenile home. Finding no one at either place fitting [defendant's] unusual physical description, they conducted a showup instead." *Id.*

The showup itself consisted of two detectives walking defendant past the victim. At the completion of the showup, the victim positively identified the defendant as the rapist. According to the victim's testimony, she had "no doubt" about her identification. *Id.*

> "A. That I have no doubt, I mean that I am sure that when I—see, when I first laid eyes on him, I knew that it was the individual, because his face—well, there was just something that I don't think I could ever forget. * * *"

During the course of the procedure (it is unclear from the trial testimony when) the victim requested the police to direct the defendant to say, "shut up or I'll kill you." According to the victim:

> "Q. What physical characteristics, if any, caused you to be able to identify him ?
> "A. First of all,—uh—his size,—next I could remember his voice.
> "Q. What about his voice ? Describe his voice to the Jury.
> "A. Well, he has the voice of an immature youth—I call it an immature youth. I have teenage boys. And that was the first thing that made me think it was the boy."

The "central question" in this case, according to the Supreme Court, was "whether under the 'totality of the circumstances' the [nurse's] identification [of defendant] was reliable even though the confrontation procedure was suggestive." *Id.* at 382.

Preliminarily, the Court noted that "the police did not exhaust all possibilities in seeking persons physically comparable to [defendant]" in order to conduct an appropriate in-person lineup. *Id.* Nonetheless, it concluded that the evidence of the showup need not be excluded so long as the suggestive procedure did not give rise to a "substantial likelihood of misidentification." *Id.*

"[T]he factors to be considered in evaluating the likelihood of misidentification include the opportunity of the witness to view the criminal at the time of the crime, the witness' degree of attention, the accuracy of the witness' prior description of the criminal, the level of certainty demonstrated by the witness at the confrontation, and the length of time between the crime and the confrontation." *Id.*

Applying and weighing all of the factors, the Court stated:

> The victim spent a considerable period of time with her as-sailant, up to half an hour. She was with him under adequate artificial light in her house and under a full moon outdoors, and at least twice, once in the house and later in the woods, faced him directly and intimately. She was no casual observer, but rather the victim of one of the most personally humiliating of all crimes. Her description to the police, which included the as-sailant's approximate age, height, weight, complexion, skin tex-ture, build, and voice * * * was more than ordinarily thorough. She had "no doubt" that [defendant] was the person who raped her. In the nature of crime, there are rarely witnesses to a rape other than the victim, who often has a limited opportunity of observation. The victim here, a practical nurse by profession, had an unusual opportunity to observe and identify her assail-ant. She testified [at one point in the proceedings] that there was something about his face "I don't think I could ever forget."

Id. at 382-83.

There was, of course, a lapse of seven months between the rape and the confrontation. According to the Court, "[t]his would be a seriously negative factor in most cases. Here, however, the testi-mony is undisputed that *the victim made no previous identification at any of the showups, lineups, or photographic showings. Her re-cord for reliability was thus a good one, as she had previously re-sisted whatever suggestiveness inheres in a showup.*" *Id.* at 383. [Emphasis added.]

Accordingly, "[w]eighing all the factors, [the Court] find[s] no substantial likelihood of misidentification. The evidence was prop-erly allowed to go to the jury." *Id.*

STOVALL v. DENNO
Supreme Court of the United States
388 *U.S.* 293, 87 *S.Ct.* 1967 (1967)

QUESTION: In the below set of circumstances, was the showup procedure performed by the police so unnecessarily suggestive that any identification made by the eyewitness must be deemed unreliable and therefore inadmissible at trial ?

CIRCUMSTANCES: Dr. Paul Behrendt was stabbed to death in the kitchen of his home at about midnight on the 23rd of August. His wife, also a physician, had followed her husband to the kitchen and jumped at the assailant who immediately knocked her to the floor and stabbed her 11 times. The police found a shirt on the kitchen floor and keys in a pocket which they traced to defendant Stovall. They arrested Stovall on the afternoon of August 24th.

On August 25th, the day after Mrs. Behrendt's surgery, the police arranged with her surgeon to permit them to bring Stovall to her hospital room for a showup. Stovall was handcuffed to one of five police officers who, with two members of the staff of the District Attorney, brought him to the hospital room. Stovall was the only black male in the room. "Mrs. Behrendt identified him from her hospital bed after being asked by an officer whether he 'was the man' and after [Stovall] repeated at the direction of the officer a 'few words for voice identification.'"

Mrs. Behrendt and the officers testified at the trial to her identification of Stovall in the hospital room, and Mrs. Behrendt also identified Stovall in the courtroom.

ANSWER: NO. On the facts of this case Stovall "was not deprived of due process of law in violation of the Fourteenth Amendment." *Id.* at 1969.

RATIONALE: Using a well-recognized ground of attack upon his conviction, defendant asserts that the confrontation (showup) conducted in Mrs. Behrendt's hospital room "was so unnecessarily suggestive and conducive to irreparable mistaken identification that he was denied due process of law." *Id.* at 1972. *The United States Supreme Court disagreed.*

"The practice of showing suspects singly to persons for the purpose of identification, and not as part of a lineup, has been widely condemned. However, a claimed violation of due process of law in the conduct of a confrontation depends on the totality of the circumstances surrounding it, and the record in the present case reveals that the showing of Stovall to Mrs. Behrendt in an immediate hospital confrontation was imperative." *Id.* Accepting the reasoning of the court below, the Supreme Court reiterated:

"Here was the only person in the world who could possibly exonerate Stovall. Her words, and only her words, 'He is not the man' could have resulted in freedom for Stovall. The hospital was not far distant from the courthouse and jail. No one knew how long Mrs. Behrendt might live. Faced with the responsibility of identifying the attacker, with the need for immediate action and with the knowledge that Mrs. Behrendt could not visit the jail, the police followed the only feasible procedure and took Stovall to the hospital room. Under these circumstances, the usual police station lineup, which Stovall now argues he should have had, was out of the question."

Id. at 1972-1973.

NOTE

Inadvertent courtroom corridor encounters. Accidental courtroom encounters are not unduly suggestive *per se.* For example, in *State v. Mance,* 300 *N.J.Super.* 37, 691 *A.*2d 1369 (App.Div. 1997), Captain Johnston of the New Jersey State Prison was waiting outside the courtroom to testify as to the events taking place at a prison riot. When the trial broke for lunch, the defendants, in shackles, were brought past him as they were being taken to eat. Johnston identified two defendants as the men who had attacked him on the morning of the prison riot. Earlier, Captain Johnston had been unable to identify his attackers through a photo array shown to him at the hospital, five days after the riot, at a time when he was heavily sedated. He did indicate at that time, however, that if he saw his assailants in person, he believed he could identify them.

According to the court, "the exposure of the defendants to Johnston was 'inadvertent,'" and therefore, not "so suggestive as to result in a substantial likelihood of misidentification." *Id.,* 300 *N.J.Super.* at 58, 59. Significantly, at the time of the inadvertent confrontation, no one had said or done anything to influence Johnston's identifications. The court elaborated:

> Since the encounter in the courtroom corridor was inadvertent, *Wade* is not implicated even though defense counsel was absent. * * * Nor are such accidental courthouse encounters unduly suggestive *per se. See e.g., United States v. Colclough,* 549 *F.*2d 937, 941-42 (4th Cir. 1977). Here, seven shackled defendants passed by the witness. Although he obviously knew they were the defendants in this case, there was nothing to indicate which of them were the men who attacked him. Therefore, there was no suggestibility with regard to his specific identifications of two of the seven as his attackers.

Id. at 58-59.

STATE v. CARTER
Supreme Court of New Jersey
91 N.J. 86, 449 A.2d 1280 (1982)

QUESTION: When law enforcement officers bring about a confrontation between an accused and a witness immediately after a crime, does the identification which takes place constitute an impermissibly suggestive procedure violative of the suspect's constitutional rights ?

ANSWER: NO. "Far from being conducive to misidentification, confrontation immediately after a crime promotes fairness to the accused by allowing a viewing while the witness' mental image of the perpetrator is still fresh." *Id.*, 91 *N.J.* at 130.

RATIONALE: The defendant was brought back to the scene of a fatal shooting for identification purposes. A witness at the scene had observed the defendant leaving the crime scene in a particularly described automobile, and police relayed that information to all units in the area. Within 30 minutes, officers spotted the auto with the defendant driving, stopped him, and brought him back to the scene for a "face-to-face" with the witness. Identification of the defendant was made by the witness.

The Supreme Court of New Jersey upheld the validity of the identification, finding that a "confrontation immediately after a crime promotes fairness to the accused by allowing a viewing while the witness' mental image of the perpetrator is still fresh." *Id.*

The touchstone for determining whether such identifications are admissible in court is "reliability." *Id.* at 129. The assessment of whether the "face-to-face" was, in fact, a reliable confrontation will be made in light of "the totality of the circumstances and consideration of factors such as 'the opportunity of the witness to view the criminal at the time of the crime, the witness' degree of attention, the accuracy of the witness' prior description of the criminal, the level of certainty demonstrated by the witness at the confrontation, and the length of time between the crime and the confrontation.'" *Id.* at 129, 130 (quoting *Neil v. Biggers,* 409 *U.S.* 188, 189, 93 *S.Ct.* 375, 382 (1972)). [Additional factors which may be considered influential include the length of time that the witness had to view the accused, the intensity of the observation, *i.e.*, did the witness "study" the accused's face at the time, and the degree of lighting in the area of the crime scene at the time the witness viewed the accused.]

NOTE

1. The 30-minute delay in *Carter*, between the time of the crime and the showup procedures should not be viewed as being permissible in all face-to-face confrontations. Such a period of time may be considered unreasonable if the suspect is found a great distance away from the witness and therefore might require a "lineup" or photographic identification procedure to assure the "fundamental fairness" required by due process considerations.

2. *Transporting the suspect to the victim.* An officer conducting an investigative detention for eyewitness identification should use the least intrusive investigative techniques reasonably available to verify or dispel his suspicion in the shortest period of time reasonably possible. This principle mandates that, as a general rule and in the absence of exigent circumstances or consent, the victim should be called or escorted to the place where the suspect is being detained for the showup. It contemplates probable cause to believe that an offense has occurred and reasonable suspicion that the person to be detained was a criminal participant. Exigent circumstances may be shown where, for example, "the victim of an assault or other serious offense was injured or otherwise physically unable to be taken promptly to view the suspect, or a witness was [otherwise] incapacitated." *See People v. Harris*, 15 *Cal.*3d 384, 124 *Cal.Rptr.* 536, 540 P.2d 632 (1975). *See also State v. Mitchell*, 204 *Conn.* 187, 527 A.2d 1168 (1987) (transportation of sexual assault suspects to hospital for viewing by victim upheld as a "means of investigation that was likely to confirm or dispel their suspicions quickly"); *Buckingham v. State*, 482 A.2d 327 (Del.Supr. 1984) (bringing robbery suspect back to the grocery store for identification upheld for it did not "unduly prolong the detention"). *And see State v. McNeil*, 303 *N.J.Super.* 266, 272 (App.Div. 1997) ("One-on-one 'show-up' identifications, in which a suspect is apprehended promptly after a crime and brought to the victim, are not prohibited."); *State v. Salaam*, 225 *N.J.Super.* 66 (App.Div. 1988) (transportation of robbery suspect back to the victim, a convenience store cashier, within 30 minutes of the robbery, not an issue in the case).

3. *Expert testimony on the reliability of eyewitness identification.* In *State v. Gunter,* 231 *N.J.Super.* 34, 554 A.2d 1356 (App.Div. 1989), the Appellate Division held that the admissibility of expert testimony by a psychologist explaining in general terms the factors which affect the reliability of eyewitness identification must be determined by a preliminary hearing "to determine its scientific reliability and the extent to which, if at all, it would have assisted the jury in its understanding of relevant matters beyond the common knowledge of human experience." *Id.*, 231 *N.J.Super.* at 38.

The expert was not prepared to express an opinion as to the specific reliability of the identification of Gunter, "but rather to testify in general terms, based on studies and experiments conducted by himself and others in the areas of perception and memory, about circumstantial factors which affect the perception and memory of victims of crime and impinge upon the accuracy of their identifications of their assailants." *Id.* at 41. The expert was prepared to testify that "cross-racial identifications are generally less reliable than identification of someone of the same race * * *. He was also prepared to testify about a 'weapon focus,' *i.e.,* the theory that when threatened with a deadly weapon, the victim's perceptions are so concentrated on the weapon as to detract from his attention upon and perception and memory of the person wielding the weapon." *Id.* The expert was prepared to opine that "stress impairs rather than enhances perception and memory; that memory is affected by a 'forgetting curve,' *i.e.,* that memory does not diminish at a uniform rate; that one's confidence in his perception is no indication of its accuracy; and that memory is affected by unconscious transfer and other associational factors." *Id.* Further, the expert was prepared to testify that "at least some of these factors are not commonly understood and that at least some of them affect memory and perception in a manner contrary to common understanding." *Id.*

4. *Voice identification.* In *State v. Clausell,* 121 *N.J.* 298, 580 A.2d 221 (1990), the Court held that "[t]he constitutional safeguards applicable to visual identifications apply equally to voice identifications." *Id.,* 121 *N.J.* at 328. "Consequently, a voice identification is inadmissible if its reliability is outweighed by the suggestiveness of the identification procedure. Reliability depends on such factors as the witness's opportunity to hear the accused and the consistency with prior voice identifications." *Id. See also Neil v. Biggers,* 409 *U.S.* 188, 199-201, 93 *S.Ct.* 375, 382-383 (1972) (holding that identification evidence, including voice identification, was properly admitted based on the determination that the "totality of the circumstances" indicated that the identification was reliable, even though the procedure was suggestive).

COMMONWEALTH v. BUTLER
Superior Court of Pennsylvania
354 *Pa.Super.* 533 (1986)

QUESTION: Based on the below set of circumstances, should the out-of-court identification procedure be suppressed because of its "suggestiveness" and the substantial likelihood of "misidentification"?

CIRCUMSTANCES: Two Hispanic women were standing outside of one of their houses when defendant appeared, looked at one of the women and grabbed four gold chains from the other woman's neck, knocking her to the ground. The entire incident, which occurred during daylight, lasted about five seconds.

Screams for help summoned a young Hispanic male who chased after the defendant. During the chase, a police car was spotted and flagged down for help, but the officer did not speak Spanish and the women spoke no English. Nonetheless, the officer did notice that the parties were in an "hysterical state."

Within a few moments, an English-speaking Hispanic youth appeared on the scene and translated what had happened. About fifteen to twenty seconds later, the first youth returned and told the officer that the defendant was hiding about a block away. The officer went directly to that location and found defendant and the gold chains. Although defendant was cornered and instructed not to move, he nonetheless struck out at the officer and attempted to flee. Additional officers at the scene apprehended him and seized the gold chains.

Defendant was then taken to a nearby police station while other officers brought in the two women. Upon arrival, the victim and eyewitness noticed the defendant and immediately and spontaneously identified him.

The total time between the arrest and the identification was approximately ten to fifteen minutes.

ANSWER: NO. The out-of-court identification of the defendant was entirely proper, and, as such, is admissible in evidence.

RATIONALE: While it is true that this "show-up" occurred without the presence of counsel, and that in Pennsylvania the right to counsel exists for such an identification confrontation due to the attachment of the right at the time of arrest, this fact, according to the *Butler* court, is not fatal to the admission of this identification.

The Pennsylvania courts have extended "on-the-scene" identifications to several areas, including hospitals (*Commonwealth v. Erin*, 255 *Pa.Super.* 289 (1978)), and areas located a few blocks from the scene of the crime, for example, where the defendant was handcuffed and in a police van (*Commonwealth v. Allen*, 287 *Pa.Super.* 88 (1981); *Commonwealth v. Dickerson*, 266 *Pa.Super.* 425 (1973)). "The reasoning for broadening the 'on-the-scene' requirements was based on (1) the exigent circumstances existing at the time, and (2) the minimal amount of suggestiveness surrounding the identification itself which reduces the likelihood of misidentification." *Butler* at 539. In fact, the key to determining the admissibility of an out-of-court identification is not simply the suggestiveness of the circumstances surrounding it but rather the likelihood of misidentification. As the Pennsylvania Supreme Court instructed in *Commonwealth v. Sexton,* 485 *Pa.* 17 (1979):

> It is the likelihood of misidentification which violates defendant's right to due process and it is this which is the basis of the exclusion of the evidence * * * . [S]uggest[ive] confrontations are disapproved because they increase the likelihood of misidentification, and necessarily suggestive ones are condemned for the further reason that the increased chance of misidentification is gratuitous.

Id. at 22.

In this case, the circumstances "clearly warrant the admissibility of the out-of-court identification given the attendant exigent circumstances. Additionally, the likelihood of suggestiveness is minimal as is the likelihood of misidentification." *Butler* at 540. Once the defendant was apprehended, he was taken immediately to a nearby police station which was located only four city blocks from the scene. At the same time, the victim and eyewitness were taken to that station house. "Such a procedure was necessary, since a Spanish speaking officer was present at the police station to interpret for the victim and the eyewitness who did not speak any English. As the eyewitness entered the police station she immediately noticed defendant and spontaneously identified him as the individual who robbed the victim. The total elapsed time between the arrest afterwards and his identification indoors was a mere ten to fifteen minutes." *Id.* at 540-541.

The significant part of the exigency which required the station house show-up was the fact that the witness and victim only spoke Spanish and the officers at the scene only spoke English. The nearest location to the scene of the crime where a Spanish-speaking officer was present was police headquarters, a mere four blocks from the scene. Moreover, the usual suggestive atmosphere of the police station house was not present here due to the spontaneous identification; a fortuitous circumstance which differs considerably from the normal identification procedures in police headquarters where a witness views a suspect in a lineup.

Accordingly, "the uncontrived meeting between defendant and the witness and the spontaneous identification of defendant by that witness without prompting from a police officer substantially reduced the likelihood of misidentification which is the cornerstone for determining whether an identification should be admissible." *Id.* at 541.

NOTE

Showup 30 minutes after the offense. In *In Interest of McElrath*, 405 *Pa.Super.* 431, 592 *A*.2d 740 (1991), defendant, dressed in a black jacket and light colored pants, approached the victim, produced a black gun and ordered the victim to hand over the bag he was carrying. Subsequently, the victim contacted the police and provided a full description of defendant and indicated the direction in which he fled. "A person matching the description provided by the victim was observed by a number of people, both citizens and police officers, as he travelled from the scene of the crime to his residence[.]" *Id.*, 592 *A*.2d at 741-742. The police entered the residence within a short time after the robbery and found defendant changing his clothes. The officers also observed a black-colored BB gun on a table in the hallway of the residence. Defendant was escorted out of his residence by several officers, one of whom was in uniform, and down the street where the victim was waiting in a patrol car. The victim first noticed the black gun in one of the officer's hands; he then immediately identified defendant and the weapon. The identification took place just under one-half hour after the robbery. *Id.* at 742.

Rejecting defendant's argument that the showup procedure was unduly suggestive, the court declared, "[defendant's] argument attempts to create suggestiveness where none was present." *Id.* at 743. According to the court,

> [t]he facts outlined above indicate that the victim's prompt complaint enabled the police to use the description provided so as to track down and locate [defendant] almost immediately after the perpetration of the robbery. Less than one-half hour after the crime, the police were able to present [defendant] for a viewing by the victim. This is proper procedure. *Absent some special element of unfairness, prompt, one-on-one identification is not per se violative of the accused's constitutional rights, even where the accused has been returned to the scene of the crime in a police cruiser. Commonwealth v. Clemmons*, 505 *Pa.* 356, 522-23, 479 *A*.2d 955, 960 (1984). * * * The fact that the victim in [this] case noticed [the defendant's gun in the hand of a police officer] before focusing on [defendant's] face at the prompt prearrest identification does not render it either unreliable or unduly suggestive. The victim's view of an assailant's weapon, whether before or after an identification is made, does not qualify as a special element of unfairness.

McElrath at 743. [Emphasis added.]

The court also opined that, even if the showup procedure was in some way suggestive, the subsequent in-court identification was nonetheless reliable. In this respect, the court noted that at the motion to suppress the pre-trial identification, the victim testified that defendant initially confronted him from a distance of about eight to ten feet, and that he viewed defendant's face at close range for about five seconds when he surrendered his bag. Significantly, when asked about his opportunity to view the perpetrator, the victim flatly replied, "I will never forget his face." *Id.*

Here, the court reasoned that, "although the victim only viewed the perpetrator for a short time, [defendant] closely matched the description the victim provided to the police and the victim strongly focused on the attacker's facial appearance. Further, the victim unequivocally identified [defendant] as the attacker when confronting him outside [his] residence." *Id.* Under these circumstances, the court could not say that the victim's in-court identification was unreliable.

§5.4. LINEUPS

A pretrial confrontation for the purpose of identification may take place by means of an in-person "lineup" or "identification parade." The in-person lineup is normally conducted by the presentation of a group of at least five individuals, including the suspect, for an eyewitness' viewing. Each of the individuals in the lineup must be of the same race and sex, and should have similar physical appearances. In this respect, courts have not required a "substantial" degree of similarity; rather, "a reasonable effort to harmonize the lineup is normally all that is required."[26]

Recent research conducted by the National Institute of Justice (NIJ)[27] suggests that the nonsuspects in the lineup—the "fillers"—should be chosen to match the eyewitness' description of the perpetrator rather than the features of an individual the police may have

---

[26] *See United States v. Lewis*, 547 *F.*2d 1030, 1035 (8th Cir. 1976) (police stations "are not theatrical casting offices"), *cert. denied*, 429 *U.S.* 1111, 97 *S.Ct.* 1149 (1977). *See also Herrera v. State*, 682 *S.W.*2d 313, 319 (Tex.Crim.App. 1984) ("While the better practice may be to get as many individuals as possible who fit the defendant's description, it is not essential that all the individuals be identical; 'neither due process nor common sense' requires such exactitude.") (citation omitted).

[27] In 1998, the NIJ convened the Technical Working Group for Eyewitness Evidence. The group consisted of law enforcement, legal, and psychological research professionals, who joined forces and shared information with the goal of developing improved procedures for collecting and preserving accurate and reliable eyewitness identification evidence. The findings of the Working Group were published in October 1999, in a document titled *Eyewitness Evidence: A Guide for Law Enforcement.* One key principle drawn from all the research was that the memory of an eyewitness should be viewed as "trace evidence," subject to possible contamination, and requiring "rigorous criteria for handling eyewitness evidence that are as demanding as those governing the handling of physical trace evidence." National Institute of Justice, *Eyewitness Evidence: A Guide for Law Enforcement* (1999), at 2.

apprehended as the suspect in the case. Lineups created by selecting fillers that all look substantially like the suspect tend to be unfair to the suspect as well as the witness, particularly when the police are not entirely sure that the suspect is in fact the perpetrator. This process tends to narrow the universe of options for the witness, while also creating a subtle suggestion as to what the police think the suspect looks like. If, however, the witness is unable to provide an adequate description of the perpetrator, the fillers should resemble the suspect's significant features.

At no time should police inform a witness that the perpetrator is in the lineup. Rather, the witness should be instructed that the actual suspect might not even be present in the lineup, and therefore the witness should not feel compelled to make a selection. The witness should understand that the lineup procedure is important not just to identify the guilty, but to clear the innocent as well. By informing the witness that the person who committed the crime may or may not be in the lineup, the police guard against a witness selecting an individual who looks most like the one who committed the crime, hoping that this will help move the investigation along, even if they are not certain.

It is also a good practice to display the lineup participants one at a time—sequentially—rather than in a line at the same time. This process guards against the tendency of an eyewitness to compare one member of a lineup to another, making relative judgments as to which person looks most like the perpetrator. By viewing the lineup participants separately, rather than simultaneously, the witness is in a better position to make an identification by comparing each person to his or her own memory of the crime. This lessons the witness' opportunity to engage in a process of elimination, because there is no opportunity to simultaneously compare the relative appearance of all of the lineup participants.

Moreover, it is impermissible to allow more than one witness to view the lineup at the same time; and it is also impermissible for a witness to know that a suspect in the lineup has already been identified by another witness at a previous viewing. If a witness identifies an individual in the lineup, the police should not indicate to the witness that he or she "picked the right person," or that the witness' identification "was correct" or "very helpful," or that the police "also think that the right person has been selected." The danger of making such suggestive comments lies in the fact that the opinion of the police that the individual identified by the eyewitness is, in fact, the perpetrator of the crime creates a risk that any future identifications that may need to be made by the witness would be unduly influenced by the official "stamp of approval." In this regard, the witness should be assured that the investigation will continue, whether or not the witness is able to identify anyone as the actual perpetrator.

To further enhance the reliability of the procedure, the lineup should be administered by an officer who does not know which lineup member is the suspect. This "blind" assignment technique helps avoid any inadvertent body signals or cues which may adversely impact a witness' ability to make a reliable identification. Even when unintended, verbal or nonverbal cues are sometimes given to witnesses when the identity of the actual suspect is known to the officer conducting the procedure.

As with other identification procedures, the lineup must be carefully documented, regardless of whether an identification is made. As a final precaution, the in-person lineup should be photographed or videotaped in case it becomes necessary at a future proceeding to examine or recreate the lineup.

UNITED STATES v. WADE
Supreme Court of the United States
388 *U.S.* 218, 87 *S.Ct.* 1926 (1967)

QUESTION: Is a *post-indictment*, pretrial lineup at which the accused is exhibited to identifying witnesses a "critical stage" of the criminal prosecution at which the accused has the right to the assistance of counsel ?

ANSWER: YES. A *post-indictment*, pretrial lineup at which the accused is exhibited to identifying witnesses is a "critical stage" of the prosecution; the police conduct of such a lineup without notice to and in the absence of his counsel denies the accused his Sixth Amendment right to counsel and seriously calls into question the admissibility at trial of any subsequent in-court identification of the accused by witnesses who attended the lineup. *Id.* at 1937. At trial, no evidence of an eyewitness' identification which flows from an uncounseled post-indictment lineup may be admitted. The absence of counsel at the lineup does not, however, automatically mean that no in-court identification will be permitted. In these circumstances, the Government has an opportunity to establish by clear and convincing evidence, at a pretrial hearing, that the prospective in-court identification will be "based upon observations of the suspect other than the lineup identification." *Id.* at 1939. If the Government is successful, courtroom identification is permissible. *Id.* at 1939, 1940.

RATIONALE: The Sixth Amendment guarantees an accused the right to the assistance of counsel for his defense; and since *Powell v. Alabama*, 287 *U.S.* 45, 53 *S.Ct.* 55 (1964), the Court has "recognized that the period from arraignment to trial [is] 'perhaps *the most critical period of the [criminal] proceedings*' * * * during which the accused 'requires the guiding hand of counsel,' * * * if the guarantee is not to prove [to be] an empty right." *Wade* at 1931 (quoting

224

Powell at 57, 69, 53 *S.Ct.* at 59, 64). [Emphasis added.] That principle has since been applied to require the assistance of counsel at an arraignment or similar proceeding, or at other *critical* pretrial confrontations which, as the trial itself, "operates to assure that the accused's interests will be protected consistently with our adversary theory of criminal prosecution." *Id.* at 1932.

"A major factor contributing to the high incidence of miscarriage of justice from mistaken identification has been the degree of suggestion inherent in the manner in which the prosecution presents the suspect to witnesses for pretrial identification. * * * Suggestion can be created intentionally or unintentionally in many subtle ways. And the dangers for the suspect are particularly grave when the witness' opportunity for observation was insubstantial, and thus his susceptibility to suggestion the greatest." *Id.* at 1933.

"Moreover, '[i]t is a matter of common experience that, once a witness has picked out the accused at the lineup, he is not likely to go back on his word later on, so that in practice the issue of identity may (in the absence of other relevant evidence) for all practical purposes be determined there and then, before the trial.'" *Id.* [Citation omitted.]

"Since it appears that there is grave potential for prejudice, intentional or not, in the pretrial lineup, which may not be capable of reconstruction at trial, and since presence of counsel itself can often avert prejudice and assure a meaningful confrontation at trial, there can be little doubt that [a] * * * post-indictment lineup [is] a critical stage of the prosecution at which [an accused is entitled to the assistance of counsel]." *Id.* at 1937. In this case, "both Wade and his counsel should have been notified of the impending lineup, and counsel's presence should have been a requisite to conduct of the lineup, absent an 'intelligent waiver.'" *Id.*

According to the Court, requiring counsel at a post-indictment lineup will not impede legitimate law enforcement; "on the contrary, * * * law enforcement may be assisted by preventing the infiltration of taint in the prosecution's identification evidence. That result cannot help the guilty avoid conviction but can only help assure that the right man has been brought to justice." *Id.* at 1938.

In this case, Wade moved to strike the in-court identification by the witnesses because of the absence of counsel at the pretrial lineup. This disposition, stated the Court, cannot "be justified without first giving the Government the opportunity to establish by clear and convincing evidence that the in-court identifications were based upon observations of the suspect other than the lineup identification. * * * Where, as here, the admissibility of evidence of the lineup identification itself is not involved, a *per se* rule of exclusion of courtroom identification would be unjustified." *Id.* at 1939. Quoting *Wong Sun v. United States*, 371 *U.S.* 471, 488, 83 *S.Ct.* 407, 417 (1963), the Court held that "the proper test to be applied in these situations" is: "'[W]hether, granting establishment of the primary illegality, the evidence to which [] objection is made has been come at by exploitation of that illegality or instead by means sufficiently distinguishable to be purged of the primary taint.' " *Wade* at 1939.

"Application of this test * * * requires consideration of various factors; for example, the prior opportunity to observe the alleged criminal act, the existence of any discrepancy between any pre-lineup description and the defendant's actual description, any identification prior to lineup of another person, the identification by picture of the defendant prior to the lineup, failure to identify the defendant on a prior occasion, and the lapse of time between the alleged act and the lineup identification. It is also relevant to consider those facts which, despite the absence of counsel, are disclosed concerning the conduct of the lineup." *Id.* at 1940.

As a result, Wade's conviction was vacated and the case remanded to provide the Government an opportunity to establish at a hearing that the in-court identification had a separate and independent source, *i.e.*, a basis unrelated to the improper out-of-court lineup.

NOTE

1. *The Wade hearing.* When a defendant presents "some evidence of impermissible suggestiveness" in the identification process, a "*Wade* hearing" should be conducted by the trial court. At the hearing, the first issue to be decided is whether the procedure utilized by the police was in fact "impermissibly suggestive." However, suggestiveness alone is not fatal. If suggestiveness is found, the second issue to be decided is whether the objectionable procedure resulted in a "very substantial likelihood of irreparable misidentification." The essence of the second inquiry is reliability, that is, whether the identification was prompted by the eyewitness' own recollection of the crime or by the suggestive manner in which the identification procedure was conducted.

2. *Pre-indictment identification procedures.* The Court, in *United States v. Wade,* made clear that a post-indictment, pretrial lineup at which the accused is exhibited to an identifying witness is a "critical stage" of the criminal prosecution. Police conduct of such a lineup, without notice to, and in the absence of, the accused's attorney violates the accused's right to counsel and calls into question the admissibility at trial of the in-court identification of the accused by the witness who attended the lineup. In *Gilbert v. California*, 388 *U.S.* 263, 87 *S.Ct.* 1951 (1967), the Court further emphasized that no in-court identification will be admissible in evidence if its "source" is a lineup conducted in violation of the *Wade* constitutional standard. This acts as a *per se* rule of exclusion "to assure that law enforcement authorities will respect the accused's constitutional right to the presence of counsel at the critical lineup." *Gilbert* at 273, 87 *S.Ct.* at 1957.

In *Kirby v. Illinois*, 406 *U.S.* 682, 92 *S.Ct.* 1877 (1972), the defendant argued that the *Wade-Gilbert per se* exclusionary rule should be extended "to identification testimony based upon a police station showup that took place *before* the defendant had been indicted or otherwise formally charged with any criminal offense." *Id.* at 684, 92 *S.Ct.* at 1879. [Court's emphasis.]

During an investigative detention conducted by Chicago police officers, Kirby was found to be in possession of three traveler's checks and a Social Security card, all bearing the name of Willie Shard, a victim of a robbery that had been perpetrated the day before. Kirby was taken to the police station and a police cruiser was dispatched to locate and bring the robbery victim to the station. Immediately upon entering the room in the police station where Kirby was seated, Shard positively identified him as the robber. No lawyer was present in the room, nor had Kirby asked for legal assistance, or been advised of any right to the presence of counsel.

Finding no constitutional violation, the Court explained that the *Wade-Gilbert* exclusionary rule stems from the constitutional guarantee of the right to counsel contained in the Sixth and Fourteenth Amendments, which "attaches only at or after the time that adversary judicial proceedings have been initiated against" the accused, "by way of formal charge, preliminary hearing, indictment, information, or arraignment." *Id.*, 92 *S.Ct.* at 1881, 1882. "The initiation of judicial criminal proceedings * * * marks the commencement of the 'criminal prosecutions' to which alone the explicit guarantees of the Sixth Amendment are applicable." *Id.*

Accordingly, the Court refused to inject

> into a routine police investigation an absolute constitutional guarantee historically and rationally applicable only after the onset of formal prosecutorial proceedings. * * * "[A]n accused is entitled to counsel at any 'critical stage of the *prosecution*,' and [] a post-indictment lineup is such a 'critical stage.' " [This Court] decline[s] to depart from that rationale today by imposing a *per se* exclusionary rule upon testimony concerning an identification that took place long before the commencement of any prosecution whatever.

Id. at 1882-83. [Court's emphasis.]

FOSTER v. CALIFORNIA
Supreme Court of the United States
394 *U.S.* 440, 89 *S.Ct.* 1127 (1969)

QUESTION: Did the lineup procedure conducted by the police in the below set of circumstances violate defendant's rights under the Due Process Clause of the Fourteenth Amendment ?

CIRCUMSTANCES: The day after an armed robbery of a Western Union office, one of the robbers, Clay, surrendered to the police and implicated Foster and Grice. According to Clay, he and Foster entered and robbed the Western Union office while Grice waited in a nearby car. Except for the robbers themselves, the only witness to the crime was the late-night manager of the Western Union office, Joseph David. David was called to the police station to view a police lineup. "There were three men in the lineup. One was [Foster]. He is a tall man—close to six feet in height. The other two men were short—five feet, five or six inches. [Foster] wore a leather jacket which David said was similar to the one he had seen underneath the coveralls worn by the robber."

After viewing the lineup, David could not positively identify Foster as the robber. He "thought" he was the man, but he was not sure. David then asked to speak to Foster. Shortly thereafter, Foster was brought into an office and sat across from David at a table. Except for law enforcement officials, there was no one else in the room. Even after this one-to-one confrontation, David still was uncertain whether Foster was one of the robbers.

About a week to ten days later, the police called David and asked him to come to the police department to view a second lineup. There were five men in the lineup, including Foster, who was the only person in this second lineup who had appeared in the first lineup. This time, David was "convinced" that Foster "was the man."

At trial, David testified to his identification of Foster as summarized above. He also made an in-court identification of him. Foster was convicted.

ANSWER: YES. Under the totality of the circumstances, the identification procedures conducted by the police in this case were " 'so unnecessarily suggestive and conducive to irreparable mistaken identification,' " that the resulting identification is constitutionally defective as a matter of law. *Id.* at 1128, 1128 n.2. [Citations omitted.]

RATIONALE: "[I]n some cases the procedures leading to an eyewitness identification may be so defective as to make the identification constitutionally inadmissible as a matter of law." *Id.* at 1128 n.2. This case "presents a compelling example of [such an] unfair lineup procedure[]." *Id.* at 1128.

In the first lineup arranged by the police, Foster "stood out from the other two men by the contrast of his height and by the fact that he was wearing a leather jacket similar to that worn by the robber. * * * When this did not lead to positive identification, the police permitted a one-to-one confrontation between [Foster] and the witness. * * * Even after this, the witness' identification of [Foster] was tentative. So some days later another lineup was arranged. [Foster] was the only person in this lineup who had also participated in the first lineup. * * * This finally produced a definite identification." *Id.* at 1128-1129.

"The suggestive elements in this identification procedure made it all but inevitable that David would identify [Foster] whether or not he was in fact 'the man.' * * * In effect, the police repeatedly said to the witness, 'This is the man.' " *Id.* at 1129. It is clear, therefore, that "the pretrial confrontations" were "so arranged as to make the resulting identifications virtually inevitable." *Id.* "This procedure so undermined the reliability of the eyewitness identification as to violate due process of law." *Id.*

NOTE

1. *Group viewings prohibited.* In *Gilbert v. California*, 388 *U.S.* 263, 87 *S.Ct.* 1951 (1967), Gilbert was identified by eyewitnesses in a Los Angeles auditorium. Between ten and thirteen prisoners were placed on the auditorium's stage behind bright lights which prevented those in the line from seeing the audience. "Upwards of 100 persons were in the audience, each an eyewitness to one of the several robberies charged to Gilbert." *Id.*, 87 *S.Ct.* at 1955. "State and federal officers were also present and one of them acted as 'moderator' of the proceedings." *Id.* at 1955 n.2. "Each man in the lineup was identified by number, but not by name. Each man was required to step forward into a marked circle, to turn, presenting both profiles as well as a face and back view, to walk, to put on or take off certain articles of clothing. When a man's number was called and he was directed to step into the circle, he was asked certain questions: where he was picked up, whether he owned a car, whether, when arrested, he was armed, where he lived. Each was also asked to repeat certain phrases, both in a loud and in a soft voice, phrases that witnesses to the crimes had heard the robbers use: 'Freeze, this is a stickup'; 'this is a holdup'; 'empty your cash drawer'; 'this is a heist'; 'don't anybody move.' * * * [T]he assembled witnesses were asked if there were any that they would like to see again, and told that if they had doubts, now was the time to resolve them. Several gave the numbers of men they wanted to see, including Gilbert's. * * * After the lineup, the witnesses talked to each other[, and] in each other's presence, call[ed] out the number of [each man] they could identify." *Id.* Gilbert's number was called by eleven witnesses.

Almost without discussion, the Court held the conduct of the auditorium identification wholly "illegal," and any evidence of the procedure clearly inadmissible. *Id.* at 1956-57.

2. *Significant age differences.* In *Swicegood v. State of Alabama*, 577 *F.*2d 1322 (5th Cir. 1978), Birmingham police arranged an in-person lineup consisting of six white males, including defendant Swicegood. All participants were dressed in "street clothes," their height ranged from 5'7" to 5'11" and weight from 125 to 150 pounds. Some had moustaches and some did not, and their hair color varied. All of the men in the lineup were 26 years of age or younger, except Swicegood, who was 35 at the time. After a second viewing, both strong-armed robbery victims identified Swicegood. Significantly, the identification occurred after the men in the lineup were directed to speak the phrases uttered by the intruders on the night of the robbery.

With respect to the difference in age, the court stated:

> First, there was a considerable difference in the ages of the lineup participants, with Swicegood being nine years older than the next-oldest man and 15 years older than the youngest. Although age generally manifests itself in appearance-related characteristics and courts often treat age as a physical attribute, * * * we think it should be treated as an independent element in this case. A person's age, for example, often has a decided effect on his vernacular, speech patterns, or voice characteristics, and both Mr. and Mrs. Carter identified Swicegood on the basis of his voice. * * * Further, a significant disparity in the ages of the lineup participants could influence a witness who believed that the culprit was an "older" person. Thus, a lineup with only one "older" person could impermissibly point the finger at that individual, albeit in a much more subtle fashion than in other situations.

Id. at 1327.

---

§5.5. PHOTO ARRAYS

Ideally, photographic arrays should be prepared, exhibited, and preserved by means of a standard procedure which demonstrates reliability and the absence of undue suggestiveness. In addition to the photograph of the suspect, at least five additional photographs are normally incorporated, producing an array of six. The photographs chosen for the array should depict individuals of the same race and sex, and having reasonably similar physical characteristics. Care should be exercised to avoid significant age differences, facial hair differences, and significant height differences, with particular attention given to the absence or presence of mustaches, eyeglasses, wild haircuts, closed eyes, etc.

Recent research conducted by the National Institute of Justice (NIJ)[28] suggests that the nonsuspects in the photo array—the "fillers"—should be chosen to match the eyewitness' description of the perpetrator rather than the features of an individual the police may have apprehended as the suspect in the case. Lineups created by selecting fillers that all look substantially like the suspect tend to be unfair to the suspect as well as the witness, particularly when the police are not entirely sure that the suspect is in fact the perpetrator. This process tends to narrow the universe of options for the witness, while also creating a subtle suggestion as to what the police think the suspect looks like. If, however, the witness is unable to provide an adequate description of the perpetrator, the fillers should resemble the suspect's significant features.

With respect to the type of photograph used, black and white pictures should not be mixed with color photographs, and "mugshots" should not be mixed with "snapshots." If one or more of the photographs portray some type of identifying information—either on the front or the back—the printed material should be covered to prevent sending an inappropriate suggestion to a witness. Moreover, if it becomes necessary to partially cover one photograph to eliminate printed material, all the photographs in the array should be treated similarly, regardless of whether they do or do not have identifying material on them. The photographs in the array are then numbered in sequence and the entire procedure is meticulously documented.

At no time should police inform a witness that the perpetrator's picture is in the photo lineup. Rather, the witness should be instructed that the actual suspect might not even be present in the array, and therefore the witness should not feel compelled to make a selection. The witness should understand that the photo lineup procedure is important not just to identify the guilty, but to clear the innocent as well. By informing the witness that the person who committed the crime may or may not be in the photo lineup, the police guard against a witness selecting an individual who looks *most like* the one who committed the crime, hoping that this will help move the investigation along, even if he or she is not certain.

---

[28] In 1998, the NIJ convened the Technical Working Group for Eyewitness Evidence. The group consisted of law enforcement, legal, and psychological research professionals, who joined forces and shared information with the goal of developing improved procedures for collecting and preserving accurate and reliable eyewitness identification evidence. The findings of the Working Group were published in October 1999, in a document titled *Eyewitness Evidence: A Guide for Law Enforcement.* One key principle drawn from all the research was that the memory of an eyewitness should be viewed as "trace evidence," subject to possible contamination, and requiring "rigorous criteria for handling eyewitness evidence that are as demanding as those governing the handling of physical trace evidence." National Institute of Justice, *Eyewitness Evidence: A Guide for Law Enforcement* (1999), at 2.

It is also a good practice to display the photographs one at a time—sequentially—rather than simultaneously. This process guards against the tendency of an eyewitness to compare one photo to another, making relative judgments as to which person looks most like the perpetrator. By viewing the photographs separately, rather than simultaneously, the witness is in a better position to make an identification by comparing each person to his or her own memory of the crime. This lessens the witness' opportunity to engage in a process of elimination, because there is no opportunity to simultaneously compare the relative appearance of all of the photographs in the array.

As in the case of the in-person lineup, only one witness at a time may view the photo array, and at no time should an officer suggest to the witness which photograph to pick. It is also highly inappropriate for an officer to even suggest that the perpetrator's photograph may be in the array or that someone else has already identified one of the individuals portrayed in the array as the perpetrator. If a witness identifies an individual in the photo lineup, the police should not indicate to the witness that he or she "picked the right person," selected the "right photograph," or that the witness' identification "was correct" or "very helpful," or that the police "also think that the right person has been selected." Here, again, the danger of making such suggestive comments lies in the fact that the opinion of the police that the individual identified by the eyewitness is, in fact, the perpetrator creates a risk that any future identifications that may need to be made by the witness would be unduly influenced by the official "stamp of approval." In this regard, the witness should be assured that the investigation will continue, whether or not the witness is able to identify anyone as the actual perpetrator.

To further enhance the reliability of the procedure, the photo lineup should be administered by an officer who does not know which photograph depicts the suspect. This "blind" assignment technique helps avoid any inadvertent body signals or cues which may adversely impact a witness' ability to make a reliable identification. Even when unintended, verbal or nonverbal cues are sometimes given to witnesses when the identity of the actual suspect is known to the officer conducting the photo lineup procedure.

As with other identification procedures, the photo lineup must be carefully documented, regardless of whether an identification is made. The presentation order of the photo lineup should be preserved, and the photographs themselves should be preserved in their original condition.

While the procedures appear to be clear, problems nonetheless arise in the preparation (creation), exhibition, or preservation of investigative photographic arrays.

SIMMONS v. UNITED STATES
Supreme Court of the United States
390 *U.S.* 377, 88 *S.Ct.* 967 (1968)

QUESTION: What standard will a court use to determine whether a criminal defendant's conviction should be set aside because of the improper use of a photographic array ?

ANSWER: Proceeding on a case-by-case basis, "convictions based on eyewitness identification at trial following a pretrial identification by photograph will be set aside on that ground only if the photographic identification procedure was so *impermissibly suggestive* as to give rise to a *very substantial likelihood of irreparable misidentification.*" *Id.* at 971. [Emphasis added.]

RATIONALE: "[I]mproper employment of photographs by police may sometimes cause witnesses to err in identifying criminals. A witness may have obtained only a brief glimpse of a criminal, or may have seen him under poor conditions. Even if the police subsequently follow the most correct photographic identification procedures and show him the pictures of a number of individuals without indicating whom they suspect, there is some danger that the witness may make an incorrect identification. This danger will be increased if the police display to the witness only the picture of a single individual who generally resembles the person he saw, or if they show him the pictures of several persons among which the photograph of a single individual recurs or is in some way emphasized." *Id.*

"The chance of misidentification is also heightened if the police indicate to the witness that they have other evidence that one of the persons pictured committed the crime. Regardless of how the initial misidentification comes about, the witness thereafter is apt to retain in his memory the image of the photograph rather than of the person actually seen, reducing the trustworthiness of subsequent lineup or courtroom identification." *Id.*

"Despite the hazards of initial identification by photograph, this procedure has been used widely and effectively in criminal law enforcement, from the standpoint both of apprehending offenders and of sparing innocent suspects the [stigma] of arrest by allowing eyewitnesses to exonerate them through scrutiny of photographs." *Id.* As a result, the Court is "unwilling to prohibit its employment, either in the exercise of [its] supervisory power or, still less, as a matter of constitutional requirement. Instead, * * * each case must be considered on its own facts, and [] convictions based on eyewitness identification at trial following a pretrial identification by photograph will be set aside on that ground only if the photographic identification procedure was so impermissibly suggestive as to give rise to a very substantial likelihood of irreparable misidentification." *Id.*

MANSON v. BRATHWAITE
Supreme Court of the United States
432 *U.S.* 98, 97 *S.Ct.* 2243 (1977)

QUESTION: Should evidence of a photographic identification automatically be excluded from evidence, regardless of "reliability," when the identification procedure consists of a police officer's examination of a single photograph after an undercover buy of narcotics ?

ANSWER: NO. Although in this case the police procedure of examining a single photograph "was both suggestive and unnecessary," *id.* at 2245, the " 'central question' " is " 'whether under the "totality of the circumstances" the identification was reliable even though the confrontation procedure was suggestive.' " *Id.* at 2249. [Citation omitted.] "The admission of testimony concerning a suggestive and unnecessary identification procedure does not violate due process so long as the identification possesses sufficient aspects of reliability." *Id.* In fact, *"reliability is the linchpin in determining the admissibility of identification testimony[.]" Id.* at 2253. [Emphasis added.]

RATIONALE: At about 7:45 p.m. on May 5, Trooper Glover of the Connecticut State Police Narcotics Division, accompanied by Henry Brown, an informant, went to an apartment building at 201 Westland, in Hartford, for the purpose of purchasing narcotics from "Dickie Boy" Cicero, a known narcotics dealer. Glover and Brown were both wearing ordinary street clothes. Upon arrival at the apartment building, Glover and Brown walked up the stairs and knocked on the door of one of the third-floor apartments where it was believed that Cicero was living. The area outside the apartment was illuminated by natural light from a window in the third floor hallway. In response to Glover's knock, the door opened 12 to 18 inches, and Glover observed a man standing at the door and, behind him, a woman. Brown identified himself and Glover asked for "two things" of narcotics. "The man at the door held out his hand, and Glover gave him two $10 bills. The door closed. Soon the man returned and handed Glover two glassine bags. While the door was open, Glover stood within two feet of the person from whom he made the purchase and observed his face. Five to seven minutes elapsed from the time the door first opened until it closed the second time." *Id.* at 2246. The seller was not Cicero.

Within approximately eight minutes of their arrival, Glover and Brown left the building. Glover drove to headquarters, where he described the seller to two other investigators. At the time, Glover did not know the identity of the seller. He described him as a black male, about five feet eleven inches tall, heavy build, dark complexion, black hair cut in a short Afro, and having high cheekbones. At the time of the sale, the suspect was wearing blue pants and a plaid shirt. One of the other investigators, suspecting that defendant, Nowell Brathwaite, was the seller, obtained a photograph of Brathwaite from the Records Division of the Hartford Police Department. The photograph was left at Glover's office. On May 7, while alone, Glover viewed the photograph; "he identified the person shown as the one from whom he had purchased the narcotics." *Id.*

Subsequently, Brathwaite was arrested at the apartment at which the narcotics sale had taken place. At his trial for the possession and sale of heroin, the photograph from which Glover had identified Brathwaite was received in evidence. Glover also testified that, although he had not seen Brathwaite in the eight months that had elapsed since the sale, "there [was] no doubt whatsoever" in his mind that the person in the photograph was Brathwaite. *Id.* at 2247. Glover also made a positive in-court identification. "No explanation was offered by the prosecution for the failure to utilize a photographic array or to conduct a lineup." *Id.* Brathwaite was convicted on both counts and the Connecticut Supreme Court affirmed.

Fourteen months later, Brathwaite brought a petition for habeas corpus in federal court, contending that "the admission of the identification testimony at his state trial deprived him of due process of law to which he was entitled under the Fourteenth Amendment." *Id.* Though the petition was unsuccessful at the District Court level, the Second Circuit Court of Appeals agreed with Brathwaite and held that "evidence as to the photograph should have been excluded, regardless of reliability, because the examination of the single photograph was unnecessary and suggestive." *Id. The United States Supreme Court disagreed and reversed.*

Although in this case the police procedure of examining a single photograph "was both suggestive [because only one photograph was used] and unnecessary" [because there was no emergency or exigent circumstance], *id.* at 2245, 2250, the " 'central question' " is " 'whether under the "totality of the circumstances" the identification was reliable even though the confrontation procedure was suggestive.' " *Id.* at 2249. [Citation omitted.] "The admission of testimony concerning a suggestive and unnecessary identification procedure does not violate due process so long as the identification possesses sufficient aspects of reliability." *Id.*

The standard, as required by the Due Process Clause of the Fourteenth Amendment, "is that of fairness," *id.* at 2252, and for determining the admissibility of eyewitness identification testimony, "reliability is the linchpin[.]" *Id.* at 2253. To determine whether an eyewitness identification is reliable, several factors may be considered: (1) "the opportunity of the witness to view the criminal at the time of the crime," (2) "the witness' degree of attention," (3) "the accuracy of his prior description of the criminal," (4) "the level of certainty demonstrated at the confrontation," and (5) "the time between the crime and the confrontation." *Id.* "Against these factors is to be weighed the corrupting effect of the suggestive identification itself." *Id.*

Applying the above criteria to the facts of this case:

1. *The opportunity of the witness to view.* Glover testified that for two to three minutes he stood at the apartment door, within two feet of Brathwaite. The door opened twice, and each time Brathwaite stood at the door, Glover looked directly at him. Natural light from outside entered the hallway through a window, as well as from inside the apartment. *Id.* at 2253.

2. *The witness' degree of attention.* Glover was not a casual or passing observer; he was a trained police officer on duty, engaged in a specialized and dangerous undercover buy of narcotics. "As a specially trained, assigned, and experienced officer, he could be expected to pay scrupulous attention to detail, for he knew that subsequently he would have to find and arrest his vendor. In addition, he knew that his claimed observations would be subject later to close scrutiny and examination at any trial." *Id.* Additionally, Trooper Glover was of the same race as Brathwaite and was therefore able to perceive more than mere "general features." *Id.*

3. *The accuracy of the description.* Within minutes of the undercover buy of narcotics, Glover described Brathwaite's race, height, build, color and style of hair, and the high-cheekbone facial features. The description also included the clothing Brathwaite was wearing. No claim is made that the description did not match Brathwaite's, and significantly, another investigator was able to call for Brathwaite's picture from Glover's description. *Id.*

4. *The witness' level of certainty.* "There is no dispute that the photograph in question was that of [Brathwaite]. Glover, in response to a question whether the photograph was that of the person from whom he made the purchase, testified: 'There is no question whatsoever.' " *Id.*

5. *The time between the crime and the confrontation.* Within minutes of the crime, Glover gave a description of Brathwaite to a second investigator. "The photographic identification took place only two days later. We do not have here the passage of weeks or months between the crime and the viewing of the photograph." *Id.* at 2253-2254.

"These indicators of Glover's ability to make an accurate identification are hardly outweighed by the corrupting effect of the challenged identification itself. Although identifications arising from single-photograph displays may be viewed in general with suspicion, * * * [the Court finds in this] case little pressure on the witness to acquiesce in the suggestion that such a display entails. * * * And since Glover examined the photograph alone, there was no coercive pressure to make an identification arising from the presence of another. The identification was made in circumstances allowing care and reflection." *Id*. at 2254.

Accordingly, the totality of the circumstances of this case do not present a "very substantial likelihood of irreparable misidentification." *Id*. The criteria or factors for determining the admissibility of an eyewitness' identification set forth above have been "satisfactorily met and complied with here." *Id*.

NOTE

1. *Officer's "post-buy" viewing of suspect's photograph.* The Court in *Manson v. Brathwaite* instructed that it would have been better had Glover been presented with a photographic array including "so far as practicable * * * a reasonable number of persons similar to any person then suspected whose likeness is included in the array." *Id*. at 2254. "The use of that procedure," according to the Court, "would have enhanced the force of the identification at trial and would have avoided the risk that the evidence would be excluded as unreliable." *Id*.

In *State v. Matthews*, 233 *N.J.Super*. 291, 558 *A.2d* 1329 (App.Div. 1989), defendant argued that it was error for the trial "court to admit testimony and photographs concerning an investigator's pre-trial identification." *Id*. at 294. Finding defendant's argument "clearly without merit," the Appellate Division noted "that this case did not involve an identification in the traditional sense. Rather, it dealt with review of two photographs by the undercover investigator in order to obtain the name of the person who sold him cocaine on [a particular date]. The undercover investigator indicated that he was 'unaware of the name,' not the identity, of the individual who sold him cocaine, and that he looked at the pictures so that the investigators could ascertain the name." *Id*., 233 *N.J.Super*. at 294-295.

According to the court, "there was no showing of impermissible suggestiveness in these circumstances, and that, in any event, the State showed by clear and convincing evidence that the in-court identification was not tainted by any out-of-court identification because there was never a question on the part of the undercover investigator as to the person, as opposed to the name of the person, from whom he bought drugs." *Id*. at 295.

2. *Group viewings prohibited.* In *Commonwealth v. Jarecki*, 415 *Pa.Super*. 286, 609 *A.2d* 194 (1992), approximately six weeks after an armed robbery of the Weis Market in Berks County, an officer took a photo display book containing seventy-five photographs,

including a photograph of defendant, to the market for viewing. The witnesses viewed the photographic display *collectively*, and four witnesses selected defendant's picture from the array of seventy-five photos. Although the robber's face, during the robbery, was covered by a blue scarf so that only his hair, eyes, and the underside of his chin were visible, one of the identifying witnesses, Joe G., claimed to have seen the robber's face as he fled the robbery scene. During the course of the identification procedure, three of the witnesses, each of whom had access to a previously-published composite sketch, watched as Joe G. selected a photograph. The witnesses discussed the photographs among themselves, and then selected defendant's photograph.

The conduct of this photo identification procedure, held the court, was entirely improper and made "the accuracy of the identifications highly suspect." *Id.*, 609 A.2d at 196. As a result, the court reversed defendant's conviction and remanded the matter for a new trial at which all evidence relating to the photographic identifications "shall be suppressed." *Id.* at 200. The court elaborated:

> Given the circumstances of this case, and the manner in which the identifications took place, misidentification was highly likely * * * [The officer] took the photographic display into the store and showed it to the witnesses approximately six weeks after the robbery, and at least four witnesses viewed the display at the same time. All but one of the four identifying witnesses had seen only the eyes, chin, and hair of the robber, and none of them had described the robber's eyes as distinctive prior to the photographic identification. Furthermore, the witnesses had access to the published composite sketch prior to the identification proceeding. Joe G[.], the witness who claimed to see the robber's entire face and on whose description the composite sketch was based, was the first to select a photograph from the display. The other witnesses had the opportunity to observe Mr. G[.] select a photograph, thus allowing the other witnesses to infer that the robber was pictured in the display. As Mr. G[.] claimed to have seen the robber's entire face and his description was the basis for the composite drawing, it is likely that the others searched the display for a person who matched the composite sketch and Mr. G[.]'s description, instead of relying on their own independent recollections.
>
> In addition, * * * the witnesses discussed the photographs as they perused the display. * * *
>
> In light of the above[,] * * * we are persuaded that the photo identification procedure was highly suggestive and that any reference to the photographic identifications should have been suppressed * * *.

Id. at 196-98.

3. *Voice identification.* In *Government of Virgin Islands v. Sanes*, 57 *F*.3d 338 (3rd Cir. 1995), a rape victim identified her attacker through a voice identification procedure similar to that used by police when conducting a photo array identification procedure. Using the five-part test set forth by the Supreme Court in *Neil v. Biggers* and *Manson v. Brathwaite*, the court found no evidence that the voice identification procedure was impermissibly suggestive or that there was a substantial likelihood of misidentification. In this respect, the court observed:

> Although voice identification obviously differs from eyewitness identification (for example, what is at issue in the first part of the *Neil* and *Manson* test is opportunity to view rather than opportunity to hear), we conclude that the *Neil* and *Manson* eyewitness identification test, adapted to voice identification, provides a standardized source of guidance * * * for assessing the reliability of voice identification as well.

Id. at 340.

The victim in this case was attacked on two different occasions, and on each occasion, she conversed with her attacker for ten minutes. Not only did she listen to her attacker for this considerable period of time, but she testified "that she engaged him in conversation in the hope that she could identify his voice[.]" *Id.* at 341. The court found that the victim was alert and had a sufficient opportunity to view or hear her attacker on both occasions, and she presented an accurate description of Sanes and his clothing. She identified the items taken from Sanes as looking like items the attacker had worn. In addition, she stated that she was certain that Sample No. 4 was the voice of her attacker. "During the voice identification procedure, she listened to the voice array three times. She was ready to identify Sample No. 4 after the second time, but was encouraged by the police to listen to the tape one more time. [She] then positively identified the fourth voice as that of her attacker. Sample No. 4 was Sanes' voice." *Id.* at 340. "Finally, although there was a six-month period between the incidents, only fifteen days elapsed between the last attack and her positive voice identification." *Id.* at 340-41.

The court concluded, therefore, that "the district court properly applied the *Neil/Manson* factors and properly denied Sanes' motion to suppress the voice identification." *Id.* at 341.

COMMONWEALTH v. SANDERS
Superior Court of Pennsylvania
380 *Pa.Super.* 78, 551 *A*.2d 239 (1988)

QUESTION: Will a photo array be deemed unduly suggestive, as a matter of law, when the victim is shown a display of nine photographs, including one of defendant, when the photograph of the defendant pictured him without a shirt, whereas all the other pictures except one pictured their subjects wearing shirts, and in addition, the photograph of defendant was of a "different gloss" than the others ?

ANSWER: NO. Such a photographic array is not, as a matter of law, impermissibly suggestive. The victim "was shown nine photographs and asked if any of the subjects portrayed one of the males in the robbery. * * * He was not given any information about the individuals in the photographs." *Id.* at 245. However, "even if the photographs were in some sense suggestive, [the court] find[s] that there was an independent basis for the [victim's] in-court identification." *Id.*

RATIONALE: At about 1:30 a.m., in the middle of October, a Philadelphia cab driver picked up two young males on Woodland Avenue. The cab driver looked at the males as they entered the cab and kept the interior light on so he could see them during the drive. During the course of the ten-minute ride, he periodically looked at defendant, who was seated in the rear passenger's side, through the rear-view mirror. As they arrived at the requested destination, defendant's cohort put a sharp object to the cab driver's throat while defendant reached into the driver's pocket and removed over $100.00 in cash. Defendant then ordered the cab driver out of the cab, and with defent the wheel, the two assailants drove off in the cab. Defendant and his companion were arrested the next day in Ohio.

At police headquarters, the cab driver gave a detailed description of defendant and was later shown an array of nine photographs, including one of defendant. The photograph of defendant, however, pictured him without a shirt, whereas all the other photographs except one pictured their subjects wearing shirts. Additionally, the photograph of defendant was of a "different gloss" than the others, and the two shirtless subjects were, according to defendant, the darkest males in the group.

In this appeal, defendant argued that the photographic identification "was unduly suggestive," *id.* at 245, thereby tainting his in-court identification. *The Superior Court disagreed.*

While defendant has failed to include in the record the photographs from the array, thus precluding this court from making an independent determination as to their suggestiveness, the court nonetheless notes "that the complaining witness was shown nine photographs and asked if any of the subjects portrayed one of the males involved in the robbery. * * * He was not given any information about the individuals in the photographs." *Id.*

"Furthermore, even if the photographs were in some sense suggestive, [this court] find[s] that there was an independent basis for the complaining witness' in-court identification." *Id.* As the Pennsylvania Supreme Court explained in *Commonwealth v. McGaghey,* 510 *Pa.* 225, 507 *A.*2d 359 (1986): " 'The problem with an impermissibl[y] suggestive identification is the potential for misidentification, resulting in a due process violation if that identification is admitted at trial. * * * Suggestiveness alone will not forbid the use of an identification, if the reliability of a subsequent identification can be sustained. * * * To do so, the Commonwealth must establish that the in-court identification resulted from the criminal act and not the suggestive encounter.' " *Sanders* at 245 (quoting *McGaghey* at 228-229, 507 *A.*2d at 359).

Factors which are used to determine whether a victim had an independent basis for an in-court identification include (1) " 'the opportunity of the witness to view the criminal at the time of the crime,' " (2) " 'the witness' degree of attention,' " (3) " 'the accuracy of the witness' prior description of the criminal,' " (4) " 'the level of certainty demonstrated by the witness at the confrontation,' " and (5) " 'the length of time between the crime and the confrontation.' " *Id.* (quoting *Commonwealth v. James,* 506 *Pa.* 526, 534, 486 *A.*2d 376, 380 (1985)).

At the hearing, the cab driver testified that he observed defendant at the time of the criminal incident. "He further testified that neither [defendant] nor his companion wore any covering over their faces. * * * When asked if either wore a hat or glasses or anything else, he answered, 'absolutely no.' " *Id.* at 245-246. The cab driver stated that he looked at defendant, who was seated on the passenger's side, during the ten-minute cab ride. Defendant told the cab driver to stop the cab and then he moved to the front seat next to him. The cab driver then again looked at defendant. The cab driver also described how defendant was dressed and the way he wore his hair.

The foregoing circumstances, coupled with the cab driver's detailed description of defendant given to the police after the crime and his positive identification at the preliminary hearing, lead the court to conclude "that even if the photo identification was in some sense suggestive, the victim did, indeed, crystalize his identification of [defendant] during the criminal incident." *Id.* at 246. Consequently, "[t]here is clear and convincing evidence that the in-court identification resulted from the victim's observations during the cab ride, and not from a suggestive photo array." *Id.*

NOTE

Officer's testimony as to "mug shots." Law enforcement witnesses should *never* refer to the photo array as "mug shots." Any testimonial reference to a photograph can constitute reversible error if a jury could reasonably infer therefrom that the defendant has a prior criminal history. A mere passing reference to photographs will not, however, invalidate the hearing so long as there has been no unfair prejudice as a result of the reference.

Testifying officers should therefore refrain from characterizing photo arrays as "mug shots," "mug books," "photographs from a police file," or any other type of reference which would reasonably suggest to a jury that the photographs were obtained as a result of the defendant's prior criminal activity. On the other hand, testimony that refers to these arrays merely as "photographs" has consistently been interpreted as neutral, and upheld as proper. *See e.g., Commonwealth v. Jones*, 411 *Pa.Super.* 312, 601 *A.2d* 808 (1991) (detective's testimony that, "We used the photographs that were available to us . . ." did not in and of itself warrant the grant of a new trial; at no time were the police photographs referred to as "mug shots," or in any other manner from which the jury could have inferred past criminal activity on the part of the defendant).

See also United States v. Fosher at §4.4.

STATE v. MADISON
Supreme Court of New Jersey
109 *N.J.* 223, 536 *A.2d* 254 (1988)

QUESTION: Will a photo lineup procedure be deemed impermissibly suggestive when (1) prior to displaying the lineup to the witness the police inform the witness that the suspect is included in the array, (2) the photographic array was made up of thirty-eight color photographs, thirteen or fourteen of which depicted the suspect as the center of attention at a birthday celebration held in his honor, and (3) the witness was able to identify the suspect in only one of the thirteen or fourteen color photographs ?

ANSWER: YES. "[T]he procedures followed in th[is] out-of-court identification * * * were impermissibly suggestive due to the unnecessary inclusion of multiple photographs of the defendant." *Id.*, 109 *N.J.* at 239. However, whether these impermissibly suggestive out-of-court identification procedures so "irreparably 'tainted' the out-of-court and in-court identifications of the defendant [so as to deny him] due process," is a question which was inadequately addressed by the trial court. Therefore, the case must be remanded to determine whether the eyewitness identification "had an independent reliable basis." *Id.* at 239, 244.

RATIONALE: The State's case against defendant Madison, "as one of three men who robbed a movie theatre [in Cherry Hill] is based primarily on the pretrial and in-court identification of the defendant by one of the victims, Brian Mason." *Id.* at 225.

The evidence established that at approximately 10:30 p.m., three men entered the Cherry Hill movie theatre. One of the three pulled a gun on two of the theatre's employees and, along with his two gun-toting compatriots, forced the two employees upstairs and into a storage closet, telling them "not to leave or they would be shot." *Id.* at 227. As the three robbers approached the manager's office, defendant took up the lead, entered and walked over to where Mr. Mason, the theatre manager, was counting the night's receipts. Defendant then "grabbed the money on the desk, and put a gun to Mr. Mason's head, threatening to blow his brains out if he did not open the safe." *Id.*

"After Mr. Mason opened the safe, [defendant] directed him to stand back and hand him a nearby coin bag [which he] used for gathering the money." *Id.* at 228. Mr. Mason was then ordered to sit down, as defendant placed his gun back in his coat and left the theatre with his associates.

The entire incident, according to Mr. Mason, lasted approximately ten to fifteen minutes. Mr. Mason "testified that the light in the theatre office was good and that he had a good opportunity to view the defendant," that "he was close to [him,]" but that "during the robbery he was shocked, scared and nervous[.]" *Id.* at 240, 241. Subsequently, the police were called and all of the theatre's employees gave statements.

"A few days after the robbery, Mr. Mason gave a description to the police from which a composite picture was drawn." *Id.* at 228.

Approximately two months after the robbery, Mr. Mason was called to the Cherry Hill police station, where he met with three detectives from the Philadelphia Police Department and one Cherry Hill police detective. At the meeting, Mr. Mason was informed by Cherry Hill Detective Grady that "[t]here were detectives from Philadelphia who had photographs of a man who they might believe was the man who held [you] up." *Id.* at 229.

Philadelphia Detective Rago conducted the photo lineup procedure. Significantly, when he assembled the lineup he never looked at the composite made by the Cherry Hill police nor had he been provided with any description of defendant.

After Mr. Mason was instructed not to pick a picture unless he felt "positive about it," he was first displayed three folders containing twenty-four black-and-white photographs, all of black males of similar complexion, most being between the ages of 25 and 30.

"Each folder contained eight pictures. Defendant's photograph was included in the black-and-white photographs[,]" *id.,* however, while Detective Rago testified that Mr. Mason did not select a photo from the black-and-white array, Mr. Mason insisted that he did in fact identify defendant in the array.

"Mr. Mason then was shown two albums that contained approximately thirty-eight color photographs. Detective Rago advised Mr. Mason that the photographs were in color and were of individuals in a more natural setting. The pictures were taken at defendant's birthday party. He appeared in thirteen or fourteen out of the total number of thirty-eight photographs, in ten photographs with one to two other individuals, once each with three others and four others, and twice with six others. ∗ ∗ ∗ Mr. Mason identified the defendant in only one color photograph." *Id.* at 229-230.

At trial, Mr. Mason identified the color photo of the defendant he had previously selected, and "[o]nce in the courtroom, he identified defendant as the individual in the picture and the person who robbed him." *Id.* at 231. Also at trial, the other employees of the theatre testified as to their observations.

In this appeal, defendant argued "that the out-of-court photographic identification procedures were 'so impermissibly suggestive' that he was denied due process of law[; ∗ ∗ ∗ further claiming] that both Mr. Mason's out-of-court and in-court identifications of him should have been excluded from evidence. The trial court found that the out-of-court identification procedures were not so impermissibly suggestive. Hence it did not reach the question of whether those procedures were so unduly prejudicial as to have fatally tainted Mr. Mason's pretrial and in-court identifications of the defendant." *Id.* at 226.

Whenever the reliability of an eyewitness' identification is drawn into issue, a court will conduct a two-step analysis to determine its admissibility into evidence. Step one involves an inquiry into "whether the procedure in question was in fact impermissibly suggestive. If the court does find the procedure impermissibly suggestive, [step two requires an inquiry into] whether the objectionable procedure resulted in a 'very substantial likelihood of irreparable misidentification.'" *Id.* at 232 (quoting *Simmons v. United States,* 390 *U.S.* 377, 384, 88 *S.Ct.* 967, 971 (1968)). "In carrying out the second part of the analysis, the court will focus on the reliability of the identification. If the court finds that the identification is reliable despite the impermissibly suggestive nature of the procedure, the identification may be admitted into evidence. 'Reliability is the linchpin in determining the admissibility of identification testimony[.]'" *Madison* at 232 (quoting *Manson v. Brathwaite,* 432 *U.S.* 98, 114, 97 *S.Ct.* 2243, 2253 (1977)). "The reliability determination is to be made from the totality of the circumstances adduced in the particular case." *Madison* at 233.

The New Jersey Supreme Court has "consistently followed the [United States] Supreme Court's analysis on whether out-of-court and in-court identifications are admissible into evidence." *Id.* at 233. Therefore, step one of the inquiry in this case "is whether the pretrial identification procedures used at the police station * * * were impermissibly suggestive. * * * 'Impermissive suggestibility is to be determined by the totality of the circumstances of the identification. It is to be stressed that the determination can only be reached so as to require the exclusion of the evidence where all the circumstances lead forcefully to the conclusion that *the identification was not actually that of the eyewitness, but was imposed upon him so that a substantial likelihood of irreparable misidentification can be said to exist.*' " *Id.* at 233-234 (emphasis supplied). [Citation omitted.] Applying this standard, the Court found that "the pretrial identification procedures [herein employed] were impermissibly suggestive." *Id.* at 234.

"Approximately two months after the robbery, Mr. Mason was called to the police station. Before he viewed the pictures, he was informed that 'there were detectives from Philadelphia who had photographs of a man who they might believe was the man who held [you] up.' 'A statement of the police that a suspect is included in the photographic array . . . should be considered in determining whether it was unduly suggestive. . . .' " *Id.* [Citation omitted.] There was, however, "no evidence that the detectives attempted to influence Mr. Mason's choice by any other statements. Thus, this statement alone is not sufficient to support the conclusion that the pretrial identification procedures were unduly suggestive." *Id.*

What caused the Court to conclude that the out-of-court procedures were impermissibly suggestive was "the sheer repetition of defendant's picture" in the photo array. Mr. Mason was shown "thirty-eight color photographs, thirteen or fourteen of which depicted defendant as the center of attention at a birthday celebration held in his honor." *Id.* at 235. Although the repetition of a defendant's photograph can cause a suggestive identification, courts have, on occasion, concluded that evidence of the photographic identification may nonetheless be admissible. *State v. Thompson,* 59 *N.J.* 396, 412, 414, 283 *A.2d* 513 (1971) (photo lineup admitted where defendant appeared in two photographs out of an array of seven); *State v. Andrial,* 203 *N.J.Super.* 1, 7, 8, 495 *A.2d* 878 (App.Div. 1985) (photo lineup admitted where defendant appeared in three photographs out of an array of eighty-five photographs). In those cases, however, "the witnesses have generally been able to identify the defendant in each of the pictures in which he appeared." *Madison* at 237.

In this case, "Mason was able to identify the defendant in only one of the thirteen or fourteen color photographs. This is so despite the fact that these pictures were taken at the same time and in the same context, *i.e.*, the defendant's birthday party. Mason's inability to identify defendant in all the photographs in which he appeared strongly suggests to [the Court] that his identification could have been the product of an impermissibly suggestive procedure." *Id.* at 238. Additionally, "[t]here is no claim by the State that these suggestive procedures were necessary because the law enforcement authorities were faced with an emergency that required an immediate identification." *Id. See e.g., Stovall v. Denno,* 388 *U.S.* 293, 302, 87 *S.Ct.* 1967, 1972 (1967) (one-man lineup at hospital justified due to grave illness of victim).

Accordingly, "the procedures followed in the out-of-court identification of defendant were impermissibly suggestive due to the unnecessary inclusion of multiple photographs of the defendant." *Id.* at 239.

"The danger of highly suggestive out-of-court identification procedures is that they may 'give rise to a very substantial likelihood of irreparable misidentification.'" *Id.* [Citation omitted.] Therefore, step two of the analysis requires a "determination of whether the impermissibly suggestive out-of-court procedures so irreparably 'tainted' the out-of-court and in-court identifications of the defendant that he was denied due process." *Id.* Such a determination is made by examining the totality of the circumstances in the particular case to see if " 'there are sufficient indicia of reliability [*i.e.,* an independent source] to outweigh the corrupting effect of the suggestive identification itself.' " *Id.* [Citations omitted.] According to the Court:

> This involves considering the facts of each case and weighing the corruptive influence of the suggestive identification against the "opportunity of the witness to view the criminal at the time of the crime, the witness's degree of attention, the accuracy of his prior description of the criminal, the level of certainty demonstrated at the time of the confrontation and the time between the crime and the confrontation."

Id. at 239-240 (quoting *Manson v. Brathwaite, supra,* 432 *U.S.* at 114, 97 *S.Ct.* at 2253).

The Court then weighed all the foregoing factors against the corrupting effects of the suggestive police procedures and concluded that "the likelihood of misidentification with respect to Mr. Mason's * * * identifications is great." *Id.* at 244. However, because the trial court made no findings on whether the out-of-court or in-court identifications were tainted by the suggestive procedures employed, the record does not permit the Court "to determine whether Mr. Mason's identifications had an independent, reliable basis." *Id.*

As a result, the case was remanded "to the trial court for a taint [*Wade**] hearing to determine whether the identifications of Mr. Mason had an independent source. Since [the Court] f[ound] the pretrial identification procedures to be impermissibly suggestive, the State has the burden of proving by clear and convincing evidence that the identifications by Mr. Mason had a source independent of the police- conducted identification procedures. * * * If the trial court finds that Mr. Mason's identification has an independent source, then the conviction should be affirmed. If the trial court finds that Mr. Mason's identification does not have an independent source, * * * there must be a new trial." *Id*. at 245-246.

NOTE

1. Compare *State v. Gunter,* 231 *N.J.Super.* 34, 554 A.2d 1356 (App.Div. 1989), where the court upheld a photographic array which depicted defendant in "two or three" photographs in a 15-photograph array. The photographs of defendant were "not the same," and the eyewitness was not aware that he tentatively identified the same person when he selected more than one photograph. *Id.,* 231 *N.J.Super.* at 40. In addition, the integrity of the subsequent in-court identification was found to be preserved because the police did not tell the eyewitness that he had tentatively identified the subject. *Id*.

2. *Identification based on television broadcast of defendant's photo and subsequent photo lineup.* In *State v. Clausell,* 121 *N.J.* 298, 580 A.2d 221 (1990), the Court held that an eyewitness' observation of the defendant's photograph on a television news broadcast, followed by an identification of the defendant through a photo lineup, "was not so suggestive as to give rise to a substantial likelihood of misidentification." *Id.,* 121 *N.J.* at 326. According to the Court, the eyewitness "had a substantial opportunity to view [the defendant] at a time when she was particularly interested in his identity. Her description of the assailant was consistent with [defendant's] actual appearance. The time lapse between the identification and the crime—six weeks—was not extensive, and [the eyewitness] was confident of her identification." *Id*. at 326-327.

3. *Improper notations attached to the photographs.* During the course of defendant's trial in *State v. Onysko,* 226 *N.J.Super.* 599, 545 A.2d 226 (App.Div. 1988), the State introduced into evidence a photographic lineup which included a photograph of defendant. The photograph was a mug shot which on the reverse side contained the following information:

---

* *United States v. Wade,* 388 *U.S.* 218, 87 *S.Ct.* 1926 (1967). The *Wade* hearing is held to determine the admissibility of an eyewitness' identification of the defendant.

MAHWAH POLICE DEPT.
Mahwah, N.J.

NAME	ROBERT J. ONYSKO
ALIAS	Timothy Eggers
CRIME	Violation of Probation
AGE	39 HEIGHT 5'10"
WEIGHT	170 BUILD thin
HAIR	brown EYES brown
COMP	Superior Ct. Bergen County
BORN	Jersey City 4/25/46
OCCUP.	burglar
DATE OF ARREST	7/31/85
OFFICER	McGill
REMARKS	

Id., 226 *N.J.Super.* at 601-602. After the trial, in which defendant elected not to testify, it was learned that at least one juror had read the information appearing on the reverse side of defendant's photograph. In the appeal which thereafter followed, the Superior Court, Appellate Division, granted defendant a new trial. The court agreed with defendant that the information disclosed improperly "characterized him as a professional burglar by listing his occupation as 'burglar,' and that the use of an alias reflected the magnitude of his criminal propensities." *Id.* at 605. According to the court, "[i]njection of his prior use of aliases and that he is characterized by the police as having an occupation as a 'burglar' clearly reveals to the jury precisely that, that he is a 'burglar' and thus guilty of the offense charged." *Id.* The officers in this case should have made some effort to at least cover the information on the back of defendant's photograph. *Id.* at 603.

4. *Varied backgrounds in the photographs.* In addition to the suggestive nature of the "collective" photo lineup procedure in *Commonwealth v. Jarecki*, 415 *Pa.Super.* 286, 609 *A.2d* 194 (1992), the court also noted that the photo array itself was defective. The court stated:

> [W]e have reviewed the seventy-five photographs that were contained in the display, and we observe that the background in [defend]ant's photograph varied from the background of the other photographs in the display. Also, the other photographs were primarily head shots, while [defend]ant's photograph was taken from a further distance and showed his entire torso. Finally, the date was prominently displayed in [defend]ant's photograph, but not in any of the other photographs. These differences emphasized [defend]ant's photograph, and the differences increased the risk of misidentification.

Id., 609 *A.2d* at 198-99.

Chapter 6

PROOF IN CRIMINAL CASES

§6.1. PRINCIPAL TYPES OF EVIDENCE

Evidence may be classified into two distinct principal types: (a) *direct* evidence and (b) *circumstantial* evidence.

§6.1(a). Direct Evidence

"Direct" evidence is primary or firsthand evidence which, in a single step and a completely straightforward way, establishes an alleged matter of fact. When direct evidence is used to establish a proposition of fact, there is no need for the drawing of inferences or the use of presumptions. Eyewitness testimony is a prime example. Thus, if a witness testifies that she saw the defendant shoot the victim with a handgun, the witness' testimony is direct evidence of whether the defendant did indeed shoot the victim. Such evidence, if believed, establishes the fact in issue.

§6.1(b). Circumstantial Evidence

"Circumstantial" evidence is indirect evidence; it is used to establish an alleged matter of fact inferentially. Presentation of circumstantial evidence generally requires the factfinder to examine a series of facts or chain of circumstances which suggest the acceptance of the ultimate fact in issue. In this respect, if a witness testifies that she saw the defendant run away from the scene of a shooting, the witness' testimony is circumstantial evidence of the shooting (but direct evidence as to the defendant's flight). Such evidence, if believed, requires an additional thought process to reach the ultimate fact in issue, that is, whether the defendant shot the victim. Nonetheless, in many cases, the circumstantial evidence presented may be as potent as direct evidence.

PEOPLE v. DUKES
Appellate Court of Illinois, First District
146 *Ill.App.*3d 790, 497 *N.E.*2d 351 (4th Div. 1986)

Justice JOHNSON delivered the opinion of the court.

"Defendants, Terry and Sylvester Dukes, were jointly tried before a jury in the circuit court of Cook County and convicted of arson * * *." *Id.* at 352.

"We first address the issue of whether the State proved defendants guilty of arson beyond a reasonable doubt. The parties disagree [] on the legal principles that we should apply to the facts of this case." *Id.* at 354.

"Direct evidence is proof of a fact without the necessity of inference or presumption, or evidence of a fact perceived through a witness' senses. Circumstantial evidence, however, is the proof of certain facts and circumstances in a given case from which the trier of fact may infer other connected facts that usually and reasonably follow according to common experience." *Id.*

"The opportunity for commission of an arson, the motive inducing arson and the identity of a person accused of arson may all be established through circumstantial evidence because the crime of arson is, by its very nature, secretive and usually incapable of direct proof. * * * A conviction may be sustained upon circumstantial evidence as well as direct evidence, it being necessary only that the proof of circumstances must be of a conclusive nature and tendency leading, on the whole, to a satisfactory conclusion and producing a reasonable and moral certainty that the accused and no one else committed the crime." *Id.*

"We conclude that the evidence linking defendants to the fire was entirely circumstantial. No one saw either defendant throw a molotov cocktail or anything else at the building. The State presented no evidence that defendants held a molotov cocktail, or even touched gasoline or any other flammable liquid. [Detective] McElrath arrested defendants approximately one-half hour after the fire and could not detect the odor of gasoline or anything else after examining their hands and clothing." *Id.*

Nonetheless, "the trial testimony reveals an overwhelming amount of circumstantial evidence against defendants." *Id.* at 355. The subject building was a two-story structure that contained two apartments and a gameroom. The testimony revealed that Jerry Brown, the owner of the building, "clashed with defendants on several occasions prior to the fire. On one occasion, * * * he had ejected Sylvester from his gameroom for beating a woman who was holding an infant. * * * Sylvester and another person then fought with Brown." *Id.* at 353. On another occasion, Brown saw Terry throw a stone at Brown's car, breaking a window. And on yet another occasion, Brown was driving his car toward his garage when he saw Sylvester crouching behind the garage, "lighting something." *Id.*

On the day of the fire, Minnie Williams, who lived in the upstairs apartment of the building, was sitting by her window. She testified that she "heard a loud noise and saw the reflection of flames against a large tree in front of the building. She went to another window in her apartment, raised it, and looked out. She saw the flames [and] both defendants [who stood] next to a street light for 2 or 3 seconds before they ran away." *Id.*

"While flight from the scene of a crime does not, in and of itself, prove guilt, if it is of such a character that it implicates an attempt to avoid capture and thus shows a consciousness of guilt on the part of the defendant, the trier of fact may consider it with all the other evidence in the case as a factor tending to show guilt." *Id.* at 355.

"We hold that the State proved defendants guilty beyond a reasonable doubt." *Id.*

NOTE

The "circumstantial evidence" test: Excluding any reasonable hypothesis of innocence.

(a) In *Holland v. United States*, 348 *U.S.* 121, 75 *S.Ct.* 127 (1954), the Court rejected the defendants' argument that the jury should be instructed, in cases where the Government's evidence is circumstantial, that it must be such as to exclude every reasonable hypothesis other than that of guilt. According to the Court, "the better rule is that where the jury is properly instructed on the standards for reasonable doubt, such an additional instruction on circumstantial evidence is confusing and incorrect." *Id.* at 139-40, 75 *S.Ct.* at 137. "Circumstantial evidence," explained the Court,

is intrinsically no different from testimonial evidence. Admittedly, circumstantial evidence may in some cases point to a wholly incorrect result. Yet this is equally true of testimonial evidence. In both instances, a jury is asked to weigh the chances that the evidence correctly points to guilt against the possibility of inaccuracy or ambiguous inference. In both, the jury must use its experience with people and events in weighing the probabilities. If the jury is convinced beyond a reasonable doubt, we can require no more.

Id. at 140, 75 *S.Ct.* at 137-38.

(b) A number of courts apply the "circumstantial evidence test." For example, in *State v. Harris*, 807 *S.W.* 528 (Mo.App. 1991), the court observed:

Circumstantial evidence means evidence that does not directly prove a fact in issue but gives rise to a logical inference that the fact exists. * * *

251

Where the state has adduced only circumstantial evidence, the reviewing court must apply the circumstantial evidence test * * *. Under that test, the state's evidence must exclude any reasonable hypothesis of innocence. * * * Where, however, any direct evidence exists, * * * the test of sufficiency changes. The proper test then requires that, based on all the evidence * * * the state proved all elements of the charges [beyond a reasonable doubt].

Id. at 529.

See also People v. Dukes, supra, 497 *N.E.*2d at 354 ("when a conviction is based entirely on circumstantial evidence, the facts proved must be consistent with the defendant's guilt and inconsistent with any reasonable hypothesis of innocence"); *People v. Wilson,* 400 *Ill.* 461, 473, 81 *N.E.*2d 211, 220 (1948) (if the government's case rests solely on circumstantial evidence and if a reasonable hypothesis of innocence arises from the evidence that is consistent with the innocence of the defendant, then the jury must adopt that hypothesis).

STATE v. HOPPER
Missouri Court of Appeals, Southern District
735 *S.W.*2d 429 (2nd Div. 1987)

MAUS, Judge.
[Defendant appeals his conviction of driving while intoxicated, arguing that the evidence was insufficient to support his conviction.]
"Th[e] evidence consisted of the testimony of the arresting officer, which is summarized as follows. The officer observed the pickup truck driven by the defendant weaving between traffic lanes. After he was stopped, the defendant stumbled in getting out of the pickup and had to cling to the door. The defendant directed an obscenity to the officer and was uncooperative in performing the sobriety field tests. The defendant's face was flushed, his eyes were glassy and bloodshot and his speech was slurred. The officer observed a moderate smell of alcohol on the defendant's breath. Without objection, the officer of 19 years testified that the defendant was intoxicated." *Id.* at 430.
"The defendant bases his contention upon the fact that there was no evidence of the results of a test to establish the defendant's blood alcohol level. He acknowledges that intoxication can be established in the absence of such evidence. * * * However, he argues that [his] conviction is based upon circumstantial evidence and that the evidence must be inconsistent with and exclude every reasonable hypothesis of [] innocence. * * * He argues that his physical condition

and appearance at 11:00 p.m. could have been the result of working between 10:00 a.m. and 3:00 p.m. in dismantling and hauling away a partially burned building. The defendant's contention has no merit for two reasons. First, the officer saw the defendant driving. The officer's testimony that the defendant was intoxicated is direct evidence of his guilt and the [circumstantial evidence] rule is not applicable. * * * Second, the proffered explanation is not a *reasonable* hypothesis of the defendant's innocence. * * * The evidence was sufficient to support the trial court's determination [that] the defendant was guilty." *Id.* [Court's emphasis.]

The judgment is *AFFIRMED.*

STATE v. MAYBERRY
Supreme Court of New Jersey
52 *N.J.* 413, 245 A.2d 481 (1968)

The opinion of the Court was delivered by

JACOBS, J.

* * * * *

"The defendant [] asserts that the State's proof of attempted robbery was circumstantial rather than direct and was insufficient to satisfy the requirements of *State v. Donohue*, 2 *N.J.* 381 (1949). In *Donohue* the Court expressed the sweeping view that when the State's evidence is circumstantial 'all of the circumstances not only must concur to indicate a defendant's guilt but they must also be inconsistent with any other rational conclusion' and they must exclude 'every other hypothesis except that of guilt.' * * * This broad expression was never applied literally, for if it had been it would have unreasonably defeated many legitimate prosecutions based on circumstantial evidence where it was possible 'to devise speculative hypotheses consistent with defendant's innocence.'" *Id.*, 52 *N.J.* at 436.

"The formulation found in *Donohue* has been criticized elsewhere * * * and has been abandoned in our recent opinions. * * * It should no longer be cited to us[.] * * * [For purposes of evidence which is circumstantial] the proper issue is simply whether the evidence, viewed in its entirety including the legitimate inferences therefrom, is sufficient to enable a jury to find that the State's charge has been established beyond reasonable doubt. * * * *The approach is the same though the testimony is circumstantial rather than direct; indeed in many situations circumstantial evidence may be 'more forceful and more persuasive than direct evidence.'*" *Id.* at 436-37. [Citations omitted; emphasis added.]

---

§6.1(c). Circumstantial Evidence of Ability to Commit the Crime

There are some crimes that are committed in such a manner as to suggest that the suspect had special skills or abilities that the average person would not have had. A unique running or weight-lifting ability, an expertise in the martial arts, a unique "safe cracking" skill, high-tech computer skills, an expertise in bookkeeping, locksmithing, or specialized artistic, etching or printing skills are just some examples. Naturally, the more unique or specialized the skill, the stronger the inference that the accused is the one who committed the crime, if he or she has the skill. On the other hand, if the crime was committed by a person with a unique skill or ability, the fact that the accused does not have it can be used by the defense for the inference that the accused did not commit the crime.

Although this circumstantial evidence is not conclusive, it may, when combined with other evidence in the case, be sufficient to convince the jury as to the defendant's guilt.

---

§6.1(d). Circumstantial Evidence of Means and Methods

Means. If it can be shown that the accused had the means to commit the crime, that may be used as circumstantial evidence if the average person would not have had access to those means, *e.g.,* a particular tool, specialized equipment or a location. For example, the accused owned a gun of the same caliber as a bullet found at the crime scene. Or, near the time of the crime, the accused was eating lunch at a diner located across the street from the crime scene. Another example is that of a person who was employed by a chemical company that manufactured explosives. This would show that the accused had access to the chemicals necessary to manufacture a bomb. Perhaps a more common example involves a drug-distribution investigation where the accused is found to be in possession of a large quantity of new, clear plastic baggies—circumstantial evidence of the means to distribute various quantities of drugs.

Methods. A suspect's *modus operandi*—his or her "method of operation"—may serve as circumstantial evidence relevant to the prosecution's case. In this regard, some patterns of criminal behavior are so distinctive that investigators attribute it to the work of a specific person. For example, staging a fight at a bus station may be part of a particular pickpocket's *modus operandi.* (M.O.)

It is well established that many criminals become creatures of habit. They tend to consistently and methodically commit the same crimes in the same way. When this occurs, the prosecution will be able to introduce evidence of the defendant's prior crimes which were committed in the same or substantially same manner as the current crime. This generates the inference that, in light of the defendant's unique or peculiar behavior involving earlier, similar crimes, it is likely that he is guilty of the current one.

Even if the suspect is apprehended at the scene of the crime, for example, an armed robbery, a close examination of his or her M.O. can help link the suspect to other robberies. Another example is the crime of burglary. Most burglars are convicted on circumstantial evidence, and many commit a series of burglaries. Investigators should look for patterns—M.O. factors—such as the day of week, time of day, type of property stolen, the method of entry or exit, and any peculiarities of the offense. Did the burglar vandalize or ransack the home, write with lipstick on mirrors, drink liquor from the scene, eat food from the refrigerator, or take a bath or shower? The existence of such factors may then be used to link the suspect to other, unsolved burglaries.

It is not enough to show that the suspect has previously committed the same crime. More is required. There must be a great deal of similarity in the *method* in which the crimes are committed. In all such cases, the prosecution must convince the court (and jury) that the method of committing the crime was so unusual and distinctive that it is as if the defendant put his "signature" on it.

LEAVITT v. ARAVE
United States Circuit Court of Appeals
383 *F*.3d 809 (9th Cir. 2004)

Before KOZINSKI, FERNANDEZ, and RYMER, Circuit Judges.

The events of this case began in the small town of Blackfoot, Idaho, when, on July 17th, "the victim of this brutal crime, Danette Elg, was viciously attacked in her own bedroom by a knife-wielding assailant. The relentless and merciless assault took place on her waterbed and with such implacable force that the bed itself was punctured and torn, while the victim sustained numerous cuts and slashes as she fought for her life. She was also stabbed multiple times: One thrust caused the knife to enter her right lung, another the right side of her heart, still another her left lung, and others penetrated her stomach, her chest cavity, and her neck. One even went through her eye and into her brain." *Id.* at 814.

"Another exceedingly peculiar and unique wound inflicted during this attack was a cut made by the attacker through which he then removed her sexual organs. He did that in a manner that showed that he had some knowledge of female anatomy, for it was done in a manner that is difficult to accomplish." *Id.*

The evidence pointing to the defendant, Richard A. Leavitt, "was powerful, if circumstantial—he was not caught redhanded, nor did he confess." *Id.* Nonetheless, "[t]he jury found him guilty, and an Idaho judge sentenced him to death." *Id.* at 815.

In this proceeding Leavitt asserts, among other things, that it was error for the court to permit his ex-wife to testify that "once, while hunting, she came upon him as he carefully and rather surreptitiously was cutting at the female sexual organs of a deer. He then removed those organs, examined them, and played with them because, he said, he wanted to see how they worked." *Id.* at 829.

"It will be recalled that the victim in this case (or her body if she was then deceased) was subjected to a highly unusual removal of her female organs. Other evidence showed that it would be difficult to accomplish that in the way it was done and that it would help to have knowledge of anatomy when doing it. We agree with the Idaho Supreme Court that the evidence in question was relevant to identifying the killer." *Id.* As that court stated:

> In [this] case the corpse of the victim had been brutalized by the removal of her sexual organs by a person who clearly had certain anatomical knowledge. That evidence tended to indicate that the defendant had a morbid and sadistic interest in sexual organs, had a knowledge of anatomy, a possible motive for the crime, and a *modus operandi* which tended to identify the defendant as the killer.

Id. [Citation omitted.]

---

§6.1(e). Circumstantial Evidence of the Consciousness of Guilt

"The wicked flee when no man pursueth; but the righteous are as bold as a lion."
Proverbs 28:1

A suspect's actions following a crime may provide the prosecution with circumstantial evidence of the consciousness of guilt, and hence of the fact of guilt itself. Many courts call this an "admission by conduct." Common examples include flight to avoid capture, resisting arrest, attempts to hide, dispose of, or falsify evidence, taking steps to cover up the crime or deflect the investigation, assuming a false name, changing appearance, possession of stolen property, threatening, intimidating or attempting to influence witnesses, the refusal to take a potentially incriminating test, and suicide attempts by the accused. In all cases, however, the inference of the consciousness of guilt should not be so uncertain and ambiguous that the evidence is more prejudicial than probative.

PEOPLE v. YAZUM
Court of Appeals of the State of New York
13 *N.Y.*2d 302, 246 *N.Y.S.*2d 626, 196 *N.E.*2d 263 (1963)

BURKE, J.

This appeal concerns the admissibility of evidence of flight in a criminal prosecution. Defendant's conviction for robbery rested, in part, upon testimony that he attempted to escape from custody. After the jury returned its verdict of guilty, defense counsel moved to set aside the verdict on the ground that the evidence of flight was inadmissible because, at the time of the attempted escape, defendant was also detained under an Ohio warrant for parole violation. It was urged that, when a person is detained for two or more crimes, flight is not relevant to show guilt of either." *Id.* at 303.

"It is our opinion that the evidence of defendant's attempted escape was properly admitted. It is quite true that the attempted escape might have been motivated by a consciousness of guilt of the Ohio parole violation as well as by guilt feelings over the crime involved here. Indeed, the defendant may have fled because of guilt of both, or for some other innocent reason. This spectrum of possibilities, however, does not differ materially from that present in any case in which a defendant's flight is introduced in evidence." *Id.* at 303-04.

"This court has always recognized the ambiguity of evidence of flight and insisted that the jury be closely instructed as to its weakness as an indication of guilt of the crime charged. * * * Such instructions were given here. The limited probative force of flight evidence, however, is no reason for its exclusion. The distinction between admissibility and sufficiency must be borne in mind. Flight is a form of circumstantial evidence[.] * * * Generally speaking, all that is necessary is that the evidence have relevance, that it tend to convince that the fact sought to be established is so. That it is equivocal or that it is consistent with suppositions other than guilt does not render it inadmissible * * *. *Id.* at 304.

"Evidence of flight as indicative of a consciousness of guilt is a classic example of the admissibility of equivocal circumstantial evidence[.] * * * It is common in cases of attempted flight to find that the defendant is charged with several crimes, or, at the time of flight, was guilty of some other offense, such as parole violation. To require as a matter of law that the admissibility of flight evidence depends on its unequivocal connection with guilt feelings over the particular crime charged would, therefore, operate to exclude such evidence from many cases in which it has always been regarded as admissible as a matter of course." *Id.* at 304-05.

"The suggested distinction would mean that only alternative innocent explanations of the flight are matters of rebuttal within the supposedly general rule, while the special dispensation of absolute exclusion is reserved for those who could show multiple guilt. We think there is obviously no justification for distinguishing in such a

257

manner between an explanation urging that flight was not motivated by consciousness of guilt at all, and one which urges that it was prompted by consciousness of a different guilt. Such a distinction not only lacks support in the principles and theory of evidence, but would create a practical preference in favor of persons who act from guilty reasons over those who act from innocent motives." *Id.* at 305.

PEOPLE v. CINTRON
Court of Appeals of the State of New York
95 *N.Y.2d* 329, 717 *N.Y.S.2d* 72, 740 *N.E.2d* 217 (2000)

WESLEY, J.

"On the evening of January 12th, two police officers parked in an unmarked car on a one-way street in Brooklyn spotted defendant, Carlos Cintron, when he drove past them in a green 1990 Acura Legend and sounded its horn. When the officers entered the license plate number into their police vehicle's computer console, they discovered that the insurance on the car had been suspended. The officers then decided to follow the car." *Id.* at 331.

"After defendant went through a red light at an intersection, forcing pedestrians to jump out of the way, the officers turned on their flashing lights and siren. Defendant did not stop but instead accelerated, leading the officers on a high-speed car chase during which he wove in and out of traffic and executed various evasive maneuvers. He eventually crashed the vehicle into a guardrail. When the officers approached, defendant jumped from the car and ran. A foot-chase ensued and the officers ultimately apprehended defendant. The officers later learned that the car had been stolen three days earlier." *Id.*

"The jury found defendant guilty of criminal possession of stolen property in the third and fourth degrees, unauthorized use of a vehicle in the third degree and reckless endangerment in the second degree." *Id.*

In this appeal, defendant argues, among other things that "the circumstantial evidence pertaining to his flight was insufficient as a matter of law to establish that he knew that the vehicle was stolen and that he did not have the consent of the car's owner to operate the vehicle. We disagree." *Id.* at 332.

"In order to establish defendant's guilt of criminal possession of stolen property, the People must prove that the defendant knowingly possessed stolen property[.] Unauthorized use of a vehicle requires the People to prove that the defendant knew that he did not have the owner's consent to operate the vehicle. On this record, the jury could reasonably conclude from both the direct and the circumstantial evidence presented at trial that all the essential elements of these crimes were proven beyond a reasonable doubt." *Id.*

"Knowledge that property is stolen can be established through circumstantial evidence, 'such as by evidence of recent exclusive possession, defendant's conduct or contradictory statements from which guilt may be inferred. * * * Here, defendant was caught red-handed in exclusive possession of an automobile stolen three days earlier. In addition, the jury could reasonably have inferred defendant's knowledge that the car was stolen from defendant's flight from the police officers * * *." *Id.*

"The jury was also entitled to find consciousness of guilt if they disbelieved defendant's explanation for his conduct. While we have noted that evidence of consciousness of guilt, such as flight, has limited probative value, * * * we have also recognized that its probative weight is highly dependent upon the facts of each particular case." *Id.* at 333.

"In this case, defendant attempted to flee from the police officers' vehicle when they turned on their lights and siren, nearly knocking down pedestrians and leading the officers on a high speed chase. He continued to flee on foot after crashing the car into a guardrail. Moreover, he gave an improbable explanation for his conduct at trial. These facts are sufficient to support the reasonable inference that defendant knew that the vehicle was stolen and that he did not have the owner's consent to operate it." *Id.*

NOTE

In *Occhicone v. State*, 570 *So.*2d 902 (Fla. 1990), evidence that the defendant had refused to allow his hands to be swabbed for an atomic absorption test was introduced by the State to refute the defendant's claim that his intoxication prevented him from knowing what he was doing. On appeal, defendant argued that allowing the State to comment on his refusal to take the hand swab test penalized him for exercising his *Miranda* rights. The court disagreed.

In a special concurrence, Justice Grimes wrote that the refusal to take the test was not protected by the constitutional privilege against self-incrimination: Just as he could have been required to submit to fingerprinting, photographing, or blood tests, . . . Occhicone could have been compelled to undergo the hand-swab test. Having refused to taking the test, evidence of this fact was admissible for any relevant purpose. In this regard, Justice Grimes stated:

"What happens if a defendant refuses to cooperate in an identification procedure which requires his active participation? One possibility is that the prosecutor may be permitted to comment on the refusal to cooperate. If the identification procedure in which the defendant has refused to participate or cooperate, such as a lineup or taking of exemplars, is not protected by the Fifth Amendment, then of course there is no right to refuse and thus the act of refusal is not itself a compelled communication. Rather, that refusal is considered *circumstantial evidence of consciousness of guilt* just as is escape from custody, a false alibi, or flight."

Id. at 907. [Citation omitted.]

STATE v. TAYLOR
Supreme Court of Florida
648 *So.*2d 701 (1995)

SHAW, Judge.

"We have for review a decision presenting the following certified question of great public importance: *Is a DUI suspect's refusal to submit to pre-arrest field sobriety tests admissible in evidence?* * * * We answer in the affirmative as explained below[.]" *Id.* at 702.

During the course of a motor vehicle stop for a traffic violation, Officer Quant asked defendant, James Taylor, to produce his driving credentials and to exit his vehicle. "Quant noted that Taylor 'staggered out' of the vehicle, and had a 'strong odor of alcoholic beverages, slurred speech, and watery, bloodshot eyes.' Taylor asked if he would be requested to do any field sobriety tests, which are simple physical tasks designed to test coordination, *e.g.*, finger-to-nose, walk-the-line, stand-on-one-foot, etc. Quant responded that he would be, and Taylor replied that he had been told by his lawyer not to perform any tests and he was going to follow that advice." *Id.* at 702-03.

"Officer Quant explained the purpose of the tests and Taylor again refused. Quant arrested him. At the stationhouse, Taylor was read Florida's implied consent law, which provides that once a person is arrested for any crime while operating a motor vehicle, he or she may be asked to submit to alcohol or substance tests. * * * These post-arrest tests are sophisticated blood, urine, and breath tests, which differ substantially from the simple pre-arrest field sobriety tests noted above. Taylor acknowledged that he understood the law, but refused to take a breath test." *Id.* at 703.

"Taylor was charged with driving under the influence of an intoxicating substance (DUI) and, prior to trial, moved to suppress his refusal to take the field sobriety tests." *Id.*

"The county court granted the motion to suppress, ruling that Taylor had not been told the tests were compulsory or that refusal would have adverse consequences. The circuit court reversed. The district court then quashed the circuit court order, ruling that 'it would be unfair to admit an individual's refusal to submit to a test as circumstantial evidence of his consciousness of guilt where he was not advised of the consequences attaching to his refusal.' The court certified the above question." *Id.*

Regarding the evidentiary issues, the Florida Evidence Code provides:

> **90.401 Definition of relevant evidence.** Relevant evidence is evidence tending to prove or disprove a material fact.

> **90.402 Admissibility of relevant evidence.** All relevant evidence is admissible, except as provided by law.

" 'The concept of "relevancy" has historically referred to whether the evidence has any logical tendency to prove or disprove a fact. If the evidence is logically probative, it is relevant and admissible unless there is a reason for not allowing the jury to consider it.' " *Id.* [Citation omitted.]

"Taylor argues that his refusal to take the tests is not probative of the issue of guilt because his refusal may have been motivated by a factor other than guilt, such as a simple desire to end the encounter with Officer Quant. We reject this argument. When Officer Quant confronted Taylor, he watched him stagger out of his car and noticed a strong odor of alcohol, slurred speech, and watery, bloodshot eyes. Officer Quant asked him twice to take the field sobriety tests, explained the purpose of the tests, and warned Taylor that if he refused to take the tests he, Quant, would be forced to make a decision concerning arrest based on his observations up to that point." *Id.*

"Taylor had ample incentive to take the tests: He was aware of the circumstances surrounding the officer's request; he knew the purpose of the tests; and he had ample warning of possible adverse consequences attendant to refusal. * * * Given the strong incentives to take the tests, Taylor's claim that his refusal was an innocent act loses plausibility. In short, he knew that refusal was not a 'safe harbor' free of adverse consequence and acted in spite of that knowledge. *His refusal thus is relevant to show consciousness of guilt.* If he has an innocent explanation for not taking the tests, he is free to offer that explanation in court." *Id.* [Emphasis added.]

"We hold that Taylor's refusal to take the field sobriety tests was not elicited in violation of his statutory or constitutional rights and its use at trial does not offend constitutional principles. We further hold that the refusal is probative of the issue of consciousness of guilt. We quash the decision of the district court and answer the certified question in the affirmative as explained in this opinion. We remand for proceedings consistent with this opinion." *Id.* at 705.

---

§6.2. MISCELLANEOUS TYPES OF EVIDENCE

§6.2(a). Cumulative Evidence

"Cumulative" evidence is additional evidence on matters as to which direct or circumstantial evidence has already been received. It merely adds to, or repeats, other evidence which has been previously received by the court.

---

§6.2(b). Corroborative Evidence

"Corroborative" evidence consists of probative material which is related to matters upon which direct or circumstantial evidence has already been received by the court. It is offered to strengthen, verify or substantiate evidence which has been previously received, or to bolster or enhance the reliability or trustworthiness of that evidence or the credibility of its source.

STATE v. KING
Superior Court of New Jersey, Appellate Division
215 N.J.Super. 504, 522 A.2d 455 (1987)

The opinion of the court was delivered by

KING, P.J.A.D.

* * * * *

"The present case involves a bank robbery and a subsequent chase, [and] a shooting while trying to elude pursuing police officers. * * *

"During testimony by Officer Lowery the State sought to admit a taped recording of Lowery's high speed chase along the New Jersey Turnpike. Over defense counsel's objections, the judge ruled the tape admissible so that the jury would 'have the insight as to the atmosphere and the conditions that were prevailing at the time of the chase engaged by Officer Lowery.'" *Id.*, 215 *N.J.Super.* at 516.

"Although not admissible to bolster Lowery's credibility, the tape was properly admitted as independent evidence of what was going on during the chase. It was an accurate, though dramatic, reproduction of the criminal episode which corroborated the State's [] version. * * * [T]he tape was 'being played for the purpose *not* to corroborate the testimony of Officer Lowery but' * * * as independent evidence to allow insight into the 'atmosphere' of the car chase. This use is analogous to a movie of a criminal episode, which would certainly be admissible * * * [as] highly probative evidence[.]" *Id.* at 517-18. [Court's emphasis.]

---

§6.2(c). Prima Facie Evidence

"*Prima facie*" (at first view) evidence consists of probative matter which is sufficient in itself to establish an alleged matter of fact as true, so long as it is permitted to stand unrebutted or without contradiction. Stated another way, once received by a court, *prima facie* evidence will suffice as proof of a given fact proposition until its effect is overcome by some other evidence.

---

§6.2(d). The Corpus Delicti

The term "*corpus delicti*" is used to refer to the body, substance or operative basis of a criminal offense. In the trial of a criminal case, the prosecution always bears the burden of establishing the *corpus delicti*, which may be done either through direct or circumstantial evidence, by demonstrating that (1) an act or omission prohibited by public law occurred, and (2) the unlawful act or omission caused injury or harm that the law sought to prevent.

"The *corpus delicti* may not be established by a confession or admission standing alone.[1] As a general rule, a confession or admission must be corroborated by independent evidence of the *corpus delicti*[2] or at least by the introduction of "independent corroborative proof of facts and circumstances tending to generate a belief in the trustworthiness" of the admission or confession.[3] The corroboration requirement is rooted in "a long history of judicial experience with confessions and the realization that sound law enforcement requires police investigations which extend beyond the words of the accused."[4]

---

[1] Wharton, 1 *Criminal Law*, §28 (C.E. Torcia 14th ed. 1978), at 144. The rule's underlying theory evinces a concern that a criminal conviction should not be based solely on a confession which may be false, inaccurate or coerced. *See* 7 Wigmore, *Evidence* §2070 (Chadbourn rev. 1978), at 510. *See also City of Bremerton v. Corbett*, 106 *Wash.*2d 569, 576, 723 *P.*2d 1135, 1139 (1986).

[2] *Wharton, supra* at 144. *See also State v. Bishop*, 753 *P.*2d 439, 478 (Utah 1988) (*corpus delicti* must be established by clear and convincing evidence).

[3] *State v. Lucas*, 30 *N.J.* 37, 57, 152 *A.*2d 50 (1959). For federal prosecutions, *see Opper v. United States*, 348 *U.S.* 84, 93, 75 *S.Ct.* 158, 164 (1954) (the "better rule" would not require that the corroborating evidence establish the *corpus delicti* but rather that it be "substantial independent evidence which would tend to establish the trustworthiness of the [defendant's] statement"); *Wong Sun v. United States*, 371 *U.S.* 471, 489-90, 83 *S.Ct.* 407, 418 (1963) (the corroboration requirement may be established by "extrinsic proof" that " 'merely fortifies the truth of the confession, without independently establishing the crime charged' ").

[4] *Smith v. United States*, 348 *U.S.* 147, 153, 75 *S.Ct.* 194, 197 (1954).

COMMONWEALTH v. McCABE
Superior Court of Pennsylvania
345 *Pa.Super.* 495, 498 *A.2d* 933 (1985)

WIEAND, Judge.

"The information charged [defend]ant with concealing or destroying relevant evidence in the nature of a note found at the scene of a robbery. The police learned of the existence of the note from [defend]ant, who told them he had destroyed it. At trial, the Commonwealth was unable to produce independent evidence that the note existed. Because the Commonwealth was unable to prove the *corpus delicti* of this offense, the trial court sustained an objection to a testimonial reference to [defend]ant's oral statement by Trooper Bordenaro, a witness for the prosecution." *Id.*, 345 *Pa.Super.* at 498.

"[Defendant took the stand in his own defense, however,] and testified to the same facts which he had related to Trooper Bordenaro on the night of the robbery. [Defend]ant testified 'that at the scene of the robbery he had picked up a piece of paper, put it into his pocket, that he had read the note ∗ ∗ ∗ and had later told the State Police that he had gotten rid of the note—had thrown it in the garbage.' " *Id.* at 499.

"As a general rule, a naked extrajudicial ["out of court"] confession of crime, uncorroborated by independent evidence establishing the *corpus delicti*, is not sufficient to warrant or support a conviction. ∗ ∗ ∗ 'The grounds on which the rule rests are the hasty and unguarded character which is often attached to confessions and admissions and the consequent danger of a conviction where no crime has in fact been committed.' " *Id.* [Citation omitted.]

"The rule that an extrajudicial confession does not warrant a conviction unless corroborated by independent evidence of a *corpus delicti* has no application to judicial admissions. ∗ ∗ ∗ Judicial admissions are deliberately made under oath during formal proceedings and are generally free from the inherent infirmity of verbal confessions made out of court." *Id.* at 499-500.

"[Defend]ant's in-court testimony was neither hasty nor unguarded. It was made after consulting with counsel, was made under oath during trial, and was exculpatory with respect to the more serious charges which had been brought against him. His testimony, which admitted the destruction of evidence, was sufficient, if believed, to warrant a finding that he had concealed and destroyed evidence." *Id.* at 500.

"The judgment of sentence is *AFFIRMED.*"

NOTE

Exploring the "corpus delicti" rule.

(a) In *State v. Discher*, 597 A.2d 1336 (Me. 1991), the court similarly explained: "In order to withstand a motion for acquittal in a manslaughter prosecution, the *corpus delicti* rule requires the State to prove that the victim died and that a criminal agency was responsible for that death. Moreover, the *corpus delicti* cannot be established solely by post-crime admissions or confessions which are unsupported by any other evidence." *Id.* at 1339.

(b) The rule that a confession without more cannot sustain a conviction can be traced back through the decisional law to as early as 1818. *See State v. Lucas*, 30 *N.J.* 37, 51, 152 A.2d 50 (1959). Though the rule requiring corroboration is firmly settled, there is a conflict among the authorities concerning the *quantum* of proof independent of the confession or admission which the prosecution must present before the confession or admission may be admitted in evidence. "One view is that the State must proffer independent proof of the *corpus delicti*." *Id.*, 30 *N.J.* at 52.

"The other view is that extrinsic corroborative proofs need not touch upon the *corpus delicti* but must be of such a nature as to give the confession an aura of authenticity. [Under this view,] it is sufficient corroboration if the State introduces independent proof of such facts and circumstances as would tend to generate a belief that the confession is true[.]" *Id.* at 52.

"Before resolving the question of what the New Jersey corroboration rule requires it will be helpful to define the term *corpus delicti*. There are three basic elements in the proof of any crime. [] First, the occurrence of loss or injury (a death in murder, a burnt dwelling house in common law arson, etc.); secondly, criminal causation of the loss or injury as opposed to accident (*i.e., some one* committed a crime), and lastly, the defendant's identity or connection with the crime (*i.e.,* that the defendant in fact was the perpetrator of the crime). * * *

"[I]n its correct meaning, the term *corpus delicti* has reference [] to [the first two elements set forth above,] namely, the fact of the specific loss or injury sustained * * * and 'somebody's criminality[,' *i.e.,* the] criminal agency causing the loss or injury[.]" *Id.* at 53-54. [Emphasis in original.]

"In *State v. Geltzeiler*, [101 *N.J.L.* 415 (E. & A. 1925),] the court declared:

> In the history of the law so many persons are known to have confessed the commission of crimes they never committed, even including murder, that the rule requiring proof of the *corpus*

delicti has been evolved. However, when there is a voluntary confession of the offense by the defendant in a criminal case, full proof of the body of the crime is not required in addition to the confession, but sufficient proof thereof may arise out of evidence corroborating some fact or facts in the confession itself. (101 *N.J.L.*, at page 416.)

"In our view," held the *Lucas* court, the rule which requires "the State [to] introduce independent proof of facts and circumstances which strengthen or bolster the confession and tend to generate a belief in its trustworthiness, plus independent proof of loss or injury, affords ample protection for the accused and is the rule best designed to serve the ends of justice in the administration of the criminal law." *Lucas* at 56.

"It might be argued that the State ought also to prove criminal agency before a confession be considered as evidential, in order to assure that confession was not the imaginary product of a mentally diseased or deficient mind. But if criminal agency must be proven * * * why not the defendant's connection with the crime ? * * * [N]o jurisdiction imposes such a requirement[, and for purposes of an out-of-court confession, the State need only] introduce such independent corroborative proof of facts and circumstances tending to generate a belief in the trustworthiness of the confession[. Requiring] independent proof of the *corpus delicti* [is not necessary]." *Id.* at 57.

"The corroborative proofs need only establish the trustworthiness of the confession and not the *corpus delicti*." *Id.* at 62.

---

§6.2(e). "Sui Generis" Evidence

In law enforcement, there are some procedures or investigative actions that are so unique, or so peculiar, that the courts tend to treat the procedure and the evidence it produces in a class of its own—as *"sui generis."*

UNITED STATES v. PLACE
Supreme Court of the United States
462 *U.S.* 696, 103 *S.Ct.* 2637 (1983)

JUSTICE O'CONNOR delivered the opinion of the Court.
"This case presents the issue whether the Fourth Amendment prohibits law enforcement authorities from temporarily detaining personal luggage for exposure to a trained narcotics detection dog on the basis of reasonable suspicion that the luggage contains narcotics. Given the enforcement problems associated with the detection of narcotics trafficking and the minimal intrusion that a properly limited detention would entail, we conclude that the Fourth Amendment does not prohibit such a detention." *Id.* at 2639.

* * * *

"The purpose for which [defendant's] luggage was seized, of course, was to arrange its exposure to a narcotics detection dog. Obviously, if this investigative procedure is itself a search requiring probable cause, the initial seizure of [defendant's] luggage for the purpose of subjecting it to the sniff test—no matter how brief—could not be justified on less than probable cause." *Id.* at 2644.

"The Fourth Amendment 'protects people from unreasonable government intrusions into their legitimate expectations of privacy.' * * * We have affirmed that a person possesses a privacy interest in the contents of personal luggage that is protected by the Fourth Amendment. * * * A 'canine sniff' by a well-trained narcotics detection dog, however, does not require opening the luggage. It does not expose noncontraband items that otherwise would remain hidden from public view, as does, for example, an officer's rummaging through the contents of the luggage. Thus, the manner in which information is obtained through this investigative technique is much less intrusive than a typical search. Moreover, the sniff discloses only the presence or absence of narcotics, a contraband item. Thus, despite the fact that the sniff tells the authorities something about the contents of the luggage, the information obtained is limited. This limited disclosure also ensures that the owner of the property is not subjected to the embarrassment and inconvenience entailed in less discriminate and more intrusive investigative methods. In these respects, the canine sniff is *sui generis*. We are aware of no other investigative procedure that is so limited both in the manner in which the information is obtained and in the content of the information revealed by the procedure. Therefore, we conclude that the particular course of investigation that the agents intended to pursue here—exposure of [defendant's] luggage, which was located in a public place, to a trained canine—did not constitute a 'search' within the meaning of the Fourth Amendment." *Id.* at 2644-45. [Citation omitted.]

NOTE

1. *See also Illinois v. Caballes,* ___ *U.S.* ___, 125 *S.Ct.* 834, 838 (2005), where the Court reaffirmed that a canine sniff by a well-trained narcotics detection dog should be treated as *"sui generis"* because "it discloses only the presence or absence of narcotics, a contraband item."

2. *Drug field tests.* In *United States v. Jacobsen,* 466 *U.S.* 109, 104 *S.Ct.* 1652 (1984), the Court determined that, similar to a canine sniff by a well-trained narcotics detection dog, a drug field test discloses only the presence or absence of narcotics. The Court said:

> The field test at issue could disclose only one fact previously unknown to the agent—whether or not a suspicious white powder was cocaine. It could tell him nothing more, not even whether the substance was sugar or talcum powder. * * *.

> A chemical test that merely discloses whether or not a particular substance is cocaine does not compromise any legitimate interest in privacy. This conclusion is not dependent on the result of any particular test. It is probably safe to assume that virtually all of the tests conducted under circumstances comparable to those disclosed by this record would result in a positive finding; in such cases, no legitimate interest has been compromised. But even if the results are negative—merely disclosing that the substance is something other than cocaine—such a result reveals nothing of special interest.

Id. at 1661-62.

Thus, like the canine sniff in *United States v. Place,* the drug field test is *sui generis.*

---

§6.2(f). After-Discovered Evidence

Generally, evidence obtained or discovered after trial which relates to a relevant issue in that trial is termed "after discovered" or "newly discovered" evidence. Such evidence may form the basis for a court granting a new trial when "(1) it could not have been obtained at or prior to the conclusion of the trial through due diligence; (2) it is not merely corroborative or cumulative; (3) it will not be used for the sole purpose of impeaching the credibility of a witness; and (4) it will likely result in a different verdict if a new trial were held."[5]

---

[5] *Commonwealth v. Lambert,* 529 *Pa.* 320, 603 *A.2d* 568, 579 (1992). *See also Commonwealth v. Colson,* 507 *Pa.* 440, 490 *A.2d* 811 (1985), *cert. denied,* 476 *U.S.* 1140, 106 *S.Ct.* 2245 (1986).

PEOPLE v. DUNN
Appellate Court of Illinois
306 *Ill.App.*3d 75, 713 *N.E.*2d 568 (1999)

PRESIDING JUSTICE GORDON delivered the opinion of the court.

Defendant, Maurice Dunn, stands convicted of rape and aggravated battery. In this appeal, he contends primarily that he is entitled to DNA testing.

At trial, the prosecution's evidence established that, on the day in question, at about 7:45 a.m., "the victim was attacked by defendant as she was walking to a southside Chicago train station. Defendant forced her into a secluded area where the victim was able to clearly see defendant's face when he got on top of her and began choking her. During the attack, the victim was able to see defendant's face a few more times. Despite the victim's struggle, defendant raped her. When the victim identified defendant in court as her attacker, the victim said, 'And I looked right at your face. I saw your face. I'll never forget your face. Ever.' " *Id.* at 77. Defendant presented an alibi claim that he was in Harvey, Illinois, at the time the crime was committed.

Defendant contends, among other things, that "the trial court erred in dismissing his post-conviction petition because it raised a free-standing claim of innocence based on newly discovered evidence. He asserts that DNA testing would cast doubt on whether he was the offender in this case." *Id.* at 78.

Defendant alleges that the "tests performed on blood and sperm samples taken from the victim and contained in the Vitullo kit did not link him to the crime. We note, however, that defendant has offered no proof of these allegations, and we have found no support for them in the record." *Id.* at 79.

"The Illinois Supreme Court has recently noted the viability of a free-standing post-conviction claim of innocence based on newly discovered evidence. * * * Free-standing claims of innocence based on newly discovered evidence are to be resolved as any other claims brought under the [law]. The supporting evidence of actual innocence must be new, material, noncumulative and of such conclusive character as would probably change the result on retrial." *Id.* at 79-80. [Citations omitted.]

"Newly discovered evidence must be evidence which was not available at defendant's trial and which defendant could not have discovered sooner through diligence. * * * Moreover, the evidence offered by defendant must be of such convincing character that it would likely change the outcome of the trial." *Id.* at 80.

"Defendant has provided no supporting evidence of his actual innocence, but only asserts that such testing would 'cast doubt on his identity as the offender.' Nor is a request for genetic testing itself evidence. However, defendant's appeal specifically raises the issue of whether DNA testing can be granted as post-conviction relief when it was unavailable at the time of defendant's trial." *Id.*

"Post-conviction forensic DNA testing has recently been authorized in Illinois by statute. Section 116-3 of the Code of Criminal Procedure was recently enacted to allow a defendant to seek genetic testing in a motion before the trial court that entered the judgment of conviction in his case. 725 *IL.C.S.* 5/116-3 (a). That section allows a motion to be made in instances where the technology for the testing was not available at the time of trial. * * * That section further provides that the defendant must present a *prima facie* case that identity was the issue in his trial and that the evidence to be tested has been subject to a chain of custody sufficient to establish that it has not been substituted, tampered with, replaced, or altered in any material aspect. 725 *IL.C.S.* 5/116-3(b)(1), (2). The trial court shall allow the testing if it determines that the testing has the scientific potential to produce new, noncumulative evidence materially relevant to the defendant's assertion of actual innocence and that the requested testing uses a scientific method generally accepted within the relevant scientific community. 725 *IL.C.S.* 5/116-3(c)(1), (2)." *Id.*

"Here, defendant has petitioned this court for genetic testing of the Vitullo kit that was taken in his original proceedings. Nearly all of the decisions which have considered whether DNA test results are admissible, including those in Illinois, have permitted such evidence to be admitted. * * * Based on the accuracy and definitiveness of DNA testing, and the recent enactment of section 116-3 of the Code of Criminal Procedure, we agree with defendant that he is entitled to such testing, provided that the required *prima facie* case has been made. Accordingly, we remand this matter to the trial court for consideration of defendant's motion for genetic testing. The court shall determine whether defendant has made a *prima facie* case for such testing and order further proceedings, if necessary, consistent with those results." *Id.* at 80-81.

STATE v. ROCHE
Court of Appeals of Washington, Division One
114 *Wn.App.* 424, 59 *P.*3d 682 (2002)

KENNEDY, J.

"Soon after James Roche and Roy Sweeney were convicted and sentenced for methamphetamine possession, it became public knowledge that Michael Hoover, a chemist at the Washington State Patrol Crime Laboratory, had been using heroin sent to the crime lab for testing purposes. Hoover was the chemist who had tested the substances recovered in both Roche and Sweeney's cases and reported them to be methamphetamine. Roche moved for, and was denied, a new trial based on this newly-discovered evidence. Sweeney filed a personal restraint petition raising the same issue, after his request for court appointed counsel to help him move for a new trial was denied by the trial court. Because we agree that this newly-discovered evidence of Hoover's malfeasance broke the chain of custody and tainted the integrity of Roche and Sweeney's trials, we reverse both convictions and remand for new trials, if the State should elect to retry them." *Id.* at 428.

FACTS

"Michael Hoover began working as a chemist for the Washington State Patrol crime laboratory in 1989. At some point in 1998 or 1999, chemists James Boaz and David Northrop, who worked with Hoover at the crime laboratory in Marysville, noticed that Hoover was assigning himself a disproportionately large number of heroin cases. Hoover was also removing heroin cases from other chemist's file drawers and reassigning them to himself. * * * Boaz observed that Hoover's lab data seemed sloppy. Boaz also suspected that Hoover was reducing his workload by testing a single purified sample and applying the results across a number of cases, a practice known as 'dry labbing.' Boaz suspected that Hoover was dry labbing because, in Boaz's professional opinion, Hoover's spectra for separate criminal cases were too similar to have come from different samples. Boaz documented at least 14 possible dry labbing incidents from August to October 2000, including several for methamphetamine from Snohomish County cases. One of these 14 cases was Sweeney's." *Id.* at 428-29

"Northrop and Boaz also noticed that Hoover behaved furtively around his workstation, attempted to conceal his activities from them, and kept a large amount of white powder in an evaporating dish on his desk. Boaz would sometimes hear scraping sounds coming from Hoover's desk area, followed by snorting sounds. Boaz also noticed that Hoover continually turned down the lights in the lab, that Hoover had taken to wearing long sleeved shirts and never rolled back his cuffs, that Hoover's face often appeared flushed at the end of the day, and that he often slipped out early at the end of the day. Northrop and Boaz reported their concerns to Erik Neilson, the supervisor at the lab." *Id.* at 429-30.

Subsequent investigation into Hoover's conduct revealed that he had been taking heroin samples from evidence sent to the lab, purifying the samples and using the purified heroin. "Hoover was given a urine test, which tested positive for heroin. Detectives found 7 test tubes at the back of Hoover's workstation that appeared to contain controlled substances. The vials had various labels, including 'meth' and 'heroin.' Testing revealed that 6 of the test tubes contained heroin, and one contained methamphetamine. Hoover was charged with evidence tampering and official misconduct." *Id.* at 430-31. Ultimately, he pleaded guilty to both charges.

In James Roche's case, Hoover was the state crime lab chemist who tested the alleged substances found at the Roche residence. He was also called as a witness at trial. Similarly, Hoover tested the substances in Roy Sweeney's case.

271

DISCUSSION

"We have linked Roche and Sweeney's cases so that we need only issue one opinion concerning the effect of the newly discovered-evidence of Hoover's malfeasance."

"To obtain a new trial based on newly-discovered evidence, a defendant must demonstrate that the evidence: (1) will probably change the result of the trial; (2) was discovered after the trial; (3) could not have been discovered before trial by the exercise of due diligence; (4) is material; and (5) is not merely cumulative or impeaching. * * * The absence of any one of these five factors is grounds to deny a new trial. * * *" *Id.* at 435.

"The State concedes factors (2), (3), and (4), *i.e.*, that the evidence was discovered after the trial, could not have been discovered before trial by the exercise of due diligence, and is material. However, the State argues that Roche has failed to establish that the evidence would probably change the result of the trial, and the State also contends that the evidence is merely impeaching. Roche contends that the evidence would probably change the result of the trial because Hoover's malfeasance broke the chain of custody and so devastated Hoover's credibility as to undermine the State's ability to prove by his testimony that the substance recovered from his residence was methamphetamine." *Id.* at 435-36.

"Before a physical object connected with the commission of a crime may properly be admitted into evidence, it must be satisfactorily identified and shown to be in substantially the same condition as when the crime was committed. * * * Evidence that is unique and readily identifiable may be identified by a witness who can state that the item is what it purports to be. * * * However, where evidence is not readily identifiable and is susceptible to alteration by tampering or contamination, it is customarily identified by the testimony of each custodian in the chain of custody from the time the evidence was acquired. This more stringent test requires the proponent to establish a chain of custody with sufficient completeness to render it improbable that the original item has either been exchanged with another or been contaminated or tampered with." *Id.* at 436.

"Factors to be considered include the nature of the item, the circumstances surrounding the preservation and custody, and the likelihood of tampering or alteration. * * * The proponent need not identify the evidence with absolute certainty and eliminate every possibility of alteration or substitution. * * * '[M]inor discrepancies or uncertainty on the part of the witness will affect only the weight of the evidence, not its admissibility.' " *Id.*

In these cases, "Hoover's credibility has been totally devastated by his malfeasance. Not only did Hoover steal heroin from the crime lab, he also admitted that he regularly used heroin on the job. He repeatedly lied about his activities until he was finally confronted * * *." *Id.* at 437.

"Furthermore, Hoover's co-workers thought that his work seemed sloppy and even suspected, with some scientific basis to support their suspicions, that he might have been dry labbing some methamphetamine cases. These events are serious enough that a rational trier of fact could reasonably doubt Hoover's credibility regarding his testing of any alleged controlled substances, not just heroin, and regarding his preservation of the chain of custody during the relevant time period." *Id.*

"Moreover, the evidence of Hoover's malfeasance is more than 'merely' impeaching; it is *critical*, with respect to Hoover's own credibility, the validity of his testing, and the chain of custody." *Id.* at 438.

"The record establishes that after Hoover's malfeasance became known, the State dismissed dozens of pending 'Hoover cases' involving drugs other than heroin, including methamphetamine cases, because of the devastating damage to Hoover's credibility and to the chain of custody. * * * Indeed, the record reflects that if the newly-discovered evidence had been known to the State at the time of Roche's trial, Hoover never would have been called as a witness." *Id.* at 438-39.

We "conclude that in a case such as this where the defendant would not have been tried or sentenced at all if the newly-discovered evidence had come to light before he was tried, convicted, or sentenced, the question of whether the result at trial would have been different if the evidence had come to light earlier becomes effectively moot. We thus conclude that the trial court should have granted Roche's motion for a new trial, leaving it up to the State to decide whether to retry Roche or to dismiss the charges. Accordingly, we reverse Roche's conviction and remand so that the State can decide whether to retry Roche, or to dismiss the charges against him." *Id.* at 439.

Regarding Roy Sweeney's matter, the "State argues that Sweeney has failed to present sufficient competent, admissible evidence to sustain his petition." *Id.* at 442. We disagree.

The standard is identical to that previously discussed for Roche's case: (1) the evidence must be such that the results will probably change if a new trial were granted; (2) the evidence must have been discovered since the trial; (3) the evidence could not have been discovered before the trial by exercising due diligence; (4) the evidence must be material; and (5) the evidence cannot merely be cumulative or impeaching. *Id.* at 444.

As in Roche's case, the "evidence of Hoover's malfeasance is so corrupting that Snohomish County instructed its prosecutors not to call Hoover as a witness to testify in court, and not to try to reconstruct the chain of custody by having the substances retested. This evidence is *critical* and not 'merely' impeaching." *Id.* at 445. Therefore, in the interests of justice, "we grant Sweeney's personal restraint petition, and vacate his conviction. We do so for the same reasons that we have reversed Roche's conviction[.]" *Id.* at 446.

CONCLUSION

"The most important consideration for us now is the preservation of the integrity of the criminal justice system. We must handle these two cases now before us in such a fashion that the public, the defense bar, the prosecuting attorneys, and the courts of Washington will clearly understand that we will not tolerate criminal convictions based on tainted evidence, but will insist upon proper standards of conduct and procedure." *Id.* at 447.

---

§6.3. PRINCIPAL BARRIERS TO THE ADMISSIBILITY OF EVIDENCE

Before any evidence may be deemed worthy of a factfinder's consideration—before it may be properly received "in evidence"—it must make it past three hurdles or barriers. First, the evidence must be of a sort that is legally receivable by a court; if it is, it makes it past the barrier of "competence." Next, the evidence must relate to a necessary and important aspect of the case, the "materiality" barrier. Finally, the evidence must be probative of a material issue, that is, it must tend to prove a material aspect of the case; if it does, it has made it past the final barrier to the admissibility of evidence, that of "relevance."

---

§6.3(a). Competence

Evidence will be deemed "competent" when it is sufficiently reliable and trustworthy so as to be eligible to be received "in evidence." The requirement of competence generally refers to both real and documentary evidence, as well as witnesses. Real or documentary evidence will be deemed competent to be received in evidence when it is shown to possess those qualities which render it trustworthy or reliable, such as in the way it was obtained (from whatever person or place), the way it was maintained or preserved, and its present form or condition.

As a general rule, evidence obtained in violation of the law is deemed untrustworthy and therefore incompetent to be received by the court. For example, in a search and seizure context, evidence obtained in violation of a criminal defendant's Fourth Amendment rights is inadmissible in the prosecution's case-in-chief because of the exclusionary rule. The law of evidence would deem that evidence unreliable and untrustworthy, and therefore incompetent to be received in evidence.

A witness will be deemed competent (or eligible) to take the witness stand so long as he or she possesses the basic attributes required of a witness: (1) the ability to accept and appreciate the obligation to testify truthfully; (2) perception; (3) recollection; and (4) the ability to communicate.

Crime-scene evidence will be deemed competent when it is discovered, collected and preserved in a reliable and trustworthy way. What the initial responding officers do or do not do at the scene of a crime will determine how successful the criminal investigation will be, and may determine whether crime-scene evidence will be admitted *as evidence* in court. Moreover, a quick response to the scene of the crime is essential, not only for the discovery and preservation of evidence, but also to the overall successful outcome of the criminal investigation. As one commentator has observed:

> The outcome of the preliminary investigation is governed by the passage of time. As a general principle, the probability of a successful case decreases with the passage of time, starting from when the suspect commits the offense. When officers arrest a suspect at the scene, or in close proximity to the scene, the probability of a successful conviction is at its highest. The longer the interval without an arrest, the lower the probability of success. Mary factors play a part in this phenomenon. The longer a suspect remains at large, the greater the likelihood of:

> 1) physical escape from the scene;

> 2) inaccurate witness or victim identification;

> 3) destruction or disposal of evidence taken from the scene by the suspect;

> 4) victims or witnesses who are unwilling to testify in court;

> 5) police suspension of the case;

> 6) construction of credible alibis by suspects; and

> 7) possible contamination or loss of physical evidence.[6]

---

[6] Gilbert, *Criminal Investigation* 62 (2d ed 1986).

Indeed, it may be said that the crime scene, in and of itself, *is evidence*, and must be treated as such. "It is not strictly a location or geographical area, but a tangible object that possesses information that can be presented for prosecution."[7] Thus, perhaps the most important first action of the investigator upon his or her arrival at the scene of a crime is to refrain from taking any physical action. Instead, the most advisable first step for the investigator to take at the scene of a crime is a careful preliminary survey of the scene. Before stepping onto the crime scene, it is best to determine where not to step.

_____

§6.3(b). Materiality

Evidence will be "material" when it has a legitimate and effective influence on an important and necessary issue in, or aspect of, the case. It constitutes that evidence which has a bearing on a matter that is of consequence to the case in general or a specific issue in the case. While from an academic standpoint, the concept of materiality is of concern, from a practical standpoint, it is usually not raised as an objection for it is embodied in the concept of relevance.

_____

§6.3(c). Relevance

"Relevant" evidence may be defined as "evidence having any tendency to make the existence of any fact that is of consequence to the determination of the action more probable or less probable than it would be without the evidence."[8] So long as a given item of evidence has any tendency in logic or reason to prove a desired fact, it is relevant. Under the federal rules,

> [a]ll relevant evidence is admissible, except as otherwise provided by the Constitution of the United States, by Act of Congress, by these rules, or by other rules prescribed by the Supreme Court pursuant to statutory authority. Evidence which is not relevant is not admissible.[9]

"There are two components to relevant evidence: materiality and probative value."[10] In this respect, evidence will be relevant

_____

[7] Mauriello, *Criminal Investigation Handbook: Strategy, Law and Science*, at 7-2 (Matthew Bender 1998).

[8] *Fed.R.Evid.* 401. As can be seen, under the federal rules, the "basic standard of relevance [] is a liberal one." *Daubert v. Merrell Dow Pharmaceuticals, Inc.*, 509 *U.S.* 579, 587, 113 *S.Ct.* 2786, 2794 (1993).

[9] *Fed.R.Evid.* 402.

[10] 1 McCormick, *Evidence* §185 (4th ed. 1992), at 773.

when (1) "the inference sought to be raised by the evidence bears upon a matter at issue in the case," and (2) the evidence "renders the desired inference more probable than it would be without the evidence."[11] In the main, relevancy questions are concerned with three elements: (a) time (relating to the particular day and period of time at issue); (b) event (relating to the correct phenomenon, that is, the correct event or transaction which has been drawn into court by the parties); and (c) person (relating to the particular individual who is the subject of the case or at least one of the necessary issues in the case).

The concept of relevancy "is not an inherent characteristic of any item of evidence but exists as a relation between an item of evidence and a proposition sought to be proved. If an item of evidence tends to prove or disprove any proposition, it is relevant to that proposition."[12] "Whether the relationship exists depends upon principles evolved by experience or science, applied logically to the situation at hand."[13]

The familiar, yet critical, question to ask for relevancy determinations is, *"What is the evidence being offered to prove ?"* If the evidence is being offered to prove a fact which is immaterial to the case, a relevancy objection posed by opposing counsel would be successful. And if the evidence is being offered to prove a fact which is material to the case, but the evidence has no tendency in logic or reason to prove that fact, that evidence is, again, irrelevant.

---

§6.3(d). Logical Versus Legal Relevance

Once it is determined that an item of evidence is probative of a material fact—that it makes the existence of a material fact in the case more probable or less probable—that evidence may be said to be logically relevant: in some degree that evidence "advances the inquiry."[14] As such it would seem to be admissible, at least preliminarily. Yet, logically relevant evidence is *not always* admissible. "There remains the question of whether its value is worth what it costs. A great deal of evidence is excluded on the ground that the costs outweigh the benefits."[15]

---

[11] *Commonwealth v. Haight*, 514 *Pa.* 438, 440, 525 *A.*2d 1199, 1200 (1987).

[12] James, *Relevancy, Probability and the Law*, 29 Calif.L.Rev. 689, 690-91 (1941).

[13] *Advisory Committee's Note to Rule* 401, 56 *F.R.D.* 183, 215.

[14] 1 McCormick, *Evidence* §185 (4th ed. 1992), at 779.

[15] *Id.*

There is, therefore, a sub-barrier to the admissibility of logically relevant evidence: the test of "legal" relevancy. Determinations of legal relevancy are matters which are left to the sound discretion of trial judges, and primarily address the question whether the particular evidence offered is "more prejudicial than probative." Thus, a trial court has the discretion to exclude logically relevant evidence

if its probative value is substantially outweighed by the danger of unfair prejudice, confusion of the issues, or misleading the jury, or by considerations of undue delay, waste of time, or needless presentation of cumulative evidence.[16]

COMMONWEALTH v. DUNKLE
Supreme Court of Pennsylvania
529 Pa. 168, 602 A.2d 830 (1992)

The opinion of the Court was delivered by

CAPPY, Justice.

"We are called upon to decide whether the trial court erred in permitting expert testimony about the behaviors exhibited by children who have been sexually abused [] in a case in which the [defendant] was charged with sexual abuse of a minor. Additionally, we must decide whether the expert testimony was properly admitted to explain why sexually abused children may not recall certain details of the assault, to explain why they may not give complete details, and to explain why they may delay reporting the incident. * * *

"We hold that [such] testimony [is] not * * * admissible[.]" *Id.* at 831.

[Preliminarily, the Court determined that testimony concerning the uniformity of behaviors exhibited by sexually abused children "is not 'sufficiently established to have gained scientific acceptance in the particular field in which it belongs.' " *Id.* at 834. (*see* §7.1.).]

"Intertwined with the notion of 'general acceptance in the particular field' is the understanding of what constitutes relevant and therefore admissible evidence. We have long held that '[a]ny analysis of the admissibility of a particular type of evidence must start with a threshold inquiry as to its relevance and probative value.' * * * Relevant evidence 'is evidence that in some degree advances the inquiry[.' First, it must be determined] 'if the inference sought to be raised by the evidence bears upon the matter in issue in the case and, second, whether the evidence "renders the desired inference more probable than it would be without the evidence." ' * * *" *Id.* [Citations omitted.]

---

[16] *Fed.R.Evid.* 403. For further discussion of the distinction between logical and legal relevance, *see* Trautman, *Logical or Legal Relevance—A Conflict in Theory*, 5 Vand.L.Rev. 385, 389-90 (1952).

"The expert testimony about the behavior patterns exhibited by sexually abused children does not meet this threshold determination. While it may 'bear upon a matter in issue,' it does not render the desired inference more probable than not. It simply does not render any inference at all. Rather, it merely attempts—in contravention of the rules of evidence—to suggest that the victim was, in fact, exhibiting symptoms of sexual abuse. This is unacceptable." *Id.*

"The expert witness also testified that sexually abused children exhibit the following behaviors: Runaway behavior, anger, rebellion, acting out, becoming promiscuous, getting involved with drugs, alcohol, not doing school work, regression to earlier behavior, suicide attempts or thoughts of suicide, depression, eating disorders, nightmares, and bed wetting. It is virtually impossible to clinically describe the elements of the 'child abuse syndrome' with any realistic degree of specificity." *Id.*

"We do not believe that the testimony in question was probative. Clearly, drug and alcohol abuse, eating disorders, low self-esteem and not doing school work are common phenomena not solely related to child abuse. To permit the jury to speculate that they might be, however, violates every notion of what constitutes probative and relevant evidence. It is neither scientifically supportable nor legally supportable. Such a laundry list of possible behaviors does no more than invite speculation and will not be condoned." *Id.* at 834 35.

ESTELLE v. McGUIRE
United States Supreme Court
502 *U.S.* 62, 112 *S.Ct.* 475 (1991)

THE CHIEF JUSTICE delivered the opinion of the Court.

[Defendant Mark McGuire was found guilty in a California state court of second-degree murder for the killing of his infant daughter, Tori. At trial, the prosecution introduced statements made by McGuire to police (that Tori's injuries resulted from a fall off the family couch), and medical evidence, including evidence of prior rectal tearing (which was at least six weeks old), evidence of partially healed rib fractures, 17 contusions on the baby's chest, 29 contusions in her abdominal area, a split liver, a split pancreas, a lacerated large intestine, and damage to her heart and one of her lungs. Two physicians testified that Tori was a "battered child."]

"The California Court of Appeal affirmed McGuire's conviction. The court observed that the evidence of prior rib and rectal injuries was introduced to prove 'battered child syndrome.' That syndrome exists when a child has sustained repeated and/or serious injuries by nonaccidental means. * * * After reviewing California authority on the subject, the court concluded that 'proof of Tori's "prior injuries" tending to establish the "battered child syndrome" was patently proper.' [] The California Supreme Court denied review." *Id.* at 479.

"We [] turn to the question whether the admission of the evidence violated McGuire's federal constitutional rights. California law allows the prosecution to introduce expert testimony and evidence related to prior injuries in order to prove 'battered child syndrome.' * * * The demonstration of battered child syndrome 'simply indicates that a child found with [serious, repeated injuries] has not suffered those injuries by accidental means.' * * * Thus, evidence demonstrating battered child syndrome helps to prove that the child died at the hands of another and not by falling off a couch, for example; it also tends to establish that the 'other,' whoever it may be, inflicted the injuries intentionally. When offered to show that certain injuries are a product of child abuse, rather than accident, evidence of prior injuries is relevant even though it does not purport to prove the identity of the person who might have inflicted those injuries. * * * Because the prosecution had charged McGuire with second-degree murder, it was required to prove that Tori's death was caused by defendant's intentional act. Proof of Tori's battered child status helped to do just that; although not linked by any direct evidence to McGuire, the evidence demonstrated that Tori's death was the result of an intentional act by *someone,* and not an accident. * * * We conclude that the evidence of prior injuries presented at McGuire's trial, whether it was directly linked to McGuire or not, was probative on the question of the intent with which the person who caused the injuries acted." *Id.* at 480. [Court's emphasis.]

"[T]he prosecution must prove all the elements of a criminal offense beyond a reasonable doubt. In this second degree murder case, for example, the prosecution was required to demonstrate that the killing was intentional. * * * By eliminating the possibility of accident, the evidence regarding battered child syndrome was clearly probative of that essential element, especially in light of the fact that McGuire had claimed prior to trial that Tori had injured herself by falling from the couch. * * * The evidence of battered child syndrome was relevant to show intent, and nothing in the Due Process clause of the Fourteenth Amendment requires the State to refrain from introducing [such] relevant evidence * * *." *Id.* at 480-81.

"We hold that McGuire's due process rights were not violated by the admission of the evidence." *Id.* at 481.

STATE v. WILLIAMS
Supreme Court of Connecticut
227 *Conn.* 101, 629 A.2d 402 (1993)

SANTANEILLO, Associate Justice.

"The defendant, Bernard Williams, was convicted, after a jury trial, of one count of felony murder." *Id.* at 403. In this appeal, he argues, among other things, that "the trial court improperly * * * allowed the state to introduce into evidence a videotape of the crime scene * * * because the probative value of the videotape was outweighed by its prejudicial effect on the jury. We disagree." *Id.* at 403, 407.

"At approximately 7:45 p.m., [] one of the police officers arrived at the crime scene with a video camera. The officer was instructed to videotape the crime scene, beginning outside the parking garage, proceeding inside and ending at the location of the body. By the time the officer reached the location of the body, the medical examiner had turned the body over to a face-up position. The videotape, therefore, showed the body in the face-up position, rather than the face-down position in which it had been found." *Id.* at 407.

"The defendant contends that the changed position of the body in the videotape created an inaccurate portrayal of the crime scene and 'highlighted the gruesomeness of the crime.' Although the defendant emphasizes that the videotape should have been excluded as excessively prejudicial, that claim is best addressed by first reviewing the reasons why photographic evidence is admissible." *Id.*

" '[P]hotographic evidence is admissible where the photograph has "a reasonable tendency to prove or disprove a material fact in issue or shed some light upon some material inquiry. * * *" There is no requirement in this state that a potentially inflammatory photograph be essential to the state's case in order for it to be admissible; rather, 'the test for determining the admissibility of the challenged evidence is relevancy and not necessity.' " *Id.* [Citations omitted.]

"A potentially inflammatory photograph may be admitted if the court, in its discretion, determines that the probative value of the photograph outweighs the prejudicial effect it might have on the jury. * * * The determination of the trial court will not be disturbed unless the trial court abused its discretion." *Id.*

"After viewing both the black and white photographs and the videotape, the trial court stated that the videotape was the most accurate, truthful and representative evidence of the crime scene. The trial court did not find the videotape so inflammatory that it would unduly prejudice the defendant and influence the jury's ultimate decision. The court also stated that any inaccuracy in the videotape resulting from movement of the body went to the weight given by the jury to the videotape, not to the admissibility of the videotape. '[T]he prosecution, with its burden of establishing guilt beyond a reasonable doubt, is not to be denied the right to prove every essential element of the crime by the most convincing evidence it is able to produce.' * * *

Accordingly, we conclude that the trial court did not abuse its discretion by allowing the videotape into evidence." *Id.* at 407-08.

COMMONWEALTH v. WHARTON
Supreme Court of Pennsylvania
530 *Pa.* 127, 607 *A.*2d 710 (1992)

The opinion of the Court was delivered by

ZAPPALA, *Justice.*
"The victims in this case, Bradley and Ferne Hart, husband and wife, were subjected to a reign of terror by Robert Wharton, the [defend]ant, and others, commencing in the summer of 1983, and ending tragically in their deaths on January 30, 1984." *Id.* at 712.
"[Defendant] asserts that the trial court erred in permitting the jury to view photographs of the bodies of the murder victims. In *Commonwealth v. Buehl*, 510 *Pa.* 363, 391-92, 508 *A.*2d 1167, 1181-82 (1986), we stated:

> The question of admissibility of photographs of a corpse in a homicide case is a matter within the discretion of the trial judge and only an abuse of that discretion will constitute reversible error. * * * A photograph of a bloody corpse in a homicide trial is not inflammatory *per se.* * * * Whether the photographs are admissible depend[s] on a two step analysis. First, the court must decide whether a photograph is inflammatory in nature. "If, but only if, the photograph is deemed to be inflammatory, the court must then apply the balancing test . . . *i.e.*, is the photograph of 'such essential evidentiary value that [its] need clearly outweighs the likelihood of inflaming the minds and passions of the jurors.' " * * *

"The black and white photographs of the victims shown to the jury in [this] case were certainly not pleasant, as they showed the bodies from various angles and depicted the manner in which their hands and feet had been bound, their faces covered with tape, the ligations around their throats and the water in which their heads had been submerged. The jury saw each photograph only briefly (55-70 seconds each to circulate among all the jurors) after first being instructed by the court to 'view them quickly, observe what you see, move on and fight the impulse to be controlled by your emotion.' * * * The court stated that: 'These photographs were extremely relevant in establishing the intent and malice with which the defendant acted and this far outweighed any inflammatory or prejudicial effects which might have attended their admission.' * * * We agree. The court did not err in admitting these photographs." *Wharton* at 720. [Citations & footnote omitted.]

"The photographs were of essential evidentiary value in establishing the manner of death, malice, the premeditation and planning and the specific intent to kill, and the court did not abuse its discretion in holding that their probative value outweighed any prejudicial effects." *Id.* at 720-21.

STATE v. ALLISON
Superior Court of New Jersey, Appellate Division
208 *N.J.Super.* 9, 504 *A.2d* 1184 (1985)

PER CURIAM
[Defendants were the subjects of a joint indictment charging various offenses, including conspiracy to commit aggravated arson and first-degree arson in violation of *N.J.S.* 2C:5-2, 2C:17-1a and 2C:17-1d. At trial, defendants produced a witness, Douglas Williams, and advised the trial judge that Williams was prepared to testify that two months before one of the fires allegedly set by defendant Allison, Williams was doing some carpentry work at the premises and observed "flammable" drug paraphernalia on the roof of the building. The point of origin of the first fire was in a third floor stairway leading to the roof.]

* * * * *

"Defendants contended that Williams' evidence was relevant to their theory that drug addicts habitually used the building and probably started the fires for which both defendants stood accused. The judge viewed this proffered evidence as too remote in time and too far removed in space from the place where the first fire originated." *Id.*, 208 *N.J.Super.* at 16.

"Defendants produced no witnesses to establish that drug paraphernalia, 'flammable' or otherwise, was observed in the building at any other time." *Id.*

"The argument made by defendants on appeal is that Williams' proffered testimony was admissible because it was 'relevant' under *Evid.R.* 1(2) and had 'some probative weight' as to a cause for the fires." *Id.*

"Relevancy is composed of two parts: materiality and probative value. * * * 'Materiality looks to the relation between the propositions for which the evidence is offered and the issues in the case.' [] 'Probative value' is 'the tendency of evidence to establish the proposition that it is offered to prove.' [] Direct evidence 'offered to help establish a provable fact can never be irrelevant' but circumstantial evidence may be 'so unrevealing as to be irrelevant.' * * * '[T]o say that [circumstantial] evidence is irrelevant in the sense that it lacks probative value is to say that [the] evidence does not justify any reasonable inference as to the fact in question.' * * * A determination of relevancy lies in 'the judge's own experience, his general knowledge, and his understanding of human conduct and motivation.' " *Id.* at 17. [Citations omitted.]

"It is apparent that the proffered testimony was material to the central issue of the case in that it was directed to the cause of the fire. It is, however, a closer question as to whether the proffered testimony satisfies the 'probative value' test and 'renders the desired inference (that drug addicts started the fire) more probable than it would be without the evidence.' * * * The [trial] court was of the view that evidence of drug paraphernalia on the building's roof * * * was not probative evidence in regard to the cause of the first [] fire. Although the relevancy test is broad, this conclusion is, in these circumstances, sustainable. The presence of drug paraphernalia at a location other than that where the fire originated two months prior to the fire does not provide probative evidence of the fire's cause." *Id.*

STATE v. MATHIS
Supreme Court of New Jersey
47 *N.J.* 455, 221 A.2d 529 (1966)

The opinion of the Court was delivered by

WEINTRAUB, C.J.

"Defendant was convicted of murder in the first degree, and the jury not having recommended life imprisonment, he was sentenced to die. He appeals directly to this Court.

"The deceased, Stanley Caswell, had an insurance debit route which took him to North Ninth Street in Kenilworth. The residents there knew him as 'the insurance man.' " *Id.*, 47 *N.J.* at 459.

[At trial, during cross-examination, the prosecutor asked defendant] "how much money he had and when he last worked. The examination suggested strongly that the State might be urging that defendant was in financial need, and hence was likely to commit a robbery. * * * This the State could not do." *Id.* at 469.

"[I]f the testimony elicited on cross-examination is not relevant upon the issues in the case, or directly upon the witness's trustworthiness, *i.e.*, his knowledge, interest, bias, or criminal record, [the prosecutor may not continue to pursue this line of questioning] lest the trial become the pursuit of sundry[,] extraneous and distracting subjects[.]" *Id.* at 471.

"But what emerged was something more than a mere trial of something extraneous. The point the State in truth made * * * was that defendant lied when he said he worked[,] and hence[,] * * * being otherwise essentially unemployed, he must have been destitute and therefore he likely would rob. [This was] impermissible." *Id.*

"Undoubtedly, a lack of money is logically connected with a crime involving financial gain. The trouble is that it would prove too much against too many. * * *

The *lack of money* by A might be relevant enough to show the probability of A's desiring to *commit a crime* in order to obtain money. But the practical result of such a doctrine would be to put a poor person under so much unfair suspicion and at such a relative disadvantage that for reasons of fairness this argument has seldom been countenanced as evidence of the graver crimes, particularly of violence.

The relationship between the deceased and defendant of creditor and debtor may be competent as to motive, * * * but, in general terms, *there must be something more than poverty to tie a defendant into a criminal milieu.*" *Id.* at 471-72. [Citations omitted; emphasis added.]

[In this case, the State exceeded the bounds of fair play when it] "projected before the jury the forbidden theme that defendant had no apparent means of income and hence was likely to commit a crime for dollar gain. This was improper and injurious." *Id.* at 472.

NOTE

1. In *Commonwealth v. Burkelbaugh*, 526 *Pa.* 133, 584 *A.*2d 927 (1990), the prosecutor made the following closing remarks to the jury:

I think that [defendant's] own testimony establishes to you the motive to commit the robbery. He is an unemployed man; the last job he ever had was seven years ago. He had no income. He lives with his brother. Yet, he had the ability to Christmas-shop, as he testified. * * *

Id., 584 *A.*2d at 929.

Finding the prosecutor's remarks unduly prejudicial, the court held that it was entirely improper for her to attempt to ascribe unemployment as a motive for committing a crime. The court emphasized that evidence offered to demonstrate "that one in need of money is more likely to steal is impermissible evidence." *Id.* at 929.

2. *Unfair prejudice.* Under Rule 403, the trial judge is authorized to exclude relevant evidence when its "probative value is substantially outweighed by the danger of unfair prejudice, confusion of the issues, or misleading the jury, or by considerations of undue delay, waste of time, or needless presentation of cumulative evidence." In *Old Chief v. United States*, 519 *U.S.* 172, 117 *S.Ct.* 644 (1997), the United States Supreme Court explained that the term

"unfair prejudice," as to a criminal defendant, speaks to the capacity of some concededly relevant evidence to lure the factfinder into declaring guilt on a ground different from proof specific to the offense charged. * * * [As] the Committee Notes to Rule 403 explain, " 'Unfair prejudice' within its context means an undue tendency to suggest decision on an improper basis, commonly, though not necessarily, an emotional one."

Id. at 180, 117 *S.Ct.* at 650. [Citations omitted.]

STATE v. SONTHIKOUMMANE
Supreme Court of New Hampshire
145 *N.H.* 316, 769 *A.2d* 330 (2000)

PER CURIAM.

[During the course of a drug investigation, an undercover narcotics detective employed the services of an informant to purchase crack cocaine from defendant. On four separate occasions, the detective gave the informant a sum of money for the drug purchases, and on each occasion, the detective recorded the serial numbers of the currency. On each occasion, the informant entered the defendant's residence, made the purchase, and, upon his return, handed the detective or another undercover officer the crack cocaine. The last two purchases produced a total of $600 worth of crack cocaine. After the last purchase, undercover officers obtained and executed a search warrant for defendant's residence.]

"During the search of the defendant's residence, the officers discovered: (1) $2,800 hidden in a stereo speaker; (2) $540 in the possession of the defendant and his wife; (3) three late model motor vehicles; (4) airline tickets valued in excess of $3,500; (5) jewelry; (6) a large screen television; (7) a stereo system; (8) a cellular telephone; (9) a pager; (10) a photocopier; (11) a loaded handgun; (12) a large suitcase filled with new clothing; and (13) a key to a safety deposit box. Mixed in with the $2,800 found in the stereo speaker was $580 of the money used by the undercover officers in their last two purchases of cocaine * * *. A subsequent search of the safety deposit box revealed $4,000 in cash and additional jewelry. The total value of jewelry found in the two searches was approximately $20,000." *Id.* at 332.

"This evidence, along with evidence of the defendant's history of unemployment, relatively low family income, and possession of food stamps was presented to the jury during trial." *Id.*

In this appeal, defendant argues, among other things, that the trial court erred by allowing the State to submit evidence of his "unexplained wealth," contending that "such evidence was irrelevant and unfairly prejudicial." *Id.* at 336.

"To be relevant, evidence must tend 'to make the existence of any fact that is of consequence to the determination of the action more probable than it would be without the evidence.' Generally, when a defendant is charged with a conspiracy that includes a profit motive, evidence of 'unexplained wealth' is relevant to the existence of the conspiracy. * * * This may be true even if there is another explanation for the extra money. * * * The mere fact that a defendant has unexplained wealth is not enough, however, for the evidence of wealth to be relevant. Such evidence must also have a nexus to the charges." *Id.*

"In this case, the defendant was indicted and convicted of three conspiracies to sell drugs. At trial, the defendant denied involvement in any conspiracy, and the State offered evidence of the conspiracies that was independent of the unexplained wealth. This evidence included the fact that $580 of the money used by the undercover police officers was found mixed in with the $2,800 hidden in the defendant's stereo speaker. Additionally, the evidence of unexplained wealth in relation to the defendant's lack of employment over the prior year supported the factual assertion that the defendant was conspiring to sell cocaine for a profit. [] Therefore, the evidence of unexplained wealth was linked with other evidence showing the existence of the charged conspiracies and tended to increase the probability that the conspiracies existed. Thus, the trial court did not err in concluding that the evidence was relevant." *Id.*

Defendant next argues that the "evidence of unexplained wealth was unfairly prejudicial," contending that "it 'may have led the jury to speculate that [he] was a drug dealer and therefore must have committed the charged offenses.' In support of his argument, the defendant points to the fact that no cocaine was ever found in his residence and no officer ever observed him with anything that could be construed as contraband." *Id.* at 336-37.

"Under Rule 403, evidence of the defendant's unexplained wealth was admissible if its probative value was not substantially outweighed by the danger of unfair prejudice to the defendant. 'Under [this] rule, evidence is unfairly prejudicial if its primary purpose or effect is to appeal to a jury's sympathies, arouse its sense of horror, provoke its instinct to punish, or trigger other mainsprings of human action that may cause a jury to base its decision on something other than the established propositions of the case.' " *Id.* at 337. [Citation omitted.]

"The indictments in this case alleged three discrete acts, yet the trial court allowed the State to introduce evidence of 'unexplained wealth' far in excess of any profits that could have resulted from the three charges. By its nature, this evidence suggested that the defendant was involved in many more drug sales than the three charged by the State. 'When, however, [evidence] is material to show the intent or the malice with which an act is done, other acts than those charged in the indictment are oftentimes competent evidence.' " *Id.* [Citations omitted.]

"The existence of any conspiracy was contested by the defendant at trial. The trial court, therefore, would 'have been justified in assigning the evidence a high probative value' for both the defendant's motive and his intent to enter into the charged conspiracies. * * * This is especially true when, as here, the circumstantial unexplained wealth evidence was a significant factor in corroborating the testimony of [two witnesses] that the defendant was supplying the crack cocaine for them to sell on his behalf." *Id.*

"The evidence of unexplained wealth supports a reasonable inference that the defendant intended to enter into the charged conspiracies. Additionally, it has a factual nexus to the charges in the indictments. Under these circumstances, the evidence of unexplained wealth was highly relevant. Therefore, the trial court did not abuse its discretion in admitting the 'unexplained wealth' evidence." *Id.*

NOTE

1. *The "logical connection" test of relevance.* In a typical case, the relevancy of an item of evidence will be tested by its probative value with respect to the points at issue. The true test is the logical connection of the proffered evidence to a fact in issue, *i.e.*, whether the thing sought to be established is more logical with the evidence than without it.

For evidence to be relevant, it need not by itself support or prove a fact proposition. As one court put it, "it is not necessary that every piece of evidence admitted should be sufficient by itself to prove the crime. Evidence which would be colorless if it stood alone may get a new complexion from other facts which are proved, and, in turn, may corroborate the conclusion which would be drawn from other facts." *Commonwealth v. Mulrey*, 170 *Mass.* 103, 49 *N.E.* 91, 94 (1898) (opinion by Justice Holmes).

Thus, in *State v. Smollok*, 148 *N.J.Super.* 382, 372 *A.*2d 1105 (App.Div. 1977), a case in which the defendant was charged with taking large cash bribes, the court held that evidence demonstrating five large cash deposits over seven months in a new bank account was clearly admissible and "highly relevant" to the bribery issue. *Id.* at 386. *See also People v. Connolly*, 171 *N.E.* 393, 397 (N Y 1930) (admission of unexplained wealth justified "by elementary principles governing the admissibility of evidence"); *Commonwealth v. Mulrey*, 49 *N.E.* 91, 94 (Mass. 1898) (wealth evidence admissible if it tends to show the existence of conspiracy); *United States v. Thompson*, 925 *F.*2d 234, 237 (8th Cir. 1991) (presence of cash, drugs, and firearms relevant to intent); *United States v. Grandison*, 783 *F.*2d 1152, 1156 (4th Cir. 1986) (wealth when unemployed relevant to intent); *United States v. Jackskion*, 102 *F.*2d 683, 684 (2d Cir. 1939) (untraced wealth relevant if it has a "logical tendency to prove criminal misconduct"); 1 C. Torcia, *Wharton's Criminal Evidence* §153, at 623 (14th ed. 1985) ("significant improvement in . . . financial condition is admissible").

2. *Crimes involving pecuniary gain as a motive.* In *State v. Coruzzi,* 189 *N.J.Super.* 273, 460 A.2d 120 (App.Div. 1983), the court observed: "It is the general view that where a defendant is on trial for a crime in which pecuniary gain is the motive, evidence of the sudden acquisition of money by defendant is admissible, even though the source of the money is not traced. The State is not required to establish, however, defendant's financial status prior to the crime, only the sudden acquisition or rise in his financial condition subsequent thereto." *Id.,* 189 *N.J.Super.* at 304.

3. *Possession of money in the same denominations as that which was taken.* It is clear that the mere possession of a sum of money is, in itself, no indication that the possessor is the thief. However, where the denominations of the money possessed and the money taken correspond in a reasonably close way, the fact of the possession of that specific money will have probative value, and should be found relevant because the money so possessed is fairly recognized as virtually the same as the money taken. *See e.g., United States v. Rouse,* 494 *F.*2d 45, 46 (5th Cir. 1974) (where $49,000 was stolen from a bank, $29,000 of which was in $100 bills, testimony showing the defendant's recent purchase of a new Cadillac for $11,000, paid for in $100 bills was relevant and admissible); *State v. Mihoy,* 98 *N.H.* 38, 93 *A.*2d 661, 662 (1953) (evidence that burglary defendant gave his female companion two or three dollars in quarters, dimes and nickels on the morning of the burglary held to be relevant and admissible after the owner of the burglarized diner testified that a coin box, which had also been broken into, contained approximately two dollars in nickels, dimes and quarters).

COMMONWEALTH v. FOY
Supreme Court of Pennsylvania
531 *Pa.* 322, 612 A.2d 1349 (1992)

The opinion of the Court was delivered by

ZAPPALA, *Justice.*
The question in this case is one of first impression: Did the trial court err in admitting into evidence testimony that following defendant's arrest, "no further crimes of the type that [defend]ant was accused of were reported. We find that the admission of such evidence was error * * *." *Id.* at 1350.

"Between February 2 and August 25, 1987, four elderly women in the Borough of Homestead, Pennsylvania, were sexually assaulted in the bedrooms of their homes. The unique pattern of these crimes indicated that the assaults were the work of a single perpetrator since all the victims ranged in age from 65 to 85 years old and lived alone within a densely populated two and one-half block area. These early morning attacks, which occurred after the victims had gone to sleep, began with the assailant covering the victim's head with a blanket, tying the victim's hands and feet with clothing, bed-clothes or other objects found in the house, sexually assaulting her, and then burglarizing the residence." *Id.* at 1350-51.

At defendant's trial, the prosecutor posed the following question to the chief of police:

Q. Chief [], have you gotten any reports of crimes that involve the early morning burglaries including rapes and robberies in that burglary involving the homes of elderly women living alone since September 3, 1987?

A. No, sir, none.

Id. at 1351.

Defendant contends that the trial court erred in permitting the police chief to testify that no further crimes of the type which defendant was accused were reported following defendant's arrest.

"In determining whether certain evidence is admissible, the trial court must first inquire into the relevancy of that evidence. Evidence which tends to establish some fact material to the case or which tends to make a fact at issue more or less probable is relevant." *Id.*

The evidence elicited by the Commonwealth "is inherently unreliable." As the Superior Court noted:

[T]here are many possible reasons for an absence of additional reported crimes that are consistent with the defendant's innocence. Police testimony concerning the reports could be inaccurate. Further signature crimes may have been committed but never reported to the police. The true culprit may have died, or left the community, or been incarcerated on unrelated charges about the time of the defendant's arrest. Or perhaps the true culprit has decided to refrain from further acts of violence in order to shift suspicion onto the defendant and thereby escape detection.

Id. [Citation omitted.]

"Because [the chief's] testimony did not establish some fact material to the case or tend to make a fact at issue more or less probable, we find that such evidence was not relevant." *Id.* at 1351-52.

"Even assuming [that the chief's] testimony is relevant, it remains clear that his statement should have been excluded. Relevant evidence is subject to exclusion if its probative value is substantially outweighed by the danger of unfair prejudice or confusion. * * * The jury may well have concluded that [defend]ant was guilty because [the police chief] testified that no further crimes had occurred since [defend]ant's arrest. Certainly, this possibility of prejudice outweighs any probative value of the evidence in light of the variety of explanations noted above for the cessation of the crimes." *Id.* at 1352.

---

§6.4. THE EXCLUSIONARY RULE

The Fourth Amendment to the United States Constitution safeguards the "right of the people to be secure in their persons, houses, papers and effects, against unreasonable searches and seizures[.]" Additionally, the Amendment commands that "no Warrants shall issue, but upon probable cause, supported by Oath or affirmation, and particularly describing the place to be searched, and the persons or things to be seized."

Generally, the United States Supreme Court has viewed a search and seizure as *"per se* unreasonable within the meaning of the Fourth Amendment unless it is accomplished pursuant to a judicial warrant issued upon probable cause and particularly describing the [places to be searched and] the items to be seized."[17] As a fundamental principle of constitutional criminal procedure, search warrants are strongly favored under both the federal constitution and all state constitutions. The judicial preference which underscores the written warrant requirement is predicated upon the proposition that the necessity, validity and reasonableness of a prospective search or seizure can best be determined by a "neutral and detached magistrate" instead of a law enforcement officer. As the Supreme Court has stated, the warrant procedure serves primarily "to advise the citizen that the intrusion is authorized by law and [is] limited in its permissible scope[,] and to interpose a neutral magistrate between the citizen and the law enforcement officer 'engaged in the often competitive enterprise of ferreting out crime.' "[18]

The warrant procedure is not a mere formality. As the Court put it in *McDonald v. United States:* [19]

> The presence of a search warrant serves a high function. Absent some grave emergency, the Fourth Amendment has interposed a magistrate between the citizen and the police. This was done not to shield criminals nor to make the home a safe haven for illegal activities. It was done so that an objective

---

[17] *United States v. Place*, 462 *U.S.* 696, 701, 103 *S.Ct.* 2637, 2641 (1983).

[18] *National Treasury Employees Union v. Von Raab*, 489 *U.S.* 656, 109 *S.Ct.* 1384, 1391 (1989) (quoting *Johnson v. United States*, 333 *U.S.* 10, 14, 68 *S.Ct.* 367, 369 (1948)).

[19] 335 *U.S.* 451, 455-456, 69 *S.Ct.* 191 (1978).

mind might weigh the need to invade that privacy in order to enforce the law. The right of privacy was deemed too precious to entrust to the discretion of those whose job is the detection of crime and the arrest of criminals. . . . And so the Constitution requires a magistrate to pass on the desires of the police before they violate the privacy of the home. We cannot be true to that constitutional requirement and excuse the absence of a search warrant without a showing by those who seek exemption from the constitutional mandate that the exigencies of the situation made that course imperative.

The driving force behind the Fourth Amendment, along with the history of its application, demonstrates that the Amendment's purpose and design is the protection of the "people" against arbitrary action by their own Government.

While the courts consistently hold that searches and seizures conducted without warrants are disfavored, the reality is that the vast majority of searches and seizures performed by law enforcement officers are accomplished without a written warrant. Nonetheless, the strong judicial preference for the acquisition of a search warrant by a law enforcement officer is not to be dispensed with lightly. Once a search or seizure is conducted without a warrant, the burden is upon the Government, as the party seeking to validate the warrantless search, to bring it within one of the recognized exceptions created by the United States Supreme Court.

The Constitution does not prohibit all warrantless searches or seizures; the Constitution only " 'forbids * * * unreasonable searches and seizures.' "[20] Thus, over the course of time, the United States Supreme Court has carved out of the Fourth Amendment several carefully tailored exceptions to its warrant requirement. Those formally recognized include: (1) searches conducted as an incident to a lawful arrest; (2) probable-cause based searches conducted in the face of exigent circumstances; (3) searches of motor vehicles based on probable cause; (4) searches conducted for the purpose of cataloging a person's property through established inventory procedures; (5) searches conducted pursuant to a valid consent; and those law enforcement activities which are not considered searches or seizures within the meaning of the Constitution either because the property in question is situated in the (6) open fields, or has been (7) abandoned, or the areas of concern are within (8) plain view.

Although the Constitution contains no express provision which specifically prohibits the use of evidence seized in violation of its terms, the Supreme Court has created a tool which is designed ultimately to safeguard Fourth Amendment rights. The tool is called the *Exclusionary Rule*, and since 1961 it has been disallowing the

---

[20] *Terry v. Ohio*, 392 *U.S.* 1, 9, 88 *S.Ct.* 1868, 1873 (1968) (quoting *Elkins v. United States*, 364 *U.S.* 206, 222, 80 *S.Ct.* 1437, 1446 (1960)).

use of evidence obtained in violation of the Fourth Amendment in state as well as federal prosecutions.[21] Rather than a personal constitutional right belonging to the victim of an illegal search or seizure, the exclusionary rule operates as a judicially created remedy which protects Fourth Amendment rights generally by deterring wrongful police conduct.[22] "Deterrence," then, is the linchpin of the exclusionary rule.[23] Simply stated, *the exclusionary rule is a judicially created device which is employed by the courts to prohibit the use of evidence at a criminal trial when that evidence has been seized by law enforcement officials in violation of the Constitution.*

The remedy of exclusion applies generally to criminal prosecutions, prohibiting the use of evidence obtained in violation of federal or state constitutional rights.[24] The exclusionary rule has never been interpreted, however, to prohibit the use of illegally seized evidence in all proceedings or against all persons. "As with any remedial device, the application of the rule has been restricted to those areas where its remedial objectives" are thought to be best served.[25] If application of the exclusionary rule in a particular situation does not result in appreciable deterrence, its use may be unwarranted. Thus, it has been held that the exclusionary rule would not bar the use of illegally seized evidence in a federal civil tax proceeding,[26] in grand jury proceedings,[27] to impeach the credibility of a defendant who takes the stand and testifies,[28] or in civil deportation proceedings.[29]

Moreover, the exclusionary rule applies only to unlawful actions by government officials. It has no application to searches and seizures by private individuals. Illegally obtained evidence, which would be subject to suppression if secured by a government official, need not be suppressed when obtained by a private citizen acting on his or her own behalf.[30]

---

[21] *See Mapp v. Ohio,* 367 *U.S.* 643, 81 *S.Ct.* 1684 (1961) ("all evidence obtained by searches and seizures in violation of the Constitution is, by that same authority, inadmissible in a state court").

[22] *United States v. Leon,* 468 *U.S.* 897, 104 *S.Ct.* 3405 (1984).

[23] *See United States v. Janis,* 428 *U.S.* 433, 96 *S.Ct.* 3021 (1976) ("the 'prime purpose' of the [exclusionary] rule, if not the sole one, 'is to deter future unlawful police conduct' "); *United States v. Calandra,* 414 *U.S.* 338, 94 *S.Ct.* 613 (1974) (the exclusionary rule is not "a personal constitutional right of the party aggrieved").

[24] *James v. Illinois,* 493 *U.S.* 307, 311, 110 *S.Ct.* 648, 651 (1990).

[25] *See United States v. Calandra,* 414 *U.S.* 338, 348, 94 *S.Ct.* 613, 620 (1974).

[26] *United States v. Janis,* 428 *U.S.* 433, 459-60, 96 *S.Ct.* 3021, 3034 (1976).

[27] *United States v. Calandra, supra* at 350-52, 94 *S.Ct.* at 621-22.

[28] *United States v. Havens,* 446 *U.S.* 620, 627, 100 *S.Ct.* 1912, 1916-17 (1980).

[29] *I.N.S. v. Lopez-Mendoza,* 468 *U.S.* 1032, 104 *S.Ct.* 3479 (1984).

[30] *See e.g., United States v. Jacobsen,* 466 *U.S.* 109, 113-14, 104 *S.Ct.* 1652, 1656 (1984) (exclusionary rule is "wholly inapplicable" to "a search or seizure, even an unreasonable one, effected by a private individual not acting as an agent of the Government or with the participation or knowledge of any governmental official").

When confronted with an unreasonable search and seizure, a state court is free, and indeed encouraged, to rely on its own constitution to provide greater protection to the privacy interests of its citizens than that afforded under parallel provisions of the federal Constitution. As a well-established principle of our federalist system, state constitutions may be the source of "individual liberties more expansive than those conferred by the federal Constitution."[31] This means that a state court is free as a matter of its own law to impose greater restrictions on police activity than those the United States Supreme Court holds to be necessary under federal constitutional standards. The federal Constitution, then, represents the base-line floor of protection, and of course, a state may not drop below the federal floor; it may, however, rely on its own state constitution to heighten that floor of protection.

State law enforcement officers are cautioned, therefore, that their state may establish, as a matter of its own law, a ceiling of protection for its citizens which may have the effect of placing additional restrictions upon, or requiring the exercise of additional precautions by, its officers. A review of local rules in this area is strongly recommended.

---

§6.4(a). The Motion to Suppress Evidence

Evidence seized in violation of the Constitution is not "automatically" excluded from a criminal trial. Rather, a defendant with "standing" must invoke the protection of the exclusionary rule—state or federal—by formally objecting to the introduction of that evidence. This is accomplished by the filing of a timely "motion to suppress evidence," which conforms to the particular jurisdiction's procedural requirements concerning how such motions should be made.

As a preliminary matter, in order to contest the admission of evidence obtained by a search or seizure, a defendant must first demonstrate that he or she has "standing." This requires a showing that the defendant's *own* Fourth Amendment rights have been violated.[32] As explained by the United States Supreme Court in *Baker v. Carr*, the defendant must establish "a personal stake in the outcome of the controversy * * * to assure that concrete adverseness which sharpens the presentation of issues upon which the court so largely depends for illumination of difficult constitutional issues."[33]

---

[31] *Pruneyard Shopping Center v. Robins*, 447 *U.S.* 74, 81, 100 *S.Ct.* 2035, 2040 (1980).

[32] *See United States v. Salvucci*, 448 *U.S.* 83, 87, 100 *S.Ct.* 2547, 2550 (1980); *Rakas v. Illinois*, 439 *U.S.* 128, 134, 99 *S.Ct.* 421, 425 (1978).

[33] 369 *U.S.* 186, 204, 82 *S.Ct.* 691, 703 (1962). *See also O'Shea v. Littleton*, 414 *U.S.* 488, 493, 94 *S.Ct.* 669, 674 (1974).

Thus, a defendant has "standing" when evidence alleged to have been unconstitutionally seized is being offered against him in a criminal case.[34] On the other hand, "a person whose Fourth Amendment rights were violated by a search or seizure, but is not a defendant in a criminal action in which the illegally seized evidence is sought to be introduced, would not have standing to invoke the exclusionary rule to prevent use of that evidence in that action."[35]

In many respects, the hearing on the motion to suppress evidence (the "suppression hearing"), is very much like a "mini trial." Both the State and the defendant have the opportunity to present witnesses, cross-examine their adversaries, introduce documentary evidence, and offer legal argument. The hearing has been described as "the mechanism specifically designed to afford a defendant his most significant opportunity to participate in a process which vindicates the constitutionally-declared right against an unlawful search."[36] Unlike the trial on the criminal charge itself,

> "[t]he very purpose of a motion to suppress is to escape the inculpatory thrust of evidence in hand, not because its probative force is diluted in the least by the mode of seizure, but rather as a sanction to compel enforcement officers to respect the constitutional security of all of us under the Fourth Amendment."[37]

The focus and scope of the suppression hearing center upon Fourth Amendment issues. Unlike a criminal trial, however, credible hearsay evidence is admissible.[38]

Generally, a hearing is only required if material facts are disputed. As to who shoulders the burden of proof, most jurisdictions follow the federal approach: if the search or seizure was conducted under the authority of a search warrant, the defendant has the burden of proof; if the search and seizure occurred in the absence of a warrant, the prosecution bears the burden of proof.

This approach takes into account the constitutional principle that warrantless searches and seizures are "presumptively unreasonable." Therefore, at a motion to suppress evidence seized without

---

[34] When, to establish standing, "a defendant testifies in support of a motion to suppress evidence on Fourth Amendment grounds, his testimony may not thereafter be admitted against him at trial on the issue of guilt[.]" *Simmons v. United States,* 390 *U.S.* 377, 394, 88 *S.Ct.* 967, 976 (1968).

[35] *Rakas v. Illinois,* 439 *U.S.* 128, 132 n.2, 99 *S.Ct.* 421, 424 n.2 (1978); *United States v. Calandra,* 414 *U.S.* 338, 352 n.8, 94 *S.Ct.* 613, 622 n.8 (1974). *See also Alderman v. United States,* 394 *U.S.* 165, 174, 89 *S.Ct.* 961, 966 (1969) ("Fourth Amendment rights are personal rights which * * * may not be vicariously asserted.").

[36] *State v. Fariello,* 71 *N.J.* 552, 559, 366 *A.2d* 1313 (1976).

[37] *McCray v. Illinois,* 386 *U.S.* 300, 307, 87 *S.Ct.* 1056, 1060 (1967) (citation omitted).

[38] *See United States v. Matlock,* 415 *U.S.* 164, 173-75, 94 *S.Ct.* 988, 994-95 (1974).

a warrant, the burden is on the prosecution to prove, in most cases by a preponderance of the evidence,[39] that the search or seizure was lawful; that the police action fell within one of the recognized exceptions to the written warrant requirement.[40] The prosecution is not required to prove that the search fell within more than one recognized exception. So long as "the validity of the search can be sustained independently on objective grounds demonstrating reasonableness" that is, on the basis of one specific exception to the written warrant requirement, the fact that it does not meet the requirements of some other ground or some other exception will not serve to invalidate the search.[41]

Searches and seizures conducted under the authority of a warrant are presumptively lawful. Even in marginal cases, courts tend to resolve any doubts as to the constitutionality of the challenged police action in favor of sustaining the search and seizure. In this regard, when the police have conducted a search and seizure with a warrant, "an independent determination on the issue of probable cause has already been made by a magistrate, thereby giving rise to a presumption of legality."[42] As a result, at the suppression hearing, once the prosecution introduces the search warrant into evidence, the more difficult burden shifts to the defendant to establish the invalidity of the warrant, and, in turn, the unlawfulness of the search and seizure. If a defendant succeeds in establishing the invalidity of the warrant, the context of the suppression hearing changes to one involving a warrantless search and seizure, with the burden now placed on the prosecution to establish that the challenged police action was justified by one of the recognized exceptions to the written warrant requirement.

At the conclusion of the hearing, if the defendant's motion to suppress is granted, the judge will enter an order suppressing the evidence seized. The evidence will be "inadmissible" at defendant's criminal trial. If the motion is denied, the judge's order will provide that the evidence seized is admissible for trial use.

---

[39] *See United States v. Matlock*, 415 *U.S.* 164, 94 *S.Ct.* 988 (1974) (the controlling burden of proof at suppression hearings is by a "preponderance of evidence").

[40] *See e.g., United States v. Carhee*, 27 *F.*3d 1493 (10th Cir. 1994); *United States v. Roach*, 5 *F.*3d 894 (5th Cir. 1993). *See also Rouse v. United States*, 359 *F.*2d 1014, 1016 (1966); *United States v. Burhannon*, 388 *F.*2d 961 (7th Cir. 1968); *Rogers v. United States*, 330 *F.*2d 535 (5th Cir. 1964); *Cervantes v. United States*, 263 *F.*2d 800 (9th Cir. 1959).

[41] *See Scott v. United States*, 436 *U.S.* 128, 138-39 & n.13, 98 *S.Ct.* 1717, 1723-24 & n.13 (1978).

[42] *See Malcolm v. United States*, 332 *A.*2d 917, 918 (D.C.App. 1975). *See also Chin Kay v. United States*, 311 *F.*2d 317 (9th Cir. 1962); *Wilson v. United States*, 218 *F.*2d 754 (10th Cir. 1955).

MAPP v. OHIO
Supreme Court of the United States
367 *U.S.* 643, 81 *S.Ct.* 1684 (1961)

Mr. Justice CLARK delivered the opinion of the Court.

* * * * *

"On May 23, 1957, three Cleveland police officers arrived at [defendant's] residence in that city pursuant to information that 'a person [was] hiding out in the home, who was wanted for questioning in connection with a recent bombing, and that there was a large amount of policy paraphernalia being hidden in the home.' Miss Mapp and her daughter by a former marriage lived on the top floor of the two-family dwelling. Upon their arrival at that house, the officers knocked on the door and demanded entrance but [defendant], after telephoning her attorney, refused to admit them without a search warrant. They advised their headquarters of the situation and undertook a surveillance of the house." *Id.* at 1685.

"The officers again sought entrance some three hours later when four or more additional officers arrived on the scene. When Miss Mapp did not come to the door immediately, at least one of the several doors to the house was forcibly opened and the policemen gained admittance. Meanwhile Miss Mapp's attorney arrived, but the officers, having secured their own entry, and continuing in their defiance of the law, would permit him neither to see Miss Mapp nor to enter the house. It appears that Miss Mapp was halfway down the stairs from the upper floor to the front door when the officers, in this highhanded manner, broke into the hall. She demanded to see the search warrant. A paper, claimed to be a warrant, was held up by one of the officers. She grabbed the 'warrant' and placed it in her bosom. A struggle ensued in which the officers recovered the piece of paper and as a result of which they handcuffed [Miss Mapp] because she had been 'belligerent' in resisting their official rescue of the 'warrant' from her person. Running roughshod over [Miss Mapp], a policeman 'grabbed' her, 'twisted [her] hand,' and she 'yelled [and] pleaded with him' because 'it was hurting.' [Mapp], in handcuffs, was then forcibly taken upstairs to her bedroom where the officers searched a dresser, a chest of drawers, a closet and some suitcases. They also looked into a photo album and through personal papers belonging to [her]. The search spread to the rest of the second floor including the child's bedroom, the living room, the kitchen and a dinette. The basement of the building and a trunk found therein were also searched. The obscene materials for possession of which she was ultimately convicted were discovered in the course of that widespread search." Id. at 1686.

"At the trial no search warrant was produced by the prosecution, nor was the failure to produce one explained or accounted for.

At best, '[t]here is, * * * considerable doubt as to whether there ever was any warrant * * *.' " *Id.*

"The State says that even if the search were made without authority, or otherwise unreasonably, it is not prevented from using the unconstitutionally seized evidence at trial, citing *Wolf v.* [*Colorado,* 338 *U.S.* 25, 33, 69 *S.Ct.* 1359, 1364 (1949)], in which this Court did indeed hold 'that in a prosecution in a State court for a State crime the Fourteenth Amendment does not forbid the admission of evidence obtained by an unreasonable search and seizure.' " *Id.*

"Seventy-five years ago, in *Boyd v. United States,* 116 *U.S.* 616, 630, 6 *S.Ct.* 524, 532 [] (1886), considering the Fourth and Fifth Amendments as running 'almost into each other' on the facts before it, this Court held that the doctrines of those Amendments

> apply to all invasions on the part of the government and its employes of the sanctity of a man's home and the privacies of life. It is not the breaking of his doors, and the rummaging of his drawers, that constitutes the essence of the offence; but it is the invasion of his indefeasible right of personal security, personal liberty and private property * * *. Breaking into a house and opening boxes and drawers are circumstances of aggravation; but any forcible and compulsory extortion of a man's own testimony or of his private papers to be used as evidence to convict him of crime or to forfeit his goods, is within the condemnation * * * [of those Amendments].

The Court noted that

> constitutional provisions for the security of person and property should be liberally construed. * * * It is the duty of courts to be watchful for the constitutional rights of the citizen, and against any stealthy encroachments thereon.

Boyd at 635, 6 *S.Ct.* at 535.

"Less than 30 years after *Boyd,* this Court, in *Weeks v. United States,* 232 *U.S.* 383, 34 *S.Ct.* 341 (1914), stated that

> the Fourth Amendment * * * put the courts of the United States and Federal officials, in the exercise of their power and authority, under limitations and restraints [and] * * * forever secure[d] the people, their persons, houses, papers and effects against all unreasonable searches and seizures under the guise of law * * * and the duty of giving to it force and effect is obligatory upon all entrusted under our Federal system with the enforcement of the laws."

Weeks at 391-92, 34 *S.Ct.* at 344.

"Specifically dealing with the use of the evidence unconstitutionally seized, the Court concluded:

> If letters and private documents can thus be seized and held and used in evidence against a citizen accused of an offense, the protection of the Fourth Amendment declaring his right to be secure against such searches and seizures is of no value, and, so far as those thus placed are concerned, might as well be stricken from the Constitution. The efforts of the courts and their officials to bring the guilty to punishment, praiseworthy as they are, are not to be aided by the sacrifice of those great principles established by years of endeavor and suffering which have resulted in their embodiment in the fundamental law of the land."

Weeks at 393, 34 *S.Ct.* at 344.

"Finally, the Court in that case clearly stated that use of the seized evidence involved 'a denial of the constitutional rights of the accused.' * * * Thus, in the year 1914, in the *Weeks* case, this Court 'for the first time' held that 'in a federal prosecution the Fourth Amendment barred the use of evidence secured through an illegal search and seizure.' [*See Wolf v. Colorado*, 338 *U.S.* 25, 69 *S.Ct.* 1359 (1949).] This Court has ever since required of federal law officers a strict adherence to that command which this Court has held to be a clear, specific, and constitutionally required—even if judicially implied—deterrent safeguard without insistence upon which the Fourth Amendment would have been reduced to 'a form of words.' * * * It meant, quite simply, that 'conviction by means of unlawful seizures and enforced confessions * * * should find no sanction in the judgments of the courts['] * * *, and that such evidence 'shall not be used at all.' " *Mapp* at 1688.

"There are in the cases of this Court some passing references to the *Weeks* rule as being one of evidence. But the plain and unequivocal language of *Weeks*—and its later paraphrase in *Wolf*—to the effect that the *Weeks* rule is of constitutional origin, remains entirely undisturbed." *Id.*

"The Court, in *Olmstead v. United States*, 277 *U.S.* 438, 48 *S.Ct.* 564 (1928), in unmistakable language restated the *Weeks rule:*

> The striking outcome of the *Weeks* case and those which followed it was the sweeping declaration that the Fourth Amendment, although not referring to or limiting the use of evidence in courts, really forbade its introduction if obtained by government officers through a violation of the Amendment."

Olmstead at 462, 48 *S.Ct.* at 567.

"Today, we once again examine *Wolf*'s constitutional documentation of the right to privacy free from unreasonable state intrusion, and after its dozen years on our books, are led by it to close the only courtroom door remaining open to evidence secured by official lawlessness in flagrant abuse of that basic right, reserved to all persons as a specific guarantee against that very same unlawful conduct. ***We hold that all evidence obtained by searches and seizures in violation of the Constitution is, by that same authority, inadmissible in a state court.***" *Mapp* at 1691. [Emphasis added.]

"*Since the Fourth Amendment's right of privacy has been declared enforceable against the States through the Due Process Clause of the Fourteenth, it is enforceable against them by the same sanction of exclusion as is used against the Federal Government.* Were it otherwise, then just as without the *Weeks* rule, the assurance against unreasonable federal searches and seizures would be 'a form of words,' valueless and undeserving of mention in a perpetual charter of inestimable human liberties * * *." *Id.* [Emphasis added.]

"* * * [I]n extending the substantive protections of due process to all constitutionally unreasonable searches—state or federal—it was logically and constitutionally necessary that the exclusion doctrine—an essential part of the right to privacy—be also insisted upon as an essential ingredient of * * * [due process]. * * * To hold otherwise is to grant the right but in reality to withhold its privilege and enjoyment. Only last year the Court itself recognized that the purpose of the exclusionary rule 'is to deter—to compel respect for the constitutional guaranty in the only effectively available way—by removing the incentive to disregard it.' " *Id.* at 1692 (quoting *Elkins v. United States*, 364 *U.S.* 206, 217, 80 *S.Ct.* 1437, 1444 (1960)).

"[O]ur holding that the exclusionary rule is an essential part of both the Fourth and Fourteenth Amendments is not only the logical dictate of prior cases, but it also makes very good sense. There is no war between the Constitution and common sense. Presently, a federal prosecutor may make no use of evidence illegally seized, but a State's attorney across the street may, although he supposedly is operating under the enforceable prohibitions of the same Amendment. Thus the State, by admitting evidence unlawfully seized, serves to encourage disobedience to the Federal Constitution which it is bound in uphold. * * * In non-exclusionary States, federal officers, being human, were by it invited to and did, as our cases indicate, step across the street to the State's attorney with their unconstitutionally seized evidence. Prosecution on the basis of that evidence was then had in a state court in utter disregard of the enforceable Fourth Amendment. If the fruits of an unconstitutional search had been inadmissible in both state and federal courts, this inducement to evasion would have been sooner eliminated. * * * " *Id.* at 1693.

"There are those who say, as did Justice (then Judge) Cardozo, that under our constitutional exclusionary doctrine '[t]he criminal is to go free because the constable has blundered.' * * * In some cases this will undoubtedly be the result. But, * * * 'there is another consideration—the imperative of judicial integrity.' The criminal goes free, if he must, but it is the law that sets him free. Nothing can destroy a government more quickly than its failure to observe its own laws, or worse, its disregard of the charter of its own existence." *Id.* at 1694. [Citations omitted.]

"Having once recognized that the right to privacy embodied in the Fourth Amendment is enforceable against the States, and that the right to be secure against rude invasions of privacy by state officers is, therefore, constitutional in origin, we can no longer permit that right to remain an empty promise. Because it is enforceable in the same manner and to like effect as other basic rights secured by the Due Process Clause, we can no longer permit it to be revocable at the whim of any police officer who, in the name of law enforcement itself, chooses to suspend its enjoyment. Our decision, founded on reason and truth, gives to the individual no more than that which the Constitution guarantees him, to the police officer no less than that to which honest law enforcement is entitled, and, to the courts, that judicial integrity so necessary in the true administration of justice." *Id.*

UNITED STATES v. LEON
Supreme Court of the United States
468 *U.S.* 897, 104 *S.Ct.* 3405 (1984)

Justice WHITE delivered the opinion of the Court.

"This case presents the question whether the Fourth Amendment exclusionary rule should be modified so as not to bar the use in the prosecution's case in chief of evidence obtained by officers acting in reasonable reliance on a search warrant issued by a detached and neutral magistrate but ultimately found to be unsupported by probable cause. To resolve this question, we must consider once again the tension between the sometimes competing goals of, on the one hand, deterring official misconduct and removing inducements to unreasonable invasions of privacy and, on the other, establishing procedures under which criminal defendants are 'acquitted or convicted on the basis of all the evidence which exposes the truth.'" *Id.* at 3409. [Citation omitted.]

[In this case, Burbank police officers conducted an extensive drug investigation which led to the issuance of a warrant for the search of several residences and automobiles. The searches uncovered large quantities of cocaine and other evidence. Ultimately, at defendants' motions to suppress the evidence seized, the search warrant was held invalid because the supporting affidavit was insufficient to establish probable cause. Consequently, the District Court granted the motions to suppress, and the Court of Appeals affirmed. At the request of the prosecution, the lower court made clear that investigating officers had acted in good faith, but it rejected the prosecution's position that the Fourth Amendment's exclusionary rule should be modified so as to not apply where evidence is seized in reasonable, good-faith reliance on a search warrant.]

"We granted certiorari to consider the propriety of such a modification * * * [and] have concluded that, in the Fourth Amendment context, the exclusionary rule can be modified somewhat without jeopardizing its ability to perform its intended functions. Accordingly, we reverse the judgment of the Court of Appeals." *Id.* at 3411.

"The Fourth Amendment contains no provision expressly precluding the use of evidence obtained in violation of its commands, and an examination of its origin and purposes makes clear that the use of fruits of a past unlawful search or seizure 'work[s] no new Fourth Amendment wrong.' * * * The wrong condemned by the Amendment is 'fully accomplished' by the unlawful search or seizure itself, [] and the exclusionary rule is neither intended nor able to 'cure the invasion of the defendant's rights which he has already suffered.' * * * The rule thus operates as 'a judicially created remedy designed to safeguard Fourth Amendment rights generally through its deterrent effect, rather than a personal constitutional right of the party aggrieved.' " *Id.* at 3411-12. [Citations omitted.]

"Whether the exclusionary sanction is appropriately imposed in a particular case, our decisions make clear, is 'an issue separate from the question whether the Fourth Amendment rights of the party seeking to invoke the rule were violated by police conduct.' * * * Only the former question is currently before us, and it must be resolved by weighing the costs and benefits of preventing the use in the prosecution's case in chief of inherently trustworthy tangible evidence obtained in reliance on a search warrant issued by a detached and neutral magistrate that ultimately is found to be defective." *Id.* at 3412.

"The substantial social costs exacted by the exclusionary rule for the vindication of Fourth Amendment rights have long been a source of concern. 'Our cases have consistently recognized that unbending application of the exclusionary sanction to enforce ideals of governmental rectitude would impede unacceptably the truth-finding functions of judge and jury.' * * * An objectionable collateral consequence of this interference with the criminal justice system's truth-finding function is that some guilty defendants may go free or receive reduced sentences as a result of favorable plea bargains. Particularly when law enforcement officers have acted in objective good faith or their transgressions have been minor, the magnitude of the benefit conferred on such guilty defendants offends basic concepts of the criminal justice system. * * * Indiscriminate application of the exclusionary rule, therefore, may well 'generat[e] disrespect for the law and administration of justice.' * * * Accordingly, '[a]s with any remedial device, the application of the rule has been restricted to those areas where its remedial objectives are [best] served." *Id.* [Citations omitted.]

"Proposed extensions of the exclusionary rule to proceedings other than the criminal trial itself have been evaluated and rejected under the same analytic approach. In *United States v. Calandra*, [414 *U.S.* 338, 348, 94 *S.Ct.* 613, 620 (1974)], for example, we declined to allow grand jury witnesses to refuse to answer questions based on evidence obtained from an unlawful search or seizure since '[a]ny incremental deterrent effect which might be achieved by extending the rule to grand jury proceedings is uncertain at best.' * * * Similarly, in *United States v. Janis*, [428 *U.S.* 433, 96 *S.Ct.* 3021 (1976)], we permitted the use in federal civil proceedings of evidence illegally seized by state officials since the likelihood of deterring police misconduct through such an extension of the exclusionary rule was insufficient to outweigh its substantial social costs. In so doing, we declared that, '[i]f . . . the exclusionary rule does not result in appreciable deterrence, then, clearly, its use in the instant situation is unwarranted.' " *Leon* at 3413 (quoting *Janis* at 454, 96 *S.Ct.* at 3032).

"Even defendants with standing to challenge the introduction in their criminal trials of unlawfully obtained evidence cannot prevent every conceivable use of such evidence. Evidence obtained in violation of the Fourth Amendment and inadmissible in the prosecution's case in chief may be used to impeach a defendant's direct testimony." *Id.* at 3413-14 (citing *Walder v. United States*, 347 *U.S.* 62[, 74 *S.Ct.* 354] (1954), and *Oregon v. Hass*, 420 *U.S.* 714[, 95 *S.Ct.* 1215] (1975)).

"The same attention to the purposes underlying the exclusionary rule also has characterized decisions not involving the scope of the rule itself. We have not required suppression of the fruits of a search incident to an arrest made in good-faith reliance on a substantive criminal statute that subsequently is declared unconstitutional." *Id.* at 3414 (citing *Michigan v. DeFillippo*, 443 *U.S.* 31, 99 *S.Ct.* 2627 (1979)).

"As yet, we have not recognized any form of good-faith exception to the Fourth Amendment exclusionary rule. But the balancing approach that has evolved during the years of experience with the rule provides strong support for the modification currently urged upon us. * * * [O]ur evaluation of the costs and benefits of suppressing reliable physical evidence seized by officers reasonably relying on a warrant issued by a detached and neutral magistrate leads to the conclusion that such evidence should be admissible in the prosecution's case in chief." *Id.* at 3415.

"Because a search warrant 'provides the detached scrutiny of a neutral magistrate, which is a more reliable safeguard against improper searches than the hurried judgment of a law enforcement officer "engaged in the often competitive enterprise of ferreting out crime," ' * * * we have expressed a strong preference for warrants and declared that 'in a doubtful or marginal case a search under a

warrant may be sustainable where without one it would fall.' * * *
Reasonable minds frequently may differ on the question whether a
particular affidavit establishes probable cause, and we hare thus
concluded that the preference for warrants is most appropriately
effectuated by according 'great deference' to a magistrate's determination." *Id.* at 3415-16.

"[Naturally, the law enforcement officer must present 's]ufficient
information * * * to the magistrate to allow that official to determine
probable cause; his action cannot be a mere ratification of the bare
conclusions of others.' * * * *Id.* at 3416. [Citations omitted.]

"To the extent that proponents of exclusion rely on its behavioral effects on judges and magistrates in these areas, their reliance is misplaced. First, the exclusionary rule is designed to deter
police misconduct rather than to punish the errors of judges and
magistrates. Second, there exists no evidence suggesting that
judges and magistrates are inclined to ignore or subvert the Fourth
Amendment or that lawlessness among these actors requires application of the extreme sanction of exclusion." *Id.* at 3417.

"Judges and magistrates are not adjuncts to the law enforcement team; as neutral judicial officers, they have no stake in the
outcome of particular criminal prosecutions. The threat of exclusion thus cannot be expected significantly to deter them. * * * " *Id.*

"If exclusion of evidence obtained pursuant to a subsequently
invalidated warrant is to have any deterrent effect, therefore, it
must alter the behavior of individual law enforcement officers or
the policies of their departments. * * * We have frequently questioned whether the exclusionary rule can have any deterrent effect when the offending officers acted in the objectively reasonable belief that their conduct did not violate the Fourth Amendment. * * * " *Id.* at 3418.

"In short, where the officer's conduct is objectively reasonable,

> excluding the evidence will not further the ends of the exclu-
> sionary rule in any appreciable way; for it is painfully apparent
> that . . . the officer is acting as a reasonable officer would and
> should act in similar circumstances. Excluding the evidence can
> in no way affect his future conduct unless it is to make him less
> willing to do his duty.

Id. at 3419. [Citation omitted.]

"This is particularly true, we believe, when an officer acting
with objective good faith has obtained a search warrant from a
judge or magistrate and acted within its scope. In most such cases,
there is no police illegality and thus nothing to deter. It is the magistrate's responsibility to determine whether the officer's allegations establish probable cause and, if so, to issue a warrant com-
porting in form with the requirements of the Fourth Amendment.

In the ordinary case, an officer cannot be expected to question the magistrate's probable-cause determination or his judgment that the form of the warrant is technically sufficient. '[O]nce the warrant issues, there is literally nothing more the policeman can do in seeking to comply with the law.' * * * Penalizing the officer for the magistrate's error, rather than his own, cannot logically contribute to the deterrence of Fourth Amendment violations." *Id.* [Citation omitted.]

"We conclude that the marginal or nonexistent benefits produced by suppressing evidence obtained in objectively reasonable reliance on a subsequently invalidated search warrant cannot justify the substantial costs of exclusion. We do not suggest, however, that exclusion is always inappropriate * * *. [An] officer's reliance on the magistrate's probable-cause determination and on the technical sufficiency of the warrant he issues must be objectively reasonable, * * * and it is clear that in some circumstances the officer[a] will have no reasonable grounds for believing that the warrant was properly issued." *Id.* at 3420.

"Suppression therefore remains an appropriate remedy if the magistrate or judge in issuing a warrant was misled by information in an affidavit that the affiant knew was false or would have known was false except for his reckless disregard of the truth. * * * The exception we recognize today will also not apply in cases where the issuing magistrate wholly abandoned his judicial role * * *; in such circumstances, no reasonably well trained officer should rely on the warrant. Nor would an officer manifest objective good faith in relying on a warrant based on an affidavit 'so lacking in indicia of probable cause as to render official belief in its existence entirely unreasonable.' * * * Finally, depending on the circumstances of the particular case, a warrant may be so facially deficient—*i.e.*, in failing to particularize the place to be searched or the things to be seized—that the executing officers cannot reasonably presume it to be valid." *Id.* at 3421.

"We have now reexamined the purposes of the exclusionary rule and the propriety of its application in cases where officers have relied on a subsequently invalidated search warrant. Our conclusion in that the rule's purposes will only rarely be served by applying it in such circumstances." *Id.* at 3422.

"In the absence of an allegation that the magistrate abandoned his detached and neutral role, suppression is appropriate only if the officers were dishonest or reckless in preparing their affidavit or could not have harbored an objectively reasonable belief in the existence of probable cause. Only [defendant] Leon has contended that

---

[a] This "good-faith inquiry is confined to the objectively ascertainable question whether a reasonably well-trained officer would have known that the search was illegal despite the magistrate's authorization. In making this determination, all of the circumstances—including whether the warrant application had previously been rejected by a different magistrate—may be considered." *Id.* at 3420 n.23.

no reasonably well trained police officer could have believed that there existed probable cause to search his house; significantly, the other [defendants] advance no comparable argument. Officer Rombach's application for a warrant clearly was supported by much more than a 'bare bones' affidavit. The affidavit related the results of an extensive investigation and * * * provided evidence sufficient to create disagreement among thoughtful and competent judges as to the existence of probable cause. Under these circumstances, the officers' reliance on the magistrate's determination of probable cause was objectively reasonable, and application of the extreme sanction of exclusion is inappropriate." *Id.*

"Accordingly, the judgment of the Court of Appeals is

Reversed."

NOTE

Tampering with illegally seized evidence. In most jurisdictions, a defendant's tampering with or "spoliation" of illegally seized physical evidence may result in his subsequent prosecution for evidence tampering, notwithstanding the fact that the exclusionary rule will bar the admission of the evidence in the pending prosecution. In this respect, consider the following hypothetical: A bank robbery defendant, who is out on bail, becomes concerned that the note he passed to the bank teller during the robbery will be used against him by the prosecution. In order to eliminate the possibility of the note being used at his trial, the defendant breaks into the police evidence room and destroys the note. Unbeknownst to the defendant, the note was inadmissible as evidence, because it was obtained during the course of an unlawful police search and seizure.

Under the foregoing circumstances, the defendant may be prosecuted for evidence tampering, notwithstanding the inadmissibility of the note. Most criminal statutes require only that the defendant *believe* that an official proceeding or investigation is pending or about to be instituted, and that he destroy or remove the item *with the purpose* to impair its availability in such proceeding or investigation. *See e.g.*, M.P.C. §241.7. *See also* N.J.S. 2C:28-6a(l).

NEW YORK v. QUARLES
Supreme Court of the United States
467 *U.S.* 649, 104 *S.Ct.* 2626 (1984)

Justice REHNQUIST delivered the opinion of the Court.

"[In this case, we conclude that] overriding considerations of public safety justify the officer's failure to provide *Miranda* warnings before he asked questions devoted to locating the abandoned weapon." *Id.* at 2629.

"[At about 12:30 a.m., Officers Kraft and Scarring were on road patrol in Queens, New York] when a young woman approached their car. She told them that she had just been raped by a black male, approximately six feet tall, who was wearing a black jacket with the name 'Big Ben' printed in yellow letters on the back. She told the officers that the man had just entered an A & P supermarket located nearby and that the man was carrying a gun." *Id.*

"The officers drove the woman to the supermarket, and Officer Kraft entered the store while Officer Scarring radioed for assistance. Officer Kraft quickly spotted [defendant], who matched the description given by the woman, approaching a checkout counter. Apparently upon seeing the officer, [defendant] turned and ran toward the rear of the store, and Officer Kraft pursued him with a drawn gun. When [defendant] turned the corner at the end of an aisle, Officer Kraft lost sight of him for several seconds, and upon regaining sight of [defendant], ordered him to stop and put his hands over his head." *Id.*

"Although more than three other officers had arrived on the scene by that time, Officer Kraft was the first to reach [defendant]. He frisked him and discovered that he was wearing a shoulder holster which was then empty. After handcuffing him, Officer Kraft asked him where the gun was. [Defendant] nodded in the direction of some empty cartons and responded, 'the gun is over there.' Officer Kraft thereafter retrieved a loaded .38-caliber revolver from one of the cartons, formally placed [defendant] under arrest, and read him his *Miranda* rights from a printed card. [Defendant] indicated that he would be willing to answer questions without an attorney present. Officer Kraft then asked [defendant] if he owned the gun and where he had purchased it. [Defendant] answered that he did own it and that he had purchased it in Miami[.]" *Id.* at 2629.

"In the subsequent prosecution of [defendant] for criminal possession of a weapon, the judge excluded the statement, 'the gun is over there,' and the gun because the officer had not given [] the warnings required by our decision in *Miranda v. Arizona*[43], * * * before asking him where the gun was located. The judge excluded the other statements about [defendant]'s ownership of the gun and the place of purchase, as evidence tainted by the prior *Miranda* violation." *Id.*

---

[43] 384 *U.S.* 436, 86 *S.Ct.* 1602 (1966)

"For the reasons which follow, we believe that this case presents a situation where concern for public safety must be paramount to adherence to the literal language of the pro- phylactic rules enunciated in Miranda." *Id.* at 653-54. [Emphasis added.]

"The Fifth Amendment guarantees that '[n]o person . . . shall be compelled in any criminal case to be a witness against himself.' In *Miranda,* this Court for the first time extended the Fifth Amendment privilege against compulsory self-incrimination to individuals subjected to custodial interrogation by the police. * * * The Fifth Amendment itself does not prohibit all incriminating admissions; '[a]bsent some officially coerced self-accusation, the Fifth Amendment privilege is not violated by even the most damning admissions.' * * * The *Miranda* Court, however, presumed that interrogation in certain custodial circumstances is inherently coercive and held that statements made under those circumstances are inadmissible unless the suspect is specifically informed of his *Miranda* rights and freely decides to forgo those rights. The prophylactic *Miranda* warnings therefore are 'not themselves rights protected by the Constitution but [are] instead measures to insure that the right against compulsory self-incrimination [is] protected.' * * * Requiring *Miranda* warnings before custodial interrogation provides 'practical reinforcement' for the Fifth Amendment right." *Id.* at 2630. [Citations omitted.]

"In this case we have before us no claim that [defendant]'s statements were actually compelled by police conduct which overcame his will to resist. * * * Thus the only issue before us is whether Officer Kraft was justified in failing to make available to [defendant] the procedural safeguards associated with the privilege against compulsory self-incrimination since *Miranda*." *Id.* at 2630-31.

"We hold that on these facts there is a 'public safety' exception to the requirement that *Miranda* warnings be given before a suspect's answers may be admitted into evidence, and that the availability of that exception does not depend upon the motivation of the individual officers involved. In a kaleidoscopic situation such as the one confronting these officers, where spontaneity rather than adherence to a police manual is necessarily the order of the day, the application of the exception which we recognize today should not be made to depend on *post hoc* findings at a suppression hearing concerning the subjective motivation of the arresting officer. Undoubtedly most police officers, if placed in Officer Kraft's position, would act out of a host of different, instinctive, and largely unverifiable motives * * *." *Id.* at 2631.

"Whatever the motivation of individual officers in such a situation, we do not believe that the doctrinal underpinnings of *Miranda* require that it be applied in all its rigor to a situation in which police officers ask questions reasonably prompted by a concern for the public safety." *Id.* at 2631-32.

"The police in this case, in the very act of apprehending a suspect, were confronted with the immediate necessity of ascertaining the whereabouts of a gun which they had every reason to believe the suspect had just removed from his empty holster and discarded in the supermarket. So long as the gun was concealed somewhere in the supermarket, with its actual whereabouts unknown, it obviously posed more than one danger to the public safety: an accomplice might make use of it, a customer or employee might later come upon it." *Id.* at 2632.

"In such a situation, if the police are required to recite the familiar *Miranda* warnings before asking the whereabouts of the gun, suspects in Quarles' position might well be deterred from responding. Procedural safeguards which deter a suspect from responding were deemed acceptable in *Miranda* in order to protect the Fifth Amendment privilege; when the primary social cost of those added protections is the possibility of fewer convictions, the *Miranda* majority was willing to bear that cost. Here, had *Miranda* warnings deterred Quarles from responding to Officer Kraft's question about the whereabouts of the gun, the cost would have been something more than merely the failure to obtain evidence useful in convicting Quarles. Officer Kraft needed an answer to his question not simply to make his case against Quarles but to insure that further danger to the public did not result from the concealment of the gun in a public area." *Id.*

"We conclude that the need for answers to questions in a situation posing a threat to the public safety outweighs the need for the prophylactic rule protecting the Fifth Amendment's privilege against self-incrimination. We decline to place officers such as Officer Kraft in the untenable position of having to consider, often in a matter of seconds, whether it best serves society for them to ask the necessary questions without the *Miranda* warnings and render whatever probative evidence they uncover inadmissible, or for them to give the warnings in order to preserve the admissibility of evidence they might uncover but possibly damage or destroy their ability to obtain that evidence and neutralize the volatile situation confronting them." *Id.*

"[We] believe that the exception which we recognize today * * * will not be difficult for police officers to apply because in each case it will be circumscribed by the exigency which justifies it. We think police officers can and will distinguish almost instinctively between questions necessary to secure their own safety or the safety of the public and questions designed solely to elicit testimonial evidence from a suspect." *Id.* at 2633.

"The facts of this case clearly demonstrate that distinction and an officer's ability to recognize it. Officer Kraft asked only the question necessary to locate the missing gun before advising [Quarles] of his rights. It was only after securing the loaded revolver and giving the warnings that he continued with investigatory questions about the ownership and place of purchase of the gun. The exception which we recognize today, far from complicating the thought processes and the on-the-scene judgments of police officers, will simply free them to follow their legitimate instincts when confronting situations presenting a danger to the public safety." *Id.*

"We hold that the [court below] erred in excluding the statement, 'the gun is over there,' and the gun because of the officer's failure to read [Quarles] his *Miranda* rights before attempting to locate the weapon. Accordingly, we hold that it also erred in excluding the subsequent statements as illegal fruits of a *Miranda* violation. We therefore reverse and remand for further proceedings not inconsistent with this opinion." *Id.*

It is so ordered.

---

§6.5. EXPLORING PROOF IN CRIMINAL CASES

STATE v. WANCZYK
Superior Court of New Jersey, Law Division
196 *N.J.Super.* 397, 482 *A.2d* 964 (1984)

The opinion of the Court was delivered by

MENZA, J.S.C.

"By pretrial motion, defendant seeks an order barring expert testimony from a state witness regarding the use of a bloodhound to track defendant after the alleged commission of a crime." *Id.*, 196 *N.J.Super.* at 400.

"The defendant is charged with the crime of arson. After his arrest and while in custody, the police removed from defendant's person his shoe and shirt and presented the items to a bloodhound dog, for the purpose of familiarizing the dog with the defendant's odor or scent. The dog thereafter followed a certain trail allegedly marked by the scent. The State seeks to offer evidence of the trail followed by the dog as circumstantial evidence corroborative of other evidence offered by the State." *Id.*

"The great weight of authority [in other jurisdictions] is that the evidence is admissible if a proper foundation is first laid. The theory upon which bloodhound evidence is offered is based upon the proposition that the bloodhound has an acute sense of smell, which enables him to follow the scent of a particular individual. *See Evidence of Trailing by Dogs in Criminal Cases*, 18 *A.L.R.*3d 1221, *et seq.* The proponents of its admissibility contend that it is competent and reliable evidence where a proper preliminary foundation has been met." *Id.* at 400-01.

"The detractors of bloodhound evidence argue that the many variables involved in this type of evidence make it uncertain and unreliable. * * * For example, they argue that the evidence is hearsay; that the defendant would be placed in jeopardy by the actions of the animal; that a defendant is unable to cross-examine a dog; and that a jury might be overly impressed by such testimony. * * * None of these additional arguments has substance. It is the handler, not the dog, who is the witness, and his testimony falls within the category of opinion testimony. I am confident that the jury, given proper instructions, would be able to afford such evidence its due weight." *Id.* at 401.

"The question of the admissibility of bloodhound evidence in the final analysis turns on whether it is reliable. The opponents are correct in their assertions that there are many variables involved in this type of evidence. Bloodhound evidence depends on such factors, for example, as atmospheric conditions, the time lapse between the commission of the crime and the tracking, the number of people who were in a particular area at the time of the commission of the crime, and perhaps even how the dog may feel or behave on a particular day. Certainly, the bloodhound is not infallible. However, these factors go to the weight of the evidence, not its competence. Indeed in almost every case where expert opinion is offered, there are some variables which may affect the ultimate conclusion of the expert. * * * The standard for the admissibility of expert testimony is not whether it is unassailable and totally reliable, but whether it has a substantial degree of reliability and would be 'an aid to the court or jury in determining the question in issue.' * * * 'In order to introduce scientific evidence, the proponent must demonstrate that the expert's technique has *sufficient* scientific basis to produce uniform and *reasonably reliable results* and will contribute materially to the ascertainment of the truth.' " *Id.* at 402. [Citations omitted; emphasis added.]

"It is a matter of common knowledge, of which courts may take notice, that dogs of some varieties, such as bloodhounds, foxhounds and bird dogs, are remarkable for the acuteness of their sense of smell, which enables them to follow a trail upon which they are laid, even though this trail be crossed by others. * * * A *per se* exclusion of bloodhound evidence is unreasonable." *Id.* at 402-03.

"*Evid.R.* 56(2), dealing with the testimony of an expert in the form of an opinion, * * * allow[s] much latitude in the admission of [such] testimony[, and] clearly permits the admission of testimony regarding bloodhound tracking, as long as the proper foundation is first laid." *Id.* at 403.

"Thus, the handler of the dog must first qualify as an expert. It must be shown that the handler has sufficient skill, training, knowledge or experience to be able to evaluate the actions of the dog.

Second, the handler, once qualified as an expert, must give testimony regarding the particular dog that he used and the facts. These facts must include testimony

> . . . that the dog is of a stock characterized by acuteness of scent and power of discrimination and that the dog in question is possessed of these qualities; that the particular dog used was trained and tested in the tracking of human beings and that the dog was reliable in the tracking of human beings; that he was laid on the trail where the circumstances tended to show that the guilty party has been, or on a track which the circumstances indicated to have been made by him; that he followed such scent or track to or towards the location of the accused, and that he was properly handled. [*C.J.S., Criminal Law 2d* § 646 at 531]."

Id. at 403-04.

"Lastly, after the foundation has been laid, the handler may testify as to what the dog did regarding the tracking and his interpretation and opinion as to what the dog's actions mean." *Id.* at 404.

"I am satisfied from the testimony [presented in this case] that the witness has sufficient knowledge and experience to be qualified as an expert in bloodhound tracking and that the other [requirements have been met]." *Id.*

"It is to be noted, in conclusion, that the testimony of the dog handler is not dispositive of the guilt or innocence of the defendant. It is, at best, circumstantial and corroborative evidence, which the jury may accept or reject. It is permitted to be offered because it is basically reliable and may be useful to the jury in assisting it in reaching a determination. Simply stated, it is this Court's function to determine the admissibility of the evidence. It is for the jury to determine the weight it is to be given." *Id.*

"The proffered testimony of the dog handler regarding the bloodhound tracking of the defendant is permitted." *Id.*

NOTE

In *State v. Parton*, 251 *N.J.Super.* 230, 597 A.2d 1088 (App.Div. 1991), the defendant was also charged with arson. The State's proofs revealed that Ronald Parton set fire to a building in which there resided a female acquaintance. The trial court allowed testimony by a bloodhound handler that "the dog tracked defendant from a mattress where it was suspected that he slept to the building which had been set on fire." *Id.*, 251 *N.J.Super.* at 233. In its first reported opinion on the subject, the Appellate Division held that expert dog-tracking testimony "is admissible when a proper preliminary foundation has been established." *Id.* The court declared: "We agree with the ruling in *Wanczyk* for the reasons set forth by Judge Menza and see no reason to rewrite his comprehensive analysis and conclusions on the subject." *Parton* at 233.

Adopting the principles set forth in *Wanczyk*, the court held that the following preconditions must be satisfied before testimony regarding dog tracking may be admitted in a criminal case:

1. The dog's handler must have sufficient knowledge, skill, training or experience to evaluate the dog's actions.

2. Once qualified as an expert, the handler must give testimony about the particular dog used and that the dog:

   a. is of a stock characterized by acute scent and power of discrimination and that this particular dog possessed those qualities;

   b. was trained and tested and proved to be reliable in the tracking of human beings;

   c. was laid on a trail where circumstances tended to show that the suspect has been, or a track which circumstances indicated was made by the suspect; and

   d. followed the scent or track to or towards the suspect's location and was properly handled during the tracking.

3. After this foundation has been laid, the handler may testify as to what the dog did during the tracking and give his interpretation and opinion of the dog's actions.

Id. at 233-34 (citing *Wanczyk* at 403-04).

In light of the sufficient foundation laid by the State here in *Parton*, the court held that the police K-9 officer's testimony, regarding the results of the drug-tracking procedures employed, was properly admitted. The testimonial foundation indicated that

[t]he dog's handler had been a member of the police K-9 unit since 1984. He had first trained in tracking with bloodhounds and thereafter attended numerous seminars and other courses on handling and training. Jackson, the dog he used for the tracking, was a purebred bloodhound, a breed which has extremely acute scent abilities. Jackson was first trained by practicing on eight different [types of] trails. His success was rewarded with liverwurst. The technique was repeated approximately fifty times, with the dog being rewarded and praised for success. The difficulty of the trails was gradually increased.

The handler had worked with Jackson on approximately twenty-five investigations. He testified that there were several cases in which the dog successfully tracked suspects.

[In this case, t]he starting point of the tracking was a mattress behind a pharmacy on which it was believed that defendant slept. The dog was on a fifteen-foot lead. He was not pointed in any particular direction and the handler was not given the location of the fire. The dog picked up a scent which the handler testified was four to five days old, which he followed to the front door of the building which had been set on fire. According to the handler, bloodhounds sometimes can follow tracks as much as two weeks old. Although inclement weather would cause the scent to diminish, the day of this tracking was sunny and clear.

Based on his observations of the dog, the handler testified that the track was made by someone leaving the scene of the fire and going to the mattress[, and that that individual] was moving quickly and perspiring.

Id. at 234-35.

The *Parton* court concluded that, in light of the "ample evidence of defendant's presence in the area of the mattress[,]" and the fact that "[t]he dog was properly handled[, i]t was proper for the handler to testify about the dog's actions during the trailing and his understanding of those actions." *Id.* at 235.

The court also agreed with the *Wanczyk* court's instruction that dog-tracking evidence "is not dispositive of [a criminal] defendant's guilt or innocence, but, at best, circumstantial and corroborative evidence which the jury is free to accept or reject." *Parton* at 235. In this case, however,

[t]here was ample circumstantial evidence pointing to defendant as the arsonist. One of the building's victims had refused to go out with him after he showed up over an hour late for a date. A short time after the fire started, defendant was seen in the area of the building acting in a peculiar manner. One day after the fire, defendant was arrested for soliciting money for its victims, specifically mentioning the woman who had earlier rebuffed his advances. Later, defendant told the police that "someone would have to be demented to walk past an open door and throw in a fire bomb because the fire definitely started in the hallway." The police had not yet made public any information about the cause or origin of the fire.

Id. at 235.

PEOPLE v. BADIA
Supreme Court of New York, Appellate Division
163 *A.D.*2d 4, 558 *N.Y.S.*2d 500 (1st Dept. 1990)

MEMORANDUM DECISION.

"The defendant was convicted of sodomizing and sexually abusing his daughter's five-year-old playmate while she was in [his] home * * *. Because we find that there was insufficient evidence introduced by the People at trial corroborating the unsworn testimony of the infant complainant[,] we reverse the conviction and dismiss the indictment." *Id.* at 501.

"The defendant's family lived in the same apartment building as Mr. and Mrs. S. and their two daughters, one of whom is the five-year-old complainant." *Id.*

"At trial, Mrs. S. testified that on Saturday, June 4[th,] at about 2:30 p.m., [defendant's daughter] Jeannette came to the S. apartment in order to take the complainant to the Badia apartment to play. One hour later, she telephoned the Badia apartment and spoke with Jeannette. At about 4:00 p.m. or 4:30 p.m., Jeannette returned complainant to the S. apartment and left immediately. According to Mrs. S., the complainant appeared 'nervous' and 'frightened.' Over defense objection, Mrs. S. was permitted to testify that upon questioning, the child expressed fear of defendant and stated that defendant had put his finger and tongue into her vagina. The child also complained about burning and itching in her vaginal area." *Id.*

"The only direct evidence as to the crimes was provided by the complainant. Her testimony was detailed and cogent, but unsworn." *Id.*

"Mr. S. testified, over defense objection, that when he returned home * * * that evening, the complainant told him that defendant had put his tongue against her tongue and had put his finger and tongue into her vagina. The next day, he and his wife took the complainant to the police precinct to report the incident." *Id.*

[The complainant repeated her account of the events to the police and then, later, to a pediatrician. Both the police officer and the doctor testified as to what the complainant told them.]

"The People were required to produce evidence independent of the unsworn testimony of the complainant 'tending to establish the crime and connecting the defendant with its commission.' * * * The medical evidence and testimony as to the child's behavior and complaints of burning and itching were independent evidence tending to show that the crimes were committed. However, the People did not present any independent evidence even remotely connecting [defend]ant with the time and place within which it is alleged that the crimes occurred." *Id.* at 502.

"The repetition of the complainant's account of the incident to her mother, her father, the police and a doctor similarly do not possess the 'independence' required of corroborative evidence. * * * Corroborative evidence may not rely to any extent on the complaining witness' testimony for to do so would be bootstrapping." *Id.*

"Moreover, we note that the testimony of Mrs. and Mr. S. and of Officer Cabrera detailing the statements made to them by the complainant were improperly admitted. When admitted as evidence of a prompt complaint or recent outcry, such testimony should be limited to the fact of the complaint and to the declarant's state of mind at the time. * * * Evidence of the victim's detailed statements is not admissible unless the statements would qualify as spontaneous declarations, excited utterances or as a prior consistent statement in the face of a claim of recent fabrication. * * * No claim of recent fabrication was made herein * * *." *Id.* at 502-503.

"The infant's complaint to her mother was sufficiently close in time to the occurrence to constitute recent outcry. However, Mrs. S.' testimony should have been limited to the fact that the child had made a complaint. The statements made by the child to her father, several hours after the occurrence, and to the police officer and physician the following day, were too remote in time to be considered a prompt complaint." *Id.* at 503.

"Because the evidence before the jury was legally insufficient, we reverse the conviction and dismiss the indictment." *Id.*

UNITED STATES v. JAMES
United States Court of Appeals
764 *F.*2d 885 (D.C. Cir. 1985)

BORK, *Circuit Judge.*

[During the course of a narcotics investigation, police developed probable cause to believe that Jerry James was selling cocaine from his Washington D.C. residence. A search warrant was secured and entry was attempted at approximately one o'clock in the afternoon. As the officers knocked on the door, they heard someone inside the house running down the back stairs. The door was forced, and once inside, the officers spread out to search different parts of the home.

Officer Stumbo ran down a hallway to the rear of the house and down stairs into a dark basement.] "After a few moments searching in the dark, one of the two officers who had followed Stumbo to the basement found and switched on an overhead light. * * * Stumbo saw a bookcase with a curtain hanging behind it and an arm reaching from behind the bookcase." *Id.* at 887. Stumbo drew his revolver and told the individual, later identified as Jerry James' brother, Thomas, to put his hands up. Rather than following the officer's instructions, Thomas grabbed for Stumbo's gun, pulled down on it and caused it to discharge. Thomas was quickly subdued. At the time, Thomas was dressed in his underwear. "When asked to get dressed, he put on clothes taken from a rack of clothes on the other side of the room. After taking Thomas James to the first floor where the other officers were assembling all the persons found in the house, the police began a search of the basement."

316

The basement consisted of two distinct areas; a laundry area and a sleeping area. The laundry area contained a washer, a dryer, and a sink. The officers described the sleeping area as containing a bookcase and curtain, and behind the curtain, a bed which had been recently slept in and a nightstand. On top of the nightstand was a toothbrush, toothpaste, a razor, and an alarm clock. Opposite the bed was the metal clothing bar from which Thomas had selected his clothing. Several items of men's clothing of similar size hung there. Initially, the officers searched the clothing and discovered "a plastic bag containing 10,780 milligrams of marijuana laced with PCP in one of the jackets, and in another seven tin foil packets containing a total of 2,420 milligrams of marijuana laced with PCP." *Id.*

"When the officers first entered the basement they heard water running. In the sink was found a jar with water from the spigot running into it. On the walls of the jar and around the base of the sink there remained flecks of a material that resembled marijuana. * * * When tested[,] the flecks proved to be marijuana laced with PCP." *Id.*

"In several holes in the basement ceiling, running generally from the area of the sink to that of the bed, were found two bags of cocaine, several bags of marijuana, marijuana seeds, and marijuana laced with PCP. * * * Also in the ceiling holes were procaine and mannitol [substances used to dilute cocaine], starch, syringes, a cut card used to mix cocaine, and a spoon with a white powder residue." *Id.* at 887-88.

"Partially partitioned off from the rest of the basement, but without a door, was a small room in which the officers found a variety of drug processing and user materials including mannitol, measuring spoons, pipes used to 'free base' cocaine, glassine bags with a white powder residue, the tops of acetylene torches, * * * a triple beam Ohaus scale used to measure weight to within a tenth of a gram, sheets of plastic, and a heat sealer * * *." *Id.* at 888.

In this appeal, Thomas James "contends that because the government showed him only to be in 'proximity' to the contraband he could not be convicted as a possessor." *Id.* at 889. *This court disagrees.*

"[P]roximity may, under certain circumstances, amount to constructive possession.

"Possession of a narcotic drug may be either actual or constructive. . . . Constructive possession may be shown through direct or circumstantial evidence of dominion and control over the contraband . . ., and may be found to exist where the evidence supports a finding that the person charged with possession was knowingly in a position, or had the right to exercise 'dominion or control' over the drug."

Id. (quoting *United States v. Lawson*, 682 *F.*2d 1012, 1017 (D.C.Cir. 1982)). The evidence presented by the government in this case "was clearly adequate to show that [Thomas James] was knowingly in a position to exercise dominion or control over the drugs. Thomas [] was found in a basement that [clearly appeared to be] an operating drug-processing factory. The spigot water running into a jar that still contained flecks of illegal narcotics indicated that the destruction of evidence of narcotics had just been attempted by somebody in the basement. There was nobody in the basement but [Thomas]. Moreover, Thomas James was not simply standing in the room or passing through. He was in his underwear, hiding behind a bookcase, and the evidence indicates he tried to disarm the arresting officer. These facts alone, which indicate consciousness of guilt, * * * would seem to be amply sufficient to sustain the conviction for possessing drugs, but there was more." *Id*.

Not only was Thomas James found in his underwear, but next to where he was found was a bed which had been recently slept in. "On the nightstand were articles showing that somebody regularly used the basement as a bedroom. [Thomas] dressed himself in clothing hanging in the room and the remaining clothing, according to a police witness, appeared also to be of the size that fit [Thomas]. Two of the jackets contained large amounts of marijuana laced with PCP. The drugs and paraphernalia in the small room without a door were only a short distance from the bed and were within view." *Id*. In light of this evidence, it would be entirely reasonable to conclude that Thomas James "often slept in the bedroom and, quite aside from the evidence of his consciousness of guilt, could not have been unaware of the narcotics and processing equipment around him." *Id*.

"The only contraband not in plain sight was that in the holes in the ceiling, though the holes themselves were clearly visible. Given the clear pattern revealed by the evidence, it [is] entirely reasonable * * * to infer possession of that contraband as well. [Thomas James'] apparent use of the basement as a residence, the fact that the basement was an operating drug-processing factory, that he had tried to destroy evidence of narcotics possession, and that he had demonstrated consciousness of guilt so clearly tied him into the entire drug operation that it would be idle to speculate that he might not have known of a particular quantity of narcotics merely because it was not in plain view. Were [this court] to rule otherwise, narcotics dealers and possessors could always avoid responsibility for illegal drugs hidden from sight on their premises." *Id*. 890.

Accordingly, defendant Thomas James' conviction was based on sufficient evidence of guilt. His proximity to the illegal drugs, when combined with the other evidence against him, clearly supports the finding that he was in constructive possession of the contraband seized.

UNITED STATES v. BRETT
United States Court of Appeals
872 *F*.2d 1365 (8th Cir. 1989)

LAY, Chief Judge.

[In early November, Kansas City Police Detective Rosilyn Morrison, while working in an undercover capacity, went to a house at 4039 Park Avenue and purchased crack cocaine from two unknown males. On the basis of this purchase, Morrison obtained a warrant to search the 4039 premises. When the search team arrived at the premises, one officer observed a black male, later identified as defendant Gray, run out the back of the building and head north. The officer immediately entered the rear of the house, arrested and secured the two other occupants (defendants Williams and Brett), and then went searching for Gray. Two houses north of the 4039 Park Avenue residence, Gray was found hiding under a porch. Also found under the porch next to Gray was $300 in currency. Gray was placed under arrest and a subsequent search of his person disclosed $3,746 in additional currency and the key to the front door of 4039 Park Avenue.]

"A search of 4039 Park Avenue revealed the existence of a fortified drug house. While the utilities were on, the house did not appear to be lived in. It had no refrigerator, no stove, no food, no telephone, and there was no clothing present. The windows were covered and the doors were reinforced. The back door was reinforced with plywood and had two locks on it as well as a chain lock at the top. The front door had metal brackets on either side of the frame which were fitted with a two-by-four board across the door." *Id.* at 1368.

Defendant Williams was found to be in possession of a 9 millimeter pistol with thirteen rounds of ammunition in the magazine and one round in the chamber, $1,465 in cash, and a large plastic bag, later determined to contain 82 small ziplock bags of crack cocaine totalling 46.66 grams in weight. Brett was found to be in possession of $1,300 in currency.

After his arrest, Gray told the officers that his name was "James Monroe," and that he did not work at the crack house. He stated that he was unemployed, but maintained that the $4,046 seized from him was "not drug money."

In this appeal, defendant Gray contends, among other things, that the Government did not present sufficient evidence to prove his possession of the contraband. *This court does not agree.*

"Proof of constructive possession is sufficient to satisfy the element of knowing possession under 21 *U.S.C.* §841(a)(1). *Brett* at 1369. "A person has constructive possession of contraband if he has 'ownership, dominion or control over the contraband itself, *or dominion over the premises in which the contraband is concealed.*'" *Id.* [Emphasis in original; citations omitted.] Moreover, "constructive possession may be joint among several defendants; it need not be exclusive." *Id.*

The circumstances in this case sufficiently demonstrate Gray's constructive possession of the evidence seized from Williams and Brett during the course of their arrest at the crack house. It is undisputed that Gray (1) fled from the scene at the time police officers initially approached the house; (2) falsely identified himself at the time of arrest; (3) had in his possession $3,746 at the time of his arrest and claimed ownership to an additional $300 recovered from the location where he was apprehended; and (4) stated that he was unemployed, but would not explain how he obtained the money which he claimed was his. "While it may be that, standing alone, each piece of this evidence would perhaps be insufficient to convict, its cumulative effect cannot be ignored." *Id.*

Perhaps the most "significant link" showing Gray's participation in the criminal possession of the evidence "was his possession of a key to the front door of 4039 Park. This house was a fortified, operational crack house where over 46 grams of cocaine, large amounts of cash, a gun and ammunition were concealed." *Id.* And in this respect, Gray's argument—that Brett and Williams were the ones in control of the contraband—is "unpersuasive." *Id.* "[C]onstructive possession may be joint among several defendants; it need not be exclusive." *Id.*

Accordingly, the Government's proof of Gray's "possession of the key to the front door of the [crack] house * * * sufficient[ly established Gray's] 'knowing possession'" of the evidence seized from Williams and Brett at the house. *Id.*

Chapter 7

ALTERNATIVES TO FORMAL PROOF

§7.1. JUDICIAL NOTICE

It is well settled that not every matter of fact must be established by the formal presentation of evidence. There are some matters which are so notorious, manifest, beyond dispute, or well settled that judicial economy and efficiency require that those matters be taken for granted; that they be accepted as true without proof. When a court accepts a fact as true because of its notorious, manifest, indisputable or well-settled nature, it takes "judicial notice" of that fact. In this respect, judicial notice may be regarded as an alternative to the formal presentation of evidence; a judicial short-cut which recognizes certain facts as true without the need for proof.[1] As one court put it:

> The doctrine of judicial notice is one of common sense. The theory is that, where a fact is well known by all reasonably intelligent people in the community, or its existence is so easily determinable with certainty from unimpeachable sources, it would not be good sense to require formal proof.[2]

§7.1(a). Notorious Facts

A judge may take judicial notice of a notorious fact when the fact, by its very nature, is (a) indisputable, and (b) a matter of

---

[1] *See Varcoe v. Lee*, 180 *Cal.* 338, 344, 181 *P.* 223, 226 (1919) ("Judicial notice is a judicial short cut, a doing away with the formal necessity for evidence because there is no real necessity for it."); *Petro v. Kennedy Tp. Bd. of Com'rs*, 49 *Pa.Cmwlth.* 305, 411 *A.2d* 849 (1980) (judicial notice avoids the necessity of presenting evidence in those limited circumstances where the fact sought to be proved is so well known in the jurisdiction that evidence in support thereof is unnecessary).

[2] *Harper v. Killion*, 345 *S.W.2d* 309, 311 (Tex.Civ.App. 1961).

common knowledge or notoriety within the territorial jurisdiction of the court (or where the crime occurred),[3] or universally.[4]

For example, a court may take judicial notice that a particular city or town is located within a certain county.[5] Judicial notice may be taken of the geographical distance between places.[6]

There are times that notorious events or facts of common knowledge—even if not unique to the particular territorial jurisdiction of the trial court—will be taken for granted.[7] In this respect, judicial notice of extra-territorial notorious events generally will be limited to current events attracting attention either nationwide or worldwide.[8] Courts have also taken notice of universally known facts which may or may not be unique to any particular jurisdiction. For example, in *Romero v. United States*,[9] the court held

---

[3] *See Fed.R.Evid.* 201(b)(1). *See also Commonwealth v. Casper*, 481 *Pa.* 143, 392 *A.*2d 287, 296-97 (1978) (A "judicially noticed fact" must be " 'one not subject to reasonable dispute in that it is either (1) generally known within the territorial jurisdiction of the trial court or (2) capable of accurate and ready determination by resort to sources whose accuracy cannot reasonably be questioned.' ") (quoting *Fed.R.Evid.* 201(b)). *See also Varcoe v. Lee*, 180 *Cal.* 338, 181 *P.* 223 (1919) (in a wrongful death case, judicial notice taken of the fact that Mission Street, between Twentieth and Twenty-second Streets is a "business district" having a maximum speed limit of 15 miles per hour); *DeTore v. Local No. 245*, 511 *F.Supp.* 171 (D.N.J. 1981) (judicial notice taken that Jersey City is a municipality of New Jersey); *State v. Richards*, 106 *N.J.Super.* 55, 59 (Law Div. 1979) (judicial notice taken of the fact that the New Jersey Highway Authority "collects tolls in the 'barrier'-type toll areas by means of toll collectors or automatic machines" on the Garden State Parkway).

[4] *See Indoor Recreation Enterprises, Inc. v. Douglas*, 194 *Neb.* 715, 719, 235 *N.W.*2d 398, 401-02 (1975) (a judicially noticed fact "must be *'known'*—that is, well *established* and *authoritatively settled*, without qualification or contention")(emphasis added). *See also Cohen v. Rodenbaugh*, 162 *F.Supp.* 748 (E.D.Pa. 1958) (judicial notice taken that "even the most tranquil horse may on occasion give a kick"); *Vallillo v. Muskin Corp.*, 212 *N.J.Super.* 155, 162 (App.Div. 1986) (judicial notice taken of the inherent danger of diving into shallow water: a fact universally recognized); *Loigman v. Keim*, 250 *N.J.Super.* 434, 436 (Law Div. 1991) (judicial notice taken of the fact "that most credit cards do not charge interest on sums paid within 30 days"); *Dunn v. Durso*, 219 *N.J.Super.* 383, 392-94 (Law Div. 1986) (judicial notice taken of the universally recognized fact that wearing seat belts serves to prevent or minimize injuries); *Kutner Buick, Inc. v. Strelecki*, 111 *N.J.Super.* 89, 100 (Ch.Div. 1970) (judicial notice taken of the universally recognized fact that stolen vehicles are a problem in this state as well as across the country).

[5] *See e.g., Goff v. Armbrecht Motor Truck Sales, Inc.*, 284 *Pa.Super.* 544, 426 *A.*2d 628, 630 n.4 (1980); *Emert v. Larami Corp.*, 414 *Pa.* 396, 200 *A.*2d 901 (1964).

[6] *See e.g., Goff v. Armbrecht Motor Truck Sales, Inc., supra*, 426 *A.*2d at 630 n.4 (judicial notice taken that Youngstown, Ohio, was about ten miles from the Ohio-Pennsylvania border).

[7] *See supra* Note 4. *See also EEOC v. Delta Airlines, Inc.*, 485 *F.Supp.* 1004 (N.D.Ga. 1980) (judicial notice taken of the fact that only women can become pregnant).

[8] *See e.g., Miller v. Fowler*, 200 *Miss.* 776, 28 *So.*2d 837 (1947) (judicial notice taken that on August 14, 1945, acts of war between the United States and Japan were continuing); *Fatemi v. Fatemi*, 371 *Pa.Super.* 101, 537 *A.*2d 840 (1988) (judicial notice taken of the ongoing conflict between Iran and Iraq, with the court noting that, "[g]enerally, matters of history, if sufficiently notorious to be the subject of general knowledge, will be judicially noticed").

[9] 318 *F.*2d 530 (5th Cir.), *cert. denied*, 375 *U.S.* 946, 84 *S.Ct.* 357 (1963).

that "mothballs are frequently used in the trade to counteract the aroma given off by marihuana."[10] In *Commonwealth v. Patterson*,[11] the Pennsylvania Superior Court declared: "Today we [] join the growing number of courts who have taken judicial notice of the fact drug dealers are likely to be armed and dangerous."[12] Courts have also taken judicial notice of the fact that "beer, in sufficient quantity, is an intoxicating beverage,"[13] and of the fact that "brewed beverages that have an appearance and flavor similar to beer, but do not contain one half of one percent or more of alcohol by volume, are available for sale."[14]

Courts have even taken judicial notice of the fact that:

> Police occupy a unique position in the community, and the people have a compelling interest in imposing strict requirements on the selection of police, inasmuch as the lives of the members of the community are entrusted to the protection of those who serve as police officers.[15]

---

[10] *Id.* at 532 n.2.

[11] 405 *Pa.Super.* 17, 591 *A.2d* 1075 (1991).

[12] *Patterson*, 591 A.2d at 1078. *See also Commonwealth v. Rodriguez*, 387 *Pa.Super.* 271, 280-81, 564 A.2d 174, 179 (1989) (suspicion of narcotics distribution should give rise to "an inference of dangerousness"), *rev'd on other grounds*, 532 Pa. 62, 614 A.2d 1378 (1992); *Commonwealth v. Johnson*, 429 Pa.Super. 159, 631 A.2d 1335, 1340 (1993) (Because ample cause existed for suspecting defendant of drug dealing, this court "may take judicial notice of the reasonable suspicion that [he] was armed and dangerous."). *And see Baker v. Monroe Tp.*, 50 *F.*3d 1186, 1191 (3rd Cir. 1995) ("The dangerousness of chaos is quite pronounced in a drug raid, where the occupants are likely to be armed [and] where the police are certainly armed * * *."); *United States v. Clark*, 24 *F.*3d 299, 304 (D.C.Cir. 1994) ("Twenty-five years ago, when the Supreme Court issued its opinion in *Terry*, it might have been unreasonable to assume that a suspected drug dealer in a car would be armed; today it could well be foolhardy for an officer to assume otherwise."); *United States v. Adams*, 759 F.2d 1099, 1109 (3rd Cir. 1985); *United States v. Barlin*, 686 F.2d 81 (2nd Cir. 1982) (an officer's actions should be measured against a background which includes the violent nature of narcotics crimes); *United States v. Wiener*, 534 F.2d 15 (2nd Cir. 1976); *United State v. Morales*, 549 F.Supp. 217 (S.D.N.Y. 1982) (to substantial dealers in narcotics, firearms are as much tools of the trade as are most commonly recognized articles of narcotics paraphernalia).

[13] *In re Steerman's Liquor License*, 185 *Pa.Super.* 214, 138 A.2d 292 (1958). *See also Rau v. People*, 63 *N.Y.* 277 (1875) (judicial notice taken that whiskey is an intoxicating beverage).

[14] *Commonwealth v. Epsilon*, 530 *Pa.* 416, 609 A.2d 791, 793 n.2 (1992).

[15] *Petro v. Kennedy Tp. Bd. of Com'rs*, 49 *Pa.Cmwlth.* 305, 411 A.2d 849 (1980). The court concluded that "[n]o amount of testimony could have proved this statement more nor could testimony have disproved it. * * * [T]he role of the police in the community is *common knowledge* * * *." *Id.* [Emphasis added.] *See also Connell v. Board of Review*, 216 *N.J.Super.* 403, 407 (1987) (taking notice of the "implicit standard of good behavior which devolves upon one who stands in the public eye as an upholder of that which is morally and legally correct"); *State v. Stevens*, 203 *N.J.Super.* 59, 65 (Law Div. 1984) ("Every police officer has an inherent duty to obey the law and to enforce it.").

A judge may not, however, take judicial notice of a fact merely because it is personally known to him or her.[16]

---

§7.1(b). Manifest Facts

A judge may take judicial notice of "manifest" or "almanac-type" facts. These facts may be the subject of judicial notice because they are capable of immediate and accurate verification or determination by resort to readily available sources of reasonably indisputable accuracy.[17] Examples may include the astronomical facts found in an almanac (the time of sunrise or sunset on a given date, state of the moon on a given night, etc.), calendar facts (the day of the week upon which January 10, 1984, fell), the overt acts of history (on what day Iraq invaded Kuwait), geographical facts found in a road atlas, and other easily-verifiable facts found in authoritative texts such as encyclopedias, dictionaries, and the like.

---

§7.1(c). Court Records

A judge may take judicial notice of the records of the court in which the action is pending, including the present trial and any preceding hearings or proceedings related thereto.[18] It would be improper, however, for a court to take judicial notice of records in one action while deciding another and different one because a party is entitled to have his case decided upon evidence introduced at trial and not upon evidence that the party has had no opportunity to refute or explain.[19]

---

[16] *See* 2 McCormick, *Evidence* §329 (West 4th ed. 1992), at 390 ("the doctrine is accepted that actual private knowledge by the judge is no sufficient ground for taking judicial notice of a fact as a basis for a finding or a final judgment"); 9 Wigmore, *Evidence*, §2569 (1981), at 723 (judge may not take judicial notice of facts that he knows only as an individual observer). *See also Varcoe v. Lee*, 180 *Cal.* 338, 181 *P.* 223 (1919) ("the fact that the trial judge knew what the actual fact was, and that it was indisputable, would not of itself justify him in recognizing it"); *State v. LiButti*, 146 *N.J.Super.* 565, 571 (App.Div. 1977) (improper to take judicial notice of those things which the judge "knows only as an individual observer"); *Vaughn v. Shelby Williams of Tennessee, Inc.*, 813 *S.W.*2d 132, 133 n.2 (Tenn. 1991) ("It is not appropriate to judicially notice facts that are beyond the scope of the knowledge of the general public, but are known instead to the judge through his personal, extrajudicial experience.").

[17] *See Fed.R.Evid.* 201(b)(2).

[18] *See Fed.R.Evid.* 201(b)(2); *See also In re Aughenbaugh*, 125 *F.*2d 887, 890 (3rd Cir. 1954) (papers within the court's file are "admissible as court records without other proof"); *Collins v. Leahy*, 347 *Mo.* 133, 146 *S.W.*2d 609 (1940) (judicial notice taken of a city map which had been made a part of the record in a prior appeal). *Compare In re Bach's Estate*, 81 *Misc.*2d 479, 365 *N.Y.S.*2d 454 (1975) (though a court may take judicial notice of its own court records, it may not take notice of the records of other courts without formal proof).

[19] *See In Interest of C.M.W.*, 813 *S.W.*2d 331, 333 (Mo.App. 1991).

§7.1(d). Law

Judicial notice will, as a matter of course, be taken of the decisional, constitutional, and public statutory law and rules of the courts of the state in which the action is pending, and of the United States.[20] In addition, given sufficient advance notice, judges may take judicial notice of such law or rules of the courts of other states or territories of the United States.[21]

---

§7.1(e). Scientific Methods and Devices

Whenever the law enforcement or legal profession begins to use a newly-invented scientific device or technique, and the results stemming from the use of the device or technique ultimately become part of a court case in some way, the party offering the results as evidence will generally prove to the court that (a) the device or technique has a scientific basis and (b) there is general acceptance in the relevant scientific community of the reliability of the particular device or technique. The proponent's proofs in this regard will generally incorporate the presentation of expert scientific testimony, authoritative scientific and legal writings, and any available legal precedent in a special hearing.[22]

In the well-known case of *Frye v. United States*,[23] the (then) Court of Appeals for the District of Columbia remarked:

> Just when a scientific principle or discovery crosses the line between the experimental and demonstrable stages is difficult to define. Somewhere in this twilight zone the evidential force of the principle must be recognized, and while courts will go a long way in admitting expert testimony deduced from a well-recognized scientific principle or discovery, *the thing from which the deduction is made must be sufficiently established to have gained general acceptance in the particular field in which it belongs.*[24]

Should, however, the proponent of such evidence be unable to prove the technique or device has gained "general acceptance" in the relevant scientific community, the United States Supreme Court has indicated that the evidence may nonetheless be admissible if

---

[20] *See e.g., N.J.Evid.R.* 201(a). *See also United States v. Ferri*, 778 *F.*2d 985, 989 (3rd Cir. 1985).

[21] *See Fed.R.Crim.P.* 26.1.

[22] *See Fed.R.Evid.* 104(a).

[23] 54 *App.D.C.* 46, 293 *F.* 1013 (1923).

[24] *Frye* at 47, 293 *F.* at 1014. [Emphasis added.]

the proofs demonstrate that the proposed evidence "rests on a reliable foundation," is "relevant," and is "based on scientifically valid principles."[25] In this regard, the proposed scientific evidence must emanate from "scientific knowledge"—it "must be supported by appropriate validation, *i.e.*, 'good grounds,' based on what is known."[26] The proposed evidence or testimony must also "assist the trier of fact to understand the evidence or to determine a fact in issue."[27]

There comes a point in time, however, when the courts have seen the same offer of scientific proof so often that such proof (of the device's or technique's scientific reliability and validity) will be taken for granted; it will become the subject of judicial notice. When that time comes, the proponent of the evidence will no longer have to call the experts to explain the technology or scientific method upon which the device or technique is based; nor will the proponent need to demonstrate that the device or technique rests upon scientifically reliable and valid principles or is generally accepted in the relevant scientific community. The proponent will, however, still need to prove that (1) the scientific device was operating properly on the given occasion, (2) the device was operated, or the technique was conducted, by a qualified person, and (3) the device was operated, or the technique was conducted, in a proper manner.

---

[25] *Daubert v. Merrell Dow Pharmaceuticals, Inc,* 509 *U.S.* 579, 588, 113 *S.Ct.* 2786, 2794 (1993) (holding for the first time that the *Frye* "general acceptance" standard is not an "absolute prerequisite" to the admission of scientific evidence). In *Daubert,* the Court declared: " 'General acceptance' is not a necessary precondition to the admissibility of scientific evidence under the Federal Rules of Evidence, but the Rules of Evidence—especially Rule 702—do assign to the trial judge the task of ensuring that an expert's testimony both rests on a reliable foundation and is relevant to the task at hand. Pertinent evidence based on scientifically valid principles will satisfy those demands." *Id.* at 597, 113 *S.Ct.* at 2799. *See also General Electric Co. v. Joiner,* 522 *U.S.* 136, 142, 118 *S.Ct.* 512, 517 (1997) ("while the Federal Rules of Evidence allow district courts to admit a somewhat broader range of scientific testimony than would have been admissible under *Frye,* they leave in place the 'gatekeeper' role of the trial judge in screening such evidence.").

[26] *Daubert* at 590, 113 *S.Ct.* at 2795. In direct response to the *Daubert* case, *Fed.R.Evid.* 702 has been amended to permit scientific testimony by an expert, "provided that (1) the testimony is sufficiently based upon reliable facts or data, (2) the testimony is the product of reliable principles and methods, and (3) the witness has applied the principles and methods reliably to the facts of the case." For a further discussion of the rules governing the admission of expert scientific testimony, refer to Section 4.1.

[27] *Fed.R.Evid.* 702. *See also Daubert* at 591, 113 *S.Ct.* at 2795. "Rule 702's 'helpfulness' standard requires a valid scientific connection to the pertinent inquiry as a precondition to admissibility." *Daubert* at 2796. Determining whether the proposed scientific evidence or testimony will be helpful to the trier of fact necessarily will require "a preliminary assessment of whether the reasoning or methodology underlying the [evidence or] testimony is scientifically valid and of whether that reasoning or methodology properly can be applied to the facts in issue." *Id.*

PEOPLE v. DONALDSON
Supreme Court of New York, Appellate Division
36 *A.D.*2d 37, 319 *N.Y.S.*2d 172 (4th Dept. 1971)

GABRIELLI, Justice.

"[W]e are called upon to determine the admissibility of the results of a blood-alcohol test as measured by an apparatus known as a 'Breathalyzer.' " *Id.* at 174.

"Defendant's main thrust on this appeal is his claim that the results of the [Breathalyzer] test were improperly received, asserting that there was no showing that the Breathalyzer is scientifically reliable and that there was no proof that the test was properly conducted by a qualified operator in accordance with required rules and regulations." *Id.*

"In approaching the question of admissibility of the results of the chemical test we examine the history and experience of its use as well as its methodology and manner of operation. The Breathalyzer has been in public use since 1954 and has been widely accepted and adopted by law enforcement agencies for use in testing blood-alcohol content. It operates on the firmly established principle that at normal body temperature the concentration of alcohol in the blood circulating through the lungs is 2,100 times greater than in the air discharged from the lungs. (4 Gray, *Attorney's Textbook of Medicine*, §133.73[1]). The apparatus is a semi-automatic analyzer designed to test blood-alcohol percentage present in any breath sample. Scientifically, the breathalyzer wastes all but the last portion of a long exhalation, trapping a measured volume which is then forced through a reagent and is ultimately photometrically measured resulting in a calculated reading of the subject's blood-alcohol percentage. Studies have shown that this device is considered to be 'fail safe' and that as a general rule its readings are slightly lower than those obtained in a corresponding blood test; and any slight error caused either by mechanical defect or operator fault will usually produce lower rather than higher readings. (45 *North Carolina Law Review* 34, 56)." *Id.* at 175-76.

"[W]e take note of an absence of any appellate determinations dealing with the scientific reliability of apparatus used to analyze one's breath in order to determine the percentage of alcohol in the blood. In noting its long usage and wide acceptance as an instrument for making a chemical analysis of alcohol in the blood, we * * * [hold] that it is no longer necessary to require expert testimony to establish the general reliability of the machine. We liken the question presented to that raised in *People v. Magri*, 3 *N.Y.*2d 562, 170 *N.Y.S.*2d 335, 147 *N.E.*2d 728, as it related to the use of radar in speed detection. There, in determining that it was no longer necessary to require expert testimony in each case as to the nature, function or scientific principles underlying the radar speedmeter, the

327

court observed * * * that 'almost daily, reproductions by photography * * *, X-rays, electroencephalograms, electrocardiograms, speedmeter readings, time by watches and clocks, identity by fingerprints, and ballistic evidence, among a variety of kindred scientific methods, are freely accepted in our courts for their general reliability, without the necessity of offering expert testimony as to the scientific principles underlying them.' Hence, we think the time has come when we may recognize the general reliability of the Breathalyzer as a device for measuring the concentration of alcohol in the blood, and that it is not necessary to require expert testimony as to the nature, function or scientific principles underlying it. (Watts, *Some Observations on Police-Administered Tests for Intoxication*, 45 *North Carolina Law Review* 34, 56 [1966]; Dobowski, *Measurement of Ethyl Alcohol in Breath*, pp. 326-333; *Pruitt v. State*, 216 *Tenn.* 686, 393 *S.W.*2d 747; *People v. Garnier*, 20 *Ill.App.*2d 492, 156 *N.E.*2d 613). Moreover, by providing that the results of the chemical analysis of breath tests are admissible in evidence, (Vehicle and Traffic Law §1192[3], now §1195), the Legislature has obviously determined that breath tests, if conducted in accordance with proper procedures, are scientifically reliable for determining the percentage of alcohol in the blood." *Donaldson* at 176.

"The evidence as to the operation of the Breathalyzer was adequate. The officer who administered the test was qualified in that respect by his training received at the State Police School given by personnel of the New York State Police Laboratory. He had administered the test on many occasions and further testified in detail regarding the required procedures to be performed, all of which were accomplished in the manner required by the standard instruction manual and the operational check list. * * * Additionally, there was ample proof that the instrument was properly calibrated and that the chemicals used in the test were of the proper kind, and mixed in the proper proportion. There is also adequate proof that the entire test had been administered in accordance with the rules and regulations of the State Police Department. Accordingly, it was not error to have admitted into evidence the results of the breath test." *Id.* at 177.

"The judgment should be *AFFIRMED*."

ROMANO v. KIMMELMAN
Supreme Court of New Jersey
96 N.J. 66, 474 A.2d 1 (1984)

The opinion of the Court was delivered by

HANDLER, J.

* * * * *

"In New Jersey, the results of scientific tests are admissible at a criminal trial only when they are shown to have 'sufficient scientific basis to produce uniform and reasonably reliable results and will contribute materially to the ascertainment of the truth.' * * * Scientific acceptability need not be predicated upon a unanimous belief or universal agreement in the total or absolute infallibility of the techniques, methodology or procedures that underlie the scientific evidence. * * * Reliability of such evidence must be demonstrated by showing that the scientific technique has gained general acceptance within the scientific community. * * * The fact that a possibility of error exists does not preclude a conclusion that a scientific device is reliable. * * * 'Practically every new scientific discovery has its detractors and unbelievers, but neither unanimity of opinion nor universal infallibility is required for judicial acceptance of generally recognized matters.' * * * Once the showing of general acceptability has been made, courts will take judicial notice of the given instrument's reliability and will admit in evidence the results of tests from the instrument without requiring further proof." *Id.*, 96 N.J. at 80. [Citations omitted.]

"[Breathalyzer] models 900 and 900A [are] considered in New Jersey to be scientific instruments generally accepted in the scientific community as reliable, and to be an appropriate subject of judicial notice. * * * In order to use breathalyzer test results as evidence in a trial charging a violation of *N.J.S.[]* 39:4-50, the State [must] clearly [] establish that (1) the equipment was in proper order—that it was periodically inspected in accordance with accepted procedures; (2) the operator was qualified to administer the instrument—that these qualifications as a breathalyzer operator were properly certified; and (3) the test was given correctly—that it was administered in accordance with the official instructions for the use of the instrument." *Id.* at 80-81.

"We hold that in its totality * * * [t]he Smith and Wesson Breathalyzer Models 900 and 900A are [] scientifically reliable and accurate devices for determining the concentration of blood alcohol. Such scientific reliability shall be the subject of judicial notice in the trial of all cases under *N.J.S.[]* 39:4-50[.]" *Id.* at 82.

NOTE

1. *See also State v. Vega*, 12 *Ohio St.*3d 185, 186 (1984) (taking judicial notice of "the reliability of intoxilyzers in general"); *State v. Downie*, 117 *N.J.* 450, 468, 569 *A.*2d 242, *cert. denied sub nom.*, *Downie v. New Jersey*, 498 *U.S.* 819, 111 *S.Ct.* 63 (1990) ("Judicial notice serves 'to provide a speedy and efficient means of proving matters which are not in genuine dispute.' * * * We are convinced that as long as proper procedures are followed, the [reliability of] breathalyzer results should remain a subject of judicial notice."); *People v. Alvarez*, 70 *N.Y.*2d 375, 380, 521 *N.Y.S.*2d 212, 515 *N.E.*2d 898 (1987) ("the scientific reliability of breathalyzers is no longer open to question").

2. The scientific bases of some techniques or devices have become so well settled that the admissibility of evidence derived therefrom has been recognized by numerous state legislatures and, as a result, regulated by statute. *See State v. Bender*, 382 *So.*2d 697, 699 (Fla. 1980) (listing statutes); Uniform Vehicle Code and Model Traffic Ordinance §11-902.1 (1984 Supp.). *See also*, McKinney's N.Y. Vehicle and Traffic Law §§1194-1195 (chemical tests to determine blood-alcohol content); 75 *Pa.C.S.* §1547(c) (chemical tests performed on an intoxicated motorist's blood); 75 *Pa.C.S.* §3368 (speed timing devices).

3. *The gas chromatograph mass spectrometer.* In *State v. Cathcart*, 247 *N.J.Super.* 340, 589 *A.*2d 193 (App.Div. 1991), the court held that the "gas chromatograph mass selector detector" is a scientifically reliable instrument on which the testimony of an expert may be based. According to the court: "Given the extensive prior use of the machine, the fact that we can take judicial notice of decisions establishing its reliability, * * * including cases in other jurisdictions so holding, we find no error in the trial judge's ruling admitting testimony regarding test results in the absence of any evidence proffered by defendant as to the machine's lack of reliability." *Id.*, 247 *N.J.Super.* at 362.

4. *Speed measuring devices.* Radar, as a device for detecting speed, is a scientific principle so soundly established that courts routinely take judicial notice of it. *See e.g.*, *State v. Graham*, 322 *S.W.*2d 188 (Mo.Ct.App. 1959).

(a) In *State v. Dantonio*, 18 *N.J.* 570, 115 *A.*2d 35, (1955), the Court addressed, for the first time, the subject of the police use of radar as a speed measuring device. The Court said:

Although there have been no appellate decisions in our own State, there have been several decisions in courts of other states and numerous articles in legal publications which have dealt comprehensively with the evidential problems presented by the use of radar speedmeters. * * * "In principle, its admission as legal evidence is based upon the theory that the evolution in practical affairs of life, whereby the progressive and scientific tendencies of the age are manifest in every other department of human endeavor, cannot be ignored in legal procedure, but that the law, in its efforts to enforce justice by demonstrating a fact in issue, will allow evidence of those scientific processes which are the work of educated and skillful men in their various departments, and apply them to the demonstration of a fact, leaving the weight and effect to be given to the effort and its results entirely to the consideration of the jury."

Id., 18 *N.J.* at 576. [Citation omitted.]

Since World War II, members of the public have become generally aware of the widespread use of radar methods in detecting the presence of objects and their distance and speed; and while they may not fully understand their intricacies they do not question their general accuracy and effectiveness. Dr. Kopper has pointed out that, in contrast to other radar methods, the method actually used in the speedmeter is rather simple and has been adopted by many law enforcement bodies; a recent tabulation indicates that speedmeters are being used in 43 states by almost 500 police departments. * * *

The writings on the subject assert that when properly operated they accurately record speed (within reasonable tolerances of perhaps two or three miles per hour) and nothing to the contrary has been brought to our attention; under the circumstances it would seem that evidence of radar speedmeter readings should be received in evidence upon a showing that the speedmeter was properly set up and tested by the police officers without any need for independent expert testimony by electrical engineers as to its general nature and trustworthiness. * * *

Id. at 578.

Under the Uniform Rules of Evidence, * * * judicial notice "shall be taken without request by a party * * * of such specific facts and propositions of generalized knowledge as are so universally known that they cannot reasonably be the subject of dispute." Radar speed meters are now in this category. Why should the time of experts be wasted and the expenses of litigation be increased by compelling such men to appear in court after court telling the same truths over and over? While it is agreed that every reasonable doubt about the accuracy of new developments should promptly be resolved against them in the absence of expert evidence, there is no longer any such doubt concerning radar. Rather, the applicable maxim should now be, "What the world generally knows a court of justice may be assumed to know."

Id. at 578-79. [Citation omitted.]

In this case, the state police officers were "sufficiently qualified," and the evidence demonstrated that the radar device was properly "tested for accuracy" before its use, was "properly set up" and operated, and was found to be functioning properly—that is, it was found to be in "regular working order" on the day in question. *Id.* at 581. The Court concluded, therefore, that "its readings constituted legal evidence to support the finding of guilt." *Id.*

(b) Today, even though the scientific basis of radar may be judicially noticed, the prosecution must still demonstrate that the device was working properly on the given occasion, and that it was operated correctly by a qualified person. *See State v. Wojtkowiak,* 174 *N.J.Super.* 460, 416 A.2d 975 (App.Div. 1980). *See also State v. Abeskaron,* 326 *N.J.Super.* 110, 740 A.2d 690 (App.Div. 1999) (upholding the admissibility of the speed readings produced by the LTI Marksman 20-20 Laser Speed Detection System).

(c) The following questions are representative of what is typically required of the prosecution in laying a foundation for the admission of speed registered on a K-55 radar device.

Q. Officer _____, how long have you been employed by the _____ Police Department?

A:

Q. And were you so employed and on duty on _____ ?
                                                    (Date)

A:

Q. What was your duty assignment on that date?

A:

Q. Now, drawing your attention to _____ on that date, did you have occasion to see a _____ (Time)

_____ ?
            (Vehicle; make, model, description)

A:

Q. Was there anything about the operation of this vehicle that caught your attention?

   A:

Q. And where did this vehicle operation take place?

   A:_____
                 (Road/City/Town)

Q. Did you ultimately identify the operator of this vehicle?

   A:

Q. And who was that?

   A:

Q. Is _____ in court today?
              (Defendant)

   A:

Q. Would you point him out for the court?

   A:_____**[IDENTIFICATION OF DEFENDANT]**

Q. Now officer, at the time of this motor vehicle stop, did you have a speed measuring device in your patrol car?

   A:

Q. Would you tell the court the type of device and its serial number?

   A:

Q. Have you been trained in the use of the radar instrument?

   A:

Q. What was the nature of your initial training?

   A:

Q. And did you receive an operator's card after that initial training?

   A:

Q. On what date?

   A:

Q. Have you received any refresher training, and if so, what were the dates?

   A:

Q. Do the dates listed on your operator's card accurately correspond to each date your training was completed?

   A:

Q. Now, prior to commencing your duty assignment, did you determine the working order of the unit?

   A:

Q. Did you perform the light tests, the internal calibration tests, and the tests using the tuning forks, in unison and in combination?

A:

Q. Did you obtain the requisite readings in the patrol windows and target windows?

A:

Q. And when you finished your tour of duty, did you run through the same battery of tests?

A:

Q. Did you receive the same test results?

A:

Q. Are those tests conducted in the regular course of _____
Police Department business?   (Agency Name)

A:

Q. Is the information reflecting the results of such tests recorded at or near the time of testing?

A:

Q. Is the information that is recorded taken from the radar instrument itself?

A:

Q. And is the person recording the information under a duty to record it accurately and correctly?

A:

Q. And is the information kept under the control of the_____
Police Department in the regular course of business?   (Agency Name)

A:

Q. Would you identify the tuning forks that you used along with the serial number of each?

A: 35 mph _____   80 mph _____
                    (identifying #)   (identifying #)

Q. Were the tuning forks calibrated prior to the date of this motor vehicle stop?

A:_____
                    (Affirmative Answer should Include Date)

Q. And you have the certificates with you?

A:

Q. Do you know if those certificates are produced in the regular course of business, at or near the time of testing by the State Superintendent's Office of Weights and Measures?

A:

Q. Now officer, at the time of the observation of defendant's vehicle, were you moving or stationary?

A:

MOVING MODE (If operated in the "moving mode," include the following questions ("Qm"))

Qm. What was the number of the patrol vehicle you were operating at the time?

A:

Qm. Had its speedometer been calibrated prior to the date of this motor vehicle stop?

A:

Qm. What was the date, and by whom was it calibrated?

A:_____ **Person:** _____

Qm. Do you know _____?

A:

Qm. And do you know if he is qualified to conduct "fifth wheel" calibration?

A:

Qm. And are the speeds that he obtained from 35 mph through 75 mph reflected on the Speedometer Test Chart?

A:

Qm. Was the speedometer calibrated after the date of this motor vehicle stop?

A:

Qm. The date?

A:

Qm. By whom?

A:

Qm. And do you know if he is qualified to conduct "fifth wheel" calibration?

A:

Qm. Are the speeds that he obtained from 35 mph through 75 mph reflected on the Speedometer Test Chart?

A:

Qm. Are both of these Speedometer Test Charts produced in the regular course of Police Department Business?

A:

Qm. Is the information that is recorded on those charts recorded at or near the time of the testing or calibration?

A:

Qm. And is the person recording the information under a duty to record it accurately and correctly?

A:

Qm. Now, during the course of your operation of the radar instrument on this date, did you have occasion to compare the radar instrument's display of the patrol car's speed with the speed registered on the car's speedometer?

A:

Qm. And how did the two readings compare?

A:

YOUR HONOR, AT THIS TIME I WOULD LIKE TO MOVE INTO EVIDENCE

- **THE RADAR TEST CHARTS**
- **THE TUNING FORK CALIBRATION CHARTS, AND**
- **THE OFFICER'S TRAINING CERTIFICATE**

Q. Now officer, directing your attention to the circumstances of this motor vehicle stop, when you first observed this vehicle, was it moving toward you or away from you?

A:

Q. Did you have the radar instrument turned on?

A:

Q. Was the instrument in the manual or automatic position?

A: MANUAL

Q. Did the defendant's vehicle pass into the beam of influence?

A:

Q. And at that time, did you activate the radar device?

A:

Q. Did you have the audible portion on, as well, at that time?

A:

Q. How do you know it was on?

A:

Q. Now, based on your training and experience and your visual observation of defendant's vehicle, could you estimate the speed at which defendant was traveling?

A: YES, IT WAS AT LEAST _____

Q. And at this time, did you make any observations related to defendant's speed and the radar instrument in the form of a tracking history?

A:

Q. What was that tracking history?

A:

Q. Did you lock in the speed at which defendant was traveling?

A:

Q. At the time, were you near any low-strung, high-tension wires?

A:

Q. Officer, you are familiar with what a "ghost reading" is?

A:

Q. Did you obtain any "ghost readings" the day of this motor vehicle stop?

A:

Q. Have you ever obtained "ghost readings" in the area of this motor vehicle stop?

A:

Q. Were there any other vehicles near the defendant's vehicle which could have affected the readings obtained on the radar instrument?

A:

Q. What was the posted speed at this location?

A:

Q. And what were the speeds you obtained on the radar instrument when defendant passed into its zone of influence?

A:_____(defendant's vehicle) _____ (patrol vehicle)

Q. Was your visual estimate of defendant's speed consistent with the radar reading?

A:

Q. Did you cause defendant's vehicle to come to a stop?

A:

Q. And did you advise him of the reason for the stop?

A:

Q. Was there any response?

A:

* * * *

STATE v. BLOME
Superior Court of New Jersey, Appellate Division
209 *N.J.Super.* 227, 507 A.2d 283 (1986)

The opinion of the court was delivered by

COLEMAN, J.H., J.A.D.
"The crucial question raised by this appeal is whether the State should have been permitted to argue to the jury that defendant could have buttressed the credibility of her insanity defense by submitting to sodium amytal." *Id.*, 209 *N.J.Super.* at 229.

"One of the main avenues of attack upon the defense of insanity was defendant's failure or refusal to submit to [the] sodium amytal drug which is popularly known as 'truth serum.' * * * The prosecution's argument, when boiled down, was: do not believe defendant's insanity defense because she hid the truth which the sodium amytal would have disclosed." *Id.* at 237.

"The results of scientific tests are admissible in a criminal trial only when they are shown to have 'sufficient scientific basis to produce uniform and reasonably reliable results and will contribute materially to the ascertainment of the truth.' * * * '[T]ruth serum' drugs may be valuable diagnostic aids because they tend to diminish the inhibitions of the subject being interviewed, but 'they do not in any wise provoke a certainty of truth-telling on his part.' [Moreover, it has been held that 'u]nder the present state of scientific knowledge, testimony elicited from a person while he is under the influence of a "truth serum" type drug is inadmissible.' " *Id.* at 238. [Citations omitted.]

"It is therefore clear that sodium amytal test results are inadmissible as evidence [] because they have not been established to be scientifically reliable. Hence it would be highly improper for the prosecutor to argue to the jury that defendant's defense of insanity and alleged amnesia should not be believed because she refused to take a sodium amytal test. The results of the test would have been inadmissible even if she had taken one." *Id.*

NOTE

1. The scientific basis of technical evidence, along with its general acceptance, may be established by:

(1) expert testimony as to the general acceptance, among those in the profession, of the premises on which the proffered expert witness based his or her analysis;

(2) authoritative scientific and legal writings indicating that the scientific community accepts the premises underlying the proffered testimony; and

(3) judicial opinions that indicate the expert's premises are reliable and valid.

See Giannelli, *The Admissibility of Novel Scientific Evidence,* 80 *Colum.L.Rev.* 1197, 1215 (1980). *See also State v. Kelly,* 97 *N.J.* 178, 210, 478 *A.*2d 364 (1984); *Commonwealth v. Nazarovitch,* 496 *Pa.* 97, 436 *A.*2d 170 (1981).

2. *Truth serum tests revisited.* In *State v. Pitts,* 116 *N.J.* 580, 630, 562 *A.*2d 1320 (1989), the New Jersey Supreme Court reiterated that "testimony derived from a sodium-amytal-induced interview is inadmissible to prove the truth of the facts asserted." The ruling stemmed, in part, from the expert testimony adduced at a pre-trial hearing which "indicated that the scientific community continues to view testimony induced by sodium amytal as unreliable to ascertain the truth." *Id.,* 116 *N.J.* at 630. *See also Commonwealth v. Stark,* 363 *Pa.Super.* 356 (1987) (the results of truth serum tests are not admissible "because they lack scientific reliability").

3. *Fingerprints & handprints.* The scientific reliability of fingerprint and handprint evidence has long been the subject of judicial notice. Today, the reliability of identifications made through the use of fingerprint evidence is virtually never challenged on the ground that the scientific basis of such evidence—the "uniqueness" of a person's fingerprint—is questionable. As one court put it: "It can be judicially noticed that there is, as yet, no other means of identification which affords the same assurance of correctness that fingerprinting does." *Roesch v. Ferber,* 48 *N.J.Super.* 231, 239, 137 *A.*2d 61 (App.Div. 1957). *See also State v. Miller,* 71 *N.J.L.* 527, 534 (E. & A. 1904) (accepting the use of handprint evidence); *State v. Cerciello,* 86 *N.J.L.* 309, 315 (E. & A. 1914) (accepting the use of fingerprints in a criminal case); *Lamble v. State,* 96 *N.J.L.* 231, 236 (E. & A. 1921) (recognizing that "[t]here is a scientific basis for the system of fingerprint identification[,]" and holding that because "[t]his method of identification is in such general and common use [] the courts cannot refuse to take judicial cognizance of it"); *State v. Watson,* 224 *N.J.Super.* 354, 361, 540 *A.*2d 875 (App.Div. 1988) ("a conviction may be based solely on fingerprint evidence as long as the attendant circumstances establish that the object upon which the prints are found was generally inaccessible to the defendant"); *Commonwealth v. Crawford,* 468 *Pa.* 565, 364 *A.*2d 660 (1976).

Footprints. In *United States v. Ferri,* 778 *F.*2d 985 (3rd Cir. 1985), the trial court permitted the government to introduce the expert testimony of Dr. Louise Robbins, a physical anthropologist. Dr. Robbins testified that she compared the impressions inside the two pairs of shoes found at the crime scene with those seized from the defendants' residences, along with their inked footprints. On the basis of these comparisons, Dr. Robbins testified that the shoes found at the crime scene belonged to the two defendants. On appeal, the Third Circuit held that the trial court "committed no abuse of discretion when it determined that Dr. Robbins' testimony was sufficiently reliable to be admitted at trial." *Id.* at 989. *See also People v. Knights*, 166 *Cal.App.*3d 46, 212 *Cal.Rptr.* 307, 312 (1985) (holding that Dr. Robbins' work "is best characterized as an extension of well-established techniques traditionally used by physical anthropologists"); *State v. Bullard*, 312 *N.C.* 129, 322 *S.E.*2d 370 (1984) (approving Dr. Robbins' testimony identifying the defendant on the basis of footprints left at the crime scene); *State v. Maccia*, 311 *N.C.* 222, 316 *S.E.*2d 241 (1984) (approving expert testimony identifying the defendant on the basis of inner sole impressions from shoes found at the crime scene).

4. *Voice prints.* In the early 1960s, Lawrence G. Kersta developed a scientific technique and device for making a visual picture or "voiceprint" of a person's voice from a tape recording. According to Kersta, no two persons will produce identical voiceprints, and the technique and voiceprint device is as accurate as fingerprint identification. *See* Kersta, *Speaker Recognition and Identification by Voiceprints*, 40 Conn.B.J. 586 (1966). *See also State v. Cary*, 49 *N.J.* 343, 351-52, 230 *A.*2d 384 (1967) (voiceprint identification can be a "highly desirable aid to judicial determinations of truth" and may be admissible so long as its proponent can establish that it "has a sufficient scientific basis to produce uniform and reasonably reliable results and will contribute materially to the ascertainment of the truth"). *See also United States v. Williams*, 583 *F.*2d 1194 (2nd Cir. 1978); *United States v. Baller*, 519 *F.*2d 463 (4th Cir. 1975); *United States v. Franks*, 511 *F.*2d 25 (6th Cir. 1975). *Compare Commonwealth v. Topa*, 471 *Pa.* 223, 369 *A.*2d 1277 (1977) (voice print evidence is inadmissible in a Pennsylvania court).

5. *Hypnosis.* Generally, testimony which has been hypnotically refreshed will be deemed incompetent and inadmissible when the witness had no memory of the event or facts prior to the hypnotic session. *Commonwealth v. Nazarovitch*, 496 *Pa.* 97, 436 *A.*2d 170 (1981). A witness who has been previously hypnotized may, however, be permitted to testify so long as the testimony relates information *not* derived from the hypnotic session, and the following requirements are met: the party offering the witness "must so advise the court, and show that the testimony to be presented was established and existed previous to any hypnotic process; that the person conducting the hypnotic session [had been] trained in the process and is neutral of any connection with the issue or the parties;

and, the trial judge shall instruct the jury that the testimony of a witness previously hypnotized should be carefully scrutinized and received with caution." *Commonwealth v. Smoyer*, 505 *Pa.* 83, 89-90, 476 *A.*2d 1304, 1308 (1984).

In *State v. Hurd*, 86 *N.J.* 525, 432 *A.*2d 86 (1981), the Court observed: "The purpose of using hypnosis is not to obtain the truth, as a polygraph or 'truth serum' is supposed to do. Instead, hypnosis is employed as a means of overcoming amnesia and restoring the memory of a witness. * * * In light of this purpose, hypnosis can be considered reasonably reliable if it is able to yield recollections as accurate as those of an ordinary witness, which likewise are often historically inaccurate." *Id.*, 86 *N.J.* at 537-38. As a result, the Court held that "testimony enhanced through hypnosis is admissible in a criminal trial if the trial court finds that the use of hypnosis in the particular case was reasonably likely to result in recall comparable in accuracy to normal human memory. If the testimony is admissible, the opponent may still challenge the reliability of the particular procedures followed in the individual case by introducing expert testimony at trial, but the opponent may not attempt to prove the general unreliability of hypnosis. The trier of fact must then decide how much weight to accord the hypnotically refreshed testimony." *Id.* at 543. *See also id.* at 543-547, for the requirements for the admissibility of hypnotically-refreshed testimony.

6. *Amylase test results. See State v. Zola*, 112 *N.J.* 384, 412-413, 548 *A.*2d 1022 (1988) (upholding the scientific reliability of amylase test results, provided by the State's serologist, which established a reasonable inference that bodily fluids consistent with saliva were found in the victim's vagina).

7. *Human Leukocyte Antigen (HLA) testing.* HLA testing has been recognized as a reliable means of addressing issues relating to nonpaternity, *see e.g., Jordan v. Mace*, 144 *Me.* 351, 69 *A.*2d 670 (1949); *Houghton v. Houghton*, 179 *Neb.* 275, 137 *N.W.*2d 861 (1965); *R.K. v. Dept. of Human Services*, 215 *N.J.Super.* 342, 346-47, 521 *A.*2d 1319 (App.Div. 1987); *Malvasi v. Malvasi*, 167 *N.J.Super.* 513, 516 (Ch.Div. 1979); *Williams v. Milliken*, 351 *Pa.Super.* 567, 506 *A.*2d 918 (1986), and to the exclusion of someone from sexual contact, *State v. Hammond*, 221 *Conn.* 264, 604 *A.*2d 793, 800 (1992). *See also State v. Spann*, 130 *N.J.* 484, 617 *A.*2d 247 (1993).

8. *Horizontal gaze nystagmus (HGN) testing.* "Nystagmus is an involuntary rapid movement of the eyeball, which may be horizontal, vertical, or rotatory." *People v. Ojeda*, 225 *Cal.App.*3d 404, 275 *Cal.Rptr.* 472 (1st Dist. 1990). "An inability of the eyes to maintain visual fixation as they are turned from side to side (in other words, jerking or bouncing) is known as horizontal gaze nystagmus, or

HGN. ∗ ∗ ∗ Some investigators believe alcohol intoxication in-creases the frequency and amplitude of HGN and causes HGN to occur at a smaller angle of deviation from the forward direction." *Id. See also State v. Bresson*, 51 *Ohio St*.3d 123, 554 *N.E*.2d 1330, 1332-33 (1990).

HGN testing has yet to be universally accepted by the courts as a sufficiently reliable method of determining whether a person is under the influence of an intoxicant. *Compare People v. Loomis*, 156 *Cal.App*.3d Supp. 1, 203 *Cal.Rptr.* 767 (1984) (HGN has not been shown to meet the *Frye* criterion of general acceptance); *Common-wealth v. Apollo*, 412 *Pa.Super.* 453, 603 *A*.2d 1023, 1027-28 (1992) (HGN principles have not been shown to be generally accepted in the appropriate scientific community); *State v. Reed*, 83 *Or.App.* 451, 732 *P*.2d 66, 68 (1987) (*same*); *State v. Superior Court*, 149 *Ariz.* 269, 718 *P*.2d 171, 178 (1986) (*same*), with *People v. Ojeda*, 225 *Cal.App*.3d 404, 275 *Cal.Rptr.* 472 (1st Dist. 1990) (finding HGN not to be inherently more "scientific" than the more familiar field sobriety tests; holding that, while a police officer may not be quali-fied to make a numerical correlation between HGN and blood alco-hol level, the officer may testify, "based on his or her own experi-ence with the relationship between HGN and alcohol intoxication, to an opinion that a subject was or was not under the influence"); *State v. Murphy*, 451 *N.W*.2d 154, 156 (Iowa 1990) (*same*); *State v. Nagel*, 40 *Ohio App*.3d 80, 506 *N.E*.2d 285, 286 (1986) (*same*).

9. *Lead bullet analysis.* Lead bullet analysis is performed by a complex process known as "inductively coupled plasma atomic emission spectroscopy (ICP analysis)." *See State v. Noel*, 157 *N.J.* 141, 144, 729 *A*.2d 602 (1999). The process is based on the premise that lead bullets are made from an initial source of molten lead, sometimes called a "batch" or "pouring." According to the experts, there is a variation in each batch of the presence and percentage of six trace elements other than lead—copper, antimony, bismuth, arsenic, tin, and silver—and it is highly improbable that any two pourings or batches could have the identical composition. Conse-quently, through ICP analysis, an expert may provide his or her opinion that two sets of bullets have identical composition and come from the same batch of lead, or, stated another way, that a defendant possessed bullets of the same caliber and manufacture as those used in a particular crime.

ICP analysis of lead bullets is a method that has been accepted by the scientific community, and is one which produces sufficiently reliable results to warrant the admission of expert testimony re-garding the methodology and test results. *See e.g., Commonwealth v. Daye*, 411 *Mass.* 719, 587 *N.E*.2d 194, 207 (1992) (permitting FBI agent's testimony that the bullets in the victim's body and those found on the defendant came from "the same box of ammunition or from different boxes that were manufactured at the same place on or about the same date"); *State v. Noel, supra,* 157 *N.J.* at 147 (permitting expert testimony that the compositional match among the bullets increased the probability that the bullets in the victim and those found at the crime scene were from the defendant); *State v. Krummacher,* 269 *Or.* 125, 523 *P.*2d 1009, 1012-13 (1974) (permitting expert testimony that bullets probably came from the same batch of metal, noting that the defendant's expert properly pointed out the weaknesses of the evidence). *See also United States v. Davis,* 103 *F.*3d 660, 673 (8th Cir. 1996); *State v. Grube,* 883 *P.*2d 1069 (Idaho 1994); *People v. Johnson,* 499 *N.E.*2d 1355 (Ill. 1986); *State v. Freeman,* 531 *N.W.*2d 190 (Minn. 1995); *Bryan v. State,* 935 *P.*2d 338, 360 (Okla.Crim.App. 1997); *State v. Strain,* 885 *P.*2d 810 (Utah Ct.App. 1994).

10. *DNA testing.* Deoxyribonucleic acid (DNA) "is an organic substance found in the chromosomes contained in the nucleus of a cell. It provides the genetic blueprint that determines the physical structures and individual characteristics of every living organism—humans, animals, plants, and even bacteria. In humans, DNA exists in all cells that have a nucleus, including white blood cells, sperm, cells surrounding hair roots, and the cells in saliva. These are the cells most often discovered at crime scenes and are most useful in forensic DNA analysis." *State v. Vandebogart,* 616 *A.*2d 483, 485 (N.H. 1992)

By and large, DNA "does not vary within an individual, *i.e.,* the DNA contained in one cell in an individual will be identical to the DNA contained in every other cell of that individual. For forensic purposes, the important characteristic of DNA is that, excepting identical twins, no two persons have the same DNA structure." *Id.* at 485-86.

"The DNA molecule is shaped like a double helix which resembles a twisted ladder. Each component strand of the helix, similar to the rungs on a ladder, consists of a sequence of nucleotides. The nucleotides are sometimes referred to as bases. There are four types of nucleotides in the DNA molecule, and they are designated as Adenine (A), Guanine (G), Cytosine (C), and Thymine (T). The nucleotides bond in predictable patterns, A to T and C to G. A pair of complementary bases—A-T, T-A, C-G, or G-C—is designated as a base pair. The order in which these base pairs appear on the DNA ladder constitutes the genetic code for the cell. This code carries the necessary information to produce the many proteins which comprise the human body. A sequence of base pairs responsible for producing a particular protein is called a 'gene.' A gene, the basic unit of heredity, consists of a sequence of between 1,000 and 2 million nucleotides. Scientists estimate that the human genome, the complete genetic makeup of a person, contains 50,000 to 100,000 genes and that in a human set of 23 chromosomes there are about 3 billion nucleotides." *Id.* at 486.

"DNA profiling primarily involves the scientific disciplines of molecular biology and population genetics." *Id.* at 492. Such profiling can "inculpate a criminal suspect by comparing the suspect's genetic material with genetic material obtained from human tissue left at the crime scene. DNA profiling involves two distinct procedures." *Id.* at 486. First, an analysis of fragments of the DNA is made to determine if there is a match. This is called RFLP analysis or an analysis of the "restriction fragment length polymorphisms." The second part of the procedure involves a population frequency calculation, which "generates a ratio which accompanies a match in order to express the statistical likelihood that an unrelated individual chosen at random from a particular population could have the same DNA profile as the suspect." *Id.*

To date, the majority of jurisdictions that have ruled on the admissibility of DNA evidence have found that the DNA profiling theory and procedures for declaring a match to be generally accepted as reliable. *See e.g., Vandebogart* at 491; *State v. Montalbo*, 73 *Haw.* 130, 144-46, 828 *P.*2d 1274, 1283 (1992); *State v. Brown*, 470 *N.W.*2d 30, 32 (Iowa 1991); *Smith v. Deppish*, 248 *Kan.* 217, 239, 807 *P.*2d 144, 159 (1991); *State v. Davis*, 814 *S.W.*2d 593, 602-03 (Mo. 1991); *State v. Pennington*, 327 *N.C.* 89, 100, 393 *S.E.*2d 847, 854 (1990); *State v. Pierce*, 597 *N.E.*2d 107 (Ohio 1992); *State v. Ford*, 301 *S.C.* 485, 488-90, 392 *S.E.*2d 781, 783-84 (1990); *State v. Wimberly*, 467 *N.W.*2d 499, 505-06 (S.D. 1991); *Glover v. State*, 825 *S.W.*2d 127 (Tex.Crim.App. 1992); *Spencer v. Commonwealth*, 238 *Va.* 275, 290, 384 *S.E.*2d 775, 783 (1989); *State v. Woodall*, 182 *W.Va.* 15, 385 *S.E.*2d 253, 260 (1989). *See also United States v. Jacobetz*, 955 *F.*2d 786 (2nd Cir. 1992).

DNA profiling is presently, however, a procedure "so novel that its reliability is still debated." *State v. Hammond*, 221 *Conn.* 264, 604 *A.*2d 793, 801 (1992). In *State v. Thomas*, 245 *N.J.Super.* 428, 586 *A.*2d 250 (App.Div. 1991), the court observed: "Within the last two years, the acceptance of the methodology of DNA testing by the scientific community has led to virtual judicial unanimity, despite some earlier reservations, in ruling that DNA test results are admissible if they are supported by an adequate evidential base. * * * Th[e] recent literature leaves little doubt of the enormous utility of DNA testing, suggesting that the time may be close at hand when genetic blueprint evidence will be as routine and decisive as fingerprint evidence[.]" *Id.*, 245 *N.J.Super.* at 433-34. [Citations omitted.] The court did not, however, decide whether DNA test results should be received in evidence in a criminal trial.

In *Commonwealth v. Rodgers*, 413 *Pa.Super.* 498, 605 *A.*2d 1228 (1992), the court upheld the admission of the results of "deoxyribonucleic acid restriction fragment length polymorphism" (DNA / RFLP) analyses performed by Lifecodes Corporation of Valhalla, New York, on bloodstains found on both the victim's clothing and that worn by the defendant at the time of the homicide. The Pennsylvania Superior Court agreed with the trial judge's conclusions that

> (1) it is generally accepted in the academic community as a sound scientific principle that individuals have unique DNA patterns; (2) techniques and experiments which currently exist and are widely employed in the scientific community are generally regarded as capable of producing reliable results in DNA identification; and (3) Lifecodes Corporation, Valhalla, N.Y., the laboratory at which the tests were conducted, utilized accepted scientific techniques in analyzing the forensic samples in this case.

Id., 605 *A.*2d at 1234.

In light of (1) the expert evidence developed during the four-day, extended pre-trial hearings in this case, (2) the extensive documentation (provided to the trial court in the form of reproductions of numerous published studies) of the general acceptance of DNA / RFLP analyses, (3) the large number of appellate courts throughout the country that have found DNA testing, and the surrounding scientific techniques used to obtain DNA identification results, to be admissible, and (4) the opportunity the defense had for full and fair cross-examination of the Commonwealth's experts, the court held that

> DNA / RFLP analysis has gained general acceptance in the national scientific community[, and] that * * * evidence adduced by DNA / RFLP analysis is scientifically valid and satisfies the *Frye* standard made applicable in Pennsylvania by *Commonwealth v. Topa, supra.*

Rodgers at 1235.

Courts that have rejected DNA evidence have done so generally on the ground that the estimates provided, as to the improbability of there being a match between the DNA sample found at the crime scene or on the victim and the one taken from the defendant, are based on weak population statistical databases or on the improper use of calculation methods. *See e.g., United States v. Two Bulls*, 925 *F.*2d 1127 (8th Cir. 1991). *See also Vandebogart, supra* at 494 (in light of the considerable debate among geneticists "concerning the possibility of significant population substructure, we conclude that the FBI's method for estimating population frequencies, which relies on the product rule, has not found general acceptance in the field of population genetics"); *Commonwealth v. Lanigan*, 413 *Mass.* 154, 162-63, 596 *N.E.*2d 311, 316 (1992) (finding the FBI's method for calculating frequency of defendant's DNA profiles not generally accepted in the scientific community). These courts emphasize the fact that "[a] match is virtually meaningless without a statistical probability expressing the frequency with which a match could occur." *See Vandebogart* at 494. *See also People v. Barney*, 8 *Cal.App.*4th 798, 10 *Cal.Rptr.*2d 731, 742 (1992) (describing statistical calculation as the "pivotal element" of DNA analysis).

11. *Bloodhounds and other tracking dogs. See State v. Wanczyk*, 196 *N.J.Super.* 397, 402, 482 *A.*2d 964 (Law Div. 1984), where the court held that "[i]t is a matter of common knowledge, of which courts may take notice, that dogs of some varieties, such as bloodhounds, foxhounds and bird dogs, are remarkable for the acuteness of their sense of smell, which enables them to follow a trail upon which they are laid, even though this trail be crossed by others." *See also Cook v. State*, 374 *A.*2d 264, 270 (Del. 1977); *Terrell v. State*, 3 *Md.App.* 340, 239 *A.*2d 128 (1968); *State v. Parton*, 251 *N.J.Super.* 230, 597 *A.*2d 1088 (App.Div. 1991); *State v. Rowland*, 263 *N.C.* 353, 139 *S.E.*2d 661 (1965); *Copley v. State*, 153 *Tenn.* 189, 281 *S.W.* 460 (1926).

STATE v. HAWKINS
Court of Appeals of Maryland
326 *Md.* 270, 604 *A.*2d 489 (1992)

CHARLES E. ORTH, Jr., Judge, Specially Assigned.
"This appeal is about murder * * * and the word 'polygraph,' which, when it crops up in a criminal prosecution, raises a red flag." *Id.* at 491.

Hawkins claims "that the prosecution of her should have aborted in the middle of the trial. The heart of her contention is that she was denied the fair trial to which she is entitled. * * * The basis for her contention is that during the examination of two of the witnesses against her, the verboten word 'polygraph' crept into their testimony." *Id.*

"The red flag was raised when a police officer, Trooper [] Mitchell, was testifying for the State on direct examination. He was recounting his interrogation of Hawkins in the police station." *Id.* at 491-92. At one point in his testimony he stated:

> I went out of my office into Sergeant Bane's office and told him what had happened. He came back into the polygraph suite— (witness slapped hand on witness table)—I'm sorry—came back into my office and said, told the Detective that she was under arrest.

Id. at 492.

"The word 'polygraph' next popped up during the State's direct examination of another police officer * * * [who] was describing Hawkins' reaction to her arrest:

> She became very emotional. She began crying. It was necessary for Trooper Mitchell and I to physically carry the Defendant from the area next to the polygraph room to a cell area where she was placed."

Id. "At this point, defense counsel heeded the warning of the red flag. He moved for a mistrial." *Id.*

" '[I]t is universally held that evidence of the defendant's willingness or unwillingness to submit to a lie detector examination is inadmissible.' * * * The reliability of such tests has not been established to our satisfaction, and we have consistently refused to permit evidence with regard to them. * * * In our system of criminal justice, the trier of fact is the lie detector, and we have been steadfast in disallowing that function to be usurped by a process we have not found to be trustworthy. Mention at a criminal trial of the results of a polygraph test, or the taking of the test, or the willingness or unwillingness to take the test, raises the specter of reversal. In criminal prosecutions, the polygraph test is a pariah; 'polygraph' is a dirty word." *Id.* [Citations omitted.]

"We have reversed judgments of conviction when mention was made of the taking of a polygraph test or of the willingness or unwillingness of a defendant to take the test. * * * Despite its status as a pariah, however, not all references to polygraph tests warrant reversal. * * * The question is one of prejudice to the defendant. * * * We note that the fact that reference to a polygraph test is inadvertent does not alone insure that it is not prejudicial." Id.

The trial judge denied Hawkins' motion for a mistrial. "In so doing, he put the word, 'polygraph' in the context in which it was mentioned. He observed that when the words passed Trooper Mitchell's lips, the officer 'paused in giving his testimony and reacted in a very unusual, shall we say, fashion.' The judge noted that '[o]ne of the members of the court stated that he looked like he had been electrocuted.' On the other hand, when Sergeant Bane used the word, he 'did not react at all.' * * * The judge concluded:

> Considering the totality of the circumstances in this case, I believe there has been no irrefutable prejudice to the Defendant by the combination of the two references. The one that troubles me the most is by Trooper Mitchell, but it was very oblique. It was not clear to the jury, I believe, what he was referring to. * * * I don't think there's been any prejudice to the Defendant[.]"

Id. at 492-93.

"The trial judge characterized the utterances of the word 'polygraph' as 'blurts,' and we are in full accord with that view. We are content with the finding of the trial judge * * * that each officer's mention of the word 'polygraph' was inadvertent, uttered abruptly and impulsively, with no nefarious intent." *Id.* at 493.

"Supporting the denial of the motion by the judge here was that the references to 'polygraph' were not solicited by the prosecutor. All that the officers voiced, without embellishment, was the taboo word, 'polygraph.' Neither officer stated that Hawkins had taken a polygraph test or had expressed her willingness or unwillingness to take it. The officers did not even indicate that Hawkins had been placed in a room containing a polygraph machine." *Id.*

"We have no quarrel with the trial judge's conclusion that Hawkins was not prejudiced. In the light of the lack of prejudice, there was no abuse of discretion, there was no error in the judge's exercise of his discretion. There being no error, the judge's action was proper. Hawkins was entitled to a fair, not a perfect, trial. * * * We hold that in the particular circumstances of this case, she received the fair trial to which she was entitled." *Id.* at 494.

NOTE

The polygraph (Greek for "many writings"), commonly known as a lie-detector, is generally recognized by the courts as a basic investigatory tool. It detects and records certain physiological changes or responses in the body of an examinee as he answers questions put to him by an examiner. Significantly, the instrument itself does *not* detect lies. Rather, it measures physiological responses in the human body that the examiner must then interpret as being either consistent or inconsistent with the stress and fear of detection that an examinee might harbor in his attempt to conceal the truth.

The instrument's supporters contend that "the polygraph accurately records these bodily changes, thus enabling a skilled examiner to make an analysis of the truth or falsehood of the answers on a scientific basis. * * * On the other hand, it has been said that the scientific basis of the polygraph is questionable for two reasons: (1) there appears to be little evidence supporting the conclusion that lying causes a reaction which can be accurately measured; and (2) the techniques of the process enhance the possibility of error from interpretation. * * * The reason most commonly assigned for the exclusion of such evidence is that the lie detector has not as yet attained scientific acceptance as a reliable means of ascertaining the truth." *State v. Walker*, 37 *N.J.* 208, 215, 181 *A.2d* 1 (1962). Indeed, "[t]o this day, the scientific community remains extremely polarized about the reliability of polygraph techniques." *United States v. Scheffer*, 523 *U.S.* 303, 309, 118 *S.Ct.* 1261, 1265 (1998).

Historically, the criminal courts have been distrustful of polygraph evidence, and as a result, have held the results of such tests inadmissible in a criminal trial because the polygraph has not yet attained general scientific acceptance of its accuracy or reliability. *See Scheffer, supra*, 118 *S.Ct.* at 1265 ("there is simply no consensus that polygraph evidence is reliable"); *State v. Carter*, 91 *N.J.* 86, 116, 449 *A.2d* 1280 (1982); *Quigley v. Civil Service Com'n*, 528 *Pa.* 195, 596 *A.2d* 144, 147 (1991) (because the polygraph has not yet attained general scientific or legal acceptance of its accuracy or reliability, the results of tests administered by it are inadmissible for any purpose). *See also State v. Christopher*, 149 *N.J.Super.* 269, 275, 373 *A.2d* 705 (App.Div. 1977) ("While we take judicial notice of the fact that polygraph testing is used extensively by police and law enforcement agencies for investigative purposes, polygraph evidence has not attained that degree of accuracy to warrant our taking judicial notice of its reliability as an aid to learning the truth."); *Commonwealth v. Johnson*, 441 *Pa.* 237, 272 *A.2d* 467 (1971) (notwithstanding the fact that the actual results of the lie detector test were never mentioned, the mere reference to the fact that the test was taken required reversal and remand for new trial); *United States v. Frye*, 293 *F.* 1013, 1015 (D.C.Cir. 1923) (polygraph testing has "not yet gained such standing and scientific recognition among physiological and psychological authorities as would justify the court in admitting expert testimony deduced from the discovery, development, and experiments thus far made").

Polygraph evidence is, therefore, generally inadmissible regardless of whether it is favorable to an accused. "The only exception to this rule occurs when the State and the defendant enter into a stipulation to have defendant submit to a polygraph test and have the results introduced in evidence. In such instances, effect is given to the stipulation and the polygraph evidence is held admissible." *Christopher*, 149 *N.J.Super.* at 274. As one court explained,

> polygraph testing has been developed to such a point of reliability that in a criminal case when the State and defendant enter into a stipulation to have defendant submit to a polygraph test, and have the results introduced in evidence, such stipulation should be given effect. Polygraph testing has sufficient probative value to warrant admission under these circumstances.

State v. McDavitt, 62 *N.J.* 36, 46, 297 *A.2d* 849 (1972). The Court in *McDavitt* emphasized, however, that "it must appear that the stipulation is clear, unequivocal and complete, freely entered into with full knowledge of the right to refuse the test and the consequences involved in taking it." *Id.* at 46.

STATE v. COMMINS
Appellate Court of Connecticut
83 *Conn.App.* 496, 850 A.2d 1074 (2004)

McLACHLAN, J.
"The defendant, John J. Commins, appeals from the judgment of conviction, rendered after a jury trial, of operating a motor vehicle while under the influence of intoxicating liquor * * *. He claims that the trial court improperly admitted into evidence testimony concerning a horizontal gaze nystagmus test * * *. We affirm the judgment of the trial court." *Id.* at 1076-77.

Early in the morning of August 16th, "Officer Steven Santucci of the Newtown police department was on patrol on Route 34 in Newtown and observed the defendant, who was driving a truck, approach an intersection, enter a left turn only lane and activate the truck's left turn signal. Instead of turning left at the intersection, however, the defendant continued through the intersection, and drove along the median line and into the oncoming traffic lane. On the basis of those observations, Santucci initiated a traffic stop." *Id.* at 1077.

"During the traffic stop, the defendant informed Santucci both that he was on his way home and that he was coming from his home. While speaking with the defendant, Santucci detected the odor of alcohol on his breath. In view of the defendant's erratic driving and the odor of alcohol, Santucci proceeded to administer three field sobriety tests to the defendant." *Id.*

"The first test administered was the horizontal gaze nystagmus test. Nystagmus is the inability of the eyes to maintain visual fixation on a stimulus when the eyes are turned to the side, often resulting in a lateral jerking of the eyeball. * * * The premise of the horizontal gaze nystagmus test is that as alcohol consumption increases, the closer to the midline of the nose the onset of nystagmus occurs. To administer the test, the officer positions a stimulus approximately twelve to eighteen inches away from and slightly above the subject's eyes. The stimulus, usually a pen or the officer's finger, is then moved slowly from the midline of the nose to maximum deviation, the farthest lateral point to which the eyes can move to either side. The officer observes the subject's eyes as he tracks the stimulus and looks for six clues, three for each eye, to determine whether the subject passes or fails the test. The officer looks for (1) the inability of each eye to track movement smoothly, (2) pronounced nystagmus at maximum deviation and (3) the onset of nystagmus at an angle less than forty-five degrees in relation to the center point. A finding of four clues indicates failure of the test and is a sign of intoxication. Santucci testified that the defendant possessed all six clues and that those results indicated that the defendant was under the influence of alcohol." *Id.*

"Santucci also administered the walk and turn test and the one-leg stand test. Santucci testified that the defendant's performance on both tests indicated that he was under the influence of alcohol." *Id.*

On the basis of the defendant's performance on the three tests, his erratic driving and the odor of alcohol on his breath, Santucci placed the defendant under arrest and transported him to the police station, where the defendant refused to submit to a breath test." *Id.* at 1077-78.

"Prior to trial, the defendant filed a motion for a hearing * * * to challenge the admission of evidence concerning the horizontal gaze nystagmus test. Specifically, the defendant challenged both the methodology underlying horizontal gaze nystagmus testing and Santucci's qualifications to testify as to his administration and grading of the test." *Id.* at 1078.

At the hearing, "the state called Constantine Forkiotis, a behavioral optometrist, as its sole witness. Forkiotis testified that horizontal gaze nystagmus testing is generally accepted in the scientific community, has been comprehensively tested and subjected to peer review, can be explained to jurors in a manner that will assist them in executing their task and was not developed solely for the purpose of use in court. At the conclusion of the hearing, the defendant asked that evidence of the test be excluded on the ground that it does not satisfy the standards * * * for the admissibility of scientific evidence[.]" *Id.* The trial court rejected that argument, concluding that horizontal gaze nystagmus testing is generally accepted by the scientific community. After trial, the jury found the defendant guilty[.]" *Id.*

In this appeal, defendant argues that the court below should have excluded evidence of the horizontal gaze nystagmus test, specifically because "the state (1) failed to establish a proper foundation for the admission of horizontal gaze nystagmus evidence * * *, and (2) failed to establish an adequate foundation for Santucci's testimony as to his administration and grading of the test. *We disagree.*" *Id.* at 1078-79.

-A-

"In determining whether the court properly admitted the horizontal gaze nystagmus evidence at issue, we employ [a] three part test[.] That test requires that the state (1) satisfy the criteria for admission of scientific evidence, (2) lay a proper foundation with regard to the qualifications of the individual administering the test and (3) demonstrate that the test was conducted in accordance with relevant procedures." *Id.* at 1079-80.*

---

* This test for the admission of horizontal gaze nystagmus evidence is substantially in accord with the approach of the majority of other jurisdictions that have addressed the issue. *See e.g., Ballard v. State,* 955 *P.*2d 931 (Alaska App. 1998); *State v. Superior Court,* 149 *Ariz.* 269, 718 *P.*2d 171 (1986); *Zimmerman v. State,* 693 *A.*2d 311 (Del. 1997); *Williams v. State,* 710 *So.*2d 24 (Fla.App. 1998); *Hawkins v. State,* 223 *Ga.App.* 34, 476 *S.E.*2d 803 (Ga. App. 1996); *State v. Ito,* 90 *Haw.* 225, 978 *P.*2d 191 (Haw. App. 1999); *People v. Buening,* 229 *Ill.App.*3d 538, 592 *N.E.*2d 1222 (1992); *State v. Murphy,* 451 *N.W.*2d 154 (Iowa 1990); *State v. Armstrong,* 561 *So.*2d 883 (La. App. 1990); *State v. Taylor,* 694 *A.*2d 907 (Me. 1997); *Schultz v. State,* 106 *Md.App.* 145, 664 *A.*2d 60 (1995); *People v. Berger,* 217 *Mich.App.* 213, 551 *N.W.*2d 421 (1996); *State v. Hill,* 865 *S.W.*2d 702 (Mo. App. 1993), *overruled on other grounds, State v. Carson,* 941 *S.W.*2d 518 (Mo. 1997); *State v. Baue,* 258 *Neb.* 968, 607 *N.W.*2d 191 (2000); *Ellis v. State,* 86 *S.W.*3d 759 (Tex.App. 2002); *State v. Zivcic,* 229 *Wis.*2d 119, 598 *N.W.*2d 565 (1999). Many of those courts have either taken judicial notice of the validity and reliability of horizontal gaze nystagmus testing or concluded that horizontal gaze nystagmus test results are admissible as scientific evidence as a matter of law and, therefore, those courts do not engage in a separate analysis of the first prong." *Commins* at 1079 n.6.

Before such scientific evidence may be admitted, "the court must determine that the evidence is scientifically valid and demonstrably relevant to the facts of the case, not simply valid in the abstract." *Id.* at 1080. Factors to consider "include: (1) whether the methodology has been tested and subjected to peer review, (2) the known or potential rate of error, (3) the prestige and background of the expert witness supporting the evidence, (4) the extent to which the scientific technique in question relies on subjective interpretations and judgments by the testifying expert, and (5) whether the testifying expert can present the methodology underlying his scientific testimony in such a manner that the fact finder can reasonably draw its own conclusions therefrom. *Id.*

The court below found that "the horizontal gaze nystagmus test and its underlying methodology is generally accepted in the scientific community. * * * Our review of the relevant transcript reveals that Forkiotis' testimony * * * provided a factual basis for the court to find that (1) the methodology has been tested and subjected to peer review, (2) there is a known or potential rate of error, (3) Forkiotis was credible and (4) the methodology is explainable to the jury in a manner from which it reasonably could draw its own conclusions. We accordingly conclude that the court properly determined that the horizontal gaze nystagmus evidence adduced at the hearing satisfied the [proper] test for the admission of scientific evidence." *Id.* at 1080-81.

-B-

"The defendant next argues that the state failed to establish that Santucci was qualified to administer and to grade the horizontal gaze nystagmus test[.] The defendant conducted a *voir dire* at trial as to Santucci's training and qualifications. Santucci testified that he had been a police officer for approximately two years and had spent six months at the police academy where he received training in the detection and apprehension of individuals operating motor vehicles while under the influence of liquor. He testified that he successfully completed an advanced detection class on the subject, in which he was taught how to administer and to evaluate the horizontal gaze nystagmus test. In particular, Santucci offered detailed explanations of the theory underlying the test, the mechanics of administering the test and the method used to evaluate a subject's performance. Santucci also demonstrated the test in the courtroom on one of the state's attorneys." *Id.* at 1081.

"As this appeal presents the first opportunity for a Connecticut court to consider whether a police officer was qualified to administer and to grade a horizontal gaze nystagmus test, we look for guidance to other jurisdictions that have considered the issue. In assessing whether a proper foundation has been laid respecting the qualifications of an officer to administer the test, courts have evaluated both the officer's training and experience. Although no mechanical factor test has emerged as dispositive, courts have considered a number of factors, including the length of time the individual has been a police officer, the approximate number of stops the officer has made in that time for operating a motor vehicle while under the influence of intoxicating liquor and any specialized training the officer has received relative to the horizontal gaze nystagmus test." *Id.*

"Applying those factors to the present case, we note that although Santucci's tenure as a police officer was not particularly lengthy and that there was no testimony regarding the approximate number of drunken driving stops he had made during his tenure, he did receive specialized training in horizontal gaze nystagmus testing at the police academy. That training later was reinforced at advanced detection classes and tested through written examinations, which he successfully completed. Santucci also demonstrated his competence by testifying in detail as to how the test was administered, what clues he looked for in grading the test and how the defendant performed. On the basis of the foregoing, we conclude that Santucci's specialized training established that he was qualified to administer and evaluate horizontal gaze nystagmus tests." *Id.* at 1081-82.

-C-

Next is "the question of whether the horizontal gaze nystagmus test was performed properly and in accordance with prevailing standards. We look again for guidance to other jurisdictions that have considered the issue. Those courts indicate that in determining whether a horizontal gaze nystagmus test has been administered properly, a primary consideration is whether a police officer has demonstrated an accurate understanding of the grading system. * * * Courts also have examined whether the test was administered in accordance with the specialized training the officer received. * * * We consider those factors in our analysis." *Id.* at 1082.

"At trial, Santucci both testified as to and demonstrated how he administered the horizontal gaze nystagmus test to the defendant. He explained to the jury the six clues one looks for when grading the test and the number of clues that indicates failure of the test. Furthermore, the defendant neither alleged nor presented evidence indicating that Santucci had administered or graded the test in a manner inconsistent with his specialized training. On the basis of Santucci's uncontroverted testimony, we conclude that the horizontal gaze nystagmus test was performed properly and in accordance with his training." *Id.*

"In light of the foregoing determinations that under the circumstances of this case, (1) the horizontal gaze nystagmus test evidence satisfied the requirements [for the admissibility of scientific evidence], (2) Santucci was qualified to administer the test and (3) the test was performed properly, we conclude that the court properly admitted evidence of the horizontal gaze nystagmus test[.]" *Id.*

---

§7.2. STIPULATIONS

A "stipulation" may be defined as an express agreement, voluntarily entered by the opposing parties, regarding the regulation or disposition of some relevant issue in, or aspect of, a particular case, for the purpose of eliminating the need for formal proof on that aspect or issue.[28] For example, at a suppression hearing, if the only disputed facts are those surrounding the way in which an officer secured a defendant's consent to search his automobile, the parties may eliminate the need for formal proof on the lawfulness of the motor vehicle stop itself by stipulating, for example, that the officer stopped the defendant because he was traveling 70 miles per hour in a 55 mile-per-hour zone.

One unique use of a stipulation was highlighted by the court in *State v. McDavitt.*[29] In open court, McDavitt declared that he was willing to submit to a lie detector test to establish the truth of his claims. Thereafter, the prosecutor and defendant stipulated to a polygraph examination. Ruling the results admissible, the court stated:

> We conclude that polygraph testing has been developed to such a point of reliability that in a criminal case when the State and defendant enter into a stipulation to have defendant submit to a polygraph test, and have the results introduced in evidence, such stipulation should be given effect. Polygraph testing has sufficient probative value to warrant admission under these circumstances.[30]

The court emphasized, however, that "it must appear that the stipulation is clear, unequivocal and complete, freely entered into with full knowledge of the right to refuse the test and the consequences involved in taking it."[31]

---

[28] Stipulations have also been called "judicial admissions." *See* 2 McCormick, *Evidence* §254 (4th ed. 1992), at 142.

[29] 62 *N.J.* 36, 297 *A.*2d 849 (1972).

[30] *Id.,* 62 *N.J.* at 46.

[31] *Id.*

§7.3. PRESUMPTIONS

A "presumption" may be defined as an evidentiary device which permits the factfinder to infer the existence of one fact from proof of others. For example, in a case where the prosecution must prove a crime having four elements, A, B, C and D, a rule of law which permits the establishment of element D to be inferred from proof of A, B and C, is generally described as a presumption. In a criminal case, such a presumption does not, however, relieve the prosecution of its burden of proof of element D. Rather, the presumption operates only to permit the prosecution to make out a *prima facie* case by proof of A, B and C alone. Thereafter, the law instructs the factfinder that it may, but is not required to, infer the existence of element D from proof of elements A, B and C.[32]

Many presumptions exist "to correct an imbalance resulting from one party's superior access to the proof."[33] A classic example is the presumption which arises from proof of facts that a person has disappeared from his home for at least seven years, that during this time those who would be expected to hear from him have heard nothing, and that a reasonably diligent effort has been made to locate him. In such a case, a presumption arises that the person is dead. In a criminal case, an example may be found in the statutory provision which permits the factfinder to infer the existence of a defendant's knowledge of an item's stolen character by proof of the facts that the item was stolen property, that the defendant is in the business of buying or selling property of that sort, and that the defendant failed to ascertain, through reasonable inquiry, that the person from whom he obtained the item had a legal right to possess and dispose of it.[34] Another example may be found in statutes which provide that the presence of a weapon in an automobile is presumptive evidence that it is possessed by all the occupants of the vehicle.[35] In criminal cases, however, presumptions may not be treated as conclusive, they may not shift the burden of proof of any element of the offense onto the defendant, nor may the fact finder give them mandatory effect.[36]

---

[32] McCormick, *Evidence* §346 (West 4th ed 1992), at 481.

[33] *McCormick* §343, at 454.

[34] *See e.g., N.J.S.* 2C:20-7b.(3).

[35] *See County Court of Ulster County v. Allen*, 442 *U.S.* 140, 99 *S.Ct.* 2313 (1979).

[36] *See Sandstrom v. Montana*, 442 *U.S.* 510, 99 *S.Ct.* 2450 (1979) (jury instruction that the "law presumes that a person intends the ordinary consequences of his voluntary acts," by itself, held unconstitutional, for a jury could interpret such an instruction as either shifting the burden of proof upon the defendant or as a conclusive presumption); *Francis v. Franklin*, 471 *U.S.* 307, 105 *S.Ct.* 1965 (1985) (presumptions violate the Due Process Clause if they relieve the State of the burden of proof on an element of the offense).

STATE v. INGRAM
Supreme Court of New Jersey
98 *N.J.* 489, 488 *A.2d* 545 (1985)

The opinion of the Court was delivered by

O'HERN, J.

[*N.J.S.* 2C:39-5b. establishes a third-degree crime for "[a]ny person who knowingly has in his possession any handgun * * * without first having obtained a permit to carry the same as provided in section 2C:58-4."]

"Based upon the definition of the offense in our Code as well as the Code's definition of 'elements of an offense' and 'affirmative defense,' we hold that the absence of a permit is an essential element of the offense [set forth above], and thus, one to be determined by the jury." *Id.*, 98 *N.J.* at 494-95.

"We turn next to the question whether the State may rely upon the statutory presumption of *N.J.S.[]* 2C:39-2 to establish the essential element of the absence of a required permit. Presumptions vary in form, and there is disagreement as to precisely how they operate." *Id.* at 495. [In relevant part, *N.J.S.* 2C:39-2 provides:

> When the legality of a person's conduct under this chapter depends on his possession of a license or permit * * * it shall be presumed that he does not possess such a license or permit * * * until he establishes the contrary.]

"Generally speaking, a presumption is an evidentiary device that enables 'the trier of fact to determine the existence of an element of the crime—that is, an "ultimate" or "elemental" fact—from the existence of one or more "evidentiary" or "basic" facts.' * * * The use of a presumption in a particular criminal case must conform to several requirements that have been established to ensure that the burden always remains upon the prosecution to prove every element of the crime charged beyond a reasonable doubt." *Id.* at 495-96. [Citation omitted.]

"The Code is cautious in directing the application of presumptions. It provides that '[w]hen the code or other statute defining an offense establishes a presumption with respect to any fact which is an element of an offense, it has the meaning accorded it by the law of evidence.' *N.J.S.[]* 2C:1-13e. * * * [Because *Evid.R.* 15] specifically declined to state the meaning to be accorded statutory presumptions in criminal cases[, t]he 'law of evidence' in this context will be found in the judicial authority dealing with criminal presumptions." *Id.* at 496.

" 'The establishment of presumptions favorable to the government in criminal cases and *quasi*-criminal cases raises delicate issues of due process[.]' * * * In general, inquiry as to whether a particular presumption meets constitutional requirements has focused on the degree to which the presumed fact tends, in reality, to flow from the established fact. In *Tot v. United States*, 319 *U.S.* 463, [467-68], 63 *S.Ct.* 1241[, 1245] (1943), that standard was stated as follows:

> [A] statutory presumption cannot be sustained if there be no rational connection between the fact proved and the ultimate fact presumed, if the inference of the one from proof of the other is arbitrary because of lack of connection between the two in common experience. * * *

Ingram at 496.

"While in New Jersey we have employed a similar standard, * * * we have tended to focus upon the jury function as the central issue. In criminal cases, '[t]he ultimate test of any [presumptive] device's constitutional validity remains constant: the device must not undermine the factfinder's responsibility at trial, based on the evidence adduced by the State, to find the ultimate facts beyond a reasonable doubt.' " *Id.* at 497.

"In sum, the validity of a statutory presumption with respect to a criminal offense rests upon two basic criteria: '[t]he first is simply that there must be a rational connection in terms of logical probability between the proved fact and the presumed fact. The second is that the presumption may not be accorded mandatory effect.' " *Id.* at 498.

"Thus, 'the meaning accorded * * * by the law of evidence,' * * * to the statutory presumption of *N.J.S.[]* 2C:39-2 is that *a jury may be permitted to infer, until the defendant comes forward with some evidence to the contrary, that the defendant does not possess the required license or permit to carry a dangerous weapon.* Permitting the jury to make such an inference does not offend our notions of due process." *Id.* at 498. [Emphasis added.]

"[Gun permits are] issued in written form. *N.J.S.[]* 2C:58-4. The current form of the permit required under *N.J.A.C.* 13:54-2.2 states that the owner must be in possession of the permit when carrying the handgun. There is nothing irrational about inferring that it would be produced if it in fact existed." *Id.* at 499.

"In sum, we hold that (1) the absence of a required permit is an essential element of a weapons offense as defined under *N.J.S.[]* 2C:39-5; (2) once possession of a weapon is shown and an accused fails to come forward with evidence of a permit, the State may employ the statutory presumption of *N.J.S.[]* 2C:39-2 to establish that absence of the required permit; and (3) a jury should be instructed that although such a statute authorizes the inference that there is no such permit, the ultimate burden of persuasion rests on the State, with the jury being at liberty to find the ultimate fact one way or the other." *Id.* at 500.

NOTE

1. *Jury to be instructed in terms of "inferences," not "presumptions."*

(a) During the course of its opinion in *Ingram*, the Court emphasized that "[c]entral to the validity of a statutory presumption is the way that the matter is presented to the jury." *Id.* at 499. In this regard, the Court reiterated, " '[t]he jury should be instructed in terms of inferences which may or may not be drawn from a fact, the jury being at liberty to find the ultimate fact one way or the other.' " *Id.* [Citation omitted.] *See also State v. Humphreys*, 54 *N.J.* 406, 255 *A.*2d 273 (1969), where the Court instructed: "[t]he jury must be carefully informed that an inference of one fact from another is never binding; the use of the term 'presumptive evidence' could have been misleading[.] * * * Jury instructions employing the term 'presumption' instead of describing an inference have been held to be reversible error, since they shift a burden from the State to the defendant." *Id.*, 54 *N.J.* at 415-16.

(b) *N.J.S.* 2C:39-2a. provides in pertinent part: "When a * * * weapon * * * is found in a vehicle, it is presumed to be in the possession of the occupant if there is but one. If there is more than one occupant in the vehicle, it shall be presumed to be in the possession of all, except [under certain circumstances]." In *State v. Bolton*, 230 *N.J.Super.* 476, 553 *A.*2d 881 (App.Div. 1989), defendant was charged with fourth-degree possession of a knife under circumstances not manifestly appropriate for such lawful uses as it may have, under *N.J.S.* 2C:39-5d. An officer observed the knife protruding from an ashtray of the car which defendant was driving. Defendant testified that the knife belonged to a passenger in the car.

According to the court, at no time should the jury be instructed that it "may 'presume' that a knife in an ashtray of a motor vehicle is possessed by all the occupants. Rather, the jury may be advised that it can draw an inference if it finds it more probable than not that the inference is true." *Id.*, 230 *N.J.Super.* at 480.

2. *The unexplained possession of recently stolen property.* As a general rule, the exclusive and unexplained possession of recently stolen property gives rise to an inference that the possessor is the thief. *See e.g., State v. Alexander*, 215 *N.J.Super.* 523, 530, 522 *A.*2d 464 (App.Div. 1987). *Cf. Barnes v. United States*, 412 *U.S.* 837, 93 *S.Ct.* 2357 (1973) (approving an instruction that "[p]ossession of recently stolen property, if not satisfactorily explained, is ordinarily a circumstance from which [the jury may infer] that the person in possession knew the property had been stolen"). Moreover, it is widely recognized that even where the defendant and other alleged perpetrators are found in "joint possession"

of recently stolen property, the inference still obtains. *See e.g.,*
United States v. Johnson, 563 *F.*2d 936, 941-42 (8th Cir. 1977);
State v. Cobb, 444 *S.W.*2d 408, 412 (Mo. 1969); *People v. Haggart,*
188 *Colo.* 164, 533 *P.*2d 488, 491 (1975); *Snyder v. State,* 661 *P.*2d
638, 641-42 (Alaska Ct.App. 1983). As the court explained in
Flamer v. State, 227 *A.*2d 123, 126-27 (Del. 1967):

> [T]he requirement that "possession" must be exclusive, in order
> to incriminate, does not mean that the possession must neces-
> sarily be separate from all others. An "exclusive possession"
> may be the joint possession of two or more acting in concert.
> Where the only persons having control of, or access to, the sto-
> len property are the defendant and his co-conspirators, joint
> possession of the stolen property may incriminate the defen-
> dant as well as his confederates.

Id. at 127.

COMMONWEALTH v. DiFRANCESCO
Supreme Court of Pennsylvania
458 *Pa.* 188, 329 *A.*2d 204 (1974)

POMEROY, Justice.
"These four consolidated appeals challenge the constitutionality
of [that section] of the Vehicle Code, which provides that if the
amount of alcohol by weight in the blood of a person accused of driving under the influence is shown by chemical analysis to be ten one-
hundredths percent (.10%) or more, 'it shall be presumed that the
defendant was under the influence of intoxicating liquor.'" *Id.* at 205.

"[W]e note that nothing in [the statute] relieves the Commonwealth of its burden of laying a proper foundation for the introduction of the test results showing the amount of alcohol in the defendant's blood. Nor does the statute compel a verdict of guilty on the
basis of such test results alone." *Id.* at 207.

"What the statute refers to as a 'presumption' is, strictly speaking, only a standardized inference. Although the terms 'inference'
and 'presumption' are often used interchangeably, this Court has
adhered to the prevailing view among legal commentators and
drawn a distinction between these two concepts. * * * According to
this view, an inference is merely a logical tool which permits the
trier of fact to proceed from one fact to another. A presumption, on
the other hand, is a procedural device which not only permits an
inference of the 'presumed' fact, but also shifts the burden of producing evidence to disprove the presumed fact. Failure to meet this burden of production will normally result in binding instructions on the

issue of the presumed fact's existence in favor of the party invoking the presumption. But the notion of a directed verdict against a criminal defendant is contrary to accepted tenets of criminal justice. Placing the burden of production on a defendant under the threat of such a sanction would run afoul of the presumption of innocence. * * * Thus, where the presumed fact comprises an element of the crime charged, the inference authorized by a presumption can never be compelled by the court. * * * From this perspective, all so-called 'criminal presumptions' are really no more than permissible inferences." *Id.* at 207-08 n. 2.

In enacting this section of the Motor Vehicle Code, "the legislature considered evidence demonstrating that, in virtually all drivers, driving ability is significantly affected by a blood-alcohol content of 0.10 percent or more. * * * [However, what this section of the Code describes] as a 'presumption' is really no more than an inference which the jury may accept or reject in the light of all the evidence in the case." *Id.* at 210, 211. "The statute does not, of course, prevent defendants from calling expert witnesses to rebut the statutory inference." *Id.* at 210 n. 12.

Accordingly, "[t]he jury should be instructed that the test results are evidence that the defendant was under the influence of intoxicating liquor, and permit a finding to that effect; but that such a finding is not mandatory; that the test results should be considered together with all the other evidence in the case; and that if there is a reasonable doubt in the minds of the jurors as to whether the defendant was under the influence of intoxicating liquor, they should return a verdict of 'not guilty.' " *Id.* at 211.

Chapter 8

PRIVILEGES

§8.1. GENERAL CONSIDERATIONS

As a matter of sound public policy, the law seeks to preserve and foster between people certain relationships which would be placed in jeopardy if confidential communications between them were disclosed to uninvited ears. To further this end, a body of law has developed which protects confidential communications by providing a "privilege" from disclosure in a court proceeding when such communications are genuinely made "in confidence" and during the course of one of the "formal relationships" protected under the law.

Unlike other aspects of the criminal law and rules of evidence, the principles and rules pertaining to privileges do not promote "the truth, the whole truth, and nothing but the truth."[1]

[T]he rules of privilege, of which the most familiar are the rule protecting against self-incrimination and those shielding the confidentiality of communications between husband and wife, attorney and client, and physician and patient, are not designed or intended to facilitate the fact-finding process or to safeguard its integrity. Their effect instead is clearly inhibitive; rather than facilitating the illumination of truth, they shut out the light.[2]

Because privileges have a tendency to hide, rather than reveal, the truth, courts will construe them "narrowly in an attempt to promote, at once, the goals of the privilege and the truthseeking role of the courts."[3]

"A unique characteristic of privilege is that the right to assert the privilege, and thus cause the exclusion of privileged evidence, belongs to the person (or persons) vested with the interest or relationship protected by the privilege—the holder(s)."[4] The holder of the privilege may or may not be a party in the case. If the holder is

---

[1] *See* 1 McCormick, *Evidence* §72 (4th ed. 1992), at 269.

[2] *Id. See also State v. Schreiber,* 122 *N.J.* 579, 582, 585 *A.2d* 945 (1991).

[3] *State v. Schreiber,* 122 *N.J.* at 582-83. *See also United States v. Nixon,* 418 *U.S.* 683, 710, 94 *S.Ct.* 3090, 3108 (1974) ("Whatever their origins, these exceptions to the demand of every man's evidence are not lightly created nor expansively construed, for they are in derogation of the search for the truth.").

[4] Lilly, *An Introduction to the Law of Evidence* §9.1 (2nd ed. 1987), at 382.

a party in the case, he or she is conveniently situated to assert the privilege. If the holder is not a party in the case, then neither party has standing to object to the use of privileged information. Thus, the privilege "is reserved for the holder, who may or may not wish to exercise it."[5] Naturally, like many legal rights, the privilege may be waived by its holder.

The drafters of the *Federal Rules of Evidence* originally proposed a number of rules relating to privilege. Those rules, however, were never formally adopted. Yet, the "proposed" rules of privilege remain in the text of the federal rules as guides for interpretation, and many jurisdictions have either treated them as persuasive rules to follow in construing their own common law of privilege, or have adopted the proposed rules.[6] As a result, the basic rules of privilege are reasonably consistent across jurisdictional lines.

In the sections that follow, a number of privileges have been selected for discussion. Those selected represent the more common privileges with which a law enforcement official may be confronted.[7]

---

§8.2. PRIVILEGE AGAINST SELF-INCRIMINATION

In addition to the testimonial privileges which arise as a result of certain confidential communications made during the course of a protected relationship, is the Fifth Amendment privilege, which requires no particular type of interpersonal "relationship." In this respect, the Self-Incrimination Clause of the Fifth Amendment commands that no person "shall be compelled in any criminal case to be a witness against himself."[8] As can be seen, the words of the Amendment do not describe the various ways in which a person may be "a witness against himself." The United States Supreme Court has held, however, that the privilege to be free from compelled self-incrimination does not protect a criminal suspect from being compelled by the prosecution to produce "real or physical

---

[5] *Id.* at 382.

[6] *See Lilly* at 384-85; *McCormick* at 283. As originally proposed, the *Federal Rules of Evidence* contained nine non-constitutional privileges: required reports (502), attorney-client (503), psychotherapist-patient (504), husband-wife (505), clergyman-communicant (506), political vote (507), trade secrets (508), secrets of state and other official information (509), and identity of informer (510).

[7] "A general word of caution: care must be taken to examine statutory materials whenever a question of privilege is raised. Most privileges are now embodied in statutory provisions," while others may still be found in the case law. *Lily* at 384.

[8] *U.S.Const. Amend. V.* The privilege against self-incrimination is applicable to the states through the Fourteenth Amendment. *Malloy v. Hogan*, 378 *U.S.* 1, 84 *S.Ct.* 1489 (1964).

evidence."[9] "Rather, the privilege 'protects an accused only from being compelled to testify against himself, or otherwise provide the State with evidence of a testimonial or communicative nature.' "[10] In order to be "testimonial or communicative" in nature, the "accused's communication must itself, explicitly or implicitly, relate a factual assertion or disclose information. Only then is a person compelled to be a 'witness against himself.' "[11]

The privilege to be free from self-incrimination is not limited to communications uttered in a courtroom from the witness stand. The privilege additionally protects criminal suspects from the inherent pressures which attach to custodial interrogation.[12] "Of course, voluntary statements offered to police officers 'remain a proper element in law enforcement.' "[13]

---

§8.3. HUSBAND-WIFE PRIVILEGE

"An accused in a criminal proceeding has a privilege to prevent his spouse from testifying against him."[14] "The privilege may be claimed by the accused or by the spouse on his behalf," and "[t]he authority of the spouse to do so is presumed in the absence of evidence to the contrary."[15] The privilege will not apply, however, in proceedings in which "one spouse is charged with a crime against the person or property of the other, or with a crime against the person or property of a third person committed in the course of committing a crime against the other."[16] Nor will the privilege protect

---

[9] *Schmerber v. California*, 384 *U.S.* 757, 764, 86 *S.Ct.* 1826, 1832 (1966).

[10] *Pennsylvania v. Muniz*, 496 *U.S.* 582, 110 *S.Ct.* 2638, 2643 (1990) (quoting *Schmerber* at 761, 86 *S.Ct.* at 1830.

[11] *Doe v. United States*, 487 *U.S.* 201, 210, 108 *S.Ct.* 2341, 2347 (1988).

[12] *See Miranda v. Arizona*, 384 *U.S.* 436, 461, 86 *S.Ct.* 1602, 1620-21 (1966). *Miranda* protects the privilege against compelled self-incrimination during pretrial questioning by requiring law enforcement officials to adhere to certain "procedural safeguards." The Court held that "[p]rior to any questioning, the person must be warned that he has a right to remain silent, that any statement he does make may be used as evidence against him, and that he has a right to the presence of an attorney, either retained or appointed." *Id.* at 444, 86 *S.Ct.* at 1612. Unless the accused "voluntarily, knowingly and intelligently waives these rights," *id.*, any statements obtained, as a result of custodial interrogation, will be inadmissible at trial in the prosecution's case-in-chief.

[13] *Pennsylvania v. Muniz, supra*, 110 *S.Ct.* at 2644 (quoting *Miranda* at 478, 86 *S.Ct.* at 1630).

[14] *See Proposed Fed.R.Evid.* 505(a).

[15] *See Proposed Fed.R.Evid.* 505(b).

[16] *Proposed Fed.R.Evid.* 505(c)(1).

those "matters occurring prior to the marriage."[17] The traditional justifications for this aspect of the husband-wife privilege—the marital "privilege against adverse testimony"—have been "the prevention of marital dissension and the repugnancy of requiring a person to condemn or be condemned by his spouse."[18]

Another aspect of the husband-wife privilege is the privilege for "confidential marital communications." While the proposed federal rules do not recognize a privilege for confidential communications, such a privilege is recognized in numerous jurisdictions. In order for a marital communication to be considered privileged, the communication must have been (1) a *confidential* statement, (2) made *between spouses*, (3) during the course of a *legal marriage*.[19] This aspect of the husband-wife privilege is most often

> justified on the ground that it promotes marital harmony. The theory usually invoked by courts is that the privilege encourages marital partners to share their most closely-guarded secrets and thoughts, thus adding an additional measure of intimacy and mutual support to the marriage.[20]

Before a trial court will permit this aspect of the privilege to be invoked, there must be a showing that the statement or communication was made "in confidence." Communications made "in private between husband and wife are assumed to be confidential."[21] Marital communications made in the known presence of a third party, however, will fail for lack of confidentiality.[22] Moreover, "the privilege does not attach unless the court finds from all of the surrounding circumstances that the statements were intended to be imparted in confidence."[23] The court must also find that the confidential communication was made "between spouses" during a "legal marriage." Confidential communications made prior to marriage or after divorce do

---

[17] *Proposed Fed.R.Evid.* 505(c)(2). *Rule* 505(c)(3) further provides that the privilege will not apply in proceedings in which a spouse is charged with importing an alien for prostitution or other immoral purpose, or with transporting a female in interstate commerce for immoral purposes.

[18] *Advisory Committee's Note to Proposed Fed.R.Evid.* 505. *See also* 8 Wigmore, *Evidence* §§2228, 2241 (McNaughton Rev. 1961).

[19] Lilly, *An Introduction to the Law of Evidence* §9.3 (2nd ed. 1987), at 387.

[20] *Lilly* at 386.

[21] 1 McCormick, *Evidence* §80 (4th ed. 1992), at 299.

[22] *See Pereira v. United States*, 347 *U.S.* 1, 74 *S.Ct.* 358 (1954) ("The presence of a third party negatives the presumption of privacy."); *People v. Ressler*, 17 *N.Y.*2d 174, 269 *N.Y.S.*2d 414, 216 *N.E.*2d 582 (1966) (privilege denied to communication between husband and wife in presence of homicide victim prior to the husband killing the victim).

[23] *Lilly* at 388.

not qualify. The privilege may also be denied to confidential communications uttered between "permanently separated couples,"[24] and unmarried couples merely "living together."[25] Once it is determined that the confidential communication is privileged, most courts hold that the privilege remains intact, notwithstanding the subsequent termination of the marriage by divorce or death.[26]

Accordingly, it is important to distinguish between the husband-wife privilege which relates to adverse testimony, and the privilege which protects confidential communications. The privilege which allows a witness-spouse to refuse to testify, or a defendant-spouse to block testimony, is concerned not necessarily with confidential information, but with knowledge of damaging information (confidential or otherwise) which, if told on the witness stand, would likely damage or destroy the marriage. The testimonial privilege will block "adverse testimony based on knowledge gained in any way, at any time, even if it is common knowledge, if the accused and the proposed witness are married at the time of trial."[27] Unlike the privilege for confidential communications, the privilege of each spouse against adverse testimony terminates when the marriage ends by death or divorce.[28]

---

§8.4. MARRIAGE COUNSELOR PRIVILEGE

In some jurisdictions, a privilege is recognized for confidential communications exchanged between a marriage counselor and the person counseled. The following is one example:

> Any communication between a marriage counselor and the person or persons counseled shall be confidential and its secrecy preserved. This privilege shall not be subject to waiver, except where the marriage counselor is a party defendant to a civil, criminal or disciplinary action arising from such counseling, in which case, the waiver shall be limited to that action.[29]

---

[24] *See United States v. Byrd*, 750 *F*.2d 585 (7th Cir. 1984).

[25] *McCormick*, §81, at 301.

[26] *See e.g., United States v. Pensinger*, 549 *F*.2d 1150 (8th Cir. 1977).

[27] *Lilly* at 392.

[28] *McCormick*, §85, at 308.

[29] *N.J.Evid.R.* 510; *N.J.S.* 45:8B-29.

§8.5. ATTORNEY-CLIENT PRIVILEGE

It has been said that the "attorney-client" privilege is the oldest of the privileges for confidential communications known to the common law.[30] "Its purpose is to encourage full and frank communication between attorneys and their clients and thereby promote broader public interests in the observance of the law and administration of justice. The privilege recognizes that sound legal advice or advocacy serves public ends and that such advice or advocacy depends upon the lawyer being fully informed by the client. * * * '[It] rests on the need for the advocate and counselor to know all that relates to the client's reasons for seeking representation if the professional mission is to be carried out.' "[31] Thus, the privilege seeks to " 'encourage clients to make full disclosure to their attorneys.' "[32]

In *State v. Toscano*,[33] the court further explained that though the early origins of the attorney-client privilege

> involved consideration for the oath and honor of the attorney it is now universally recognized as resting upon the policy in favor of affording to the client freedom from apprehension in consulting his legal advisor. * * * Since the protection of the privileged communication is not for the lawyer but for the client[,] * * * waiver thereof rests with the client.[34]

Proposed *Fed.R.Evid.* 503 grants a privilege to a "client" to "refuse to disclose and to prevent any other person from disclosing confidential communications made for the purpose of facilitating the rendition of professional legal services to the client[.]"[35] The privilege protects confidential communications exchanged between the client

> or his representative and his lawyer or his lawyer's representative, or (2) between his lawyer and the lawyer's representative, or (3) by him or his lawyer to a lawyer representing another in a matter of common interest, or (4) between representatives of the client or between the client and a representative of the client, or (5) between lawyers representing the client.[36]

---

[30] *UpJohn Co. v. United States*, 449 *U.S.* 383, 389, 101 *S.Ct.* 677, 682 (1981).

[31] *Id.* at 389, 101 *S.Ct.* at 682. [Citation omitted.]

[32] *Id.* [Citations omitted.]

[33] 13 *N.J.* 418, 100 *A.*2d 170 (1953).

[34] *Id.*, 13 *N.J.* at 424. [Citations omitted.]

[35] *Proposed Fed.R.Evid.* 503(b).

[36] *Id.*

The rule defines "client" as any person, corporation, or other entity "who is rendered professional legal services by a lawyer, or who consults a lawyer with a view to obtaining professional legal services from him."[37] The consultation must concern a *legal* matter, that is, the client must be seeking *legal advice*. The privilege will not attach to confidential communications between a lawyer and client over matters of business, accounting, banking, sporting events, friendship or the like.

"Attorney" or "lawyer" is defined as "a person authorized, or reasonably believed by the client to be authorized, to practice law."[38] In order for the privilege to attach, the client must *reasonably believe* he or she is consulting a lawyer for the purpose of obtaining legal advice. If it is later learned that the person consulted was not a lawyer, the privilege nonetheless remains intact. For example, in *People v. Barker,*[39] the attorney-client privilege was successfully invoked to shield from disclosure a suspect's confession to a detective who pretended to be a lawyer.

A communication will be deemed "confidential" so long as it is "not intended to be disclosed to third persons other than those to whom disclosure is in furtherance of the rendition of professional legal services to the client."[40] Recent cases require the client to take "all reasonable precautions to keep the information in question confidential; if this is done, the privilege will survive an *unintended* disclosure to third persons."[41] Information disclosed to the attorney's law clerk, paralegal, investigator or similar representative is treated as a communication made directly to the attorney. Those individuals are considered to be included under the umbrella of the privilege.

The attorney-client privilege thus "prevents testimonial disclosure, discovery, or seizure by subpoena of confidential communications between an attorney and his client, unless the client waives the privilege."[42] The privilege first attaches when a prospective client initially consults a lawyer about a legal matter. "These preliminary discussions remain privileged even if the attorney is not retained. The privilege applies during any representation that follows and persists after the attorney-client relationship ends."[43] Moreover, "[t]he privilege belongs only to the client, and therefore the lawyer

---

[37] *Proposed Fed.R.Evid.* 503(a)(1). Payment of a fee, or the promise of payment, is not required. *See United States v. Costanzo,* 625 *F.*2d 465 (3rd Cir. 1980).

[38] *Proposed Fed.R.Evid.* 503(a)(2).

[39] 60 *Mich.* 277, 27 *N.W.* 539, 546 (1886).

[40] *Proposed Fed.R.Evid.* 503(a)(4).

[41] Lilly, *An Introduction to the Law of Evidence* §9.6 (2nd ed. 1987), at 399. [Emphasis added.] *See also In re Grand Jury Proceedings Involving Berkley & Co.,* 466 *F.Supp.* 863, 869 (D.Minn. 1979).

[42] *Lilly* at 396.

[43] *Id.* If, however, during the course of preliminary discussions the services of the attorney are turned down, statements made thereafter are not protected. *See McGrede v. Rembert Nat. Bank,* 147 *N.W.*2d 580 (Tex.Civ.Ct.App. 1941).

may not claim the privilege when the client waives it, nor waive the privilege without the client's consent."[44]

There are several exceptions to the attorney-client privilege. There is no privilege under the rule if a client seeks an attorney's services for the purpose of committing a crime or facilitating a fraud.[45] The privilege will not attach to communications relevant to an issue involving a breach of duty owed by the attorney to the client or by the client to the attorney.[46] Nor will the privilege protect a communication relevant to an issue concerning an attested document to which the attorney is an attesting witness.[47]

NIX v. WHITESIDE
Supreme Court of the United States
475 U.S. 157, 106 S.Ct. 988 (1986)

Chief Justice BURGER delivered the opinion of the Court.

[Whiteside was convicted of the second-degree murder of a Cedar Rapids, Iowa, man.] "Whiteside and two others went to one Calvin Love's apartment late [one] night, seeking marihuana. Love was in bed when Whiteside and his companions arrived; an argument between Whiteside and Love over the marihuana ensued. At one point, Love directed his girlfriend to get his 'piece,' and at another point got up, then returned to his bed. According to Whiteside's testimony, Love then started to reach under his pillow and moved toward Whiteside. Whiteside stabbed Love in the chest, inflicting a fatal wound." *Id.* at 990-91.

Gary Robinson was appointed to represent Whiteside. Whiteside told Robinson in confidence that he had never "actually seen a gun, but that he was convinced that Love had a gun. No pistol was found on the premises * * *. Robinson advised Whiteside that the existence of a gun was not necessary to establish the claim of self-defense, and that only a reasonable belief that the victim had a gun nearby was necessary even though no gun was actually present." *Id.* at 991.

"About a week before trial, during preparation for [his testimony,] Whiteside for the first time told Robinson * * * that he had seen something 'metallic' in Love's hand. When asked about this, Whiteside responded: * * * 'If I don't say I saw a gun, I'm dead.' Robinson told Whiteside that such testimony would be perjury and repeated

---

[44] *Lilly* at 405-06.

[45] *Proposed Fed.R.Evid.* 503(d)(1). Communications about "past" crimes, however, are protected by the privilege.

[46] *Proposed Fed.R.Evid.* 503(d)(3).

[47] *Proposed Fed.R.Evid.* 503(d)(4).

that it was not necessary to prove that a gun was available but only that Whiteside reasonably believed he was in danger." *Id.* Whiteside insisted that he would testify that he saw "something metallic" in Love's hand. Robinson again told Whiteside that such testimony would be perjury and advised Whiteside that if he did testify in that way the judge would have to be told. "Robinson also indicated that he would seek to withdraw from the representation if Whiteside insisted on committing perjury." *Id.* Whiteside did not commit perjury. He was, however, convicted of second-degree murder.

In this appeal, Whiteside argues that he had been denied a fair trial because his attorney did not allow him to testify that he "saw a gun or something metallic" in Love's hand.

"[T]o obtain relief * * * on a claim of a deprivation of effective assistance of counsel under the Sixth Amendment, the [defend]ant must establish both serious attorney error and prejudice." *Id.* 993.

The question in this case concerns "the definition of the range of 'reasonable professional' responses to a criminal defendant client who informs counsel that he will perjure himself on the stand." *Id.* at 994.

"[We have] recognized counsel's duty of loyalty and his 'overarching duty to advocate the defendant's cause.' [] Plainly, that duty is limited to legitimate, lawful conduct compatible with the very nature of a trial as a search for truth. Although counsel must take all reasonable lawful means to attain the objectives of the client, counsel is precluded from taking steps or in any way assisting the client in presenting false evidence or otherwise violating the law. This principle has * * * been recognized * * * since the first Canons of Professional Ethics were adopted by the American Bar Association in 1908. The 1908 Canon 32 provided:

> 'No client, ... however powerful, nor any cause, ... however important, is entitled to receive, nor should any lawyer render, any service or advice involving disloyalty to the law whose ministers we are, or disrespect of the judicial office, which we are bound to uphold, or corruption of any person or persons exercising a public office or private trust, or deception or betrayal of the public. ... He must ... observe and advise his client to observe the [] law. ... ' "

Id.

"Similarly, Canon 37, adopted in 1928, explicitly acknowledges as an exception to the attorney's duty of confidentiality a client's announced intention to commit a crime:

> 'The announced intention of a client to commit a crime is not included within the confidences which [the attorney] is bound to respect.' "

Id.

"These principles have been carried through to contemporary codifications of an attorney's professional responsibility. Disciplinary Rule 7-102 of the Model Code of Professional Responsibility * * * provides:

'(A) In his representation of a client, a lawyer shall not:

* * * * *

(4) Knowingly use perjured testimony or false evidence.

* * * * *

(7) Counsel or assist his client in conduct that the lawyer knows to be illegal or fraudulent.' "

Id. The rules clearly articulate a "specific exception from the attorney-client privilege for disclosure of perjury that his client intends to commit or has committed." *Id.* at 995.

"These standards confirm that the legal profession has accepted that an attorney's ethical duty to advance the interests of his client is limited by an equally solemn duty to comply with the law and standards of professional conduct; it specifically ensures that the client may not use false evidence. This special duty of an attorney to prevent and disclose frauds upon the court derives from the recognition that perjury is as much a crime as tampering with witnesses or jurors by way of promises and threats, and undermines the administration of justice." *Id.*

"Considering Robinson's representation of [Whiteside] in light of these accepted norms of professional conduct, we discern no failure to adhere to reasonable professional standards that would in any sense make out a deprivation of the Sixth Amendment right to counsel." *Id.* at 996.

---

§8.6. ACCOUNTANT-CLIENT PRIVILEGE

Confidential communications made to an accountant are privileged in some states. Pennsylvania's statute is illustrative:

> Except by permission of the client[,] * * * a certified public accountant, public accountant, partnership or corporation, * * * or a person employed by [the same], * * * shall not be required to, and shall not voluntarily, disclose or divulge information of which he may have become possessed relative to and in connection with any professional services as a certified public accountant, public accountant, partnership or corporation. The information derived from or as the result of such professional services shall be deemed confidential and privileged[.]"[48]

The privilege does not, however, prohibit disclosure of information required to be disclosed to a court of law or in a disciplinary investigation or proceeding when the professional services of the accountant, partnership or corporation are at issue.[49]

---

[48] 63 *P.S.* §9.11(a).

[49] *Id.*

§8.7. PHYSICIAN-PATIENT PRIVILEGE

The physician-patient privilege is more a creature of statute than of common law.[50] Beginning as far back as, perhaps, 1828,[51] state legislatures across the country began adopting statutes designed to protect confidential communications made to a physician for purposes of diagnosis and treatment of illness, disease or injury. The privilege is designed to encourage patients to fully and honestly disclose information regarding their physical or mental conditions so as to assist their treating physicians in the process of diagnosis and treatment. The privilege spares the patient from being placed in the potentially embarrassing position of having his or her most "private details concerning health and bodily condition" exposed in a courtroom.[52]

In order for the physician-patient privilege to attach, the individual calling on the doctor must be a "patient." To meet this requirement, it is sufficient if the individual consulted the physician for the purpose of seeking medical treatment or diagnosis.[53] "If the patient's purpose in the consultation is an unlawful one, as to obtain narcotics in violation of law, or as * * * a fugitive from justice to have his appearance disguised by plastic surgery, the law withholds the shield of the privilege."[54] Next, the individual consulted must be a "physician." The statutes generally require the individual to be a licensed medical doctor. In this respect, court decisions have excluded from the privilege such practitioners as dentists, optometrists, and chiropractors.[55] Further, like the attorney-client privilege, the communication or disclosure made to the physician must have been made in "confidence." The presence of casual third parties, excluding nurses, other doctors, technicians, etc., will destroy the privilege.[56]

The privilege has generally been held to apply in both civil and criminal cases. There are several states, however, that deny the privilege in criminal cases,[57] or limit its application to certain offenses.[58]

---

[50] See State v. Schreiber, 122 N.J. 579, 583, 585 A.2d 945 (1991). See also 1 McCormick, Evidence §98 (4th ed. 1992), at 368 ("The common law knew no privilege for confidential information imparted to a physician.").

[51] N.Y.Rev.Stat. 1828, vol. II, Part III, c. 7, Tit. 3, art. 8, §73.

[52] McCormick, §98, at 369.

[53] Court-ordered medical examinations, examinations for the purpose of securing life insurance, and examinations designed to facilitate litigation are generally outside the scope of the privilege. See generally, McCormick at § 99; Lilly at §9.10.

[54] McCormick at 374-75.

[55] See id. at 372-73 n.1 (cataloging cases).

[56] See e.g., State v. Phillips, 213 N.J.Super. 534, 541, 517 A. 1204 (App.Div. 1986) (Had the police chief wanted his conversation with the doctors to remain confidential, he should have told the officers standing by him to leave the room.).

[57] See e.g., Cal.Evid.Code §998; Idaho Code §9-203(4); Commonwealth v. Ellis, 415 Pa.Super. 220, 608 A.2d 1090, 1092 (1992) ("in Pennsylvania, the physician-patient privilege does not apply in criminal proceedings").

[58] See e.g., Kan.Stat. §60-427(b) (privilege inapplicable to felonies).

STATE v. SCHREIBER
Supreme Court of New Jersey
122 N.J. 579, 585 A.2d 945 (1991)

The opinion of the Court was delivered by

GARIBALDI, J.

"The narrow issue in this appeal is whether the patient-physician privilege * * * precludes the admission into evidence, at defendant's trial for driving while under the influence of alcohol, of defendant's blood test, which was voluntarily disclosed to the police by an emergency room physician. That ultimate question, whether or not the doctor's revelations violated the patient-physician privilege, depends on our answer to the penultimate question of whether defendant's violation of the Motor Vehicles Act, more particularly, *N.J.S.[]* 39:4-50, driving while under the influence of alcohol (DWI), is 'a crime or violation of the disorderly persons law[.]' " *Id.*, 122 *N.J.* at 580-81. [Citation omitted.]

"[D]efendant, Linda Schreiber, driving alone, was involved in a one-car accident. Her car skidded back and forth off of and onto the roadway. Finally, it left the roadway, flipped over and came to rest upside down in a grassy area near the roadway. Ms. Schreiber was thrown from the car, sustaining serious injuries that necessitated a one-month hospital stay." *Id.* at 581.

"Because of Ms. Schreiber's extensive injuries, the rescue squad rushed her to the Princeton Medical Center. The police officers, Sergeant Erdelsky and Patrolman Simonelli, therefore, were not able to speak to her at the scene." *Id.*

"Ms. Schreiber, injured and unconscious, was admitted to the hospital through its emergency room, where the medical staff conducted several tests, including a blood test. Although neither police officer was present nor requested such a test, the medical staff administered it for diagnostic reasons." *Id.*

Almost a month later, "an emergency-room physician at the Princeton Medical Center called the [] Police Department and revealed that the blood test showed Ms. Schreiber's blood alcohol level to be .26% at the time of her admission to the hospital. * * * Based on this new information, Sergeant Erdelsky then issued Ms. Schreiber additional summonses for DWI * * * and careless driving." *Id.*

The hospital record containing the results of the blood-alcohol test was introduced at trial and Ms. Schreiber was found guilty of DWI. In this appeal, she argues that the blood test results should have been suppressed due to a violation of the patient-physician privilege. *We disagree.*

"Of privileges, it has been noted that 'their effect . . . is clearly inhibitive; rather than facilitating the illumination of truth, they shut out the light.' * * * Nonetheless, for reasons considered important by society, witnesses are permitted to withhold relevant,

often invaluable, evidence from the search for truth." *Id.* at 582.
[Citation omitted.]

Because privileges have such effect, courts here and elsewhere
have long construed them narrowly in an attempt to promote, at
once, the goals of the privilege and the truthseeking role of the
courts." *Id.* at 582-83.

"The patient-physician privilege, which did not exist at common
law, was added to New Jersey's legal landscape by statute in 1968.
The relevant portion of that statute reads:

> *Communications between physician and patient considered
> privileged under certain circumstances.* Except as otherwise
> provided in this act, a person, whether or not a party, has a
> privilege in a civil action or in a prosecution for a *crime or viola-
> tion of the disorderly persons law or for an act of juvenile delin-
> quency* to refuse to disclose, and to prevent a witness from dis-
> closing, a communication, if he claims the privilege and the
> judge finds that (a) the communication was a confidential com-
> munication between patient and physician * * *.

Id. at 583 (quoting *N.J.S.* 2A:84A-22.2) (court's emphasis).

"Crimes in New Jersey are defined by the Code of Criminal Justice * * *. This court has recently reaffirmed that motor vehicle violations, including violations of a DWI statute, are not offenses under that Code. * * * [Therefore,] violation of a DWI statute is not a
crime in New Jersey." *Id.* at 584.

Moreover, since 1921, the Legislature has not considered motor
vehicle violations to be disorderly persons offenses.

Accordingly, because the statutory patient-physician privilege
"does not cover DWI offenses, like the present one, * * * [Ms.
Schreiber's] statutorily-created and -defined interest has not been
infringed[.]"

"Nevertheless, our decision here, although outside the legally-
applicable privilege, does potentially affect the patient-physician
relationship. We understand that

> [p]hysicians must often elicit extremely confidential and poten-
> tially embarrassing information from patients in order to diag-
> nose and treat a physical ailment. Patients might hesitate to
> communicate that information to physicians if they believed
> disclosure could be compelled by a court. For instance, when
> New York required doctors to report to a state agency the
> names of all patients who were prescribed certain narcotic
> medications, a few patients discontinued use of the medications
> or began obtaining them in another state. This evidence sug-
> gests that some patients might forgo treatment rather than risk

the public stigma that might follow from disclosure of medical information. [*Developments in the Law—Privileged Communications*, 98 *Harv.L.Rev.* 1450, 1543 (1985).]

The patient-physician privilege, as enacted by the Legislature, is but one method of promoting and strengthening a relationship that is valued by society." *Id.* at 587.

"Notwithstanding recurrent concerns over the application of a testimonial privilege, we have long understood that the law should acknowledge the ethical duties imposed on physicians by their profession while the judicial system engages in the search for the truth. * * * However, we are not called upon to decide whether the emergency-room physician violated any ethical duty imposed on him by his profession. He volunteered the information to police without any prompting or pressure. Although we can caution law-enforcement officers not to cajole hesitant hospital doctors to violate confidences absent some preceding justification, we cannot expect diligent, conscientious officers like Sergeant Erdelsky to ignore evidence voluntarily placed before them." *Id.*

"In sum, we find *N.J.S.*[] 2A:84A-22.2, which defines the patient-physician privilege, is to be strictly construed and by its language does not apply to a prosecution for violation of the motor vehicle laws." *Id.* at 588.

NOTE

1. The physician-patient privilege, as a creature of statute, can, of course, be removed or curtailed by its creator. Thus, notwithstanding the existence of the privilege, various statutes generally require consulting or treating physicians to report

[e]very case of a wound, burn or any other injury arising from or caused by a firearm, destructive device, explosive[, fire accelerant,] or weapon * * * at once to the police authorities.

See e.g., N.J.S. 2C:58-8. *See also Freeman v. State*, 258 *Ark.* 617, 527 *S.W.*2d 909 (1975); *People v. McAlpin*, 50 *Misc.*2d 579, 270 *N.Y.S.*2d 899 (Nassau Co. Ct. 1966). Other required disclosures cover such matters as venereal disease and child abuse.

2. Generally, the physician-patient privilege will not survive the patient. *See e.g., Estate of Green v. St. Clair Co. Rd. Comm.*, 175 *Mich.App.* 478, 438 *N.W.*2d 630 (1989) (physician-patient privilege held not to apply to the results of tests taken during autopsy, finding that no doctor-patient relationship arises when the patient is dead).

§8.8. PSYCHOTHERAPIST-PATIENT PRIVILEGE

It has been said that among all physicians,

the psychiatrist has a special need to maintain confidentiality. His capacity to help his patients is completely dependent upon their willingness and ability to talk freely. This makes it difficult if not impossible for him to function without being able to assure his patients of confidentiality and, indeed, privileged communication * * *. Psychiatrists not only explore the very depths of their patients' conscious, but their unconscious feelings and attitudes as well. Therapeutic effectiveness necessitates going beyond a patient's awareness and, in order to do this, it must be possible to communicate freely. A threat to secrecy blocks successful treatment.[59]

Although the common law historically did not recognize a physician-patient privilege, "it had indicated a disposition to recognize a psychotherapist-patient privilege."[60] As originally proposed in the federal rules, and recognized in numerous jurisdictions, a patient has "a privilege to refuse to disclose and to prevent any other person from disclosing confidential communications, made for the purposes of diagnosis or treatment of his mental or emotional condition, including drug addiction, among himself, his psychotherapist, or persons who are participating in the diagnosis or treatment under the direction of the psychotherapist, including members of the patient's family."[61] For purposes of this privilege, a "patient" includes any "person who consults or is examined or interviewed by a psychotherapist."[62] A person "authorized to practice medicine," or "reasonably believed by the patient so to be, while engaged in the diagnosis or treatment of a mental or emotional condition, including drug addiction," is a "psychotherapist."[63] In addition, any person licensed or certified as a psychologist while similarly engaged is also considered a psychotherapist for purposes of the privilege.[64]

The psychotherapist-patient privilege "may be claimed by the patient, by his guardian or conservator, or by the personal representative

---

[59] Report No. 45, *Group for the Advancement of Psychiatry* 92 (1960). *See also* Slovenko, *Psychiatry and a Second Look at the Medical Privilege, 6 Wayne L.Rev.* 175, 184 (1960).

[60] *Advisory Committee's Note to Proposed Fed.R.Evid.* 504. *See also* Note, *Confidential Communications to a Psychotherapist: A New Testimonial Privilege, 47 Nw.U.L.Rev.* 384 (1952).

[61] *Proposed Fed.R.Evid.* 504(b).

[62] *Proposed Fed.R.Evid.* 504(a)(1).

[63] *Proposed Fed.R.Evid.* 504(a)(2).

[64] *Id.*

of a deceased patient. The person who was the psychotherapist may claim the privilege but only on behalf of the patient."[65]

There are three exceptions to the rule of nondisclosure: (1) commitment proceedings; (2) court-ordered examinations; and (3) where, in any proceeding, the patient raises and relies upon his mental or emotional condition as a claim or defense.[66]

JAFFEE v. REDMOND
Supreme Court of the United States
518 U.S. 1, 116 S.Ct. 1923 (1996)

Justice STEVENS delivered the opinion of the Court.

"After a traumatic incident in which she shot and killed a man, a police officer received extensive counseling from a licensed clinical social worker. The question we address is whether statements the officer made to her therapist during the counseling session are protected from compelled disclosure in a federal civil action brought by the family of the deceased. Stated otherwise, the question is whether it is appropriate for federal courts to recognize a 'psychotherapist privilege' under Rule 501 of the Federal Rules of Evidence." *Id.* at 1925.

"The United States courts of appeals do not uniformly agree that the federal courts should recognize a psychotherapist privilege under Rule 501. * * * Because of the conflict among the courts of appeals and the importance of the question, we granted *certiorari.*" *Id.* at 1927.

"Rule 501 of the Federal Rules of Evidence authorizes federal courts to define new privileges by interpreting 'common law principles . . . in light of reason and experience.' * * * The Senate Report accompanying the 1975 adoption of the Rules indicates that Rule 501 'should be understood as reflecting the view that the recognition of a privilege based on a confidential relationship . . . should be determined on a case-by-case basis.' * * * The Rule thus did not freeze the law governing the privileges of witnesses in federal trials at a particular point in our history, but rather directed federal courts to 'continue the evolutionary development of testimonial privileges.' " *Id.* at 1927-28. [Citations omitted.]

"Like the spousal and attorney-client privileges, the psychotherapist-patient privilege is 'rooted in the imperative need for confidence and trust.' * * * Treatment by a physician for physical ailments can often proceed successfully on the basis of physical examination, objective information supplied by the patient, and the

---

[65] *Proposed Fed.R.Evid.* 504(c).

[66] *Proposed Fed.Rs.Evid.* 504(d)(1) - (3).

results of diagnostic tests. Effective psychotherapy, by contrast, depends upon an atmosphere of confidence and trust in which the patient is willing to make a frank and complete disclosure of facts, emotions, memories, and fears. Because of the sensitive nature of the problems for which individuals consult psychotherapists, disclosure of confidential communications made during counseling sessions may cause embarrassment or disgrace. For this reason, the mere possibility of disclosure may impede development of the confidential relationship necessary for successful treatment. * * * By protecting confidential communications between a psychotherapist and her patient from involuntary disclosure, the proposed privilege thus serves important private interests." *Id.* at 1928.

"The psychotherapist privilege serves the public interest by facilitating the provision of appropriate treatment for individuals suffering the effects of a mental or emotional problem. The mental health of our citizenry, no less than its physical health, is a public good of transcendent importance." *Id.* at 1929.

"That it is appropriate for the federal courts to recognize a psychotherapist privilege under Rule 501 is confirmed by the fact that all 50 States and the District of Columbia have enacted into law some form of psychotherapist privilege. * * * " *Id.*

"The uniform judgment of the States is reinforced by the fact that a psychotherapist privilege was among the nine specific privileges recommended by the Advisory Committee in its proposed privilege rules. * * * " *Id.* at 1930.

"Because we agree with the judgment of the state legislatures and the Advisory Committee that a psychotherapist-patient privilege will serve a 'public good transcending the normally predominant principle of utilizing all rational means for ascertaining truth, * * * we *hold that confidential communications between a licensed psychotherapist and her patients in the course of diagnosis or treatment are protected from compelled disclosure under Rule 501 of the Federal Rules of Evidence.*" *Id.* at 1931. [Emphasis added.] ["Like other testimonial privileges, the patient may of course waive the protection." *Id.* at 1931 n.14.]

"All agree that a psychologist privilege covers confidential communications made to licensed psychiatrists and psychologists. We have no hesitation in concluding in this case that the federal privilege should also extend to confidential communications made to licensed social workers in the course of psychotherapy. The reasons for recognizing a privilege for treatment by psychiatrists apply with equal force to treatment by a clinical social worker such as [the one who counseled the officer in this case]. Today, social workers provide a significant amount of mental health treatment. * * * Their clients often include the poor and those of modest means who could not afford the assistance of a psychiatrist or psychologist, * * * but whose counseling sessions serve the same public goals." *Id.*

"[Accordingly, the] conversations between Officer Redmond and [her licensed clinical social worker] and the notes taken during their counseling sessions are protected from compelled disclosure under Rule 501 of the Federal Rules of Evidence." *Id.* at 1932.

---

§8.9. VICTIM COUNSELOR PRIVILEGE

Some jurisdictions confer a privilege upon a victim counselor so as to preclude his or her examination "as a witness in any civil or criminal proceeding with regard to any confidential communications."[67] A communication will be deemed confidential, and therefore protected, when it involves an exchange of information between a victim and a victim counselor in private, or in the presence of a third person who is necessary to the counseling process, and which is disclosed in the course of the counselor's treatment of the victim for any emotional or psychological condition resulting from an act of violence.[68] In addition to the privilege attaching to confidential communications, neither the victim counselor nor the victim may be compelled to provide testimony in any criminal or civil proceeding "that would identify the name, address, location, or telephone number of a domestic violence shelter or any other facility that provided temporary emergency shelter to the victim of the offense or transaction that is the subject of the proceeding unless the facility is a party to the proceeding."[69] The privilege must be claimed by the counselor unless he or she has the

---

[67] *See e.g., N.J.S.* 2A:84A-22.15. In enacting this privilege, the New Jersey State Legislature made the following findings: (a) "The emotional and psychological injuries that are inflicted on victims of violence are often more serious than the physical injuries suffered;" (b) "Counseling is often a successful treatment to ease the real and profound psychological trauma experienced by these victims and their families;" (c) In the counseling process, victims of violence openly discuss their emotional reactions to the crime. These reactions are often highly intertwined with their personal histories and psychological profile; (d) Counseling of [victims of violence] is most successful when the victims are assured their thoughts and feelings will remain confidential and will not be disclosed without their permission; and (e) Confidentiality should be accorded all victims of violence who require counseling whether or not they are able to afford the services of private psychiatrists or psychologists." *N.J.S.* 2A:84A-22.13.

See also 42 *Pa.C.S.* §5945.1 ("No sexual assault counselor may, without the written consent of the victim, disclose the victim's confidential oral or written communications to the counselor nor consent to be examined in any court or criminal proceeding."); *Commonwealth v. Wilson / Aultman,* 529 *Pa.* 268, 602 *A.2d* 1290, 1295 (1992) (sexual assault victim - counselor privilege "is intended to be absolute").

[68] *N.J.S.* 2A:84A-22.14(b). This privilege will not, however, "prevent the disclosure to a defendant in a criminal action of statements or information given by a victim to a county victim-witness coordinator, where the disclosure of the statements or information is required by the Constitution[.]" *See N.J.S.* 2A:84A-22.16.

[69] *N.J.S.* 2A:84A-22.15.

prior written consent of the victim to disclose protected communications, or unless the privilege is waived by the victim.[70]

---

§8.10. COMMUNICATIONS TO CLERGYMEN

Virtually all states recognize a person's "privilege to refuse to disclose and to prevent another person from disclosing a confidential communication by the person to a clergyman in his professional character as spiritual advisor."[71] A "clergyman" is "a minister, priest, rabbi, or other similar functionary of a religious organization, or an individual reasonably believed so to be by the person consulting him."[72] "The privilege may be claimed by the person, by his guardian or conservator, or by his personal representative if he is deceased. The clergyman may claim the privilege on behalf of the person."[73]

While the privilege protects confidential information exchanged between a clergyman and communicant, it has been held not to protect information regarding the manner in which a religious institution conducts its affairs or information acquired by such institution as a result of independent investigations not involving confidential communications between a clergyman and communicant.[74]

STATE v. CARY
Superior Court of New Jersey, Appellate Division
331 *N.J.Super.* 236, 751 A.2d 620 (App.Div. 2000)

LEFELT, Judge

Does the cleric-penitent privilege apply when a defendant confesses to a Baptist deacon, who is also a New Jersey State Trooper? This court concludes that "the privilege does not apply to the communication in this case between the defendant and the deacon-trooper, and we reverse the motion judge's suppression of the statement." *Id.*, 331 *N.J.Super.* at 238.

The facts are as follows: On February 5th or 6th, "an altercation occurred between defendant David Cary and at least one other individual

---

[70] *Id.*

[71] *See e.g., Proposed Fed.R.Evid.* 506(b).

[72] *Proposed Fed.R.Evid.* 506(a). While the definition of "clergyman" seems broad, "it is not so broad as to include all self-denominated 'ministers.' " *See Advisory Committee's Note to Proposed Fed.R.Evid.* 506.

[73] *Proposed Fed.R.Evid.* 506(c).

[74] *See Hutchison v. Luddy*, 414 *Pa.Super.* 138, 606 A.2d 905, 909 (1992).

near a Country Fried Chicken restaurant in Newark. After this altercation, the State claimed that defendant returned to Country Fried Chicken and fired several gun shots into the store, striking two bystanders, Andre Dean and Salvatore Johnson. Johnson survived, but Dean died from his injuries." *Id.* at 238.

On Sunday, February 7th, "Cary visited the Second Baptist Church in Belleville to speak with his pastor, Lucious Williams. After attending the morning service, Cary met privately with Pastor Williams, apparently to seek spiritual guidance regarding the altercation and how he should proceed. After meeting with the pastor, Cary indicated that he wanted to surrender to the police. Therefore, Pastor Williams summoned a recently ordained deacon, John Perry, because Perry was also a state trooper and the pastor needed assistance in [deciding what to do to help Cary]." *Id.*

Perry and Pastor Williams met with Cary in the pastor's study. Perry introduced himself as a deacon in the church and also mentioned that he was a state trooper. During this meeting, Cary related certain events that had occurred in Newark, and at some point during the conversation, Perry reminded Cary of his right to remain silent. After receiving this warning, Cary continued to talk about the incident. "At some point in the meeting all three men prayed together." *Id.* at 239.

At one point during the meeting, Perry searched Cary by having him stand against the wall and spread his arms and legs in a traditional frisk posture. "When Cary finished his statement, Perry called the Newark and Belleville police departments. * * * The Newark police arrived and transported Cary to the Newark Police Department. Shortly thereafter, both Pastor Williams and Perry arrived at the Newark Police Department. Cary refused to speak to the police following his arrest, so Detective Michael DeMaio of the Newark Police Department asked Perry to give a statement regarding his knowledge of the incident that led to the shooting of Andre Dean." *Id.* at 239. During the course of his statement, Perry revealed that "Cary admitted shooting a gun during an altercation and that Cary believed he had killed someone." *Id.* at 240.

At the hearing on the motion to suppress Perry's statement, the motion judge "concluded that the cleric-penitent privilege applied to Cary's statement to Perry because Perry was a cleric pursuant to [rules of evidence], and, as such, is prohibited from waiving the privilege without defendant's consent. * * * Thus, the judge [ruled that] defendant's statement to Perry was inadmissible and must be suppressed." *Id.*

Currently, *N.J.R.E.* 511 defines the cleric-penitent privilege, in pertinent part, as follows:

> Any communication made in confidence to a cleric in the cleric's professional character, or as a spiritual advisor in the course of the discipline or practice of the religious body to which the cleric belongs or of

the religion which the cleric professes, shall be privileged. Privileged communications shall include confessions and other communications made in confidence between and among the cleric and individuals, couples, families or groups in the exercise of the cleric's professional or spiritual counseling role.

The rule requires three elements to be present for the cleric-penitent privilege to apply; "a person's communication must be made: (1) in confidence; (2) to a cleric; and (3) to the cleric in his or her professional character or role as a spiritual advisor. Considering the privilege language, and the circumstances of this case, the first issue presented is whether Deacon Perry is a 'cleric' as defined by the privilege." *Id.* at 241-42.

"The applicable [] rule defines 'cleric' as 'a priest, rabbi, minister or other person or practitioner authorized to perform similar functions of any religion.' The defendant argues that Perry qualified as a 'cleric' because he was authorized to perform functions similar to those performed by a priest, minister or rabbi." *Id.* at 242.

"Pastor Williams testified that deacons prayed with individuals, saved souls and administered and read scripture and responsive readings. The pastor added that in his absence, deacons 'are the ones who are responsible for filling the pulpit. They are the ones who are responsible for seeing the sick. As a matter of fact, they are the next in line * * *.'" *Id.* at 243.

"In this case, [it is unnecessary for this court] to decide definitively whether all deacons are clerics. Even assuming that Perry was a cleric, we conclude that the motion judge erred by protecting a statement that did not meet the third element required to sustain the privilege, *i.e.*, that the communication was made in confidence in the cleric's 'professional character, or as a spiritual advisor.'" *Id.* at 244.

As a general matter, "privileges are narrowly construed * * * because they are obstacles in the path of the normal trial objective of a search for the ultimate truth. * * * They are accepted only because in the particular area concerned, they are regarded as serving a more important public interest than the need for full disclosure. Therefore, privileges should always be construed and applied in a sensible accommodation to the aim of a just result. Our interpretation, therefore, should protect the policy driving the privilege without too broadly impairing the trial's search for the truth." *Id.* at 244-45.

"To be privileged, confidential communications must be made to a cleric 'in the cleric's professional character, or as a spiritual advisor in the course of the discipline . . . of the religious body to which the cleric belongs or . . . the cleric professes.' * * * When the communication is not made in such capacity, it is not privileged." *Id.* at 245.

In this case, the uncontested evidence "reflects a dual role played by Perry in his relationship with Cary; he acted as both deacon and police officer. Pastor Williams did not summon Deacon Perry for help until Cary had decided he wanted to surrender.

Perry indicated that part of his role in meeting with defendant was spiritual in nature. Yet, Perry also testified that he introduced himself to Cary as both a deacon and state trooper. During their conference, despite praying with Cary, Perry reminded defendant of his right to remain silent and, in fact, at one point, searched Cary. It is obvious that Perry acted in both capacities during his meeting with Cary and understood that he was present to perform the secular function of assisting defendant's surrender to the police. Moreover, given the fact that Cary knew Perry was a State Trooper and that Perry warned Cary of his right to remain silent and searched Cary, it is difficult to comprehend how Cary could have 'reasonably expected' that his communications with Perry would remain confidential. * * * Therefore, given Perry's dual capacity during Cary's confession, Cary's communications to Perry were not made in a deacon's 'professional character, or as a spiritual advisor in the course of the discipline or practice of the religious body. . . .' The communications were made to Perry when he was at least partially performing a secular function as a law enforcement official, and are not privileged." *Id.* at 246-47.

"For the above explained reasons, we reverse the motion judge's decision and rule that defendant Cary's communications with Deacon Perry, under the circumstances of this case, are not protected under the cleric-penitent privilege. In the course of this decision we have made some reference to *Miranda v. Arizona*, 384 *U.S.* 436, 86 *S.Ct.* 1602 (1966). We do not reach the question whether the communication might be inadmissible under *Miranda* or for any other reason. We hold only that Cary's communications to Deacon Perry were not made in confidence in the deacon's professional character or as a spiritual advisor, and are not privileged under [] *N.J.R.E.* 511." *Cary* at 247.

Reversed and remanded for further proceedings in accordance with this decision.

---

§8.11. POLITICAL VOTING PRIVILEGE

"Secrecy in voting is an essential aspect of effective democratic government, insuring free exercise of the franchise and fairness in elections."[75] Moreover, maintaining secrecy "after the ballot is cast is as essential as secrecy in the act of voting."[76] Consequently, it is recognized in all jurisdictions that "[e]very person has a privilege to

---

[75] *Advisory Committee's Note to Proposed Fed.R.Evid.* 507.

[76] *Id.*

refuse to disclose the tenor of his vote at a political election conducted by secret ballot unless the vote was cast illegally."[77]

---

§8.12. NEWSPERSON'S PRIVILEGE

An increasing number of jurisdictions are recognizing a privilege which shields journalists from being compelled to divulge the identities of their news sources.[78] Known as "shield" laws, the statutory provisions generally permit persons employed by the news media "for the purpose of gathering, procuring, transmitting, compiling, editing or disseminating news for the general public,"[79] to refuse to disclose the source of their information in any legal or *quasi*-legal proceeding or before any investigative body. The privilege "is designed to protect the confidential sources of the press as well as information so obtained by reporters and other media representatives."[80] It is "motivated by concern that forced disclosure of sources would make potential informants less willing to talk to newsgatherers, and would thus deprive the public of important information."[81]

The newsperson's privilege is not absolute. As one commentator observed:

> [I]t seems unacceptable that reporters should be entirely excused from the general duty to give whatever evidence one has to aid the state in the pursuit of justice and the suppression of crime.[82]

Consequently, the newsperson's privilege "is accorded less respect in criminal prosecutions, where the cost of withholding evidence seems higher than in the civil context, * * * and is least likely to succeed when a journalist's evidence is sought by a criminal defendant."[83]

---

[77] *See e.g., Proposed Fed.R.Evid.* 507.

[78] The newsperson's privilege was not recognized at common law and, as a creature of statute, is of relatively recent origin. *See Branzburg v. Hayes,* 408 *U.S.* 665, 92 *S.Ct.* 2646 (1972).

[79] *See e.g., N.J.S.* 2A:84A-21.

[80] *See In re Schuman,* 114 *N.J.* 14, 20, 552 *A.2d* 602 (1989).

[81] Lilly, *An Introduction to the Law of Evidence* §9.12 (2nd ed. 1987), at 448.

[82] *Lilly* at 448-49.

[83] *Id.* at 449. *Compare In re Schuman, supra* at 16 (newsperson's shield prohibited the State from compelling a reporter to testify at trial concerning a confession made to him during the pursuit of his professional activities by a criminal defendant after the confession had been published in the newspaper).

The privilege has been held not to extend to any situation in which a newsperson is an eyewitness to, or participant in, an accident or any criminal act or act involving physical violence or property damage.[84] It has been held that in order to bypass the privilege and obtain shielded information, a party must first demonstrate that:

> he has made an effort to obtain the information from other sources. Second, he must demonstrate that the only access to the information sought is through the journalist and her sources. Finally, the [party] must persuade the Court that the information sought is crucial to the claim.[85]

The privilege belongs to the newsperson, who may claim it or waive it "irrespective of the wishes of the news source."[86]

---

§8.13. POLICE INFORMER'S PRIVILEGE

"What is usually referred to as the informer's privilege is in reality the Government's privilege to withhold from disclosure the identity of persons who furnish information of violations of law to officers charged with enforcement of that law. * * * The purpose of the privilege is the furtherance and protection of the public interest in effective law enforcement. The privilege recognizes the obligation of citizens to communicate their knowledge of the commission of crimes to law-enforcement officials and, by preserving their anonymity, encourages them to perform that obligation."[87]

"The scope of the privilege is limited by its underlying purpose. Thus, where the disclosure of the contents of a communication will not tend to reveal the identity of an informer, the contents are not

---

[84] *See e.g., N.J.S.* 2A:84A-21. *See also Miami Herald Pub. Co. v. Morejon*, 561 *So.*2d 577, 581 (Fla. 1990) (journalist required to testify concerning observations made of an arrest and search of defendant); *Lightman v. State*, 15 *Md.App.* 713, 294 *A.*2d 149 (requiring reporter to testify to observations of drugs being sold), *aff'd*, 266 *Md.* 550, 295 *A.*2d 212 (1972); *Matter of Woodhaven Lumber & Mill Work*, 123 *N.J.* 481, 497, 589 *A.*2d 135 (1991) (eyewitness exception to the newsperson's privilege includes only the observation of the act, not the resultant consequences of the act; thus, photographs taken after reporter's arrival at an already-burning building were privileged); *Ex parte Grothe*, 687 *S.W.*2d 736 (Tex.Crim.App. 1984) (news reporter stands on same footing as a layperson with regard to personal observations of alleged criminal activity, and therefore must testify).

[85] *United States v. Cuthbertson*, 651 *F.*2d 189, 195-96 (3rd Cir. 1981).

[86] *See* 1 *McCormick, Evidence* §76.2 (4th ed. 1992), at 288.

[87] *Roviaro v. United States*, 353 *U.S.* 53, 59, 77 *S.Ct.* 623, 627 (1957).

privileged."[88] "Likewise, once the identity of the informer has been disclosed to those who would have cause to resent the communication, the privilege is no longer applicable. A further limitation on the applicability of the privilege arises from the fundamental requirements of fairness. Where the disclosure of an informer's identity, or of the contents of his communication, is relevant and helpful to the defense of an accused, or is essential to a fair determination of a cause, the privilege must give way. In these situations the trial court may require disclosure and, if the Government withholds the information, dismiss the action."[89]

There is, however, no fixed rule respecting disclosure. "The problem is one that calls for balancing the public interest in protecting the flow of information against the individual's right to prepare his defense."[90] Consequently, a court's decision to compel the disclosure of an informant's identity will depend on "the particular circumstances of each case, taking into consideration the crime charged, the possible defenses, the possible significance of the informer's testimony, and other relevant factors."[91]

As originally proposed, the federal rules contained a provision providing a privilege to the government "to refuse to disclose the identity of a person who has furnished information relating to or assisting in an investigation of a possible violation of law to a law enforcement officer."[92]

---

[88] *Id.* at 60, 77 *S.Ct.* at 627. *See also Grodjesk v. Faghani*, 104 *N.J.* 89, 96, 514 *A.*2d 1328 (1986) ("contents of informer's communications with a law enforcement official are not privileged unless disclosure of the communications would probably reveal the identity of the informer").

[89] *Roviaro* at 60-61, 77 *S.Ct.* at 627-628.

[90] *Id.* at 62, 77 *S.Ct.* at 628-629.

[91] *Id.* at 62, 77 *S.Ct.* at 629. *See also Commonwealth v. Carter*, 427 *Pa.* 53, 58, 233 *A.*2d 284, 287 (1967) (adopting and applying the *Roviaro* balancing test.)

[92] *Proposed Fed.R.Evid.* 510.

STATE v. OLIVER
Supreme Court of New Jersey
50 N.J. 39, 231 A.2d 805 (1967)

The opinion of the Court was delivered by

WEINTRAUB, C.J.

"Defendant Oliver was convicted of bookmaking * * *. The Appellate Division reversed because the trial court refused to order the State to disclose the identity of an informer. * * * We granted certification [and now reverse the order of the Appellate Division]." *Id.*, 50 N.J. at 40.

At trial, undercover State Trooper Walter Decker was the principal witness for the State. Decker testified to defendant's bookmaking activities which took place at a tavern in New Brunswick. The trooper made no reference to an informant. On cross-examination, the defense elicited the fact that on all occasions the trooper was in the company of an informant. The informant did not, however, place any bets. Rather, it appears that the informant accompanied Decker only because the informant was a familiar figure at the bar and therefore his presence tended to shield the undercover trooper from suspicion. The informant was not there to be a witness but instead to make Decker less conspicuous.

This Court rejects defendant's contention that the identity of the informant should have been disclosed. Such disclosure is not required where the informant "was no more than a witness to the criminal event." *Id.* at 46.

When a court must determine whether the identity of a confidential police informant must be disclosed in a particular case, the determination requires a "balancing [of] the public interest in protecting the flow of information against the individual's right to a fair determination of the issues." *Id.* at 46 (citing *Roviaro v. United States*, 353 U.S. 53, 77 S.Ct. 623 (1957)). In this State, the *Roviaro* balancing approach has been codified at N.J.S. 2A:84A-28[,] which provides

> A witness has a privilege to refuse to disclose the identity of a person who has furnished information purporting to disclose a violation of a provision of the laws of this State or of the United States to a representative of the State or the United States or a governmental division thereof, charged with the duty of enforcing that provision, and evidence thereof is inadmissible, *unless the judge finds that (a) the identity of the person furnishing the information has already been otherwise disclosed or (b) disclosure of his identity is essential to assure a fair determination of the issues.* (emphasis added).

In this case, "the informer played no part whatever in the criminal event. He did not bet, or induce defendant to accept a bet from anyone. Nor did the State attempt to get into the record of the trial anything the informer may have seen or said. It was the defense that brought out his presence at the scene, obviously to raise the immediate issue. *But the defense was unable to show that the informer's testimony was necessary for a fair determination of the issues in the case.*" *Id.* [Emphasis added.] "The defense could advance nothing more than an ungrounded hope that if the informer were called as a defense witness, he would say something which would somehow discredit the trooper and lead to an acquittal. [The law does not, however, allow] disclosure of a nonparticipating informer upon that rootless speculation." *Id.* Were it otherwise, "[u]pon that sheer speculation, a demand for disclosure would be routinely made, not really with any expectation that defendant will call the informer, but rather to obtain the dismissal to which the prosecution would have to submit to honor its obligation to protect him." *Id.* at 47.

Consequently, "[i]n dealing with the informer privilege, we must be mindful of the ease with which the privilege would be destroyed if disclosure were required *without a substantial showing of a need for it.*" *Id.* [Emphasis added.] In this case, defendant has failed to demonstrate a substantial showing of a need for the disclosure of the informant's identity. The informant was not an active participant. Unlike the informant in *Roviaro*, he was not the principal actor in the offense; he did not help set up the criminal occurrence or play a prominent part in it. "[T]he risk of loss to defendant[] is pure conjecture, while the loss to society in its efforts to cope with crime would be real and substantial. The balance contemplated by *Roviaro* must be struck in favor of law and order." *Id.* at 48.

NOTE

1. During the course of its opinion in *Oliver*, the Court explained that the "informer's privilege"

> exists to secure a flow of vital information which can be had only upon a confidential basis. Not all such information comes from people of high motivation. The police must have the aid of men of lesser quality who respond to selfish inducements, including money. These men are needed [not only] for what they know, but also for what they can learn because of their associations. This is especially true with respect to crimes of a consensual nature as to which there is little likelihood that a victim will complain. * * * The informer, paid or not, is subject to risks of retaliation which a regular member of a police force need not fear and hence, whether paid or not, he comes within the protection of the privilege.

Id. at 42.

2. *The informant as an active participant in the crime.* In *State v. Roundtree*, 118 *N.J.Super.* 22, 285 A.2d 564 (App.Div. 1971), the court observed that the disclosure of an informer's identity will normally be compelled where the informer was an active participant in bringing about the crime for which the defendant is charged. *Id.*, 118 *N.J.Super.* at 32. In *Roundtree*, a narcotics agent "insinuated himself into [a drug] society with the help of an informer." *Id.* at 25. On the day of the offense, the agent and the informer met defendant at a bar and asked him where they could purchase some narcotics. Defendant took them to a nearby house where defendant purchased the drugs while the agent and the informer waited outside in the car. Although the narcotics agent testified that it was he who had asked defendant for the drugs and for the name of defendant's supplier, the agent's handwritten notes indicated that it was the informer who had done so.

Appealing his conviction for the unlawful possession and sale of heroin, defendant argued, among other things, that his conviction should be set aside because of the State's failure to disclose the identity of its informant and because the trial court refused to allow any cross-examination concerning the informant's role in the narcotics transaction. The appellate court agreed, finding that the

> trial court erred in extending the scope of the privilege to cover anything that the informer might have said or done during the time that criminal activity was alleged to have taken place. The participation of the informer was certainly relevant not only on the basis of [the officer's] credibility but also on the issue of possible entrapment. Although [the officer's] notes written at the time stated that the informer initiated the transaction, he indicated in his direct testimony that the transaction was initiated by him. In view of the fact that defendant could not remember what he had been doing on the day of the alleged offense, the fact that the informer was present at the time of the offense, and the fact that [the officer's] handwritten notes gave clear indication that the informer was an actor in the transaction, the limitation on cross-examination was prejudicial error for which the judgment must be reversed.

Id. at 30-31.

Respecting the issue of disclosure, the court stated: "Disclosure is normally compelled where the informer was an *actual participant [in] the crime for which the defendant is being charged.*" *Id.* at 31. [Emphasis added.] The informer in this case did "far more than merely set up or witness the meeting between [the undercover officer] and defendant. The informer was an active participant bringing about the violation[,] * * * and a material witness on the issue of defendant's guilt. As such his identity should have been disclosed. The failure to require disclosure under the circumstances of this case was prejudicial error, a denial of fundamental fairness." *Id.* at 32.

BODIN v. STATE
Court of Criminal Appeals of Texas
807 *S.W.*2d 313 (1991)

Before the court en banc.

MILLER, Judge.
[Officer Price of the Houston Police Department, along with his partner, Officer Mitchell, arranged a controlled buy of narcotics after receiving information from a confidential informant that defendant was engaged in drug trafficking at his home. The officers provided their informant with twenty-five dollars and watched as he entered defendant's apartment. Four or five minutes later, the informant emerged from the apartment and handed the officers a quantity of methamphetamine just purchased from defendant. After receiving a description of defendant from the informant, Officer Price prepared an affidavit and search warrant which was later approved and signed by Judge Kolenda. A search of defendant's apartment uncovered an additional quantity of methamphetamine, which formed the basis of defendant's conviction for the possession of less than 28 grams of methamphetamine.]

In this appeal, defendant argues "that the trial court erred in refusing to order disclosure of the informer's identity under Texas Rule of Criminal Evidence 508(c)(2), which provides in part:

> If it appears from the evidence in the case or from other showing by a party that an informer may be able to give testimony necessary to a fair determination of the issues of guilt [or] innocence and the public entity invokes the privilege, the judge shall give the public entity an opportunity to show in camera facts relevant to determining whether the informer can, in fact, supply that testimony.

Id. at 315.

It is defendant's contention that a man named James brought the drugs into his apartment on the day in question. Defendant states that James "did some drugs" there while defendant was in the bathroom, and left fifteen minutes later. According to defendant, the methamphetamine found by the police was left by, and belonged to, James.

"In order to adequately address [defendant's] claims, a review of the law relating to informer's identity is necessary. Under federal law, the government has a privilege not to disclose the identity of its informers. This privilege was applied in *Scher v. United States*, 305 U.S. 251, 59 *S.Ct.* 174 [] (1938), when the Supreme Court observed that public policy forbids disclosure of an informer's identity unless it is essential to the defense. The privilege was later discussed in *Roviaro [v. United States]*, in which the Supreme Court stated:

> The purpose of the privilege is the furtherance and protection of the public interest in effective law enforcement. The privilege recognizes the obligation of citizens to communicate their knowledge of the commission of crimes to law-enforcement officials and, by preserving their anonymity, encourages them to perform that obligation."

Bodin at 316 (quoting *Roviaro* at 59, 77 *S.Ct.* at 627).

"Wigmore explained the basis for the rule as follows:

> Whether an informer is motivated by good citizenship, promise of leniency or prospect of pecuniary reward, he will usually condition his cooperation on an assurance of anonymity—to protect himself and his family from harm, to preclude adverse social reactions and to avoid the risk of defamation or malicious prosecution actions against him. . . . Revelation of the dual role played by [professional informers] . . . ends their usefulness to the government and discourages others from entering into a like relationship."

Id. (quoting 8 Wigmore, *Evidence*, § 2374 (McNaughton Rev. 1961).

"In *Roviaro*, the Supreme Court held that no fixed rule could be formulated as to when identity had to be disclosed. Rather, the public interest in protecting the flow of information had to be weighed against the accused's right to prepare a defense. Under cases interpreting *Roviaro*, however, disclosure may be deemed appropriate in several situations." *Bodin* at 316. "For instance, identity may be disclosed when an informer is likely to be a 'material witness' because he or she has information critical to the defense on such issues as identity of the culprit, events in the crime, or defensive matters such as entrapment. *See United States v. Barnes*, 486 *F.*2d 776 (8th Cir. 1973). *See also United States v. Ordonez*, 737 *F.*2d 793 (9th Cir. 1984); *United States v. Gonzales*, 606 *F.*2d 70 (5th Cir. 1979)." *Bodin* at 316.

"Texas Rule of Criminal Evidence 508 establishes the state informer's identity privilege." *Id.* at 317.

"Generally, the Texas Rules of Criminal Evidence were patterned after the Federal Rules of Evidence. Cases interpreting federal rules [may, consequently,] be construed for guidance. * * * [We will therefore use [the] federal cases when such cases are helpful to resolution of state informer privilege issues." *Id.*

Under Rule 508, "[t]he privilege does not apply if the informer's identity has been voluntarily disclosed, if the informer may be able to give testimony necessary to a fair determination of guilt, or if a judge is not satisfied that information was obtained from an informer reasonably believed to be reliable." *Id.*

"[B]efore enactment of Rule 508, courts acknowledged the informer identity privilege, as established in *Roviaro*, and held that disclosure was not required unless:

1. The informer participated in the offense;

2. Was present at the time of the offense or arrest; or

3. Was otherwise shown to be a material witness to the transaction or as to whether the defendant knowingly committed the offense charged.

* * * The informer had to be placed within one of the three categories before disclosure could be compelled." *Id.*

"Under current law, however, Rule 508(c)(2) requires only that the testimony be 'necessary to a fair determination of the issues of guilt [or] innocence.' Thus, the new rule is broader than that applicable under the prior law[ ]" *Id.* at 317-18.

"The informer's potential testimony must significantly aid the defendant and mere conjecture or supposition about possible relevancy is insufficient." *Id.* at 318

"The defendant has the threshold burden of demonstrating that identity must be disclosed. * * * Since the defendant may not actually know the nature of the informer's testimony, however, he or she should only be required to make a plausible showing of how the informer's information may be important." *Id.*

"Evidence from any source, but not mere conjecture or speculation, must be presented to make the required showing that the informer's identity must be disclosed."

"We now turn to the issue of whether, in th[is] case, there was sufficient information presented to show that the informer could give testimony necessary to a fair determination of guilt. The State's evidence showed that the informer told the police that [defendant] was engaged in drug trafficking. The police arranged for the informer to go into defendant's apartment * * *. The informer emerged with methamphetamine and told police he had purchased it from [defendant]. Police used the informer's information to procure a search warrant, which, when executed the next day, led to discovery of the methamphetamine [defendant] was charged with possessing. [Defendant] testified that James left the drugs in the apartment the day before the search. [Defendant] wanted to know the informer's identity so that if James were the informer, [defendant] could pursue an entrapment defense. Also, since the informer stated he bought drugs from [defendant], and since [defendant] claims James left the drugs in the apartment, the informer may have had information material to the defense." *Id.*

"Based on these facts, we hold that [defendant] made a plausible showing that the informer could give testimony necessary to a fair determination of guilt. The informer had information material to [defendant's] possession of drugs, and could have information relevant to possible entrapment. The trial court should have therefore conducted an in camera hearing to determine whether the informer could, in fact, supply such information." *Id.*

"We reject the [lower court's] finding that since [defendant] knew James and where to find him, [defendant] had no need of the informer's identity. Whether James was the informer was the precise information [defendant] needed. He could use the other information concerning James and his location once [defendant] knew whether James was, in fact, the informer. Thus, [defendant] was missing the key link in the chain." *Id.* at 318-19.

NOTE

1. *The informant as an eyewitness to the crime charged.*

(a) In *Anderson v. State*, 817 *S.W.*2d 69 (Tex.Cr.App. 1991), the court emphasized that whenever it is shown that "an informant was an eyewitness to an alleged offense," it is clear that the informant can in fact give testimony necessary to a fair determination of the issues of guilt or innocence. *Id.* at 72. *See also Commonwealth v. McGinn*, 251 *Pa.Super.* 170, 173, 380 *A.*2d 431, 433 (1977), where the court observed that the disclosure of an informer's identity may be required where "the evidence against the defendant proceeds solely from the testimony of police officers, and the only relatively neutral eyewitness to the crime is the informant."

(b) *Compare State v. Milligan*, 71 *N.J.* 373, 365 *A.*2d 914 (1976). In *Milligan*, undercover State Trooper Roberson was involved in an extensive narcotics investigation. During the course of the investigation, the trooper accompanied a police informant to a street corner where the informant introduced the trooper to defendant Milligan. A conversation about drugs took place and when defendant stated that he had some "good stuff for sale," the officer agreed to purchase a quantity of heroin from defendant. Although the informant was present throughout the meeting and did participate in the general discussion, he did not negotiate the sale.

At the conclusion of the negotiations, Roberson, defendant and the informant drove to defendant's home. "The informer then left the others alone in the living room and went to the bathroom." *Id.*, 71 *N.J.* at 378. While the informer was out of the room, defendant sold Roberson eleven glassine envelopes of heroin. No other person was in the living room during the sale. Significantly, the informant neither witnessed nor participated in the transaction. After the sale, the informant re-entered the room and the trio then departed. Roberson drove the defendant back to the corner where they had first met.

In the appeal which followed his conviction for the unlawful possession and distribution of heroin, defendant argued that the trial judge erred in denying his motion for disclosure of the informant's identity. *The New Jersey Supreme Court disagreed.*

"Because informers serve an indispensable role in police work, it is important to encourage their continued cooperation. For this reason, the * * * 'informer's privilege' has long been considered essential to effective enforcement of the criminal code[,]" *id.* at 381, and "the use of informers is particularly important in the enforcement of the narcotics laws." *Id.* at 381 n.3. "Thus, it is generally agreed that the informer's privilege 'is well-established, and its soundness cannot be questioned.' " *Id.* at 383. [Citation omitted.]

"The privilege, however, is not absolute." *Id.* Beyond the limitations set forth by the United States Supreme Court in *Roviaro v. United States*, 353 *U.S.* 53, 60-61, 77 *S.Ct.* 623, 627-628 (1957), "the privilege is inapplicable where the informer is an essential witness on a basic issue in the case." *Milligan* at 383. The privilege is also inapplicable "where the informer is an active participant in the crime for which defendant is prosecuted, * * * where a defense of entrapment seems reasonably plausible, * * * or where disclosure is mandated by fundamental principles of fairness to the accused." *Id.* at 383-384.

In determining whether the disclosure of an informant's identity is appropriate in a particular case, most courts will accommodate the competing interests of criminal defendants and the State by reference to the balancing test set forth in *Roviaro*:

> "We believe that no fixed rule with respect to disclosure is justifiable. The problem is one that calls for balancing the public interest in protecting the flow of information against the individual's right to prepare his defense. Whether a proper balance renders nondisclosure erroneous must depend on the particular circumstances of each case, taking into consideration the crime charged, the possible defenses, the possible significance of the informer's testimony, and other relevant factors."

Milligan at 384 (quoting *Roviaro* at 62, 77 *S.Ct.* at 628).

Applying the *Roviaro* balancing test to this case, the Court concluded that "the interests of the State must prevail." *Id.* at 385. Contrary to defendant's contention, the informant was not an "active participant" in the illegal transaction; nor did he play an "instrumental role" in its occurrence. "[I]t was the narcotics agent, not the informer, who actually purchased drugs from the defendant. Moreover, there is no evidence that the informer induced defendant to make the sale or in any other way entrapped defendant. Finally, the informer was not even present in the room when the sale was consummated." *Id.* at 390.

"[A]bsent a strong showing of need, courts generally deny disclosure where the informer plays only a marginal role, such as providing information or 'tips' to the police or participating in the preliminary stage of a criminal prosecution." *Id.* at 387. It has also been held that "[p]roof that the informer witnessed the criminal transaction, without more, is * * * insufficient to justify disclosure." *Id.* at 388. Consequently, where, as here, the role of the informer is confined to introducing the undercover agent to the defendant and accompanying the officer and defendant to the place where the sale is transacted, the informer's role does not rise to the level of "active participation" to warrant disclosure of his identity. *Id.* at 388-389.

"Nonetheless, even when the informer's involvement falls short of active participation in a criminal offense, the privilege of nondisclosure will yield where the defendant can show that the testimony of the informer is essential to preparing his defense or to assuring a fair determination of the issues. Thus, on a motion for disclosure, courts must examine the nature of the accused's defenses and the purposes for which the informer's testimony is sought, as well as the extent of the informer's involvement." *Id.* at 390.

In this case, defendant has not demonstrated "a substantial showing of need" for disclosing the identity of the informant. *Id.* at 390, 393 n.12. He "has made no special showing of how disclosure of the informer's identity would be helpful to his defense. * * * Nor has he asserted a defense of entrapment which might also justify disclosure." *Id.* at 390-391.

The Court emphasized that while trial judges "*must* remain sensitive to the legitimate needs of defendants and to fundamental principles of fairness, they should not honor frivolous demands for information on unsubstantiated allegations of need. This is especially true where such demands would jeopardize the protection afforded police informers. Something more than speculation should be required of a defendant before the court overrules an informer's privilege of nondisclosure." *Id.* at 393. [Emphasis in original.]

Accordingly, the Court concluded that the informer's "limited involvement in the crime, the speculative significance of his testimony and the reasons offered for disclosure d[id] not sufficiently outweigh the State's interest in protecting the free flow of information." *Id.* at 394. Milligan was therefore denied disclosure.

2. *Supplying information only.* In *State v. Foreshaw*, 245 *N.J.Super.* 166, 584 *A.2d* 832 (App.Div. 1991), the court emphasized that, "[u]nder most circumstances, * * * an informer's identity will be kept secret and will not be revealed for insignificant or transient reasons." *Id.*, 245 *N.J.Super.* at 181. Here, the informant advised the police that a silver or gray Eldorado Cadillac with New Jersey license plates and a spare tire mounted on the back had departed the Camden area around 10:00 a.m. and was heading toward New York City to pick up cocaine. The informant stated that the vehicle would be returning to Camden at approximately 4:30 p.m. Additionally, the informant advised that three people would be inside the car—a Jamaican male named Arthur Brown, a second Jamaican male and a Spanish female. Independent police investigation corroborated every detail of the data supplied by the informant, and a search of the vehicle produced 502 grams of cocaine. Rejecting defendant Foreshaw's contention that, "because the informant mentioned only Brown's name to the police, it can be inferred that the informant" was in possession of exculpatory information "and, therefore, his identity should have been disclosed," the court stated:

> * * * the informant here was not at all involved in the events which took place. The informant did not contact defendants, accompany the police or participate in any meetings, sales or arrests. The informer only gave a detailed description of defendants and their vehicle to the police. Surely such action does not rise to the level of participation necessary for disclosure. This case bears no relationship to *Roviaro v. United States, supra,* and *State v. Roundtree, supra.* In those cases, the informants played integral roles in the subject transactions and were actually present during the criminal activity. *Here, by contrast, the informant only relayed incriminating information to the police and took no further part in the case.* * * *
>
> Moreover, and more importantly, because he did not accompany defendants or the police, the informant had no knowledge of the incriminating events. The informant could neither testify as to Foreshaw's knowledge or intent nor could he offer evidence on Foreshaw's behalf. Because Foreshaw's criminal activity took place outside of the informer's presence, the identity of the informer was irrelevant.

Id. at 184. [Emphasis added.]

STATE v. GARCIA
Supreme Court of New Jersey
131 *N.J.* 67, 618 A.2d 326 (1993)

The opinion of the Court was delivered by

CLIFFORD, J.
   "We granted certification [] to decide whether New Jersey should recognize a 'surveillance location privilege,' under which the State can refuse to disclose the exact location from which law-enforcement officers observe criminal activity. We hold that *Evidence Rule* 34 [now 515], the 'official information privilege,' permits the State to withhold that information in appropriate circumstances." *Id.*, 131 *N.J.* at 70.
   Garcia and an accomplice were observed by Newark police officers Farina and McCauley apparently selling drugs in the area of Clark Street and Broadway within 1,000 feet of a school. "The officers were conducting a surveillance at that location based on an informer's tip that two males were dealing 'Dope-P-Dope' (a street name for heroin) near that corner. The officers observed an unknown male, believed to be a drug buyer, approach Garcia's accomplice and speak briefly with him. After a short conversation with the accomplice, Garcia crossed the street and retrieved something from an abandoned freezer in a vacant lot. When he returned, Garcia handed the 'frozen goods' to either the 'buyer' or the accomplice [the officer's testimony was unclear on this point] and the 'buyer' gave the money to the accomplice." *Id.* at 71
   "The officers witnessed the transaction with the aid of binoculars from a distance of approximately sixty feet. After leaving their observation post in an unsuccessful attempt to locate the buyer, the officers returned to the vacant lot, where they saw defendant and his accomplice. Garcia fled, but Officer Farina apprehended and arrested him. The officers also arrested the accomplice. Officer McCauley searched the freezer and found nine glassine envelopes of heroin marked 'white monster' in a cardboard box. A search of the accomplice yielded $23. The police found no drugs or money on Garcia." *Id.* at 71.
   Prior to trial, the prosecution moved for a protective order prohibiting disclosure of the officers' surveillance location. At the pretrial hearing, one of the officers testified that "he had observed defendant from an elevated position in an occupied building on Broadway, fifty to seventy-five feet south of the intersection of Broadway and Clark, and fifty to sixty feet from the site of the alleged drug transaction." *Id.* The officer told the court that "the police still used the building as a surveillance site because of extensive drug activity in that area. He expressed concern that drug dealers might retaliate against the building owner or burn down

the block if they learned of the surveillance site." *Id.* at 72. The officer also testified that "persons often hesitate to allow the use of their properties for surveillance activities because they fear reprisal." *Id.* The trial court issued the protective order.

This court upholds the lower court's decision to withhold the location of the surveillance site, and determines, pursuant to *Evidence Rule* 34, "that a surveillance location falls within the type of information that a court may conceal in the public interest." *Garcia* at 73. *Evidence Rule* 34, the "official information privilege," provides:

> No person shall disclose official information of this State or of the United States (a) if disclosure is forbidden by or pursuant to any Act of Congress or of this State, or (b) if the judge finds that disclosure of the information in the action would be harmful to the interests of the public.

The " 'surveillance location,' qualifies as 'official information' that becomes privileged, in the absence of a defendant's demonstration of need, if the State can show that disclosure would be 'harmful to the interests of the public.' " *Garcia* at 74.

"Failure to protect the confidential locations from which police have witnessed criminal activity would harm several important public interests. First, non-disclosure avoids compromising ongoing surveillances. Police officers often experience difficulty in finding places from which to observe criminal conduct unobtrusively. * * * Failure to conceal exact locations may force the State to choose between dropping the charges against a defendant or losing future interests. Also, disclosure of the information might cause criminal offenders simply to relocate their activities to a place not visible from that surveillance location." *Id.* at 74-75.

"Second, the privilege protects police officers and private citizens from reprisal. * * * If those bent on crime were to learn of the location of surveillance activities, they might resort to violence or engage in vandalism to render that site useless." *Id.* at 75.

"Third, and related to the second reason, the privilege encourages citizens to cooperate with police. If citizens know that a defendant charged with an offense can learn the exact surveillance location, many will not permit use of their property." *Id.*

In order to maintain the confidentiality of the surveillance location, the State bears the burden of first convincing a court that "disclosure would compromise an important public interest." *Id.* at 77. In this respect, the surveillance location privilege is different from the informer's privilege, which automatically recognizes the privilege to withhold the informer's identity unless the party seeking disclosure makes a "substantial showing of need." *Id.* at 77-78. Because the official information privilege shields information only if its disclosure would be "harmful to the interests of the public," the State "must demonstrate a realistic possibility that revealing the location would compromise present or future prosecutions or would possibly endanger lives or property." *Id.* at 78. At a pre-trial hearing, the State bears the burden of justifying application of the surveillance location privilege. Defense counsel is not permitted to attend the hearing. The court must, however, "make a sealed record sufficiently detailed to facilitate appellate review." *Id.*

Once the State has met its burden, the court must ensure that application of the privilege does not deprive a defendant of the right to a fair trial. *Id.* at 79. "Like the informer's privilege, the surveillance location privilege must yield when it infringes on a defendant's constitutional rights." *Id.* In this respect, "[a] defendant's right to cross-examine adverse witnesses is one of the most important protections afforded by the Sixth Amendment to the United States Constitution and Article I, Paragraph 10 of our Constitution." *Id.* at 80.

The determination of whether the location of a surveillance site should be disclosed should proceed on a case-by-case basis. "The balancing test outlined in *Roviaro* * * * to determine the applicability of the informer's privilege should apply in this context as well. If the State meets its preliminary burden for application of the privilege, the court should permit disclosure if the information sought is relevant and helpful to the defense or essential to a fair determination of the case. * * * In deciding whether to require disclosure, a court must focus on the negative effect that such disclosure may have on the public good. * * * '[C]ourts * * * should not honor frivolous demands for information or unsubstantiated allegations of need. * * * Something more than speculation should be required of a defendant * * *.' [A] defendant must make a substantial showing of need to defeat the State's proper assertion of the privilege." *Id.* at 80-81. [Citation omitted.]

"Therefore, if the trial court finds that the State has met its initial burden of showing that the information should be protected, a defendant may then request [a hearing] to attempt to show substantial need for the information." *Id.* at 81.

Even if a court should deny a defense request for the exact location of a surveillance site, there is some information that is "so vital" that in the vast majority of cases a defendant may nonetheless have access to it. "For instance, a defendant may always inquire about the distance from which the observation was made because that information closely relates to the ability of the witness to see what he or she claims to have seen. Second, a defendant may always ask if the witness used some vision-enhancing article, *e.g.*, binoculars or a telescope, because disclosure of that information bears substantially on the witness's ability to perceive without sacrificing any public interest." *Id.* at 81-82.

"As a general rule, a defendant should be permitted to explore whether the officer observed the alleged crime from an elevated position. That fact often has great importance, given the better view that normally accompanies an elevated vantage point. Passing cars and pedestrians that block the view from the street level may not hamper an officer who views a transaction from a raised position. Likewise, in many instances buildings in an area will be of comparable size, and revealing whether the view was elevated will not automatically divulge the surveillance point. In most situations, disclosing those facts will not sacrifice any public interests." *Id.* at 82.

"Finally, in most cases a defendant may inquire into the officer's angle of sight. Conditions such as the position of the sun at the time of the observation could bear on the witness's ability to see. The line of sight may also reveal whether the officer saw the activity across a crowded roadway or a vacant lot. In most, but not all, cases that information will not pinpoint the surveillance location. Therefore, unless the State establishes some good reason for nondisclosure, a defendant may examine a witness concerning line of sight." *Id.*

In some cases, "particularly those in which the only evidence offered against a defendant is the testimony of the surveillance officer, a court may determine that disclosure is warranted." *Id.* at 82. The circumstances of this case, however, demonstrated a sufficient opportunity to cross-examine the State's witnesses without inquiring about the exact location of the surveillance site. In addition, "the State presented a substantial amount of corroborating evidence." *Id.* "Furthermore, defendant has failed to show how the concealment of the surveillance location deprived him of effective cross-examination." *Id.* at 83. In fact, defendant "failed to show that disclosure of the exact location was essential or even helpful to a fair determination of his case." *Id.* Consequently, the trial court's decision to issue the protective order, prohibiting disclosure of the exact location of the surveillance site, was appropriate.

Judgment affirmed.

Appendix

FEDERAL RULES
OF EVIDENCE

This Appendix consists of the Federal Rules of Evidence in unannotated form, currently including the amendments promulgated by the Supreme Court through H.D. 109-6, Jan. 17, 2005, and by the Congress through P.L. 109-37, July 22, 2005.

RULES

ARTICLE I. GENERAL PROVISIONS

NOTES

Rule 101. Scope

These rules govern proceedings in the courts of the United States and before United States bankruptcy judges and United States magistrate judges, to the extent and with the exceptions stated in rule 1101.
(Amended by H.D. 100-41, Mar. 2, 1987, eff. Oct. 1, 1987; H.D. 100-187, Apr. 25, 1988, eff. Nov. 1, 1988; H.D. 103-76, Apr. 22, 1993, eff. Dec. 1, 1993.)

Rule 102. Purpose and Construction

These rules shall be construed to secure fairness in administration, elimination of unjustifiable expense and delay, and promotion of growth and development of the law of evidence to the end that the truth may be ascertained and proceedings justly determined.

Rule 103. Rulings on Evidence

(a) Effect of erroneous ruling. Error may not be predicated upon a ruling which admits or excludes evidence unless a substantial right of the party is affected, and

(1) Objection. In case the ruling is one admitting evidence, a timely objection or motion to strike appears of record, stating the specific ground of objection, if the specific ground was not apparent from the context; or

(2) Offer of proof. In case the ruling is one excluding evidence, the substance of the evidence was made known to the court by offer or was apparent from the context within which questions were asked.

Once the court makes a definitive ruling on the record admitting or excluding evidence, either at or before trial, a party need not renew an objection or offer of proof to preserve a claim of error for appeal.

(b) Record of offer and ruling. The court may add any other or further statement which shows the character of the evidence, the form in which it was offered, the objection made, and the ruling thereon. It may direct the making of an offer in question and answer form.

(c) Hearing of jury. In jury cases, proceedings shall be conducted, to the extent practicable, so as to prevent inadmissible evidence from being suggested to the jury by any means, such as making statements or offers of proof or asking questions in the hearing of the jury.

(d) Plain error. Nothing in this rule precludes taking notice of plain errors affecting

substantial rights although they were not brought to the attention of the court.
(Amended by H.D. 106-225, Apr. 17, 2000, eff. Dec. 1, 2000.)

Rule 104. Preliminary Questions

(a) Questions of admissibility generally. Preliminary questions concerning the qualification of a person to be a witness, the existence of a privilege, or the admissibility of evidence shall be determined by the court, subject to the provisions of subdivision (b). In making its determination it is not bound by the rules of evidence except those with respect to privileges.

(b) Relevancy conditioned on fact. When the relevancy of evidence depends upon the fulfillment of a condition of fact, the court shall admit it upon, or subject to, the introduction of evidence sufficient to support a finding of the fulfillment of the condition.

(c) Hearing of jury. Hearings on the admissibility of confessions shall in all cases be conducted out of the hearing of the jury. Hearings on other preliminary matters shall be so conducted when the interests of justice require, or when an accused is a witness and so requests.

(d) Testimony by accused. The accused does not, by testifying upon a preliminary matter, become subject to cross- examination as to other issues in the case.

(e) Weight and credibility. This rule does not limit the right of a party to introduce before the jury evidence relevant to weight or credibility.
(Amended by H.D. 100-41, Mar. 2, 1987, eff. Oct. 1, 1987.)

Rule 105. Limited Admissibility

When evidence which is admissible as to one party or for one purpose but not admissible as to another party or for another purpose is admitted, the court, upon request, shall restrict the evidence to its proper scope and instruct the jury accordingly.

NOTES

NOTES

Rule 106. Remainder of or Related Writings or Recorded Statements

When a writing or recorded statement or part thereof is introduced by a party, an adverse party may require the introduction at that time of any other part or any other writing or recorded statement which ought in fairness to be considered contemporaneously with it.
(Amended by H.D. 100-41, Mar. 2, 1987, eff. Oct. 1, 1987.)

ARTICLE II. JUDICIAL NOTICE

Rule
201.   Judicial Notice of Adjudicative Facts.
    (a) Scope of rule.
    (b) Kinds of facts.
    (c) When discretionary.
    (d) When mandatory.
    (e) Opportunity to be heard.
    (f) Time of taking notice.
    (g) Instructing jury.

Rule 201. Judicial Notice of Adjudicative Facts

(a) Scope of rule. This rule governs only judicial notice of adjudicative facts.

(b) Kinds of facts. A judicially noticed fact must be one not subject to reasonable dispute in that it is either (1) generally known within the territorial jurisdiction of the trial court or (2) capable of accurate and ready determination by resort to sources whose accuracy cannot reasonably be questioned.

(c) When discretionary. A court may take judicial notice, whether requested or not.

(d) When mandatory. A court shall take judicial notice if requested by a party and supplied with the necessary information.

(e) Opportunity to be heard. A party is entitled upon timely request to an opportunity to be heard as to the propriety of taking judicial notice and the tenor of the matter noticed. In the absence of prior notification, the request may be made after judicial notice has been taken.

(f) Time of taking notice. Judicial notice may be taken at any stage of the proceeding.

(g) Instructing jury. In a civil action or proceeding, the court shall instruct the jury to accept as conclusive any fact judicially noticed. In a criminal case, the court shall instruct the jury that it may, but is not required to, accept as conclusive any fact judicially noticed.

ARTICLE III. PRESUMPTIONS IN CIVIL ACTIONS AND PROCEEDINGS

Rule 301. Presumptions in General in Civil Actions and Proceedings

In all civil actions and proceedings not otherwise provided for by Act of Congress or by these rules, a presumption imposes on the party against whom it is directed the burden of going forward with evidence to rebut or meet the presumption, but does not shift to such party the burden of proof in the sense of the risk of non persuasion, which remains throughout the trial upon the party on whom it was originally cast.

Rule 302. Applicability of State Law in Civil Actions and Proceedings

In civil actions and proceedings, the effect of a presumption respecting a fact which is an element of a claim or defense as to which State law supplies the rule of decision is determined in accordance with State law.

NOTES

Rule 401. Definition of "Relevant Evidence"

"Relevant evidence" means evidence having any tendency to make the existence of any fact that is of consequence to the determination of the action more probable or less probable than it would be without the evidence.

Rule 402. Relevant Evidence Generally Admissible; Irrelevant Evidence Inadmissible

All relevant evidence is admissible, except as otherwise provided by the Constitution of the United States, by Act of Congress, by these rules, or by other rules prescribed by the Supreme Court pursuant to statutory authority. Evidence which is not relevant is not admissible.

Rule 403. Exclusion of Relevant Evidence on Grounds of Prejudice, Confusion, or Waste of Time

Although relevant, evidence may be excluded if its probative value is substantially outweighed by the danger of unfair prejudice, confusion of the issues, or misleading the jury, or by considerations of undue delay, waste of time, or needless presentation of cumulative evidence.

Rule 404. Character Evidence Not Admissible To Prove Conduct; Exceptions; Other Crimes

(a) **Character evidence generally.** Evidence of a person's character or a trait of character is not admissible for the purpose of proving action in conformity therewith on a particular occasion, except:

(1) **Character of accused.** Evidence of a pertinent trait of character offered by an accused, or by the prosecution to rebut the same, or if evidence of a trait of character of the alleged victim of the crime is offered by an accused and admitted under Rule 404(a)(2), evidence of the same trait of character of the accused offered by the prosecution;

(2) **Character of alleged victim.** Evidence of a pertinent trait of character of the alleged victim of the crime offered by an accused, or by the prosecution to rebut the same, or evidence of a character trait of peacefulness of the alleged victim offered by the prosecution

NOTES

in a homicide case to rebut evidence that the alleged victim was the first aggressor;

(3) Character of witness. Evidence of the character of a witness, as provided in rules 607, 608, and 609.

(b) Other crimes, wrongs, or acts. Evidence of other crimes, wrongs, or acts is not admissible to prove the character of a person in order to show action in conformity therewith. It may, however, be admissible for other purposes, such as proof of motive, opportunity, intent, preparation, plan, knowledge, identity, or absence of mistake or accident, provided that upon request by the accused, the prosecution in a criminal case shall provide reasonable notice in advance of trial, or during trial if the court excuses pretrial notice on good cause shown, of the general nature of any such evidence it intends to introduce at trial.
(Amended by H.D. 100-41, Mar. 2, 1987, eff. Oct. 1, 1987; H.D. 102-76, Apr. 30, 1991, eff. Dec. 1, 1991; H.D. 106-225, Apr. 17, 2000, eff. Dec. 1, 2000.)

Rule 405. Methods of Proving Character

(a) Reputation or opinion. In all cases in which evidence of character or a trait of character of a person is admissible, proof may be made by testimony as to reputation or by testimony in the form of an opinion. On cross-examination, inquiry is allowable into relevant specific instances of conduct.

(b) Specific instances of conduct. In cases in which character or a trait of character of a person is an essential element of a charge, claim, or defense, proof may also be made of specific instances of that person's conduct.
(Amended by H.D. 100-41, Mar. 2, 1987, eff. Oct. 1, 1987.)

Rule 406. Habit; Routine Practice

Evidence of the habit of a person or of the routine practice of an organization, whether corroborated or not and regardless of the presence of eyewitnesses, is relevant to prove that the conduct of the person or organization on a particular occasion was in conformity with the habit or routine practice.

Rule 407. Subsequent Remedial Measures

When, after an injury or harm allegedly caused by an event, measures are taken that, if taken previously, would have made the injury or harm less likely to occur, evidence of the subsequent measures is not admissible to prove negligence, culpable conduct, a defect in a product, a defect in a product's design, or a need for a warning or instruction. This rule does not require the exclusion of evidence of subsequent measures when offered for another purpose, such as proving ownership, control, or feasibility of precautionary measures, if controverted, or impeachment.
(Amended by H.D. 105-69, April 11, 1997, eff. Dec. 1, 1997.)

Rule 408. Compromise and Offers to Compromise

Evidence of (1) furnishing or offering or promising to furnish, or (2) accepting or offering or promising to accept, a valuable consideration in compromising or attempting to compromise a claim which was disputed as to either validity or amount, is not admissible to prove liability for or invalidity of the claim or its amount. Evidence of conduct or statements made in compromise negotiations is likewise not admissible. This rule does not require the exclusion of any evidence otherwise discoverable merely because it is presented in the course of compromise negotiations. This rule also does not require exclusion when the evidence is offered for another purpose, such as proving bias or prejudice of a witness, negativing a contention of undue delay, or proving an effort to obstruct a criminal investigation or prosecution.

NOTES

NOTES

Rule 409. Payment of Medical and Similar Expenses

Evidence of furnishing or offering or promising to pay medical, hospital, or similar expenses occasioned by an injury is not admissible to prove liability for the injury.

Rule 410. Inadmissibility of Pleas, Plea Discussions, and Related Statements

Except as otherwise provided in this rule, evidence of the following is not, in any civil or criminal proceeding, admissible against the defendant who made the plea or was a participant in the plea discussions:

(1) a plea of guilty which was later withdrawn;

(2) a plea of nolo contendere;

(3) any statement made in the course of any proceedings under Rule 11 of the Federal Rules of Criminal Procedure or comparable state procedure regarding either of the foregoing pleas; or

(4) any statement made in the course of plea discussions with an attorney for the prosecuting authority which do not result in a plea of guilty or which result in a plea of guilty later withdrawn.

However, such a statement is admissible (i) in any proceeding wherein another statement made in the course of the same plea or plea discussions has been introduced and the statement ought in fairness be considered contemporaneously with it, or (ii) in a criminal proceeding for perjury or false statement if the statement was made by the defendant under oath, on the record and in the presence of counsel.

Rule 411. Liability Insurance

Evidence that a person was or was not insured against liability is not admissible upon the issue whether the person acted negligently or otherwise wrongfully. This rule does not require the exclusion of evidence of insurance

against liability when offered for another purpose, such as proof of agency, ownership, or control, or bias or prejudice of a witness.
(Amended by H.D. 100-41, Mar. 2, 1987, eff. Oct. 1, 1987.)

Rule 412. Sex Offense Cases; Relevance of Alleged Victim's Past Sexual Behavior or Alleged Sexual Predisposition

(a) Evidence generally inadmissible. The following evidence is not admissible in any civil or criminal proceeding involving alleged sexual misconduct except as provided in subdivisions (b) and (c):

(1) Evidence offered to prove that any alleged victim engaged in other sexual behavior.

(2) Evidence offered to prove any alleged victim's sexual predisposition.

(b) Exceptions.

(1) In a criminal case, the following evidence is admissible, if otherwise admissible under these rules:

(A) evidence of specific instances of sexual behavior by the alleged victim offered to prove that a person other than the accused was the source of semen, injury or other physical evidence;

(B) evidence of specific instances of sexual behavior by the alleged victim with respect to the person accused of the sexual misconduct offered by the accused to prove consent or by the prosecution; and

(C) evidence the exclusion of which would violate the constitutional rights of the defendant.

(2) In a civil case, evidence offered to prove the sexual behavior or sexual predisposition of any alleged victim is admissible if it is otherwise admissible under these rules and its probative value substantially outweighs the danger of harm to any victim and of unfair prejudice to any party. Evidence of an alleged victim's reputation is admissible only if it has been placed in controversy by the alleged victim.

NOTES

NOTES

(c) Procedure to determine admissibility.

(1) A party intending to offer evidence under subdivision (b) must—

(A) file a written motion at least 14 days before trial specifically describing the evidence and stating the purpose for which it is offered unless the court, for good cause requires a different time for filing or permits filing during trial; and

(B) serve the motion on all parties and notify the alleged victim or, when appropriate, the alleged victim's guardian or representative.

(2) Before admitting evidence under this rule the court must conduct a hearing in camera and afford the victim and parties a right to attend and be heard. The motion, related papers, and the record of the hearing must be sealed and remain under seal unless the court orders otherwise.
(Amended by P.L. 100-690, title VII, §7046(a), Nov. 18, 1988, 102 Stat. 4400; H.D. 103-250, Apr. 29, 1994, eff. Dec. 1, 1994; P.L. 103-322, §40141(b), Sept. 13, 1994, 108 Stat. 1919, eff. Dec. 1, 1994.)

Rule 413. Evidence of Similar Crimes in Sexual Assault Cases

(a) In a criminal case in which the defendant is accused of an offense of sexual assault, evidence of the defendant's commission of another offense or offenses of sexual assault is admissible, and may be considered for its bearing on any matter to which it is relevant.

(b) In a case in which the Government intends to offer evidence under this rule, the attorney for the Government shall disclose the evidence to the defendant, including statements of witnesses or a summary of the substance of any testimony that is expected to be offered, at least fifteen days before the scheduled date of trial or at such later time as the court may allow for good cause.

(c) This rule shall not be construed to limit the admission or consideration of evidence under any other rule.

(d) For purposes of this rule and Rule 415, "offense of sexual assault" means a crime under Federal law or the law of a State (as defined in section 513 of title 18, United States Code) that involved—

(1) any conduct proscribed by chapter 109A of title 18, United States Code;

(2) contact, without consent, between any part of the defendant's body or an object and the genitals or anus of another person;

(3) contact, without consent, between the genitals or anus of the defendant and any part of another person's body;

(4) deriving sexual pleasure or gratification from the infliction of death, bodily injury, or physical pain on another person; or

(5) an attempt or conspiracy to engage in conduct described in paragraphs (1)-(4).
(Added by P.L. 103-322, §320935(a), Sept. 13, 1994, 108 Stat. 2135.)

Rule 414. Evidence of Similar Crimes in Child Molestation Cases

(a) In a criminal case in which the defendant is accused of an offense of child molestation, evidence of the defendant's commission of another offense or offenses of child molestation is admissible, and may be considered for its bearing on any matter to which it is relevant.

(b) In a case in which the Government intends to offer evidence under this rule, the attorney for the Government shall disclose the evidence to the defendant, including statements of witnesses or a summary of the substance of any testimony that is expected to be offered, at least fifteen days before the scheduled date of trial or at such later time as the court may allow for good cause.

(c) This rule shall not be construed to limit the admission or consideration of evidence under any other rule.

(d) For purposes of this rule and Rule 415, "child" means a person below the age of fourteen, and "offense of child molestation" means

NOTES

413

NOTES

a crime under Federal law or the law of a State (as defined in section 513 of title 18, United States Code) that involved—

(1) any conduct proscribed by chapter 109A of title 18, United States Code, that was committed in relation to a child;

(2) any conduct proscribed by chapter 110 of title 18, United States Code;

(3) contact between any part of the defendant's body or an object and the genitals or anus of a child;

(4) contact between the genitals or anus of the defendant and any part of the body of a child;

(5) deriving sexual pleasure or gratification from the infliction of death, bodily injury, or physical pain on a child; or

(6) an attempt or conspiracy to engage in conduct described in paragraphs (1)-(5).
(Added by P.L. 103-322, §320935(a), Sept. 13, 1994, 108 Stat. 2135.)

Rule 415. Evidence of Similar Acts in Civil Cases Concerning Sexual Assault or Child Molestation

(a) In a civil case in which a claim for damages or other relief is predicated on a party's alleged commission of conduct constituting an offense of sexual assault or child molestation, evidence of that party's commission of another offense or offenses of sexual assault or child molestation is admissible and may be considered as provided in Rule 413 and Rule 414 of these rules.

(b) A party who intends to offer evidence under this Rule shall disclose the evidence to the party against whom it will be offered, including statements of witnesses or a summary of the substance of any testimony that is expected to be offered, at least fifteen days before the scheduled date of trial or at such later time as the court may allow for good cause.

(c) This rule shall not be construed to limit the admission or consideration of evidence under any other rule.
(Added by P.L. 103-322, §320935(a), Sept. 13, 1994, 108 Stat. 2135.)

ARTICLE V. PRIVILEGES

Rule
501.   General Rule.

Rule 501. General Rule

Except as otherwise required by the Constitution of the United States or provided by Act of Congress or in rules prescribed by the Supreme Court pursuant to statutory authority, the privilege of a witness, person, government, State, or political subdivision thereof shall be governed by the principles of the common law as they may be interpreted by the courts of the United States in the light of reason and experience. However, in civil actions and proceedings, with respect to an element of a claim or defense as to which State law supplies the rule of decision, the privilege of a witness, person, government, State, or political subdivision thereof shall be determined in accordance with State law.

ARTICLE VI. WITNESSES

Rule
601.   General Rule of Competency.
602.   Lack of Personal Knowledge.
603.   Oath or Affirmation.
604.   Interpreters.
605.   Competency of Judge as Witness.
606.   Competency of Juror as Witness.
        (a) At the trial.
        (b) Inquiry into validity of verdict or indictment.
607.   Who May Impeach.
608.   Evidence of Character and Conduct of Witness.
        (a) Opinion and reputation evidence of character.
        (b) Specific instances of conduct.

NOTES

NOTES

Rule 601. General Rule of Competency

Every person is competent to be a witness except as otherwise provided in these rules. However, in civil actions and proceedings, with respect to an element of a claim or defense as to which State law supplies the rule of decision, the competency of a witness shall be determined in accordance with State law.

Rule 602. Lack of Personal Knowledge

A witness may not testify to a matter unless evidence is introduced sufficient to support a finding that the witness has personal knowledge of the matter. Evidence to prove personal knowledge may, but need not, consist of the witness' own testimony. This rule is subject to the provisions of rule 703, relating to opinion testimony by expert witnesses.
(Amended by H.D. 100-41, Mar. 2, 1987, eff. Oct. 1, 1987; H.D. 100-187, Apr. 25, 1988, eff. Nov. 1, 1988.)

Rule 603. Oath or Affirmation

Before testifying, every witness shall be required to declare that the witness will testify truthfully, by oath or affirmation administered in a form calculated to awaken the witness' conscience and impress the witness' mind with the duty to do so.
(Amended by H.D. 100-41, Mar. 2, 1987, eff. Oct. 1, 1987.)

Rule 604. Interpreters

An interpreter is subject to the provisions of these rules relating to qualification as an expert and the administration of an oath or affirmation to make a true translation.
(Amended by H.D. 100-41, Mar. 2, 1987, eff. Oct. 1, 1987.)

Rule 605. Competency of Judge as Witness

The judge presiding at the trial may not testify in that trial as a witness. No objection need be made in order to preserve the point.

Rule 606. Competency of Juror as Witness

(a) At the trial. A member of the jury may not testify as a witness before that jury in the trial of the case in which the juror is sitting. If the juror is called so to testify, the opposing party shall be afforded an opportunity to object out of the presence of the jury.

(b) Inquiry into validity of verdict or indictment. Upon an inquiry into the validity of a verdict or indictment, a juror may not testify as to any matter or statement occurring during the course of the jury's deliberations or to the effect of anything upon that or any other juror's mind or emotions as influencing the juror to assent to or dissent from the verdict or indictment or concerning the juror's mental processes in connection therewith, except that a juror may testify on the question whether extraneous prejudicial information was improperly brought to the jury's attention or whether any outside influence was improperly brought

NOTES

to bear upon any juror. Nor may a juror's affidavit or evidence of any statement by the juror concerning a matter about which the juror would be precluded from testifying be received for these purposes.
(Amended by H.D. 100-41, Mar. 2, 1987, eff. Oct. 1, 1987.)

Rule 607. Who May Impeach

The credibility of a witness may be attacked by any party, including the party calling the witness.
(Amended by H.D. 100-41, Mar. 2, 1987, eff. Oct. 1, 1987.)

Rule 608. Evidence of Character and Conduct of Witness

(a) Opinion and reputation evidence of character.— The credibility of a witness may be attacked or supported by evidence in the form of opinion or reputation, but subject to these limitations: (1) the evidence may refer only to character for truthfulness or untruthfulness, and (2) evidence of truthful character is admissible only after the character of the witness for truthfulness has been attacked by opinion or reputation evidence or otherwise.

(b) Specific instances of conduct.— Specific instances of the conduct of a witness, for the purpose of attacking or supporting the witness' character for truthfulness, other than conviction of crime as provided in rule 609, may not be proved by extrinsic evidence. They may, however, in the discretion of the court, if probative of truthfulness or untruthfulness, be inquired into on cross-examination of the witness (1) concerning the witness' character for truthfulness or untruthfulness, or (2) concerning the character for truthfulness or untruthfulness of another witness as to which character the witness being cross-examined has testified.

The giving of testimony, whether by an accused or by any other witness, does not operate as a waiver of the accused's or the witness'

privilege against self-incrimination when examined with respect to matters which relate only to character for truthfulness.
(Amended by H.D. 100-41, Mar. 2, 1987, eff. Oct. 1, 1987; H.D. 100-187, Apr. 25, 1988, eff. Nov. 1, 1988; H.D. 108-57, eff. Dec. 1, 2003.)

Rule 609. Impeachment by Evidence of Conviction of Crime

(a) **General rule.** For the purpose of attacking the credibility of a witness,

(1) evidence that a witness other than an accused has been convicted of a crime shall be admitted, subject to Rule 403, if the crime was punishable by death or imprisonment in excess of one year under the law under which the witness was convicted, and evidence that an accused has been convicted of such a crime shall be admitted if the court determines that the probative value of admitting this evidence outweighs its prejudicial effect to the accused; and

(2) evidence that any witness has been convicted of a crime shall be admitted if it involved dishonesty or false statement, regardless of the punishment.
(Amended by H.D. 101-142, Jan. 26, 1990, eff. Dec. 1, 1990.)

(b) **Time limit.** Evidence of a conviction under this rule is not admissible if a period of more than ten years has elapsed since the date of the conviction or of the release of the witness from the confinement imposed for that conviction, whichever is the later date, unless the court determines, in the interests of justice, that the probative value of the conviction supported by specific facts and circumstances substantially outweighs its prejudicial effect. However, evidence of a conviction more than 10 years old as calculated herein, is not admissible unless the proponent gives to the adverse party sufficient advance written notice of intent to use such evidence to provide the adverse party with a fair opportunity to contest the use of such evidence.

NOTES

NOTES

(c) Effect of pardon, annulment, or certificate of rehabilitation. Evidence of a conviction is not admissible under this rule if (1) the conviction has been the subject of a pardon, annulment, certificate of rehabilitation, or other equivalent procedure based on a finding of the rehabilitation of the person convicted, and that person has not been convicted of a subsequent crime which was punishable by death or imprisonment in excess of one year, or (2) the conviction has been the subject of a pardon, annulment, or other equivalent procedure based on a finding of innocence.

(d) Juvenile adjudications. Evidence of juvenile adjudications is generally not admissible under this rule. The court may, however, in a criminal case allow evidence of a juvenile adjudication of a witness other than the accused if conviction of the offense would be admissible to attack the credibility of an adult and the court is satisfied that admission in evidence is necessary for a fair determination of the issue of guilt or innocence.

(e) Pendency of appeal. The pendency of an appeal therefrom does not render evidence of a conviction inadmissible. Evidence of the pendency of an appeal is admissible.
(Amended by H.D. 100-41, Mar. 2, 1987, eff. Oct. 1, 1987; H.D. 101-142, Jan. 26, 1990, eff. Dec. 1, 1990.)

Rule 610. Religious Beliefs or Opinions

Evidence of the beliefs or opinions of a witness on matters of religion is not admissible for the purpose of showing that by reason of their nature the witness' credibility is impaired or enhanced.
(Amended by H.D. 100-41, Mar. 2, 1987, eff. Oct. 1, 1987.)

Rule 611. Mode and Order of Interrogation and Presentation

(a) Control by court. The court shall exercise reasonable control over the mode and order of interrogating witnesses and presenting evidence so as to (1) make the interrogation and presentation effective for the ascertainment of the truth, (2) avoid needless consumption of time, and (3) protect witnesses from harassment or undue embarrassment.

(b) Scope of cross-examination. Cross-examination should be limited to the subject matter of the direct examination and matters affecting the credibility of the witness. The court may, in the exercise of discretion, permit inquiry into additional matters as if on direct examination.

(c) Leading questions. Leading questions should not be used on the direct examination of a witness except as may be necessary to develop the witness' testimony. Ordinarily leading questions should be permitted on cross-examination. When a party calls a hostile witness, an adverse party, or a witness identified with an adverse party, interrogation may be by leading questions.
(Amended by H.D. 100-41, Mar. 2, 1987, eff. Oct. 1, 1987.)

Rule 612. Writing Used To Refresh Memory

Except as otherwise provided in criminal proceedings by section 3500 of title 18, United States Code, if a witness uses a writing to refresh memory for the purpose of testifying, either—

(1) while testifying, or

(2) before testifying, if the court in its discretion determines it is necessary in the interests of justice, an adverse party is entitled to have the writing produced at the hearing, to inspect it, to cross-examine the witness thereon, and to introduce in evidence those portions which relate to the testimony of the witness. If it is claimed that the writing contains matters not related to the subject matter of the testimony the court shall examine the writing in camera, excise any portions not so related, and order delivery of the remainder to the party entitled thereto. Any portion withheld over objections shall be preserved and made available to the appellate court in the event of an appeal. If a writing is not produced or delivered pursuant

NOTES

to order under this rule, the court shall make any order justice requires, except that in criminal cases when the prosecution elects not to comply, the order shall be one striking the testimony or, if the court in its discretion determines that the interests of justice so require, declaring a mistrial.
(Amended by H.D. 100-41, Mar. 2, 1987, eff. Oct. 1, 1987.)

Rule 613. Prior Statements of Witnesses

(a) Examining witness concerning prior statement. In examining a witness concerning a prior statement made by the witness, whether written or not, the statement need not be shown nor its contents disclosed to the witness at that time, but on request the same shall be shown or disclosed to opposing counsel.

(b) Extrinsic evidence of prior inconsistent statement of witness. Extrinsic evidence of a prior inconsistent statement by a witness is not admissible unless the witness is afforded an opportunity to explain or deny the same and the opposite party is afforded an opportunity to interrogate the witness thereon, or the interests of justice otherwise require. This provision does not apply to admissions of a party-opponent as defined in rule 801(d)(2).
(Amended by H.D. 100-41, Mar. 2, 1987, eff. Oct. 1, 1987; H.D. 100-187, Apr. 25, 1988, eff. Nov. 1, 1988.)

Rule 614. Calling and Interrogation of Witnesses by Court

(a) Calling by court. The court may, on its own motion or at the suggestion of a party, call witnesses, and all parties are entitled to cross-examine witnesses thus called.

(b) Interrogation by court. The court may interrogate witnesses, whether called by itself or by a party.

(c) Objections. Objections to the calling of witnesses by the court or to interrogation by it may be made at the time or at the next available opportunity when the jury is not present.

Rule 615. Exclusion of Witnesses

At the request of a party the court shall order witnesses excluded so that they cannot hear the testimony of other witnesses, and it may make the order of its own motion. This rule does not authorize exclusion of (1) a party who is a natural person, or (2) an officer or employee of a party which is not a natural person designated as its representative by its attorney, or (3) a person whose presence is shown by a party to be essential to the presentation of the party's cause, or (4) a person authorized by statute to be present.
(Amended by H.D. 100-41, Mar. 2, 1987, eff. Oct. 1, 1987; H.D. 100-187, Apr. 25, 1988, eff. Nov. 1, 1988; P.L. 100-690, title V11, §7075(a), Nov. 18, 1988, 102 Stat. 4405; H.D. 105-268, Apr. 24, 1998, eff. Dec. 1, 1998.)

ARTICLE VII. OPINIONS AND EXPERT TESTIMONY

Rule 701. Opinion Testimony by Lay Witnesses

If the witness is not testifying as an expert, the witness' testimony in the form of opinions or inferences is limited to those opinions or inferences which are (a) rationally based on the perception of the witness, and (b) helpful to a clear understanding of the witness' testimony or the determination of a fact in issue, and (c) not based on scientific, technical, or other specialized knowledge within the scope of Rule 702.
(Amended by H.D. 100-41, Mar. 2, 1987, eff. Oct. 1, 1987; H.D. 106-225, Apr. 17, 2000, eff. Dec. 1, 2000.)

NOTES

NOTES

Rule 702. Testimony by Experts

If scientific, technical, or other specialized knowledge will assist the trier of fact to understand the evidence or to determine a fact in issue, a witness qualified as an expert by knowledge, skill, experience, training, or education, may testify thereto in the form of an opinion or otherwise, if (1) the testimony is based upon sufficient facts or data, (2) the testimony is the product of reliable principles and methods, and (3) the witness has applied the principles and methods reliably to the facts of the case. (Amended by H.D. 106-225, Apr. 17, 2000, eff. Dec. 1, 2000.)

Rule 703. Bases of Opinion Testimony by Experts

The facts or data in the particular case upon which an expert bases an opinion or inference may be those perceived by or made known to the expert at or before the hearing. If of a type reasonably relied upon by experts in the particular field in forming opinions or inferences upon the subject, the facts or data need not be admissible in evidence in order for the opinion or inference to be admitted. Facts or data that are otherwise inadmissible shall not be disclosed to the jury by the proponent of the opinion or inference unless the court determines that their probative value in assisting the jury to evaluate the expert's opinion substantially outweighs their prejudicial effect. (Amended by H.D. 100-41, Mar. 2, 1987, eff. Oct. 1, 1987; H.D. 106-225, Apr. 17, 2000, Dec. 1, 2000.)

Rule 704. Opinion on Ultimate Issue

(a) Except as provided in subdivision (b), testimony in the form of an opinion or inference otherwise admissible is not objectionable because it embraces an ultimate issue to be decided by the trier of fact.

(b) No expert witness testifying with respect to the mental state or condition of a defendant in a criminal case may state an opinion or inference as to whether the defendant did or did not have the mental state or condition constituting an element of the crime charged or of a defense thereto. Such ultimate issues are matters for the trier of fact alone.

Rule 705. Disclosure of Facts or Data Underlying Expert Opinion

The expert may testify in terms of opinion or inference and give reasons therefor without first testifying to the underlying facts or data, unless the court requires otherwise. The expert may in any event be required to disclose the underlying facts or data on cross-examination. (Amended by H.D. 100-41, Mar. 2, 1987, eff. Oct. 1, 1987; H.D. 103-76, Apr. 22, 1993, eff. Dec. 1, 1993.)

Rule 706. Court Appointed Experts

(a) Appointment. The court may on its own motion or on the motion of any party enter an order to show cause why expert witnesses should not be appointed, and may request the parties to submit nominations. The court may appoint any expert witnesses agreed upon by the parties, and may appoint expert witnesses of its own selection. An expert witness shall not be appointed by the court unless the witness consents to act. A witness so appointed shall be informed of the witness' duties by the court in writing, a copy of which shall be filed with the clerk, or at a conference in which the parties shall have opportunity to participate. A witness so appointed shall advise the parties of the witness' findings, if any; the witness' deposition may be taken by any party; and the witness may be called to testify by the court or any party. The witness shall be subject to cross-examination by each party, including a party calling the witness.

(b) Compensation. Expert witnesses so appointed are entitled to reasonable compensation in whatever sum the court may allow. The compensation thus fixed is payable from funds which may be provided by law in criminal cases and civil actions and proceedings involving just compensation under the fifth

NOTES

NOTES

amendment. In other civil actions and pro-ceedings the compensation shall be paid by the parties in such proportion and at such time as the court directs, and thereafter charged in like manner as other costs.

(c) Disclosure of appointment. In the exercise of its discretion, the court may autho-rize disclosure to the jury of the fact that the court appointed the expert witness.

(d) Parties' experts of own selection. Nothing in this rule limits the parties in call-ing expert witnesses of their own selection. (Amended by H.D. 100-41, Mar. 2, 1987, eff. Oct. 1, 1987.)

ARTICLE VIII. HEARSAY

Rule
801.   Definitions.
    (a)   Statement.
    (b)   Declarant.
    (c)   Hearsay.
    (d)   Statements which are not hearsay.
        (1)   Prior statement by witness.
        (2)   Admission by party-opponent.
802.   Hearsay Rule.
803.   Hearsay Exceptions; Availability of Declarant Immaterial.
    (1)   Present sense impression.
    (2)   Excited utterance.
    (3)   Then existing mental, emotional, or physical condition.
    (4)   Statements for purposes of medical diagnosis or treatment.
    (5)   Recorded recollection.
    (6)   Records of regularly conducted activity.
    (7)   Absence of entry in records kept in accordance with the provisions of paragraph (6).
    (8)   Public records and reports.
    (9)   Records of vital statistics.
    (10) Absence of public record or entry.
    (11) Records of religious organizations.
    (12) Marriage, baptismal, and similar certificates.
    (13) Family records.
    (14) Records of documents affecting an interest in property.
    (15) Statements in documents affecting an interest in property.
    (16) Statements in ancient documents.
    (17) Market reports, commercial publications.

Rule 801. Definitions

The following definitions apply under this article:

(a) Statement. A "statement" is (1) an oral or written assertion or (2) nonverbal conduct of a person, if it is intended by the person as an assertion.

(b) Declarant. A "declarant" is a person who makes a statement.

(c) Hearsay. "Hearsay" is a statement, other than one made by the declarant while testifying at the trial or hearing, offered in evidence to prove the truth of the matter asserted.

(d) Statements which are not hearsay. A statement is not hearsay if—

(1) Prior statement by witness. The declarant testifies at the trial or hearing and is subject to cross-examination concerning the statement, and the statement is (A) inconsistent with the declarant's testimony, and was given under oath subject to the penalty of perjury at a trial, hearing, or other proceeding, or in a deposition, or (B) consistent with the declarant's testimony and is offered to rebut

NOTES

NOTES

an express or implied charge against the declarant of recent fabrication or improper influence or motive, or (C) one of identification of a person made after perceiving the person; or

(2) Admission by party-opponent. The statement is offered against a party and is (A) the party's own statement, in either an individual or a representative capacity or (B) a statement of which the party has manifested an adoption or belief in its truth, or (C) a statement by a person authorized by the party to make a statement concerning the subject, or (D) a statement by the party's agent or servant concerning a matter within the scope of the agency or employment, made during the existence of the relationship, or (E) a statement by a coconspirator of a party during the course and in furtherance of the conspiracy. The contents of the statement shall be considered but are not alone sufficient to establish the declarant's authority under subdivision (C), the agency or employment relationship and scope thereof under subdivision (D), or the existence of the conspiracy and the participation therein of the declarant and the party against whom the statement is offered under subdivision (E). (Amended by H.D. 100-41, Mar. 2, 1987, eff. Oct. 1, 1987; H.D. 105-69, Apr. 11, 1997, eff. Dec. 1, 1997.)

Rule 802. Hearsay Rule

Hearsay is not admissible except as provided by these rules or by other rules prescribed by the Supreme Court pursuant to statutory authority or by Act of Congress.

Rule 803. Hearsay Exceptions; Availability of Declarant Immaterial

The following are not excluded by the hearsay rule, even though the declarant is available as a witness:

(1) Present sense impression. A statement describing or explaining an event or condition made while the declarant was perceiving the event or condition, or immediately thereafter.

(2) Excited utterance. A statement relating to a startling event or condition made while the declarant was under the stress of excitement caused by the event or condition.

(3) Then existing mental, emotional, or physical condition. A statement of the declarant's then existing state of mind, emotion, sensation, or physical condition (such as intent, plan, motive, design, mental feeling, pain, and bodily health), but not including a statement of memory or belief to prove the fact remembered or believed unless it relates to the execution, revocation, identification, or terms of declarant's will.

(4) Statements for purposes of medical diagnosis or treatment. Statements made for purposes of medical diagnosis or treatment and describing medical history, or past or present symptoms, pain, or sensations, or the inception or general character of the cause or external source thereof insofar as reasonably pertinent to diagnosis or treatment.

(5) Recorded recollection. A memorandum or record concerning a matter about which a witness once had knowledge but now has insufficient recollection to enable the witness to testify fully and accurately, shown to have been made or adopted by the witness when the matter was fresh in the witness' memory and to reflect that knowledge correctly. If admitted, the memorandum or record may be read into evidence but may not itself be received as an exhibit unless offered by an adverse party.

(6) Records of regularly conducted activity. A memorandum, report, record, or data compilation, in any form, of acts, events, conditions, opinions, or diagnoses, made at or near the time by, or from information transmitted by, a person with knowledge, if kept in the course of a regularly conducted business activity, and if it was the regular practice of that business activity to make the memorandum, report, record or data compilation, all as shown by the testimony of the custodian or other qualified witness, or by certification that complies

NOTES

with Rule 902(11), Rule 902(12), or a statute permitting certification, unless the source of information or the method or circumstances of preparation indicate lack of trustworthiness. The term "business" as used in this paragraph includes business, institution, association, profession, occupation, and calling of every kind, whether or not conducted for profit.

(7) Absence of entry in records kept in accordance with the provisions of paragraph (6). Evidence that a matter is not included in the memoranda reports, records, or data compilations, in any form, kept in accordance with the provisions of paragraph (6), to prove the nonoccurrence or nonexistence of the matter, if the matter was of a kind of which a memorandum, report, record, or data compilation was regularly made and preserved, unless the sources of information or other circumstances indicate lack of trustworthiness.

(8) Public records and reports. Records, reports, statements, or data compilations, in any form, of public offices or agencies, setting forth (A) the activities of the office or agency, or (B) matters observed pursuant to duty imposed by law as to which matters there was a duty to report, excluding, however, in criminal cases matters observed by police officers and other law enforcement personnel, or (C) in civil actions and proceedings and against the Government in criminal cases, factual findings resulting from an investigation made pursuant to authority granted by law, unless the sources of information or other circumstances indicate lack of trustworthiness.

(9) Records of vital statistics. Records or data compilations, in any form, of births, fetal deaths, deaths, or marriages, if the report thereof was made to a public office pursuant to requirements of law.

(10) Absence of public record or entry. To prove the absence of a record, report, statement, or data compilation, in any form, or the nonoccurrence or nonexistence of a matter of which a record, report, statement, or data compilation, in any form, was regularly made and preserved by a public office or agency, evidence in the form of a certification in accordance with rule 902, or testimony, that diligent search failed to disclose the record, report, statement, or data compilation, or entry.

(11) Records of religious organizations. Statements of births, marriages, divorces, deaths, legitimacy, ancestry, relationship by blood or marriage, or other similar facts of personal or family history, contained in a regularly kept record of a religious organization.

(12) Marriage, baptismal, and similar certificates. Statements of fact contained in a certificate that the maker performed a marriage or other ceremony or administered a sacrament, made by a clergyman, public official, or other person authorized by the rules or practices of a religious organization or by law to perform the act certified, and purporting to have been issued at the time of the act or within a reasonable time thereafter.

(13) Family records. Statements of fact concerning personal or family history contained in family Bibles, genealogies, charts, engravings on rings, inscriptions on family portraits, engravings on urns, crypts, or tombstones, or the like.

(14) Records of documents affecting an interest in property. The record of a document purporting to establish or affect an interest in property, as proof of the content of the original recorded document and its execution and delivery by each person by whom it purports to have been executed, if the record is a record of a public office and an applicable statute authorizes the recording of documents of that kind in that office.

(15) Statements in documents affecting an interest in property. A statement contained in a document purporting to establish or affect an interest in property if the matter stated was relevant to the purpose of the document, unless dealings with the property since the document was made have been inconsistent with the truth of the statement or the purport of the document.

NOTES

(16) Statements in ancient documents. Statements in a document in existence twenty years or more the authenticity of which is established.

(17) Market reports, commercial publications. Market quotations, tabulations, lists, directories, or other published compilations, generally used and relied upon by the public or by persons in particular occupations.

(18) Learned treatises. To the extent called to the attention of an expert witness upon cross-examination or relied upon by the expert witness in direct examination, statements contained in published treatises, periodicals, or pamphlets on a subject of history, medicine, or other science or art, established as a reliable authority by the testimony or admission of the witness or by other expert testimony or by judicial notice. If admitted, the statements may be read into evidence but may not be received as exhibits.

(19) Reputation concerning personal or family history. Reputation among members of a person's family by blood, adoption, or marriage, or among a person's associates, or in the community, concerning a person's birth, adoption, marriage, divorce, death, legitimacy, relationship by blood, adoption, or marriage, ancestry, or other similar fact of personal or family history.

(20) Reputation concerning boundaries or general history. Reputation in a community, arising before the controversy, as to boundaries of or customs affecting lands in the community, and reputation as to events of general history important to the community or State or nation in which located.

(21) Reputation as to character. Reputation of a person's character among associates or in the community.

(22) Judgment of previous conviction. Evidence of a final judgment, entered after a trial or upon a plea of guilty (but not upon a plea of nolo contendere), adjudging a person guilty of a crime punishable by death or imprisonment in excess of one year, to prove any fact essential to sustain the judgment, but not including, when offered by the Government in a criminal prosecution for purposes other than impeachment, judgments against persons other than the accused. The pendency of an appeal may be shown but does not affect admissibility.

(23) Judgment as to personal, family, or general history, or boundaries. Judgments as proof of matters of personal, family or general history, or boundaries, essential to the judgment, if the same would be provable by evidence of reputation.

(24) [Transferred to Rule 807.]
(Amended by H.D. 100-41, Mar. 2, 1987, eff. Oct. 1, 1987; H.D. 105-69, April 11, 1997, eff. Dec. 1, 1997; H.D. 106-225, Apr. 17, 2000, eff. Dec. 1, 2000.)

Rule 804. Hearsay Exceptions; Declarant Unavailable

(a) Definition of unavailability. "Unavailability as a witness" includes situations in which the declarant—

(1) is exempted by ruling of the court on the ground of privilege from testifying concerning the subject matter of the declarant's statement; or

(2) persists in refusing to testify concerning the subject matter of the declarant's statement despite an order of the court to do so; or

(3) testifies to a lack of memory of the subject matter of the declarant's statement; or

(4) is unable to be present or to testify at the hearing because of death or then existing physical or mental illness or infirmity; or

(5) is absent from the hearing and the proponent of a statement has been unable to procure the declarant's attendance (or in the case of a hearsay exception under subdivision (b)(2), (3), or (4), the declarant's attendance or testimony) by process or other reasonable means.

A declarant is not unavailable as a witness if exemption, refusal, claim of lack of memory, inability, or absence is due to the procurement or wrongdoing of the proponent of a statement for the purpose of preventing the witness from attending or testifying.

(b) Hearsay exceptions. The following are not excluded by the hearsay rule if the declarant is unavailable as a witness:

(1) *Former testimony.* Testimony given as a witness at another hearing of the same or a different proceeding, or in a deposition taken in compliance with law in the course of the same or another proceeding, if the party against whom the testimony is now offered, or, in a civil action or proceeding, a predecessor in interest, had an opportunity and similar motive to develop the testimony by direct, cross, or redirect examination.

(2) *Statement under belief of impending death.* In a prosecution for homicide or in a civil action or proceeding, a statement made by a declarant while believing that the declarant's death was imminent, concerning the cause or circumstances of what the declarant believed to be impending death.

(3) *Statement against interest.* A statement which was at the time of its making so far contrary to the declarant's pecuniary or proprietary interest, or so far tended to subject the declarant to civil or criminal liability, or to render invalid a claim by the declarant against another, that a reasonable person in the declarant's position would not have made the statement unless believing it to be true. A statement tending to expose the declarant to criminal liability and offered to exculpate the accused is not admissible unless corroborating circumstances clearly indicate the trustworthiness of the statement.

(4) *Statement of personal or family history.* (A) A statement concerning the declarant's own birth, adoption, marriage, divorce, legitimacy, relationship by blood, adoption, or marriage, ancestry, or other similar fact of personal or family history, even though declarant had no means of acquiring personal knowledge of the matter stated; or (B) a statement concerning

the foregoing matters, and death also, of another person, if the declarant was related to the other by blood, adoption, or marriage or was so intimately associated with the other's family as to be likely to have accurate information concerning the matter declared.

(5) [Transferred to Rule 807.]

(6) *Forfeiture by wrongdoing.* A statement offered against a party that has engaged or acquiesced in wrongdoing that was intended to, and did, procure the unavailability of the declarant as a witness.
(Amended by H.D. 100-41, Mar. 2, 1987, eff. Oct. 1, 1987; P.L. 100-690, title VII, §7075(b), Nov. 18, 1988, 102 Stat. 4405; H.D. 105-69, Apr. 11, 1997, eff. Dec. 1, 1997.)

Rule 805. Hearsay Within Hearsay

Hearsay included within hearsay is not excluded under the hearsay rule if each part of the combined statements conforms with an exception to the hearsay rule provided in these rules.

Rule 806. Attacking and Supporting Credibility of Declarant

When a hearsay statement, or a statement defined in Rule 801(d)(2)(C), (D), or (E), has been admitted in evidence, the credibility of the declarant may be attacked, and if attacked may be supported, by any evidence which would be admissible for those purposes if declarant had testified as a witness. Evidence of a statement or conduct by the declarant at any time, inconsistent with the declarant's hearsay statement, is not subject to any requirement that the declarant may have been afforded an opportunity to deny or explain. If the party against whom a hearsay statement has been admitted calls the declarant as a witness, the party is entitled to examine the declarant on the statement as if under cross-examination.
(Amended by H.D. 100-41, Mar. 2, 1987, eff. Oct. 1, 1987; H.D. 105-69, Apr. 11, 1997, eff. Dec. 1, 1997.)

NOTES

Rule 807. Residual Exception

A statement not specifically covered by Rule 803 or 804 but having equivalent circumstantial guarantees of trustworthiness, is not excluded by the hearsay rule, if the court determines that (A) the statement is offered as evidence of a material fact; (B) the statement is more probative on the point for which it is offered than any other evidence which the proponent can procure through reasonable efforts; and (C) the general purposes of these rules and the interests of justice will best be served by admission of the statement into evidence. However, a statement may not be admitted under this exception unless the proponent of it makes known to the adverse party sufficiently in advance of the trial or hearing to provide the adverse party with a fair opportunity to prepare to meet it, the proponent's intention to offer the statement and the particulars of it, including the name and address of the declarant. (Added by H.D. 105-69, Apr, 11, 1997, eff. Dec. 1, 1997.)

ARTICLE IX. AUTHENTICATION AND IDENTIFICATION

Rule
901.   Requirement of Authentication or Identification.
    (a) General provision.
    (b) Illustrations.
        (1) Testimony of witness with knowledge.
        (2) Nonexpert opinion on handwriting.
        (3) Comparison by trier or expert witness.
        (4) Distinctive characteristics and the like.
        (5) Voice identification.
        (6) Telephone conversations.
        (7) Public records or reports.
        (8) Ancient documents or data compilation.
        (9) Process or system.
      (10) Methods provided by statute or rule.

NOTES

Rule 901. Requirement of Authentication or Identification

(a) General provision. The requirement of authentication or identification as a condition precedent to admissibility is satisfied by evidence sufficient to support a finding that the matter in question is what its proponent claims.

(b) Illustrations. By way of illustration only, and not by way of limitation, the following are examples of authentication or identification conforming with the requirements of this rule:

(1) Testimony of witness with knowledge. Testimony that a matter is what it is claimed to be.

(2) Nonexpert opinion on handwriting. Nonexpert opinion as to the genuineness of handwriting, based upon familiarity not acquired for purposes of the litigation.

(3) Comparison by trier or expert witness. Comparison by the trier of fact or by expert witnesses with specimens which have been authenticated.

(4) Distinctive characteristics and the like. Appearance, contents, substance, internal patterns, or other distinctive characteristics, taken in conjunction with circumstances.

(5) Voice identification. Identification of a voice, whether heard firsthand or through mechanical or electronic transmission or recording, by opinion based upon hearing the voice

NOTES

at any time under circumstances connecting it with the alleged speaker.

(6) Telephone conversations. Telephone conversations, by evidence that a call was made to the number assigned at the time by the telephone company to a particular person or business, if (A) in the case of a person, circumstances, including self-identification, show the person answering to be the one called, or (B) in the case of a business, the call was made to a place of business and the conversation related to business reasonably transacted over the telephone.

(7) Public records or reports. Evidence that a writing authorized by law to be recorded or filed and in fact recorded or filed in a public office, or a purported public record, report, statement, or data compilation, in any form, is from the public office where items of this nature are kept.

(8) Ancient documents or data compilation. Evidence that a document or data compilation, in any form, (A) is in such condition as to create no suspicion concerning its authenticity, (B) was in a place where it, if authentic, would likely be, and (C) has been in existence 20 years or more at the time it is offered.

(9) Process or system. Evidence describing a process or system used to produce a result and showing that the process or system produces an accurate result.

(10) Methods provided by statute or rule. Any method of authentication or identification provided by Act of Congress or by other rules prescribed by the Supreme Court pursuant to statutory authority.

Rule 902. Self-authentication

Extrinsic evidence of authenticity as a condition precedent to admissibility is not required with respect to the following:

(1) Domestic public documents under seal. A document bearing a seal purporting to be that of the United States, or of any State, district, Commonwealth, territory, or insular possession thereof, or the Panama Canal Zone, or the Trust Territory of the Pacific Islands, or of a political subdivision, department, officer, or agency thereof, and a signature purporting to be an attestation or execution.

(2) Domestic public documents not under seal. A document purporting to bear the signature in the official capacity of an officer or employee of any entity included in paragraph (1) hereof, having no seal, if a public officer having a seal and having official duties in the district or political subdivision of the officer or employee certifies under seal that the signer has the official capacity and that the signature is genuine.

(3) Foreign public documents. A document purporting to be executed or attested in an official capacity by a person authorized by the laws of a foreign country to make the execution or attestation, and accompanied by a final certification as to the genuineness of the signature and official position (A) of the executing or attesting person, or (B) of any foreign official whose certificate of genuineness of signature and official position relates to the execution or attestation or is in a chain of certificates of genuineness of signature and official position relating to the execution or attestation. A final certification may be made by a secretary of an embassy or legation, consul general, consul, vice consul, or consular agent of the United States, or a diplomatic or consular official of the foreign country assigned or accredited to the United States. If reasonable opportunity has been given to all parties to investigate the authenticity and accuracy of official documents, the court may, for good cause shown, order that they be treated as presumptively authentic without final certification or permit them to be evidenced by an attested summary with or without final certification.

(4) Certified copies of public records. A copy of an official record or report or entry therein, or of a document authorized by law to be recorded or filed and actually recorded or filed in a public office, including data compilations in

NOTES

NOTES

any form, certified as correct by the custodian or other person authorized to make the certification, by certificate complying with paragraph (1), (2), or (3) of this rule or complying with any Act of Congress or rule prescribed by the Supreme Court pursuant to statutory authority.

(5) Official publications. Books, pamphlets, or other publications purporting to be issued by public authority.

(6) Newspapers and periodicals. Printed materials purporting to be newspapers or periodicals.

(7) Trade inscriptions and the like. Inscriptions, signs, tags, or labels purporting to have been affixed in the course of business and indicating ownership, control, or origin.

(8) Acknowledged documents. Documents accompanied by a certificate of acknowledgment executed in the manner provided by law by a notary public or other officer authorized by law to take acknowledgments.

(9) Commercial paper and related documents. Commercial paper, signatures thereon, and documents relating thereto to the extent provided by general commercial law.

(10) Presumptions under Acts of Congress. Any signature, document, or other matter declared by Act of Congress to be presumptively or prima facie genuine or authentic.

(11) Certified domestic records of regularly conducted activity. The original or a duplicate of a domestic record of regularly conducted activity that would be admissible under Rule 803(6) if accompanied by a written declaration of its custodian or other qualified person, in a manner complying with any Act of Congress or rule prescribed by the Supreme Court pursuant to statutory authority, certifying that the record

(A) was made at or near the time of the occurrence of the matters set forth by, or from information transmitted by, a person with knowledge of those matters;

(B) was kept in the course of the regularly conducted activity; and

440

(C) was made by the regularly conducted activity as a regular practice. A party intending to offer a record into evidence under this paragraph must provide written notice of that intention to all adverse parties, and must make the record and declaration available for inspection sufficiently in advance of their offer into evidence to provide an adverse party with a fair opportunity to challenge them.

(12) Certified foreign records of regularly conducted activity. In a civil case, the original or a duplicate of a foreign record of regularly conducted activity that would be admissible under Rule 803(6) if accompanied by a written declaration by its custodian or other qualified person certifying that the record

(A) was made at or near the time of the occurrence of the matters set forth by, or from information transmitted by, a person with knowledge of those matters;

(B) was kept in the course of the regularly conducted activity; and

(C) was made by the regularly conducted activity as a regular practice. The declaration must be signed in a manner that, if falsely made, would subject the maker to criminal penalty under the laws of the country where the declaration is signed. A party intending to offer a record into evidence under this paragraph must provide written notice of that intention to all adverse parties, and must make the record and declaration available for inspection sufficiently in advance of their offer into evidence to provide an adverse party with a fair opportunity to challenge them.
(Amended by H.D. 100-41, Mar. 2, 1987, eff. Oct. 1, 1987; H.D. 100-187, Apr. 25, 1988, eff. Nov. 1, 1988; H.D. 106-225, Apr. 17, 2000, eff. Dec. 1, 2000.)

Rule 903. Subscribing Witness' Testimony Unnecessary

The testimony of a subscribing witness is not necessary to authenticate a writing unless required by the laws of the jurisdiction whose laws govern the validity of the writing.

NOTES

NOTES

ARTICLE X. CONTENTS OF WRITINGS, RECORDINGS, AND PHOTOGRAPHS

Rule 1001. Definitions

For purposes of this article the following definitions are applicable:

(1) Writings and recordings. "Writings" and "recordings" consist of letters, words, or numbers, or their equivalent, set down by handwriting, typewriting, printing, photostating, photographing, magnetic impulse, mechanical or electronic recording, or other form of data compilation.

(2) Photographs. "Photographs" include still photographs, X-ray films, video tapes, and motion pictures.

(3) Original. An "original" of a writing or recording is the writing or recording itself or any counterpart intended to have the same effect by a person executing or issuing it. An "original" of a photograph includes the negative or any print therefrom. If data are stored in a computer or similar device, any printout or other output readable by sight, shown to reflect the data accurately, is an "original".

(4) Duplicate. A "duplicate" is a counterpart produced by the same impression as the original, or from the same matrix, or by means of photography, including enlargements and miniatures, or by mechanical or electronic rerecording, or by chemical reproduction, or by other equivalent techniques which accurately reproduces the original.

Rule 1002. Requirement of Original

To prove the content of a writing, recording, or photograph, the original writing, recording, or photograph is required, except as otherwise provided in these rules or by Act of Congress.

Rule 1003. Admissibility of Duplicates

A duplicate is admissible to the same extent as an original unless (1) a genuine question is raised as to the authenticity of the original or (2) in the circumstances it would be unfair to admit the duplicate in lieu of the original.

Rule 1004. Admissibility of Other Evidence of Contents

The original is not required, and other evidence of the contents of a writing, recording, or photograph is admissible if—

(1) Originals lost or destroyed. All originals are lost or have been destroyed, unless the proponent lost or destroyed them in bad faith; or

(2) Original not obtainable. No original can be obtained by any available judicial process or procedure; or

(3) Original in possession of opponent. At a time when an original was under the control of the party against whom offered, that party was put on notice, by the pleadings or otherwise, that the contents would be a subject of proof at the hearing, and that party does not produce the original at the hearing; or

(4) Collateral matters. The writing, recording, or photograph is not closely related to a controlling issue.

(Amended by H.D. 100-41, Mar. 2, 1987, eff. Oct. 1, 1987.)

NOTES

Rule 1005. Public Records

The contents of an official record, or of a document authorized to be recorded or filed and actually recorded or filed, including data compilations in any form, if otherwise admissible, may be proved by copy, certified as correct in accordance with rule 902 or testified to be correct by a witness who has compared it with the original. If a copy which complies with the foregoing cannot be obtained by the exercise of reasonable diligence, then other evidence of the contents may be given.

Rule 1006. Summaries

The contents of voluminous writings, recordings, or photographs which cannot conveniently be examined in court may be presented in the form of a chart, summary, or calculation. The originals, or duplicates, shall be made available for examination or copying, or both, by other parties at reasonable time and place. The court may order that they be produced in court.

Rule 1007. Testimony or Written Admission of Party

Contents of writings, recordings, or photographs may be proved by the testimony or deposition of the party against whom offered or by that party's written admission, without accounting for the nonproduction of the original. (Amended by H.D. 100-41, Mar. 2, 1987, eff. Oct. 1, 1987.)

Rule 1008. Functions of Court and Jury

When the admissibility of other evidence of contents of writings, recordings, or photographs under these rules depends upon the fulfillment of a condition of fact, the question whether the condition has been fulfilled is ordinarily for the court to determine in accordance with the provisions of rule 104. However, when an issue is raised (a) whether the asserted writing ever existed, or (b) whether another writing, recording, or photograph produced at the trial is the original, or (c) whether other evidence of contents correctly reflects the contents, the issue is for the trier of fact to determine as in the case of other issues of fact.

ARTICLE XI. MISCELLANEOUS RULES

Rule 1101. Applicability of Rules

(a) Courts and judges. These rules apply to the United States district courts, the District Court of Guam, the District Court of the Virgin Islands, the District Court for the Northern Mariana Islands, the United States courts of appeals, the United States Claims Court, and to United States bankruptcy judges and United States magistrate judges, in the actions, cases, and proceedings and to the extent hereinafter set forth. The terms "judge" and "court" in these rules include United States bankruptcy judges and United States magistrate judges.

(b) Proceedings generally. These rules apply generally to civil actions and proceedings, including admiralty and maritime cases, to criminal cases and proceedings, to contempt proceedings except those in which the court may act summarily, and to proceedings and cases under title 11, United States Code.

(c) Rule of privilege. The rule with respect to privileges applies at all stages of all actions, cases, and proceedings.

(d) Rules inapplicable. The rules (other than with respect to privileges) do not apply in the following situations:

(1) Preliminary questions of fact. The determination of questions of fact preliminary to admissibility of evidence when the issue is to be determined by the court under rule 104.

NOTES

NOTES

(2) Grand jury. Proceedings before grand juries.

(3) Miscellaneous proceedings. Proceedings for extradition or rendition; preliminary examinations in criminal cases; sentencing, or granting or revoking probation; issuance of warrants for arrest, criminal summonses, and search warrants; and proceedings with respect to release on bail or otherwise.

(e) Rules applicable in part. In the following proceedings these rules apply to the extent that matters of evidence are not provided for in the statutes which govern procedure therein or in other rules prescribed by the Supreme Court pursuant to statutory authority: the trial of misdemeanors and other petty offenses before United States magistrate judges; review of agency actions when the facts are subject to trial de novo under section 706(2)(F) of title 5, United States Code; review of orders of the Secretary of Agriculture under section 2 of the Act entitled "An Act to authorize association of producers of agricultural products" approved February 18, 1922 (7 U.S.C. 292), and under sections 6 and 7(c) of the Perishable Agricultural Commodities Act, 1930 (7 U.S.C. 499f, 499g(c)); naturalization and revocation of naturalization under sections 310-318 of the Immigration and Nationality Act (8 U.S.C. 1421-1429); prize proceedings in admiralty under sections 7651-7681 of title 10, United States Code; review of orders of the Secretary of the Interior under section 2 of the Act entitled "An Act authorizing associations of producers of aquatic products" approved June 25, 1934 (15 U.S.C. 522); review of orders of petroleum control boards under section 5 of the Act entitled "An Act to regulate interstate and foreign commerce in petroleum and its products by prohibiting the shipment in such commerce of petroleum and its products produced in violation of State law, and for other purposes," approved February 22, 1935 (15 U.S.C. 715d); actions for fines, penalties, or forfeitures under part V of title IV of the Tariff Act of 1930 (19 U.S.C.

1581-1624), or under the Anti-Smuggling Act (19 U.S.C. 1701-1711); criminal libel for condemnation, exclusion of imports, or other proceedings under the Federal Food, Drug, and Cosmetic Act (21 U.S.C. 301-392); disputes between seamen under sections 4079, 4080, and 4081 of the Revised Statutes (22 U.S.C. 256-258); habeas corpus under sections 2241-2254 of title 28, United States Code; motions to vacate, set aside or correct sentence under section 2255 of title 28, United States Code; actions for penalties for refusal to transport destitute seamen under section 4578 of the Revised Statutes (46 U.S.C. 679);* actions against the United States under the Act entitled "An Act authorizing suits against the United States in admiralty for damage caused by and salvage service rendered to public vessels belonging to the United States, and for other purposes," approved March 3, 1925 (46 U.S.C. 781- 790), as implemented by section 7730 of title 10, United States Code.

Repealed and reenacted as 46 U.S.C. 11104(b)-(d) by P.L. 98-89, §§1, 2(a), 4(b), Aug. 26, 1983, 97 Stat. 500.

(Amended by H.D. 100-41, Mar. 2, 1987, eff. Oct. 1, 1987; H.D. 100-187, Apr. 25, 1988, eff. Nov. 1, 1988; P.L. 100-690, title VII, §7075(c), Nov. 18, 1988, 102 Stat. 4405; H.D. 103-76, Apr. 22, 1993, eff. Dec. 1, 1993.)

Rule 1102. Amendments

Amendments to the Federal Rules of Evidence may be made as provided in section 2072 of title 28 of the United States Code.

(Amended by H.D. 102-76, Apr. 30, 1991, eff. Dec. 1, 1991.)

Rule 1103. Title

These rules may be known and cited as the Federal Rules of Evidence.

NOTES

TABLE OF CASES

References are to pages in this volume. Principal cases are in **bold** type. Page numbers of extended discussions of cases are in *italic* type. For In re _____, and In the Matter of _____, see the name of the party. For Commonwealth v. _____, People v. _____, State v. _____, and United States v. _____, see the name of the other party. Where a case is discussed in another case, reference is made only to the first page at which it is cited.

449

Index

(References are to Sections)

NOTES

NOTES

NOTES

NOTES

NOTES

NOTES

NOTES

NOTES

NOTES

NOTES

NOTES

NOTES

NOTES

NOTES